Children of God's Fire

Children of God's Fire

A Documentary History of Black Slavery in Brazil

Robert Edgar Conrad

THE PENNSYLVANIA STATE UNIVERSITY PRESS
University Park, Pennsylvania

First published in 1984 by Princeton University Press

Reissued in paperback, with corrections and an updated bibliography, in 1994
by The Pennsylvania State University Press, University Park, Pennsylvania 16802

ISBN 0-271-01321-4

Third printing, 1997

Printed in the United States of America

CONTENTS

Part Five. Relations between the Races

Part Six. "Peculiar Legislation": Slavery and the Law

Part Nine. "A State of Domestic War": How Slaves Responded

Part Ten. "The Noblest and Most Sacred Cause": The Abolition Struggle

ILLUSTRATIONS

PREFACE

THE DOCUMENTS collected in this book are intended to create a realistic portrait of black slavery in Brazil, a system of human exploitation that lasted for centuries and caused immeasurable suffering to millions of human beings. The legal and philosophical origins of this system lie in antiquity and in the medieval world, but the form of slavery depicted here, based as it was on tropical agriculture and explicit racial distinctions, was something quite different from ancient slavery. When Europeans, led by the Portuguese, spread into Africa and tropical America, they happened upon the components of a new economic and social order which they hastened to establish: large non-white, non-European populations who could be forcibly enslaved and vast new lands where valuable agricultural products and precious minerals could be produced. The outcome of these circumstances was the swift unleashing of a great deal of cruel and even mindless behavior which was quickly institutionalized and then steadfastly maintained and defended for nearly four hundred years.

The Portuguese initiated the direct maritime slave trade from the African coast in the fifteenth century (see Document 1.1), experimented for decades thereafter with black slavery both in Portugal and in their newly colonized Atlantic islands, and finally established in Brazil one of the most enduring slave systems in the history of the world. In fact, slavery as an institution was a fundamental factor in Brazil's entire historical development from the beginnings of colonization, when the victims were mostly native Indians, until it was finally abolished by law in 1888, and today the legacies of slavery continue to influence Brazil in basic ways. Thus this collection of documents should advance not only our understanding of slavery in one important country, but also our comprehension of that country's broader historical development.

These documents will take on even greater significance, however, if it is recognized that the slave system from which they emerged was similar in many ways to other New World slave systems. There were obvious affinities between the exploitation of human beings in Portuguese and Spanish colonies in the first phases of settlement, but the similarities did not end with the consolidation of the Iberian conquests, or when other

Europeans appeared on the scene some decades later. The latecomers to American colonial enterprise—the English, French, and Dutch—came from national environments that were different from those of Catholic Portugal and Spain, but the opportunities and circumstances that they encountered in the Guianas, in the Caribbean islands, and, in the case of the Dutch, in seventeenth-century Brazil itself, were not very different from those that attracted their predecessors. Thus, with little hesitation and few moral doubts, and with useful Iberian models to guide them, these new colonizers emulated their predecessors, adopting the plantation system wherever it was suitable, and setting in motion the same kinds of brutal exploitation of black people, even spreading that system—or something very much like it—into the colder regions of North America.

Moreover, tropical slave systems continued to show striking resemblances even in more recent times. There were pronounced similarities, for example, between the slave systems of Brazil and Cuba during the nineteenth century, although those two countries had little contact or trade and little popular awareness of their parallel development.[1] Economic opportunities and the availability of non-white, non-Christian peoples, whose enslavement was still not totally unacceptable to European mores, permitted continuation of the same forms of human exploitation witnessed in earlier centuries. Indeed, although there were obvious local differences, a book of documents telling a story much like this one could be assembled to portray slavery in such European colonies as Saint Domingue (Haiti), Jamaica, or Venezuela in the eighteenth century, or Cuba in the nineteenth century. Thus, although originating specifically with the Brazilian experience, these documents will provide insights into American tropical slavery wherever it appeared.

It must be pointed out here that the slavery which developed in the English colonies of mainland North America, while resembling slavery in Brazil and other tropical regions, took on quite distinct characteristics of its own. It is dangerous to generalize on the nature of slavery even in limited geographical areas, where the word "slave" might have been used, for example, to refer to both a tormented field hand and a pampered *mulata* favorite draped in rich ornaments and surrounded by servants of her own. However, after years of concentrated study of Brazilian slavery and abolition, and after reading extensively on slavery in the United States, I have become convinced that the *physical conditions* endured by slaves in Brazil made life there considerably more precarious and uncomfortable—again in the physical sense—than it was for most

[1] For a study of Cuba describing a society much like that revealed by the documents in this book, see Franklin W. Knight, *Slave Society in Cuba during the Nineteenth Century* (Madison, Wis., 1970).

slaves in the United States. Eugene D. Genovese has distinguished between three basic meanings of the word "treatment," as it applies to slaves, including "day-to-day living conditions." As used here, the term "physical conditions" has roughly the same meaning, which must be distinguished from Genovese's other two categories of treatment, "conditions of life" and "access to freedom and citizenship," which are quite different things.[2]

Among the main reasons for this basic difference between Brazilian and British North American slavery, in my opinion, were the differing economies and societies that developed in the two countries.[3] In Brazil, plantation economies almost exclusively devoted to production for export quickly developed and remained the dominant economic arrangement, despite the slow growth of subsidiary free populations. In North America, in contrast, such plantation economies did indeed appear in subtropical regions of the South, but collateral settler colonies emphasizing production for local or regional consumption also developed and powerfully influenced the kind of broad society that eventually emerged. Because Virginia, the Carolinas, and Georgia—to cite examples—were settlement colonies as well as plantation colonies, they quickly developed larger white populations, relative to the number of blacks, than did Brazil, and for cultural and economic reasons these white populations were both more productive and made greater demands on producers of goods and services than did Brazil's marginal and impoverished free populations of largely mixed racial origin. Itself more developed economically than Brazil, the American South was also attached politically, culturally, and economically to the even more highly developed northern colonies or states, whereas Brazil's slave society lacked such an internal driving force. As a result of these factors, the overall standard of living in the American South was unquestionably higher than that of Brazil—or of other tropical colonies or countries—and, needless to say, something of that higher standard of living "trickled down" to the slaves. In the American South there was a greater consumption of material goods, including both food and clothing, by *every* segment of the population than in Brazil. For example, while a comparatively large amount of food for internal consumption was generated by the demands and productive

[2] "The Treatment of Slaves in Different Countries: Problems in the Application of the Comparative Method," in Laura Foner and Eugene D. Genovese, *Slavery in the New World* (Englewood Cliffs, N.J., 1969), pp. 202-210.

[3] For Brazil's colonial development and how it differed from that of temperate regions of North America, see Caio Prado, Jr., *The Colonial Background of Modern Brazil* (Berkeley, 1967), pp. 13-22, 133-147. For the United States, see Douglass C. North, *The Economic Growth of the United States, 1790-1860* (New York, 1966).

activities of a large free white population in the South, that demand helping to stimulate even the rich farming economies of the Midwest, in Brazil the low productivity and buying power of the population as a whole encouraged landholders to continue concentrating their efforts on production of commodities for foreign markets, at the obvious expense of the nation. The resulting scarcity and high cost of food were among Brazil's most serious economic problems, and a major cause of the inadequate diet and high mortality rate among the nation's slave population.

The comparative *physical* advantages that slaves in North America derived from living in a more highly developed society extended even beyond material things. For example, the high literacy rate among slaves in North America, which is reflected in the comparative abundance of slave narratives, sermons, and other writings by North American blacks, is the result, I believe, of the greater access to education enjoyed by white North Americans compared with free Brazilians. In the United States, where institutions of higher learning were founded in towns and cities in every region, teaching a slave to read and write was sometimes prohibited by law, presumably because of the fear of the power that education brought to an oppressed element of society. In contrast, such a prohibition was not even dreamt of in Brazil, since few slaves and only a small minority of free people had access to formal education of any kind. As late as 1872 only about 1,400 slaves in a total Brazilian slave population of over 1,500,000—less than one in a thousand—were registered as literate.[4] In comparison, by 1860 probably one of every twenty slaves in the United States—perhaps some 200,000 people—could read and write.[5]

This situation, incidentally, has even influenced the contents of this book. Compilers of documents on slavery in the United States have made much use of the writings of blacks themselves.[6] Indeed, some years ago the historian of American Negro slave revolts, Herbert Aptheker, published a book of more than five hundred pages made up entirely of selections written or spoken by black people, and more recently John W. Blassingame produced an even larger volume of "slave testimony."[7] In

[4] *Recenseamento da população do Imperio do Brasil a que se procedeu no dia 1º de Agosto de 1872* (Rio de Janeiro, 1872), XIX, 2.

[5] See Eugene D. Genovese, *Roll, Jordan, Roll: The World the Slaves Made* (New York, 1972), pp. 561-566.

[6] See, for example, Willie Lee Rose, *A Documentary History of Slavery in North America* (New York, 1976).

[7] Herbert Aptheker, *A Documentary History of the Negro People in the United States from Colonial Times through the Civil War* (New York, 1971); John W. Blassingame, *Slave Testimony: Two Centuries of Letters, Speeches, Interviews and Autobiographies* (Baton Rouge, 1977).

contrast, this collection of documents on Brazil includes only seven items written, dictated, or spoken by persons who had experienced slavery (Part One, Docs. 4 and 6; Five, Doc. 7; Eight, Docs. 4, 10, and 20; and Nine, Doc. 12), and only four additional selections written by known descendants of blacks (Part Four, Doc. 2; Five, Doc. 9; and Ten, Docs. 5 and 8). The reason for this lack of testimony by slaves or their descendants is simple: there were very few documents available from which to choose. According to my late colleague, Gilbert Osofsky, *thousands* of slave narratives, including those published in the abolitionist press, were written in the United States, and about eight full-length autobiographies were published before the Civil War.[8] Again in contrast, aside from sketchy accounts of their lives hastily written by the mulatto abolitionists, Luís Gama and José do Patrocinio,[9] I know of only one autobiography of a black man giving a detailed account of life in Brazil. Significantly, this *Biography of Mahommah G. Baquaqua, Native of Zoogoo, in the Interior of Africa* (see Document 1.4) was published in the United States in 1854 after Baquaqua had sailed as a crewman on a Brazilian ship to New York, where he was befriended and freed. In the last thirty years literally dozens of collections of original documents on slavery and the black experience in the United States have been published, including the many volumes of interviews of ex-slaves carried on in the 1930s by the W.P.A.'s Federal Writers Project.[10] In contrast, as far as I know only one major collection of original documents on the experience of black slaves in Brazil, Edison Carneiro's *Antologia do negro brasileiro*, has been made available to the reading public of that country in recent years.[11]

One more illustration of the differences between Brazilian and North American slavery will be useful. Carl N. Degler has argued that slaves in the United States received milder treatment than those in Brazil because the African slave trade to the United States ended earlier, making it essential to provide better care for existing slaves.[12] While this theory is not wrong as far as it goes, the situation will be better understood if we reverse the argument: the African slave trade to the United States ended earlier because, aside from various religious and moral pressures, the physical conditions of slaves in the United States, including a bal-

[8] Gilbert Osofsky, *Puttin' on Ole Massa* (New York, 1969), pp. 9-10.

[9] See Sud Menucci, *O precusor do abolicionismo no Brasil (Luiz Gama)* (São Paulo, 1938), pp. 19-26; Edison Carneiro, *Antologia do negro brasileiro* (Rio de Janeiro, 1967), pp. 398-404.

[10] See James M. McPherson et al., *Blacks in America: Bibliographical Essays* (New York, 1972); George P. Rawick, *The American Slave: A Composite Autobiography* (Westport, Conn., 1972-).

[11] See note 9.

[12] *Neither Black nor White: Slavery and Race Relations in Brazil and the United States* (New York, 1971).

anced ratio of females to males, allowed a rapid natural growth of the slave population, thereby contributing to the abolition of a traffic that had become practically superfluous. The slave population of British North America was growing naturally before the slave trade was abolished in 1807, whereas in Brazil the slave population failed to grow naturally even after the traffic ended in 1851.[13] In fact, once that major source of slaves had been eliminated, Brazil's slave population rapidly declined, helping to bring about abolition in less than forty years.[14] No comparison of Brazilian slavery with slavery in the United States should be expected, of course, in a book of documents on Brazil alone. I hope, however, that this collection will give students opportunities to make comparisons of their own, aided perhaps by the observations that I have occasionally included in my introductions which are intended to stimulate further reflection. Thus this book can make a contribution to the comparative-slavery controversy on the side of those scholars who reject the concept of a "milder" Brazilian or Latin American slavery which was put forward some years ago by such writers as Gilberto Freyre and Frank Tannenbaum.[15]

At this point, however, something must be said about the origins and development of the durable myth of the good-natured Brazilian master and his contented slave, if only because these concepts are out of step with the evidence in this book. This theory is firmly rooted in nineteenth-century efforts to defend slavery from its critics. As the antislavery movements of the United States and Britain began to call the world's attention to the horrors of their own domestic and colonial slave systems in the decades after the American Revolution—in the process threatening Brazilian slavery as well—the Luso-Brazilian world began to wage its own systematic campaign both at home and abroad to defend and exonerate slavery and the slave trade. The writings of the Brazilian Bishop, José Joaquim da Cunha de Azeredo Coutinho, are merely the most obvious evidence of this campaign,[16] which lasted until slavery

[13] See, for example, Peter H. Wood, " 'More Like a Negro County': Demographic Patterns in Colonial South Carolina, 1700-1741," in Stanley L. Engerman and Eugene D. Genovese, *Race and Slavery in the Western Hemisphere: Quantitative Studies* (Princeton, N.J., 1975), pp. 131-171; and Allan Kullikoff, "A 'Prolifick' People: Black Population Growth in the Chesapeake Colonies, 1700-1790," in *Southern Studies* 16 (1977), 391-428.

[14] See Robert Conrad, *The Destruction of Brazilian Slavery, 1850-1888* (Berkeley, 1972).

[15] See Gilberto Freyre, *The Masters and the Slaves: A Study in the Development of Brazilian Civilization* (New York, 1946); Frank Tannenbaum, *Slave and Citizen: The Negro in the Americas* (New York, 1963).

[16] See Sergio Buarque de Holanda, ed., *Obras econômicas de J. J. da Cunha de Azeredo Coutinho (1794-1804)* (São Paulo, 1966).

ended and was thereafter eagerly taken up by a number of influential historians.

Opponents of slavery, both Brazilian and foreign, commented on this type of misrepresentation. In 1837 an early Brazilian abolitionist observed: "Horrid punishments are common among us. Nevertheless, *the false opinion has been propagated* that we are the best of masters. If we are the most merciful, what must others be!" (See Document 6.10.) Nearly half a century later the abolitionist, Joaquim Nabuco, said much the same thing. "One finds . . . ," he wrote in his book, *O Abolicionismo*, in 1883, "*repeated declarations that slavery among us is a very mild and pleasant condition for the slaves*, better for him, in fact, than for the master, a situation so fortunate, according to these descriptions, that one begins to suspect that, if slaves were asked, they would be found to prefer slavery to freedom, which merely proves that newspapers and articles are not written by slaves or by persons who for one moment have imagined themselves in their condition." (See Document 10.6.) William Christie, the British minister to Brazil during the slave trade crisis of 1850, hinted at what was going on when he wrote: "the '*Brazilian agents*' have, I believe, succeeded in establishing a general impression that slaves are very well treated in Brazil. . . . But I am sure that there, as in all slave-countries, there are bad masters; and that Brazilian nature would not be human nature, if . . . slavery . . . did not produce a large crop of vice, cruelty, and crime. *Brazil is not known in England*. The general English public have, for many years past, had little or nothing before them but *the flattering pictures of Brazilian agents*."[17]

This pro-slavery propaganda, though perhaps intended mainly for foreigners, influenced the thinking of many Brazilians, resulting in one memorable contradiction which is reproduced in this book. In a speech opposing the Free Birth Law of 1871 (see Document 10.4), a member of the Brazilian Chamber of Deputies, José Inacio de Barros Cobra, told his fellow legislators: "It is known that, thanks to the generous and humane character of the Brazilians, slavery among us is so mild that the condition of our slaves is preferable to that of the working classes of some European countries. . . ." Earlier in this same speech, nevertheless, Barros Cobra had argued that, by freeing the newborn children of slave women, the Free Birth Law would eliminate the masters' incentive to support those same children, and they would therefore be abandoned "on the greatest imaginable scale." The claim that slaves in Brazil were treated better than European workers was also put forward by the noted play-

[17] William D. Christie, *Notes on Brazilian Questions* (London, 1865), pp. xlvi-xlvii. Italics added in this and the two previous citations.

wright, José de Alencar, one of Barros Cobra's legislative colleagues who also rejected the Free Birth Law; and, significantly, Alencar's assertion was the source of a similar claim on the part of Gilberto Freyre at the outset of his scholarly career.[18]

Referring to the persecution of Indians, Africans, and their descendants, the historian, José Honório Rodrigues, recently wrote that Brazilian society, "which trampled on the vanquished and ridiculed the defeated, never was kindly, cordial, humanitarian, tolerant, and respectful of human rights, like the official image of itself which it sought to portray."[19] Nevertheless, after abolition, this "official image" was not changed. While intellectuals of the First Republic (1889-1930) were giving new credence to scientific racism and applying its theories to the Brazilian situation, certain historians, aided by a few foreigners,[20] were elevating the theory of a milder Brazilian slavery to the level of historical science.

One of the most influential of these writers was João Ribeiro, author of a history of Brazil which was selected in 1900 to serve as an advanced textbook, a function it still served as late as 1966, the year it appeared in its nineteenth edition.[21] For Ribeiro, whose work was read by generations of Brazilian students, the Brazilian master was humane and philanthropic. The African (after surviving the miseries of the slave trade) found a new and happier life in Brazil. "Beautiful" Brazilian customs and sentiments of brotherly love worked in favor of the blacks, who were often liberated, given free time to work for themselves, granted the pleasures of religion and family life, and the right to choose their own masters and even to take their masters' surnames. Slavery in Brazil was rehabilitation, he claimed, a new fatherland, peace, and freedom which could never have been enjoyed in barbaric Africa.

In 1911, one of Ribeiro's professed admirers, Manoel de Oliveira Lima, expressed almost identical views on the subject before an audience at the Sorbonne: "The condition of slaves in Brazil [said Oliveira Lima] was infinitely more tolerable than in almost all the other countries in which the institution of slavery existed. There racial hostility is, so to speak, nonexistent, and charity is not only practised as a public activity, but rather as a social virtue." Later the same writer generalized that Brazilian "gentleness, which is one of the special qualities of the national charac-

[18] Raymond S. Sayers, *The Negro in Brazilian Literature* (New York, 1956), p. 146, n. 32.

[19] *Independência: Revolução e contra-revolução* (Rio de Janeiro, 1975), II, 104.

[20] See especially Harry H. Johnston, *The Negro in the New World* (New York, 1910).

[21] *História do Brasil*, 19th ed., revised by Joaquim Ribeiro (Rio de Janeiro, 1966).

ter, . . . made the slaves' lot in Brazil less rigorous, just as the absence of racial prejudice made that of the freedmen less humiliating."[22]

Such writers contributed greatly to Gilberto Freyre's theories regarding Brazilian social and historical development, and it was Freyre's impressive scholarly works that inspired Frank Tannenbaum's brief comparative study of slavery and race relations in the Americas, which in turn stimulated a virtual school of American scholarship eager to prove, or at least to believe, that slavery in the United States was particularly inhumane.[23] One wonders how many historians who welcomed these ideas understood that they were based in part at least upon the inventions of former defenders and apologists of Brazilian slavery.[24]

WHILE SELECTING the documents in this book I have been guided by certain principles. First of all, of course, I have sought to reveal historical truth. Secondly, clarity of style has been an important criterion. While not sacrificing accuracy and truth for literary niceties, I have naturally preferred documents that are dramatic, colorful, and well-written, because I sincerely want them to be read. Third, for certain parts of the book, those dealing, for example, with the Catholic Church, race relations, and the abolition controversy (Parts Four, Five, and Ten), I have deliberately chosen items that reveal the conflicting opinions of the day, since controversy, whether we like it or not, is also interesting. Fourth, I have made an effort to assemble material on a wide variety of topics with the intention of creating not only a many-faceted account of the Brazilian slave system, but also a portrait of the society in which that system existed. I have hoped, moreover, to assemble a record of Brazilian slavery that is not limited to a narrow geographical area or to a brief period of time. Therefore I have included items dealing with all major parts of the country and both the colonial and national periods. In view of my own research interests and the relative abundance of documentation for the nineteenth century, most of the selections naturally derive from the latter period. However, seeking to be as all-inclusive as possible, whenever I had an opportunity to choose between two documents from the colonial and national eras, I normally chose the former if the

[22] Manoel de Oliveira Lima, *Formação historica da nacionalidade brasileira* (Rio de Janeiro, 1944), pp. 41, 252.

[23] For Freyre's works, see Robert Conrad, *Brazilian Slavery: An Annotated Research Bibliography* (Boston, 1977), pp. 65-66, 132-133.

[24] For valuable recent analyses of the question of comparative slavery, see John V. Lombardi, "Comparative Slave Systems in the Americas: A Critical Review," in Richard Graham and Peter H. Smith, eds., *New Approaches to Latin American History* (Austin, 1974), pp. 156-174; and Jacob Gorender, *O escravismo colonial* (São Paulo, 1978), pp. 348-358.

items were otherwise equal in value. As a result, about 28 percent of the selections published here were written before the establishment of the independent Brazilian Empire in 1822, a fifth before the nineteenth century. Thus I believe the earlier periods are reasonably well represented, especially the eighteenth century. Obviously Brazilian slavery differed substantially over the centuries, but I am convinced that it exhibited certain basic characteristics throughout, and these are well reflected in the selections.

There is, however, one major gap. It was clearly impossible to deal with every variety of Brazilian slavery. Thus this collection, as the title suggests, neglects Indian slavery, which in fact during most of the sixteenth century was more prevalent in Brazil than black slavery. In my opinion the subjugation and destruction of Brazil's indigenous population was an historical event of such great importance that it deserves to be treated separately by someone with specialized knowledge of it.[25] Something of the way Indians were dealt with may be seen, however, in Document 7.1.

While making these selections I have tried to include as much testimony as possible on the special situation of slave women, and for a time I planned to include a separate chapter on women. Eventually I concluded however, that such a division would be artificial, since female slaves were an integral part of the Brazilian population and did not act out their lives on some separate stage. Although males almost always outnumbered females on slave ships and on plantations, all participated equally in the hardships and drudgery of slave life throughout Brazil, and so references to slave women are found in every chapter of this book. Nevertheless, since female slaves tended to be concentrated in cities and towns where they were made to work as household servants, washerwomen, ironers, seamstresses, wet nurses, prostitutes, peddlers, water carriers, and in other occupations traditionally assigned to women, Part Three, which deals with slave life in urban areas, contains a cluster of documents reflecting the special problems of female slaves.

While attempting to deal with a wide variety of topics, I have also tried to use a wide variety of sources. In addition to published and unpublished archival materials, the selections are drawn from memoirs, personal letters, diaries, agricultural and medical handbooks, doctoral theses, medical and legal journals, political pamphlets, abolitionist tracts, pro-slavery writings and speeches, travel accounts, newspaper articles and advertisements, and ecclesiastical writings. Among the government sources

[25] Persons eager to learn more about this topic might read John Henning's outstanding study, *Red Gold: The Conquest of the Brazilian Indians* (London, 1978).

used are British documents on the slave trade, ministerial reports, speeches of provincial presidents, the annals of the Brazilian General Assembly, special government publications on slavery, and Portuguese, imperial, and provincial law collections. Although two fragments of verse and one of Padre Antônio Vieira's impressive sermons are also included, this work has not drawn significantly on literary works. These too might better be collected by a specialist in that area.[26]

As a look at the table of contents will show, the selections have been arranged both topically and chronologically. The first part deals with the Atlantic slave trade in its several phases, from the backlands and ports of Africa to the marketplaces of Brazilian coastal cities. Parts Two and Three, concerned with depicting the lives of rural and urban slaves respectively, reveal the kinds of hardships and indignities that were regularly imposed upon both men and women, unquestionably shortening their difficult lives and contributing to their usual failure to put surviving progeny into the world. Part Four contains selections exhibiting the Catholic Church's longstanding contradictory attitudes and policies toward slavery, proving the Church's importance both as a nominal protector of slaves and as a defender of the slave system. It also provides clear evidence of the Church's deep and customary involvement as participant and beneficiary of slavery.

The items in Part Five hint at the multitude of compromises which evolved over the centuries between people of different social and racial backgrounds in a society where sincere exhibitions of friendliness and good will masked deep and endemic racial hostility and class conflict. Part Six offers first-hand information on the laws and legal concepts which evolved over the ages to keep a tyrannized racial group under control. The documents in Part Seven reveal the brutal forms of corporal punishment which were regularly inflicted upon slaves as part of that system of legal repression, and include analyses of slave punishment from several distinct points of view. Part Eight deals both with liberation and with the peculiar problems inherent in being an African or having a dark skin in a land where these personal characteristics were popularly accepted evidence of slave status, and includes selections concerned with the interprovincial slave trade and its effects.

The ninth part, one of the longest and most important, reveals how courageous and desperate victims of slavery resisted or evaded oppression over the centuries, along with the tactics and attitudes of their oppressors. And finally, Part Ten offers some key documents from the nine-

[26] For a good introduction to the topic, see Raymond S. Sayers, *The Negro in Brazilian Literature* (New York, 1956).

teenth-century abolition struggle which expose the conflicting attitudes of the time and show the major role that black people played in their own liberation. Many of the selections in this part confirm, I believe, the impressions which emerge from the rest of the book: that Brazilian slavery comprises one of the harsher chapters in human history, comparable in ferocity to some of the cruel events in our own historical period; but that nevertheless the slaves of Brazil were not just passive victims, but human beings who fought and schemed and compromised in order to reduce their level of misery or even escape entirely from bondage.

Some additional explanations are needed. Portuguese and Brazilian currency denominations included the *conto, milréis*, and the *real* (plural *réis*). One thousand *réis* were a *milréis* (written 1$000), and a thousand *milréis* were a *conto* (written 1:000$000). A *pataca*, referred to in some documents, was a minor coin often valued at 320 *réis*. The buying power of this currency changed, or course, over time, but in 1844 a *conto* was worth about 125 pounds sterling. At that time a healthy male African cost about 650$000 (650 *milréis*) and a female about 400$000. Popular measurements include the league or *liga*, about four miles, the *alqueire*, a dry measure of about thirteen liters, and the *arroba*, approximately thirty-two pounds. For these and other foreign terms, see the Glossary.

In regard to the introductions to the Parts and the individual documents, these are generally intended to provide just enough information to place them in their historical context, to identify their authors, to enumerate some of their most significant points, and to offer occasional contrasts with slavery in the United States which might contribute to the ongoing comparative discussion. I hope they will also help to stimulate discussion among readers who encounter this book in history courses. Some of the selections are given in their entirety, but many others are excerpts from books or other lengthy sources, or are shorter pieces which I have abbreviated to save space or to eliminate irrelevant or repetitious passages. When this was done, I always tried to select the parts of the document that best conveyed the author's message or best revealed a specific historical condition or situation. At times I have placed explanatory or informative notes within texts, but always in brackets to differentiate them from original insertions, which usually appear in parentheses. All italics contained in the texts are original.

ACKNOWLEDGMENTS

I WISH TO EXPRESS my thanks for the help I have received from many people and institutions, not merely to fulfill a conventional obligation, but to convey my genuine appreciation.

Many libraries and archives have given me access to their facilities, including some dusty, little-frequented stacks, and I am thankful to every one of them. Those that have been most useful include the Biblioteca Nacional (especially the Seção de Livros Raros, the Seção de Manuscritos, and the Seção de Iconografia), the Arquivo Nacional, the Instituto Histórico e Geográfico Brasileiro, the libraries of the Arquivo Histórico do Itamarati, the Museu de História, and the Ministério da Fazenda, all in Rio de Janeiro. Also useful were the Biblioteca da Faculdade de Direito in Recife, which allowed me to use their complete collection of published provincial laws, the Biblioteca Municipal in São Paulo, and the Biblioteca Pública in Niterói. In the United States the main libraries used were the Library of Congress, the New York Public Library, the Newberry Library in Chicago, and the university libraries of Chicago, Columbia, Harvard, Northwestern, Princeton, Rutgers, and the University of Illinois at Chicago Circle. My thanks go as well to the Iberoamerikanisches Institut in West Berlin.

I am also most grateful to colleagues, friends, and students whose help and encouragement have aided me immensely. Tony and Nancy Naro must receive special thanks for their unending hospitality in Rio de Janeiro. The students who took part in my seminar on Brazilian slavery during the summer semester of 1980 at the Free University of Berlin carefully read some of the first parts and offered a multitude of useful comments which affected both content and organization. Professors Eugene D. Genovese, Stuart B. Schwartz, and Mary Karasch and Marilyn Campbell of Princeton University Press all read the manuscript in its entirety, offering many valuable suggestions, for which I am especially grateful. My thanks go as well to Professors Paul Harper, Diana Soares de Galliza of João Pessoa, Paraíba, and Linda Lewin of Princeton University, all of whom have kindly offered useful suggestions. I am also grateful to Professors Thomas E. Skidmore, Gregory Rabassa, Raymond

S. Sayers, Warren Dean, and E. Bradford Burns for their timely encouragement and support. I also wish to thank the following persons and institutions for granting me permission to publish documents and copyrighted materials: Professor Charles R. Boxer, Warren Dean, and Stuart B. Schwartz for Documents 5.1, 8.4, and 9.12, respectively, the University of Illinois Press for 10.6, the University of Wisconsin Press for 8.4, Editora Conquista, Rio de Janeiro, for 9.11, and the Universidade Estadual Paulista, Campus de Assis, São Paulo, for 8.2. The sources of all the documents are, of course, given in the text. My wife, Ursula, deserves special thanks for her involvement in the growth and organization of this project over the years and her many valuable suggestions.

The financial aid which I have received since 1964 was essential to the long evolution of this book. This included two NDFL-Fulbright-Hays fellowships which helped me to get started with my research on Brazilian slavery, as well as later grants from Columbia University, the American Council of Learned Societies, the American Philosophical Society, and the University of Illinois at Chicago Circle. I am also grateful to the Free University of Berlin for allowing me to take time away from teaching to work on this book, and to my esteemed colleagues, Volker Lühr and Manfred Nitsch, for encouraging me to do so.

Finally I wish to thank the National Endowment for the Humanities, an independent Federal Agency, for a translation grant without which this book would not exist. I am of course responsible for all errors and misconceptions that appear here, except of course those of the "contributors," some of whom were guilty of a multitude of errors and misconceptions. Like an archaeologist trying to assemble an antique mosaic from many scattered stones, I have tried to patch together an impression of a complex and unfortunate institution. I hope I have located most of the essential pieces.

Robert Edgar Conrad

You are the brothers of God's preparation and the children of God's fire. —*Padre Antônio Vieira*

ATLANTIC OCEAN
Macapá
Manaus
Santarém
Belém
São Luís
Fortaleza
Baturité
Natal
AMAZONAS
AMAZONAS
P A R Á
MARANHÃO
CEARÁ
RIO GRANDE do NORTE
PARAIBA
Paraíba
Olinda
PIAUÍ
PERNAMBUCO
Recife
ALAGOAS
Palmares
Maceió
SERGIPE
Aracajú
SÃO FRANCISCO
Cachoeira
B A H I A
Salvador da Bahia
Bahia de Todos os Santos
Ilheus
MATO GROSSO
Cuiabá
G O I Á S
Goiás
M I N A S G E R A I S
Diamantina
ESPIRITO SANTO
Sabará
Mariana
Barbacena
Ouro Prêto
S. João del Rei
Vitória
Campos
SÃO PAULO
Campinas
RIO de JANEIRO
São Paulo
Cabo Frio
Petrópolis
Niterói
Rio de Janeiro
Santos
São Vicente
PARANÁ
Curitiba
SCALE
0
500
Miles
SANTA CATARINA
Destêrro
RIO GRANDE do SUL
Porto Alegre
Pelotas
BRAZILIAN EMPIRE 1822-89

ONE

"Men of Stone and of Iron": The African Slave Trade

THE PORTUGUESE-African-Brazilian traffic in black slaves began during the Age of Exploration and ended in the Age of Steam Power. During two-thirds of Brazil's recorded history it was an established and nearly unquestioned practice to uproot black people from their native societies and transport them across the Atlantic to Brazil, there to be sold to planters, miners, and town dwellers to do the harsh work of a frontier society. Once referred to by a slave trader as "the most lucrative trade under the sun," this trafficking in human beings was a fully integrated component of African cultures, of the Portuguese Atlantic system, and of the Brazilian colonial economy.

Never—not even in its earliest experimental phase—was the slave trade looked upon as merely a temporary way to supply needed workers under transitional conditions, and rarely until the slave trade's final years was it suggested that natural population growth might replace the African traffic as the main source of workers. Economically this trade was looked upon for hundreds of years as an essential means of replacing a constantly diminishing work force, and ideologically it was seen as a gratifying means of rescuing pagan souls for Christianity. In the words of one early nineteenth-century writer (see Document 10.2), God had evidently "created just opposite Brazil in the interior of Africa men who were deliberately constructed to serve on this continent." Writing as he did after three centuries of the Portuguese Atlantic slave trade, he was obviously convinced that such an act of Divine Providence was not intended to satisfy only passing needs.

To better understand the effects of the African slave trade upon Brazil, some comparisons with the United States will be useful. Though Indians performed most of the hard labor for the Portuguese pioneers during the first decades of Brazilian colonization after 1500, already by 1551, with the founding or a permanent sugar colony at Bahia and the strengthening of other newly established settlements, African slaves began to reach Brazil in substantial numbers, and by 1675, *before the traffic to British North America had fully gotten under way*, more slaves had already arrived in Brazil than would ever reach British North America from abroad. Then during the next 175 years (from 1676 until 1851), over 3,000,000 additional slaves went to Brazil from Africa, more than a million during the first half of the nineteenth century alone, during which time, for the sake of comparison, the slave population of the United States grew from about 900,000 to over 3,000,000 without much further assistance from the slave trade.

Thus in Brazil, among every generation of slaves, there were many persons who had passed through the harsh experiences of the African slave trade. As the documents in this part reveal, this meant that they had suffered enslavement in their native regions, long treks through the African interior bound in chains, and the pain of multiple brandings: that they had been forced to endure weeks or even months in African coastal depots, more weeks or months at sea on overcrowded ships, naked, diseased, and deprived of adequte food and water, and finally more days and weeks of waiting and recuperating in Brazilian coastal markets before being sold to some new owner and marched off to a distant place of labor. The slave trade was an unforgettable part of the life experience of millions of slaves in Brazil, which stamped deep and lasting impressions on their minds and bodies.

1.1. The Beginnings of the Portuguese-African Slave Trade in the Fifteenth Century, as Described by the Chronicler Gomes Eannes de Azurara

The following excerpt from the chronicle of African discovery and conquest by the official Portuguese historian, Gomes Eannes de Azurara, is probably the first and certainly one of the best descriptions of the onset of the Portuguese-African slave trade in the fifteenth century. It vividly reveals that, while early Portuguese slave traders were motivated in part by a desire to serve God and the Portuguese Kingdom, their alleged higher intentions did not prevent them from employing unscrupulous methods in the capture of slaves, or from later treating them with the brutality that became characteristic of the international slave trade. As Azurara shows, for example, the captured "Moors" arrived in Portugal in a miserable state, and little respect was shown for their personal feelings when, in the presence of Prince Henry the Navigator, they were divided up among their new owners. Similarly, although Prince Henry is described here as pleased by the slaves' opportunity to save their souls in a Christian land, his quick partition of the forty-six persons who made up his royal share was also apparently carried out with little regard for any wish the slaves might have had to remain with friends or loved ones. From the very beginning of the traffic, making profits and saving souls were more important than the welfare and happiness of human beings.

Source: *Chronica do descobrimento e conquista de Guiné, escrita por mandada de Elrei D. Affonso V, sob a direcção scientifica e segundo as instrucções do Illustre D. Henrique pelo chronista Gomes Eannes de Azurara* (Paris: J. P. Aillaud, 1841), pp. 103-135.

Since Prince [Henry the Navigator] was normally to be found in the Kingdom of the Algarve after his return from Tangier because of the town he was having built there, and since the prisoners whom [his captains] brought back were landed at Lagos [the town where Henry established his headquarters], it was the people of this place who first persuaded the Prince to grant them permission to go to that land from which the Moorish captives came. . . .

The most important captain was Lançarote, and the second Gil Eannes, who, as we have written, was the first to round Cape Bojador. Aside from these, there were Stevam Affonso, a nobleman who died later in the Canary Islands, Rodrigo Alvarez, Joham Dyaz, a shipowner, and Joham Bernaldez, all of whom were very well qualified. Setting out on their voyage, they arrived at the Island of Herons [Ilha das Garças] on the eve of Corpus Christi, where they rested for a time, living mainly from the many young birds they found there, since it was the breeding season. . . .

And so these two captains [Martim Vicente and Gil Vasquez] made preparations, and they took five boats manned by thirty men, six in each boat, and set out at about sunset. Rowing the entire night, they arrived about daybreak at the island they were looking for. And when they recognized it by signs the Moors had mentioned, they rowed for awhile close to the shore until, as it was getting light, they reached a Moorish village near the beach where all the island's inhabitants were gathered together. Seeing this, our men stopped for a time to discuss what they should do. . . . And after giving their opinions, they looked toward the village where they saw that the Moors, with their women and children, were leaving their houses as fast as they could, for they had seen their enemies. The latter, crying the names of St. James, St. George, and Portugal, attacked them, killing and seizing as many as they could. There you could have seen mothers forsaking their children, husbands abandoning their wives, each person trying to escape as best he could. And some drowned themsleves in the water; others tried to hide in their huts; others, hoping they would escape, hid their children among the sea grasses where they were later discovered. And in the end our Lord God, who rewards every good deed, decided that, for their labors undertaken in His service, they should gain a victory over their enemies on that day, and a reward and payment for all their efforts and expenses. For on that day they captured 165 [Moors], including men, women, and children, not counting those who died or were killed. When the battle was over, they praised God for the great favor He had shown them, in wishing to grant them such a victory, and with so little harm to themselves. After their captives had been put in the boats, with others securely tied up on land, since the boats were small and could not hold so many people, they ordered a man to go as far as he could along the coast to see if he could sight the caravels. He set out at once, and, going more than a league from where the others were waiting, he saw the caravels arriving, because, as he had promised, Lançarote had sailed at dawn.

And when Lançarote, with those squires and highborn men who accompanied him, heard of the good fortune which God had granted to that handful of men who had gone to the island, and saw that they had accomplished such a great deal, it pleasing God to bring the affair to such a conclusion, they were all very happy, praising God for wishing to aid those few Christians in this manner. . . .

On the next day, which was a Friday, they prepared their boats, since the caravels had to remain where they were, and loaded into them all the supplies needed for two days only, since they did not intend to stay away from their ships any longer than that. Some thirty men departed in the boats, namely Lançarote and the other captains of the caravels, and with them squires and highborn men who were there. And they took with them two of those Moors whom they had captured, because they had told them that on the island of Tiger, which was five leagues distant, there was a Moorish village of about 150 persons. And as soon as it was morning, they set out, all very devoutly commending themselves to God, and asking His help in guiding them so that He might be served and His Holy Catholic Faith exalted. And they rowed until they reached the said island of Tiger; and as soon as they had leaped upon the shore the Moor who was with them led them to a village, where all the Moors, or at least most of those on the island, had earlier assembled . . . ; and Lançarote, with fourteen or fifteen men, went toward the place where the Moor led them. And walking half a league . . . they saw nine Moors, both men and women, with ten or twelve asses loaded with turtles, who hoped to cross over to the island of Tiger, which would be a league from there, it being possible to cross from one island to the other on foot. And as soon as they saw them, they pursued them, and, offering no effective defense, they were all captured except one, who fled to inform the others in the village. And as soon as they had captured them, they sent them to the place where Gil Eannes was, Lançarote ordering him to place a guard over the Moors, and then to set out after them, using all the men he had, because he believed that they would find someone to fight with.

And as soon as the captives reached them, they bound them securely and put them in the boats, and leaving only one man with them, they set out at once behind Lançarote, following constantly in his footsteps until they reached the place where Lançarote and his followers were. After capturing the Moors whom they had sent to the boats, they followed the Moor to a village that its inhabitants had abandoned, having been warned by the Moor who had escaped when the others were taken prisoner.

And then they saw all the people of the island on a smaller island where they had gone in their canoes; and the Christians could not reach them except by swimming, nor did they dare to retreat for fear of encouraging their enemies, who were much more numerous than they were. And thus they remained until all the other men had reached them; and seeing that even when they were all together they could not do them any harm, because of the water that lay between them, they decided to return to their boats which were a good two leagues away.

And, upon their return, they entered the village and searched everything to see if they might find something in the houses. And, while searching, they found seven or eight Moorish women, whom they took with them, thanking God for their good fortune which they had received through His grace; and thus they returned to their boats, which they reached at about sunset, and they rested and enjoyed themselves that night like men who had toiled hard throughout the day. . . .

The needs of the night forced them to spend it mainly in sleep, but their minds were so fixed upon the tasks that lay before them that they could think of nothing else. And so they discussed what they would do the next day, and, after hearing many arguments, which I will omit in order not to make my story too long, they decided to go in their boats to attack the settlement before daybreak. . . . Having reached this decision, they set out in the dark, rowing their boats along the shore. And as the sun began to rise, they landed and attacked the village, but found no one in it, because the Moors, having seen their enemies leaving, had returned to the village, but, not wanting to sleep in it, they had gone to stay a quarter of a league away near a crossing point by which they went over to Tiger. And when the Christians recognized that they could find nothing in the village, they returned to their boats and coasted along that island on the other side of Tiger, and they sent fifteen men overland to see if they could find any Moors or any trace of them. And on their way they saw the Moors fleeing as fast as they could, for they had already observed them, and then all our men leaped out on land and began to pursue them. They were not able to reach the men, but they took seventeen or eighteen of the women and small children who could not run so fast. And one of the boats, in which Joham Bernaldez was traveling, one of the smallest, went along the coast of the island; and the men in the boat saw some twenty canoes which were moving toward Tiger, in which Moors of both sexes were traveling, both adults and children, four or five in each boat. And they were very pleased when they first saw this, but later greatly saddened. Their pleasure came from seeing the profit and honor that lay before them, which was their reason for going there; their sadness came when they recognized that their boat was so small that they could put only a very few aboard. And with their few oars, they pursued them as well as they could, until they were among the canoes; and, stirred by pity, even though the people in the canoes were heathens, they wished to kill very few of them. However, there is no reason not to believe that many of them, who in their terror abandoned the boats, did not perish in the sea.

And some of them were on the left and some on the right, and, going in among them, they selected the smallest, because this way they could load more into their boats, of which they took fourteen, so that those who were captured in those two days, not including some who died, totaled forty-eight. . . .

The caravels arrived at Lagos, from where they had set out, enjoying fine weather on the voyage, since fortune was no less generous in the mildness of the weather than it had been to them in the taking of their prizes. And from Lagos the news reached the Prince, who just hours before had arrived there from other places where he had spent some days. . . . And the next day, Lançarote, as the man who had had the main responsibility, said to the Prince: "Sir! Your Grace knows full well that you must accept the fifth of these Moors, and of everything which we took in that land, where you sent us in the service of God and yourself. And now these Moors, because of the long time we have been at sea, and because of the obvious sorrow in their hearts at finding themselves far from their birthplace and held in captivity, without possessing any knowledge of what their future will be; as well as because they are not used to sailing on ships; for all these reasons they are in a rather poor condition and sickly; and so it seems to me that it will be useful for you to order them removed from the caravels in the morning and taken to that field that lies outside the city gate, and there divided up into five parts, according to custom, and that Your Grace should go there and select one of the parts which best suits you." The Prince said that he was well pleased, and very early the next day Lançarote ordered the masters of the caravels to bring them outside and to take them to that field, where they were to be divided up, as stated before; but, before doing anything else, they took the best of the Moors as an offering to the church of that place, and another little one who later became a friar of St. Francis they sent to São Vicente do Cabo, where he always lived as a Catholic Christian, without any knowledge or feeling for any other law but the holy and true doctrine, in which all Christians await our salvation. And the Moors of that conquest numbered 235. . . .

On the next day, which was August 8, the seamen began to prepare their boats very early in the morning, because of the heat, and to bring out those captives so that they could be transferred as ordered. And the latter, placed together in that field, were a marvelous thing to behold, because among them there were some who were reasonably white, handsome, and genteel; others, not so white, who were like mulattoes; others as black as Ethiopians, so deformed both in their faces and bodies, that it seemed to those who guarded them that they were gazing upon images of the lowest hemisphere. But what human heart, no matter how hard, would not be stabbed by pious feelings when gazing upon such a company of people? For some had their heads held low and their faces bathed in tears, as they looked upon one another. Others were moaning most bitterly, gazing toward heaven, fixing their eyes upon it, as if they were asking for help from the father of nature. Others struck their faces with the palms of their hands, throwing themselves prostrate upon the ground; others performed their lamentations in the form of a chant, according to the custom of their country, and, although our people could not understand the words of their language, they were fully appropriate to the level of their sorrow. But to increase their suffering even more, those responsible for dividing them up arrived on the scene and began to separate one from another, in order to make an equal division of the fifths; from which arose the need to separate children from their parents, wives from their husbands, and brothers from their brothers. Neither friendship nor kinship was respected, but instead each one fell where fortune placed him! Oh powerful destiny, doing and undoing with your turning wheels, arranging the things of this world as you please! do you even disclose to those miserable people some knowledge of what is to become of them, so that they may receive some consolation in the midst of their tremendous sorrow? And you who labor so hard to divide them up, look with pity upon so much misery, and see how they cling to each other, so that you can hardly separate them! Who could accomplish that division without the greatest toil; because as soon as they had put the children in one place, seeing their parents in another, they rose up energetically and went over to them; mothers clasped their other children in their arms, and threw themselves face down upon the ground with them, receiving blows with little regard for their own flesh, if only they might not be parted from them!

And so with great effort they finished the dividing up, because, aside from the trouble they had with the captives, the field was quite full of people, both from the town and from the surrounding villages and districts, who for that day were taking time off from their work, which was the source of their earnings, for the sole purpose of observing this novelty. And seeing these things, while some wept, others took part in the separating, and they made such a commotion that they greatly confused those who were in charge of dividing them up.

The Prince was there mounted upon a powerful horse, accompanied by his retinue, distributing his favors, like a man who wished to derive little material advantage from his share; for of the forty-six souls who belonged to his fifth, he quickly divided them up among the rest, since his main source of wealth lay in his own purpose; for he reflected with great pleasure upon the salvation of those souls that before were lost.

And his thoughts were certainly not in vain, because, as we have said, as soon as they gained a knowledge of our language, they turned Christian without much difficulty; and I who have brought this history together in this volume saw boys and girls in the town of Lagos, the children and grandchildren of those people, born in this land, Christians as good and true as though they were descended from the beginnings of Christ's law, through the generation of those who were first baptized.

1.2. The Enslavement Process in the Portuguese Dominions of King Philip III of Spain in the Early Seventeenth Century

The following selection is another early description of slave-hunting in Portuguese overseas conquests. Part of an advisory message by an unnamed author addressed almost certainly to King Philip III of Spain (Philip II of Portugal), it was probably written in 1612, since its author refers to an expulsion of Christians from Japan (probably that ordered by Hideyoshi in 1587) as having occurred twenty-five years before. This urgently written statement shows that by the early years of the seventeenth century the fragile medieval Christian, Roman, and African legalities upon which the Iberian empires had based their enslavement of non-European peoples—the concept of a "just war" in which "infidels" might be enslaved, the right of a local ruler to enslave his delinquent subjects, the individual's right to sell himself into slavery, and a needy father's privilege of selling his own children—had been much abused on the lawless frontiers of Portugal's empire. (See Document 1.3 for later "legal" grounds for enslavement.) Clearly, in fact, with a growing demand for laborers in America, new justifications for slavery had been invented, and manhunting had become an unlicensed free-for-all wherever Portuguese influence had reached, not only in Brazil and Africa, but also in India and the Far East.

Source: "Proposta a Sua Magestade sobre a escravaria das terras da Conquista de Portugal," Document 7, 3, 1, No. 8, Seção de Manuscritos, Biblioteca Nacional, Rio de Janeiro.

❧ Modern theologians in published books commonly report on, and condemn as unjust, the acts of enslavement which take place in the Provinces of this Royal Empire, employing for this purpose the same principles by which the ancient theologians, doctors of canon law, and jurists have regulated legitimate and just acts of enslavement. According to these principles, only infidels who are captured in just wars, or who because of serious crimes have been condemned by their Rulers may be held as legitimate slaves, or if they sell themselves, or if they are sold by their own fathers who have legitimate need. And because, by the use of these four principles, great injustices are committed in the buying and selling of slaves in our Empire, as will later be seen, it is also certain that most of the slaves of this Empire are made so upon other pretexts, of which some are notoriously unjust, and others with great likelihood may be presumed to be so as well. Because on the entire Guinea Coast and at Cape Verde those persons called *tangosmãos* and other dealers in this merchandise, men of loose morals with no concern other than their own interests, commonly carry out their raiding expeditions up the rivers and in the remote interior far from these areas that are frequented by the Portuguese, by His Majesty's officials, and by the priests of those regions. They collect as many pieces [*peças*] as they can, sometimes through deception, at other times through violence, capturing them in ambushes aided by other local people who share in the profits. And sometimes when our ships arrive the natives themselves go out to hunt each other, as if they were stags, with the intention of selling them to us.

At other times our own people enslave many free persons as substitutes for the slaves who flee from them, merely because they are brothers or relatives of the runaways. And this wickedness is carried to the point that even the authorities seize the children and relatives of those who give them reasons to do so.

Also the blacks themselves falsely assert that the persons whom they bring to be sold are captured in a just war, or they say that they will butcher and eat them if they are not purchased. So that, of every thousand slaves who are captured, scarcely one-tenth will be justly enslaved, which is a notorious fact confirmed by all God-fearing men who reside or have resided in those places.

Not even the merchants themselves deny that they collect these slaves in the ways described, but they defend themselves saying that they transport them so that they may become Christians, and so that they may wear clothes and have more to eat, failing to recognize that none of this is sufficient to justify so much theft and tyranny, because, as St. Paul says, those who perform evil acts in order to bring about some good are justly condemned before God. How much more is this true in a matter as serious as the freedom of human beings.

The same methods are used in a large part of the land of the Kaffirs [term used for inhabitants of eastern and southern Africa], and were also used in Brazil before King Sebastian in 1570 promulgated the law forbidding the enslavement of the natives of Brazil, except in a just war to be carried on with his authority: although after the law was made practically the same thing has been done under new pretexts, and with entirely unjust methods which they search for, as will be shown below.

Also in parts of East India many Kings hold their vassals tyrannically as captives, and they sell them themselves or through other heathens to the Portuguese, and many of those nations are accustomed to attacking the Indians, Javanese, Malayans, and others, and they sell them as slaves to the Portuguese. And for these and other causes which are much the same to disinterested and impartial persons, the enslavement that goes on in those parts of India is generally looked upon as unjust. And, aroused by their consciences, many men grant freedom to their slaves, others set them free at the time of their deaths, and others make use of them for only a few years.

Finally, all these methods of enslavement are notoriously unjust, as are any others that are not those referred to above. And in those places even these may be commonly presumed to be unjust in the following ways:

Concerning the principle of just war, it is known that, since they are infidels and barbarians, the Kings and private Lords of the entire Conquest are not normally motivated by reason when they make war, but rather by passion, nor do they examine or consult others about their right to do so. Therefore most of their wars are unjust wars carried on merely for greed, ambition, and other unjust causes. Often the same may be presumed about the wars carried on by individual Portuguese captains, because, greedy as they are to capture slaves and other prizes, they often do so without any concern for their consciences.

The principle of condemning persons to perpetual slavery must be looked upon as a very questionable principle in the same places, and especially in Guinea and the land of the Kaffirs, because an infinite number of persons are unjustly condemned to servitude for very trifling reasons, or because of some passion of their masters. Because, just as when among us someone displeases a King he is cast out of Court or loses his favored status, among them, his freedom is attacked, and he and his whole family are enslaved, and all too often with a thousand tricks and much false testimony. . . .

Concerning the other two principles: the need to sell oneself to seek release from an unjust death or some other great misery; or being sold by one's father who is in dire need—these are the causes of many unjust acts of enslavement in those places. Because in some places, as has been said, some persons make a pretense of wanting to eat others, or of wishing to slaughter them, so that they can be sold. Many fathers sell their sons for almost nothing, without being in any dire need which might justify such a sale, which is invalid and without any force in law, because the power is not given to a father to sell his minor son, except in dire need, according to common scholarly doctrine. And also in place of their children they sell other relatives who are close at hand, and other strangers using tricks which they invent for the purpose, saying, or making them say, that they are their sons. And in Brazil before the abovementioned law of King Sebastian, the Portuguese persuaded the Indians to sell themselves, and since, because of their ignorance, they didn't understand how important this was, they sold themselves for a cotton jacket and some breeches, which later they wore out in the service of their own masters. And when they later understood the trick, if it was not possible for them to run away, some died from their misery and others lived in a state of perpetual grief. And one may suspect that in all likelihood the same thing happens in other places, such as Guinea, the land of the Kaffirs, etc.

And this ill-treatment and enslavement is scandalous to everybody, and especially to those same heathens, because they abandon our religion, seeing that those who are supposed to convert them are the same persons who enslave them in such unjust ways, as is witnessed every day.

And this is felt especially by those of greater understanding, such as the Japanese. So much is this so that this comprised the principal chapter of the Decree with which twenty-five years ago the tyrant Cambucodono, Universal Lord of all Japan, ordered the exile of all those who accepted that conversion, claiming that they went about buying and making slaves in those ports, on the pretext of Religion, because little by little they were plotting to subjugate all those States and to make them tributary to Portugal.

The same scandal exists in China, as can be proved by unquestionable facts, and it reached the point that the Bishop of Macao issued a directive by which he ordered that no one in those places, under penalty of excommunication, might enslave any Chinese, and this because our people did not possess any of the justifications that our laws grant to enslave people of that nation. Because, concerning the pretext of just war, they do not make war, except with the Tartars, and the latter do not engage in commerce with the Portuguese, nor do the Chinese sell the Tartars to our people.

And in regard to the justification of slavery through condemnation for a crime committed, the laws of China do not condemn people to slavery for any crime. And, concerning the title by which one sells himself or allows himself to be sold to escape an unjust death, as in Brazil and Guinea, where human flesh is eaten, there they do not have the custom of men selling themselves, nor does it appear that fathers there sell their children during periods of great famine, as happens sometimes in Cambodia, since general famines do not occur in China, the laws of China not permitting them, everyone there being given what he needs to maintain himself, and without working.

So that on many occasions the people of that nation are shocked by the way the Portuguese make slaves of them against the law of their land, knowing that they do not buy them from anybody except pirates and thieves, who are not their legitimate masters. To which reasonable shock and dismay Your Majesty and your Ministers have an obligation to make a positive response.

It is also known that in Angola when they take the slaves to the ships the natives weep a great deal and are shocked and grieved by the violence that is inflicted upon them. They observe that, aside from being cruelly enslaved, they are treated most inhumanely on the ships, where in large numbers they die of suffocation in their own stink, and from other kinds of ill-treatment. There was a night when thirty died on one ship while it was still in port, because the hatchway was not opened for fear they would run away. Below they screamed that it be opened because they were dying, but they got no response except to be called dogs and other names of that kind.

And on another ship in which 500 were being transported from Cape Verde to New Spain, on a single night 120 died from suffocation because there was fear that they would revolt against those who were transporting them. . . .

These acts of enslavement are together the cause of great scandal, and they are the source of very great sins on the part of the heathens and Moors of those places. Seeing that the Portuguese deal in that merchandise in every way they can, they also take up that life, robbing and tricking men, women, and children in order to sell them, and they search for other tricks with which to make their profits.

All the other provinces of Europe are also shocked by us, saying that the Portuguese, who look upon themselves as pious and devoted, commit such extraordinary acts of injustice and inhumanity.

1.3. A Portuguese Doctor Describes the Suffering of Black Slaves in Africa and on the Atlantic Voyage (1793)

The following description of the Portuguese Atlantic slave trade by a Portuguese medical doctor with personal experience in Africa and Brazil emphasizes the physical effects of that traffic on its victims. Delivered as a lecture in Portugal in 1793, it gives frank and detailed information on four phases of the Portuguese slave trade: the enslavement process in the African interior, the march to the Atlantic, confinement on the coast, and the sea voyage to Brazil. At the outset the author lists several circumstances in which persons could be legally enslaved in Africa, showing, as did the author of Document 1.2 some 180 years before, that legal or customary justifications for slavery were regularly abused in order to meet the great demand for laborers in New World colonies.

Source: Luiz Antonio de Oliveira Mendes, *Discurso academico ao programa: determinar com todos os seus symptomas as doenças agudas, e chronicas, que mais frequentemente accometem os pretos recem tirados da Africa* (Lisbon: Real Academia, 1812), pp. 8, 18-32.

According to their laws there are six ways in which the black Africans can be enslaved. However, the fifth and sixth ways do not have their origin in those laws, since they result from piracy, force, and treachery for the most part, and from the will and judgment of the fathers and husbands when they punish their wives and children.

We have already said that those rude peoples have adopted polygamy. Among them, according to their established laws, the most serious crime a man can commit is to meddle with a woman who has been admitted among the concubines of another man. . . . When the crime is proved, the criminal is punished.

For this purpose, and for others, in each of their fortified places they choose judges from among themselves whom they call *sobas*, whose task it is to judge them. . . . The ultimate punishment on that continent is slavery, and in civil and criminal cases witnesses are questioned, and the debtor or adulterer condemned to slavery. He is at once put in irons, and awarded to the creditor or person who has been offended, who can sell him as his own, since as a result of the judgment and sentence, he will remain a slave as his form of punishment.

Among those people there is the custom that when someone is condemned to slavery, he can name others to suffer slavery in his place; however, this can only be done to persons over whom the condemned person has a claim. For example, he can name his children, his wives, or his nephews.

The women, however, who are adulterous, and who are sentenced to slavery for their sins, do not have the right to name a substitute, because it is assumed that they will have nobody to name. Here another custom of the Romans is maintained, and from them transferred to our time, that women are the end-all and the be-all of the family.

One substitute alone is not acceptable, but, according to the gravity of the offense and the amount of the debt, six, seven, eight, and more are named. Once these have been appointed by the condemned man, they are put in irons, and these new slaves are divided up among the *sobas* and the offended persons or creditors, and each one of these can trade or sell the slaves who are granted to him.

When a black is seen stealing the harvest or fruits of another, and taking what is not his, the crime having been proved in the *soba*'s presence, he is condemned to slavery. However, he too can offer substitutes in the manner we have mentioned. . . .

When a kingdom makes war against another kingdom and is victorious, possessing the right to kill their conquered enemies, this right is transformed into that of slavery, and thus the captives can be bartered. This is how in this center of heathenism the rights of war are interpreted.

The fifth way in which the free man is innocently brought into slavery is by force and treachery. Certain pirates among them deceptively persuade others to go with them to certain places, and there rushing upon those they wish to enslave, they seize them and then sell them to backlanders when these are in certain places to barter for slaves, their trade fairs, for example. This happens ordinarily to persons of minor age who are more susceptible to trickery and fraud, and for this reason expose themselves to treachery, and does not happen as often to adults. And when these same crimes are proved, the pirates are themselves sentenced by the *sobas* to slavery. . . .

Sometimes it happens that needy family fathers, who have not themselves been sentenced, willfully desiring to punish their children and concubines, sell their own concubines and children to the backlanders, thus delivering them into slavery. . . .

Having been reduced to slavery in Africa, either because he was so condemned, or as a result of piracy and treachery, this once free black human being is the most unhappy person imaginable; because he is immediately placed in irons, and in this condition he eats only what the tyrants, the worst enemies of humanity, wish to give him.

In that moment in which he loses his freedom, he also loses everything which for him was good, pleasant, and enjoyable. In the presence of everything which he must suffer, how could we compare even the suffering of Adam when he was banished from Paradise?

Since all those fortified places are spread inland at a distance of a hundred, two hundred, three hundred and more leagues, such as Ambaque and others, and since it is always expected that there will be slaves there who have been condemned and imprisoned in order to be bartered, there are backlanders, who in some places are called *funidores* and in other places *tumbeiros*, who are always journeying through those interior areas for the purpose of acquiring slaves condemned to captivity through the

exchange of the merchandise . . . which they most prefer, including glass beads, coral, tobacco, rum, some iron instruments which they use, and muskets, powder, and lead.

After the deal has been concluded and the purchased article delivered over, there is a cruel scene, because the *funidores* or *tumbeiros* carry in their *manpas* or baggage the needed *libambo*, [an iron chain used to bind the slaves together]. And the slaves leave the stocks or shackles or any other sort of confinement for the *libambo*. Each of the slaves is attached to this iron chain at regular intervals in the following manner; the backlanders and those persons who accompany the convoy pass a piece of iron through the ring of the chain in the proper place, and out of this piece of iron they pound out another ring, placing the iron points one above the other so that the slave's hand is imprisoned in this new iron ring. Normally the *libambo* is attached to the right hand, because the *funidores* fear that if the right hand is free the slaves can use another piece of iron or even a stick to open the ring that binds them. The slave women are placed in a separate *libambo*, and the children, whom they refer to as *crias* [colts or fillies], are allowed to run free.

When the *funidores* are told in the towns, or by those who bartered them, that a slave is rebellious, and too strong-willed, they attach the *libambo* ring to his neck, and it often happens that because of their fear of these slaves, they make them wear the *libambo* on the neck as well as the hand.

Only the imagination can give an idea of the treatment that the slaves suffer when they are put in those *libambos*, and there are some who resist, fearing its hardness, banishment from their native land, or the uncertainty of where they will be taken. And in order to attach them to the *libambo*, they must be thrown to the ground.

The backlanders or *funidores* pass from fortress to fortress, taking with them in the convoy the slaves they have purchased. Each slave carries on his back a provision sack, which the backlanders have bought for them to feed themselves until they arrive at another settlement, where they are resupplied. . . .

This brutal and laborious trek lasts from one to six, seven, or eight months. On the way they do not drink water whenever they wish, but only when they reach some pool or pond. They camp wherever the *funidor* decides. Their bed is the earth, their roof the sky, and the blanket they cover themselves with the leaves of the trees, which do not cover them completely. The morning dew falls upon them. Their pillows are the trunks of the trees and the bodies of their companions. After the camping place has been selected, the slaves are arranged in a circle, and a bonfire is lit to provide heat and light. This lasts until dawn, when having warmed the earth with their bodies, their journey is resumed.

The night is passed in a state of half sleep and watchfulness, because even during the hours intended for rest and sleep, they are constantly aroused by their black guards, who, fearing an uprising, scream at them and frighten them, when in fact the exhausted and mistreated travelers are more disposed to sleep and to die than to resist. All this results from the unreasonable fear that, with so many slaves together, some might open the iron ring that attaches them to the *libambo*. And because of an even greater prejudice, and this is common to all, that the captive slaves know of a plant that causes iron to soften and break. . . .

During this unhappy time everything conspires toward the mistreatment of these people, who are so much like ourselves. Everything is scarce, and what is given to them, aside from being badly seasoned and badly cooked, is also badly chosen; because they receive a scanty ration, enough only to keep them from dying.

The backlanders treat them this way for several reasons. First, they are convinced that spending more to feed their slaves is not good business, that this will only result in greater expense, when, besides, many of them will die anyway. Secondly, because owing to the distance from one place to another, the food supply must be managed with economy, so that they can make the distance to the next settlement in time to obtain a new supply, which they usually do not achieve. Thirdly, because the slaves cannot carry more food than they do, weakened as they are by the journey and by bad treatment. . . .

For this same reason the food which is prepared for them is disagreeable and bad-tasting, since they lack the necessary spices, including salt. This is required most of all, but, since it is a heavy item, it overloads them too much. The reason their food is badly cooked is that on the treks everything is done in a hurry, and their food consists of nothing but Indian corn, beans, and manioc flour, all badly prepared and only half cooked. In their exile and wandering, rarely do they experience their own African foods, such as *anfunge, mutete*, and *quenga*, of which they are so very fond. They lack pepper; they lack oil, without which they eat only to remain alive. In this situation, with their memories of the comforts of their own country, they eat, drink, sleep, and live in much discomfort.

Among the slaves themselves can be observed charitable and obliging qualities which are not seen among the backlanders or any of the other free people. If the slave is carrying pepper, rum, or oil in his sack, he shares some of it with the others who are in the same condition as he.

If on the way a slave should claim that he is sick and can no longer continue, he is taken for a liar, so that, instead of seeking to cure him, he receives a beating to force him to march. So that, attached again to the *libambo*, he must either continue the journey, whether able to or not, or he must die on the *libambo*, becoming the unfortunate victim of those who traffic in their lives.

When the slaves coming from many different parts of the interior reach the maritime ports of Africa, they are there once more traded for goods and merchandise to the many agents or merchants who have their houses established there for that purpose. Acquiring the slaves by means of such trading, they keep them for a time in the same *libambo*, and if they are not kept this way they are closed up in a secure ground-level compound surrounded by high walls, from which they cannot escape.

Here takes place the second round of hardships that these unlucky people are forced to suffer. By these new tyrants they are terribly handled and most scantily provided for, and for them they are like mere animals, their human nature entirely overlooked. The dwelling place of the slave is simply the dirt floor of the compound, and he remains there exposed to harsh conditions and bad weather, and at night there are only a lean-to and some sheds or warehouses, also on the gound level, which they are herded into like cattle.

Their food continues scarce as before, and without any seasoning except salt, which in the ports is more abundant. There is meat in these ports, but it is expensive, and so it is not purchased for the slaves. Their food is limited at times to badly cooked beans, at other times to corn, also boiled, and at other times to beans mixed with corn to provide variety. They also add to the diet a small amount of salted fish, which abounds in Luanda and the Kingdom of Angola. . . .

Simply because the slaves are close to the sea, after eating their breakfast at about ten in the morning they are sent in lots to wash themselves in the ocean. With the slaves there is no outlay for clothing at all, because they make them keep the few things they might have brought with them, and if this is lacking they remain nearly naked. They do not want to pay out more for clothing, since they are convinced that this makes their slaves more expensive, and because from hour to hour they are hoping to begin trading with those who will transport them to Brazil. . . .

They suffer in other ways. When they are first traded, they are made to bear the brand mark of the backlander who enslaved them, so that they can be recognized in case they run away. And when they reach a port . . . they are branded on the right breast with the coat of arms of the king and nation, of whom they have become vassals and under whom they will live subject to slavery. This mark is made with a hot silver

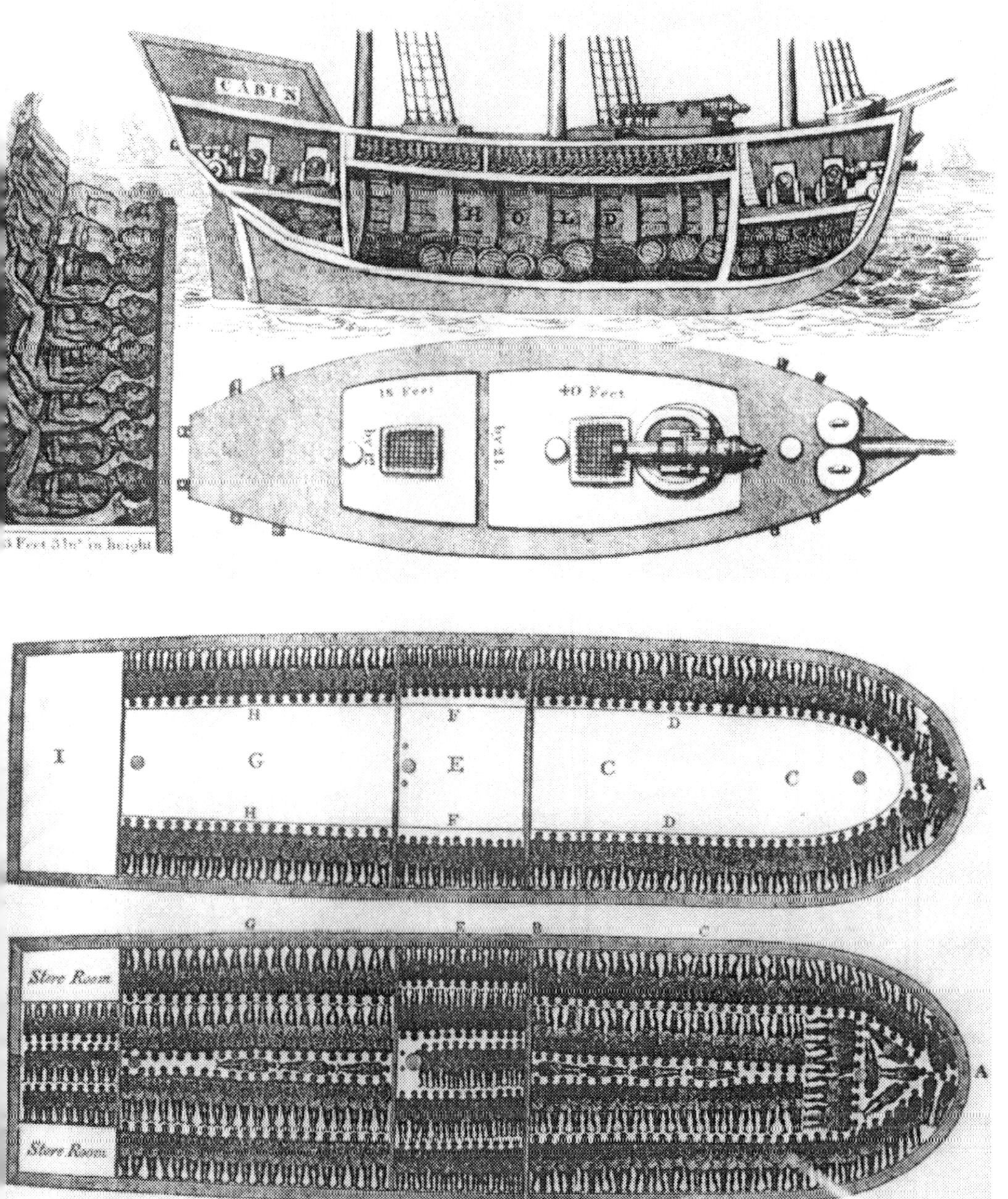

1. Sections of a Slave Ship

instrument in the act of paying the king's duties, and this brand mark is called a *carimbo*.

They are made to bear one more brand mark. This one is ordered by their private master, under whose name they are transported to Brazil, and it is put either on the left breast or on the arm, also so that they may be recognized if they should run away. . . .

In this miserable and deprived condition the terrified slaves remain for weeks and months, and the great number of them who die is unspeakable. With some ten or twelve thousand arriving at Luanda each year, it often happens that only six or seven thousand are finally transported to Brazil. . . .

Shackled in the holds of ships, the black slaves reveal as never before their robust and powerful qualities, for in these new circumstances they are far more deprived than when on land. First of all, with two or three hundred slaves placed under the deck, there is hardly room enough to draw a breath. No air can reach them, except through the hatch gratings and through some square skylights so tiny than not even a head could pass through them. . . .

The captains, aware of their own interests, recognize the seriousness of the problem, and they try to remedy it to some extent. Twice a week they order the deck washed, and, using sponges, the hold is scoured down with vinegar. Convinced that they are doing something useful, each day they order a certain number of slaves brought on deck in chains to get some fresh air, not allowing more because of their fear of rebellion. However, very little is accomplished in this way, because the slaves must go down again into the hold to breathe the same pestilent air. . . .

Second, the slaves are afflicted with a very short ration of water, of poor quality and lukewarm because of the climate—hardly enough to water their mouths. The suffering that this causes is extraordinary, and their dryness and thirst cause epidemics which, beginning with one person, soon spread to many others. Thus, after only a few days at sea, they start to throw the slaves into the ocean.

Third, they are kept in a state of constant hunger. Their small ration of food, brought over from Brazil on the outward voyage, is spoiled and damaged, and consists of nothing more than beans, corn, and manioc flour, all badly prepared and unspiced. They add to each ration a small portion of noxious fish from the African coast, which decays during the voyage. . . .

The law of 1647 which was intended to prevent these scandals clearly reveals the extent to which these conditions already existed in that period.

With good reason, then, we may speak of these black Africans, who resist so much and survive so many afflictions, as men of stone and of iron.

1.4. A Young Black Man Tells of His Enslavement in Africa and Shipment to Brazil about the Middle of the Nineteenth Century

The following document is one of the few in this book dictated or written by a slave or former slave. Its author, Mahommah Gardo Baquaqua, a former Moslem turned Christian, was a native of a place called Zoogoo (Soulougou?) located south of the great bend of the Niger River, perhaps in the region now known as Upper Volta. A privileged attendant of the local king or "massa-sa-ba," Baquaqua was seized, he claimed, by envious persons, sold as a slave, and forced to travel, mostly on foot, to an unidentified coastal location. From this place, probably a Portuguese possession, Baquaqua was shipped to Brazil, arriving in Pernambuco some time in the 1840s. This account of his ordeal, which was told to a publisher named Samuel Moore, fortunately includes detailed impressions of every phase of the slave trade, from seizure in Africa to illegal sale in Brazil.

Baquaqua's story would not have been published had he not traveled to New York, still in the capacity of a slave, on a Brazilian merchant vessel. There, evidently with the aid of some sympathetic free blacks and other abolitionists, he was given his freedom and sent to Haiti. In Haiti he was aided by American Baptist missionaries, eventually returning to the United States where he studied for several years under Baptist tutelage. For Baquaqua's brief account of his experiences as a slave in Brazil, see Ann M. Pescatello, *The African in Latin America* (New York, 1975)

Source: *Biography of Mahommah G. Baquaqua, A Native of Zoogoo, in the Interior of Africa . . . Written and Revised from His Own Words, by Samuel Moore . . .* (Detroit, Geo. E. Pomeroy & Co., 1854), pp. 34-45.

❧ It has already been stated, that when any person gives evidence of gaining an eminent position in the country, he is immediately envied, and means are taken to put him out of the way; thus when it was seen that my situation was one of trust and confidence with the king, I was of course soon singled out as a fit object of vengeance by an envious class of my countrymen, decoyed away and sold into slavery. I went to the city one day to see my mother, when I was followed by music (the drum) and called to by name, the drum beating to the measure of a song which had been composed apparently in honor of me, on account of, as I supposed, my elevated position with the king. This pleased me mightily, and I felt highly flattered, and was very liberal, and gave the people money and wine, they singing and gesturing the time. About a mile from my mother's house, where a strong drink called Bah-gee, was made out of the grain Har-nee; thither we repaired; and when I had drunk plentifully of Bah-gee, I was quite intoxicated, and they persuaded me to go with them to Zar-ach-o, about one mile from Zoogoo, to visit a strange king that I had never seen before. When we arrived there, the king made much of us all, and a great feast was prepared, and plenty of drink was given to me, indeed all appeared to drink very freely.

In the morning when I arose, I found that I was a prisoner, and my companions were all gone. Oh, horror! I then discovered that I had been betrayed into the hands of my enemies, and sold for a slave. Never shall I forget my feelings on that occasion; the thoughts of my poor mother harassed me very much, and the loss of my liberty and honorable position with the king grieved me very sorely. I lamented bitterly my folly in being so easily deceived. . . .

The man in whose company I found myself left by my cruel companions, was one, whose employment was to rid the country of all such as myself. The way he secured me, was after the following manner:—He took a limb of a tree that had two prongs, and shaped it so that it could cross the back of my neck; it was then fastened in front with an iron bolt; the stick was about six feet long.

Confined thus, I was marched forward towards the coast, to a place called Ar-oo-zo, which was a large village; there I found some friends, who felt very much about my position, but had no means of helping me. We only stayed there one night, as my master wanted to hurry on, as I had told him I would get away from him and go home. He then took me to a place called Chir-a-chur-ee, there I also had friends, but could not see them, as he kept very close watch over me, and he always stayed at places prepared for the purpose of keeping the slaves in security; there were holes in the walls in which my feet were placed (a kind of stocks). He then took me on to a place called Cham-mah (after passing through many strange places, the names of which I do not recollect) where he sold me. We had then been about four days from home and had traveled very rapidly. I remained only one day, when I was again sold to a woman, who took me to Efau; she had along with her some young men, into whose charge I was given, but she journeyed with us; we were several days going there; I suffered very much traveling through the woods, and never saw a human being all the journey. There was no regular road, but we had to make our passage as well as we could. . . . After passing through the woods, we came to a small place, where the woman who had purchased me, had some friends; here I was treated very well, indeed, during the day, but at night I was closely confined, as they were afraid I would make my escape; I could not sleep all night, I was so tightly kept.

After remaining there for the space of two days, we started on our journey again, traveling day after day; the country through which we passed continued quite hilly and mountainous; we passed some very high mountains, which I believe were called the mountains of Kong. . . . At length we arrived at Efau, where I was again sold; the woman seemed very sorry to part with me, and gave me a small present on my leaving them. Efau is quite a large place, the houses were of different construction to those in Zoogoo, and had not so good an appearance.

The man to whom I was again sold, was very rich, and had a great number of wives and slaves. I was placed in charge of an old slave; whilst there a great dance was held and I was fearful they were going to kill me, as I had heard they did in some places, and I fancied the dance was only a preliminary part of the ceremony; at any rate I did not feel at all comfortable about the matter. I was at Efau several weeks and was very well treated during that time; but as I did not like the work assigned me, they saw that I was uneasy, and as they were fearful of losing me, I was locked up every night. . . .

After leaving Efau, we had no stopping place until we reached Dohama; we remained in the woods by night and traveled during the day, as there were wild beasts in great abundance, and we were compelled to build up large fires at night to keep away the ferocious animals, which otherwise would have fallen upon us and torn us to pieces; we could hear them howling round about during the night. . . . Dohama is about three days journey from Efau, and is quite a large city; the houses being built differently to any I had previously seen. . . . When we arrived here I began to give up all hopes of ever getting back to my home again, but had entertained hopes until this time of being able to make my escape, and by some means or other of once more seeing my native place, but at last hope gave way; the last ray seemed fading away, and my heart felt sad and weary within me, as I thought of my home, my mother! whom I loved most tenderly, and the thought of never more beholding her added very much to my perplexities. . . .

We then proceeded to Gra-fe, about a day and half's journey; the land we passed was pretty thickly settled and generally well cultivated; but I do not recollect that we passed any streams of water after entering upon this level country. At Gra-fe, I saw the first white man, which you may be sure took my attention very much; the windows in the houses also looked strange, as this was the first time in my life that I had ever seen houses having windows. They took me to a white man's house, where we remained until the morning, when my breakfast was brought in to me, and judge my astonishment to find that the person who brought in my breakfast was an old acquaintance, who came from the same place; . . . his name was Woo-roo, and had come from Zoogoo, having been enslaved about two years; his friends could never tell what had become of him. . . .

Woo-roo seemed very anxious that I should remain at Gra-fe, but I was destined for other parts; this town is situated on a large river. After breakfast I was taken down to the river and placed on board a boat; the river was very large and branched off in two different directions, previous to emptying itself into the sea. The boat in which the slaves were placed was large and propelled by oars, although it had sails as well, but the wind not being strong enough, oars were used as well. We were two nights and one day on this river, when we came to a very beautiful place; the name of which I do not remember; we did not remain here very long, but as soon as the slaves were all collected together, and the ship ready to sail, we lost no time in putting to sea. Whilst in this place, the slaves were all put into a pen, and placed with our backs to the fire, and ordered not to look about us, and to insure obedience, a man was placed in front with a whip in his hand ready to strike the first who should dare to disobey orders; another man then went round with a hot iron, and branded us the same as they would the heads of barrels or any other inanimate goods or merchandise.

When all were ready to go aboard, we were chained together, and tied with ropes round about our necks, and were thus drawn down to the sea shore. The ship was lying some distance off. I had never seen a ship before, and my idea of it was, that it was some object of worship of the white man. I imagined that we were all to be slaughtered, and were being led there for that purpose. I felt alarmed for my safety, and despondency had almost taken sole possession of me.

A kind of feast was made ashore that day, and those who rowed the boats were plentifully regaled with whiskey, and the slaves were given rice and other good things in abundance. I was not aware that it was to be my last feast in Africa. I did not know my destiny. Happy for me, that I did not. All I knew was, that I was a slave, chained by the neck, and that I must readily and willingly submit, come what would, which I considered was as much as I had any right to know.

At length, when we reached the beach, and stood on the sand, oh! how I wished that the sand would open and swallow me up. My wretchedness I cannot describe. It was beyond description. . . . I was then placed in that most horrible of places,

THE SLAVE SHIP.

Its horrors, ah! who can describe. None can so truly depict its horrors as the poor unfortunate, miserable wretch that has been confined within its portals! . . . We were thrust into the hold of the vessel in a state of nudity, the males being crammed on one side, and the females on the other; the hold was so low that we could not stand up, but were obliged to crouch upon the floor or sit down; day and night were the same to us, sleep being denied us from the confined position of our bodies, and we became desperate through suffering and fatigue.

Oh! the loathsomeness and filth of that horrible place will never be effaced from my memory; nay, as long as memory holds her seat in this distracted brain, will I remember that. My heart even at this day, sickens at the thought of it. . . .

The only food we had during the voyage was corn soaked and boiled. I cannot tell how long we were thus confined, but it seemed a very long while. We suffered very much for want of water, but was denied all we needed. A pint a day was all that was allowed, and no more; and a great many slaves died upon the passage. There was one poor fellow so very desperate for want of water, that he attempted to snatch a knife from the white man who brought in the water, when he was taken up on deck and I never knew what became of him. I supposed he was thrown overboard.

When any one of us became refractory, his flesh was cut with a knife, and pepper or vinegar was rubbed in to make him peaceable (!) I suffered, and so did the rest of us, very much from sea sickness at first, but that did not cause our brutal owners any trouble. Our sufferings were our own, we had no one to share our troubles, none to care for us, or even to speak a word of comfort to us. Some were thrown overboard before breath was out of their bodies; when it was thought any would not live, they were got rid of in that way. Only twice during the voyage were we allowed to go on deck to wash ourselves—once whilst at sea, and again just before going into port.

We arrived at Pernambuco, South America, early in the morning, and the vessel played about during the day, without coming to anchor. All that day we neither ate or drank anything, and we were given to understand that we were to remain perfectly silent, and not make any out-cry, otherwise our lives were in danger. But when [night came], the anchor dropped, and we were permitted to go on deck to be viewed and handled by our future masters, who had come aboard from the city. We landed a few miles from the city, at a farmer's house, which was used as a kind of slave market. The farmer had a great many slaves, and I had not been there very long before I saw him use the lash pretty freely on a boy, which made a deep impression on my mind, as of course I imagined that would be my fate ere long, and oh! too soon, alas! were my fears realized.

When I reached the shore, I felt thankful to Providence that I was once more permitted to breathe pure air, the thought of which almost absorbed every other. I cared but little then that I was a slave, having escaped the ship was all I thought about. Some of the slaves on board could talk Portuguese. They had been living on the coast with Portuguese families, and they used to interpret to us. They were not placed in the hold with the rest of us, but come down occasionally to tell us something or other.

These slaves never knew they were to be sent away, until they were placed on board the ship. I remained in this slave market but a day or two, before I was again sold to a slave dealer in the city, who again sold me to a man in the country, who was a baker, and resided not a great distance from Pernambuco.

When a slaver comes in, the news spreads like wild-fire, and down come all those that are interested in the arrival of the vessel with its cargo of living merchandise, who select from the stock those most suited to their different purposes, and purchase the slaves precisely in the same way that oxen or horses would be purchased in a market; but if there are not the kind of slaves in the one cargo, suited to the wants and wishes of the slave buyers, an order is given to the Captain for the particular sorts required, which are furnished to order the next time the ship comes into port. Great numbers make quite a business of this, and do nothing else for a living, depending entirely upon this kind of traffic.

1.5. An Ex-Slavetrader's Account of the Enslavement Process in Africa and the Illegal Traffic to Brazil (1848-1849)

On two occasions in 1848 and 1849, as part of a parliamentary investigation of the international slave trade, members of the British Parliament questioned an American-born fomer slave trader, Dr. Joseph Cliffe. A naturalized Brazilian subject and a trained physician, Cliffe had spent many years in Brazil and Africa. He had served Brazil in her war for independence in the early 1820s, had worked in the interior province of

Minas Gerais as a gold and diamond prospector, and, while trafficking in slaves, had made voyages to Portuguese African colonies. His frank responses to questions concerning conditions in Africa and on slave ships, while confirming the testimony of Baquaqua and Oliveira Mendes, add details which apply especially to the years after 1830. In that year the British-Brazilian treaty of 1826, which banned the traffic, went into effect, and the slave trade to Brazil was henceforth illegal.

Source: *Second Report from the Select Committee on the Slave Trade Together with the Minutes of Evidence and Appendix* (London, 1848), pp. 42-46, 51-53, *Report from the Select Committee of the House of Lords, Appointed to Consider the Best Means which Great Britain Can Adopt for the Final Extinction of the African Slave Trade. Session 1849* (London, 1849), pp. 153-154, 160.

❧ 2180. From what you have heard from {Africans}, and seen yourself on the coast, can you tell the Committee anything as to the mode in which they are collected in the interior?—They are captured generally; many of them have been captured, some bought by means of domestic goods, dry goods, cloths, linen, handkerchiefs, snuff-boxes, beads and ornaments of any kind; a man takes a certain portion of them, and makes slaves of them, and sends them down; others will retaliate upon him in the same way. Frequently, from what I can judge, or from what I know, I believe that it has been often a thing agreed upon between them, consequently the loss of life has been very small upon those occasions. Frequently it has arisen from an actual state of war; all the older ones are then killed, and the younger ones, or the saleable ones, are brought down to the coast; those who are not considered worth bringing down, or worth making slaves of, are oftentimes put to death by having their brains beaten out.

2181. What part of the coast are you speaking of?—I am now speaking of north of Loango, west of the Portuguese settlements.

2182. At what age are they generally brought down for sale?—From seven to eight up to 20 or 25.

2183. You would not buy a man older than 25?—At the present time almost any age sells, but when it was a fair {legal} trade, not older than 25, and rarely, indeed, so old.

2184. Would a man's brains be beaten out if he was older than 25?—They say so.

2185. How are the slaves collected in the interior; are they collected by African agents of the Portuguese slave-traders?—The king or the chief having them for sale, send them down, or did send them down in the olden time, as far as was within his territory; they are a quarrelsome

2. A Slave Market in the City of Recife

people; he probably could not pass over a neighboring chief's territory, but he sold them to him; he traded with him for a certain amount of goods; this one then took them as far as he could carry them, and so ultimately they reached the sea-coast; in fact, they were living money.

2186. They were not paid for originally with money furnished by the Portuguese slave-trader?—In many cases they have been, and in many cases they have not been; many of the blacks themselves consider that if they had not had someone to buy them, they would have been put to death; many and many have stated that to me.

2187. Do the Africans generally treat the slaves kindly or brutally in carrying them down to the coast?—Unless you saw it, you could not suppose the small amount of value which is attached to human life. . . .

2191. Can you tell the committee anything as to the proportion of the sexes in the Africans who are brought into Brazil?—About one to ten.

2192. You are speaking of the present time?—I am speaking of the present time. In looking back, I do not think that there has been a very great difference; perhaps the lowest would be one to seven, and it has not at any time, I think, exceeded one to fourteen, excepting the years 1829 and 1830, and then expecting that the Slave Trade was to have been stopped, everything was brought over that could be brought; the lame, the blind, the deaf, and everything; princes, priests and patriarchs, everything that could swell the number was brought over then.

2193. And were there more women then?—Everything that could be bought, young and old; women with little babies, and women that were pregnant; everything was brought over then. . . .

2314. You spoke of the mortality in the barracoons, when you were estimating the mortality from the first capture of the slaves to their landing in Africa; have you seen much of the condition of the slaves in the African barracoons?—I have seen some little of them; I know that they suffer occasionally from want of food; instances have occurred in which they have suffered much from want of food.

2315. Are not the barracoons always near the sea?—Generally.

2316. Or near some point of embarkation?—Near some point of embarkation; they are simple things; they are merely half-a-dozen poles stuck up, and thatched over with palm; you can make them in a few hours.

2317. But simple as they are, they add very much to the comfort of the slaves on the coast?—Certainly they protect them from the heat, sun and rain, and from the evening dew the effect of which is very bad. . . .

4196. I wish to ask you some questions relative to the sufferings of the slaves on board the slave ships and in the barracoons; is there much suffering generally in the barracoons on the coast of Africa where the slaves are in a state of detention?—Not in the ordinary course of business. At present, from what I know. I believe that at times there is a great deal of suffering. We will say, for example, that there are 500 slaves waiting for a vessel; a cruiser is in the neighbourhood, and the vessel cannot come in; it is very difficult to get, on the coast of Africa, sufficient food to support them, and they are kept upon the smallest possible ration on which human life can subsist, waiting for an opportunity of putting them on board the vessel or vessels. Therefore there is a great deal of suffering now in the barracoons that did not formerly exist.

4197. It would be generally very difficult in Africa to subsist such a body as 2,000 or 3,000 slaves assembled in a barracoon, and detained there for any lenth of time?—I do not think that you really could support so many; 500 or 600, from what I know of the parts with which I am acquainted, would be with great difficulty supported for 20 days.

. . .

4208. Do the slaves in consequence of insufficient accomodation and other causes, perish in large numbers on board the vessels?—Occasionally they do; in many cases they do.

4209. Generally speaking, is there a large mortality?—There is.

4210. Is the suffering of such slaves as escape death very great?—Exceedingly so; almost beyond the powers of description. I have seen them when brought ashore, when life had been reduced to the lowest possible ebb; when they have been simply alive; nothing more than that could be stated of them; there was a complete wasting of the animal system, and a mere mass of bones, but still alive.

4211. To what causes is that attributable?—To a long passage, to a want of sufficiency of food, and to the confinement and foul air.

4212. Is the heat in the hold of a slaver very great?—Yes, I should think from 120 to 130 degrees, taking the Fahrenheit thermometer, and perhaps more.

4213. What would that thermometer stand at on deck?—Probably not more than 100.

4214. Supposing that the air was not fetid from the crowd of persons and other causes, would that degree of heat expose the slaves to suffering?—Not to a great deal; no. Heat alone would be nothing for their constitution; no injury to them.

4215. What they suffer from then really, is the fetid state of the atmosphere?—The fetid state of the atmosphere, and not having a sufficiency of food and water.

4216. Although the Africans would not suffer from that high degree of temperature, would it not promote a great deal for drink?—Of course it would under those circumstances.

4217. What quantity of water do you consider that an African would require for his sustenance per day?—A boy of 10 or 12 years of age would drink more than a gallon.

4218. What quantity do they usually get?—It is horrid almost to say; the quantity is very small. I have known from hearsay, within the last two years, that a teacup-full given once in three days, will support life for 20 to 30 days.

4219. Even in that temperature?—Yes; but the loss of life must be great on those occasions.

4220. Is the agony occasioned by desire for water very great?—Indescribable. There are no words that I can make use of that will describe the sufferings in the tropics from the want of water; it is ten times more horrible than the want of food. A man may suffer from the want of food four or five days and think nothing of it, but the sufferings from want of water for two days in the tropics is almost beyond endurance.

4221. Did you ever experience it yourself?—Yes, I have suffered it; I speak from what I have felt. . . .

4223. The slaver, I suppose, is in a very dirty condition?—It must be, because the slaves are jammed in, as I observed before. They are packed in upon their sides, laid in heads amongst legs and arms, so that it is very difficult frequently, until they become very much emaciated so as to leave room, for them to get up alone without the whole section moving together.

4224. Are they permitted to get up?—Small boys would be. Small boys are never confined; but the way in which they are put in now is, that they are generally jammed in in such masses that, even allowing that there was elevation sufficient for them to rise up, they could not rise without the whole section rising. They make two or three slave decks in a vessel which has perhaps six feet between her deck and the beams above. There would be three tiers of slaves stowed away.

4225. In six feet?—Yes; 16 to 18 inches would stow them in; then the timber, or whatever you term it, of which it is built, would occupy the rest of the space; so that you would have three tiers of them in a common deck; therefore there is not room for a very small boy to sit. They are put like books upon a shelf; consequently there is plenty of room for them to lie flat, but not enough for them to elevate.

4226. Do they lie upon their backs?—No; all upon their sides.

4227. Mr. *Gladstone*: Can they turn from side to side?—By the whole section turning, not otherwise until they have become a good deal emaciated, and some have died out; that of course, makes more room for the remainder.

4228. *Chairman*: Are they so placed for the convenience of stowage?—Yes, for the possibility of stowing larger numbers.

4229. By what means is the food supplied to them in that way?—By a man going down amongst them, passing down a calabash with a quantity of rice or beans, or whatever the description of food may be, and passing it round, a little portion to each one.

4230. The slaves are not brought on deck and fed there?—In a vessel where it was well conducted, the old plan used to be to bring them on deck by sections, and let them feed and let them wash themselves, and do what was necessary, and then to take them below again; but now when they are so jammed up it is impossible to do so; in addition to which, the want of water is so great that if they were to see water alongside a great number of them no doubt would jump overboard, without considering that it was salt water, therefore they are fed between decks as much as they possibly can be; a few who are suffering more than the others are occasionally brought on deck, but the object is to keep as many below as possible. . . .

4237. From the circumstances of dispatch under which you have described that the slaves are constantly embarked, are they not occasionally embarked when they are infected with dysentery, and ophthalmia, and fever?—They are brought down now from the interior of the country, and frequently remain for some length of time in the barracoons, upon a very small or imperfect allowance of food; they become much debilitated by it; consequently, when they are packed on board the mortality will be greater in consequence of their sufferings having been so much prolonged. In addition to which the voyage now, in consequence of having to run out of the usual line where cruisers are, in the place of being 20 or 25 days, may occupy sometimes from two months to as much as four months; and no doubt a great deal of this suffering from the want of food and the want of water, where there has been a sufficiency on board for the usual run of 20 days, may have arisen from being compelled to make such a very long passage of it.

4238. The slaves being packed in those large numbers, and exposed to a long voyage after a considerable detention, are very liable to suffer from diseases?—Yes; those are the cases in which the mortality is much the greatest, where they have been detained for some length of time in the barracoons, not having had an opportunity to be shipped; those are the cases in which the mortality is the greater, because their systems have been worn down previously to being put on board the vessel.

4239. Did you ever know an instance of a vessel losing one half of her cargo?—Yes; a good deal more than that. There was an instance in which, out of 160, which was but half the cargo, only 10 escaped, and those 10 were sold for 300 milreis, about 37£. I know that personally to be a fact. . . .

4243. *Chairman*: The slaves being packed on board ship in the way which you have described, which precludes the possibility of removing them upon deck, of course all the excrement of those wretched creatures during the whole of the voyage remains in the vessel?—In a certain measure. As far as I am aware, it is found almost impossible to keep them clean.

4244. It must remain altogether in the vessel if they do not go on deck?—Yes. Many vessels after they come in are abandoned from the impossibility of getting any person to clean the vessel. I can mention the case of an Austrian-built vessel, a very fine vessel, in which there had been some French seamen on board; she was cast adrift. The Brazilian government had her brought in and cleaned out by galley slaves.

4245. Of course if that is done with regard to a fine vessel, namely abandonment, it would be frequently done with regard to a vessel which was of small value?—Yes. This vessel was worth about 9,000£, but the immense number of slaves that she brought over gave the parties such a famous profit that there was no need of troubling themselves about the vessel. . . .

4250. There is one cause to which you have not called attention, and that is the nature of the decks; I believe that it has been the practice to pack the slaves away frequently upon the casks, has it not, without the intervention of a slave deck?—Yes, that is very frequently done; but as the African is not accustomed to sleep in a feather bed, from sleeping on a hard cask no injury arises.

4251. Do not they suffer from bruises from being jammed together between the casks?—When they are first put on board, they do bruise; but afterwards they become so emaciated, and are so very light, that the bruising is very trifling then. . . .

4302. *Chairman*: With respect to the condition of the slaves when they are landed, are they in a state of great suffering?—They certainly are.

4303. Have you seen many cases of the slaves landed from the slavers on their arrival?—Yes.

4304. In what condition did you find them?—I do not know I could describe it, to be intelligible to you. I do not think that I have power of description enough to describe it.

4305. Mr. *Gladstone*: You have told us these three things, that they are, very many of them, in a situation of acute suffering and at the same time of great physical reduction and torpidity of the animal functions?—Yes; so that the knee bones appear almost like the head of a person; from the arm you may slip your fingers and thumb up; the muscular part of the arm is gone; it is a mere bone covered with a bit of skin; the abdomen is highly protuberant; it is very much distended; very large. I am speaking of them just as they are landed. A man takes them up in his arms and carries them out of the vessel; you have some slave or some person that must do it if they are not capable of walking; they are pulled out, and those that are very dirty are frequently washed.

4306. Lord *H. Vane*: Do they recover very rapidly after they are once landed?—That is according to the treatment. In those establishments in which they are kept, where they have a clever medical man, by putting them into a warm bath, and by giving them a suitable diet, and suitable regimen, those that will recover do recover quickly.

4307. Mr. *Gladstone*: Are they for the most part lifted up on deck?—A great many of them are; a good many make attempts; they could not stand even if they were not so much emaciated. From not having perhaps stood upright for a month or two, the muscles have lost the power of supporting them.

4308. *Chairman*: The eye has lost its speculation?—Precisely so; it has an idiotic appearance; a leaden appearance; in fact, a sunken appearance. It is almost like the boiled eye of a fish.

4309. In fact, nature is reduced to the very last stage consistent with life?—To the lowest stage in which it is possible to say that they are living.

4310. Do they suffer much from bruises and sores?—Many become bruised; and there are many cases in which a gangrene probably takes place, or a very large ulcer takes place from lying so long in such putrid materials they have to lie in. Many no doubt die from it.

4311. Do they suffer very much from a sort of disease called craw-craws?—Yes, but that is not on board the ships; that is a land disease.

4312. Is it not very rapidly communicated from the contact in which they are placed?—Yes, it passes like the itch would pass. . . .

4316. The slaves usually require some period of time before they can be sufficiently recovered to be brought into the market?—Frequently three months; they require to be fed and taken care of before any person would take the trouble of buying them.

4317. When they are first landed where are they placed?—In a species of barracoon.

4318. In a species of hospital, in fact?—No, a mere barracoon.

4319. Lord *Courtenay*: A barrack?—A barrack.

4320. *Chairman*: They are disposed of in the barracoon, in order that they may recover their health and strength before coming into the market?—The reason of putting them into such a place is this: no owner of an establishment would permit a new cargo of slaves to be taken to his property, because a species of itch, or a disease of the skin which they have very much, would be propagated throughout the whole establishment; therefore no person would have them in a settled place. Those barracoons are in remote places by themselves, where there is no danger of the slaves running away; the object is to have a species of hospital where they are treated till those that get well do get well, and those that die there are buried.

4321. But as a matter of commercial policy, I presume that it is considered desirable to restore them to some degree of health and physical strength before they are exhibited in the market?—Yes. If you did not, when a purchaser took them, unless he had the convenience of taking them by water, he could not take them away; they could not walk; therefore the sooner you can get them into good condition the better; because a purchaser will take them as soon as he sees that they are able to walk, and not before.

1.6. "It Was the Same as Pigs in a Sty": A Young African's Account of Life on a Slave Ship (1849)

Two days after the ex-slavetrader, Joseph Cliffe, was interrogated, the Select Committee of the House of Lords questioned one Augustino, an African who in 1830, while still a child, had been included in a cargo of slaves transported to Brazil. Cliffe had told the committee that before the traffic had become illegal in March, 1830, conditions on slave ships had been comparatively comfortable. The questions put to Augustino, which were evidently intended to test whether or not this was true, partially refute this part of Cliffe's testimony. Africans rarely had an opportunity to put their impressions of slavery into the written record, and so this brief document, like Baquaqua's testimony (Doc. 1.4), is of unusual interest.

Source: *Report from the Select Committee of the House of Lords, Appointed to Consider the Best Means which Great Britain Can Adopt for the Final Extinction of the African Slave Trade. Session 1849* (London, 1849), pp. 162-163.

AUGUSTINO is called in, and examined as follows, through Mr. Herring, as Interpreter.

2353. How old are you?—I do not know

2354. When you were brought over from Brazil?—I do not know.

Mr. Herring. It was in 1830; I bought him myself in the month of July; we estimated his age at that time at about 12.

2355. (*To Augustino.*) Have you any recollection of your being brought over to Brazil?—I recollect when I arrived, and I recollect also when I came on board ship.

2356. Do you recollect anything which happened while you were on board ship?—I do.

2357. Can you remember whether, while you were so on board, your countrymen who were with you were brought over laid in packs, or in what way they were treated on board?—They were so closely packed together that there was no room to get anything at all in between them.

2358. Were you yourself, as a boy, brought on deck during the time that you were on board?—Yes, because I was so young.

2359. Were the grown slaves taken on deck?—No, they were not.

2360. They could not be, from the number which were packed together?—No; because they were chained down below to the sides of the vessel.

2361. Do you know whether many died on board ship?—When they were first put on board, they were so very thick together that a great many died in a day; five, six, ten, sometimes even a dozen died in a day, in consequence of the excessive heat and of the want of water. Their food was twice a week salt meat, and for the general meals of the day farina, a stuff like saw-dust—baked flour. In consequence of having a very insufficient supply of water, their thirst became so intense that many, from absolute suffocation, from the want of drink, died.

2362. Then, at that time they were not brought over in comfortable berths as emigrants were?—No.

2363. This was in 1830?—

Mr. Herring. It was before the expiration of the Treaty in 1830.

2364. But it was in 1830?—Yes.

Augustino. So far from there being cabins, if you call them cabins, it was the same as pigs in a sty, they were so thick.

2365. Do you know whether there was any difference between the state in which you were brought over and what had been the custom before?—As far as I know, it was the same thing.

Mr. Herring. But then he was up the country 30 leagues.

2366. (*To Augustino.*) Do you remember anything in Africa of your being made a prisoner before you were put on board?—Yes.

2367. Will you state anything that you remember?—A merchant sold my uncle some merchandise, and, before it was paid for, my uncle died;

the merchant came and seized us all, and made us all prisoners, and took us down to the coast; we were there about a week or 10 days, when we were put on board ship. The clothes of all the negroes going on board ship were stripped off them, even to the last rag.

2368. To what country in Africa did you belong?—Sefala.

2369. How far from the coast?—About a fortnight; at about three leagues a day.

Mr. Herring. Those leagues of which he speaks are Brazilian leagues, of four miles, very nearly.

Augustino. We always travelled by night, because they were afraid to travel by day.

2370. Why?—They were afraid that the relations of those who were taken prisoners might come, perhaps to the rescue. When we were on board ship, several had the liberty of coming on deck, in consequence of their youth; I was one, but the powerful ones were fastened below. The young ones had the right of coming on deck, but several of those jumped overboard, for fear they were being fattened to be eaten. The greater part of those that died on board died from thirst.

2371. What put the idea into their heads of being eaten; are they eaten in their own country?—They do not know for what object they are taken, and the idea comes into their head that it is from being made food of. Sometimes, when they are very ill indeed, and perhaps the white man thinks that one of them is dead, he comes and pinches his ear, to see if he feels the pain, and he finds that he is not dead; and then a man will take hold of his rope's end, and give him a good basting with it, and say, "There is nothing at all the matter with you; get up, get up."

Augustino is directed to withdraw.

1.7. A Slave Revolt at Sea and Brutal Reprisals (1845)

The previous documents show that traders in Africans feared revolts among their slaves both on land and at sea, and at times, of course, rebellions occurred. When such revolts were successful there was obviously little chance that anyone involved would have had an opportunity to record what he had seen. As a result, those slave uprisings about which we are informed, whether they happened in Africa, at sea, or in Brazil, were generally without success.

The following sworn testimony of William Page, a British sailor, given before the American consul in Rio de Janeiro, concerns the violent events that occurred aboard an American ship, the *Kentucky*, in 1845.

Under the protection of the American flag, the *Kentucky* had sailed from Rio de Janeiro in 1844 equipped for the slave trade. Reaching Inhambane on the coast of Mozambique, it took on a cargo of slaves and a Brazilian crew. Then, with the original crew members, including Page, traveling as passengers, it returned to Brazil where it landed its surviving cargo. The following section of Page's testimony deals mainly with the revolt and the Brazilian crew's fierce response to it, but it also includes some valuable details on the more normal daily routine of a slave ship in the final phase of the Brazilian traffic.

Source: *Class A. Correspondence with the British Commissioners at Sierra Leone, Havana, Rio de Janeiro, Surinam, Cape of Good Hope, Jamaica, Loanda, and Boa Vista, Relating to the Slave Trade. From January 1 to December 31, 1845, Inclusive* (London, 1846), pp. 517-518.

❧ Deponent . . . said, that a majority of the slaves were brought on board during the night in launches, near the fort at Inhambane. There were about 500 in all that came on board. About a dozen died on the passage, and 46 men and one woman were hung and shot during the passage; and 440 or about, were landed at Cape Frio. When the slaves came on board they were put down on the slave deck, all in irons. Across the vessel, aft, a bulkhead was run, aft of which, and in the cabin, the women, 150 to 200 in number, were put, and the men and boys forward of the bulkhead. When it was good weather, a good many of the negroes were on deck during the night and day. In stormy weather, only those that were kept at work were on deck, but all the others below. The vessel had not a full cargo. It was intended to have 700, but they could not get them. The negroes slept scattered about the slave-deck, as they chose. They were fed twice a day with beans, farina, rice, and dried beef, all boiled together. At the first meal they had beans, farina, and rice together, and at the second meal dried beef and farina. They eat in messes, as on board of a man-of-war, having their food in their dishes. All were provided with wooden spoons, made on board by the seamen, at Inhambane. The cooking apparatus was rigged in the galley, and so arranged and painted that it could not be discovered without coming on board. The cooking was going on all the time, excepting when near a sail, when the fires were damped, and all the negroes put below.

And deponent further said, that the next day after the vessel crossed the bar on leaving Inhambane, as aforesaid, the negroes rose upon the officers and crew; a majority of the men, all of whom were in irons, got their irons off, broke through the bulkhead in the females department, and likewise into the forecastle. Upon this, the Captain armed the crew with cutlasses, and got all the muskets and pistols, and loaded them, and the crew were firing down amongst the slaves for half an hour or more. In the meantime deponent was nailing the hatches down, and used no musket or pistol; and there was no occasion, as the Brazilian sailors seemed to like the sport. In about half an hour they were subdued, and became quiet again.

The slaves were then brought on deck, eight or ten at a time, and ironed afresh. They were all re-ironed that afternoon, and put below, excepting about seven, who remained on deck. None were killed on this occasion, and but eight or ten more or less wounded. They fired with balls in the pistols and shot in the muskets. Supposes the reason none were killed is, that they had to fire through the grates of the hatches, and the slaves got out of the way as much as they could.

On the next day they were brought upon deck two or three dozens at a time, all being well ironed, and tried by Captain Fonseca and officers; and within two or three days afterwards forty-six men and one woman were hung and shot, and thrown overboard. They were ironed or chained two together, and when they were hung a rope was put round their necks, and they were drawn up to the yard-arm clear of the sail. This did not kill them, but only choked or strangled them. They were then shot in the breast, and the bodies thrown overboard. If only one or two that were ironed together was to be hung, a rope was put round his neck and he was drawn up clear of the deck, beside of the bulwarks, and his leg laid across the rail and chopped off, to save the irons and release him from his companion, who, at the same time, lifted up his leg till the other's was chopped off as aforesaid, and he released. The bleeding negro was then drawn up, shot in the breast, and thrown overboard as aforesaid. The legs of about one dozen were chopped off in this way. When the feet fell on deck, they were picked up by the Brazilian crew and thrown overboard, and sometimes at the body, while it still hung living; and all kinds of sport was made of the business. When two that were chained together were both to be hung, they were hung up together by their necks, shot, and thrown overboard, irons and all. When the woman was hung up and shot, the ball did not take effect, and she was thrown overboard living, and was seen to stuggle some time in the water before she sunk.

And deponent further said that, after this was over, they brought up and flogged about twenty men and six women. When they were flogged they were laid flat upon the deck, and their hands tied, and secured to one ring bolt, and their feet to another. They were then whipped by two men at a time—by the one with a stick about 2 feet long, with five or six strands of raw hide secured to the end of it (the hide was dry and hard and about 2 feet long); and by the other with a piece of the hide of a sea-horse; this was a strip about 4 feet long, from half an inch to an inch wide, as thick as one's finger or thicker, and hard as whalebone, but more flexible. The flogging was very severe. Deponent and another Englishman on board, named Edward Blake, were obliged to assist in the flogging, as the Brazilians got tired. Deponent flogged four, but he got clear of the hanging and shooting business. All the women that were flogged at this time died, but none of the men. Many of them, however, were sick all the passage, and were obliged to lie on their bellies during the remainder of the voyage, and some of them could hardly get on shore on arrival at Cape Frio. The flesh of some of them where they were flogged (which was not generally on their backs, but on their posteriors) putrified and came off, in some cases 6 or 8 inches in diameter, and in places half an inch thick. Their wounds were dressed and filled up by the Contramestre with farina and cachaça [rum] made into poultice, and sometimes with a salve made on board. When the farina and cachaça were applied to the poor creatures, they would shiver and tremble for half an hour, and groan and sob with the most intense agony. They were a shocking and horrible sight during the whole passage. There was no disturbance on board after this, and no flogging, excepting of the boys for stealing water, farina, and so forth, when it was not allowed them.

Deponent further said that the ages of the negroes were from nine or ten up to thirty years. They were generally healthy, as sickly ones were not bought. Most of them were generally entirely without any article of clothes or covering, though at times they had strips of cloths around their loins, and some had handkerchiefs tied around them. The women were not so frequently naked as the men. Both the men and women frequently would get lousy, and be obliged to take off their strips of cloth to cleanse themselves. They were all brought on deck at different times during the voyage, say fifty at a time, and washed, by having water thrown over them, &c. They were washed four or five times each, and twice they had vinegar given to them to wash their mouths, and scrub their gums with brushes. In good weather the negroes themselves were obliged to sweep and wash down the slave deck every day, and thus kept it clean; but at night, and in hot weather, the hold of the vessel smelt very badly. But a few of them were sick during the passage, excepting those that were so badly flogged. The sick were doctored by the Contramestre, and the wounds of those that were flogged were dressed with aguardiente and farina, and a salve that was made on board.

1.8. A British Physician Describes the State of Africans upon Their Arrival in Brazil (1841-1843)

From the early years of the nineteenth century until after 1850 the British Royal Navy captured hundreds of slave ships at sea as part of Britain's long campaign to stop the international slave trade. The Africans found aboard those ships were taken either to a British colony or, when seized near Brazil or Cuba, delivered over to the doubtful protection of the government in those countries.

Obviously, after their hard journeys, the rescued slaves required assistance of every kind, especially food, quartering, and medical care. To meet these needs locally, in 1840 the British government stationed a frigate, the *Crescent*, in the harbor of Rio de Janeiro, and during the next five or six years eight shiploads of slaves seized off the Brazilian coast, some 3,000 Africans, received help aboard the *Crescent*.

Assigned to this arduous and dangerous duty was a British medical doctor, Thomas Nelson, who kept a written account of what he saw, with an emphasis on the physical conditions of the Africans and their diseases. The following descriptions of Africans who came under Nelson's professional care in 1841 and 1843 are taken from his sensitive account of the Brazilian slave trade published in 1846. The sections within quotation marks are of particular importance, since they were written on the scene while Nelson's impressions were still fresh.

Source: Thomas Nelson, *Remarks on the Slavery and Slave Trade of the Brazils* (London: J. Halchard and Son, 1846), pp. 43-56.

"A few minutes after the vessel dropped her anchor, I went on board of her, and although somewhat prepared by the previous inspection of two full slavers to encounter a scene of disease and wretchedness, still my experience, aided by my imagination, fell short of the loathsome spectacle which met my eyes on stepping over the side. Huddled closely together on deck, and blocking up the gangways on either side, cowered, or rather squatted, three hundred and sixty-two negroes, with disease, want, and misery stamped upon them with such painful intensity as utterly beggars all powers of description. In one corner, apart from the rest, a group of wretched beings lay stretched, many in the last stage of exhaustion, and all covered with the pustules of small-pox. Several of these I noticed had crawled to the spot where the water had been served out, in the hope of procuring a mouthful more of the precious liquid; but unable to return to their proper places, lay prostrate around the empty tub. Here and there, amid the throng, were isolated cases of the same loathsome disease in its confluent or worst form, and cases of extreme emaciation and exhaustion, some in a state of perfect stupor, others looking piteously around, and pointing with their fingers to their parched mouths whenever they caught an eye whom they thought would relieve them. On every side, squalid and sunken visages were rendered still more hideous by the swollen eyelids and the puriform discharge of a virulent ophthalmia [a dangerous eye inflamation], with which the majority appeared to be afflicted; added to this were figures shrivelled to absolute skin and bone, and doubled up in a posture which originally want of space had compelled them to adopt, and which debility and stiffness of the joints compelled them to retain.

"On looking more leisurely around, after the first paroxysm of horror and disgust had subsided, I remarked on the poop another wretched group, composed entirely of females. Some were mothers with infants who were vainly endeavouring to suck a few drops of moisture from the lank, withered, and skinny breasts of their wretched mothers; others were of every intermediate age. The most of them destitute even of the decency of a rag, and all presenting as woeful a spectacle of misery as it is possible to conceive. . . .

"While employed in examining the negroes individually, and separating and classifying the sick, who constituted by far the majority, I obtained a closer insight into their actual condition. Many I found afflicted with confluent small-pox, still more with purulent ophthalmia, and the majority of what remained, with dysentery, ulcers, emaciation, and exhaustion. In several, two or three of these were met. Not the least distressing sight on that pest-laden deck was the negroes whom the ophthalmia had struck blind, and who cowered in seeming apathy to all that was going on around. This was indeed the ultimatum of wretchedness, the last drops in the cup of bitterness. Deprived of liberty, and torn from their native country, there was nothing more left of human misery but to make them the victims of a physical darkness as deep as they had already been made of a moral one.

"The stench on board was nearly overwhelming. The odour of the negroes themselves, rendered still stronger by their filthy and crowded condition, the sickening smell of the suppurative stage of small-pox, and the far more disgusting effluvium of dysenteric discharge, combined with bilge water, putrid jerked beef, and numerous other matters to form a stench, it required no little exertion of fortitude to withstand. To all this, hunger and thirst lent their aid to finish the scene; and so poignant were they, that the struggles to obtain the means of satisfying them were occasionally so great as to require the interference of the prize crew. The moment it could be done, water in abundance and a meal was provided them; and none but an eye-witness could form an idea of the eagerness with which the former luxury was coveted and enjoyed. For many days, it seems, the water had not only been reduced in quantity, but so filled with impurities, and so putrid, that nothing but the most stringent necessity could have induced the use of it. . . ."

Of another, called the "Vencedora," the following are the notes which are taken.

"Early yesterday morning (11th of September, 1843) the decks of the Crescent were again thronged by a miserable crowd of liberated Africans. The vessel in which they had been conveyed from the 'coast' was captured a few days ago by one of the boats belonging to H.M.S. Frolic, a little to the northward of Rio.

"Previously to the removal of the negroes, Dr. Gunn (the surgeon of the Crescent) and myself went on board the slaver, and on stepping over the side, were astonished at the smallness of the vessel, and the number of wretched negroes who had been thrust on board of her. Below, the hold was crowded to excess; and above, the deck was so closely packed with the poor creatures, that we had to walk along the top of the low bulwarks in order to get aft. Of the appearance of the negroes, no pen can give an adequate idea. In numbers, the different protuberances and anatomical peculiarities of the bones can be distinctly traced by the eye, and appear, on every motion, ready to start through the skin, which is, in fact, all that covers them. Nor has this been confined to appearance; in many, at the bend of the elbows and knee-joints, over the hip-joints and lower part of the spine, the integuments have given way, and caused the most distressing and ill-conditioned sores. A great number of the Africans, especially the younger, cannot stand upright even when assisted, and the moment they are left to themselves, they double up their knees under their chins, and draw their legs so closely to their bodies, that they scarcely retain the form of humanity. So weak and so cramped are the most of them that they had to be carried in the arms of the seamen, one by one, up the Crescent's ladder. All those not affected with contagious diseases are now on board the Crescent, and the most of them look like animated skeletons. From one of the Portuguese crew, who is at present under treatment for small-pox, I learn that the name of the vessel is the Vencedora, and that she left Benguela on the coast of Africa with four hundred and sixty slaves on board. But of this number only three hundred and thirty-eight have been counted over the side, a circumstance which will appear the less surprising when the space in which they were stowed comes to be considered. . . ."

Just as the negroes who remained of the Vencedora had entirely re-

3. Sick Slaves

covered their wonted health and vigour, and were fit to be sent to one of our colonies, H.M.S. Dolphin, on the 15th of November, 1843, brought into harbour a full slaver, which she had captured a day or two before, a little to the northward of Rio. The crew of the slaver had actually run her ashore, and had begun to throw the negroes overboard into the sea, in order that they might be induced to swim for the land, when the boats of the Dolphin came up and obliged them to stop and effect their own escape.

This vessel is the largest I have yet seen employed in this traffic, and is better fitted and found than the common run of slavers; she is American built, and several of her fittings bear the name of American tradesmen. But, as usual, the Africans benefit nothing from the greater size of the vessel. The additional room has not been devoted to give increased accommodation, but to carry a greater number from the coast. The hold, instead of being fitted with one slave-deck, has two; so that, in fact, the negroes have been as badly off, if not worse, than they would have been in a smaller vessel.

On attempting to go down into the hold, and satisfy myself with an examination before the Africans were removed, I was forced, after one or two unsuccessful attempts, to give it up;—the effluvium was perfectly overwhelming, and the heat so great, that the moment I left the square of the hatchway, the sensation approached suffocation. . . . The decks furnish a melancholy spectacle of disease and wretchedness; but the most prominent and widely-spread scourge is purulent ophthalmia. Numbers of poor creatures are squatting down in corners or groping about the deck, deprived of all sight. Their immensely swollen eyelids, contrasting with their haggard and wasted features, and the discharge which keeps constantly trickling down their cheeks, and which they have not even a rag to wipe away, gives them an appearance of ghastly murky misery which it is impossible for me to describe.

Many eyes, I am afraid, are irretrievably lost, and several poor wretches must remain forever totally blind. Dysentery, too, that fellest of all diseases in the negro race, is at work amongst them, and will doubtless commit fearful ravages. Five hundred and seventy-two Africans were found on board. What the number was at starting there is no means of ascertaining. One of the crew, a slave, who acted on board in the capacity of a cook, and who preferred being captured by Englishmen to escaping with his master, told me that many had died and were thrown overboard during the passage. The exact number taken on board, however, he could not tell. In all probability, it was not under seven hundred; but of course this is only mere conjecture. The cargo, he told me, was shipped at

Angola, and is composed of five distinct tribes, who converse in dialects differing entirely from each other. . . .

"21st Nov. The eyes of the negroes afflicted with the ophthalmia are beginning to take on a more favourable aspect generally. We have been highly delighted with the magical effects of the nitrate of silver in these cases. Under its influence, the profuse discharge is rapidly disappearing, and the numerous ulcers on the cornea assuming a healthier and healing appearance. Our hopes are considerable, that we shall not have many totally blind after all. Several eyes are irretrievably lost; but, thanks be to Heaven, this disaster has seldom visited both eyes in the same person.

"It is astonishing to witness the sagacity, if I may so call it, and fortitude with which the poor creatures submit, nay, press to be treated with the different remedies. Not only do they appear perfectly aware that their interest is consulted, and give no trouble, but exhort each other to stand firm while the necessary painful operations of scarifying and of touching the inflamed and ulcerated parts are performed. I could not help being struck, on more than one occasion, while a dingy group of some hundred and more surrounded me on the lower deck of the hulk, which had been hired for their accommodation, all waiting eagerly yet patiently to have their eyes attended to. Children not more than five or six years old will go down on their knees, and opening their swollen eyelids with their own fingers, will remain firm and unflinching whilst the pungent remedies are applied to their eyes."

But while the local affection was thus yielding to the remedies employed, dysentery, in spite of every effort and precaution, continued to spread. Unlike the acute complaint in the white man, in the negro its approach is insidious, and attended with so little pain, that its poor victims, ignorant of its nature, often do not complain until the most fatal lesions have taken place. Day after day fresh cases would present themselves, or be selected where the disease was suspected to exist; but it mattered comparatively little whether they were got early or late: the disease once established clung to the wasted bodies of the wretched sufferers. Apathetic, from exhaustion, to acute suffering, and with scarce any rallying powers of constitution left—and seldom indeed did it quit its hold until death closed the scene.

1.9. A British Clergyman's Impressions of the Valongo Slave Market in Rio de Janeiro (1828)

Most of the foreign travelers who wrote accounts of life in Brazil during the early decades of the nineteenth century devoted at least a few paragraphs to that intriguing commercial phenomenon, the Valongo slave market in Rio de Janeiro. One of the most valuable of these descriptions was written by Robert Walsh, a British clergyman who traveled widely in Brazil in 1828 and 1829 and wrote sympathetically and intelligently about many aspects of the nation's social life. Like many Europeans with little previous acquaintance with black Africans, Walsh revealed some underlying racist attitudes. However, his Christian humanism was also well developed, and so in this description of conditions in the Valongo market Walsh compassionately revealed the human dignity which the slaves maintained despite the hardships and humiliation that they were made to endure day after day in a new and hostile environment.

Source: Robert Walsh, *Notices of Brazil in 1828 and 1829*, 2 vols. (London: Frederick Westley and A. H. Davis, 1830), II, 323-328.

❧ The place where the great slave mart is held, is a long winding street called the Vallongo, which runs from the sea, at the northern extremity of the city. Almost evey house in this place is a large ware-room, where the slaves are deposited, and customers go to purchase. These ware-rooms stand at each side of the street, and the poor creatures are exposed for sale like any other commodity. When a customer comes in, they are turned up before him; such as he wishes are handled by the purchaser in different parts, exactly as I have seen butchers feeling a calf; and the whole examination is the mere animal capability, without the remotest inquiry as to the moral quality, which a man no more thinks of, than if he was buying a dog or mule. I have frequently seen Brazilian ladies at these sales. They go dressed, sit down, handle and examine their purchases, and bring them away with the most perfect indifference. I sometimes saw groups of well-dressed females here, shopping for slaves, exactly as I have seen English ladies amusing themselves at our bazaars.

There was no circumstance which struck me with more melancholy reflections than this market, which I felt a kind of morbid curiosity in seeing, as a man looks at objects which excite his strongest interests, while they shock his best feelings. The ware-rooms are spacious apartments, where sometimes three or four hundred slaves, of all ages and both sexes, are exhibited together. Round the room are benches on which the elder generally sit, and the middle is occupied by the younger, particularly females, who squat on the ground stowed close together, with their hands and chins resting on their knees. Their only covering is a small girdle of cross-barred cotton, tied round the waist.

The first time I passed through this street, I stood at the bars of the window looking through, when a cigano [gypsy] came and pressed me to enter. I was particularly attracted by a group of children, one of

4. New Africans Waiting to Be Sold

whom, a young girl, had something very pensive and engaging in her countenance. The cigano observing me look at her, whipped her up with a long rod, and bade her with a rough voice to come forward. It was quite affecting to see the poor timid shrinking child standing before me, in a state the most helpless and forlorn, that ever a being, endowed, like myself, with a reasonable mind and an immortal soul, could be reduced to. Some of these girls have remarkably sweet and engaging countenances. Notwithstanding their dusky hue, they look so modest, gentle and sensible, that you could not for a moment hesitate to acknowledge, that they are endowed with a like feeling and a common nature with your own daughters. The seller was about to put the child into all the attitudes, and display her person in the same way, as he would a man; but I declined the exhibition, and she shrunk timidly back to her place, and seemed glad to hide herself in the group that surrounded her.

The men were generally less interesting objects than the women; their countenances and hues were very varied, according to the part of the African coast from which they came; some were soot black, having a certain ferocity of aspect that indicated strong and fierce passions, like men who were darkly brooding over some deep-felt wrongs, and meditating revenge. When any one was ordered, he came forward with a sullen indifference, threw his arms over his head, stamped with his feet, shouted to show the soundness of his lungs, ran up and down the room, and was treated exactly like a horse, put through his paces at a repository; and when done, he was whipped to his stall.

The heads of the slaves, both male and female, were generally half shaved; the hair being left only on the fore part. A few of the females had cotton handkerchiefs tied round their heads, which, with some little ornaments of native seeds or shells, gave them a very engaging appearance. A number, particularly the males, were affected with eruptions of a white scurf, which had a loathsome appearance, like a leprosy. It was considered, however, a wholesome effort of nature, to throw off the effects of the salt provisions used during the voyage; and, in fact, it resembles exactly a saline concretion.

Many of them were lying stretched on the bare boards; and among the rest, mothers with young children at their breasts, of which they seemed passionately fond. They were all doomed to remain on the spot, like sheep in a pen, till they were sold; they have no apartment to retire to, no bed to repose on, no covering to protect them; they sit naked all day, and lie naked all night, on the bare boards, or benches, where we saw them exhibited.

Among the objects that attracted my attention in this place were some young boys, who seemed to have formed a society together. I observed several times in passing by, that the same little group was collected near a barred window; they seemed very fond of each other, and their kindly feelings were never interrupted by peevishness; indeed, the temperament of a negro child is generally so sound, that he is not affected by those little morbid sensations, which are the frequent cause of crossness and ill-temper in our children. I do not remember, that I ever saw a young black fretful, or out of humour; certainly never displaying those ferocious fits of petty passion, in which the superior nature of infant whites indulges. I sometimes brought cakes and fruit in my pocket, and handed them in to the group. It was quite delightful to observe the generous and disinterested manner in which they distributed them. There was no scrambling with one another; no selfish reservation to themselves. The child to whom I happened to give them, took them so gently, looked so thankfully, and distributed them so generously, that I could not help thinking that God had compensated their dusky hue, by a more than usual human portion of amiable qualities.

TWO

"A Hell for Blacks": Slavery in Rural Brazil

FROM THE BEGINNINGS of Brazilian slavery early in the sixteenth century until its end in 1888, slaves were primarily employed in the production of agricultural products for export to Europe, Asia, Africa, or North America. Although brazilwood was the first important export product (even giving the nation its name), early in the colonial period European demand quickly placed the raising of sugar cane in the forefront of economic activity. This was the first important crop planted in the captaincies of São Vicente, Bahia, Pernambuco, and Rio de Janeiro in the sixteenth century, and the first to stimulate a serious importation of slaves from Africa. Soon joined by tobacco, cotton, cacao, and other agricultural products, sugar retained its great importance until modern times, employing hundreds of thousands of slaves on the great sugar plantations of the Northeast and other regions of the country over several centuries.

In the last decades of slavery, however, coffee achieved even greater importance than sugar cane. Planted in the northern captaincy of Pará in the early eighteenth century, by the advent of Brazilian independence in 1822, coffee was already becoming Brazil's most valuable export product, like sugar and the mining industry before it, stimulating an immense importation of Africans (and later Creole slaves from the Northeast and other regions), most destined for the major coffee-producing provinces of Rio de Janeiro, Minas Gerais, and São Paulo. Hundreds of thousands of Brazil's slaves worked as personal servants, miners, craftsmen, day laborers, and even as sailors and fishermen, but assignment to agricultural work was always an African's most likely fate. As late as 1872, for example, over 70 percent of the employed slaves in Brazil, over 812,000 people, were registered as agricultural workers.

The documents included in this section are intended to reveal how rural slaves lived, worked, and suffered, and why it was that they could not proliferate naturally on Brazilian soil as slaves did in North America. Aside from broader glimpses into the class structure and social relationships of rural society, there is information here about the African origins of plantation workers, their occupations, their food and how they acquired it, their housing, clothing, hygiene, family life, entertainment, and religious practices, their relationships with their masters and mistresses, the special roles of mulatto slaves, their punishments, discipline and time for rest, the status and plight of women and children, their diseases, medical treatment, and causes of death. Finally, these documents also reveal that plantation slavery was not always the same, but rather varied from place to place, depending upon local circumstances and the character of individual masters. As a whole, however, they leave little doubt that life in rural Brazil was indeed "a hell for blacks," even if it was not exactly, in the words of the first of these authors, "a paradise for mulattoes."

2.1. An Italian Jesuit Advises Sugar Planters on the Treatment of Their Slaves (1711)

Despite the great importance of sugar to the history of colonial Brazil, few accounts of slave conditions on colonial sugar plantations exist. Among those that do is the following excerpt from an eighteenth-century analysis of Brazil's sugar, tobacco, gold, and cattle industries which was published in Lisbon in 1711 by João Antônio Andreoni, a Jesuit father who employed the pseudonym André João Antonil. Writing as a Catholic clergyman, Andreoni revealed concern for the spiritual life of the slaves as well as their treatment at the hands of their owners. Thus his account contains his views on the religious training of slaves, their marriages or lack of them, their family life, food, clothing, recreation, and punishments. Andreoni was also a practical man, however, and his essay was in fact a series of suggestions to sugar planters on the management of their workers. Thus it also includes businesslike advice on the African origins of slaves, their alleged attributes, weaknesses, qualifications for plantation occupations, and practical advice on master-slave relationships. Andreoni's generalizations on the various racial groups in Brazil, especially the mulattoes, undoubtedly echo the beliefs and attitudes of many of his white contemporaries.

Source: André João Antonil, *Cultura e opulência do Brasil por suas drogas e minas* (São Paulo: Companhia Melhoramentos, 1922), pp. 91-97.

How the Sugar-Mill Owner Ought to Treat His Slaves

The slaves are the hands and the feet of the sugar-mill owner [*senhor de engenho*], because without them it is not possible in Brazil to set up, maintain, and develop a plantation, nor to have a functioning mill. And whether they are available for labor in good condition or not depends on how they are treated. To maintain permanent service, it is necessary to purchase some pieces [peças] each year and to distribute them over the property: some to the mill, others to field work, woodcutting, and boat service. And since they are usually of various nations and some are ruder than others and of different physical development, this sorting out of personnel ought to be done carefully and not blindly. Those who come to Brazil are of the Ardas [Adras or Dahomeans], Minas [persons said to have been shipped from São Jorge da Mina or Elmina, a Gold Coast port], and Congo nations. Others are from São Tomé, Angola, Cape Verde, and Mozambique, the latter arriving on ships from India. The Ardas and Minas slaves are robust, whereas those from Cape Verde and

São Tomé are weaker. Slaves from Angola who grow up in Luanda are more capable of learning mechanical trades than those from the other places mentioned. Among the Congos, there are also some who are rather industrious and useful not only for field service, but also for the various crafts and for household management.

Many reach Brazil in a very rude condition and quite unable to communicate, and so they remain for the rest of their lives. Others in a few years grow skillfull and learn to find their way about. They learn Christian doctrine and how to make the best of their situation: how to take command of a boat, for example, how to receive orders and to apply themselves in all the ways that are usually required of them. The women handle the scythe and the hoe, like the men, but only the male slaves make use of the axe to cut down the forests. Boilermen, carpenters, and caulkers are chosen from among the acculturated slaves, as well as the keepers of the vats, boatmen, and sailors, since these occupations require more careful attention. Newly arrived slaves who have been established on a plantation should not be sent elsewhere against their will, because they can easily succumb to grief and die. Those who are born in Brazil or are brought up from childhood in the home of the white people take on the qualities of their masters and turn themselves to good account; and any one of them is worth four new slaves.

Mulattoes serve even better in the various crafts. However, many of them take too much advantage of their masters' favors, and thus are proud and vicious, boast of their bravery, and are prone to insolent behavior. Nevertheless, they and the women of the same color usually have the greatest opportunities in Brazil, because with the blood of the whites flowing in their veins (the blood perhaps of their own masters), they charm them to the point that some masters will put up with anything they may do and pardon them every act; and it appears that, unless they are brave enough to correct them, these mulattoes can engage in every kind of pleasure and indulgence. And it is hard to decide whether the masters or the mistresses are more at fault in this regard. Whatever the case, there are some owners among both sexes who allow themselves to be dominated by mulattoes of the worst kind, so that we find confirmed the proverb which states that Brazil is a hell for blacks, purgatory for whites, and paradise for mulattoes of both sexes—except when, as a result of some suspicion or jealousy, love is transformed into hatred and armed with every type of brutality. It is useful to take advantage of the talents that the mulattoes possess, as some people do. However, no one ought to bestow as much as a hand upon them, for in that case they will take an arm, and will then transform themselves from slaves into masters. To liberate troublesome *mulatas* is obviously harmful, because the money that they pay to free themselves rarely comes from any source other than their own bodies, as a result of constant sins; and once they are liberated they continue to be the downfall of many people.

Some masters oppose marriage among their slaves, and not only are they not much bothered by their loose sex life, but they even clearly consent to it. In fact, they even initiate their irregular relationships, saying to them: "You, So-and-So, someday you will marry So-and-So," and from then on they are permitted to live together as though they were husband and wife. Masters claim that they do not arrange marriages among their slaves because they fear that once they have grown tired of the relationship they will murder each other with poisons or witchcraft, and there are some among them, in fact, who are well-known masters of this art. Other slaveholders, after arranging marriages for their slaves, separate them for years, so that they live in fact as if they were single, and masters cannot do this in good conscience. Others exercise so little care concerning their slaves' salvation that they keep them in the cane fields or in the mills for long periods of time without having them baptized. And among those who are baptized, many do not even know who their Creator is, what they ought to believe in, what law they should keep, how they should surrender themselves to God, why Christians go to church, why they adore the Church, what they should say to the priest when they kneel before him and he asks if they have a soul, or whether or not the soul dies, and where it goes when it leaves the body. What even the most recent arrivals learn, however, is the name and identity of their masters. And they know how many holes of manioc they must plant each day, how many bundles of sugar cane they must cut, how many loads of firewood they must collect, and other matters concerning their masters' service. And they also learn to ask his pardon when they make mistakes, to beg his mercy when he threatens them with punishment, and how to promise that they will better their ways. Their masters say that they are incapable of learning to confess, of asking God's pardon, of saying their beads, or of learning the Ten Commandments. All this is due to lack of education among the masters, and to their failure to think about the great reckoning regarding these questions which they must make with God. As St. Paul says, being Christians and failing to take care of their slaves, it will be worse for them than if they were infidels. Nor do they order them to attend mass on holy days; instead they keep them so busy that they have no time for mass. Nor do they order the chaplain to indoctrinate them, granting him if necessary a larger stipend for his efforts.

Concerning food, clothing, and moderate labor, these obviously should not be denied to them, because it is nothing more than right for a master to give his servants adequate food, medication when they are sick, and the means to cover themselves decently as their condition requires, so that they do not go about nearly naked in the streets. Work should also be kept to a reasonable amount so that it is not more than their strength can bear.

It is customary to say in Brazil that three "p's" are required for slaves, that is: *pão, páo*, and *pano* [bread, a stick, and a piece of cloth]. Even when they start out with the stick, which means, of course, punishment, they should also offer proof to God that their food and clothing are as abundant as their punishment often is. Slaves are often falsely accused, and punishment is often inflicted without much proof of guilt. And even when crimes are proved, the instruments they use to punish them with are too harsh, for they would not employ such devices against brute animals. Masters, in fact, sometimes give more care and attention to a single horse than they do to half a dozen slaves. The horse receives careful grooming; he has someone to bring him hay; he has a blanket when he perspires, a saddle, and a gilded bridle.

The new slaves should receive special care because, unlike those older slaves who plant their own gardens or acquire goods through their own efforts, new slaves lack ways to make their own living. It is not right that they should be noticed only when work is assigned, and that they should be forgotten when sick or when clothes are passed out. Sundays and holy days should belong to them, and when masters deprive them of those days and make them work as on ordinary days, they suffer greatly, and call down a thousand plagues upon them. Some masters customarily grant their slaves one day a week to plant food for themselves, sometimes ordering the overseer to accompany them so that they will not neglect this work. This is done so that they will not go hungry, or so that they will not go each day to their master's house to beg for a portion of manioc flour. Not to give them flour or a day to plant it, and to require that they work from sunup to sundown in the fields, and day and night in the mill with little rest—how can a master who treats them in this way be admitted to God's tribunal without suffering His retribution? If to deny alms to the needy person who requests it is to deny it to Christ Himself, as Our Lord Himself says in the Gospel, what shall we say about a person who denies food and clothing to his slave? And what account can he give of himself who bestows fine wool and silk and other splendid garments upon those women who are the cause of his downfall, and then denies four or five yards of cotton and a few yards of rough cloth to the person who sweats away his life in his service, and has only enough time left to himself to hunt a few roots or crabs for his food? And if in addition to all this their punishment is frequent and excessive, they will either run away into the forests or take their own lives by stopping their breath or hanging themselves, which they commonly do. Or they will try to take the life of the person who has brought so much evil upon them, resorting if necessary to the arts of the devil. Or they will cry out so loud to God that He will hear them, and will do to these masters what He did to the Egyptians when they subjected the Hebrews to such extraordinary toil, sending terrible plagues upon their plantations and upon their children, as we read in Holy Scripture. As He allowed the Hebrews to be taken captive into Babylonia as punishment for the harsh captivity that they imposed upon their slaves, in the same way might He allow some brutal enemy to carry these masters to their own country where they will experience the kind of wretched existence that they impose upon their slaves.

Not to punish the excesses that slaves commit would be most offensive. However, the charges against them must be looked into so that the innocent are not punished. Once their guilt has been established, they should be whipped moderately, or locked for a time in irons or in the stocks. But to punish with violence and a vengeful spirit, with one's own hand and with terrible instruments, and to go at these poor people with fire or hot wax, or to brand them on the face, would not be tolerated among barbarians, much less among Catholic Christians. Obviously if a master treats his slaves as a father would his children, giving them what they need for their sustenance and dress, and some respite from their labors, they will also respond generously to him. Aware as they are of their own guilt, they will not be so surprised when they receive the punishment they deserve, if it is administered with compassion and justice. If after they have made some mistake, as weak people are apt to do, they go voluntarily to their master to ask his pardon, or if they seek a protector to accompany them, it is the custom in Brazil in such cases to forgive them. They are aware that here at least they possess some advantage, because otherwise they might flee to some runaway settlement in the forest, and, if recaptured, might take their own lives before their master can whip them. Or some relative might take revenge upon them, using either witchcraft or poison. To totally deny them their amusements, their sole relief in their slavery, is to wish them miserable and melancholy, apathetic and sick in body. For this reason masters should not object when on a few days each year they appoint their kings and sing and dance decently for a few hours, or when they seek some honest pleasure in the afternoon after they have passed the morning celebrating the feasts of Our Lady of the Rosary, of St. Benedict, and of the patron saint of the plantation chapel. And these festivals should be without cost to the slaves, the master himself supporting the festival officials with his generosity, giving them some reward for their continuing efforts. Because if the men and women who organize the festivals have to spend their own money, this will cause much inconvenience and will be offensive to God, since they cannot lawfully accumulate much money of their own.

What ought to be particularly avoided on plantations is that the slaves intoxicate themselves with sour cane wine or brandy. Sweet wine, which does them no harm, is adequate, and this they can use to trade for flour, beans, sweet manioc, and potatoes.

If masters take the trouble to give leftovers from their tables to their slaves' small children, this will be enough to make them serve with good will, and to take pleasure in increasing the number of slaves, both male and female. Otherwise slave women deliberately attempt to abort themselves so that the children inside their bodies will not be made to suffer what they have suffered.

2.2. A Royal Decree on the Feeding of Slaves and Their Days Off (1701)

There is a large body of evidence that indicates that many plantation owners customarily gave their slaves no food, but instead granted them one day in the week, usually Sunday, free from plantation labor so that they might plant and cultivate their own. (See, for example, Document 4.1, Paragraphs 377ff.) The worst effects of such a policy, of course, were malnutrition and an almost total absence of free time, and, in the minds of some government and Church leaders, the inability of the slaves to attend religious services and to keep the Sabbath holy. The following decree of King Pedro II (the original is in the Arquivo Público da Bahia) shows that Portuguese authorities sometimes tried to stop this common abuse for both religious and humanitarian reasons.

Source: Carlos B. Ott, *Formação e evolução étnica da cidade do Salvador*, 2 vols. (Bahia: Tipografia Manú, 1955, 1957), II, 95-96.

❧ To Dom João de Lencastro, Friend. I the King send you greetings. Having consulted with my Overseas Council concerning the suggestion of the Council of Missions that the sugar-mill owners give Saturday free to their slaves for the cultivation of their gardens, Sundays and saints' days thus being unencumbered so that they might take part in Christian doctrine and divine services, and recognizing that this matter is of the greatest importance and that every effort ought to be made to remedy it, because the slaves being obliged as they are to serve their masters, the masters are also obliged to give them the necessary sustenance so that they will not die. I have therefore decided to order you to force the mill owners either to give their slaves the required sustenance, or a free day in the [work] week, so that they can themselves cultivate the ground, in the event that mill owners should choose this alternative. Written in Lisbon on January 31, 1701. THE KING

2.3. "I Doubt that the Moors Are So Cruel to Their Slaves": The Feeding of Slaves in Late Colonial Bahia

The following except from a personal letter written in late eighteenth-century Salvador da Bahia by a careful observer of regional life indicates that the royal decree of 1701 intended to assure adequate provisioning for plantation slaves (see previous document) was no longer seriously enforced by that period. In fact, there is no reason to doubt that the brutal neglect, punishment, and mismanagement here described were commonplace during much of the long history of Brazilian plantation slavery.

Source: Luis dos Santos Vilhena, *Recopilação de noticias soterpolitanas e brasilicas contidas em XX cartas que da cidade do Salvador, Bahia de Todos os Santos, escreve hum a outro amigo em Lisboa* (Salvador: Imprensa Official do Estado, 1921-1922), II, 187-189.

❧ Aside from the agricultural methods and the treatment of cattle which I have referred to, it is only just and charitable that I say something about the barbaric, cruel, and bizarre way that the majority of masters treat their unfortunate working slaves.

There are some who provide them with no food at all, merely allowing them to work on Sundays or on a holy day on a tiny plot of ground called a "*roça*." From this work they are supposed to supply themselves with food during the entire week, their masters contributing only a drop of molasses of the worst kind during milling time. If it is discovered that one of these miserable people has stolen something from him, the master has him tied to a wagon, and, bound in this way, he is given at least two hundred strokes on the buttocks with a whip of two or three strands of coarse twisted leather, which amounts in reality to four hundred or six hundred individual blows. If their injuries bleed adequately, they have them washed with salt and vinegar to prevent gangrene, and some

mix in Indian peppers to prevent infections, and if some swelling remains they order the wounds lanced, after which they are washed in the manner stated above.

—I doubt that the Moors are so cruel to their slaves.

There are others who give them Saturday to work for themselves under the same conditions. They get no other day, but receive a quart of manioc flour and three and a half pounds of dried and salted beef to sustain themselves for ten days. Others, however, who are more humane, give them this ration as well as one free day each week. There are others, finally, and these are the poorest and least ridiculous, who supply their slaves with food in a humane, charitable, and Christian fashion.

The work of these unhappy slaves consists of digging up their little plot of land and planting manioc and some other kind of vegetable that the land can support. And despite the irregular nature of this work, they might profit from it if they were not cursed with so many enemies. In the first place, their own companions rob them, starved and indolent as they are. The many head of cattle who normally wander over the fields and fallow lands break down the slaves' flimsy fences and eat and destroy their crops. Then there are the many wild animals, notably a species of wild pig called *caitelú*, and a very destructive ant which in a single night can cut down and destroy everything they grow.

The lack of economic management on the part of the masters is the main cause of these misfortunes, not only for the slaves, but for the masters themselves, who quickly lose their workers, consumed as they are by work, hunger, and punishment.

What an improvement there would be if the owners of these rural properties were compelled by law to select some land from among their superabundant holdings, were made to have these lands cleared and tilled, according to their customs, and were forced to destroy the ant hills with which they are normally plagued, their tenants also being compelled to kill and drive away those ingenious insects. All these lands should then be enclosed by high, sturdy fences to keep the cattle out. The greater part of such tracts of land could be planted in manioc, with some also in rice, which in the right kind of soil and with the right kind of weather, produces a fine crop. Between the manioc plants or in a separate place *aipins*, a kind of sweet manioc excellent when boiled or roasted, might be grown, along with yams, potatoes, millet, sesame, gourds, and other vegetables. Finally, large and flourishing banana groves should be planted and given the greatest amount of care, since on this continent and neighboring islands the banana provides a sure form of security for the poor.

2.4. The Masters and the Slaves: A Frenchman's Account of Society in Rural Pernambuco Early in the Nineteenth Century

The following analysis of Pernambucan rural society, written by a French cotton buyer, L. F. de Tollenare, who lived in Brazil from 1816 until 1818, contains portraits of the richest masters and the poorest slaves, as well as intermediate classes. Of special interest are the author's descriptions of the housing, food, and clothing of the several groups, his analyses of the interrelationships of those classes and their economy, and his comments on the roles of women in rural life. Tollenare's "Sunday notes," which were written in both Bahia and Pernambuco, remained unpublished until translated into Portuguese by Alfredo de Carvalho and printed in two parts early in this century. This translation was done from Carvalho's Portuguese version.

Source: L. F. de Tollenare, *Notas dominicaes tomadas durante uma residencia em Portugal e no Brasil nos annos de 1816, 1817 e 1818. Parte relativa a Pernambuco* (Recife: Empreza do *Jornal do Recife*, 1905), pp. 78-87, 93-96.

I will divide the inhabitants of these regions into three classes (I am not speaking of the slaves, who are nothing but cattle). These three classes are:

1. The owners of sugar mills [*senhores de engenho*], the great landowners.
2. The *lavradores*, a type of tenant farmer.
3. The *moradores*, squatters or small cultivators.

The sugar-mill owners are those who early received land grants from the crown, by donation or transfer. These subdivided grants constitute considerable properties even today, as can be seen from the expanses of 7,000 and 10,000 acres of which I spoke earlier; the crown does not have more lands to grant; foreigners should be made aware of this.

There are some sugar-mill owners who interest themselves in the theoretical aspects of agriculture and who make some effort to improve the methods of cultivation and production. I was conscious of their existence, at least, because of the derision of which they were the object. I visited six mills and encountered few notable men.

With bare legs, clad in a shirt and drawers or a dressing gown of printed calico, the sugar-mill owner, armed with a whip and visiting the dependencies of his estate, is a king who has only animals about

5. Slaves Working at a Sugar Mill

him: his blacks; his squatters or *moradores*, slaves whom he mistreats; and some hostile vassals who are his tenants or *lavradores*.

The great distances and lack of security on the roads do not encourage contacts with neighbors. Not even in the church are there opportunities to meet, because each mill either has its own chapel, or, what is more  frequently the case, there isn't any church and no religious worship is carried on at all. The Portuguese government, which requires that a chaplain sail aboard merchant ships, would perhaps promote the progress of civilization by ordering that a priest be maintained at mills which have a certain number of blacks.

When a sugar-mill owner visits another one, the ladies do not make their appearance. I spent two days in the house of one of them, a very charming man who overwhelmed me with kindness, and I did not see his family either in the living room or at the dinner table. On a different occasion I arrived unexpectedly after supper at the house of another of them, the splendor of which promised better taste; I noticed on the floor a piece of embroidery which seemed to have been tossed there suddenly. I asked for a glass of water in order to have a chance to go into the next room, but they made me wait for a long time. The lady of the house prepared a choice meal, but I did not see her. Furthermore, the same thing happened to me in a country house near Recife that belonged to a native of Lisbon.

In these houses, where the owners reside for the whole year, one does not observe anything fashioned to make them comfortable; one does not even find the avenue which among [the French] adorn both the simple property and the sumptuous chateau, neither parks, nor gardens, nor walks, nor pavillions. Living in the midst of forests, the inhabitants seem to fear shadows; or, more precisely stated, up to the edge of the forest around the mill everything is denuded and scorched to a distance of a quarter of a league. I witnessed at Salgado [a sugar plantation near the town of Cabo] the cutting down for firewood of orange groves which the previous owner had planted near the house, either for his pleasure or his profit.

Generally the residences are elevated on pillars; the cellar serves as a stable or as a dwelling place for the blacks; a long stairway provides access to the main floor, and it is on this level, or terrace, where one can enjoy the cool air. The rooms do not have ceilings; instead the timber-work of the roof is exposed and, between its extremities and the walls that hold it up, there is a free space of five inches to increase the air currents. The interior divisions are made with simple lath partitions measuring nine to ten feet in height, so that all the rooms have the roof as a common ceiling.

Luxury consists of a great variety of silverware. When a foreigner is entertained, in order to wash himself he is given splendid vessels made of this metal, of which also the coffee trays used at table, the bridles and stirrups for the horses, and knife hilts are made. Some sugar-mill owners showed me luxurious and expensive English firearms, and I also saw porcelain tea sets from England of the most beautiful type.

I ought to say a few words about meals. Supper consists of an abundant and thick soup, in which garlic abounds, or some other plant of a very pronounced and disagreeable taste which I did not recognize. The first plate is boiled meat which is not very succulent, the tastelessness of which they try to conceal with bacon, which is always a little rancid, and with manioc flour, which each serves himself with his fingers. For a second plate they serve a chicken ragout and rice with pepper. Bread is not seen, although it is much appreciated; they could manufacture it from foreign flour, which Recife is well supplied with, but it is not the custom. The black men or mulatto women (I saw many of the latter serving at table) fill the glasses with wine as soon as they are emptied, but people do not persist in drinking; liqueurs are not served with dessert. . . .

The sugar-mill owners are the only landholders. The only exceptions I know of are some chapels erected 100 or 150 years ago by the piety of the Portuguese and endowed with 50 to 60 uncultivated acres. . . . The extension of the lands owned by the mills is therefore immense, and the capital invested in them is much less considerable than it was in the French [Caribbean] islands. Only the most important establishments have 140 to 150 blacks. One could estimate the importance of the mills by the number of slaves, if it were not for the existence of the *lavradores*.

The *lavradores* are tenants without leases. They plant cane, but do not own mills. They send the harvested cane to the mill that they are dependent upon, where it is transformed into sugar. Half of it belongs to the *lavrador* and half to the sugar-mill owner. The latter keeps the molasses, but furnishes the cases for the sugar. Each one pays his tithe separately. The *lavradores* normally possess from six to ten blacks and themselves wield the hoe. They are Brazilians of European descent, little mixed with mulattoes. I counted from two to three *lavradores* per mill.

This class is truly worthy of interest since it possesses some capital and performs some labor. Nevertheless, the law protects it less than it does the mill owners. Since they do not make contracts, once a piece of land becomes productive, the mill owner has the right to expel them without paying compensation. It should be recognized that leases of only a year are not very favorable to agriculture. The *lavrador* builds only a miserable hut, does not try to improve the soil, and makes only temporary fences, because from one year to the next he can be expelled, and then all his labor is lost. He invests his capital in slaves and cattle, which he can always take with him. . . .

If I estimate an average of eight blacks for each *lavrador*, and sugar production at fifty *arrobas* per slave, which is not too much considering the vigilance and labor of the master himself, I can calculate the annual income of each *lavrador* at four hundred *arrobas* of sugar [about 12,800 pounds], which six or seven years ago was sold for about 3,000 francs. Now, this income is clear, since the *lavrador* does not buy anything at all to feed his blacks, and he lives very frugally from the manioc he plants.

Therefore, this class of capitalists, if favored by the government, is destined some day to exercise a major role in the political economy of Brazil. Consider the influence that they would have if the govenment would guarantee leases for nine years, and especially if an agrarian law were adopted that would obligate the present owners to make concessions, at stipulated prices, of certain parts of their uncultivated lands to anyone who might wish to buy them. Yet today everything remains exactly the opposite. I was witness to a rich mill owner's expulsion from his property of *all* the *lavradores* and squatters whom his less wealthy predecessors had allowed to establish themselves there. The number of exiles reached almost 600 persons, the property measuring two square leagues in size [about thirty square miles]. . . .

The *lavradores* are quite proud to receive on a basis of equality the foreigner who comes to visit them. Under the pretext of seeking shelter, I entered the houses of several to speak with them. The women disappeared as in the homes of ladies, though I was always offered sweets. I never managed to get them to accept the little presents of cheap jewelry which I had supplied myself with for the trip. This noble pride caused me to respect the hard-working *lavradores*, a class intermediate between the haughty mill owner and the lazy, subservient, and humble squatter. The *lavrador* has a miserable house, for the reasons I have already mentioned. However, when he abandons the hoe to go to Serinhaem [a nearby town] or to church, he dresses himself up like a city man, rides a good horse, and has stirrups and spurs made of silver.

The *moradores* or squatters are small settlers to whom the sugar-mill owners grant permission to erect a hut in the middle of the forest and to farm a small piece of land. The rent they pay is very small, worth at the most a tenth part of their gross product, without an obligation to pay the royal tithe. Like the *lavradores*, they do not have a contract, and the master can send them away whenever he wishes. As a general rule they are mixtures of mulattoes, free blacks, and Indians, but Indians and pure blacks are rarely encountered among them. This free class comprises the true Brazilian population, an impoverished people because they perform little labor. It would seem logical that from this class a number of salaried workers would emerge, but this does not happen. The squatter refuses work, he plants a little manioc, and lives in idleness. His wife has a small income because, if the manioc crop is good, she can sell a bit of it and buy some clothing. This comprises their entire expense, because their furniture consists of only a few mats and clay pots. Not even a manioc scraper is found in all their houses.

The squatters live isolated, far from civil and religious authority, without comprehending, so to speak, the value of property. They replaced the Brazilian savages but have less value, since the latter at least had some political and national affiliation. The squatters know only their surroundings, and look upon all outsiders practically as enemies. The sugar-mill owners court their women for their pleasure; they flatter them greatly, but from these seductions acts of vengeance as well as stabbings result. Generally speaking, this class is hated and feared. Because they pay them little or badly and often rob them, the sugar-mill owners who have the right to dismiss the squatters fear taking this dangerous step in a country that lacks police. Assassinations are common, but do not result in any pursuit whatsoever. I knew a certain mill owner who did not travel alone a quarter of a league from his house, because of the hostility and treachery of his squatters. He had incurred their wrath, and I had similar reasons to fear them when I entered their huts. . . .

I promised to make a quick survey of the black population. I am not in possession, however, of enough information about the laws that govern them to be able to deal with the matter adequately. Here is what I can say at the moment in respect to them.

The Salgrado mill contains about 130 to 140 slaves, including those of all ages, but there is no written list of them. Deducting the children, the sick, and the people employed in domestic service and in the infirmary, there remain only about a hundred people who are fit for agricultural labor. During the four or five months that the sugar harvest lasts, the toil of the mill blacks is most violent; they alternate so as to be able to stay on their feet for eighteen hours. I said earlier that they received for food a pound of manioc flour and seven ounces of meat. Here it is distributed already cooked. There are few properties on which slaves are allowed to plant something for themselves. Passing through the forests I sometimes came upon small clearings where the blacks had come secretly to plant a little manioc. These were certainly not the lazy ones. Nevertheless, Gonçalo [a slave] told me not to speak about it to their master, because this could expose them to punishment.

Upon arrival from Africa, the blacks who have not been baptized in Angola, Mozambique, or another place where there are Portuguese governors, receive baptism upon disembarking; this is nothing but a pointless formality, because they are not given any instruction whatsoever. At certain mills I saw the blacks being married by the priest, but in others they are united only by their whims or inclinations. In either case the master may sell separately the husband and the wife and the children to another buyer, regardless of how young they may be. A black baby is worth 200 francs at birth. Some masters make their slaves hear mass, but others save the cost of a chaplain, claiming that the sacrifice of the mass is a matter too grand for such people. Finally, there are mill owners who are more or less formalistic in matters of religion, and more or less able to appreciate its influence upon the conduct and habits of their slaves. It seems to me that it is in the interest of the masters to maintain family ties.

At the Salgado mill I saw only good slave quarters; everywhere, for that matter, they are of stone and lime and well roofed. Those of Salgado are ten feet wide and fifteen feet in depth, with a small interior division forming almost two rooms. It has a door which can be locked with a key, and a round opening toward the field to provide ventilation. The brick floor is two feet above the level of the adjacent ground, which makes such houses much more healthful than those of many French peasants. Each black is supposed to have his own private room, but love and friendship generally prevent them from living alone.

A mat, a clay cup or a gourd, sometimes a few claypots, and some tatters and rags make up the furnishings of the home of a black couple. All have permission to light a fire in their rooms and they take advantage of it. Their food is furnished to them already prepared, so that they have no need to cook. However, the fire is a distraction for them and serves for preparing fish or other food which they manage to acquire, lawfully or not. I observed that they were very careful to lock their doors and that when they were barred inside their houses they opened them with great reluctance. Although I was rather friendly with them in Salgado, I had some difficulty in satisfying my curiosity regarding the interior of their huts. I also saw some of the latter that were made of mud and covered with cocoa leaves. . . .

The black women generally have a flexible and elegant figure, the shoulders and arms very well formed. Many are seen who could qualify as pretty women if their necks were longer, giving more freedom to their heads. Their breasts are firm and fleshy, and they seem to understand their value, proving themselves very wise by concealing them, since this, in fact, is the way they commit terrible sins. It is unusual to see a black woman, even seventeen or eighteen years of age, whose neck has retained the shape which we prize so much and which European art imitates more or less badly. Nevertheless, they are not without a certain ability to hide its flaccidness [goiter?] with a piece of blue or red cloth. They tie these under their armpits, arrange the draping nicely over their waists and thighs, and make a large knot over the bosom, which hides the deformity I have just mentioned. The shoulders remain naked and the knees nearly uncovered, the scantiness of the cloth, which is made even tinier because of the part reserved for creating the knot, betraying all the body's movements, and I must say that they are all attractive and very graceful. . . . Their legs are normal, but their feet are damaged by hard work and the lack of footwear. They habitually have their heads uncovered, though some are given round hats which are not very becoming to them. They are happy when they can adorn themselves with a necklace or some bits of jewelry. Many of them, lacking such ornaments, attach a feather or a small round stick of wood to their ears. A tobacco pipe a foot long is usually thrust through the knotted cloth over the breast, and there it figures majestically like the dagger belonging to a leading lady of the theater.

This is the portrait of the black women who fix themselves up a bit. One sees others in a state of abandonment which is much less picturesque, dressed in a tattered shirt and an old petticoat which leaves the part beneath the breasts uncovered. Always, however, when they wrap their bodies or heads with a piece of cloth, the result is quite agreeable. . . .

The men have a better appearance when they are naked than the women, because of the flabbiness of the breasts that disfigures the latter. They are less robust than our porters, but the habit of going about without clothing makes their movements less wooden. What they possess that is better are their arched chests and their sinewy thighs. It is rare to see gray and wrinkled persons among them. Their black, shiny-smooth skin, destitute of hair, allows one to observe the entire play of their very active muscles. The arms and especially the legs are usually weak, but I saw some blacks with Apollo-like physiques.

Those coming from Africa have their shoulders, arms, and chests covered with symmetrical marks, which seem to be made with a hot iron, and the women also display these marks. For clothing the men are given a shirt and some breeches, but these garments evidently make them uncomfortable, and few preserve them, particularly the shirts. Most of the time they are satisfied with tying a rope around their loins from which hangs, both in front and behind, a small piece of cloth with which they try to hide that which modesty does not permit them to display.

The children also get clothing, but they make quick work of it so that they can go about naked. When they reach fourteen or fifteen years of age they are beaten with switches to make them more careful. At that time some are seen wearing their shirts hung over one shoulder in the fashion of Roman patricians, and, seen thus, they are reminiscent of Greek statues.

The blacks employed in domestic service, or close to their masters, dress with less elegance and more in the European manner. They take care of their breeches and shirts and sometimes even possess a waistcoat. Gonçalo had an embroidered shirt, and when he wore his lace hat and small trinkets which I had given him his pride was greater than that of any dandy; but when we went out hunting, his greatest pleasure was to leave at home both his necessary and unnecessary items of clothing.

2.5. "The African Man Transformed into the American Beast": Slavery in Rural Pernambuco in the 1840's

The kind of treatment slaves received in rural areas was dependent in part upon local economic, social, and cultural conditions, including especially the kinds of products slaves produced, and the relative prosperity, stagnation, or decline of the areas where slaves lived and worked. Obviously, too, the personal character of masters and overseers was an important determinant of the amount of hardship and suffering that slaves endured, or of how much they might be allowed to soften their condition through pleasurable activities and relationships.

The following accounts of slavery in Pernambuco were contained in two separate reports by H. Augustus Cowper, British Consul in Recife, to the Earl of Aberdeen. Written in the mid-1840s, they were the result of Cowper's long journeys of investigation through several regions of the province and of many visits to sugar *engenhos* and cattle and cotton estates in the interior. A conscientious observer like Tollenare before him, Cowper confessed that some of his preconceived ideas about slavery were altered by personal observation. Slavery was not everywhere the same, he learned, even in a single province. In his travels he encountered an intelligent patriarch as well as sinister brutes, the harsh reality of the sugar estates and milder, even easygoing forms of slavery in the backland regions of Pernambuco.

Sources: *Class B. Correspondence with Spain, Portugal, Brazil, etc. Relative to the Slave Trade, 1843* (London, 1844), pp. 363-369; *Class B. Correspondence on the Slave Trade with Foreign Powers, Parties to Treaties, under Which Captured Vessels Are to Be Tried by Mixed Commissions. From January 1 to December 31, 1846* (London, 1847), pp. 290-292.

Dispatch of August 4, 1843

Of the 13 *engenhos* which I visited, the 4 last, Agoa Fria, Trapiche, Anjo, and Jaceru, belonging to Colonel Gaspar de Menezes Vasconcellos Drummond, afforded me the greatest interest, and, as regards the state of the slaves, may be looked upon as the locality where they are treated with the greatest humanity in the province. The proprietor of this noble property, situated within a ring fence, and bounded by two navigable rivers, the Seringhaem and Formosa, is one of the most interesting and remarkable men with whom I have had the good fortune to meet in Brazil, and I should not flatter him, indeed, if I added, in any country; he is anciently descended from a noble Scotch family, of which he is extremely proud, and the Vasconcellos rank amongst the first families of this empire; his brothers have been for many years employed in Europe, in the diplomatic service of Brazil, and he himself in its army until 8 years past, when he purchased his *engenhos*, without having visited Europe.

Colonel Drummond, possessing natural talents of the highest order, has employed them in the acquirement of knowledge of the most varied description; his physical powers are perfectly astonishing, and his habits offer the most striking contrast to the general indolence of the people. He is probably 50 years of age, slightly made, with nothing very remarkable in his appearance than an eye of astonishing brilliancy; he often rises at daybreak, mounts his horse, superintends the labours of his people, and returns at night frequently without having tasted food. He tells me that after this he sometimes dictates 20 despatches to his secretary, which his official situation as delegate of the police obliges him to attend to. His estates are the best cultivated in the province; they extend 3 leagues along the coast from the embouchures of the Seringhaem to that of the Formosa, and 7 leagues inland. They produce 1,000 cases of sugar, besides *mandioca*, Indian corn, &c., and are worked by 400 slaves, and perhaps 50 freemen. Anjo and Trapiche have 6-horse-power steam engines, and Agoa Fria and Jaceru engines worked by water-power, all of English manufacture. His stills for the distillation of rum are also British; indeed, so strongly is Colonel Drummond attached to Great Britain, that he never admits the manufactures of other countries upon his estates.

The system by which he governs the slaves is peculiar; he has drawn up a code of laws avowedly upon the principles of the martial law; each slave that is purchased, or who arrives at a discretionary age, has this code explained to him, and by it alone can he be tried or punished for his offences. No overseer or administrator can punish a slave; he dare not even strike him, he must bring him before the Colonel, who reserves the judicial power entirely in his own hands; the men are mustered at daybreak, and answer "Prompto" [Ready] to their names; the women, "Senhor." If anyone is unwell, instead of replying he steps out; and the Colonel, who to his other qualifications, adds those of an excellent physician, examines him, and prescribes accordingly; the promptos then go to their work, taking their food with them, and do not return until 8 in the evening, when they are again mustered and dismissed. An interesting ceremony takes place at this time; the children, or as the Colonel calls them, his "Caçadores," [Huntsmen] are mustered with their calabashes of food in their hands, and not being under such severe discipline as their parents, pull the Colonel about, slap him, and play all sorts of tricks; at the word of command, "Agora," [Now] they draw up, the Colonel inquires, "Está servido?" [God is served?] "Sim, senhor," they scream together; "bom está com fome?" [are you good and hungry?]. "Sim, senhor,"—"Então via comer;" [then go and eat] and away they scamper as happy as if they were not slaves.

Colonel Drummond endeavours to prevent concubinage by marrying the girls off as they attain their 18th year; he does not force this upon them, but if they afterwards commit themselves, he sends them to the fields, which they naturally dislike, for the hoe is a dreadful instrument for a female to wield; he does not allow a woman to perform labour after the 5th month of her pregnancy, and she continues her light domestic occupations for 12 months after her child is born, that she may rear it. His domestic slaves are all females, and are never allowed to pass the threshold, but sit for 15 hours a day making clothes for the rest of the slaves.

The Senzala, or slave-building, at Trapiche, is a perfect picture of comfort and neatness; but I cannot speak so favourably of this portion of his other *engenhos*. Each slave is allowed 2 suits of clothes per annum and a blanket; their rations are served out once a week, consisting of dried beef from Ceará, and farinha [manioc flour]; the quantity, the military allowance to the soldiers of the line; they work 18 hours per diem during the crop-time, and 14 hours during the season of comparative rest.

I have been thus particular in describing Colonel Drummond, not only because his system with the slaves presents a pleasing contrast to that which I have to report, but because I foresee that, in the event of Her Majesty's Government requiring information or assistance in any project of Brazilian emancipation, Colonel Drummond might prove a most valuable auxiliary, partly from his fortunately strong Anglican prejudices, and from his influence, wealth, and talents. . . .

I have spoken of "irresponsible tyranny." I propose to offer to your

Lordship one or two examples of it, which may demonstrate how a slave may be ill-treated in Brazil, and with what absolute legal impunity the most barbarous and abominable crimes may be perpetrated at the *engenhos*. . . . However improbable some of these stories may appear to your Lordship, I cannot doubt them, as I have seen some of the poor creatures [who were mutilated by Colonel Antonio Francisco de Rego Barros of the Genipapo sugar estate]. He is most positively stated to have worked his slaves, women as well as men, 20 hours per diem; to have been in the constant habit of maiming them; and he is said to have actually killed upwards of 20 in his fury. If a woman offended him, his favourite punishment was the injection of pepper vinegar into the vagina, if a man, emasculation. He killed one man, a slave of course, who, suffering under acute syphilis, disturbed him by his groans, by cutting away his parts with a razor; and he is accused of burying several persons alive, some say one of his own children.

But the following story I had confirmed by the mother and sister of the victim: having formed a strong desire to possess a very pretty child, the daughter of one of his white tenants, he caused her to be stolen from her parents and brought to Genipapo; he kept her there under the same roof as his wife, who, of course, dared not complain, until she had borne him 2 children, when he either discovered her in an intrigue with a young man, who was upon a visit at the *engenho*, or he fancied her guilty. He called 2 of his slaves and ordered them to dig a grave, and to put the girl into it: they dragged her out, but overcome by her tears, allowed her to escape. Upon their return, probably answering their master evasively, he ordered them to go with him and show him the body: it is needless to add that he discovered the fraud which had been practiced upon him, and caused the poor fellows to be castrated.

It is often urged, my Lord, that masters will not injure their slaves from motives of interest: the preceding story is an example of how much stronger some of the passions are in a man's mind than self-interest, and I will mention one other instance, as it has occurred very recently.

Some months since the owner of the *engenho* Caga Fogo, was murdered, it was asserted, by a slave, who succeeded in escaping; the family used every exertion to apprehend him, and having expended Rs. 600 in these efforts, succeeded about a fortnight since. The present owner, Senhor Vieira, a man of notorious brutality, publicly invited his acquaintances to visit him last Sunday, for the purpose of seeing the man boiled alive in the sugar boiler of the estate; and although I cannot say that I have had this horror confirmed, the answer to all inquiries is, "if Vieira said so he will do it." The invitation was so public that the authorities had time for interference; they offered none. This man has also emasculated many of his blacks, which is a favourite punishment with some proprietors.

I have here presented to your Lordship the best and the worst features of praedial slavery as they exist in this province. I fear that if there are not many proprietors to be found so brutal as Antonio Francisco de Rego Barros, or Vieira, there are still less to be met with so humane as Colonel Drummond. Upon the whole, it would be absurd to deny that there is no protection afforded by the laws to these people. They are kept in a state of the darkest ignorance; they are baptized for form's sake, but are never instructed in religion, and, no doubt, actually worship the images of the saints, as probably resembling their African gods; their daughters are always debauched when quite children; and their wives (if they are allowed them) only protected by the loss of beauty, brought on by the thousand ills they suffer. They are overworked. Who can deny it? If a well-fed horse is used for one-fourth of the time per day, that our ill-fed fellow men are worked, he will become a skeleton; and yet these people are worked 18 hours a day!

It is most monstrous, my Lord, and scarcely explicable how nature can support itself; but I verily believe that the degradations to which slavery gives rise in the majority of men actually destroys their intellect, their reason, and levels them with the brutes, leaving nothing more to direct and guide their actions than general instinct. Power being thus withdrawn from their reasoning faculties, it falls into their physical, and enables them to support treatment the most degrading, and sufferings the most acute, which under any other circumstances would annihilate them. They are ill-fed: even those few who have sufficient in quantity, would die, they could not live long upon the unwholesome and continual salt beef or fish, which is their unchangeable diet, were it not that they rob the precious limited hours allowed them for sleep, to catch rats or crabs for food, or, perhaps worse, become in secret dirt eaters, and die the most horrible of deaths. They are ill-clothed; let us take the most favourable part of my report, Colonel Drummond's property, where they have 2 suits a year: for the men, a shirt and a pair of trousers; for the women, a shift and a frock. Can persons, constantly hard at work, keep themselves clean with such a wardrobe, and in such a climate? The air is infected by the smell of their bodies, which has erroneously been attributed by ignorant prejudice to the colour of their skin; whereas I have often met with filthy white men in the tropics, with precisely the same disgusting odour; and on the contrary, in Pará, where the blacks are remarkably clean, the "catinga," as this smell is called, is almost unknown. They are denied many of the privileges of beasts, who are at least allowed to tend their young; these men are not. The birds pair at will; these are prohibited, excepting at the will of a capricious master. They are not citizens; if they are denied natural and legal rights, it is not astonishing their political are withheld from them. In a word, my Lord, all the worst features of slavery exist in this province; the endeavour of the master is to suppress alike the intellect, the passions, and the senses of these poor creatures, and the laws aid them in transforming the African man into the American beast.

Dispatch of March 2, 1846

During the last two months I have carried into effect the intention expressed in my former reports of visiting the *Sertão*, or cotton and cattle districts, with a view of completing my reports upon the state of slavery in the province, from personal observation. I was accompanied by the French Consul, my colleague and intimate friend. We left [Recife] on the 21st of January, and passed through . . . numberless villages, reaching [the same city] once more on the 37th day of continued riding on horseback, having journeyed 305 leagues. . . .

I cannot avoid expressing to your Lordship my satisfaction that I determined upon undertaking this journey. I am confirmed in my determination never to adopt the dangerous course of offering information to Her Majesty's Government upon popular rumours or generally received opinions. . . . I am amply rewarded by being enabled to do justice to the kindest, most hospitable, and generous race of men that I ever met with. This applies equally to the upper and lower classes; the latter . . . were always ready to receive us; to share all they had with us; to show us all the attention which their means enabled them; and yet who never, under their trying and pitiable circumstances, purloined the most trifling thing which we possessed, and invariably refused the slightest remuneration for their trouble. They are also by far the finest race of men that I have seen in Brazil; . . . indeed they are always on horseback, and it is truly wonderful to see one of them in chase of cattle, at full gallop through the forests. . . . A people thus free themselves can scarcely be cruel to their slaves. Indeed at the Fazendas de Gado, or cattle estates, there exist very few, and those are employed in domestic services; at the Fazendas de Algodão, or cotton estates, there are more, but infinitely less than at the *engenhos*. There the most repulsive features of slavery are unknown; the Negroes are not overworked, and the women and children are employed separating the cotton from the seed, whilst the men turn the wheel of the machinery with which this is effected. Upon the whole I saw nothing revolting in the slavery of the Sertão, always excepting the fact of its existence.

2.6. Practical Advice on the Management of Plantation Slaves (1847)

Many Brazilian planters understood that the lives of many of their slaves were too short to yield them a profit, and that most plantation work forces did not grow by natural means. Nevertheless, even in the first half of the nineteenth century, when their labor needs were still supplied from Africa, they did not dispense with the customary wasteful methods of slave management which Andreoni deplored in the eighteenth century. (See Document 2.1.) All too often this meant excessive labor, inadequate nourishment, poor hygiene, and much physical brutality.

In 1847 Francisco Peixoto de Lacerda Werneck published a handbook intended to advise the planters of Rio de Janeiro province on the management of their estates. In the following selection from that work dealing with plantation slaves, the author pointed out some of the practices he had observed on the estates of fellow planters that reduced slave efficiency and shortened lives, suggesting other methods based in part upon operations on his own properties. Since Lacerda Werneck was himself a prominent coffee planter, since his handbook's purpose was to promote the fortunes of his fellow planters, and since it may be assumed that his own slaves enjoyed the "better" treatment that he recommended, this document constitutes a particularly believable inside look at plantation living conditions.

Source: Francisco Peixoto de Lacerda Werneck, *Memoria sobre a fundação e custeio de uma fazenda na provincia do Rio de Janeiro, sua administração e epocas em que se devem fazer as plantações, suas colheitas, etc., etc.* (Rio de Janeiro: Typographia Universal de Laemmert, 1847), pp. 16-18.

The slaves should have Sundays and saints' days free. They should hear mass if it is available on the plantation, should know Christian doctrine, and confess annually. This is a restraining and controlling influence, especially if the confessor knows how to comply with his duty, and earnestly warns them to act morally, to behave well and with blind obedience to their masters, and to those who manage them.

On Sunday morning they should put on newly washed clothes, and the dirty ones should be put in a lye solution on Monday morning, and rinsed on Tuesday. If it rains and the slaves get wet, they should actually change clothes and hang up the wet ones in their quarters to be worn the following day, when they go out to work, keeping a clean set of clothes in reserve.

The planter should reserve a small plot of land as nearby as possible where the blacks can plant their gardens. Let them plant their own coffee, maize, beans, bananas, potatoes, yams, sweet cassava, etc. However, the planter should not allow them to sell their products to anyone else, but only to himself, and he should pay them a reasonable price, to prevent them from going astray and carousing in the taverns.

This money should be used for their tobacco, to buy special foods, fine clothing for their wives, if they are married, and for their children. Drunkenness, however, should be severely prohibited, and they should be put into the stocks until they have sobered up, and then be punished with 20 to 50 lashes.

Their gardens and what they produce in them cause them to acquire a certain love of the country, distract them a bit from slavery, and delude them into believing that they have a small right to property. Surely the planter will enrich his own soul with some satisfaction when he sees his slaves coming from their gardens carrying their boxes of bananas, yams, sugar cane, etc. Extreme discomfort dries up their hearts, hardens them, and inclines them to evil. The master should be severe, but just and humane.

When they are sick they should be treated with care and humanity. Even if there is an attending physician, the master should make his inspection of the infirmary to cheer the sick and give them relief, watching out for any negligence that may exist.

Nor should it be said that the black man is always the enemy of the master. This occurs only under two extreme conditions: either excessive severity, or too much leniency. The smallest excess on the part of an otherwise easygoing master makes them irritable, and too much severity brings them to a state of desperation.

There are also masters who have the very bad habit of not punishing on time, and who threaten the slave, telling him: "Wait and see, you will pay all at once."—or: "You are filling the bucket, which will overflow, and then we will see!" And when he is ready, he lays hold of the poor black man, and gives him a blow which all too often sends him to eternity. And why? Because he paid *all at once!!!* This is barbaric. The black man should be punished when he commits the offense. The punishment should fit the crime. The slave who is well corrected and punctually punished does not forget. Treat your slave with honorable and impartial justice, and, despite his brutishness, he will not fail to acknowledge it.

Do not send a childbearing black woman to the fields for a period of one year. Occupy her with household chores such as washing clothes, sorting coffee, and other work. After she has nurtured her child she should then go to the fields, leaving her little one in the care of a general nurse, who should wash him, change his clothes and give him his meals.

The black fieldworker should eat three times a day. He should have breakfast at eight o'clock, lunch at one, and dinner from eight to nine. His food should be simple and healthful. In the uplands, generally, do not give him meat; he should eat beans, seasoned with salt and lard, and corn meal, which is a very substantial food. Manioc flour is weak and has little nutritional value. When by necessity I find myself forced to give them a constant diet of manioc flour mixed with beans, they begin to feel weak and melancholy, and they ask for corn meal; at such times the most I do is to give them one meal of manioc flour and beans, to two meals of corn flour.

Do not send your sick slave to work; if he has wounds, they should be completely healed before he returns to work. On some plantations I have seen blacks at work with large ulcers, and they even go into the fields unable to make full use of their limbs at the risk of dying or being permanently crippled. This practice, aside from being inhumane, is not in the interest of the owner.

Some time ago certain farmers adopted the custom of giving their slaves only two meals: breakfast at ten or eleven, and dinner at five in the afternoon. Such planters do not understand their own interests; [under such circumstances] their slaves can do far less work, and in addition their stomachs are ruined. How is it possible for a man or a woman (who is even weaker) to manage without food from five o'clock in the afternoon until ten or eleven the following day, performing rigorous labor with a hoe, scythe, or axe? They come to their food exhausted and then put too much food into their stomachs. They fall into a state of apathy, digestion becomes difficult, and soon they are sick. Instead of these two meals, I would suggest three, even if smaller: breakfast, lunch, and dinner, and at the hours suggested above. The digestive functions will be regularly established, and the slave will become more capable, more satisfied, and healthier, rather than weaker because of the lack of necessary food.

2.7. Slave Life on a Plantation in the Province of Rio de Janeiro in the Late Nineteenth Century

Written by the French wife of a Brazilian, this selection deals with a *fazenda* or plantation in the province of Rio de Janeiro which was owned by a friend of the author's husband. Here, too, the master ruled over his slaves in patriarchal fashion, but the latter were harshly punished, overworked, poorly housed, fed and clothed. In fact, this selection is of unusual value because of the detailed and accurate information it provides on the diet of plantation slaves and other aspects of their treatment.

Included is the author's description of a *batuco* (more commonly *batuque*), a dance of African origin which was normally accompanied by drums and other percussion instruments. Madame Toussaint-Samson's account of this brief celebration suggests the enormous importance of such activities to Brazilian slaves and the perhaps equally enormous fear that such events could arouse among the white rural master class.

Source: Adèle Toussaint-Samson, *A Parisian in Brazil* (Boston: James H. Earle, 1891), pp. 76-87, 93-97.

❧ After three hours of travel, we had arrived at the *fazenda* São Jozé. It was six o'clock in the evening, and the sun was beginning to set. Hardly had we stepped in when we were led to our rooms, where a bath *a la cachaça* (molasses brandy) was awaiting us, destined for regaining our strength. The *fazendeiro*, upon arriving, had completely changed face; his countenance, usually so amiable during the whole trip, had suddenly become severe and hard; he hardly said "How do you do" to a Frenchwoman who was his housekeeper, and scarcely answered the slaves of the plantation, who pressed around him to ask for his benediction or blessing. Our bath taken, the bell rang for dinner, and we then appeared in the dining-room, with its old, blackened walls, opening on an inner court, dirty enough. This room, long and narrow, had for furniture nothing but a large square table, around which wooden benches were arranged. On the table was seen traditional *feijoada* [a meal of black beans and meat often served with rice and rum], dishes filled with manioca, a large platter of rice, and two chickens, as well as bananas and oranges. This is about the usual Brazilian dinner to be found in the interior, where fresh meat is a rare thing.

Dinner over, the host called his *feitor* (foreman), an old negro called Ventura, whom I yet can see with his good face, honest and grave. He came escorted by two other large darkies, who were his aides; all three had for clothing nothing but a course linen shirt, worn over their trousers, made of sail cloth. Over their shoulders were thrown some sort of tatters, which, in by-gone days, might have been coats or overcoats. In one hand they rolled their hats of coarse straw, while the other was ornamented by a long, stout stick, and Ventura held the *chicote* (whip), insignia of his command. Besides, each one carried an immense cutlass (a kind of little sword), with which the slaves help themselves to cut sugar-cane, or make their way through the woods. They placed themselves, all three, standing before their master, in an angle of the room, which was scarcely lit up by two candles burning in glass panes placed on the large silver chandelier. This scene has remained present in my memory in its minutest details, for to a Parisienne it did not lack strangeness.

These are the questions which were set by the master, in a short and hard tone, and the answers of the slaves, pronounced in a humble and frightened manner:

"What has been planted this week?"

"Rice, senhor."

"Begun to cut the sugar-cane?"

"Yes, master; but the *rio*" (the river) "has overflowed, and we must repair the canals."

"Send twenty negroes over there tomorrow morning. What more?"

"Henrique has escaped."

"The *cachorro*" (the dog)! "Has he been caught?"

"Sim, senhor, he is in the *tronco*" (in irons).

"Give him twenty blows with the lash, and put the iron collar around his neck."

"Yes, senhor. A troop of *porcas do mato*" (wild boars) "are ravaging all the *batatas* plantations, and a jaguar has been seen yesterday near the torrent: we ought to have guns."

"You shall have three this evening. Is this all?"

"Yes, senhor."

"[The *engenho*] is to begin to work to-morrow; is it in condition?"

"Yes, senhor."

"Very well. Call the negroes now for prayer."

The master rang a heavy bell, then called in a formidable voice, "*Salta para a resa!*" (Hurry up for prayer.)

Night had almost come. Before the house, and all around it, ranged in circle, were the *senzalas* (negro cabins), to the number of seventy about.

At the master's call, one saw rising up out of the dusk these [sic] sort of phantoms; each one came out of their [sic] cabin, a sort of hut made of clay and mud with dried banana leaves for roofing, gloomy abode, where the water penetrates when it rains, where the wind blows from everywhere, and from where a most dreadful smoke arises at the hour when the negro gets his supper, for the cabin has neither chimney nor window, so that the fire is made with a fagot, oftentimes green, which is lighted in the centre of the cabin.

The negroes cross the meadow and ascend one by one the two flights of stairs to the veranda, where a sort of cupboard has been opened,

6. A Rural Slave Hut

forming an altar in one of the corners. Here it was that the miseries of slavery appeared to me in all their horror and hideousness. Negresses covered in rags, others half naked, having as covering only a handkerchief fastened behind their back and over their bosoms, which scarcely veiled their throats, and a calico skirt, through whose rents could be seen their poor, scraggy bodies; some negroes, with tawny and besotted looks, came and kneeled down on the marble slabs of the veranda. The majority carried on their shoulders the marks of scars which the lash had inflicted; several were affected with horrible maladies, such as elephantiasis, or leprosy. All this was dirty, repulsive, hideous. Fear or hate, that is what could be read on all these faces, which I never have seen smile.

Four candles were lighted, and the two subordinate overseers placed themselves on the steps of the altar, where the Christ appeared, in the centre of four vases. These two negroes officiated after their own fashion; they had retained a smattering of Latin, which a chaplain, formerly at the plantation, had taught them, and then added their own picturesquely, which served as a beginning to the litany of saints. After the *Kyrie eleison* they began to sing in unison, *Santa Maria, mai de Deos, ora pro nobis!* Then all the saints in paradise followed, to whom they thought fit to add this, *Santa Pé de canna, ora pro nobis!* (Holy Foot made of sugar-cane, pray for us!) Finally their singing ended with this heart-rending cry, which they all gave, prostrating themselves, their faces on the ground, *Miserere nobis!* This cry touched me to the inmost recesses of my heart, and tears streamed silently from my eyes, while, after the devotions, the negroes filed past us one by one in asking our benediction, to which each white person must reply, "I bless thee."

Prayers were held every Saturday evening. I could never listen to it without remaining profoundly impressed. The aspect of these miseries and these sufferings, and that cry of despair, which seemed to me to rise way up to God,—all this was striking, and of a horrible beauty, even from the artistic point of view.

The following day scenes not less sad awaited me. Having been awakened at four o'clock in the morning by the great bell in the veranda, which the *feitor* was ringing for the rising up of the negroes, I wished to witness these proceedings, and jumped out of my bed.

Day was scarcely dawning on the horizon, a soft and melancholy color was enveloping the landscape. From the summit of the mountain, in the rear of the *fazenda*, a beautiful cascade was unrolling its sheets of silvery water, and this mountain was covered with wild woods, where fruits and flowers interlaced each other in charming confusion.

From the other side, in front of the house, immense pastures could be seen, where more than a hundred head of cattle were collected. The oxen were still sleeping.

Some of the negroes began to come out of their cabins. If one of them was late in appearing, old Ventura would shake his big whip in crying out, "*O Patife! puxa para fora!* (O good-for-nothing, get out!)

Then three gangs, each of about twenty-five negroes and negresses, were formed: one was under the direction of Ventura, and took the way to the woods; the second proceeded to the plantations with one of the subordinate superintendents; and the third drove immense wagons with wheels of solid wood, yoked by four oxen, and was getting ready to cut the sugar-cane, which the wagons were to carry back. One of the little shepherds in his turn collected all the oxen, the second followed him with a flock of sheep; the field gates were opened, and all this human live stock started with the rest for work. . . .

The *moleque* (darky) who enjoys the best health at the fazenda is, without question, the *vaqueiro* (cow-keeper), because he does not forget himself, and milks the cows for his proper benefit far from the eye of the master. It has also happened sometimes that with four cows there would hardly be the necessary milk for the house, the negroes awarding themselves a little too much, and the cow-keeper would be punished; yet when one would see the food given these poor unfortunates, one could not blame them for trying to make up.

At nine o'clock the bell would ring again; it was rung for the negroes' breakfast, and I had the curiosity to be present at the distribution of the rations. There are always two cooks at a plantation,—one for the whites and one for the blacks—and there are even two kitchens. I repaired to the large smoky room which served for the darkies' kitchen, and there I saw two negresses having before them two immense caldrons, one of them containing *feijões* [beans] and the other *angú* (a dough made of manioca flour and boiling water). Each slave soon arrived, gourd in hand. The cook would pour in a large ladleful of *feijões*, adding a little piece of *carne secca* [dried or salted beef] of the poorest quality, as also a little manioca flour sprinkled over all; the other one distributed the *angú* to the old men and children. The poor slaves would leave with this, murmuring in a low tone that the meat was rotten, and that there was not enough.

Our dogs would certainly not have eaten such food. The little darkies of three or four years, entirely naked, were returning with their rations of *feijões*, which their delicate stomachs could hardly digest; also did they nearly all have large stomachs, enormous heads, and lank arms and legs,—in short, all the signs of the rickets. It caused pity to see them; and I never understood, from a speculative stand-point even, that these merchants of human flesh did not take better care of their merchandise. Happily I was assured that it was not thus everywhere, and that in several plantations the slaves were very well treated; for myself, I tell what I have seen. . . .

[On a later occasion while we were celebrating a religious holiday] we desired that the poor slaves should have their share in the day's festivities, and their master permitted us to treat them to a small keg of *cachaça*, authorizing them after this, at my request, to dance in the evening on the meadow.

The overseer then made the distribution of the *cachaça*, giving each one but a small glass at a time, and then the *batuco* (negro's dance, accompanied with the clapping of hands) began. I wish I could give my readers an idea of this strange scene and of this wild dance. Let me try.

Large fires had been lit in the middle of the meadow. A negro of high stature, formerly king in his native country, soon appeared, armed with a long white wand,—sign apparent, to them, of his command. His head was ornamented with feathers of all colors, and little bells were fastened around his legs. Every one bowed himself down before him with respect, while he gravely walked about, dressed in this manner, filled with a supreme majesty. Near the king stood the two musicians who were to lead the *batuco*; one carried a kind of immense calabash, which contained six or seven [more calabashes] of different sizes, over which were placed a very thin little board. With the aid of little sticks, which he maneuvered with great dexterity, the negro obtained dull sounds, the monotony of which seemed sooner to provoke sleep than anything else. The second musician, squatted on his heels, had before him a piece of the hollow trunk of a tree, over which a dried lambskin was stretched. He was beating in a melancholy way on this primitive drum to re-enforce the singing. Three or four groups of dancers soon came to place themselves in the centre of the circle, which was formed by all their companions. The negresses walked harmoniously, keeping time in waving their handkerchiefs and in giving themselves up to a most accentuated movement of the hips, while their dark partners were turning around them, skipping upon one foot with the most grotesque contortions, and the old musician was walking from one group to another, speaking and singing, while shaking his sticks with frenzy. He seemed, by his expressions, desirous of exciting them for the dance, while the assistants accompanied the *batuco* with clapping of hands, which accentuated the rhythm in a strange manner, and the king was promenading in a grave manner while shaking his bells.

The negroes were dripping, and yet the musicians did not cease running from one to the other and exciting them still more. The dance had arrived at such a degree of strange over-excitement, when suddenly calling was heard from the house: "*Feitor*, let all fires be extinguished, that all noise ceases, and that all the negroes return to their cabins!"

There was some murmuring among the poor slaves, but the overseer, armed with his whip and followed by his two assistants, soon restored order everywhere.

Not knowing to what to attribute this sudden disturbance in the festival, I hastily ascended to the house, where I found the proprietor perfectly pale, and having barricaded windows and doors around him. He seemed to me laboring under a certain excitement, whose cause I asked him.

He then told me that, while his comrades were dancing, a negro had entered the house, with drunken face, and vociferating threats against his master, who immediately had him laid hold of, but who had understood that if his negroes became more excited by the *cachaça* and their national dance, his life might be in danger.

These national dances excite to such a degree these poor slaves, that they have been prohibited to them in the city. In spite of all this, however, they take place. At the risk of being cruelly beaten, the negroes go at night, when the whites are asleep, to dance on the beach in the moonlight. They assemble in groups of the same nationality, either Congo or Mozambique, or Minas; then, in dancing and singing, they forget their ills and servitude, and only remember their native country and the time that they were free.

Sometimes it has happened to me, having need of the services of my *mucama* (lady's maid) in the night, to search for her in vain all over the house: she had gone to re-join her brethren at the dance. Our doors, however, had been carefully locked. Little did it concern her: she passed through the window.

2.8. A Medical Report on Slaves on Five Coffee Plantations in the Province of Rio de Janeiro (1853)

The following document is a brief but scientific study of five large plantation work forces in the province of Rio de Janeiro which stresses such matters as age and sex composition, diseases, and birth and mortality rates. Its author, Reinhold Teuscher, was a German doctor who for five years served as a resident plantation physician. His responsibilities included the care of some 900 slaves residing on five coffee plantations, all under the control of a single owner. His study, which took the form of a medical thesis based upon his own experiences as a rural doctor, was presented in 1853 to the Medical Faculty of Rio de Janeiro as a legal verification of his Jena University medical degree.

Teuscher's account is objective and intelligently presented, but his criticisms of black mothers for their alleged poor treatment of their children perhaps fails to take their hard circumstances adequately into account, as well as their powerlessness in the face of diseases for which they could hardly have known the latest scientific cures.

Source: Reinhold Teuscher, *Algumas observações sobre a estadistica sanitaria dos escravos em fazendas de café. These apresentada á Faculdade de Medicina do Rio de Janeiro e publicamente sustentada aos 22 de Julho de 1853* (Rio de Janeiro: Villeneuve e Comp., 1853), pp. 5-11.

❧ Brazil is large; the climate, the localities, the occupations, the life styles of the slaves quite different in the various places; therefore, even if my statistics have some value, they can only serve as a point of comparison for a very small part of the Brazilian territory. Nevertheless, I will give a succinct description of the localities, the living conditions of the slaves, and the quality and quantity of the work which weighs so heavily upon them.

The nine hundred slaves that I am concerned with are divided up among five plantations situated a few leagues northeast of the town of Cantagallo, in a rather mountainous part of the country, with steep hills, narrow valleys, and fast-moving waters, in which swamps are nowhere to be found. The elevation above sea level of Santa Rita is 800 spans, and the thermometer oscillates between 26° (in January and February) and 7° Reaumur (in June and July). . . .

The slaves live in well-built houses, constructed in part of stone and lime. All have tile roofs, are dry, and well aired. The slaves get up in the morning between four and five o'clock, and go to bed at night between eight and nine. They wear clothes of coarse cotton, and each one possesses a woolen jacket. The food is prepared in common, and is so abundant that each one can eat as much as he likes. At both breakfast and lunch their meals consist of corn flour boiled in water (*angú*), beans well mixed with bacon, and dried meat every other day. Their supper is corn flour porridge (*cangica*).

Of these slaves, not counting the children, hardly half are fully and constantly engaged in agricultural work; the rest are employed in construction, transport, and other services. The amount of work they perform can be calculated by observing that each one of them manages 5,000 to 6,000 coffee trees, producing annually, on the average, 100 *alqueires* [at 13 liters to an *alqueire*] of millet, eight of beans, seven of rice, and contributes toward the construction and preservation of roads and fences, along with other services.

The five plantations of which I speak are called Santa Rita, Boa Sorte, Boa Vista, Arêas, and Itaoca. Only the plantations of Santa Rita and Arêas have regular hospitals, with a white orderly in attendance, and furnished with all necessary supplies. The most gravely ill of the other plantations are sent to these hospitals, while the less serious illnesses are treated at home; only Itaoca sends all its sick to the hospital of Arêas. This is why I can present complete data only for the populations of Santa Rita and of Arêas with Itaoca.

Statistics on the ratio of births to deaths in a group of people assembled on the orders of their owner and for his sole benefit cannot, of course, be compared with statistics on groups of people whose composition, sex, and age are in perfect equilibrium. On most plantations, in fact, the number of women is greatly inferior to that of the men, which limits reproduction. These five plantations possess, thanks to their proprietor's sentiments of humanity, a larger slave population than most such establishments in this area. The plantation of Santa Rita possesses 160 men, 106 women, and 64 children (meaning Creoles under ten to twelve years of age). Boa Sorte has 66 men, 37 women, and 32 children; Boa Vista 76 men, 49 women, and 20 children; Arêas along with Itaoca 159 men, 101 women, and 55 children. The total: 925 souls.

Unfortunately I could not obtain exact information concerning the number of children who were born in each of the last years, because the administrators' lists are compiled for only the most practical purposes. Nevertheless, it appears to me that in Santa Rita between fifteen and twenty babies are born each year, and in Arêas nine to twelve (which still does not equal one birth among ten women), and thus it seems likely that, subtracting those who die, there is a small annual increase in the population.

Mortality was as follows during the last five years: on the Santa Rita and Boa Sorte plantations five children and five adults died in 1848; ten children and six adults in 1849; nine children and ten adults in 1850; nineteen children and two adults in 1851; sixteen children and one adult in 1852; which gives an average annual mortality of 11.8 children and 4.8 adults, or 16.6 persons; and since the total number of slaves on these plantations is 465, their mortality was at a rate of 3.5 percent. The documents from the plantations of Arêas and Boa Vista pertain to the last three years only: nine children and fifteen adults died in 1850; ten children and four adults in 1851; twenty-three children and ten adults in 1852 (a year of whooping cough, measles, and dysentery), which would lift the mortality rate to 5 percent, if it was not exaggeratedly high in these three years, owing to exceptional causes. It is certain that the child mortality is less the result of the medical treatment they receive than of their physical training, which is why, the fewer the number of children brought together in one place, the easier it is to bring them up.

I will now provide information on the illnesses of the blacks in these places. Each plantation necessarily possesses a certain number of slaves who are less vigorous and who, although also assigned to much lighter work, nevertheless sicken at a much higher rate than the others. In 1847 the plantation of Santa Rita counted 516 sick, 494 in 1848, 564 in 1849, 448 in 1850, 465 in 1851, and 397 in 1852; which gives an average of 480, or 146 percent. Arêas with Itaoca sent 275 sick people to the hospital in 1850, 262 in 1851, and 284 in 1852, which makes an average of 273 sick persons per year, or 86 percent.

The number of sick has been nearly equal in all the months of the year. They were as follows:

	Jan.	Feb.	Mar.	Apr.	May	Jun.
Santa Rita	45.3	32.1	37.3	43	39.3	36.3
Arêas . . .	30	28.3	23	14.3	22	20
	75.3	60.4	60.3	57.3	61.3	56.3

	Jul.	Aug.	Sept.	Oct.	Nov.	Dec.
Santa Rita	45	44	38.6	38.5	42.3	40.3
Arêas . . .	19	16	27.3	23.3	25.6	26.3
	64	60	65.9	61.8	67.9	66.6

Only a small increase may be observed in January. A greater difference can be noted if we compare the duration of the sicknesses (which to a certain point indicates their seriousness) which appear in the various months of the year.

	Jan.	Feb.	Mar.	Apr.	May	Jun.
Santa Rita	19.4	18.2	11	17.1	15.2	12.5
Arêas . . .	19.9	18.2	18.4	19.4	15.5	9
Average Length	19.6	18.2	15.9	18.2	15.3	10.7

	Jul.	Aug.	Sept.	Oct.	Nov.	Dec.
Santa Rita	11.9	11	14.3	12.5	11.8	10
Arêas . . .	17.3	11.4	10	11.8	8.9	8.9
Average length	14.5	11.2	12.1	12.1	10.3	9.4

From which it may be seen that the most serious illnesses generally occur in the first months of the year, which is also confirmed by calculating the number of deaths in the various months: twenty-eight died in

January, fifteen in February, eleven in March, fourteen in April, twelve in May, ten in June, eight in July, seven in August, eighteen in September, nine in October, thirteen in November, and nine in December.

I will now provide some information about the diseases that are most common among the blacks in these areas. Among them intertropical anemia, or constipation, occupies the first place in importance. The symptoms are well known, but not so much its causes. The tropical climate undoubtedly predisposes people to this illness, but the localized causes that can advance it are also numerous. It does not exist equally among the slaves of all the plantations, but seems to prefer those where the earth is most humid, and therefore most fertile; for this reason it is more common in Santa Rita and Boa Sorte than in Arêas and Boa Vista, in a proportion of fifteen to six, and also more common in the rainy months of the year then in the dry season, as we see in the following statistics: January, 49; February, 26; March, 24; April, 31; May, 43; June, 37; July, 59; August, 53; September, 47; October, 44; November, 27; December, 34.

All the debilitating influences contribute toward this disease: excessive labor, poor nourishment, damp quarters, lack of sleep, sexual excesses, grave illnesses either acute or chronic, especially those that induce a loss of humors. Perhaps of notable importance is the fact that a number of women have become constipated during pregnancy, whereas children are attacked less frequently. The treatment is experimental: iron given along with other tonics is ordinarily a certain cure, if the condition is not too advanced. However, as sick people after their cure often suffer again from the same influences, victims of constipation almost always go into a relapse, and each time the disease is more stubborn, and the patient finally dies of general dropsy or of chronic diarrhea, or of the complications from some other disease, so that of all the adults who died in these five years, nearly two-thirds had suffered from constipation. Among the slaves of Santa Rita, twenty-nine developed constipation in 1848; twenty in 1849; seven in 1850; five in 1851; and seventeen in 1852 (a year of much rain); and since the treatment of this disease is always very prolonged, the average duration of illnesses in these years was in direct proportion to the number of those with constipation. This duration was 15.9 days in 1848; 14.9 in 1849; 4.8 in 1850; 10.9 in 1851; and 14.5 in 1852. . . .

The illness that sends the greatest number of sick to the hospitals is . . . an acute rheumatism, often accompanied by gastric or inflammatory symptoms. The symptoms are strong forehead pain, rheumatic pains in the trunk, arms, legs, and neck; cold chills, hot skin, aversion to food, and frequently fever. It is caused by suppression of the breathing and, in a light form, can be cured in two to three days with steam sudorifics. Its distribution during the various months of the year in Santa Rita is as follows: January, 49; February, 26; March, 24; April, 31; May, 43; June, 37; July, 59; August, 53; September, 47; October, 44; November, 27; December, 34.

Thus it was more common during the cold season; in the warm period the gastric complications are most likely to appear. Bronchitis is common and prevails in epidemic form when the seasons are changing. Diarrheas and dysenteries show themselves in greatest number during the hot season, whereas intermittent fevers only appear when imported from outside. . . .

The children are much exposed to diarrheas, caused for the most part by indigestion or intestinal worms, and they are particularly common during dentation. The greatest danger comes during the time when the canine teeth are appearing, that is, between eighteen and twenty months. Also during this period an interesting variety of hepatitis can be observed among the children, since, aside from the ordinary symptoms of liver inflammation, it almost always shows signs of passing to the chronic stage, which often creates some black, scabrous spots on the skin, mainly on the buttocks and back part of the thighs, which often develop into scratches and small superficial ulcers. These are almost always a bad sign.

If generally the medical treatment of the blacks encounters obstacles because of their lack of understanding, if the difficulty which most of them have of giving an account of their sicknesses usually limits recognition of their objective symptoms, this is true to an even greater extent when treating children. The mothers, careless and badly informed, generally contribute more toward making their children sick than toward maintaining their health, and they hinder treatment instead of assisting it.

2.9. "There Are Plantations Where the Slaves Are Numb with Hunger": A Medical Thesis on Plantation Diseases and Their Causes (1847)

Among Brazilian students of medicine and the medical profession in general, there was considerable interest in the slave population, particularly, of course, in regard to the diseases that were so rampant among them. Many doctors were obviously aware that the extraordinary mortality rate among slaves in Brazil could be reduced if masters took some elementary precautions and spent a little more money on preserving the slaves they possessed instead of using it to buy fresh ones from Africa. This concern of the medical profession is well reflected in the following excerpts from the thesis that Dr. David Gomes Jardim presented to the Medical Faculty in Rio de Janeiro in 1847. Jardim gave particular attention to the problem of poor diet, inadequate clothing, and excessive labor.

Source: David Gomes Jardim, *Algumas considerações sobre a hygiene dos escravos* (Rio de Janeiro: Typ. de Laemmert, 1847), pp. 7-12.

❧ *Foods*

Beans, corn, and in the absence of this, manioc, comprise the daily food of the slaves in Brazil. An unvaried diet such as this, often in insufficient quantity and badly prepared, must be a significant cause of the development of the diseases that ordinarily attack this class of people. On the plantations where I have gone I have observed that the feeding of the slaves was always the same. It consisted of corn which, after being ground and boiled in water, is stirred until it takes the form of a consistent mass, which is called *angú*. This constitutes the daily bread, to which are added black beans boiled and mixed with pork fat (when there is some), so that it is not unusual, in fact, to see slaves eating it cooked only in water, because their masters are convinced that they make up the herbivorous part of society. In order to give variety to their food, the slaves sometimes obtain for themselves soft substances such as *carurú* [various greens used in cooking], *ora-pro-nobis* [a cactus bearing an edible fruit], *quiabo* fruit, etc., mixing these with enormous quantities of peppers. This privilege is not granted, however, to all of them. The scarcity of foods forces the slaves to search for roots, the properties of which are not known to them, and for which reason they are often victims of bloody punishments, accused of poisoning their companions, when in fact they are entirely innocent! It would appear impossible, but there are masters in fact who allow their slaves to eat sick animals, or even animals that have died of diseases, with no concern for the possible effects of such a careless policy. If the animal was infected with a contagious disease, such as carbuncle, for example, it is not surprising that it is passed on not only to those who eat the meat, but also to those who removed its hide, an item they never fail to put to use. . . . From these and other irregular practices, gastric impediments arise, acute and chronic inflammations, tumors, cancers, and the whole retinue of internal diseases which are so common among the blacks. There are plantations where the slaves

7. Preparing Manioc at a *Fazenda*

are numb with hunger, so that their appearance fills us with sorrow. . . .

Dr. Jobim, in a lecture on the diseases of the poor people of Rio de Janeiro, claimed that the great use which our slaves make of feculent substances is the reason for their tendency to develop constipation. I believe that manioc is a particularly poor food, since it is heavy, difficult to digest, badly prepared, and without alkaline elements, in a word, unsuitable as an item of diet. . . . The manioc flour which is given to the blacks is very badly prepared, because the poisonous liquid is almost never extracted from it by pressure, and its bad quality is not improved by the action of fire.

The vessels used to prepare the slaves' food are made of copper, and the person in charge of the cooking is usually a rather negligent black man who fails to clean them, so that the foods often contain verdigris [a greenish film on metal surfaces], a poisonous substance. It is possible that many of the slaves who are poisoned are not only victims of the wickedness of their companions, but also of their masters' lack of concern for the utensils in which their food is cooked!

Slaves have a very pronounced tendency toward alcoholic beverages; there is no obstacle that can prevent them from giving themselves up to this vice. To support this assertion, I will narrate a case which I have witnessed. A black man, who was over ninety years of age and already bent under the weight of his years, went out every night to a parish a league from his place of residence, for the purpose of buying sugar brandy to satisfy his impetuous need. Note that this journey was made with a nimbleness and speed which seem incompatible with his weak physical condition. I know another slave who feigned illness so that he could get a dose of Leroy Remedy [a popular patent medicine of French origin with some alcoholic content]. . . .

We have seen the great importance of poor diet as a cause of disease. Therefore it is an absolute necessity that their foods be varied and of good quality, consisting of a mixed regimen, that is, composed of substances from both the vegetable and animal kingdoms, with restorative powers, and in such quantity that they can satisfy the needs of the organisms. The person assigned to the preparation of food should take care to keep the cooking utensils clean at all times, and it will be far better if they are manufactured of some material other than copper. They should receive a portion of brandy when the circumstances require it, for example, whenever they get wet or on feast days so that they can enjoy themselves. . . .

Clothing

The clothing of plantation blacks does not offer complete protection against the changing temperatures, since each one receives each year only one set of clothes, consisting of a shirt and a pair of trousers! Always exposed to rain and heat, how can a slave protect himself from the effects of perspiration with this single set of clothing, being compelled frequently to allow his clothes to dry while still on his body, and to wear them in a dirty condition? It is difficult, even impossible, to understand how one set of clothes is to be kept in a wearable condition for a whole year. The result of this badly conceived frugality is that the slaves go about in rags and nearly naked, exposed not only to the action of the elements, but also offending the laws of modesty. If I have touched on this point, it is because I believe that clothing is as important as food.

Daily experience teaches us the disadvantages that result from the negligence of some planters who permit their slaves to wear their clothes after they have gotten wet, and to allow them to dry on their own bodies. Is this because they are convinced that the constitutions of these beings are resistant to the action of disease-causing agents, and therefore incapable of responding to their influence? Do they not realize that pneumonias, pleurisy, catarrhal fevers, etc., frequently appear after rain, that they occur when the slaves are exposed to the hot rays of the sun, and that such illnesses never cease to assault them principally if they are bathed in sweat? And as if these evils were not sufficient to mortify the miserable blacks, there are also apoplexies and cerebral congestions which afflict them so often, since they are accustomed to work with their heads uncovered and exposed to the rays of the sun. . . .

To remedy these conditions, I suggest that the slaves be given the necessary clothes, and that they always be washed so that they are not impregnated with harmful materials; because, if they have surplus clothing, they will not be as exposed to diseases, which have such disastrous consequences. I also recommend that their clothes be made of linen or wool, depending upon the season of the year, and that the greatest precautions be taken to protect their heads from the sun's rays, which can be accomplished with the use of caps.

Labor

If idleness is harmful, the abuse of labor is even more so. We are so convinced of the truth of this principle that we do not hesitate to affirm that a third of the slaves in Brazil die as a result of the excessive labor that they are forced to endure. The slaveholding planters do not understand their own interests when, lured by badly conceived ambitions, they sacrifice their captives to the rigors of superhuman toil. Is it even believable, for example, that a slave with a weak constitution can compete in service with a strong one, when the day's toil is so hard that it exceeds even the latter's powers? We have constantly observed that work is assigned without concern for the strength of the individuals; that the weak and the strong share the work alike. From this lack of consideration can come only one result, that which daily occurs: the weakest are the first to die, and when they do they are completely emaciated. When I asked a planter why the death rate among his slaves was so exaggerated, and pointed out that this obviously did him great harm, he quickly replied that, on the contrary, it brought him no injury at all, since when he purchased a slave it was with the purpose of using him for only a single year, after which very few could survive; but that nevertheless he made them work in such a way that he not only recovered the capital employed in their purchase, but also made a considerable profit! And besides, what does it matter if the life of a black man is destroyed by one year of unbearable toil if from this we derive the same advantages which we would have if he worked at a slower pace for a long period of time? This is how many people reason.

The slaves, going off to work at five o'clock in the morning, exposed during the entire day to the effects of sun and rain, are vulnerable to the kinds of fevers which result from too much exposure to the sun. They also get violent headaches, mainly when the sun is at its zenith, and apoplexies, which also quite frequently occur at this time of the day. This we would particularly like to prevent, and therefore we strongly recommend that on very hot days slaves be allowed a little time to rest.

It is customary to force the slaves to work for some hours at night. I have seen the terrible results of this. On one plantation the slaves were attacked by a stubborn eye inflammation (ophthalmia), which ended often with blindness. Looking into the causes of this condition, I concluded that it resulted from this evening work, and when this was discontinued the ophthalmia also disappeared. After their daytime labors, it is only right that the evening be devoted to recuperating their lost strength. We therefore protest against the conduct of those persons who, denying their slaves their necessary rest, force them to perform evening work, which consists of digging trenches, leveling terraces, preparing coffee and sugar, etc. This evening work almost always causes illnesses of the kind that arise from suppressed perspiration.

Once more, owners of slaves, stop these practices. Regulate the labor of your slaves according to each one's strength. Give them their needed rest, and you will see that the observance of simple rules of personal conduct can go far toward preserving the lives of your slaves.

2.10. The Annual Work Routine on Plantations in Maranhão in the Mid-Nineteenth Century

The following description of the annual work routine on the cotton and rice plantations of Maranhão is from a book on slavery by a native of that northern province, F. A. Brandão, Júnior. A Positivist reformer with experience in France, Brandão based his account of slave labor upon youthful memories. Particularly interesting are his references to the inadequate tools which slaves used and the damaging ecological effects of the prevailing agricultural system.

Source: F. A. Brandão, Júnior, *A escravatura no Brasil precedida d'um artigo sobre a agricultura e colonisação no Maranhão* (Brussels: H. Thiry-Vern Buggenhoudt, 1865), pp. 31-38.

On the plantations there is no law but the absolute will of the master, which is rudely delegated to the overseer, usually a trusted slave. And since there is no better wedge than a chunk of the wood itself, the overseer surpasses his master's intentions when enforcing his orders, making extraordinary demands upon the workers in the tedious service in the fields.

At six o'clock in the morning the overseer forces the poor slave, still exhausted from the evening's labors, to rise from his rude bed and proceed to his work. The first assignment of the season is the chopping down of the forests for the next year's planting, using a scythe to hack down the smaller trees. This work normally goes on for two months, depending upon the type of jungle being cut and the stamina of the slaves.

The next step is destruction of the large trees, and this, like the previous work, continues for twelve hours each day. At night the slaves return home, where evening work of two or more hours awaits them, depending upon the character of the master. They set fire to the devastated jungle, and then they cut and stack the branches and smaller tree trunks which have escaped the fire and which, occupying the surface of the earth, could hinder development of the crop.

These mounds of branches are again burned, and the result is a sad and devastating scene! Centuries-old tree trunks which two months before had produced a cool, crisp atmosphere over a broad stretch of land, lie on the surface of a field ravaged by fire and covered with ashes, where the slaves are compelled to spend twelve hours under the hot sun of the equator, without a single tree to give them shelter.

This destruction of the forests has exhausted the soil, which in many places now produces nothing but grasses suitable for grazing cattle. The temperature has intensified, and the seasons have become irregular. The rains at times damage the crops, and at other times there is no rain at all. The streams and certain shallow rivers, such as the Itapucurú, have dried up or have become almost unnavigable, and lumber for building has become very rare, or is only found at a great distance from the settlements.

When it finally rains toward the end of December or early January, the slaves begin to seed the devastated fields, and the only tool they use in planting cotton is a small hoe, and for the rice and millet they use nothing but a stick with an iron point to hollow out the ground.

8. The Destruction of Forests in Preparation for Planting

After this comes the weeding. This is painful labor for the slaves, who, with nothing to work with but a weeding-hook, are forced to stand in a stooped position during the entire day, cutting the shoots or other native plants, and enduring a temperature in the sun of 40° Celsius. This work, which is the most arduous, continues as long as it takes for the plants to fully establish themselves.

The next step is the rice cutting in May or June, which each slave accomplishes with a small knife, cutting the stems one by one, and at night beating them with a branch to loosen the grains. During this phase of their labor the overseers demand a certain number of *alqueires* of rice from each slave, and if the unfortunate person does not produce what is demanded of him, the tragedy is brought to an end with *the daily bread of the slave*, that is, the lash.

There is still another kind of work no less exacting, in which the masters make even greater demands. This is the picking of the cotton crop. To accomplish this the slaves disperse themselves over a certain part of the field, collecting the pods and depositing them in a basket or sack which each slave carries for this purpose attached to his waist.

Under a brutally hot sun, the atmosphere bathed in exhausting light, the slave unsteadily forces himself to pick the nearest pod, responding only to the terrible system of injustice which condemns him, with no appeal to clemency; with no hope of reward except respite from daily labor. . . . From time to time he interrupts the silence of these deserts with his melancholy song, inspired by his slave condition, whose rhythm itself is often set to the crack of a whip!

2.11. A Brazilian Senator Comments on the High Mortality among Rural Slave Children in the First Half of the Nineteenth Century

In the following excerpts from a speech delivered before an assembly of Brazilian planters in 1871, Senator Cristiano Benedito Ottoni of Minas Gerais told his audience what many must already have known: that under conditions prevailing in Brazil before abolition of the slave trade only a tiny minority of the children born of slave women in Brazil lived long enough to grow into useful adulthood. Attempting to prove in his address that the liberation of the newborn children of slave women (then under debate in the General Assembly) would revive such awesome child mortality, Ottoni offered explanations for this high death rate based upon many years of personal observation.

Source: C. B. Ottoni, *A emancipação dos escravos* (Rio de Janeiro: Typographia Perseverança, 1871), pp. 65-68.

I know our rural districts, and I do not hesitate to affirm that at the present time, despite the better treatment of the slaves that began after workers grew scarce, not more than 25 or 30 percent of the children reach the age of eight. The scarcity of adolescent slaves is proof of great child mortality.

It is an incontestable fact that while the price of slaves was low few babies [*crias*] survived on the plantations. If you traveled through the counties of Piraí, Vassouras, Valença, Paraíba do Sul, observing the groups in service, almost all were Africans. You noticed one exception (and there were not many others), a great plantation whose orphaned owner was receiving an education in a foreign country. This one was notably populated by creoles. Why? Because, according to a contract, some of those who survived belonged to the overseer. Always personal interest. In all the discussions among the planters this kind of calculation was heard: "You buy a black for 300$000. In a year he harvests 100 *arrobas* [about 3,200 pounds] of coffee, which at least produces his cost clear. From then on everything is profit. There is no advantage in tolerating the *crias* who will be capable of similar labor only after sixteen years." As a result, pregnant black women and those nursing their babies were not excused from hoeing. In some, hard labor prevented normal development of the fetus. In others it reduced the flow of milk. In almost all, the children were neglected, and as a result sickness and death were the fate of the poor babies. How many grew up? There are no statistics to tell us, but if only 9 or 10 percent survived among those abandoned in the capital, as the Viscount Abaeté once proved in the Senate, of those born into slavery certainly not more than 5 percent survived.

The rising prices and the havoc wrought by cholera caused a greater number to be saved, but even today I doubt that the proportion exceeds 30 percent. Eliminate personal interest, and we will return to 95 percent mortality among the children.

2.12. A Bahian Sugar Planter Registers His Slaves (1872)

A list of slaves, including information on their color, age, marital status, birthplace, parentage, aptitude for labor, and occupation, was recorded on April 19, 1872, by the Bahian planter, Dr. Francisco Moreira de Carvalho, Viscount de Subahé, in accordance with the Free Birth

Law of 1871. Once more we can see here some of the disastrous results of slavery. Not one of the Viscount's slaves, for example, was listed as married, a fact not surprising when we realize that of the eighty-three individuals nineteen years of age or older, only four were women. In fact a demographer who based a population profile upon these statistics would create a very lopsided picture hardly suggesting the familiar Christmas-treelike images we are accustomed to. Instead of a broad base representing children, for example, there would be a near-void at the bottom, with only twelve persons eleven or younger and none under three. Even odder, the male side of the "tree," while outdoing the female at almost every level, would display conspicuously lengthy branches representing older males, while the complete absence of upper branches on the female side would show that this group of 104 persons did not include even one old woman.

Revealing a callous disregard for human norms, these statistics also suggest that the Viscount was guilty of a form of fraudulent slaveholding which was widespread or even looked on as normal during the last fifty years of Brazilian slavery. The large number of older males, including no fewer than forty-seven recorded as forty-six or older, was clearly the result of efforts to cover up the enslavement of Africans who had entered Brazil after the slave trade had become illegal in 1831. Although tens of thousands of African boys and young men had entered Bahia between 1831 and 1851, many of whom would hardly have reached middle age by 1872, all the forty-two Africans claimed by the Viscount were registered as forty-six or older (an average of over fifty-three). Nevertheless, all were said to be capable of "full service."

Finally, although the ratio of younger children (those under sixteen) to females of childbearing age was high (sixteen children to four women), the low ratio of children to adults as a whole reveals that the Viscount's captive population was not growing naturally (an impossibility considering the scarcity of women), but was rapidly declining. The notations in the right column under "Observations," added between 1872 and 1884, also show this rapid decline. At least a quarter of the 104 persons originally listed died in those twelve years and almost a fifth were freed, while two or three had run away and one or two had been sold. Nearly half the original number, in any case, no longer existed as slaves by 1884, and many more, especially among the Africans, had indeed reached an age when they could not have worked at full capacity. Obviously such rapid changes in slave work forces, especially in Northeastern provinces, were among the causes of abolition in 1888.

Source: Coleção Subaé. Lata 551, Document 29, Instituto Histórico e Geográfico Brasileiro.

❧ List No. 42 of the slaves belonging to the Viscount de Subahé, resident in the province of Bahia, municipality of Santo Amaro, parish of Nossa Senhora do Rosario

(Art. 2 of the Regulation No. 4835 of December 1, 1871)

List No.	Name	Color	Age	Marital Status	Birthplace
1	Adão	Black	15	Single	Alcoçaba
2	Albano	"	50	"	Africa
3	Abrahão	"	48	"	"
4	Anastasio	"	50	"	"
5	Antão	"	48	"	"
6	Alexandre	"	60	"	São Pedro, Rio Fundo
7	Angelo	"	48	"	Africa
8	Antonio	"	47	"	"
9	Adolfo	"	52	"	"
10	Bernardino	Dark	19	"	São Sebastião
11	Benedicto	Black	22	"	"
12	Benjamin	"	50	"	Africa
13	Calixto	"	50	"	"
14	Clemente	"	68	"	"
15	Damasio	Dark	22	"	Santo Amaro
16	Elias	Black	50	"	Africa
17	Euzequiel	"	50	"	"
18	Elesiario	"	36	"	Sao Sebastião
19	Francisco	"	30	"	Bom Jardim
20	Francisco Salles	Dark	30	"	São Sebastião
21	Felippe	"	23	"	"
22	Fermiano	Black	50	"	Africa
23	Fermino	"	50	"	"
24	Higino	Dark	17	"	Santo Amaro
25	Herculano	Black	25	"	São Sebastião
26	Honorato	"	52	"	Unknown
27	Jozé Januario	"	30	"	Bom Jardim
28	Jozé de Santo Amaro	"	35	"	São Sebastião
29	João	"	30	"	"
30	Jozé	"	12	"	Bom Jardim
31	Justina	"	4	"	"
32	João das Palmeiras	"	35	"	Unknown
33	Julião	"	55	"	Africa
34	Jozé	"	50	"	"
35	Justino	"	50	"	"
36	Juvencio	"	47	"	"
37	Luiz	"	46	"	"
38	Ludovico	"	67	"	"
39	Lairrianno	"	50	"	"
40	Lucas	"	50	"	"

Parentage	Aptitude for Labor	Occupation	Observations
Unknown	Light service	Agriculture	
"	Full service	"	Fled to unknown place Sept. 5, 1877
"	"	"	
"	"	"	
"	"	"	
"	"	Overseer	Freed
"	"	Butcher	Dead
"	"	"	
"	"	Potter	
Son of Domingas	"	Mason	Son of Domingas, belonging to another master
Son of Benta	"	Dyer	Son of Benta, now dead
Unknown	"	Head stableman	
"	"	Agriculture	
"	"	"	
"	"	"	
"	"	"	
"	"	"	
Son of Justina	"	"	Son of Justina, freed
Unknown	"	"	
Son of Anastasias	"	"	Son of Anastasias, freed
Son of Gertrudes	"	"	Son of Gertrudes, dead
Unknown	"	"	
"	"	"	
"	Light service	"	
	"	"	Son of Custodia, freed
"	Full service	"	Died August 15, 1876
Son of Izabel	"	"	Son of Izabel, now dead
Son of Lescadia	"	"	Son of Lescadia, today freed
Son of Jozefa	"	Butcher	Son of Jozefa, today freed
Son of Roza	Light service	Agriculture	Son of Roza, under No. 63
"	None	"	Child of Roza, under No. 63
Unknown	Full service	Cowhand	Freed
"	"	Agriculture	
"	"	"	
"	"	"	
"	"	"	
"	"	Shepherd	
"	"	"	
"	"	Agriculture	
"	"	"	

List No.	Name	Color	Age	Marital Status	Birthplace
41	Lucas	Black	50	Single	Africa
42	Ladislão	Dark	50	"	Bom Jardim
43	Luiz Paschoal	"	16	"	Unknown
44	Manuel Alves	Black	60	"	"
45	Manuel Pontes	"	42	"	"
46	Manuel Fustino	"	30	"	São Sebastião
47	Manuel do Conde	"	15	"	Santo Amaro
48	Martinho	"	23	"	São Sebastião
49	Marcelino	"	19	"	Bom Jardim
50	Malaquinan	"	55	"	Africa
51	Malheos	"	55	"	"
52	Nicaco	"	50	"	"
53	Oligario	"	50	"	"
54	Ignacio	"	47	"	"
55	Pedro Fernando	"	50	"	Bom Jardim
56	Pedro Crioulo	"	35	"	"
57	Pedro Lustoza	"	30	"	"
58	Pompeio	"	50	"	Africa
59	Pompeio	"	46	"	"
60	Purdencio	"	60	"	"
61	Rofino	Dark	35	"	São Sebastião
62	Raimundo	Black	24	"	"
63	Roza Liberta	"	35	"	Bom Jardim
64	Ricardo	"	7	"	"
65	Rodolpho	"	18	"	Rio Fundo
66	Silvano	"	50	"	Africa
67	Sabino	"	50	"	"
68	Raphael	"	48	"	"
69	Sotero	"	47	"	"
70	Fetr.	"	50	"	"
71	Thomé	"	55	"	"
72	Vicente	Dark	21	"	Unknown
73	Vintino	Black	17	"	"
74	Zacharias	"	25	"	"
75	Zeferino	"	23	"	Bom Jardim
76	Constança liberta	"	30	"	"
77	Jozé	"	11	"	São Sebastião
78	Alfeo	"	9	"	"
79	Maria liberta	"	7	"	"
80	Guilherme	"	4	"	"
81	Izabel liberta	"	3	"	"
82	Marinha liberta	"	27	"	"
83	Vidal	"	8	"	"
84	Thereza liberta	"	6	"	"
85	Roza liberta	"	2	"	"
86	Andreza liberta	"	30	"	"

Parentage	Aptitude for Labor	Occupation	Observations
Unknown	Full Service	Agriculture	Died in 1878
"	"	Carpenter	Dead
"	Light service	Agriculture	
"	Full service	"	
"	"	Stonemason	Died September 15, 1878
Son of Justina	"	Agriculture	Son of Justina, today freed
Son of Epiphania	Light service	"	Died on February 1, 1876
Unknown	Full service	Shepherd	Son of Marcollina, now dead
Son of Roza	"	"	Son of Roza under No. 63
Unknown	"	Agriculture	Freedman
"	"	"	
"	"	"	Dead
"	"	"	Died on October 5
"	"	"	
Son of Luiza	Light service	Blacksmith	Son of Luiza who died free
Son of Custodia	Full service	Agriculture	Son of Custodia, free
Unknown	"	"	Sold or fled
"	"	"	Died on July 30, 1872
"	"	"	
"	"	"	
Son of Agostinha	"	"	Son of Agostinha, now dead
Son of Jozefa	"	Shepherd	
Daughter of Benta	No service	Agriculture	Daughter of Benta, now dead
Son of Roza	"	"	Son of Roza under No. 63
Unknown	Light service	"	Ran away on Aug. 21, 1878
"	Full service	"	Died August 2, 1876
"	"	"	
"	"	Herdsman	
"	"	Agriculture	
"	"	"	
"	"	"	
"	Light service	"	
"	"	"	
"	Full service	"	
Son of Roza	"	"	Son of Roza under No. 63
Daughter of Izabel	Light service	"	Daughter of Izabel, now dead
Child of Constança	No service	"	Child of Constança under No. 76
"	"	"	"
"	"	"	"
"	"	"	"
"	"	"	"
Daughter of Delfina	Light service	"	Daughter of Delfina, a free woman
Child of Marinha	None	"	Child of Marinha under No. 82
Daughter of Maria	"	"	"
"	"	"	"
Daughter of Paulina	Light service	Inventor	Daughter of Paulina now dead

List No.	Name	Color	Age	Marital Status	Birthplace
87	Emilia liberta	Black	3	Single	São Sebastião
88	Jacob	"	47	"	Africa
89	Leão	"	50	"	"
90	Olympio	"	50	"	"
91	João	"	58	"	"
92	João (dead)	Dark	30	"	Santo Amaro
93	Jozé	"	26	"	"
94	Ernesto	"	35	"	Unknown
95	Fernando	Black	22	"	Sao Sebastião
96	Edmundo	"	12	"	Unknown
97	Manuel	"	10	"	"
98	Manuel Canuto	"	28	"	"
99	Manuel Francisco	"	20	"	Rio Fundo
100	Eznello	Dark	17	"	São Sebastião
101	Pedro Leite	"	65	"	Rio Fundo
102	Benedicto liberto	Black	24	"	B. Jardim
103	Pio	"	50	"	Africa
104	Luiz Camara	"	25	"	Sao Sebastião

Parentage	Aptitude for Labor	Occupation	Observations
Daughter of Andreza	None	Agriculture	
Unknown	Full service	Serves as a wise guy	Freed on June 21, 1884
"	"	Distiller	Freed Aug. 22, 1873
"	"	"	Died on 20 of December 1878
"	"	"	Freed on June 28, 1884
Son of Faustina	"	"	Son of Faustina, a free woman, died on Feb. 4, 1878
"	"	"	Same 1878
Unknown	Full service	Agriculture	Freed on July 20, 1873
Son of Marcelina	"	"	Son of Maria now dead
Unknown	Light service	"	Died 2-5-85
"	"	"	
"	"	"	Died on June 4, 1879
Son of Rofina	Full service	"	Son of Rofina, freed, died in 1875
Son of Tecla	Light service	"	Son of Tecla, deceased
"	Full service	"	Freedman
Son of Selveria	"	"	Son of Selveria, freed woman
Unknown	"	"	Freed on January 6, 1873
"	"	"	Sold on Oct. 1, 1876

THREE

Slave Life in Cities and at the Mines

If there were differences between the slave systems of Brazil and the United States, there were also similarities. In both countries, for example, many slaves were employed in towns and cities. In this regard, Brazilian towns like Rio de Janeiro, Bahia, Recife, and São Luis had much in common with such Southern commercial centers as Baltimore, Richmond, Savannah, and Charleston. In Brazilian cities female slaves were particularly abundant, in part because of the greater demand for men on plantations, and because women were often preferred as servants and for other normally urban occupations. Notable in this regard were the textile and clothing industries which in 1872 employed over 50,000 slaves, most of whom were women.

In Brazil owning black servants was not only a convenience, but also evidence of wealth and high social standing (see Document 3.9). Moreover, menial labor—even carrying a parcel or an umbrella—was seen as beneath the dignity of free people, and thus even persons of modest means were apt to own a personal servant or two. The staffs of wealthy households often included an army of servants and their children: *mucamas* or female retainers, a cook or two, laundresses, seamstresses, women to wait at table, *moleques* or "pickaninnies" to do odd jobs, and, if there were white children, one or two *amas de leite* or wet nurses (see Documents 3.6 through 3.9). In the American South male servants would normally have included coachmen and stable hands, but in Brazil a member of the privileged class also frequently possessed an ornamented sedan chair (cadeira) or hammock (the former sometimes sporting his coat of arms), along with some liveried but barefoot blacks whose job it was to carry him about town (see Documents in 3.4 and Fig. 14). This difference in personal transportation is perhaps symbolic of the contrasts between Brazilian and Southern slavery.

In Brazil, city slaves were employed in a wide variety of occupations

They were peddlers, carpenters, bakers, shoemakers, barbers, masons, miners, sailors, fishermen, waiters, cooks, porters, and prostitutes, to name some of the more common professions (see Document 3.1). As in the United States, slaves were often hired out to others, including industrial establishments. In Minas Gerais, to cite one example, rich slaveholders rented hundreds of slaves to British gold-mining companies (see Document 3.11). Even more often, city slaves were urged to work on their own, with the understanding that they pay for their personal needs and that each day they bring their masters a certain sum of money, the alternative being severe punishment. These *prêtos de ganho*, or earning blacks, were a common sight on Brazil's streets, selling merchandise or produce, working as craftsmen or laborers, or hiring themselves out as porters or sedan chair carriers. "We are not the least inventive," wrote a critic of slavery in 1823, "because whoever possesses a slave sends him out to earn money; it does not matter if he robs, assaults, or kills, as long as he brings the stipulated daily amount." (Cited in José Honório Rodrigues, *Independência,* II, 136.)

City slaves probably had more control over their own lives than those in the countryside, more opportunities to entertain themselves, to learn a trade, to save some money, and even to buy their freedom. However, the documents in this part also suggest that they were perhaps no less vulnerable to abuse than rural slaves, and that their struggles to earn a living and survive in a highly competitive environment were tragically difficult.

3.1. Slave Life in Rio de Janeiro as Seen through Newspaper Advertisements (1821)

One important source of information about urban slaves is the advertisements which appeared regularly in Brazil's daily newspapers during most of the nineteenth century. These blunt offers to buy, sell, or rent slaves, or to pay rewards to persons who captured and returned runaways contain much information about their African origins, clothing, occupations, skills, punishments, diseases, physical disabilities, and the clever personal adjustments that some of them managed to make in the face of extraordinary hardships. Concerning their masters, such advertisements also reveal a remarkable callousness toward their victims, many of whom, as their actions showed, were helpless, bewildered, and desperate. The following notices, selected from among dozens of the kind that appeared in a *single issue* of *O Diario do Rio de Janeiro*, give a stark impression of slave life in one of Brazil's most important and sophisticated cities.

Source: *O Diario do Rio de Janeiro*, December 17, 1821.

❧ SALES . . .

2. For sale a creole slave, a skilfull shoemaker, with a very good figure, about twenty years of age, with no vices or bad habits. His final price is 300$000 *reis*. Anyone interested in him should go to Travessa do Paço No. 11, upstairs, where he will find someone to speak to about the matter.

3. In Rua de Santa Teresa No. 36 a black man is now on sale, since his master is about to leave for Lisbon.

4. For sale, a black man of the Angola nation, about 20 to 25 years of age, a very good maker of combs, both tortoise shell and animal horn. Anyone interested should go to Rua da Quitanda, cornor of São Pedro, No. 50, where he will find someone to deal with. . . .

6. Whoever would like to buy three native slave women from Angola, who have come recently from that place, one who irons and does laundry, another a baker and laundress, and the third also a laundress, all with very good figures and the ability to do every kind of work in the house, should contact Manoel do Nascimento da Mata, Rua Direita No. 54, first floor. . . .

8. Whoever would like to buy a very good black cook and laundress, who also knows how to iron, is still young and without vices, should go to Rua dos Pescadores No. 80, where he will find someone to speak to. . . .

PURCHASES . . .

11. Whoever has a creole girl, well made, from six to eight years of age, and wishes to sell her, should contact Manoel do Nascimento da Mata, Rua Direita No. 54, first floor. He wishes to buy her to take her out of the country. . . .

RENTALS

13. Whoever is interested in renting slaves well trained in the baker's trade, who could even do every type of work in a house, should go to Rua dos Latoeiros, house No. 14, or to the textile shop on the Rua do Cano, almost at the cornor of Rua dos Latoeiros, facing house No. 51. . . .

WET NURSES

16. Whoever would like to buy a black woman with milk, who can also cook and wash, should go to Rua do Senhor dos Passos, No. 35, opposite [the statue] of the same Senhor dos Passos. . . .

PRIVATE NOTICES . . .

19. Whoever is interested in sending us any slave woman for training in ironing, sewing, and other accomplishments appropriate to a woman should direct himself to Rua São José, No. 69. In the same shop we mend silk stockings, do washing, every kind of sewing, and ironing is taken in at a reasonable price. . . .

FOUND

34. Antonio José Telles, bush captain [*capitão-do-mato*], just arriving from Santa Cruz, has captured three black men from some thieves. Two acculturated Africans [*ladinos*] have been turned over to their owners, and a beardless boy newly arrived from Mozambique has been delivered to the jail for safekeeping, and I now make known to the public through this ad that his owner can see him at the jail.

35. On the 7th of the current month about ten o'clock in the morning two residents of Minas Gerais who stayed at the marshy encampment on the road to Minas and São Paulo found a black woman in an open hut and, suspecting her of being a runaway, took her with them and turned her over to Manoel Lopes Rodrigues Guimarães, a resident at the Carova ranch, in the new parish of Campo Grande. She says she is a Benguela and that her name is Maria. She is still not very adapted to the country, but says her master is a mulatto named Alexandre, and that he lives in the Valongo. [See Document 1.9.] Her owner can find her in the aforementioned ranch, or look for her in the bakery in the Beco das Cancellas

between Rua do Ouvidor and Rua do Rosario, where she will be sent. When a precise description of her has been given, she will be surrendered to her owner, once the expenses have been paid.

ROBBERY

36. A black man of the Benguela nation named Joaquim has run away, taking with him a display case containing wares. He has been going about the city as a peddler, with a license made out in the name of Isabel Esmeria, and the wares he has stolen belong to her, his mistress. He is believed to be selling his materials in various places protected by the license which he also took with him. Whoever knows anything about the stolen goods, or the black man, should notify his mistress, who will pay a reward for the trouble. It is suggested to anyone who inspects street peddlers' licenses that if he should find this man in possession of that license he should have him arrested as a thief. It is also suggested that it will be easier to find him during daylight hours, and that the license will serve as evidence. . . .

RUNAWAY SLAVES

40. It is now two months since a black creole woman named Candida from Mozambique ran away. She is tall, full-bodied, has long hair, and four spots or marks of her nation, one between the eyes, another on the chin, and one on each cheek. She has one slightly bent leg. Whoever brings her safely to Rua de Santo Antonio, No. 10, will receive the deserved reward.

41. A slave named Joaquim ran away in September of last year from Luis Manoel de Almeida Bastos. He is of the Benguela nation, practices the profession of cook, and was also a peddler. He is tall, ugly in the face, has a flat nose, with a scar in the corner of his left eye, and another on his lower lip close to the corner of his mouth, and he has big flat feet. Anyone who has any information about him, and wishes to notify his above-mentioned master, a resident at Caju Point in the house of Captain Manoel Joaquim Bacellar, will receive three doubloons as a reward.

42. On October 30, last, a black man named Narciso fled from house No. 19 of the Rua do Lavradio. He is a trained mason, still a boy of about 18, short, well-built, has large eyes, and a very sprightly and happy face; blue trousers of cotton gingham from Minas Gerais, also carried cotton trousers. It is believed that he goes about in the city suburbs working at his trade. Project supervisors and master masons are requested to check at their construction sites to see if the said slave is

there, and to advise his master and have him taken to him by someone, with the assurance that he will receive a reward of 12$800 *réis*.

43. A boy of 13 or 14 years of age, with the following distinguishing marks, has run away: a white spot on his right eye, he is covered with scabies, has trousers of yellow cotton and a blue cotton jacket. Whoever has knowledge of him should come to Rua da Ajuda No. 57, where he will get a reward.

44. Fled the first of the current month a black man named Manoel, of the Benguela nation, of ordinary stature, small eyes, full-bodied but not badly built, a rather yellowish complexion. He is a sailor, wears cotton trousers and a blue waistcoat, carried more clothes in a bundle, including a gingham shirt. Whoever knows anything about him or has some news should go to house No. 13 Rua dos Barbones, where he will be paid for his troubles.

45. All those persons who run eating houses or even private persons who may be approached by a black from the Mina coast named Joaquim offering himself as a cook, or even as a waiter, are informed that he is a runaway, and it is requested that he be detained and his master informed, who lives in the Rua do Cano No. 143 upstairs. A reward will be paid. . . .

48. On November 20 a Mozambique slave named Martinho fled from a ranch at the Engenho Novo. He is still unacquainted with the country, a boy with a beard, and he ran away with a chain attached to his leg. Anyone knowing anything about him should come to Rua do Sabão to the house of Major Manoel dos Santos Portugal, who is his master and will pay for the trouble involved.

49. From Dona Constança Umbelina fled a slave named Anna, of the Benguela nation, who is between 18 and 20 years of age, of ordinary height, a thin face, rather pale in color, big lips, and the upper one very elevated, with some sign of a long gash made by an iron instrument on her face under her right eye. She has elevated breasts, legs that are good-looking but a little bowed. She walks fast and is a little snooty (as we say). She is a market woman, and it is supposed that she is going about on certain city streets such as Saco do Alferes, Praia Dom Manoel, etc. She wore a violet-colored dress, wine-colored, adorned with little bows, but now she is said to be wearing another dress which is covered with mud, and a kerchief of old cloth round her waist. Whoever does me the favor of capturing her will be well paid, and he can bring her to the Campo de Santa Anna between Rua dos Ciganos and Rua do Alecrim in the first house close to the wall. . . .

51. On Saturday the 7th of this month disappeared a black named Pedro, of the Caçange nation, who has been working out on his own, with the following features: youthful, short, full-bodied, and with an

ulcer which is still small on his forehead. He was dressed in large gingham trousers and an English shirt, also of gingham. He does not speak Portuguese very well except a few words, and these very badly, and he has been in this city for fourteen months. Anyone who has news of him is asked to come to Rua do Catete just past house No. 6. He will get a good reward.

52. Fled on November 29, 1821, a black man named Francisco of the Mozambique nation, with the following distinguishing features: short, large, with his toes so cut that they are hardly visible. Trousers and shirt of white cotton, his body entirely covered with welts. He has been going about selling water. Whoever has news of him should come to Rua da Prainha No. 49, where he will be well paid for his trouble. . . .

62. Disappeared on December 1 a black woman of the Angola nation by the name of Josefa. She has a scar on her left leg, and is dressed in the loincloth which she brought from the Valongo market, and has many strings of beads around her neck. She vanished when she went to get water in the Campo. Anyone who knows anything about her should go to the house of Sra. Maria Rita, Rua do Sabão No. 254, or inform this newspaper.

On the 21st of this month a new slave who recently came from Angola fled from Valongo warehouse No. 106. On his left breast he has a brand mark in the shape of an "S" set in the middle of a triangle. Anyone with news of him should go to the same warehouse, where he will find his master, who will give him a good reward.

Fled on the first of this month a young black boy of the Mina nation named Joaquim. He is a most unusual slave, thin, good-looking, and with two marks of his nation on his face, one on each side, and a scar on the left side of his forehead, and he is a bit too smug. He sold fish in the market, and at that place and all over the city he is known by the surname of Carne Seca [Dried Beef]. His usual route is along the Beach of Dom Manoel dos Mineiros, and along the Rua da Valla and the Largo do Capim. Sometimes he goes about selling vegetables, and at other times he gambles. Whoever captures him should come to the Rua dos Ourives, beneath the hospital of the Third Carmelite Order, No. 77.

3.2. A North American Describes Slave Life in Rio de Janeiro (1846)

A generation after the above advertisements were published, slave life in the Brazilian capital retained many of its former characteristics. The slave trade continued on a large scale, and the city still teemed with

9. Street Scene in Rio de Janeiro

newly imported Africans selling goods in the streets, washing clothes in public fountains, carrying huge sacks of coffee or other merchandise on their heads, or tugging badly made carts through the city's narrow streets. Some still wore chains, iron rings attached to their necks, or iron masks covering their faces; many of both sexes were still nearly naked, and others diseased or tragically deformed. Slaves still disappeared with startling frequency, some seeking liberty or respite from punishment or labor, others allegedly taking their own lives. The following descriptive account of slave life in Rio de Janeiro is taken from a book by an American traveler, Thomas Ewbank, who resided in Rio for about six months during 1846. Ewbank analyzed the life of the city in extraordinary detail, with particular emphasis on the customs of its population.

Source: Thomas Ewbank, *Life in Brazil; or a Journal of a Visit to the Land of the Cocoa and the Palm* (New York: Harper & Bros., 1856), pp. 92-95, 113-119, 277, 280-281, 436-437.

The "cries" of London are bagatelles to those of the Brazilian capital. Slaves of both sexes cry wares through every street. Vegetables, flowers, fruits, edible roots, fowls, eggs, and every rural product; cakes, pies, rusks, *doces* [sweets], confectionery, "heavenly bacon," etc., pass your windows continually. . . . If cases of cutlery, of glass ware, china, and silver have not already passed the door, they will appear anon. So of every article of female apparel, from a silk dress or shawl to a handkerchief and a paper of pins. Shoes, bonnets ready trimmed, fancy jewelry, toy-books for children, novels for young folks, and works of devotion for the devout . . . —these things, and a thousand others, are hawked about daily.

Vegetables are borne in open, fowls in covered baskets; pies, confectionery, and kindred matters are carried on the head in large tin chests, on which the owner's name and address are painted; dry-goods, jewelry, and fancy wares are exposed upon portable counters or tables, with glass cases fixed on them. These are very numerous.

Proprietors accompany silver-ware, silks, and also bread, for blacks are not allowed to touch the latter. When a customer calls, the slave brings his load, puts it down, and stands by till the owner delivers the articles wanted. The signal of dry-goods venders is made by the yard-stick, which is jointed like a two-foot rule. Holding it near the joint, they keep up a continual snapping by bringing one leg against the other. . . .

Young Minas and Mozambiques are the most numerous, and are reputed to be the smartest *marchandes*. Many a one has an infant added to her load: she secures it at her back by a wide piece of check wound round

her waist. Between the cloth and her body it nestles and sleeps; and when awake, inquisitively peeps abroad, like an unfledged swallow peering over the edge of its nest. To protect her babe from the sun, she suspends a yard of calico at the rear end of the case on her head: this serves as a screen, and, from its motions, acts somewhat as a fan. . . .

The way customers call street-venders is worth noticing and imitating. You step to the door, or open a window, and give utterance to a short sound resembling *shir*—something between a hiss and the exclamation used to chase away fowls; and it is singular to what a distance it is heard. If the person is in sight, his attention is at once arrested: he turns and comes directly to you, now guided by a signal addressed to his eyes—closing the fingers of the right hand two or three times, with the palm downward, as if grasping something—a sign in universal use, and signifying "Come." . . .

Here comes the tallest and blackest man-milliner I have yet seen; his dress, the usual brown shirt and trowsers, ending at the knees and elbows. His case contains Leghorn and fancy silk bonnets—nothing else. These he cries, and at every few steps turns to this side and that in quest of fair customers.

Yesterday a young negro came along with a couple of *Seguise*, or miniature monkeys. He stopped and held up the wicker cage, not over six inches square. "Tres milreis?" I said. "Não, senhor, seis milreis," putting forth his spread dexter hand, from which, sure enough, *six* fingers grew. This was the only itinerant Macaco [monkey] merchant I met in the streets; there are several in the market. . . .

I . . . continued on to the Campo—a spacious square, on the sides of which several national buildings stand, including the Senate-house. Covered with stunted grass, and the site of one of the principal fountains, it is the city's great washing and bleaching establishment, and is ever alive with lavandeiras [washerwomen]. More than two hundred are now scattered over the field, exclusive of crowds at the fount. From the surrounding mountain peaks they must appear like clamorous daws or restless magpies. How busy all are, each in the centre of a ring of drying garments! The huge wooden bowl, which, in coming and returning, serves as a basket, is now a washing-tub, and "the barril" a bucking-stool. Most are, like their Larangeiras sisters, slightly draped. A single vestment with most suffices, and with its purification the wearer winds up her labors. Some are Minas and Mozambique girls, as evinced by their superior forms, and attentions to attire. If others are naked to the waist, these are so seldom. Figures graceful as any seen at the wells of the East occur among them. . . .

The fountain supplies a wide district with water, and hence no small

10. A Peddler and His Slave in Rio de Janeiro

part of the colored population is constantly passing to and from it. Let us draw near. What a hubbub! A Hottentot fair cannot surpass it. These two military policemen may prevent a lusty negro squeezing in before his turn and pushing aside the half-filled barril of a weak one, but they can not silence the oral clamor. The fluid not borne off runs into two stone cisterns, thirty feet by fifteen, and keeps them knee-deep filled. They are bordered with granite coping, which, sloping outward, forms continuous washboards for the negroes within. A dozen or more are busy in each. Splash, swash, go shirts and sheetings! Plunged, pounded, twisted like a rope, swung overhead, and flap, slap, down they come upon the

11. Water Carriers at a Fountain in Rio de Janeiro

coping. A score of those thongs are whirling in the air at once, wielded by infuriates, whose laughings and screaming interjections break the monotony of the ceaseless gabble at the fount. . . . Lavandeiras have no saint assigned them, yet they deserve one, were it only to relieve them once a year from the washing-tub. . . .

I emerged from the long avenue in Direita Street, not far from the Custom-house, where street-passengers have to run amuck through piles of bales, barrels, packages, crates, trucks, and bustling and sweating negroes. Here are no carts drawn by quadrupeds for transportation of merchandise. Slaves are the beasts of draught as well as of burden. The loads they drag, and the roads they drag them over, are enough to kill both mules and horses. Formerly, few contrivances on wheels were used at the Custom-house. Every thing was moved over the ground by simply dragging it. A good deal of this kind of work is still done. See! there are two slaves moving off with a cask of hardware on a plank of wood, with a rope passed through a hole at one end, and the bottom greased or wetted! Such things were a few years ago very common.

Trucks in every variety are now numerous. Some recent ones are as heavily built and ironed as brewers' drays, which they resemble, furnished with winches in front to raise heavy goods. Each is of itself sufficient for any animal below an elephant to draw; and yet loads varying from half a ton to a ton are dragged on them by negroes. Two strain at the shafts and one or two push behind, or, what is quite as common, walk by the wheels and pull down the spokes. It is surprising how their naked feet and legs escape being crushed, the more so as those in front cannot prevent the wheels every now and then sinking into the gutters, and whirling the shafts violently one way or the other. One acts as a foreman, and the way he gives his orders is a caution to the timid. From a settled calm he in a moment rages like a maniac, and seems ready to tear his associates to pieces.

A slave was chained to one heavy truck. He had been absent when it was wanted, and his enraged owner took this method of preventing him from losing another job. The links of the chain were three quarter inch round iron.

Neither age nor sex is free from iron shackles. I met this morning a very handsome Mozambique girl with a double-pronged collar on; she could not have been over sixteen. And a few evenings ago, while standing on the balcony of a house in Custom-house Street, a little old negress, four fifths naked, toddled past, in the middle of the street, with an enormous tub of swill on her head, and secured by a lock and chain to her neck. "Explain that, Mr. C——," I said, "Oh, she is going to empty slops on the beach, and being probably in the habit of visiting vendas {taverns}, she is thus prevented, as the offensive vessel would not be admitted. Some slaves have been known to sell their 'barrils' for rum, and such are sent to the fountains and to the Praya {Beach} accoutred as that old woman is."

With a friend I went to the Consulado, a department of the Customs having charge over exports. Gangs of slaves came in continually with coffee for shipment. Every bag is pierced and a sample withdrawn while on the carrier's head, to determine the quality and duty. . . .

Every gang of coffee-carriers has a leader, who commonly shakes a rattle, to the music of which his associates behind him chant. The load, weighing 160 lbs., rests on the head and shoulders, the body is inclined forward, and the pace is a trot or half run. Most are stout and athletic, but a few are so small and slightly-made that one wonders how they manage to keep up with the rest. The average life of a coffee-carrier does not exceed ten years. In that time the work ruptures and kills them. They have so much a bag, and what they earn over the sum daily required by their owner they keep. Except four or five, whose sole dress was short canvas shirts, without sleeves, all were naked from the waist upward and from the knees below; a few had on nothing but a towel round the loins. Their rich chocolate skins shone in the sun. On returning, some kept up their previous chant, and ran as if enjoying the toil; others went more leisurely, and among them some noble-looking fellows stepped with much natural grace.

A gang of fourteen slaves came past with enormously wide but shallow baskets on their heads. They were unloading a barge of *sea-coal*, and conveying it to a foundry or forge. The weight each bore appeared equal to that of a bag of coffee (160 lbs.). . . . As with coal, so with every thing; when an article is once mounted on the head of a negro, it is only removed at the place where it is to remain.

A couple of slaves followed the coal-carriers, each perspiring under a pair of the largest sized blacksmith bellows—a load for a horse and cart with us. A week ago I stood to observe eight oxen drag an ordinary wagon-load of building stone for the Capuchins up the steep Castle hill; it was straining work for them to ascend a few rods at a time; today I noticed similar loads of stone discharged at the foot of the ascent, and borne up on negroes' heads.

No wonder that slaves shockingly crippled in their lower limbs are so numerous. There waddled before me, in a manner distressing to behold, a man whose thighs and legs curved so far outward that his trunk was not over fifteen inches from the ground. It appeared sufficiently heavy, without the loaded basket on his head, to snap the osseous stem and drop between his feet. I observed another whose knees crossed each other, and his feet prematurely apart, as if superincumbent loads had pushed his knees in instead of out. The lamplighter of the Cattete district exhibits another variety. His body is settled low down, his feet are drawn both to one side, so that his legs are parallel at an angle of thirty degrees. The heads of Africans are hard, their necks strong, and both, being perpendicular to the loads they are called to support, are seldom injured. It is the lower parts of the moving columns, where the weights are alternately thrown on and off the jointed thighs and legs, that are the weakest. These necessarily are the first to give way under excessive burdens; and here are examples of their having yielded and broken down in every direction. . . .

While waiting for Colonel F——, whose office is not far from the Matadouro [the public slaughterhouse], a dozen at least of butchers' slaves went past in the course of an hour with crushing loads of fresh-killed beef. The flesh was warm; it smoked, and all but quivered. One poor fellow had a collar, and a chain extending from it to an ankle; he belonged to a meat shop in the Cattete. Two hindquarters are a common load. Other slaves went by, awfully crippled in their feet and legs; among them two women, lame with elephantiasis, with light loads. The right leg of one was really almost as large as her waist. A purblind man, with a talha [large earthen vessel] of water on his head, crept along, feeling his way with a stick.

Some Minas girls, dealers in fowls, smartly dressed, and with tribal scars on their faces, passed on laughing. Each had a wide basket and a supplemental chicken in her hand, holding it, as the custom is here, by the wings. Of about one hundred and fifty blacks who thus passed by, all were slaves save one. His feet were thrust into a pair of old shoes or slippers—the badge of freedom. . . .

Among lithographic scenes of life in Rio [a reference to L. Buvelot and Auguste Moreau's *Rio de Janeiro Pitoresco* (Rio de Janeiro, 1845)] . . . those relating to the slaves are not the least conspicuous. There is no more fastidiousness, that I observed, about portraying them in shackles than in their labors and their pastimes.

It is said slaves in masks are not so often encountered in the streets as formerly, because of a growing public feeling against them. I met but three or four, and in each case the sufferer was a female. The mask is the reputed ordinary punishment and preventative of drunkenness. [See Fig. 22.] As the barril is often chained to the slave that bears it, to prevent him from selling it for rum, so the mask is to hinder him or her from conveying the liquor to the mouth, below which the metal is continued, and opposite to which there is no opening. . . .

On returning, I passed in the same street a short, spare, and feeble old woman, creeping along the pavement with a barril of water on her head. An iron collar grasped her shriveled throat, and from its prong a chain ran up and was secured to the handle of the vessel by a padlock—about as cruel a sight as I have yet seen.

"Is it a cause of wonder that so many of your slaves emancipate themselves by death rather than endure life on such conditions?" "To treat them in that way," replied my friend, "or to put masks on them, is forbidden, but laws respecting them are disregarded." Every day or two suicides are announced in the police reports, yet it is affirmed that not half are officially noticed. Those who plunge into the Bay and float ashore come under the cognizance of the authorities. Of such as sink and never rise, and all that pass out to sea, or are devoured by sharks before they reach it, no account is or can be kept, nor yet of those who destroy themselves in the secret places of the city or dark recesses of the neighboring forests. Many are advertised as runaways who have reached the spirit land. Suicides, it is said, have greatly increased during the last three years.

3.3. A Royal Navy Surgeon Discusses the Black Coffee Carriers of Rio de Janeiro (1848)

In 1848 the Select Committee on the Slave Trade of the House of Lords questioned one T.R.H. Thompson, a Royal Navy Surgeon who served in Brazil in the 1830s and 1840s. The following questions and answers are concerned with the hard-worked coffee carriers of Rio de Janeiro whom Ewbank also briefly described in the previous selection. In these excerpts from his testimony, Thompson provided specific information about *prêtos de ganho*, blacks who were sent out by their masters with the obligation to bring back a stated amount of money. As pointed out in the introduction to this part, such slaves were often obliged to meet their personal expenses for food and clothing with anything which might have been left over from their earnings. Failure to satisfy their masters often resulted in corporal punishment.

Source: *Second Report from the Select Committee on the Slave Trade Together with the Minutes of Evidence and Appendix* (London, 1848), p. 119.

❧ 5109. If the price [of slaves] were to fall would not the tendency be to increase the numbers that were sold in the Brazils?—That does not follow; it just depends upon the demand for labour; but the profit arising from slaves is so great that I think scarcely anything would induce the Brazilians to give it up. If you take the case of any of the slaves that are imported, and calculate the actual value of their labour, you will find it so enormous that nothing can be more profitable to them than the labour of slaves. If we take the coffee-carriers, who are the hardest worked of any of the Brazilian slaves, the average of their life is said to be about eight years after they are imported into the Brazils. They gain from 1 *s.* 4 *d.* to 2 *s.* a day carrying coffee, and they have to support themselves; taking 300 working days per annum, you have a very enormous sum realized at the end of eight years.

5110. Does the master get all that?—The master gets the whole of it. The system with the coffee-carriers is to send them out, and they have to bring home to their master a certain amount of money, and of course, to make a little over and above the sum for themselves they work remarkably hard, and drink to a fearful amount; they drink very hard; about eight years is said to be the average of the life of the coffee and sugar carriers, who are the hardest worked.

5111. Mr. *Gladstone.* What is the nature of their labour?—Merely carrying the coffee and sugar.

5112. *Chairman.* How do they carry it?—On the back.

5113. Mr. *Barkly.* From the plantations to the shipping place?—Yes, from the plantations; and also from the different localities where the sugar is brought in the town to the ships.

5114. Sir *E. Buxton.* They are porters, in fact?—They are.

5115. Mr. *Barkly.* They cannot carry a cask of coffee, can they?—Not a cask; it is all in bags.

5116. Mr. *Gladstone.* In point of fact, they are not field labourers?—No.

5117. Is that a large class?—It must be a considerable class.

5118. They do the work of beasts of burden?—Exactly; carrying the coffee, sugar, and those things, and loading of vessels; you see them in long strings.

5119. Are they task gangs?—No; they have to bring a certain amount of wages to their masters, and whatever they gain above that goes to their own subsistence.

5120. Sir *E. Buxton.* They are able to get about 2 *s.* a day, do you say?—Yes, from 1 *s.* 4 *d.* to 2 *s.* per diem, *i. e.* from 2 to 3 pataks [*pataca*, a silver coin worth 320 *reis*].

5121. One shilling and fourpence or two shillings a day, and they have to support themselves in addition?—Yes; so that the labour must be immense.

5122. Do you say that they are a large class?—They are a large class.

5123. This proves that the price of labour in the Brazils, in the towns at least, is about 2 *s.* a day?—No, it is not so much as that: I should think about 1 *s.* a day would be the average of the other, if you take the average of all classes; I have put it down, with the exception of those

12. Moving Cargo on a City Street

who have to work in this manner, and whose lives, therefore, are shorter, the average duration of them eight years.

5124. The mortality among those men is 12 per cent; 12 per cent. about kills them off in eight years?—Yes; but I have put down the others at 16 years, and supposing that one day with another they make 1 *s.* a day, the actual sum to the master, at the end of 16 years, would be 240 £.; so that if a man had a number of slaves, we will say if he could invest 5,000 £. in 100 slaves, if he had 100 coffee-carriers, earning 1 *s.* 6 *d.* daily, he would realize altogether at the end of the eight years, about 13,300 £., and so on in proportion.

3.4. The Sedan Chair and the Hammock: Urban Transportation in the Eighteenth and Nineteenth Centuries

For hundreds of years slave-borne *cadeirinhas* or sedan chairs and hammocks strung on poles were an elegant means of getting about in every major Brazilian city. Genteel Brazilians, who owned ornate sedan chairs as a means of displaying their opulence, dressed their porters in elaborate

13. Coffee Carriers in Rio de Janeiro

and outdated livery and shiny leather hats, which sometimes contrasted strangely with their bare feet, the badge of slavery. Many slaves supported their masters by hiring themselves and their chairs to the public, particularly in Bahia where the *cadeirinha* facilitated the arduous ascent from the port district to the city center high above the sea. Following are two brief descriptions by foreigners of this mode of transportation, one dealing with eighteenth-century Rio de Janeiro and the other with nineteenth-century Bahia.

Sources: René Courte de la Blanchardiere, *A Voyage to Peru* (London, 1753), pp. 114-115; Alexander Marjoribanks, *Travels in South and North America* (London: Simpkin, Marshall and Company, 1853), pp. 94-95.

Rio de Janeiro in the Eighteenth Century

The gentry here are usually carried in a kind of chair, ornamented in a very grand manner; but instead of two poles, as in Europe, they use but one, to which the chair is suspended, and this is carried upon negroes [*sic*] shoulders. This vehicle is always followed by at least one or two negro servants, dressed in a fine livery, but bare-footed. A lady is usually attended by four or five negro girls, who, besides a decent clothing, are ornamented with several rows of necklaces, and large gold earrings. If a person is carried in a hammock, he is obliged to lie along it.

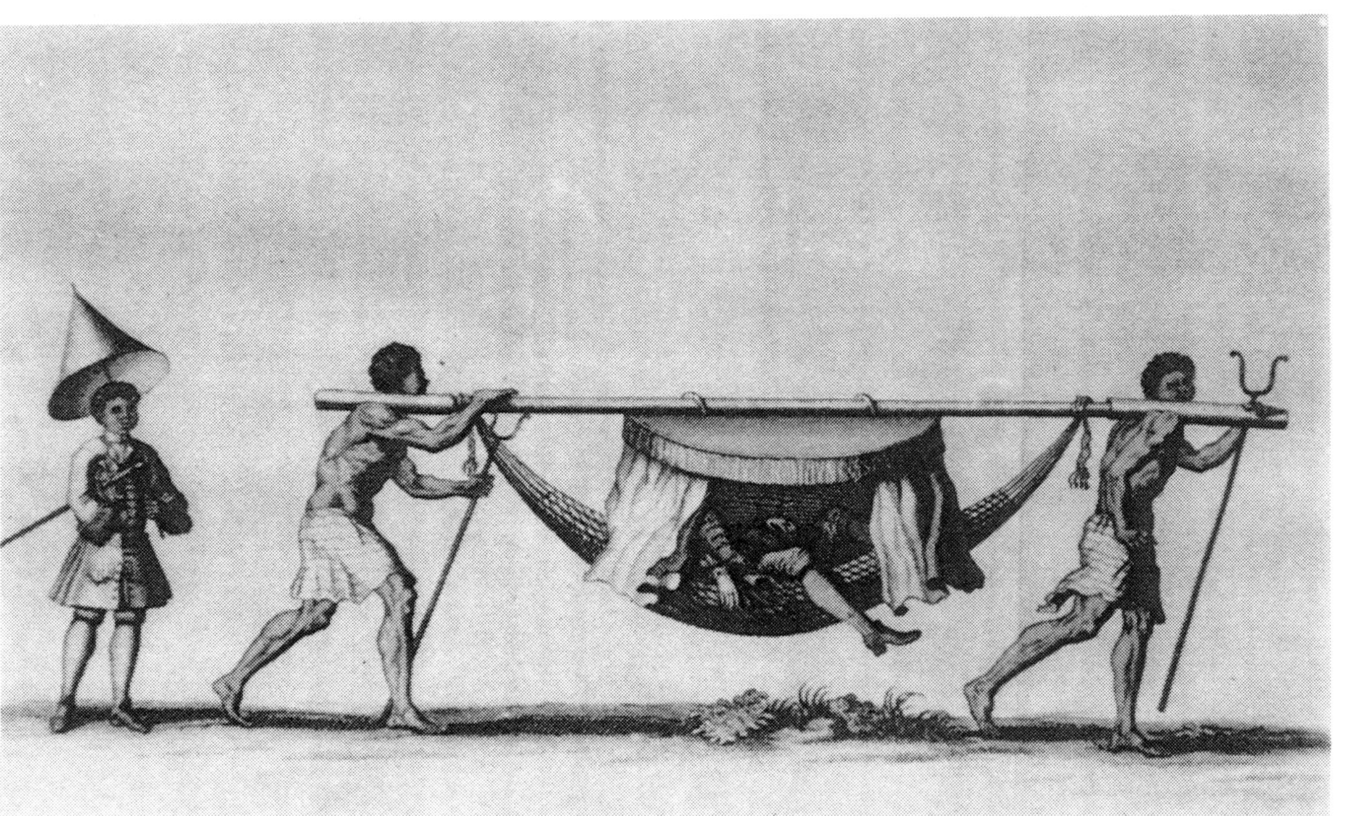

14. Slaves Bearing a Hammock in the Eighteenth Century

This hammock is suspended on a bamboo cane, and carried on the shoulders of two negroes. Over is a curtain, generally of some rich silk, which falls on both sides of the hammock, to keep off the rays of the sun, which are here excessively scorching. Those who are of a lower station and walk on foot must be poor indeed, if they are not attended by a negro carrying a large umbrella, at least of four feet and a half diameter, which is usually painted green.

Bahia in the Nineteenth Century

From the steepness of the streets of Bahia they use a curtained chair, with a pole placed along the top of it, which rests upon the shoulders of two slaves, one before and the other behind. The Cadeira, the name given to this sedan chair, is carried obliquely, so that each of the slaves may see his way before him, whilst it allows the person carried to see also, if he chooses to open the curtain at the side, as there is no glass about them. This forms the universal mode of travelling through the streets of Bahia. You meet with captains of ships, English and American sailors, fashionable ladies, bishops and fat priests, passengers from emigrant ships, the old and the young, the lame and the blind, all riding about in these cadeiras; and they are not very extravagant in their charges, as they carried me about a mile one day for ten-pence. From not being raised much more than a foot from the ground, even though they were to stumble, you could not fall far. One of our passengers who had got rather hearty, stepped into one of them, and not being able to balance himself properly, tumbled out onto the street, to the no small amusement of the slaves who were carrying him, and all those passing at the time. There are supposed to be a thousand of these cadeiras in Bahia, some of the higher classes keeping private ones of their own, so that you frequently meet cadeiras carried by two slaves dressed in livery. The cost of a cadeira is about £20 sterling. The owners of them generally let them out to their slaves at a certain sum per day, allowing them to pocket as much more as they can, and this makes them very active, and occasionally somewhat importunate, as when they see a decent person walking they are apt to ask if he wants a cadeira; but withal they are remarkably civil and obliging.

3.5. Slave Prostitutes in the Brazilian Capital (1871)

Prostitution was another cruel form of exploitation that Brazilian society permitted. As a result, many Brazilian towns contained notorious districts where demoralized and physically ravaged slave women offered themselves to the public, no doubt often against their will. Although it was not clearly illegal to use women in this fashion, it was obviously immoral, and dangerous as well to public health, and therefore urban authorities, including the police, sometimes intervened to protect the women concerned. In 1871, for example, a municipal judge, Miguel José Tavares, addressed a report to the chief of police of Rio de Janeiro on prostitution in the area of his jurisdiction and his personal crusade against it. The judge's letter and excerpts from the police chief's report to the minister of justice comprise the following selection. Together they tell much about the nature of slave prostitution in Brazil's cities and the efforts—or lack of them—on the part of responsible authorities to eliminate it.

Source: "Relatorio do Chefe de Policia da Corte," in *Relatorio apresentado á Assembléa Geral Legislativa na Terceira Sessão da Decima Quarta Legislatura pelo Ministro e Secretario de Estado dos Negocios de Justiça, Francisco de Paula de Negreiros Sayão Lobato* (Rio de Janeiro, 1871), pp. 21-22.

❧ Prostitution, which formerly, with some concern for decency, tried to conceal itself, has today reached a scandalous level and takes pride in displaying its horrid features. . . .

The matter belongs among the responsibilities of the police, and linked to it are the most delicate questions of morality, of hygiene, and of security.

The position of this authority is a most delicate one. . . .

There has been an increase in the public protests in this city against the immoral scandal of slave women prostituting themselves either by order or with the express consent of their masters, from which the latter gain exorbitant profits. These unfortunate women are forced to satisfy the hellish greed of these masters by practicing acts that are exceedingly offensive to public morality, presenting themselves at windows seminude, and arousing people on the streets to lustful acts almost forcibly by their words and gestures.

My predecessor, Counselor Luis Carlos de Paiva Teixeira, saw fit to address the Illustrious Municipal Chamber, in a letter dated November 7, 1861, concerning the need to take some action in regard to this question by means of an ordinance, in which penalties would be threatened against masters or renters of slave women who consigned them to prostitution.

Regarding the matter as one of very great importance, and the adoption of repressive measures as indispensable, I once again addressed the Illustrious Municipal Chamber on this matter, in a letter of September 15, 1869, without obtaining any result.

With the evil continuing on a large scale (and since it was verified by the reports of the Subdelegates having responsibility in this area that an excessive number of slave women are publicly consigned to prostitution by order or consent of their masters, either in their own homes, or in those of persons who rent them for such a criminal purpose) I decided to send the said reports to the Municipal Judge of the 2nd District, along with a letter dated January 18, with the aim of appointing protectors [*curadores*] for the slave women held under those conditions, so that they may demand on their behalf whatever might legally aid them.

The Municipal Judge of the 2nd District, giving the matter its deserved attention, with the zeal and energy which distinguish him, and which I regard as worthy of praise, immediately took some preliminary steps, which were crowned with great success and widely appreciated, as may be perceived from the message which he addressed to me on the 18th of the current month, and which I deem worthy of quotation.

"Municipal Judge of the 2nd District, March 18, 1871.
"Most Illustrious and Excellent Sir.

"Accepting the measure ordered by Your Excellency in your letter of January 18 of the current year, which accompanied the list of all the slave women prostituted and daily placed in view in windows by order of their owners, I appointed protectors for those unfortunate people. The protectors, who were called to such a noble purpose, accepted and even applauded with enthusiasm the measure which we took.—Two or three alone excused themselves, fortunately few.—The appointed protectors immediately demanded removal of their wards to private or public depositories. The public depository, under pretext that it did not have a guarantee for what it might spend in feeding the deposited women, refused to accept them. With great difficulty the private ones have accepted some of these unhappy people. This difficulty caused me to exert great efforts, and creates major problems for me. As soon as the press of this Court publicized the first measures which we took, some masters appeared to liberate the slave women whom they held in this sad state. The number of letters of emancipation registered in the notary offices of this Court has risen to more than one hundred and fifty. Some protectors have now found places for their wards to live, and some of them are located in family homes, earning wages. The ordinary responsibilities of this tribunal have not permitted me to order a roster of all the slave women in the depositories or being maintained in private homes; meanwhile, with no great error, I calculate at more than two hundred those who are bringing legal charges through their protectors.

"Allow me to point out to Your Excellency the dreadfulness of this cancer of the prostituted slave; a cancer with which I am completely familiar since, as a former police delegate, I made some efforts to root it out. The female slave posted at the window is not a woman; she is a machine who moves at the nod of her mistress, who forces her to laugh for the passers-by, threatened and frightened to tears by the pain of the whip, since at the end of the day she is forced to present an amount never less than ten *milréis*. Covered with syphilis, she does not get permission to abstain from these lewd acts. She must receive anyone who appears, even if nature demands abstinence. With cold liquids they are forced to suppress the lochial discharges after childbirth, and this is how their mistresses act, veritable peddlers of lust, selling for the price of a *milréis* the poison of syphilis and the health of the slave girl who, however robust she may be, cannot tolerate such excesses. What I have just narrated is a pale copy of what has been revealed in the interrogations of these unfortunate girls. Not only has there been cruelty to the body, but also to the spirit, because they prostitute the heart and the most personal and pure feeling—that of modesty and decency, to which every woman has a right, even if she is a slave. Among ancient people, where slavery was permitted by law, the master who obligated his slave woman to prostitute herself was obligated to free her. It was a great step forward for Roman Law, a subsidiary of our own in questionable cases, which Christianity and civilization have accepted. The tribunals of this Court have invariably regarded as free any slaves brutally treated by their masters; with greater reason I have understood that this favor should also be extended to the slave women who are cast into prostitution. Holding this opinion, I initiated the idea and am convinced that it will triumph. I have already achieved a great advantage: the dealers in slave women no longer sell them for three *contos de réis*. Furthermore, I have accomplished one hundred and eighty six liberations, and the slave women who find themselves in these circumstances are disappearing. These are the facts which I believed I should present to Your Excellency, who has cooperated so effectively with me in this matter.

"God Keep Your Excellency.—Most Illustrious and Most Excellent Dr. Francisco Faria Lemos, Chief of Police of the Court.—Municipal Judge of the 2nd District, *Miguel José Tavares*."

3.6. Newspaper Advertisements for Black Wet Nurses (1821-1854)

It was a common practice in Brazilian cities to purchase or rent slave women to serve as wet nurses (*amas de leite*) for infants of the more prosperous classes. The women so employed were usually teenagers or in their early twenties, both African and Brazilian-born, unmarried, and frequently without children of their own. This absence of children resulted in part, of course, from Brazil's heavy child mortality, particularly high among babies born of slave women, but it was also sometimes alleged that the unwanted babies of slave women were often abandoned or left at orphanages as a means of increasing the market value of new slave mothers. Many of these women attached themselves intimately to the families that employed them, and many were freed later in life as a gesture of respect or gratitude on the part of the masters whom they had cared for in infancy.

The following characteristically blunt advertisements for the purchase, sale, or rental of wet nurses are drawn from issues of nineteenth-century Brazilian newspapers.

❧ For rent, a wet nurse with very good milk, from her first pregnancy, gave birth six days ago, in the Rua dos Pescadores, No. 64. Be it advised that she does not have a child [*cria*].

Jornal do Comércio, Rio de Janeiro, December 10, 1827

Will trade a good black boy [moleque] 15 to 16 years of age, accustomed to the country, a good cook, does all the work of the house, makes purchases, does washing; for a wet nurse who has good milk, who also knows how to take care of a house, and who is without vices. Our reason [for trading] is that we have more need of the latter than of the former. Apply at house No. 39, Rua do Proposito. Also we will sell the said boy for no less than 350$000 *réis*.

Jornal do Comércio, Rio de Janeiro, December 10, 1827

For sale as a wet nurse or simply as a personal servant girl [*mucama*] an African who is twenty years of age, without a child, whose talents aside from the usual ones, are an ability to sew reasonably well, to iron, cook, and wash. She would be especially valuable for the service of any bachelor, or farmer, because she understands everything more or less perfectly, and alone can do all the work which normally employs many slave women. She has a good complexion, a good figure, and is for sale only because we have too many in the house. Her final price, free of tax, is 400$000, and she can be seen in the Rua dos Ferradores next to No. 385.

Jornal do Comércio, Rio de Janeiro, December 12, 1827

In the street behind Rua do Hospicio No. 27 we have for sale or for rent a black woman of the Mina nation with a six-day-old child, with very good milk and healthy. She is without vices or bad habits, since she is new in the country and does not even know how to get about in the streets.

Jornal do Comércio, Rio de Janeiro, December 13, 1827

Whoever wants to buy a creole slave, still a young girl, with good milk and in great quantity, who gave birth twenty days ago, should go to Rua das Marrecas, facing toward the public plaza.

Diario do Rio de Janeiro, June 18, 1821

For sale a black woman, wet nurse, without a child [*cria*], gave birth ten days ago from first pregnancy, 18 to 19 years of age, without any faults, knows how to wash, iron, cook, has learned the rudiments of sewing, and is capable of the full management of a house, in Rua do Sabão da Quitanda, upper section.

Diario do Rio de Janeiro, July 30, 1821

For rent two wet nurses, one Brazilian-born, the other African, both first pregnancies. One gave birth forty days ago, and the other twenty-six days ago. Both very healthy and very young with an abundance of milk. Whoever has use for them should go to Rua Estreita de São Joaquim No. 32.

O Mercantil, Rio de Janeiro, March 5, 1845

For rent an eighteen-year-old girl, wet nurse, healthy, and with much good milk for the last two months. She is for rent because her child has died. In the Rua da Candelaria No. 18A.

O Mercantil, Rio de Janeiro, April 30, 1845

In this printing office there is for rent a wet nurse, without a child, very healthy and affectionate.

O Observador, São Luis do Maranhão, March 22, 1854

3.7. A French Doctor with Twelve Years of Medical Experience in Brazil Advises Mothers on Choosing a Black Wet Nurse (1843)

Selecting a wet nurse to suckle the babies of more privileged families was obviously a serious matter, especially since many slaves were affected by chronic diseases such as syphilis or tuberculosis which might damage the children's health. Recognizing the dangers involved in the careless selection of an *ama de leite*, Dr. J.B.A. Imbert offered the following advice in his medical guide for mothers which was published in Rio de Janeiro in 1843.

Source: J.B.A. Imbert, *Guia medica das mães de familia, ou a infancia considerada na sua hygiene, suas molestias e tratamentos* (Rio de Janeiro: Typ. Franceza, 1843), pp. 51-53.

❧ *Selecting a Wet Nurse*

For the hypothetical case of a mother who cannot nurse her child without incurring the risk of endangering her own health, or that of her baby, we must obviously deal with the problem of choosing a wet nurse, and that of determining the qualities which she must possess if she is to meet fully the requirements demanded of her. Obviously this choice must be recognized as a thorny and difficult one, if we fully consider the attributes that a good and perfect wet nurse must possess. Yet this difficulty, great as it is, must never be allowed to justify the abandonment of every precaution in this respect. Thus we must inform mothers of how they may best make this choice through the enumeration of the necessary qualities, etc.

Let us recognize in the first place that white wet nurses would be preferable in every respect, if in this climate they offered the same advantages as those of the African race. The latter, organically formed to live in hot regions, in which their health prospers more than it does in any other place, acquire in this climate an ability to suckle babies which the same climate generally denies to white women, since the physical organization of the latter does not harmonize as well with the effects of the extreme temperature of these equatorial regions.

This fact being sufficiently obvious, our choice must therefore fall upon a black wet nurse, but we require that she be: 1) young, strong, and robust, that is, between twenty and twenty-four years of age, and physically well-constituted; 2) that her milk correspond as much as possible to the age of the child whom she is to suckle, so that this nourishment may conform to that which he would receive from the breast of his mother; 3) in order that the milk may be of good quality, it should be somewhat sweetish, without odor, white, and sufficiently consistent so as to form little drops when placed on a flat object; yet because the physical characteristics of the milk may vary according to the length of time since birth has occurred and because it becomes ever thicker, whiter, more buttery, and sweetish the older it gets, we must consider this circumstance when making the required appraisal of her qualities, in this way avoiding a mistaken judgment; 4) the breasts should be reasonably well developed, the nipples neither too hard nor too soft, neither very pointed nor shriveled up, but accomodated to the lips of the child; 5) we must assure ourselves that there does not exist a mark or scar on any part of the body, indications of a tubercular condition or some other illness of the body humors. In such a case we must reject her at once, and also if by the side of the breast any of those special symptoms present themselves which may cause us to fear a predisposition to pulmonary consumption, or which positively indicate the existence of the first or second stage of this terrible disease. To justify such a rejection, we should point out that in speculative medicine some doctors admit the defects of the blood and of the humors, whereas others reject them as pure fancies which exist only in the minds of those who dream them up. . . . Thus we believe in the existence of special and specific viruses . . . which possess, on the whole, the unfortunate property of transmitting themselves in a thousand ways from one individual to another by indirect or direct contact. We therefore share the opinion that a wet nurse can easily communicate to the child by means of nursing all the alterations pertaining to humors, with which she may be infected. Such a nurse should be discharged at once, because in regard to suckling children, one cannot take risks where any doubts exist. Repentance may follow, but a remedy will no longer be available. 6) The skin of the wet nurse should be smooth, soft to the touch, only slightly oily, and, most important, without a bad odor; 7) her teeth should be clean and clear, and her gums without signs of deterioration; her breath should be pure, her physiognomy agreeable, and her personality good. If a nurse is found with all these requisites, she may be assigned without fear to the physical education of the child. Nevertheless, if after a few days it is seen that her milk is insufficient for the child's nourishment, or that the child has declined owing to noticeable physical disorders, it will be necessary to replace her with another, whose milk may correspond in a more satisfactory way to the conditions of the nursing process.

3.8. Was the Black Wet Nurse a Transmitter of Disease? A Medical Debate in Rio de Janeiro (1846)

The following professional debate on the causes of high child mortality in the Brazilian capital, and its possible relationship to the use of slave wet nurses to suckle children of all classes, took place at the Imperial Academy of Medicine in Rio de Janeiro on June 18, 1846. Involved in this debate was Dr. José Pereira Rego, a noted student of epidemics and child mortality in Rio de Janeiro and author of several important articles and books on these topics (see Robert Conrad, *Brazilian Slavery*, p. 94).

Source: *Annaes de Medicina Brasiliense*, Vol. 2, No. 9 (February, 1847), pp. 193-195.

Order of the day. . . . 2nd. Part. Moving on to the questions proposed by the President as today's object of discussion:

. . . To what causes should we attribute the very high mortality among children during their first years of life? Should the custom of nursing infants at the breasts of slave women, who are very carelessly selected, be seen as one of the principal causes? . . .

Mr. Reis stated that we have in Rio de Janeiro special causes, which to a certain point explain the great mortality among children. . . . The principal ones, according to him, are the following: 1st. The custom immediately following birth of immersing babies in water, more or less hot, the result of which is an impairment of their skin circulation owing to the varying temperatures, sometimes excessively hot, and at other times colder than it should be. 2nd. The bad methods used to cut the umbilical cord and the customary use by ignorant midwives of irritating medical substances in its treatment. 3rd. Pressure on the head during delivery, aggravated further by rough handling by ignorant and unskilled midwives, along with the pressures that these careless and crude nurses exert upon the head during the suckling process, sometimes bending down over the child held in their laps, and sometimes even falling asleep in this position. 4th. The use and abuse of strong foods during the first six months, and even long after, and resulting irritations of the stomach and intestines, and gastroenteritis. These illnesses are extremely common in the first years of life and are the main causes of child mortality in this city. 5th. The failure to provide children with adequate clothing, a type of neglect that becomes more evident when children reach one year of age, children being allowed to go about the house, and even in the streets, almost naked. And, much less commonly, there are children who are excessively dressed. 6th. The delegation of the mothers' natural responsibilities to slave women, which brings on a host of problems stemming from the poor quality of the milk of these nurses, as well as all those difficulties caused by the contagious diseases which these nurses are infected with. 7th. Clothes that are too constricted, especially among girls. 8th. The effects of the bad personal behavior of slave nurses, and, at a later age, these same nurses inducing a precocious development among the children of those activities which normally begin at the age of puberty, thus exposing them at a tender age not only to the evils of immoderacy, but to the contagious diseases that result from relations inappropriate to their age. 9th. Carelessness in the choice of African nurses, or false or mistaken considerations, such as searching for nurses who appear well-fed, have very clean, smooth, and shiny skins, and an unusually black color, without visible diseases, and with milk having a good appearance; all this being done by examination at the time of selection. Parents of the children satisfy themselves with these routine measures without carefully investigating the former lives of the nurses in order to be certain, or at least to increase the likelihood, that they do not suffer from syphilitic diseases, principally chancres and scrofula. There is nothing more deceptive and misleading than all these signs, principally the appearance of the milk and the smooth, clean skin, since these conditions are often found in nurses who have suffered from chancres, scrofula, and other diseases, which will certainly appear later in the children whom they nurse. Parents should be more careful in this regard, if they do not want their children to suffer later, or to die during their earliest years. He was of the opinion that this last cause is among those having the greatest effects, and his judgment is based on many cases he has seen of strong, healthy, well-nourished babies who, delivered over to those nurses, quickly began to ail, to grow thin, and were quickly covered with skin conditions such as chancre and other syphilitic eruptions, the itch, ringworm, ulcers, etc.

Dr. [José Pereira] Rego responded negatively to the second part of the first question. According to him, most of the children who die in Rio de Janeiro do not succumb to contagious diseases. He was persuaded therefore that nursing is of little significance. One of the principal causes, according to him, is the violation of the principles of nourishment, either by giving an excessive amount, or due to a lack of adequate foods, particularly among the slaves, because there are masters who at times overburden one nurse alone with a number of children, without giving her the necessary sustenance. This last problem, however, is less common than excessive feeding, which occurs most frequently among the children of wealthy people, and among the slaves themselves, since the nurses force every kind of food available upon the children's stomachs, with the aim of keeping them well-satisfied. As a result they stuff those delicate stomachs with indigestible foods, the result of which is stomach and intestinal irritations, and later true and chronic gastroenteritis with mesenteritis and diarrheas. . . . Concerning degenerated milk [Dr. Pereira Rego] recognized its possible effects, but he did not attribute to it the importance of the other indicated causes. . . .

Mr. Reis insisted that suckling with diseased nurses is one of the most important causes of the diseases and mortality among children in Rio de Janeiro, and that this is especially true in the interior of the provinces, where the number of people affected by syphilis and elephantiasis is very considerable, and where more than elsewhere one can observe the sad results of this practice.

3.9. The Black Wet Nurse: A Status Symbol (1863)

Black servants in Brazil, including *amas de leite*, were not merely nursemaids, housekeepers, and washerwomen. They also had an important role to play in many households as friends, lovers, and confidants (see Document 5.5). Moreover, by their sheer numbers and fine attire, *mucamas* and *amas de leite* acted as living evidence of their owners' wealth and high social status. (See Fig. 19.) The following analysis of the role of the *ama de leite* as a status symbol in Rio homes is from a book by a French critic of Brazilian society whose several works reflect an unusual interest in the situation of Brazil's female inhabitants, both slave and free.

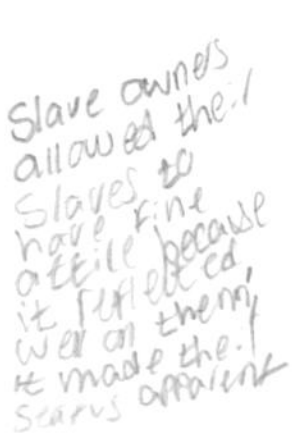

Source: Charles Expilly, *Le Brésil tel qu'il est* (Paris: Jung-Treuttel, 1863), pp. 203-205.

❧ In the homes of the merchants of the city [Rio de Janeiro] it is a matter of personal self-esteem to have a wet nurse who serves to display their insolent extravagance. Also this can conceivably take the form of a speculation. The luxury of possessing a wet nurse can reveal the prosperity of the house, if it does not in fact give the public a false impression regarding the true state of affairs. The black girl, richly and splendidly dressed, approaching with her head held high, a superb smile on her lips, as majestic as an ancient goddess, will obviously establish with her fine attire and the embroidered garment of the child she carries, the immense wealth of her masters. A magnificant get-up, but sometimes as deceptive as those grand balls given in Paris to mislead public opinion and reduce the fears of uneasy debtors the night before a "hurried" departure for Brussels. Without the proud creature even being aware of it, her rich clothing in these cases is nothing more than a dishonest lure, a bait offered cleverly to suspicious debtors, misleading evidence. Because the shining buckles on her polished shoes, her silk stockings, her coral necklace, the lace on her blouse and the many flounces on her muslin dress are intended to hide an empty cash box, behind which deceitfully lurks the hideous specter of bankruptcy.

The nurse, however, is little concerned with the role she is made to play. Gifts of every kind are displayed round her neck, on her hands, her arms; she glitters, she struts through the streets behind her mistress, breathing with full nostrils the atmosphere of flattering compliments which accompany her, humiliating her female companions with her flashy finery, drunk, finally, with all the suspect perfumes which mount to her head. If her coquettishness is fully satisfied in her new role, her greed has no cause for complaint either. The best foods served at her master's table are sent to her, and she squanders delicate morsels of every kind which are given to her, even before she has had an adequate time to desire them. . . .

And here again is one of the deadly results of slavery, that unhealthy institution which smothers all sense of decency in the woman, every moral feeling in the man. Without waiting for love to speak to her heart, the young woman seeks, not the sweet pleasures, but the benefits of motherhood. An obsession dominates her, a selfish, shameful scheme, which leads her to a disorderly life. She resolves to become a mother in order to become a wet nurse, even if to achieve her goal she is forced to abandon her child, the innocent fruit of a hateful speculation.

3.10. Slave Workers at the Diamond Washings of Tejuco, Minas Gerais, in the Early Nineteenth Century

Slaves were also employed during the eighteenth and nineteenth centuries in the diamond washings of the interior province of Minas Gerais, particularly in the so-called diamond district centered in and about the colonial town of Tejuco, the modern Diamantina. The following account of the working and living conditions of slaves employed at the diamond washings was written by the French naturalist, Auguste de Saint-Hilaire. Saint-Hilaire lived and traveled in southern and western Brazil from 1816 to 1822. His many volumes of observations are among the most important sources of information on the colony just prior to independence.

Source: Auguste de Saint-Hilaire, *Viagem pelo distrito dos diamantes e litoral do Brasil* (São Paulo: Companhia Editora Nacional, 1941), pp. 8-11.

❧ The places where diamonds are extracted are called *serviços*. Each *serviço* has a warehouse-keeper and a miller, offices of the same category and with the same salary as that of the overseers. The various *serviços* are supplied with carpenters, sawyers, etc., and these are at the same level as the overseers, having a number of slaves under their command. . . .

All the slaves occupied in the various *serviços* belong to private owners who rent them to the administration. There was a time when their number rose to three thousand, but the administration, then much in debt, was forced to reduce the number to one thousand. In the beginning they were paid at the rate 1$200 [1,200 *milréis*] per week. This amount was then reduced to $900, later to $675. The owners of the slaves dress them and treat them when they are sick, and the administration feeds them and supplies the tools that they need for their work.

For their nourishment the blacks receive each week one-fourth of an *alqueire* [about 3 1/4 pounds] of *fubá* [corn flour], a certain quantity of beans, and a little salt, and to these provisions they add yet a slice of roll tobacco. When beans are unavailable they substitute meat. The black slaves eat three times a day, in the morning, at noon, and in the afternoon. Since they have very little time at their disposal during the day, they are forced to cook their food at night, and at times they have no fuel other than dried herbs.

Forced to stand constantly in water during the time when they are panning for diamonds and consuming foods of little nutritive value, their intestinal tract is weakened and they become morose and apathetic. Aside from this, they often run the risk of being crushed by rocks which, undermined from the mineral beds by digging, loosen themselves and fall. Their work is constant and agonizing. Ever under the watchful eye of the overseers, they cannot enjoy a moment of rest. Nevertheless, almost all of them prefer the extraction of diamonds to working for their masters. The money they acquire by stealing diamonds and the hope they nourish of acquiring their freedom if they find stones of great value are undoubtedly the main reasons for this preference, and yet there are others. Brought together in large numbers, these unfortunate people entertain themselves during their work; they sing in chorus songs of their countries, and, whereas in the houses of their masters they are subjected

15. Washing for Diamonds in Minas Gerais Early in the Nineteenth Century

to all of their masters' whims, here they obey a fixed set of rules, and if they adapt themselves to those rules, they need not fear punishment.

The overseers ordinarily carry a large stick topped off by a strip of leather, which serves for the immediate punishment of any black who seeks to evade his duty. When the offense is grave the punishment is more severe. Then the guilty man is tied up, and two of his companions apply blows to his buttocks with a *bacalhau*, a whip made up of five plaits of leather. The overseers do not have permission to use this kind of whip, and only the private administrators can inflict such a severe punishment. The regulations forbid the application of more than fifty lashes with a *bacalhau*. Nevertheless, they often exceed this limit.

When a black finds a diamond which weighs one dram (an eighth of an ounce), the administrator evaluates the slave, buys him from his master, provides him with clothes, and awards him his freedom. His companions crown him and grant him a joyful demonstration, carrying him in triumph on their shoulders. He has the right to keep his job in the diamond administration, and each week he receives $600, which previously was paid to his master. When a black man finds a diamond weighing three-fourths of a dram, his freedom is guaranteed, but he is obliged to work yet for a certain time for the administration. It was Sr. da Câmara who made these additions to the regulations. In 1816 three blacks were freed, but until October, 1817, no black had yet enjoyed this benefit. For the diamonds that weigh less than three-fourths of a dram the blacks receive small rewards in proportion to the value of the stones, for example, a knife, a hat, a waistcoat, and so forth.

When a black slave finds a diamond, he shows it to the overseer, holding it between his thumb and index finger, his other fingers separated. The diamond is then guarded in a bowl which is hung from the tile-covered shed under which the diamond washing is carried on. At the end of the day the overseers together submit the results of the day's work to the private administrator.

3.11. Black Miners at a British-Owned Gold Mine in the 1860s

After Brazil achieved its independence in 1822, British capital entered the country in some force, and by 1840 six British mining companies were established at various places in the interior, employing more than 3,000 slaves in their operations. The British-owned Morro Velho mine, located in the heart of Minas Gerais, was visited in 1868 by the British explorer, Richard F. Burton, who took advantage of his position as consul at the port of Santos to make extensive journeys in the Brazilian interior. The following is his account of the British company's treatment of the hundreds of male and female slaves employed at the Morro Velho mine. Burton's testimony probably suffers from his clear racial prejudices and his obvious attempt to defend the mining company's ownership of slaves, which was contrary to British law.

Source: Richard F. Burton, *Explorations of the Highlands of the Brazil; with a Full Account of the Gold and Diamond Mines. Also Canoeing down 1500 Miles of the Great River São Francisco, from Sabará to the Sea*, 2 vols. (London: Tinsley Brothers, 1869), I, 273-277.

❧ I proceed now to give my account of the black miner as I found him at Morro Velho. Without including 130 children of hired blacks, and who are not under contract, the establishment consists of 1,450 head, thus distributed: Company's blacks, 254 (109 men, 93 women, and 52 children); Cata Branca blacks, 245 (96 men, 87 women, and 62 children); blacks hired under contract, 951.

In these numbers we may see a modification of Saint Hilaire's [see previous document] statement, "*le service des mines ne convient pas aux femmes*" [service in the mines is not fit for women]. This might have been true under the old system, it is not so now. Generally in the Brazil men are preferred upon the sugar plantations, women on those that grow coffee, and as they are wanted for domestic purposes it is not so easy to hire them.

The "Company's Blacks" consider themselves the aristocracy, and look down upon all their brethren. Both they and the Cata Brancas are known by the number on their clothing; the hired negroes wear also M. V. [Morro Velho] marked on their shirts. The establishment expends per mens. £1400 upon contracts: I need hardly remark what a benefit this must be to the large proprietors of the neighbourhood. Thus the Commendador Francisco de Paula Santos lets under contract a total of 269 (including 173 children), his son-in-law Sr. Dumont 145 (97 adults and 48 children), and the Cocaes or National Brazilian Mining Association contributes 142 negroes and 13 children.

The figures given below will show the average of hire:

Annual hire of first-class slaves	men	220$000	women	100$000
Not paying in case of death or flight	"	230$000	"	110$000
Annual hire of second-class slaves	"	150$000	"	75$000
Not paying in case of death or flight	"	160$000	"	75$000

Clothing, food, and medical treatment are at the Company's expense. Usually the agreement is for three to five years, during which period the slave cannot be manumitted. As a rule the Superintendent employs only robust men who have passed a medical examination, but he will take in doubtful lives under annual contract. The slave is insured by a deduction of 10$000 to 20$000 per annum for a fixed period; and if he dies before the lease has expired the owner still receives his money—there are actually eighty-nine cases of this kind. Pay ceases only if the negro runs away: it is issued every third or sixth month, and the contractors can obtain one year's advance, at a discount of ten per cent.

As regards labour, all are classified according to their strength into first, second, and third-class blacks. In 1847 permission to work overtime, that is to say, beyond nine hours forty-five minutes, was given to the first-rates. There is another division into surface and underground blacks. The former are smiths and mechanics, especially carpenters and masons, who work between 6 A.M. and 5 P.M., with one hour forty-five minutes of intermission for meals. The oldest and least robust are turned into gardeners, wood-fetchers, and grass-cutters. The regular work day at Morro Velho is as follows:

5 A.M. Reveillé sounded by the gong, and half an hour afterwards the Review.

6 A.M. Work.

8.15 A.M. Breakfast.

9 A.M. Work.

12.30 P.M. Dinner.

1.15 P.M. Work.

2 P.M. Change guard. Blasting in the mine.

5.30 P.M. Mechanics' work ended.

8.30 P.M. Return to quarters. The slaves cook their own meals and eat supper at home. Saturday is a half-holiday: they leave off work at 2.30 P.M., and retire at 9 P.M.

The underground labourers are borers, stope cleaners, trammers who push the wagons, kibble-fillers, and timber-men: they are divided into three corps, who enter the mine at 6 A.M., 2 P.M., and 10 P.M. On Sunday the gangs shift places, so that only one week in three is night work. A rough estimate makes the number of the gang in the mine at the same time 620, including all hands. When work is over they proceed to the changing-house, and find a tepid bath at all hours. They put on their surface-clothes, and leave the mine suits either to be dried in the open air, or by flues during the rains. The precaution is absolutely necessary, though very difficult and troublesome to be enforced: the English miners shirk it, and the free Brazilians are the most restive, though they are well aware how fatal are wet garments.

The blacks lodge in the two villages situated half-way between the bottom of the river valley and the Morro Velho hill. Thus, while they escape malaria they are saved fatigue when going to, or coming from work. They begin the day with coffee or Congonhas tea. Their weekly allowance, besides salt and vegetables, comprises 9 lb. of maize meal, 4 1/2–5 lb. of beans, 13 1/2 oz. of lard, and 2 lb. of fresh beef. Meat of the best quality here averages 3$000 per arroba [32 pounds], or two-pence a pound, and the labourers purchase, at cost prices, the heads and hoofs, the livers and internals of the bullocks killed for the use of the establishment. The industrious have their gardens and clearings: they keep poultry and pigs, fattened with bran, which they receive gratis. Part they eat, the rest they sell to procure finery and small luxuries. "Carne Seca" [dried or salted beef] and farinha [manioc flour] are issued when the doctor orders. Nursing women have something added to the six-tenths of a plate of meal, one quarter of beans, and two ounces of lard, and children when weaned claim half rations. All the articles are of good quality, and if not a report is made to the Manager of Blacks.

Drink is not issued every day, nor may it be brought into the establishment. A well-conducted negro can obtain a dram once per diem with permission of the chief feitor or overseer. Each head of a department has a supply of "restilio" [rum], which he can distribute at discretion, and the mine captain can give a "tot" [an allowance of drink] to any negro coming wet from duty. It is, however, difficult to correct the African's extreme fondness for distilled liquors, which in this light and exciting air readily affect his head, and soon prove fatal to him. He delights also in "Pango," [hashish] here called Arirí, the well-known Bhang (Cannabis sativa) of India, and of the east and west coast of Africa. He will readily pay as much as 1$000 for a handful of this poison.

I never saw negroes so well dressed. The men have two suits per annum—shirt and overalls of cotton for the hot, and of woolen for the cold season; the "undergrounds" receive, besides these, a stout woolen shirt, and a strong hat to protect the head. Each has a cotton blanket, renewed yearly, and if his dress be worn or torn, the manager supplies another. The women work in shifts of thin woolen stuff, and petticoats of stronger material; they usually wear kerchiefs round their neck, thus covering the bosom, and one shoulder, after the fashion of African "Minas," is left bare. In winter capes of red broadcloth are added to the Review costume.

The slave labourer is rewarded with gifts of money; he is allowed leave out of bounds, even to Sabará [a nearby town]; he is promoted to the offices of trust and of increased pay; he is made an overseer or a captain over his own people; at the Review he wears stripes and badges of distinction, and he looks forward to liberty. [In a note Burton included a list showing that 118 slaves had become candidates for manumission at

Morro Velho from 1848 through 1866, an average of a little more than six per year.]

The chief punishments are fines, which negroes, like Hindus, especially hate; the penalties, which now amount to 400$000, have been transferred to charitable purposes, and swell a small reserved trust-fund, intended to support the old and infirm. Other pains are, not being allowed to sell pigs, poultry, and vegetables; arrest within the establishment or confinement in a dry cell, with boards like a soldier's guard-room; fugitives are put in irons. Formerly the manager and the head captain, who required implicit obedience from the 500 hands of the underground department, could order a flogging. This was abolished, not, I believe, with good effect. Every head of a department can still prescribe the "Palmatoria" [a wooden device used to rap slaves on the hands], but he must note and report the punishment to the Superintendent. Only the latter can administer a flogging with the Brazilian cat of split hide; and this is reserved for confirmed drunkenness, disobedience of orders, mutiny, or robbing fellow-workmen. The punishment list is sent in every fortnight, and as a rule is small. I especially noticed the civil and respectful demeanour of Morro Velho blacks, who invariably touch their hats to a white stranger, and extend their hands for a blessing. They are neither impudent, nor cringing, nor surly, and, in my opinion, there is no better proof that they are well and humanely treated.

3.12. "Common Graves": How City Slaves Were Buried

The next two documents, the first composed of excerpts from the regulations of the public cemetery in Olinda, Pernambuco (1858), the second a description of the slave cemetery of the Misericórdia (Mercy Hospital) in Rio de Janeiro (about 1825), are evidence that squalor, insult, and neglect were as characteristic of the treatment of slaves after their deaths as they generally were while they were still alive.

Sources: *Collecção das leis provinciaes de Pernambuco do anno de 1858*, pp. 75, 80-81; Eduardo Theodoro Bösche, *Quadros alternados (Impressões do Brasil de D. Pedro I)*, trans. Vincente de Souza Queirós (São Paulo: Typ. da Casa Garraux, 1929), p. 120.

Regulations for the Public Cemetery of Nossa Senhora da Conceição of the City of Olinda

Art. 28. The following will be buried free of charge: . . . 2. Those bodies found in any public place, whose relatives, guardians, masters, proprietors, or employers are not located, or when no one comes to claim them. Such persons will be buried in common graves. . . .

Art. 66. Bodies buried in common graves will be placed side by side, but never on top of one another. This type of burial is especially intended for the cases dealt with in Art. 28.

Art. 67. Slaves will also be buried in common graves, but in a distinct and separate place from that which serves for the burial of free people. . . .

Art. 70. There will be two books for registering the dead: one for free persons and the other for slaves; these will be initiated, numbered, rubricated, and closed by the president of the municipal chamber, and maintained by the administrator.

Art. 71. Each entry in the registry of free deceased persons will contain a declaration of the name, place of birth, age, marital status, profession, residence, time of death, and disease that caused death, along with the number of the tomb or grave in which the individual is laid to rest.

Art. 72. Each entry in the registry of deceased slaves should contain a declaration of the individual's name, his master's name, his age, marital status, place of birth, and the disease from which he died. . . .

The Black Cemetery of Nossa Senhora da Misericórdia in Rio de Janeiro

Among the institutions of charity, the great public hospital known as the Misericordia deserves first mention. Accomodations for several thousand people exist in this beneficent institution, and the sick of every color and nation are received.

Yet a glance at its interior conditions and at the terrible diseases that are treated here is enough to fill one with horror. Behind this building, situated near the bay, is the cemetery of the blacks and of the poor people of Rio.

Nothing more wretched and nasty can be imagined than this cemetery, which in fact looks more like a trash deposit than a cemetery. Here no cypress tree mourns over expensive cenotaphs; in this place of horror and death we do not find the usual loving messages with which gratitude and dedication ornament the tombs of absent relatives. Putrefaction and decomposition have here installed their throne composed of skulls and human limbs, with empty eyes visible over the entire length of their silent and deserted realm.

The surface is of eighty square meters, and in such a small space thousands of people are buried every year. The dead do not come in coffins, but rather in most cases are as naked as the day they were born. When they arrive they are immediately thrown into a large ditch. This undecorated grave remains open until some thirty bodies have filled it up (they are known for their love of company), and then it is covered with earth.

However, this latter operation is carried out with such negligence that quite often a foot, an arm or a head remains uncovered, as if the dead still had something to do on earth, and were making an effort to return.

. . .

Under the sun's action the bodies decompose so fast and are so quickly consumed by vermin, that after a few days they open the ditches again to receive new candidates.

The bones are then piled up, and often skulls with hair may be seen. The distinguished families bury their dead in the churches. . . .

FOUR

"From Babylon to Jerusalem": Slavery and the Catholic Church

HISTORIANS who have claimed that slavery in Brazil and Spanish America was comparatively humane have usually emphasized the role of the Catholic Church in this alleged achievement (see especially Frank Tannenbaum, *Slave and Citizen*, and Herbert S. Klein, *Slavery in the Americas*, pp. 86-105). As several documents in this part in fact reveal, particularly 1, 2, and 8, such claims regarding the Church's positive role are rooted in Catholic doctrine and actual procedures and customs introduced by Portugal and Spain into their American colonies. The Catholic Church did indeed regard masters and slaves as equal in the sight of God, and looked upon blacks as human beings with souls worthy of being saved. The Church, which had the authority to intervene in the master-slave relationship, theoretically required owners of newly imported Africans to acquaint them with the fundamentals of Christian doctrine, to see to it that they were baptized and received the sacraments, that they attend mass on Sundays and Church holidays, and that on those days they refrain from all unnecessary labor. In Brazil and Spanish America slaves, free blacks, and mulattoes were encouraged to organize their own religious brotherhoods, and in Brazil some of these organizations adopted Nossa Senhora do Rosario (Our Lady of the Rosary) as their special patroness, erecting fine churches for her worship and making these churches the center of their social world (see Document 4.4 and Fig. 16). On some plantations, at least, masters and slaves attended mass together, and at many a big house slaves were made to line up at night after a day's toil to receive their masters' ceremonial blessing (see Document 2.7). Canon law stipulated that slaves were to be married in the Church, and, once married, a couple could not be *honorably* separated by their master. The Church did not actually condemn the enslavement of blacks, as authors like Tannenbaum and Klein correctly pointed out, but it did encourage manumission, and some Church leaders, aware of the abuses which slaves suffered, implored masters, both in print and in the pulpit, to treat them in a more humane and Christian way (see Documents 1, 2, and 3 in this part and 7.2).

There is, then, evidence that as a body the Catholic Church opposed the worst features of the Brazilian slave system, and that in a kinder world it would have fashioned something more commendable. Unfortunately, however, historians like Tannenbaum, perhaps too eager to emphasize the evils of Southern slavery, used that evidence uncritically, overlooking sources of the kind that fill this volume. Writing before much serious research had been done on Latin American slavery in the United States, such authors overlooked some key facts about Brazilian slave society.

In the first place, despite its great moral and civic authority, not even the Catholic Church had the power to oversee and control the great slaveholding landlords who were scattered over vast areas of Brazil and who saw themselves as all-powerful on their own estates. In the second place, clergymen in Brazil, themselves commonly members of the privileged slaveholding class, possessed and exploited slaves of their own, as did the monasteries, Catholic brotherhoods, and other Church organizations (see Documents 6 through 9 in this part), and by doing so they set an example for the lay population which strengthened the worst features of slavery.

In the third place (and here we have an important contrast with the United States), whereas Quakers, Methodists, and other Protestant churches served in the vanguard of the American anti-slavery movement, the Church in Latin America was for centuries a bulwark of slavery (see Documents 2 and 5 in this part), rarely making efforts to quicken the cause of freedom. To give just one example, the foremost Brazilian defender of the slave trade toward the end of the eighteenth century was a leading member of the Luso-Brazilian clergy, Bishop José Joaquim da Cunha de Azeredo Coutinho of Pernambuco, who in 1798 published an outspoken defense of the slave trade (see Sergio Buarque de Holanda, ed., *Obras econômicas de J. J. da Cunha de Azeredo Coutinho* [São Paulo, 1966]), inspiring many a later defender of slavery (see Document 10.2). In 1808 the same author published a second work on the topic which demonstrated the compatibility of papal bulls and Portuguese laws in support of the slave trade, thus documenting the Church's long and steadfast support of that traffic (see *Concordancia das leis de Portugal e das bullas pontificias, das quaes humas permittem a escravidão dos pretos d'Africa, e outras prohibem a escravidão dos indios do Brazil*, Lisbon, 1808).

The Church's record on the slavery issue was hardly better during slavery's last years. Characteristically, it was not until May 5, 1888, a week before Brazilian slavery ended, that Pope Leo III at last released an encyclical giving long-overdue support to the Brazilian anti-slavery cause. Before that event, most members of the Brazilian clergy had remained nearly silent on the issue. The abolitionist, Joaquim Nabuco was not far off the mark when he wrote: "Our clergy's desertion of the role which the Gospel assigned to it was as shameful as it could possibly have been. No one observed it taking the side of the slaves; no one saw it using religion to ease the burdens of their captivity, or to propose moral truths to the masters. No priest ever tried to stop a slave auction; none ever denounced the religious regimen of the slave quarters. The Catholic Church, despite its immense power in a country still greatly fanaticized by it, *never* raised its voice in Brazil in favor of emancipation." (*Abolitionism*, pp. 18-19.)

4.1. Slavery and Church Doctrine: The Archbishop of Bahia Rules on Slave Evangelization and Aspects of Their Treatment (1707)

The basic positions of the Catholic Church in regard to the slaves are stated in the following excerpts from a large volume of precepts and regulations governing the Brazilian religious community which was first issued by the Archbishop of Bahia, D. Sebastião Monteiro da Vide, in 1707. This selection shows how painfully aware Church leaders were that the slave's de facto condition and his poor understanding (as a newly imported alien) of the Portuguese language and culture and of basic Christianity stood in the way of his complete incorporation into the Church. Equal in the sight of God, the slave's disadvantages in Brazil, it was alleged, caused him to be in greater need of spiritual assistance than other communicants. Specifically, the slave was to be introduced to Christianity through expedients fashioned to meet his particular needs.

Other parts of this selection reveal the Church's positive stand on slave marriage, its general prohibition of slave labor on Sundays and holy days of obligation, and its strong opposition to the practice of forcing slaves to work on those days as a means of acquiring their own food and clothing—a practice evidently common during the colonial period, since it was often condemned by the Church and the royal government (see Documents 2.2 and 2.3). These and other provisions of the *Constituições Primeiras* suggest the Church's difficult position in the face of the basic contradiction between its teachings and the realities of the colonial slavery which it supported.

Source: *Constituições Primeiras do Arcebispado da Bahia feitas e ordinadas pelo Illustrissimo e Reverendissimo Senhor D. Sebastião Monteiro da Vide*, 3rd ed. (São Paulo: Na Typ. de Dezembro de Antonio Louzada Antunes, 1853), pp. 2-3, 20-22, 125-126, 150-152, 219-222, 272-273, 295-296, 340-341.

❧ 4. We order all persons, ecclesiastics as well as secular, to teach or have taught the Christian doctrine to their families, and especially to their slaves, who because of their ignorance are those most in need of this instruction, sending them to church so that the priest may teach them the Articles of Faith, so that they may know what to believe; the Pater Noster and Ave Maria, so that they may know how to pray; the Commandments of the Law of God and of the Holy Mother Church, and the moral sins, so that they will know how to behave; the virtues, so that they may recognize good values; and the seven Sacraments, so that they may receive them with dignity, and with them the grace which they give, and the other prayers of Christian doctrine, so that they may be instructed in everything which is important to their salvation. . . .

6. And because the slaves of Brazil are those most in need of Christian Doctrine, so numerous are their nations and so diverse their languages, we should search for every means to instruct them in the faith, or for someone who may speak to them in their languages, and in ours, when they can already understand it. And there is no more profitable way than a kind of instruction accomodated to the rudeness of their understanding and the barbarity of their speech. Thus the Parish Priests are required to have copies made . . . of the brief form of the Catechism, which is to be found in Title XXXII, for distribution to the houses of the parishioners, in order that they may instruct their slaves in the mysteries of the Faith, and Christian Doctrine, in the manner of the said instruction, and so that their questions and answers will be those examined by them when they confess and take Christian communion, and this will be easier than studying from memory the Lord's Creed; and others which those of greater ability learn. . . .

50. And for greater security in regard to the Baptism of the brute and raw slaves, and those of unknown language, such as are those who come from Mina, and many also from Angola, the following will be done. After they have acquired some knowledge of our language, or if there are interpreters, the instruction of the mysteries [special catechism] will be used, which as we said is contained in the third book [Title XXXII] number 579. [See below.] And aside from this the raw slaves referred to above will be asked only the following questions:

Do you want to wash your soul with holy water?
Do you want to eat the salt of God?
Will you cast all the sins out of your soul?
Will you commit no more sins?
Do you want to be a child of God?
Will you cast the devil out of your soul?

51. And because it has happened that some of these raw slaves have died before it could be learned whether they wished to be baptized or not, the first chance that they may be asked the above questions, either through interpreters or in our own language, they possessing some understanding of it, it is very important for the salvation of their souls that this be done, because then, in the event of death, since they have already expressed their desire, even if this was long before, they may certainly be baptized *sub conditione*, or even absolutely, depending upon the assessment of their ability which has been formed up to that time.

52. We order all our subjects who are being served by infidel slaves that they labor hard to convert them to our Holy Catholic Faith, and to

receive the Sacrament of Baptism, coming to a knowledge of the errors of their ways, and the state of perdition in which they walk, and that for this purpose they should be sent frequently to learned and virtuous persons, who will point out their errors to them and teach them what is required for their salvation. . . .

54. We order the Vicars and Curates to take great care to acquaint themselves with the slaves of both sexes in their parishes, and having learned that they do not know the Pater Noster, the Ave Maria, the Lord's Creed, the Commandments of the Law of God and of the Holy Mother Church, they being able to learn all this, they [the priests] should take steps against their masters so that they will teach them the Holy Doctrine or have it taught to them, and so that they will send them to church to learn it, and that as long as they do not know it they should not administer to them the Sacrament of Baptism, or, having already been baptized, any other Sacrament.

55. Since experience has revealed to us, however, that among the many slaves who exist in this Archbishopric there are many so coarse and rude that, although their masters make every possible effort to teach them, they always seem to know less, while pitying them for their coarseness and misery, we grant permission to the Vicars and Curates to administer to them the Sacraments of Baptism, Penance, Extreme Unction, and Matrimony, it being apparent to them that, although the masters have been diligent in teaching them, the slaves are too coarse to learn. They should first catechize them in the mysteries of the Faith, in the intentions required for receiving them, and the obligations which accompany them; so that from their replies it may be understood that they consent, possess understanding, and everything else which is needed for the said Sacraments.

56. And let the Vicars and Curates know that they should not make use too lightly of this permission to administer the Sacraments to the slaves. In fact, they should not administer them at all until they are convinced that the masters have made a great effort and that, because of the slaves' great ignorance, this was not enough, and that in the future what they have been doing will most probably not be enough. Instead they should proceed with great care, first examining them, and teaching them, to see if they can derive something from it, because they should not give the masters a chance to neglect their obligation to teach their slaves, which they perform so badly that rarely is a master found who makes the effort he should, erring also in the way they teach, because they do not teach the doctrine point by point, and at leisure, as required by ignorant people, but rather all at once, and with a great deal of haste. . . .

Brief Instruction in the Mysteries of the Faith, Accomodated to the Manner of Speaking of the Slaves of Brazil, So That They May Be Catechized by It

Questions	*Answers*
579.	
Who made this world?	God.
Who made us?	God
Where is God?	In Heaven, on earth, and in the whole world.
Do we have one God, or many?	We have only one God.
How many persons?	Three.
Tell me their names.	The Father, the Son, and the Holy Spirit.
Which of these persons took our flesh?	The Son.
Which of these persons died for us?	The Son.
How is this Son called?	JESUS Christ.
How is His Mother called?	The Virgin Mary.
Where did the Son die?	On the Cross.
After he died where did He go?	He went under the earth in search of the good souls.
And later, where did He go?	To Heaven.
Will He Return?	Yes.
What will He come to search for?	The souls of good heart.
And where will He take them?	To Heaven.
And the souls of bad heart, where will they go?	To hell.
Who is in hell?	The devil is there.
And who else?	The souls of bad heart.
And what are they doing there?	They are in the fire, which never goes out.
Will they ever leave there?	Never.
When we die, does the soul die also?	No. Only the body dies.
And the soul, where does it go?	If the soul is good, it goes to Heaven; if the soul is bad, it goes to hell.
And the body, where does it go?	It goes to the earth.
Will it leave the earth alive?	Yes.
Where will the body go which had a soul of bad heart?	To hell.

And where will the body go, which had a soul of good heart?	To Heaven.
Who is in Heaven with God?	All those who had good souls.
Will they leave Heaven, or will they be there forever?	They will be there forever.

INSTRUCTION FOR CONFESSION

580.

What is confession for?	To wash away the sins of the soul.
He who confesses, does he hide sins?	No.
He who hides sins, where does he go?	To hell.
He who sins, will he sin again?	No.
What does sin do?	It kills the soul.
After confession, does the soul live again?	Yes.
Will your soul sin again?	No.
Because of Whose love?	Because of God's love.

INSTRUCTION FOR COMMUNION

581.

Do you desire communion?	Yes.
Why?	So that Our Lord Jesus Christ may enter my soul.
And when is Our Lord Jesus Christ in the Communion?	When the Father says the words.
Where does the Father say the words?	In the Mass.
And when does he say the words?	When he takes the Host in his hands.
Before the priest says the words, is Our Lord Jesus Christ already in the Host?	No, there is only bread.
And who puts Our Lord Jesus Christ into the Host?	He Himself, after the priest speaks the words.
And what is in the Chalice when the priest takes it in his hands?	Wine is in it, before the priest speaks the words.
And after he speaks the words, what is in the Chalice?	The blood of Our Lord Jesus Christ is in it.

THE ACT OF CONTRITION FOR SLAVES AND SIMPLE PEOPLE

582. My God, my Lord, my heart only desires and loves You. I have committed many sins, and my heart aches greatly for all those I committed. Pardon me, my Lord, I will commit no more sins. I cast all of them from my heart and from my soul for the love of God.

HOW TO SPEAK TO THE DYING

Questions	*Answers*
583.	
Does your soul believe everything that God said?	Yes.
And your heart loves only God?	Yes.
Will God take you to Heaven?	Yes.
Do you want to go where God is?	Yes.
Do you want to die because God wishes it so?	Yes.

584. Repeat to him over and over the act of contrition: and keep in mind that before giving the above instruction, you should tell your listeners what Confession is, what Communion is, what the Host is, what the Chalice is, and what Mass is, and everything in course words, but in such a way that they will understand and can perceive what you are teaching them. And if you do not know the language of the person who wishes to confess, or of the dying person, and someone is present who does know it, he may translate these questions into that language, in accordance with what has been instructed. . . .

Concerning the Matrimony of the Slaves

303. In conformity with Divine and human law, the slave men and women may marry other captive or free persons, and their masters may not deny them matrimony, nor the practice of it at a convenient time and place, nor on this account may they treat them worse, or sell them to other faraway places where one of them, because of being a slave, or for some other just impediment, cannot follow; and acting in a contrary fashion they commit mortal sin, and take upon their own consciences the guilt of their slaves, and thus do they frequently fall into and remain in a state of damnation. For which reason we order and strongly charge that they not place impediments in the way of their slaves' marriages, nor, with threats and ill-treatment, oppose the practice of matrimony at a convenient time and place, nor after they are married sell them to remote outside places, where their wives, because they are slaves or because they have some other legitimate impediment, cannot follow them.

And we declare that once they are married, they remain slaves as before, and fully obligated to their masters' service.

304. But so that this Sacrament will not be administered to slaves except when they are capable and understand how it is to be used, we order the Vicars, Assistants, Chaplains, and the Priests of our Archbishopric to examine them before the said slave men and women receive matrimony, so that they may learn whether or not they know the Christian Doctrine, at least the Our Father, Ave Maria, I-Believe-in-God-the-Father-All-Mighty, Commandments of the Law of God, and of the Holy Mother Church, and whether they understand the obligations of Holy Matrimony which they wish to enter into, and whether it is their intention to remain in it for the service of God and the welfare of their Souls; and learning that they do not know and do not understand these things, they should not receive it until they do, and if they know them, they should receive it, even if their masters are opposed. . . . And, complying with the Bull of Pope Gregory XIII, given on January 25, 1585, we order that all the Parish Priests, when receiving newly converted slaves believed to be married in their country, dispense with the said earlier marriage (if it was not entered into sacramentally). . . .

989. And because the concubinage of the slaves is in need of a quick remedy, it being everywhere normal and almost common to permit them to go about in a state of damnation, which because of their ignorance and misery they are not concerned about, we order that when their concubinage is discovered they should be reprimanded; no fine should be imposed upon them, but through due course of law their masters will be informed of the bad state of their behavior; and they should be warned that if they do not take steps to turn them away from their wayward activities and ruinous condition, either through marriage (which best conforms with God's law, and which their masters cannot deny them without a great weight upon their souls), or in some other convenient way, legal steps will be taken against the said slaves, leading to imprisonment and banishment, without any regard for the loss which the said masters may incur because of the absence of the said slaves from their service, because being slaves does not exempt them from the penalty that they deserve for their offense. . . .

Concerning the Labors Which Are Prohibited on the Holy Days of Obligation, and the Penalties Which Will Be Imposed upon Those Who Perform Them

377. Because it is not good that on the few days which God reserves for his cult and veneration the faithful occupy themselves in servile la-

bors, ungratefully denying Him this little bit of time which He took for Himself, directed toward the spiritual relief of our souls, laboring or allowing those whom they have under their supervision to labor, adding to sins committed these new sins, desiring as we do in fulfillment of our pastoral function to remedy (as much as it is possible for us) the abuses and negligence which exist in this matter, we order all our subjects to abstain from all work, servile and mechanical labors on Sundays and on Holy Days of Obligation; and we order the Parish Priests to exercise the greatest vigilance in this matter, warning their parishioners about this; and our Vicar General, Visitors, District, and Parish Priests will sentence those who do not comply with the punishments later stated.

378. And because the most notable abuse which can exist in this regard is the openness with which the Lords of the Mills [senhores de engenho] order the milling done on Sundays and Holy Days, we order all our subjects of whatever category to abstain from all servile labor done either by themselves or by others, fully observing the precept of God's law which forbids work on such days; which is understood to be from midnight Saturday until the following midnight Sunday, and in the same way on Holy Days. And if some particular need exists, such as a burning cane field, or the cane being in such a condition that delay would probably result in its loss, or some other similar need, and therefore labor is performed; this may be allowed if a license is first requested from the Superior, who in our absence or in the absence of our Vicar General we declare to be the Parish Priest, to whom we grant the power and authority to issue the said license, if he convinces himself that the need exists. And anyone acting in a contrary fashion will be condemned by the Parish Priest to a fine of ten *tostões* [a *milréis*] on the first occasion, on the second to two *milréis*, and on the third to four *milréis*, which will be used to maintain the church; and if he should remain stubborn, our Vicar General will be informed, so that he may act as required by law, and the strongest action will be taken against any Parish Priest who does not comply with this decree.

379. No less detestable is the inhuman, brutal, and depraved abuse which many slaveholders have adopted to the great harm of God's service and the welfare of souls: making use of the miserable slaves during the entire week, without giving them anything for their sustenance, or any clothing with which to cover themselves; this need, which is based in natural law, is met by giving them Sundays and Holy Days free so that at that time they may obtain their required food and clothing. As a result, the miserable slaves do not hear Mass, nor keep the Law of God which forbids labor on those days. To banish such an evil abuse against God and mankind, we exhort and ask all our subjects, recalling the

wounds of Christ our Lord and Redeemer, that from now on they grant their slaves the needed support, so that they may observe the said precepts and live like Christians. And we order the Parish Priests to very carefully observe and inform themselves whether this abuse is continuing, and, when encountering guilty persons who are not complying with this provision, that they take full action against them in the manner prescribed in the previous decree in Paragraph 378.

380. The same procedure and punishment will be imposed upon the sugar cane, manioc, and tobacco planters who allow their blacks and slaves to work openly on Sundays and Holy Days, planting gardens for themselves or for others, fishing, or loading or unloading boats, or any other kind of labor service which is forbidden on those days, unless there is an urgent need, and a license is requested for this purpose (as we stated in another place). . . .

Concerning the Persons and Cases in Which the Immunity of the Church Does Not Apply

754. Although normally the immunity of the Church is valid and defends delinquent persons who seek shelter there, nevertheless there are exceptions to this rule concerning some crimes which, because of their material gravity or for other reasons or circumstances, are excepted by law, custom, and the doctrines of the Church: and they are the following:

755. The heretic, the apostate and the schismatic do not enjoy the immunity of the Church. Nor the blasphemer, the sorcerer, the making of false blessings, soothsayer, or witch. Nor does the public thief or highwayman who is in the habit of killing, wounding, or stealing. Nor those who during the night destroy fields or crops, or deliberately set fire to cane, manioc, or tobacco either already harvested or about to be harvested. . . .

757. Nor the slave (even if he is a Christian) who flees from his master to free himself from slavery. However, if he runs away from his master because the latter intends to treat him with relentless severity, the slave will not be taken back to him unless he first makes a sworn promise, when he can make no other, that he will not mistreat him, or he will be sold in cases when this is required by law.

Concerning Burials, the Bodies of the Faithful to Be Interred in Sanctified Places, and in the Graves of Their Choice

844. And because during the inspection which we made of our entire Archbishopric, we discovered (much to our heart's sorrow) that some persons, forgetful not only of other people's humanity, but also of their

own, order the burial of their slaves in the fields or forests, as if they were brute beasts: wishing to control and put an end to this wickedness, we order, under penalty of greater excommunication *ipso facto incurrenda*, and of a fine of fifty *cruzados* to be paid at the ecclesiastical prison and applied to payment of the accuser and to special prayers for the dead slave, that nobody of whatever state, condition, and quality may bury or order buried outside the consecrated place any deceased person who, according to our law, being a baptized Christian, should be given a Church burial, there existing no impediment of the kind later indicated on which grounds this should be denied. And we order the Parish Priests and our Visitors to make special and careful inquiries concerning the above-stated matter. . . .

4.2. "Children of God's Fire": A Seventeenth-Century Jesuit Finds Benefits in Slavery but Chastizes Masters for Their Brutality in a Sermon to the Black Brotherhood of Our Lady of the Rosary

The conflicting roles of the Church in regard to slavery are demonstrated in the following sermon by the noted Jesuit writer, diplomat, and adviser to the court of Portugal, Father Antônio Vieira. Speaking to both slaves and masters at the church of the black brotherhood of the Rosary in Bahia (for information on such brotherhoods, see Document 4.4), Vieira fashioned the Church's discordant doctrines on slavery into a complex baroque "harmony." Justifying slavery through scripture, especially the example of the Babylonian Captivity, he urged the slaves to submit willingly to their earthly chains. Only their bodies could be enslaved on earth, he told his black listeners, but their souls were free unless, by their own sins, they sold themselves to the devil. Lifelong slavery was hard, but when they served their masters with a good will, slaves were in reality serving God and making a place for themselves in heaven.

Himself a descendant of black Africans and a former protector of enslaved Indians, Vieira seems to have been convinced of what he preached, especially when he spoke of the cruel treatment that masters inflicted upon their slaves. He scolded them for their greed, their un-Christian behavior, their brutal punishments, and more than hinted at the likelihood that they would spend eternity in hell.

Source: *Obras completas do Padre Antonio Vieira, Sermões*, 15 vols. (Porto: Livraria Chardon, 1907-1909), XII, 301-334.

One of the remarkable things witnessed in the world today, and which we, because of our daily habits, do not see as strange, is the immense transmigration of Ethiopian peoples and nations who are constantly crossing over from Africa to this America. The fleet of Aeneas, said the Prince of Poets, brought Troy to Italy . . . ; and with greater reason can we say that the ships which one after the other are entering our ports are carrying Africa to Brazil. . . . A ship enters from Angola and on a single day unloads 500, 600, or perhaps 1,000 slaves. The Israelites crossed the Red Sea and passed from Africa to Asia, fleeing captivity; these slaves have crossed the Ocean at its widest point, passing from that same Africa to America to live and die as slaves. . . .

Now if we look at these miserable people after their arrival and at those who call themselves their masters, what was observed in Job's two conditions is what fate presents here, happiness and misery meeting on the same stage. The masters few, the slaves many; the masters decked out in courtly dress, the slaves ragged and naked; the masters feasting, the slaves dying of hunger; the masters swimming in gold and silver, the slaves weighted down with irons; the masters treating them like brutes, the slaves adoring and fearing them as gods; the masters standing erect, waving their whips, like statues of pride and tyranny, the slaves prostrate with their hands tied behind them like the vilest images of servitude, spectacles of extraordinary misery. Oh God! What divine influence we owe to the Faith You gave us, for it alone captures our understanding, so that, although in full view of such inequalities, we may nevertheless recognize Your justice and providence! Are not these people the children of Adam and Eve? Were not these souls redeemed by the blood of Christ? Are not these bodies born and do they not die as ours do? Do they not breathe the same air? Are they not covered by the same sky? Are they not warmed by the same sun? What star is it, so sad, so hostile, so cruel, that decides their fate? . . .

There is not a slave in Brazil—and especially when I gaze upon the most miserable among them—who for me is not an object of profound meditation. When I compare the present with the future, time with eternity, that which I see with that which I believe, I cannot accept the idea that God, who created these people as much in His own image as He did the rest of us, would have predestined them for two hells, one in this life and another in the next. But when today I see them so devout and festive before the altars of Our Lady of the Rosary, all brothers together and the children of that same Lady. I am convinced beyond any doubt that the captivity of the first transmigration is ordained by her compassion so that they may be granted freedom in the second.

Our Gospel mentions two transmigrations, one in which the children of Israel were driven from their country "in the transmigration of Babylon" [Matt. 1:11] . . . ; and the other in which they were brought back to their country "after the transmigration of Babylon" [Matt. 1:12]. . . . The first transmigration, that of captivity, lasted for seven years; the second, that of freedom, had no end, because it lasted until Christ's coming.

Behold in the following, black brothers of the Rosary, . . . your present condition and the hope it gives you for the future: "and Josias begot Jechonias and his brethren" [Matt. 1:11] Your are the brothers of God's preparation and the children of God's fire. The children of God's fire of the present transmigration of slavery, because in this condition God's fire impressed the mark of slavery upon you; and, granted that this is the mark of oppression, it has also, like fire, illuminated you, because it has brought you the light of the Faith and the knowledge of Christ's mysteries, which are those which you solemnly profess on the rosary. But in this same condition of the first transmigration, which is that of temporal slavery, God and His Most Holy Mother are preparing you for the second transmigration, that of eternal freedom.

It is this which I must preach to you today for your consolation. Reduced to a few words, this will be my topic: that your brotherhood of Our Lady of the Rosary promises all of you a Certificate of Freedom, with which you will not only enjoy eternal liberation in the second transmigration of the other life, but with which you will also free yourselves in this life from the most terrible captivity of the first transmigration. . . .

Although banished Children of Eve, we all possess or all expect a universal transmigration, which is that from Babylon to Jerusalem, from this world's exile to our true home in heaven. You, however, came or were brought from your homelands to these places of exile; aside from the second and universal transmigration, you have another, that of Babylon, in which, more or less moderated, you remain in captivity. And so you may know how you should conduct yourselves in it, and so that you will not yourselves make it worse, I want first to explain to you what it consists of. I will try to say it so clearly that you will all understand me. But if this does not happen (because the topic requires a greater ability than all of you can have), at least, as St. Augustine said in your own Africa, I will be satisfied if your masters and mistresses understand me, so that they may more slowly teach you what for you and for them is very important to know.

Let it be known, all of you who are slaves, that not all of what you are is a slave. Every man is composed of a body and a soul, but that which is a slave and is known as one is not the whole person, but only half of him. Even the Pagans, who had little knowledge of souls, knew this truth and made this distinction. Homer . . . stated as follows . . . : "those men whom Jupiter made slaves divided them in half and did not leave them more than half as their own"; because the other half belongs to the master whom they serve. And which is the enslaved half that has a master whom it is forced to serve? There is no doubt that it is the more abject half—the body. . . .

Speaking of slaves, and with slaves, St. Paul said: "be obedient to them that are your lords according to the flesh" [Eph. 6:5]. And who are these "lords according to the flesh"? All interpreters declare that they are the temporal masters, such as yours whom you serve during your entire life; and the Apostle calls them "lords according to the flesh" because the slave, like any other person, is made up of flesh and spirit, and the master's control over the slave is only over the flesh, that is, the body, and does not include the spirit, which is the soul.

This is why among the Greeks the slaves were called *bodies*. Thus reports St. Epiphanius, who says that their normal way of speaking was not that this or that master had so many slaves, but that he had so many bodies. The same, according to Seneca, was the Roman custom. . . .

But we do not have to go as far back as Rome and Greece. I ask you this: in your own Brazil, when you want to say that so-and-so has many or few slaves, why do you say that he has this many or that many *pieces* [*peças*]? Because the first persons who named them this way intended to signify, wisely and in a Christian manner, that the slave's subjection to the master, and the master's control over the slave, consist only in the body. Men are not made of one piece only, like the angels and the beasts. The angels and the beasts are whole, the angel because he is all spirit, the beast because he is all body. But not man. Man is composed of two pieces: the soul and the body. And because the slaveowner is the master of only one of these pieces, that which can be dominated, that is, the body, for this reason you call your slaves *pieces*. And if this derivation does not satisfy you, let us say that you call your slaves pieces just as we say *a piece of gold, a piece of silver, a piece of silk*, or of any other thing among those which do not possess a soul. And in this way it is even more proven that the name *peça* does not include the slave's soul, and is only meant to mean his body. This is the only thing that is enslaved, the only thing that is bought and sold, the only thing that you [masters] have under your jurisdiction and as part of your fortune, and this, finally, is what was taken in the transmigration of the children of Israel from Jerusalem to Babylon, and was brought from Ethiopia to Brazil in the transmigration of those who are here called slaves and here remain in captivity.

Therefore, black brothers, the slavery you suffer, however hard and grinding it may be, or seems to be to you, is not total slavery, or the enslavement of everything you are, but rather only half slavery. You are slaves in your exterior part, which is the body; however, in the other interior and nobler half, the soul, . . . you are not a slave, but free. This first point accepted, it follows that you should know a second and more important point, which I now put to you: whether that free part or half, the soul, can also in some way be enslaved, and who can enslave it. I say to you that your soul too, like anybody's, can be enslaved; and he who can enslave it is not your master, not the king himself, not any other human power, but only you yourself, and this only by your own free will. Fortunate are those of you who can so adapt yourself to the condition of your half slavery that you can take advantage of your own servitude and may know how to make use of it to gain that which you deserve! . . .

And if you ask me, as you should—in what way are souls enslaved, who are those who sell them, and to whom do they sell them, and for what price?—I respond that each person sells his own; it is the devil to whom they are sold; the price for which they are sold is sin. And because the soul is invisible, and the devil also invisible, these sales are not seen; and so that you will believe that these are not exaggerations or mere forms of speech, but rather truths of the Faith, let it be known that it is thus defined by God, and often repeated throughout the Holy Scriptures. . . .

Tell me, white people and black, do we not all condemn Adam and Eve? Do we not know that they were ignorant and more than ignorant, mad and more than mad, blind and more than blind? Are we not the same people who curse them for what they did? Then why do we do the same and sell our souls, as they sold theirs? Let the white people listen first to an example, so that they may recognize their dishonor, and then we will demonstrate others to the black people, so that they may recognize theirs. . . . Is it necessary that, in order to add another fathom of land to your cane fields, and another day's work each week on your plantation, you must sell your soul to the devil? Your own soul, however, since it is yours, you may go ahead and sell and resell. But those of your slaves, why must you sell them too, putting your lust for gold and your damned and always ill-acquired possessions ahead of their salvation? Because of this your slaves lack Christian Doctrine; because of this they live and die without the Sacraments; and because of this, even if you do not altogether prohibit the Faith to them with a level of greed which only the devil might invent (to express this in popular language), you do not wish them to come near the door of the Church. You allow the slave men and women to go about in sin, and do not permit them to marry, because you say that married slaves do not serve you as well. Oh reason (if such it is) so unworthy of your intelligence and Christianity!

Let us turn to the example most appropriate to the slaves, who for no reason at all should sell their souls, even if this might cost them their lives. . . . If the master orders a slave to do something, or wants from a slave anything that gravely harms his soul and conscience, the slave is obliged not to obey. I have told you repeatedly that you must not offend God; and if [the masters] threaten you because of this, and punish you, suffer it bravely and with a Christian spirit, even if this lasts your entire life, since these punishments are martyrdoms.

We have seen that, just as man is made up of two halves, the body and the soul, slavery is of two kinds: the first, the captivity of the body in which the bodies are the involuntary captives and slaves of men; the other, the slavery of the soul, in which the souls, by their own will, sell themselves and make themselves slaves and captives of the devil. And because I promised you that the Virgin, Our Lady of the Rosary, will free you, as one might say, from the greater form of slavery, . . . it is important that you first understand which of these two types of slavery is the better one. The soul is better than the body, the devil is a worse master than a man, however tyrannical the latter may be; enslavement by men is temporal, but that of the devil eternal; thus there can be no mind so coarse and blind who does not understand that the greater and worse captivity is that of the soul. But since the soul, the devil, and this type of slavery are, as I said, things that cannot be seen by the eyes, where shall I find a way fitting your ability to make this lesson clear? Let us base it on your own slavery, which to you is a more understandable thing. I ask you: if at this moment God freed all of you from your present slavery and you suddenly found yourselves liberated, would this not be a remarkable and admirable blessing which God would grant you? Well, the grace which the Lady of the Rosary will grant you, freeing your souls from the slavery of the devil and of sin, is . . . of a greater and higher value. We find this in the Gospel. . . .

And if we look for the basic reason why Christ, mankind's Redeemer, came only to redeem and liberate men from the slavery of the soul, and not from the slavery of the body, the clear and manifest reason is that mere men would be sufficient to liberate men from the slavery of men; [however,] to free from the enslavement of the devil and from sin, all God's power is required. These same children of Israel of whom we spoke were often enslaved by various nations; very early [they were] slaves of the Egyptians; later slaves of the Mesopotamians; slaves of the Ammonites; slaves of the Canaanites; slaves of the Midianites; slaves of the Philistines. And from all these captivities God always freed them through the power of men. . . . For the slavery of souls, to free them from the devil's yoke and from sin, only God himself had the power, and this with both His arms extended on a cross. . . . To redeem from the slavery of the body, it is enough to pay as much gold or silver as the slave costs. But to redeem from the slavery of the soul, how much gold or silver would be enough? Would a million be enough? Would two million be enough? Would all the gold of Sofala [a Mozambique seaport identified with Solomon's Ophir] and all the silver of Postosí [a rich source of silver in Upper Peru] be enough? Oh the baseness and ignorance of human conception! If the whole ocean were changed to silver, and the whole earth into gold; if God had created another world and a thousand worlds of a material more precious than gold and more desirable than diamonds, this entire price would not be enough to free a single soul for a single moment from the devil's slavery and from sin. For this it was necessary that God's son become man and die on a cross, so that with the infinite price of his blood he could redeem and did redeem the souls from the devil's captivity and from sin. And it is from this slavery, so harsh, fearsome and immense, that I offer you your Certificate of Freedom, through the devotion of the rosary of God's mother. . . .

Thus freed from the greatest and hardest slavery, that of the soul, you remain slaves of the second kind, that of the body. But you should not therefore suppose that the compassion which Our Lady of the Rosary feels for you is less complete. That Our Lady of the Rosary is able to free people from the slavery of the body has been seen in the countless examples of those who, finding themselves captives in an infidel land, were freed through devotion to the rosary, and after offering to the altars of the same Lady the broken chains and fetters of their captivity, as trophies to her power and charity, they hung them in the temples. When God descended to free His people from slavery in Egypt, why do you suppose that he appeared to Moses in a burning bush? Because the burning bush, as the saints tell us, was the figure of the Virgin, Our Lady; and already at that time God wished to make known to the world that the same Most Holy Virgin was not only the most appropriate and able instrument of Divine Omnipotence to free men from the slavery of the souls (for which reason he chose Her as His Mother when he came to redeem mankind), but also to liberate them from the slavery of the body. . . . Thus the Redeemer's Mother is also capable of freeing you from this second and lesser slavery. However, the fact that you now live as slaves and captives is by a special providence of God and of Our Lady, so that through that same temporal captivity you may more easily acquire eternal freedom.

We have arrived at the second part of the liberation which I promised you, and at a point where you lack only the knowledge of how to make good use of your condition to become this world's most fortunate people. Regarding this topic, I have only to quote the two princely Apostles, St. Peter and St. Paul, who quite deliberately dealt with it in various places, speaking with slaves as seriously as if they had spoken with emperors of Rome. . . . The Apostle Paul spoke to the slaves in two places as follows: "Servants, obey in all things your masters according to the flesh; not serving to the eye, as pleasing men, but in simplicity of heart, fearing God. Whatsoever you do, do it from the heart, as to the Lord, and not to men. Knowing that you shall receive of the Lord the reward of inheritance. Serve ye the Lord Christ" [Col. 3:22, 23, 24; Eph. 6:5, 6, 7, 8, 9].

When you serve your masters, you are neither their heirs, nor do they pay you for your labor. You are not their heirs because the inheritance belongs to the sons and not to the slaves; and they do not pay you for your labor, because the slave serves through an obligation and not for wages. A sad and miserable condition, to serve throughout life without hope of reward, and to work without hope of rest except in the grave! But there is a good remedy, says the Apostle (and this is not exaggeration, but Catholic Faith). The remedy is that when you serve your masters, you do not serve them as someone who serves men, but rather as someone who serves God; . . . because then you do not serve as captives, but rather as free persons, nor do you obey as slaves, but as sons and daughters [of God]. You do not serve as captives, but as free men, because God will pay you for your labor; . . . and you do not obey as slaves, but rather as sons and daughters [of God], because God, to whom you are similar in that fate which He gave you, will make you his heirs. . . .

Thus far according to St. Paul. And what does St. Peter say? . . . "Servants, be subject to your masters with all fear, not only to the good and gentle but also to the froward" [1 Pet. 2:18]. This is the . . . advice which the Prince of Apostles gives you, and later he adds reasons worthy of being given to the noblest and most generous spirits. Firstly, because it is the glory of patience to suffer without guilt. "For what glory is it, if committing sin, and being buffeted for it, you endure?" Secondly, because this is the way in which men make themselves more acceptable to God. "But if doing well you suffer patiently; this is thankworthy before God." Thirdly, and truly stupendous: because in that condition in which God has placed you, your vocation is similar to that of His

Son, who suffered for us, providing you the example which you are to imitate. "For unto this are you called; because Christ also suffered for us, leaving you an example that you should follow his steps" [1 Pet. 2:20, 21].

I most justly called this reason "stupendous" because who will not be amazed by the low condition of the subjects with whom St. Peter speaks, and by the highness of the most lofty comparison to which he raises them? He does not compare the slaves' vocation to another grade or condition of the Church, but to Christ Himself. "For unto this are you called; because Christ also suffered." More still: the Apostle does not stop here, but adds another new and greater prerogative of the slaves, declaring for whom Christ suffered, and why: "leaving you an example that you should follow his steps." . . .

Do you know what the condition of your servitude is if you make good use of the means it contains? It is a state not just of religion, but of one of the most austere religious orders of the entire Church. It is a religious order according to the apostolic and divine purpose, because if you do what you are obliged to do, you do not serve men, but rather God, and with the express title of servants of Christ: "as the servants of Christ, doing the will of God from the heart. With a good will serving, as to the Lord, and not to men" [Eph. 6:6, 7].

Carefully observe the wording: "With a good will serving." If you serve through force and ill will, you are apostates to your religious order, but if you serve with a good will, you are true servants of Christ. . . . Thus, just as in the Church there are two religious orders dedicated to the redemption of slaves, yours is an order of slaves without redemption, so that it will not be without perpetuity, which is a perfection of your condition. Some religious are barefoot, others wear shoes; yours is one of bare feet and rags. Your habit is of your own color; because you do not wear the skins of sheep and camels, as did Elias, but rather those which nature covered you with, or with which she left you naked, exposed to the sun's rays and the cold rain. Your poverty is poorer than that of the poorest and your obedience more complete than that of those we call the Minims [a religious order instituted by Saint Francis de Paula near the end of the fifteenth century]. Your abstinences better deserve to be called hunger than fasting, and your vigils are not from one o'clock until midnight, but the whole night without relief. Your Rule is one of many, because it is the decision or decisions of your masters. You are obligated to them because you cannot abandon your slavery, and they are not obligated to you, because they can sell you to someone else when they wish to do so. Finally, every religious order has a purpose and vocation and a special grace. The grace of yours is whips and punishments. . . .

Your vocation is the imitation of Christ's patience . . . ; and its purpose is the eternal inheritance as a reward. . . .

Believe everything I have told you, because everything, as I said before, belongs to the Faith, and upon this Faith raise up your hopes, not only for Heaven, but for what you will now hear, that preparations are being made there for you. Oh what a change of fortune will be yours at that time, and what astonishment and confusion for those who have so little humanity today, and so little understanding that they do not desire it. Tell me this: if as you serve your masters in this life, they in the other life would have to serve you, would this not be a most remarkable change and a glory for you never imagined? Then, understand that it will not happen that way, because this would be very insignificant. Does God not tell you that when you serve your masters you do not serve men, but rather God? . . . Those who will serve you in Heaven will not be your masters, many of whom will probably not be going there, but instead the one who will serve you is God Himself. It is God who will serve you in Heaven, because you served Him here on earth. . . . In this way you will be twice liberated and free: freed from the slavery of the devil, through the liberation of the souls, and free from temporal slavery, through the liberation of all eternity. . . .

This was my lesson for the slaves. And will the masters also gain something from this Babylonian Captivity? It seems not. [You may say] I, by the grace of God, am white and not black; I am free and not a captive; I am a master and not a slave; in fact I possess many slaves. And those who went as captives to Babylon, were they black or white? Were they captives or free? Were they slaves or masters? Neither in color nor in freedom nor in lordliness were they less than you. Well, if they could be lowered into slavery, having to drop so far for this to occur, you who by taking a single step could find yourselves in this condition, why do you not fear your peril? . . . Look to the two poles of Brazil, that of the North and that of the South, and see if there was ever a greater Babylon or a greater Egypt in the world, in which so many thousands of captives have been made, seizing those who were free in nature, with no more right than violence, and with no greater cause than greed, and selling them as slaves. When Joseph's brothers sold him to the Ismaelites to be taken to Egypt, they seized only one free man, but, as punishment for this one act of enslavement, God enslaved in Egypt the whole generation and descendants of those who enslaved Joseph to the number of six hundred thousand, and for a period of forty years. But why should we search for examples far from home and so long ago, if we have them in all our Conquests? Because of the existence of slavery in Africa, God subdued Mina, Santo Tomé, Angola, and Benguela; because of slavery in Asia, God subdued Malacca, Ceylon, Armuz, Muscat, and Cochin; because of slavery in America, He conquered Bahia, Maranhão, and, under the name of Pernambuco, four hundred leagues of coastline over a period of twenty-four years [a reference to the Dutch conquest of northeast Brazil during Vieira's own lifetime]. And because our own acts of enslavement began on Africa's shores, God allowed there the loss of King Sebastian, after which came the sixty-year captivity of the Kingdom itself [a reference to the death of King Sebastian of Portugal in Morocco in 1578 and the subsequent domination of Portugal by the Spanish Hapsburgs (1580-1640), sometimes called the Babylonian Captivity].

I understand full well that some of these acts of enslavement are just: those which the laws permit, and supposedly also those slaves bought and sold in Brazil, not the natives, but those brought from other places. But what theology could justify the inhumanity and brutality of the exorbitant punishments with which these same slaves are mistreated? "Mistreated," I said, but this word is totally inadequate. . . . Tyrannized, one might say, or martyrized; because they injure these miserable people, drop hot fat or wax on them, slash them, cudgel them, and inflict many other kinds of excesses upon them, of which I will not speak, these deserving more the name of martyrdoms than of punishments. Well, be certain that you should not fear such injustice less than the slaves themselves; I say rather that you should fear them more, because God feels them much more. As long as the Egyptians only enslaved the children of Israel, God accepted their captivity; but in the end Divine Justice cannot abide its own dissimulation, and after the ten plagues with which the Egyptians themselves were punished, he totally finished with them, and he destroyed them and laid them waste. And why? God Himself says it: "I have seen," says God, "the affliction of my people in Egypt, and I have heard their cry; because of the rigor of them that are over the works" [Exod. 3:7].

Observe two things: first, that God does not complain about the Pharaoh, but rather about his overseers; . . . because the overseers are often those who cruelly oppress the slaves. Secondly, that he does not give slavery as the reason for his act of justice, but rather the oppression and hardship which they inflicted upon the slaves. . . . "I have seen the affliction of my people." And God adds that he had heard their cries, which for me is a cause for great pity, and for God must be a circumstance that greatly arouses His anger. The miserable slave is being whipped, and with every lash he cries out: "Jesus! Maria! Jesus! Maria!"—and the reverence that these two names deserve is not enough to arouse pity in a man who calls himself a Christian. And how do you expect these two names to respond to you when you call upon them at the hour of your death? Know full well that God hears these cries for help which you do not hear; and though they do not touch your heart, you should know that they make your own punishment certain. . . .

4.3. A Jesuit Friar Writes on Slave Marriage and Immoral Acts Forced by Masters upon Their Slaves (1700)

Disturbed by slave conditions seen in Brazil, an Italian Jesuit, Jorge Benci, asked his Order's permission late in the seventeenth century to publish a sermon on "The Obligations of Masters to Their Slaves." The result was a small volume from which the following admonitions on slave marriages and abuse of slave women are taken. Father Benci revealed a situation that remained essentially unchanged as long as Brazilian slavery lasted. Slaveholders took advantage of their power over black slave women both to profit financially from them and to satisfy their personal desires. Benci also reveals that masters were often neglectful of their slaves' marriages, or denied them altogether, despite the Church's unchanging view, confirmed by the *Constituições do Arcebispado da Bahia* in 1707, that slave marriages were sacred and could not morally be prevented or terminated by their masters (see Document 4.1, Paragraph 303 ff). As Benci hints, there was some disagreement between Church and state on this question, and in fact as late as 1874 the Brazilian government decided that a slave wishing to marry needed his master's permission (see Augusto Texeira de Freitas, *Consolidação das leis civis*, 3rd ed. [Rio de Janeiro, 1876], p. 106).

Source: Jorge Benci, S.I., *Economia cristã dos senhores no governo dos escravos (livro brasileiro de 1700)*, 2nd ed., edited by Serafim Leite, S.I. (Porto: Livraria Apostolado da Imprensa, 1954), pp. 82-86, 90, 98-101.

89. [The Holy Eucharist] is not the only sacrament that masters deny to their slaves; they also prevent them from marrying. The state of matrimony ought to be freely available to the captives, so that no power on earth (says the most learned Father Sánchez) can impede it (Sánchez, Lib. 7, de Matrim, disp. 21, no. 3). And if it is supposed that according to Imperial Law the right to contract marriage is allowed only to free persons, Canon Law in fact revokes this provision of civil law as contrary to the holy and natural law which grants human beings the right to multiply their species, and declares that the marriage of slaves should

not be prevented, that their marriages are valid when entered into against the will of their masters. Can that which Emperors are not allowed to prohibit be prohibited by slavemasters of Brazil?

90. I ask you this: For what purpose was Holy Matrimony instituted? Not only for the propagation of the human species, but also (according to the same Sánchez previously cited) as a remedy against lust and as a means of avoiding sin. Is there perhaps a master in existence who has the power to restrain the lust of his slaves so that its effects do not appear, and so that they are not tempted and driven to sin? Certainly not. Therefore, if you cannot suppress your slaves' lust and its results, why must you deny them the remedy that God gave them against it? And do you not see that, aside from subjecting yourself to the excommunication which the Sacred Council of Trent pronounced against those who prevent matrimony, in this way you also make yourselves participants in all the sins which your slaves commit against the Sixth Commandment?

91. You will tell me that marriage is not intended for such brutish people, since as soon as the wedding ceremonies are performed both men and women abandon each other and commit the greatest sins. But if this cause seems reasonable to you, answer the following question: How many masters are there who are married to women gifted with honor and beauty who leave them, perhaps for some enormous, wicked, and vile slave woman? Should we conclude from this that it is also improper for white men and slavemasters to marry? Nobody will say that this rightly follows; because although such licentiousness does exist among the masters after they marry, they should not for this reason be deprived of marriage. Therefore, even if there are individuals among the slaves and blacks, both men and women, who overstep the bounds after they are married, it does not follow that they are therefore not suited for marriage. Allow them to marry, if they wish, because in this way you will meet your obligation. And if, once they are joined in matrimony, they turn to vice, it will be their responsibility, and not yours, to give an account to God of the sins which they have committed.

92. And since it is not right for masters to prevent marriage among their slaves, it is also wrong for them to impede the normal practices of marriage once they have entered into matrimony, separating husband from wife and leaving the one at home and ordering the sale of the other, or forcing him to live in a place so far away that the couple cannot maintain a conjugal relationship. Because, even if by depriving the slave of that which belongs to him according to natural law, you do not sin against justice, as Father Sánchez teaches, it cannot be denied that you sin at least against charity, because by separating married slaves from

ou deprive them of what is good in marriage, in which case em very serious harm, which charity forbids you to do to another person without a very good cause.

93. And this being the case, it is quite amazing how easily some masters, for insignificant reasons, order the sale to other places of either the slave man or woman, or in some other way separate married couples from each other. Who gave you the power to order these divorces, if the Church, which alone possesses this power, is so careful in this matter that it does not permit a divorce between a man and his wife without quite justifiable and urgent reasons?

94. I know quite well that a case can exist in which masters may, and perhaps should, order their slaves to be sold or to live in very distant places, even when married, especially if serious damage can be done to the souls of the slaves or to those of their masters if they keep them under their control; however, in this case the master should not act suddenly and passionately, but rather with great maturity and much consideration, consulting with the learned and pious theologians so that they may investigate and judge whether or not there are adequate reasons for this. And when it is decided that there is a sufficient cause, and it is the husband who deserves to be banished, you should ask the wife if she wishes to follow him. And if she wishes to accompany her husband, she should go with him and meet the same fate which he meets; and if she does not wish to follow him because of the serious inconveniences which she must suffer if she does, then go ahead and sell the husband alone. And if the wife is the offender, the husband should be dealt with in the same way as we have just said in regard to the wife. . . .

95. Finally, in order to bestow upon slaves their spiritual nourishment, masters ought to provide them with an example of virtue and good habits: *Bonorum omnium operum exemplo pascere.* The good doctrine which masters give their slaves is of little value when the master's good example is lacking. The best way to teach doctrine is not with words but with deeds. Deeds are seen, words are heard: and what is heard perhaps goes in one ear and out the other; and what is seen enters through the eyes and, since it lacks a door through which to leave, it penetrates to the heart. For this reason the teacher who is a teacher should teach more through what he does than what he says. . . . From which it follows that the masters who hope to lead their slaves toward an exact observance of the divine precepts should live in such a way that the slaves may see in them the model and image of a true Christian. . . .

101. From this we may surmise the main reason for the scandalous life which slave men and women normally lead in Brazil. But how can it be otherwise, if in masters and mistresses they do not see Christian

models, but rather outrageous behavior suitable for pagans? . . . However often the master may teach them that God wants them to remain chaste, how should they be persuaded to lead an honest and pure life when they see the master himself keeping a concubine in his own house. . . .

115. . . . That there should be masters who give no thought or consideration to the great offense which they commit against their slave women, permitting them to leave the house at all hours, night or day, knowing that so many offenses against God will result! Oh! If the streets and alleys of the cities and towns of Brazil could talk! How many sins would they reveal, which night conceals and day does not discover! But I will not concern myself with particulars, nor reveal what results when slave women go out on their own; because even my pen itself trembles and grows faint from writing about them.

116. That there should be masters who give no thought to the great harm they do to their slave women, either praising them as industrious when they see them dressed in fine clothes, which they have acquired by offending God; or scolding them for their lack of industry and vitality when they do not do what they see the others doing who are corrupted and damned! That there should be masters, I say, who do not ponder over this, aware that they excuse guilt in this way so that they may more easily commit it; and that they approve that which under any name is bad, as if it were good; and condemn that which under any name is good, as if it were evil. . . . "Woe to you," God threatened through the Prophet Isaiah, "that call evil good, and good evil." And against whom is this threat uttered more directly than against you, oh masters, and, with more reason, against you, oh mistresses, who approve of the elegant apparel of your slave girls, earned by sin, and who condemn them if, unwilling to offend God, they are reluctant to go out and earn.

117. That there should be masters who give no thought to the great harm they do to their slave girls, dividing up among them the provisioning of the house, and imposing a share upon each one! To one the flour or bread for the table; to another the meat or fish for the plate; this one must pay the rent on the houses; that one must provide the oil for the lamps; and each must contribute that which she is responsible for. And that this should happen among Christians! That there should be so little fear of God, that no thought is given to the consequences of these tributes which are so unworthy of a Catholic! Tell me, masters, or tell me, mistresses (and it is mainly to the latter that I speak); where should your slave girls go to satisfy these payments? Do they perhaps have some income from which to acquire that which you order them to pay? Certainly not. Thus, where should it come from, except from sin and the

wanton use of their bodies? And in supporting yourselves with this tainted money and from these sins, what are you yourself but a living, walking sin? The Philosopher said it: that each person is nothing more than that which sustains him. And since you are sustained by nothing more than sin, what must you be other than sin itself?

118. But the scandals of the masters of Brazil do not stop here; because you are not satisfied to urge, counsel, consent, and even order your slaves to sin; you go much further, forcing them with punishment and threats of punishment to offend God, and to fail in the keeping of His precepts. . . .

120. Is it not a scandal, and the most hateful in the eyes of God, for the master to establish a friendship with his slave girl? And is it not much worse yet, and more abominable, to compel her by the use of force to consent to her master's sin, and to punish her when she resists and seeks to avoid this offense against God? No Catholic will deny it. And should the master who does this expect to be saved? Such things happen in Mauritania or Barbary, where Mohammed in his sixth commandment expounded on ungodly people and produced some reasons for pardoning masters who committed such impure crimes. But that this should happen in a Christian land and to Christians who are as Christian as the Portuguese! What can we say except that, aside from the eternal suffering with which masters who thus violate and compel their slaves to sin should be punished, they also deserve the temporal death which is imposed by common law and the special laws of Portugal upon all persons who through violence or some other means compel and force women of any quality to sin, even those whom we commonly refer to as worldly.

4.4. The Black Brotherhood of Our Lady of the Rosary in Recife in the Eighteenth Century

The Church encouraged some slaves in Brazil, especially those residing in towns, to progress well beyond the basic Christianity which is implied by the catechism contained in Document 4.1. In fact, in Rio de Janeiro, Salvador, Recife, Ouro Prêto, and other major cities, slaves and free descendants of Africans were encouraged to organize their own religious brotherhoods (*irmandades*) and to construct their own churches, which were normally dedicated to Our Lady of the Rosary (Nossa Senhora do Rosario), protectress of blacks. These lay organizations played a vital role in the lives of many urban blacks and mulattoes. They gave them opportunities to assemble legally, to communicate, to worship, and to express themselves creatively, not only as builders but also as active communicants. Dedicated as they were to saints identified with their own race, the *irmandades* gave slaves opportunities to further their own dignity and self-respect. At the same time they served the dominant society as a means of diverting the energies of blacks away from rebellious behavior. The following account of the religious activities of the black brotherhood of Our Lady of the Rosary in Recife was written about 1757 by the Dominican friar, D. Domingos de Loreto Couto.

Source: D. Domingos de Loreto Couto, *Desagravos do Brasil e glorias de Pernambuco. Discursos brasilicos, dogmaticos, belicos, apologeticos, moraes, e historicos*, in *Annaes da Biblioteca Nacional do Rio de Janeiro*, Vol. 25 (1903), pp. 158-159.

The black people, and captives, have proved themselves so devoted to the service of the Mother of God, Our Lady of the Rosary, that they themselves, although poor, resolved to establish a beautiful church, in which they alone are the founders and administrators. This temple has an outstanding and sumptuous structure; its façade is a splendid edifice of white stone, an admirable example of inspirational architecture. Our Lady of the Rosary is the comfort, the consolation of these people, because all of them have recourse after their labors to the sovereign Empress of Glory. And it is with such faith and devotion that they go in quest of her and experience her favors that they are reluctant to take leave of her presence, offering up their prayers to her. It is certainly highly inspiring and touching to witness the fervor, zeal, and expense with which they serve Our Lady. Every day of the year, if some event does not prevent it, they chant in liturgy the third part of the rosary. On Saturdays at five o'clock in the afternoon they chant a recital, and at seven at night again the third part of the rosary. On holy days they all attend the mass of their chaplain, which they enrich with their singing, their recital of the rosary, and the minor office. At three o'clock in the afternoon they chant another rosary and at night at the door of the church yet another. On the second Sunday of October they worship Our Lady with great solemnity, and to increase the fervor of their devotion, they engage in dances and other licit entertainments with which they devoutly gladden the hearts of the population.

In the five chapels of the church are the images of Our Lady of the Rosary, who is the patron of the house; and those of Our Lady of Boa Hora, and Saint Dominic, as well as those of the black saints, Estebão, Moíses, Benedito, Antonio de Catalagirona, Efigenia, and His Holiness King Balthasar. Everyone is gladdened by the solemn festivities devoted to our Lord, the chanted mass and sermon. These ceremonies are preceded by novenas, which they celebrate with great devotion and a large participation. Every Saturday and on the first Sunday of each month they go into the streets singing the rosary of Our Lady with such a pleasing combination of voices that a smooth harmony results which is both agreeable and edifying.

4.5. The Archbishop of Bahia Staunchly Supports Slavery and the Slave Trade (1794)

In the fifteenth and sixteenth centuries enduring ecclesiastical doctrines and a large body of royal and canon law were developed in response to the obvious moral questions associated with the enslavement of Africans and Indo-Americans. According to these doctrines, there were clear differences between "legitimate" and "illegitimate" slavery. Slaves taken in so-called "just wars," for example, or those "redeemed" (*resgatados*) from their true masters could be legitimately held as slaves, but those who were seized without cause or captured in "unjust wars" could not be so held. (See Documents 1.2, 3.) To a limited extent such precepts protected Brazil's Indians, whose enslavement was sometimes even banned. However, enslavement of blacks eventually became so commonplace and so essential to the Luso-Brazilian economic system that royal laws or Church doctrines intended to protect Africans came to be largely neglected. How could anyone know in Brazil, it was sometimes reasoned, that a particular African had been kidnapped or seized in an unjust war? What buyer of a newly imported African could be expected to ask a slave merchant if he was legitimately held, and what merchant would have admitted that he was not? For "practical" people, both lay and ecclesiastical, to raise such questions was to threaten slavery itself.

On the other hand, human servitude was so obviously out of step with fundamental Christian beliefs that at least a few clergymen, especially foreigners, found the Church's laxity uncomfortable or even unacceptable. The following letter from the governor of Bahia to the Portuguese secretary of state for overseas affairs, written in Salvador in 1794, reveals one Italian friar's doubts concerning these questions and gives an account of the swift action taken against him when he dared to challenge illegal but common practices which conflicted with long-established but neglected Church doctrine. The letter proves that the Church's support of slavery was hardly subject to debate in 1794, and that the government could fully count on the help of the ecclesiastical community when slavery seemed threatened by one of its own members.

Source: Original in Archivo Publico do Estado da Bahia, published as "Opinião de um Frade Capuxinho sobre a escravidão no Brasil em 1794," in *Revista do Instituto Histórico e Geográfico Brasileiro* 60, Part 2 (1897), 155-157.

❧ Most Illustrious and Excellent Sir:

The Archbishop of this diocese, guided by the vigilance which he always reveals in his efforts to hinder any doctrine of a spiritual nature which might disturb the calm and tranquillity of this captaincy, or which might go counter to laws and orders of His Majesty, has informed me that the priest, Friar Joseph of Bologna, an Italian Capuchin missionary, has unwisely and indiscreetly followed an opinion in respect to slavery which, if propagated and adopted, would disturb the consciences of this city's inhabitants and bring future results disastrous to the preservation and welfare of this colony.

This monk had lived in this country for nearly fourteen years with exemplary conduct, complying with the obligations of his ministry—despite some indiscretions and odd behavior which he fell into, and from which he abstained when warned by his superiors—earning the reputation of a virtuous man, eager in the service of God. Later, however, he convinced himself, or was persuaded, that slavery was illegitimate and contrary to religion, or at least, being sometimes legitimate and other times illegitimate, the distinction ought to be made between slaves captured in just and unjust wars. He became so convinced of his belief that, acting as confessor for several persons during the feast of the Holy Spirit, he put this doctrine into practice, making them ponder this very difficult if not unresolvable question, with the purpose of freeing those slaves who were either stolen or reduced to unjust slavery. This he did without realizing that whoever buys slaves normally buys them from persons authorized to sell them, under the eyes and with the consent of the Prince, to whom it would be unheard-of, and against the peace of society, to demand of a private person, when he buys merchandise from a person authorized to sell it, that he first inform himself of its source through inquiries not only useless but obviously capable of eliminating every kind of commerce.

In a search for the source of this opinion, which this monk for so long did not follow, it was learned that some conversations that he had with the Italian fathers from the Gôa mission, who are passengers in the ship *Belém* anchored in this port and who were lodged in the Da Palma Hospice, caused the friar to accept this doctrine, not so much because of malice and bad faith, but for lack of greater talents and theological learning, and because of an extraordinary conscience.

To avoid the spread of such a pernicious doctrine, the Archbishop immediately ordered him to suspend his confessions, requesting that I deport him in the same ship, which is continuing its voyage, and that the captain not allow him to go ashore without a positive order from Your Excellency. And, conferring with the Archbishop himself on this matter so that I might take further steps which might seem prudent, I judged it convenient to call to my presence the rector of the above-mentioned missionaries from Gôa. I strongly expressed my astonishment at his indiscretion, indicating to him that this matter is extraordinarily delicate and risky, and that it was for the Prince alone to make decisions concerning it, if he should someday judge this convenient; and that finally it was extremely rash and ill-advised, in the opinion of the wise and learned prelate, and of the whole clergy of this city, to bring up such a question. The rector tried to explain himself, telling me that when the priest, Friar Joseph of Bologna, asked his opinion on this point, he had merely responded that there was legitimate and illegitimate slavery, but that he had not encouraged him to do what he did in the confessional. Prior to that he had suggested to him that if there were doubts he should discuss them first with his superior. But, despite this defense, which did not satisfy me, in order to obtain greater security I ordered that the commander of the *Belém* put the said missionaries on board, and not let them set foot on land without a positive order from me.

God protect Your Excellency.
Bahia, June 18, 1794.

4.6. Slaves as Prizes in a Lottery Benefiting the Santa Casa da Misericórdia in Ouro Prêto (1825)

To Brazilian clergymen, as to Brazilians in general, slaves were property which could be bought, sold, bartered, bequeathed, or even awarded as prizes in a lottery. This selection is an example of the latter. In 1825, following established legal practice, a priest of the Santa Casa da Misericórdia in the city of Ouro Prêto, Padre Manoel Joaquim Ribeiro, requested permission of the provincial government of Minas Gerais to hold an auction intended to benefit that charitable Catholic organization. In turn, the provincial president applied to the central government in Rio for this permission, which on August 8, 1825, was granted by Emperor Pedro I. The following is the text of the plan for this lottery as submitted by Father Manoel Joaquim, approved by the imperial government, and published in the official collection of imperial laws. It should also be noted parenthetically that black brotherhoods employed lotteries as a means of raising money, and that individual slaves played lotteries as a way to win their freedom.

Source: *Decretos, cartas imperiaes e alvarás* (Rio de Janeiro, 1825), pp. 74-77.

❧ Plan of the lottery which His Majesty the Emperor has seen fit to approve by an Imperial Order of this date, for the benefit of the Sacred House of Charity [Santa Casa de Misericórdia] of the Imperial City of Ouro Preto.

Prizes

1st		
A large country estate with grand ceremonial rooms, a park, garden, and numerous planted areas		4:000$000
2nd		
Francisco, black, Mina coast, 8 years old	300$000	
Libania Rebola, 16 years old	300$000	
Lizauro, son, 6 years old	100$000	
Lizandro, son, 4 years old	60$000	
Francisco, son, 1 year old	40$000	
1 English writing desk	28$800	
12 jacaranda chairs with inlay work	24$000	
1 wagon with iron reenforcements	40$000	
1 leather couch	7$200	
In cash	100$000	
		1:000$000
3rd		
Antonio Benguella, 21 years old	300$000	
Maria Benguella, 23 years old	200$000	
		500$000
4th		
Lourenço Benguella, 32 years old	200$000	
1 horse bridle of fine silver	60$000	
1 desk	26$000	
1 musket	8$000	
2 copper basins	6$000	
		300$000

5th

1 tea set, fine quality	60$000	
2 brass molds for printing on leather	30$000	
1 mirror and 2 branched candlesticks	10$000	
1 chest of drawers with inlay work	30$000	
2 small tables	12$000	
1 copper chafing dish	4$800	
1 walking stick with silver head	25$000	
In cash	28$200	
		200$000

6th

José Benguella, 45 years old	120$000	
1 eyeglass for nearsighted	12$800	
1 bottle holder	12$800	
2 large coffee trays, 1 small one	12$000	
1 backgammon board	6$000	
1 copper alembic lamp	4$200	
In cash	32$200	
		200$000

7th

25 campaign chairs	45$500	
1 jacaranda travel bed with inlay work	25$000	
1 chest of drawers with large upper shelf	20$000	
4 wagons for fruit peddlers	4$800	
In cash	4$700	
		100$000

8th

1 oratory in which Mass is recited, with all the large Images and decorations		100$000
4 prizes of	50$000	200$000
8 ditto of	25$000	200$000
80 ditto of	15$000	1:200$000
700 ditto of	9$000	6:300$000
The first blank ticket		50$000
The last blank ticket		50$000
802 prizes		
1,598 blank tickets at	6$000	14:400$000

Since the properties, which will be included in the lottery, are realistically priced in accordance with legal evaluations, the players must pay the 12 percent tax; however, the excise tax on the real estate, and the half taxes on the slaves should come from the profits of the Sacred House, since it does not contribute to the sale of the tickets, nor to the expenses or losses of the lottery. After they are printed, the tickets will be signed by the principal Board Members of the Sacred House, the Notary, Treasurer, and Proctor, and the latter will be obliged to attend the drawing. The raffle will take place as soon as the sale of tickets is concluded.

The Palace of Rio de Janeiro, August 8, 1825. *Estevão Ribeiro de Rezende.*

4.7. A Catholic Brotherhood Is Authorized to Buy and Sell Slaves (1842)

The Church and certain brotherhoods were obviously committed to protecting slaves and easing their troubled lives. However, as the following provincial law of Santa Catarina suggests, lay Church officials could also be quite businesslike when dealing with slave property.

Source: Lei de 16 de Abril de 1842, n. 166, *Leis de Santa Catarina* (n.p., n.d.), p. 31

Only Article. The Governing Board of the Brotherhood of Our Lord Jesus Bearing the Cross [Senhor Jesus dos Passos] is authorized to sell, in a public sale, the useless slave women of the Charity Hospital, to which they belong, the proceeds to be used to purchase male slaves; all contrary dispositions being revoked.

4.8. A British Resident of Pernambuco Describes the Beneficial Effects of Catholicism on Slaves, Notably upon Those Belonging to Plantations of the Benedictine Order (about 1815)

The Church's influence upon the personal lives of slaves in Brazil is set forth in the following selection by a British author, Henry Koster, who was a resident of Pernambuco from 1809 to 1820 and a careful observer of the society of northeastern Brazil. Koster was convinced that slaves benefited from the Church's influence in a variety of ways, but he was especially impressed by the alleged advantages of those held by the Benedictine Order, particularly in regard to marriage and religious experience. While describing these advantages, Koster also revealed that the monks of St. Benedict, like ecclesiastical slaveholders throughout Brazil, unblushingly derived the same kinds of benefits from slaveholding that were enjoyed by ordinary Brazilians, even if, as Koster writes, the slaves on the Benedictine plantations were looked upon as the personal property of St. Benedict himself. As Koster implied, for example, the monks encouraged marriage not only for religious reasons, but also because they wished to propagate new slaves on their estates. Moreover, a good mulatto overseer belonging to the Benedictine plantation adjacent to Koster's own property was unable to buy his freedom, despite his offer to pay for it with two slaves of his own, since the monks appeared to believe that his management of the property was indispensable to its economic success. Finally, like slaveholders everywhere, the Benedictine friars allegedly abused the power they had over their female slaves, adding a lighter racial element to the creole work forces on St. Benedict's Brazilian estates.

Source: Henry Koster, *Travels in Brazil*, 2 vols., 2nd ed. (London: Longman, Hurst, Rees, Orme, and Brown, 1817), II, 237-246, 262-267.

All slaves in Brazil follow the religion of their masters; and notwithstanding the impure state in which the Christian church exists in that country, still such are the beneficent effects of the Christian religion, that these, its adopted children, are improved by it to an infinite degree; and the slave who attends to the strict observance of religious ceremonies invariably proves to be a good servant. The Africans who are imported from Angola are baptized in lots before they leave their own shores, and on their arrival in Brazil they are to learn the doctrines of the church, and the duties of the religion into which they have entered. These bear the mark of the royal crown upon their breasts, which denotes that they have undergone the ceremony of baptism, and likewise that the king's duty has been paid upon them. The slaves which are imported from other parts of the coast of Africa, arrive in Brazil unbaptized, and before the ceremony of making them Christians can be performed upon them, they must be taught certain prayers, for the acquirement of which one year is allowed the master, before he is obliged to present the slave at the parish-church. This law is not always strictly adhered to as to time, but it is never evaded altogether. The religion of the master teaches him that it would be extremely sinful to allow his slave to remain a heathen; and indeed the Portuguese and Brazilians have too much religious feeling to let them neglect any of the ordinances of their church. The slave himself likewise wishes to be made a Christian, for his fellow-bondsmen will in every squabble or trifling disagreement with him, close their string of opprobrious epithets with the name of *pagam* (pagan). The unbaptized negro feels that he is considered as an inferior being, and although he may not be aware of the value which the whites place upon baptism, still he knows that the stigma for which he is upbraided will be removed by it; and therefore he is desirous of being made equal to his companions. The Africans who have been long imported, imbibe the Catholic feeling, and appear to forget that they were once in the same situation themselves. The slaves are not asked whether they will be baptized or not; their entrance into the Catholic church is treated as a thing of course; and indeed they are not considered as members of society, but rather as brute animals, until they can lawfully go to mass, confess their sins, and receive the sacrament.

The slaves have their religious brotherhoods as well as the free persons; and the ambition of a slave very generally aims at being admitted into one of these, and at being made one of the officers and directors of the concerns of the brotherhood; even some of the money which the industrious slave is collecting for the purpose of purchasing his freedom will oftentimes be brought out of its concealment for the decoration of a saint, that the donor may become of importance in the society to which he belongs. The negroes have one invocation of the Virgin (or I might almost say one virgin) which is peculiarly their own. Our Lady of the Rosary is even sometimes painted with a black face and hands. It is in this manner that the slaves are led to place their attention upon an object in which they soon take an interest, but from which no injury can proceed towards themselves, nor can any through its means be by them inflicted upon their masters. Their ideas are removed from any thought of the customs of their own country, and are guided into a channel of a totally different nature, and completely unconnected with what is practised there. The election of a King of Congo by the individuals who come from that part of Africa, seems indeed as if it would give them a bias towards the customs of their native soil; but the Brazilian Kings of Congo worship Our Lady of the Rosary, and are dressed in the dress of white men; they and their subjects dance, it is true, after the manner of their country; but to these festivals are admitted African negroes of other nations, creole blacks, and mulattos, all of whom dance after the same manner; and these dances are now as much the national dances of Brazil as they are of Africa.

The Portuguese language is spoken by all the slaves, and their own dialects are allowed to lay dormant until they are by many of them quite forgotten. No compulsion is resorted to to make them embrace the habits of their masters, but their ideas are insensibly led to imitate and

16. Festival of Our Lady of the Rosary, Patron Saint of Blacks

adopt them. The masters at the same time imbibe some of the customs of their slaves, and thus the superior and his dependent are brought nearer to each other. I doubt not that the system of baptizing the newly-imported negroes proceeded rather from the bigotry of the Portuguese in former times rather than from any political plan; but it has had the most beneficial effects. The slaves are rendered more tractable; besides being better men and women, they become more obedient servants; they are brought under the control of the priesthood; and even if this was the only additional hold which was gained by their entrance into the church, it is a great engine of power which is thus brought into action.

But in no circumstances has the introduction of the Christian religion among the slaves been of more service than in the change which it has wrought in the men regarding the treatment of their women, and in the conduct of the females themselves. . . . The slaves of Brazil are regularly married according to the forms of the Catholic church [this is the most questionable part of Koster's essay, unless we are to reject the testimony of many others, as well as abundant statistics; see, for example, Document 2.12]; the banns are published in the same manner as those of free persons; and I have seen many happy couples (as happy at least as slaves can be) with large families of children rising around them. The masters encourage marriages among their slaves, for it is from these lawful connections that they can expect to increase the number of their creoles. A slave cannot marry without the consent of his master, for the vicar will not publish the banns of marriage without the sanction. It is likewise permitted that slaves should marry free persons; if the woman is in bondage, the children remain in the same state; but if the man is a slave, and she is free, their offspring is also free. A slave cannot be married until the requisite prayers have been learnt, the nature of confession be understood, and the sacrament can be received. Upon the estates the master or manager is soon made acquainted with the predilections of the slaves for each other, and these being discovered, marriage is forthwith determined upon, and the irregular proceedings are made lawful. In towns there is more licentiousness among the negroes, as there is among all other classes of men. . . .

The sugar-plantations which belong to the Benedictine monks and Carmelite friars, are those upon which the labour is conducted with the greatest attention to system, and with the greatest regard to the comfort and ease of the slaves. I can more particularly speak of the estates of the Benedictine monks, because my residence at Jaguaribe gave me daily opportunities of hearing of the management of one of their establishments; and although sugar-works were not erected upon the estate in question, still the number of negroes which were upon it was fully adequate to this purpose. Besides, in some years canes were planted upon it, which were to be ground at some neighbouring mill. The frequent communication, likewise, which there was between the slaves of this plantation and those of the other estates, belonging to the same convent, upon which sugar is made, enabled me to ascertain that all the establishments which are owned by the Benedictines, are conducted in the same manner.

The slaves of the Jaguaribe St. Bento estate are all creoles, and are in number about one hundred. The children are carefully taught their prayers by some of the elder negroes, and the hymn to the Virgin is sung by all the slaves, male and female, who can possibly attend, at seven o'clock every evening; at this hour it is required that every person shall be at home. The young children are allowed to amuse themselves as they please during the greatest part of the day; and their only occupation for certain hours is to pick cotton for lamps, and to separate the beans which are fit for seed from those which are rotten, and other work of the same description. When they arrive at the age of ten and twelve years, the girls spin thread for making the coarse cotton cloth of the country, and the boys attend to the horses and oxen, driving them to pasture, &c. If a child evinces peculiar fitness for any trade, care is taken that his talents should be applied in the manner which he would himself prefer. A few of them are taught music, and assist in the church-festivals of the convent. Marriages are encouraged; as early as the age of seventeen and eighteen years for the men, and at fourteen and fifteen for the girls, many of these unions take place. Immediately after their entrance into this state, the people begin to labour regularly in the field for their owners; oftentimes both boys and girls request the manager to allow them to commence their life of daily toil, before the age which is pointed out by the regulations of the convent; and this occurs because they are not permitted to possess provision-grounds of their own until they labour for their masters. Almost every description of labour is done by piece-work; and the task is usually accomplished by three o'clock in the afternoon, which gives to those who are industrious an opportunity of working daily upon their own grounds. The slaves are allowed the Saturday of every week to provide for their own subsistence, besides the Sundays and holidays. Those who are diligent fail not to obtain their freedom by purchase. The provision-grounds are never interfered with by the monks, and when a negro dies or obtains his freedom, he is permitted to bequeath his plot of land to any of his companions whom he may please to favour in this manner. The superannuated slaves are carefully provided with food and clothing.

One of these old men, who was yet however sufficiently hearty to be often in a state of intoxication, and would walk to a considerable distance to obtain liquor, made a practice of coming to see me for this purpose.

He would tell me, that he and his companions were not slaves to the monks, but to St. Bento himself, and that consequently the monks were only the representatives of their master for the due administration of the Saint's property in this world. I enquired of some of the slaves, and found that this was the general opinion among them.

None of the monks reside upon the Jaguaribe estate, but one of them comes from Olinda almost every Sunday and holiday to say mass. Upon the other Benedictine estates there are resident monks. The slaves treat their masters with great familiarity; they only pay respect to the abbot, whom they regard as the representative of the Saint. The conduct of the younger members of the communities of regular clergy is well known not to be by any means correct; the vows of celibacy are not strictly adhered to. This circumstance decreases the respect with which these men might otherwise be treated upon their own estates, and increases much the licentiousness of the women. I have seen upon these plantations many light-coloured mulatto slaves; but when the approximation to white blood becomes considerable, a marriage is projected for the individual with a person of a darker tint. No compulsion is made use of to oblige any one to marry, and therefore many of the slaves, contrary to the wishes of their masters, remain single. The monks allow their female slaves to marry free men, but the male slaves are not permitted to marry free women. Many reasons are alleged in favour of this regulation. One is that they do not wish that a slave should be useless in the way of increasing the stock of the plantation; likewise the monks do not wish to have a free family residing among their slaves (for obvious reasons), which must be the case if a man marries a free woman; they have less objection to a man, because he is during the whole of the day away from their people, or is perhaps employed by the community, and thus in part dependent upon it, and he merely comes to sleep in one of the huts; besides, a stranger is contributing to the increase of the stock.

The Jaguaribe estate is managed by a mulatto slave, who married a person of his own colour, and she likewise belonged to the convent. Her husband has purchased her freedom and that of her children; he possesses two African slaves, the profits of whose labour are entirely his own; but he is himself obliged to attend to the business of the plantation, and to see that the work of his masters is properly executed. This man has offered his two Africans in exchange for himself to the monks; but they tell him that the Jaguaribe estate could not be properly managed without his assistance; and, though much against his inclination, he continues in slavery. This is one of the strongest instances of man's desire to act for himself; Nicolau enjoys the entire direction of the estate, and every comfort which a man of his description can possibly wish for; when he moves from home, he is as well mounted as the generality of the rich planters;

he is permitted to be seated in the presence of his masters, and indeed is allowed all the privileges of free men; and yet the consciousness of being under the control of another always occupies his mind, and leads him to desire the possession of those privileges as a right, which he at present only enjoys by sufferance.

4.9. A Slave Revolt at a Carmelite Estate in Pará (1865)

The following three letters written in July, 1865, give brief accounts of a rebellion of slaves belonging to a Carmelite estate near the city of Belém, Pará. Of particular interest is the revelation of the convent's prior (in Letter A) that for over a quarter of a century, the slaves of the estate, "owing to special circumstances better not mentioned at this time," had maintained a defiant and semi-independent status approaching outright mutiny. Also significant is the provincial president's disclosure in his first letter to the Minister of Justice (Letter B) that less than three months after Lee's surrender to Grant at Appomattox slaves in Pará had become aware of the Civil War in the United States and its possible effects upon their lives. A second letter from the provincial president (Letter C), written immediately after the first, also shows that ownership of the rebellious slaves by the Carmelites did not avert a violent conclusion to the crisis.

Source: *Relatorio do Ministerio da Justiça apresentado na quarta sessão da decima-segunda legislatura pelo respectivo Ministro e Secretario de Estado, José Thomaz Nabuco de Araujo* (Rio de Janeiro, 1866), pp. 8-9.

☙ *A. Letter of the Prior of the Carmelite Convent of Belém to the Provincial President*

Carmelite Convent of the Province of Pará. July 5, 1865, ten o'clock in the morning.

Most Illustrious and Excellent Sir:

A canoe bringing the disagreeable news of a serious conflict between the administrator and the slaves has just arrived from the Pernambuco plantation, which is the property of this convent.

Last March 18 I informed Your Excellency of the insubordination of those slaves, and of my wish to make them work so as to promote the interests of the convent that I administer. I also informed you of the bad state of public order which since 1838, except for brief periods, long and short, has made that place seem more like a den of assassins and deserters than an argricultural establishment. Not even the measures Your Excellency took to destroy the *mocambo* [runaway-slave settlement] of Maracanã where those who fled found a refuge (which fortunately was achieved), nor the measures which I employed and of which Your Excellency has been informed, were enough to bring order and industrious habits to a body of slaves who, owing to special circumstances better not mentioned at this time, have for many years possessed a de facto freedom, living in a state of indolence and demoralization which are hard to describe. This was the state of affairs which existed before the event that now concerns me, and that I will describe only briefly, since at the moment the information I have is not complete.

Yesterday morning the overseer assembled the convent's slaves, numbering almost two hundred individuals, and ordered the punishment of certain slaves. The others objected to this, and, possessing weapons, made it known to the administrator that he should leave the plantation immediately. Recognizing that resistance was pointless, he agreed to do so, asking them to give him a dugout canoe and someone to row it for him. In this way he left them to themselves, starting the journey with four slaves who also abandoned the estate.

The news spread that the administrator had been murdered on the way, and I feared this myself, but I now see that this was false, because he has just arrived and is now at this convent. The reason for his delay was that nobody stayed with the canoe except himself and a child, and they were not able to row the canoe quickly from that place to the capital.

This action is the beginning of a new revolt of the kind which those slaves have attempted more than once, the results of which cannot be predicted.

Bringing these facts to the high attention of Your Excellency, I am at the same time requesting speedy action so that the revolt may be stopped in its earliest stage. . . .

Manoel da Natividade, prior.

B. Letter from the Provincial President of Pará to the Minister of Justice

Communiqué. Province of Pará. Palace of the Presidency in the city of Belém, July 8, 1865.

Most Illustrious and Excellent Sir:

It is my duty to report to Your Excellency that on the 4th of this month a conflict took place on the Pernambuco plantation, which is the property of the Carmelite Convent, between the slaves and the administrator, as a result of which the latter was expelled from the plantation, and the slaves were left to their own resources and in a state of rebellion.

I was informed of this on the 5th at eleven o'clock in the morning, and I judged it of some importance not only because the condition of the province's slaves is so terrible, the war in the United States having convinced them that they will all be freed, but also because of the large number on that estate and the very bad reputation which that multitude has earned by their past behavior. I sent one of the small steamboats of the Amazon Company, transporting eighty soldiers, with orders to surround the plantation and to arrest all the male slaves older than twelve and younger than sixty years of age. . . .

Dr. *José Vieira Couto de Magalhães.*

C. Second Letter from the Provincial President of Pará to the Minister of Justice

Most Illustrious and Excellent Counselor José Thomaz Nabuco de Araujo. Belém, July 8.

In my official correspondence I informed Your Excellency of a slave revolt which took place on the Pernambuco estate, the property of the Carmelite Convent.

The steamboat which I sent there has just returned here (ten o'clock at night). The slaves resisted. One was killed, two wounded, and eighty arrested. The force suffered no casualties, and I regard the rebellion as suppressed.

I saw it as my duty to send you this news, which pleases me so much, because in our present situation the revolt seemed particularly alarming. God was well served to have it end well, and I hope that the vigor and speed with which it was suppressed will prevent repetition of such incidents.

I am with utmost respect. Your attentive servant and venerator.

Dr. *José Vieira Couto de Magalhães.*

4.10 "The Negroes Were Holding Their Saturnalia": A Popular Festival at the Church of Our Lady of Bomfim in Bahia (1860)

The following description of a religious festival at the church of Nossa Senhora do Bomfim in a suburb of Salvador da Bahia is by the Austrian Archduke Maximilian, who visited Brazil four years before his famous misadventure as Emperor of Mexico. While depicting something of the urban life style of Bahia's large black population, this selection also provides vivid impressions of the blending of African and European cultures and religious practices which had taken place in Brazil during centuries of contact and Catholic indoctrination. Shocking to a European nobleman, the kinds of accomodations between dissimilar religious and cultural traditions which are described here were not only unavoidable but perhaps also expedient from the point of view of Brazil's ruling elite, who, wherever they were, in towns or on plantations, surrounded themselves by masses of black laborers and servants.

Source: Maximilian I, *Recollections of My Life*, 3 vols. (London: Richard Bentley, 1868), III, 170-176.

❧ The road brought us to the hill of Nossa Senhora do Bom Fim, which is surrounded by palms and watered by the spray of the sea. Our four horses dashed across the square in front of a church of brilliant whiteness in the rococo style, standing on a broad handsome terrace, up to which was a wide flight of steps, and on which were some houses. In the square and round the church all was confusion, as though it were a fair-day; black people in their gayest holiday attire were passing to and fro, and chattering noisily; carriages filled with well-dressed senhoras and inquisitive citizens were endeavouring to steer a path through the human waves to the terrace near the church; glass cases, filled with eatables, hovered above the heads of the crowd; little groups of people selling cachaça formed, as it were, islands in the sea of people; a wooden stage similar to that erected in the Theatre Square for the Emperor, announced marvels for the coming afternoon.

Our chariot was drawn safely by its four foaming steeds through the thronging crowd; we alighted and were borne along by the stream to the large building, we pressed through a side door as though passing the lock of a canal, and found ourselves in a long, cheerful, handsomely ornamented gallery; beautiful copper engravings in gilt frames were suspended against the walls, and the light which streamed in through the large windows danced on the sparkling lustres. Mirth and gaiety pervaded the hall. Many young damsels were seated in rows by the wall; their dusky charms not concealed, but enhanced by kerchiefs of transparent light-coloured gauze. In the most graceful and becoming attitudes, and amid incessant chattering, they were selling all kinds of reliques, amulets, torches, and eatables, partly from their baskets and partly from glass cases. To a good Catholic the whole of this proceeding could not but appear most blasphemous; for at this festival the blacks mingled

17. Black Women Going to Church to Have Their Children Baptized

heathen notions to a most improper extent with their ideas of pilgrimage. All went on merrily in the hall: the negro crowd pressed round the saleswomen, laughing and joking; the latter jested in return, behaved in a very coquettish manner, and ogled at the black clowns. The whole scene presented a wild, oriental appearance, though mixed with a certain amount of civilization. . . .

We fought our way on, and reached a spacious apartment filled with rich ornaments; the furniture of which showed it to be a sacristy. A jovial, yellow-faced clergyman was leaning on a chest, with a chasuble and chalice close behind him, and was talking to some senhoras in a lively and agreeable strain. It was indeed a most comfortable, pleasant sacristy.

The stream of people again pressed us on, driving us forward, and pressing us with ever-increasing force, into a spacious hall, from the ceiling of which various chandeliers were hanging, filled with lighted tapers; the walls were of white and gold and were adorned with gay pictures. An atmosphere of festivity seemed to pervade the place; a joyous expectation; as though nothing were wanting in this brilliant hall but the drums and fiddles for the dance. It was crammed with black, brown, yellow figures: with lovely women, sometimes complete giantesses, whose bare necks and beautifully formed shoulders were ornamented with beads, coral, gold chains, and amulets. These women all had shrill voices, rendered mirthful by the influence of cachaça; and for festival trophies, they carried ornamented brooms.

This was an excellent opportunity for studying dusky complexions and negro costume. The negroes were holding their saturnalia; slavery had ceased for the moment; and by the unrestrained movements and the wild merriment of both blacks and mulattoes, by their rich and picturesque attire, one could see that they were, for this day, perfectly happy. There were specimens of every size, every form of the negro race: from the matron, with her gilt ornaments, her almost portly figure and proud gait, to the graceful, joyous, gazelle-like maiden, scarce yet developed: from the white-headed, ape-like, good-tempered old negro, to the roguish chattering boy.

All moved hither and thither in a confused mass. Here, were two acquaintances greeting and kissing each other; there, two negro slaves from distant parts of the town were shaking hands; here a matron shouted "Good day," over the heads of those around her, to an approaching Amazon; there groups of people had collected and were chattering merrily over the events and love-adventures of this happy day. Mirth and unrestrained happiness reigned everywhere: one could see that it was a long-looked-for festival, at which the negroes felt quite at home. The whole company was unanimous on one point; namely, the pleasure of keeping up a loud unceasing chatter.

We pushed forward into the hall in gay spirits, and likewise talking loudly. I was gazing here and there with curiosity, anxious to impress on my mind, as clearly as possible, all the scenes of this black witches' sabbath; when at the farther end of the hall my eye was attracted to a figure on a daïs, who continually looked anxiously up and down in a book, then cast a glance around him, vanished, and reappeared again. I could not believe my eyes; I fixed them on him once more and saw him in the same place. Suddenly a light flashed across my mind and a thrill of horror succeeded. It was the yellow-complexioned priest, who was going through the ceremony of the mass (I cannot call it celebrating mass), as though he were giving an oration at this public festival. I could no longer doubt; we were in the church; the large, mirthful dancing-hall was a Brazilian temple of God, the chattering negroes were baptized Christians, were supposed to be Catholics, and were attending mass.

The Brazilian priests maintain that it is necessary to lead the negroes into the paths of religion by these means: that they understand nothing higher, and can only be brought to the church by mirth and gaiety and when plied with cachaça. This is certainly a very convenient view of the question for slave-owners to take; for it stamps the negro as being half a beast, and gives a sort of sanction to slavery. We spent only the morning in the church; but in the afternoon, and especially towards evening, when the cachaça has raised hilarity to its height, every bound of pious reverence is said to be broken through, and a wild bacchanalia celebrated, in which vice remains victor of the day.

The proper object of this festival is a pilgrimage of the women to this church in order that by washing the entrance on the terrace and the stone pavement, they may obtain the blessing of children; hence the ornamented broom that each woman brings with her, and the emptying of water and careful sweeping which, to our amusement, we noticed everywhere among the crowd. Whether this washing and sweeping be of much avail, I do not know. In any case the miracle is not always worked, but appears to be confined to some isolated instances; for (to the despair of the slave oligarchy) the statistics show that the negro population diminishes considerably every year. The principal reasons probably are the ill-treatment of the slaves, their immorality, the necessity laid upon the expectant mother to continue her work as long as possible, and the excessive use of cachaça. There are also the fearful instances of slave women committing child-murder in order to revenge themselves on their cruel masters, and to rob him of valuable capital. These saturnalia are really only occasions of public rejoicing, like that of the dearly-prized feast of St. Bridget in Vienna. . . . But it is not left to negroes only to amuse themselves in this way; it is a genuine national pastime.

On our return, we saw unceasing streams of negroes and negresses carrying glass cases on their heads, of carriages filled with white people, and of white men riding on mules whom curiosity had attracted to Bom Fim.

FIVE

Relations between the Races

THIS VOLUME of documents would be incomplete if it failed to deal at least briefly with the comparatively elastic Brazilian racial attitudes which have so often been confused with the way Brazilians treated their slaves. As the documents in this part suggest, the subject is far from simple.

It should be clear at the outset, however, that racial discrimination has existed in Brazil since the Portuguese arrived there in the sixteenth century, and that its most obvious manifestation has been the limiting of slave status to non-whites, first Indians and then imported blacks. For nearly as long as slavery existed in Brazil, it should be remembered, the word "African" was practically synonymous with "slave," and a dark skin was always a formidable impediment to economic advancement and personal safety—when it was not an outright pretext for reenslavement (see Part Eight). Discrimination and prejudice also manifested themselves in less obvious ways. To cite some examples, colonial and nineteenth-century laws banning or restricting various kinds of dress, weapons, entertainment and moneymaking activities often lumped free blacks and mulattoes together with slaves, while excluding whites from their provisions (see Part Six); in the colonial period and into the nineteenth century, soldiers were assigned to separate units on the basis of race, in part because whites were unwilling to serve with blacks (see Document 5.2); many religious brotherhoods barred blacks and mulattoes from membership, and the founding of black and mulatto brotherhoods was itself a form of segregation. More clearly harmful was the barring of blacks and even mulattoes from institutions of learning and high government and ecclesiastical appointments, though such discrimination was sometimes remedied by the government itself (see the documents in 5.4). Obviously too, whites attempted to impede entry of blacks and mulattoes into their legitimate families, not always of course with complete success (see Document 5.5).

Despite obvious racial discrimination, however, Brazil did not erect an exclusive color bar such as existed in the United States (see Document 5.9). Relations between the races were not determined by race alone, but were influenced as well by an individual's class and economic status. With luck, ability, perseverance, hard work, the right connections, and a skin not too dark, Brazilians descended in part from non-Europeans were often able to overstep some of the barriers which society normally placed before them. Once this was achieved, however, even wealth, education, and high social standing did not give complete immunity from insults and scorn, sometimes more or less disguised (see Document 5.6). Brazilian blacks and even mulattoes thus suffered serious discrimination which, though often different in mood and degree from that suffered by "Negroes" in the United States, was perhaps no less destructive to the personalities and lives of those concerned.

5.1. "The Fact Remains that They Are Black": Racial Attitudes in Eighteenth-Century Portugal and Brazil

The following selection is the full text of an anonymous pamphlet which the British historian, Charles R. Boxer, purchased from a Lisbon bookseller in 1962 and two years later published in English translation in the British scholarly journal, *Race*. Originally published in Lisbon in 1764 under the title *Nova e Curiosa Relação*, this pamphlet might best be evaluated by its modern discoverer. "One of the few works printed in the eighteenth century which criticize the mistreatment of Negro slaves in Brazil," wrote Boxer in his introduction, ". . . this little pamphlet accurately reflects the climate of opinion in the Portuguese-speaking world at the time that it was written. It shows that there were a number of people (here represented by the Lawyer) who were aware of the evils inherent in any system of slavery. It also shows that the views of these enlightened people were not shared by the great majority of their contemporaries (here represented by the Miner), with whom it was an article of faith that the black man was born to serve the white, and that the latter could do what he liked with his own. The allegations made by the anonymous author concerning the ill-treatment of Negro slaves in colonial Bahia are amply borne out by the testimony of reliable and contemporary observers, as I have shown elsewhere." All of the brief insertions contained in the text in brackets, except the final one, have been adopted from Professor Boxer's original footnotes.

Source: C. R. Boxer, "Negro Slavery in Brazil: A Portuguese Pamphlet (1764)," *Race: The Journal of the Institute of Race Relations* 5 (1964), 38-47.

New and Curious Relation of a Grievance Redressed, or Evidences of the Right Adduced in Favour of the Black Men in a Dialogue between a Lawyer and a Miner

Miner: Learned Sir, I come here to sit at your feet and seek your advice concerning a most important matter.

Lawyer: Sit down, dear Sir. The problem is whether my scanty qualifications will be sufficient to advise you as wisely as I hope to do.

Miner: The fact is that I have a Negro whom I suppose must have been sent into this world for my Purgatory.

Lawyer: Well, let us continue; for it is always true that whoever deals with youths and with slaves needs patience.

Miner: Slowly, learned Sir. That patience is necessary in dealing with youths, I agree; for after all they are somebody's children, and they are white like ourselves. But I cannot endure to hear it said that patience is necessary in dealing with slaves; for after all they are Negroes, and as their owner has bought them for money he can do whatever he likes with them.

Lawyer: You seem to be very offended with the Negroes; but, withal, however, one cannot deny the truth.

Miner: I am going to deny everything.

Lawyer: Whew, Sir! That is crazy! How can you deny that which is right?

Miner: Yes, Sir. If it is anything in favor of Negroes or slaves, I deny it absolutely.

Lawyer: Truly you seem to be of a terrible disposition. But I presume that the ill behavior of one of your slaves has annoyed you so much that you feel compelled to give vent to this great excess. However, I hope that, all passion spent, you will be prepared to agree with me, if perchance you should understand and realize that what I am going to say is the truth.

Miner: Agreed. You have your say, and we will see if I can agree with it.

Lawyer: Now, Sir. One of the reasons which you give me for being patient with youths is that they are somebody's children?

Miner: Yes, Sir.

Lawyer: Well, then. This reason is equally applicable to our being patient with slaves, as they are also somebody's children.

Miner: But with a difference. For we whites are descended from Adam, and the Negroes are descended from Cain, who was black, and who died cursed by God himself, as the Scripture relates.

Lawyer: It is certain that all the whites are descended from Adam, and it is equally certain that all rational beings are likewise descended from him, whether they are black, or dark, or swarthy, or red, or green, or blue etc. Whatever color a man may have, it is certain that he is a son of Adam. Even according to what you yourself say, the blacks are descended from Adam. For if the blacks are descended from Cain, and Cain was the son of Adam, it follows that they likewise descend from and are sons of Adam. Now that Cain was accursed is scriptural truth; but that he was a Negro, and the Negroes are his descendants—I would like to know where you found this information?

Miner: It is something which I have always heard ever since I was a boy.

Lawyer: Ah, well, in that case you are bound to believe in a lot of foolish things! If you are one of those people who implicitly believe whatever they have heard tell since boyhood, then there will hardly be anything so ridiculous but that you will believe it.

Miner: But this is something which is staring one straight in the face.

Lawyer: What, Sir! Since you quoted the Bible at me, listen to this. It is certain, and a scriptural truth, that all men, women, and children were drowned in the universal flood, with the exception of only eight persons who were left alive: Noah, his wife, their three sons, and three women who were wives of the said sons. It is also certain that the Bible does not state that any of them were black. Therefore, the blacks are not black because they are descendants of Cain.

Miner: Well then; why have they got that color, and not we?

Lawyer: That problem, my good Sir, is a very intricate one and hard to resolve. Very learned men have exhausted themselves in trying to find the reason for it, and up to now we still do not know.

Miner: I have heard say that the blackness of the blacks is due to their being born in a very hot climate, and much nearer the sun.

Lawyer: That is a boys' tale. If that was really so, then anybody who was born in the country of the blacks would be black, while on the other hand everybody born in the country of the whites would be white. However, this is not so, since we see that black parents always give birth to black children, whereas white parents always give birth to white children. This is something which we can see at every turn. In Ethiopia itself, where nearly all the natives of the country are black, there are villages of very white people, and the climate is the same all over. So we have not yet been able to ascertain the reason for the blackness of the black people.

Miner: Whatever the reason may be, the fact remains that they are black.

Lawyer: And what do you deduce from that?

Miner: I deduce that the Negroes are not people like ourselves.

Lawyer: Sir, the blackest man in all Africa, because he is a man, is just as much a man as is the whitest German in all Germany. There have been very famous black men and women, of whom we read in History. From the Bible, we learn of the wisdom and greatness of the Queen of Sheba. One of the Magi, who worshipped the Babe born in Bethlehem, was a black. Saint Elesbaan, the Emperor, and his daughter, the Princess Saint Ephigenia, were both Ethiopes and both black. Saint Benedict was black, and so were many others who could be named. What does not Portugal owe to the blacks in its conquests in Brazil! They were the ones who threw the Dutch out of Pernambuco and Rio de Janeiro [the Dutch occupation was confined to northeast Brazil and did not include Rio de Janeiro]; and Lord the King Dom Pedro II granted a habit of the Order of Christ to a black, who on that occasion successfully led the others [it was King John IV, not Pedro II, who knighted the black military leader, Henrique Dias]; for that great king did not wish that the accident of color should deprive him of the honor to which his merits entitled him. And what have you got to say in view of these facts?

Miner: In this way you are arguing that a black is just as good as a white.

Lawyer: Undoubtedly he is, in the sense in which I am speaking.

Miner: Well, if the blacks are just as good as we are, what is the reason that they are our slaves, and we whites are not their slaves?

Lawyer: I now see that you are very far from perceiving the truth. Sir, the blacks are not our slaves just because they are black. The Moors can likewise be enslaved, and what is more they are not black. Mulattoes, Kanarese, Chinese, and others can be enslaved, and they are not black. Once upon a time the Tapuyas of Pará were reputed as slaves, and what is more they are not black. I have seen in this city a boy who was about ten years old, with all the features of his face and the shape of his hair just as if he was a black, but his hair was very blond and his body exceedingly white, yet this boy [an albino] was a slave. So that it is not owing to their color that the blacks are enslaved. There are other lawful and political reasons why they can be enslaved. Once upon a time the Romans enslaved all their prisoners of war, and this custom formerly prevailed among some of the European nations; but this abuse is now extinct. Only the Moors still treat the Europeans whom they capture as slaves.

Miner: I am amazed at what you have told me about this matter; but I have always observed that in Brazil the Negroes are treated worse than animals, being punished very severely, and called by very insulting names, yet withal the blacks endure this.

Lawyer: From what I can see, you must be a miner, and have lived in Brazil. However, you must now have the patience to listen to me. All those punishments and insulting, or rather, scandalous names, if they exceed the limits of needful correction are all sinful, criminal and unjust.

Miner: Oh now, you must be joking! On a certain plantation in Bahia, I saw two Negroes killed in one day, their master standing by and ordering them to be flogged to death by other slaves. And on a farm in Rio de Janeiro, I saw a master kill a Negro with his own hands. Moreover, none of these men were punished for killing their slaves, nor did anybody take the slightest notice of it. For after all, if they killed the Negroes, they were the ones who lost their money thereby, and a man can do what he likes with his own.

Lawyer: Excuse me, Sir, because I simply must tell you that I cannot believe everything you say. I do not doubt but that those sugar-planters killed their slaves, in fact I can very readily believe it. But what I cannot believe is that they went unpunished for those crimes, save only if the crime was not known; and in that case, what you have told me proves nothing to the point. It is also quite true, as you say, that these men lost their money when they killed their slaves. But what do you mean by this? Do you mean to imply that they did not commit murder? That they should not be severely punished? That they were not cruel? That they did not commit mortal sin? Ah, Sir! how badly do they treat the wretched slaves in Brazil! But who treats them thus? Avaricious people! Godless people! People with the hearts of wild beasts!

Miner: How I would like, learned Sir, to see *you* trying to cope with 100 or 200 disobedient, treacherous, lazy, and thieving slaves, and to see how you would treat them then.

Lawyer: I would probably treat them worse than does anybody else there. But what each one of us ought to do, is to treat his servants with charity, with zeal, and for the love of God. Whoever does not have the patience to take trouble with slaves should seek some other way of life. For it is more important not to offend God than to gain profit from any worldly concern whatsoever.

Miner: I see that you have become a missionary in favor of the Negroes; but this is because you have no experience of what they are really like. In short, Sir, let us drop this futile argument and come to the point of the purpose for which I came; although I can see from our preliminary discussion that you will decide against me.

Lawyer: I can assure you, and if necessary on oath, that I will never advise you to do anything that will go against my conscience, nor have I done so in anything that I have told you hitherto.

Miner: Learned Sir, the fact of the matter is that I have a Negro whom I bought about ten or eleven years ago. At first he served me as he ought, and in view of this I promised him that if he would continue to serve me well, I would give him his freedom at the end of ten years.

Lawyer: So far you did, if not what you were obliged to do, at any rate something just and praiseworthy. For I assure you that I cannot help feeling sorry for the wretched slaves who have to toil all their life in perpetual bondage.

Miner: What would you do, Sir, if you saw the Negroes in Brazil working almost continually day and night, and this while going naked? As a rule, they are only given a little bit of manioc flour to eat; and they have Sundays and some Saints' days off, so that they can earn something to keep themselves from starving.

Lawyer: Although I have never actually seen such, I am reasonably well informed about the hardships that those wretches endure. But let us come to the principal point of your visit.

Miner: As I was saying, seeing that the Negro served me loyally and readily in everything, and that even after my promise his zeal was still greater, I secretly resolved never to give him his certificate of manumission.

Lawyer: This was quite contrary to all justice. The very reason that you were the more obliged to keep your word to free him, you used as an excuse to go back on your word.

Miner: Even so, am I obliged to keep a promise which I made to my own Negro?

Lawyer: If your promise, or your word, was given for a just cause, who can doubt it?

Miner: But surely there is no reason why I should not deceive my own black?

Lawyer: On the contrary, Sir! We are always obliged to keep faith with everyone without exception.

Miner: Oh, nobody can tell me that! For in this way, I would be placed on a level with a Negro.

Lawyer: Then do you think that the privilege of being white gives you the right to lie as much as you like? But let us leave this matter and come to the point of your visit.

Miner: The Negro, seeing that I was not performing what I had promised, began to cool off in his zeal to serve me; and he displeased me so much that I resolved to sell him as a slave in Brazil, with the sole object of getting him killed by the harsh punishments in vogue there. The Negro, perceiving this, and having been so advised by others, went and enrolled as a Brother in one of their Brotherhoods, which they say has the privilege that the blacks belonging to this Brotherhood cannot be sold as slaves for overseas [probably the Brotherhood of the Most Holy Rosary of Our Lady of the Black Men of São Salvador da Matta of Lisbon]. However, I, as soon as I heard of this, gave him a severe beating; and notwithstanding this, I resolved to sell him secretly and send him to Minas Gerais. However, last Sunday I went to confession and telling this to the confessor, he raised objections to it, telling me that I could not in conscience do such a thing. I now come to sit at your feet, so that you may reassure me on this point.

Lawyer: Sir, your confessor, like a wise and prudent man, has already told you what you ought to do. I can only add two words in confirmation of what he has already said. It is certain that anyone who disobeys the laws which the sovereigns lay on their vassals commits a mortal sin. The privilege, which our lord kings granted to the blacks of that Brotherhood is a law by which our monarchs order that such Brothers cannot be sold as slaves for overseas. It therefore follows that whoever violates this privilege commits a mortal sin. This is most certain; and thus it seems to me that this is a case of restitution, both to the said Brotherhood, in so far as it is concerned with that Brother, as with the said Brother, in so far as he is concerned as a member of the said Brotherhood.

Miner: Well, learned Sir, does this mean that I am not master of what is mine?

Lawyer: You can be, yes Sir, and you are; but with those restrictions and conditions stipulated by just laws.

Miner: I have a friend, who has done the same thing, and nothing of all this happened to him.

Lawyer: Of all this what?

Miner: There was no talk of sinning nor of restitutions.

Lawyer: I confess and believe that it is likely that your friend did not make restitution. But I would like you to tell me how you know that he was under no obligation to make restitution, nor did he sin?

Miner: Because in that case there would be many sins and much to be restituted.

Lawyer: And who doubts it? Sir, what I feel is that you want to find someone who will approve of all your desires, or rather all your excesses. However, I will say what I believe: what you ought to do, is to fulfill your promise; or, at the very least, inflict no further affliction on your slave, who is sufficiently unfortunate in being one. It is a very common error to believe that the blacks were born solely in order to serve as slaves, but Nature itself loves men of all races without distinction. The way in which many masters treat their slaves is unjust. The latter ought to be punished when they do wrong, but the punishment should be in proportion to the fault. Children are likewise punished by their parents, but in moderation. I do not argue from this that slaves who disobey their masters should not be punished at all, but I only affirm that the punishment ought not to degenerate into cruelty. A conditional promise has the force of law. You promised to free your slave if he continued to serve you well; he not only continued to serve you well, but better still. You are, therefore, obviously bound to free him. You are likewise bound to respect the privilege which he enjoys as a member of his Brotherhood. Hence, if you take my advice, you should either give your slave a certificate of manumission, or else you should treat him kindly, so that he does not lead a dog's life. In this way you will avoid sinning before God, and do what you ought to do.

Miner: Tell me, learned Sir, won't it be enough if I give this Negro his freedom in fifteen or twenty years time?

Lawyer: Better late than never. But tell me, how old is this Negro?

Miner: When I bought him he would have been about twenty-eight years old. I have had him about fourteen or fifteen years [earlier he said ten or eleven], so he must be over forty years old now.

Lawyer: And you want to give him his certificate of manumission fifteen or twenty years hence? In other words, when he will no longer be able to work at all! In this way you are not doing a favor to your black, but merely trying to escape the responsibility of feeding him when he can no longer work. And in that case you are not only very far from keeping your promise but you are rather behaving in a tyrannical way. Now tell me, what can be more contrary to reason, than to make use of a man as a slave for so long as he can work, and then when he can no longer do so, dismiss him and let him die of hunger! In short, I have told you what I think, and now you can go and do what you like.

Miner: I soon saw at the beginning that you would give your decision in favor of the Negro. How is it possible that you, being a white man and a learned one, should favor Negroes rather than white men! I cannot conceive what ground or reason you have for this.

Lawyer: The reason on which I ground myself is following the truth. For I look more to my conscience than to my convenience: and for this reason I have always disabused those persons who come to seek my advice.

Miner: I have heard what you say and I will do what I think best. Excuse me, Sir, here are eight testoons, which may serve to buy a watermelon as a dessert for your dinner.

Lawyer: Thank you kindly, Sir. I remain ready to serve you in any way I can be of use.

LISBON
In the office of Francisco Borges de Sousa
Anno MDCCLXIV
With all the necessary licenses.

5.2. "Even a Considerable Tinge Will Pass for White": A British Resident of Pernambuco Analyses Brazilian Racial and Social Categories Early in the Nineteenth Century

Something of the complicated nature of the Brazilian racial situation is suggested by the following observations of the British writer, Henry

Koster (see introduction to Document 4.8). While Koster's analysis informs us that many Brazilians held liberal or even benevolent attitudes toward non-whites, he also shows us that the "ideal" racial type to which people aspired, and which people most respected, was the European. On the other hand, while an individual's social acceptance and economic and amorous opportunities were clearly related to the color of his or her skin, a tiny minority of lucky, ambitious or well-placed mulattoes and even blacks were not prevented by their appearance from acquiring certain positions of respect and responsibility among whites, or even status and wealth, once some intricate personal and societal bargains had been made. As Koster also cleverly demonstrated, by improving his social status, acquiring a high position, or getting rich, a man could (in an abstract sense) "lighten" the color of his skin—or that of his descendants.

Source: Henry Koster, *Travels in Brazil*, 2 vols., 2nd ed. (London: Longman, Hurst, Rees, Orme, and Brown, 1817), II, 208-22.

❧ Notwithstanding the relationship of the mulattos on one side to the black race, they consider themselves superior to the mamalucos [offspring of Indians with whites]; they lean to the whites, and from the light in which Indians are held, pride themselves upon being totally unconnected with them. Still the mulattos are conscious of their connection with men who are in a state of slavery, and that many persons even of their own colour are under these degraded circumstances; they have therefore always a feeling of inferiority in the company of white men, if these white men are wealthy and powerful. This inferiority of rank is not so much felt by white persons in the lower walks of life, and these are more easily led to become familiar with individuals of their own colour who are in wealthy circumstances. Still, the inferiority which the mulatto feels is more that which is produced by poverty than that which his colour has caused, for he will be equally respectful to a person in his own cast who may happen to be rich. The degraded state of the people of colour in the British colonies is most lamentable. In Brazil, even the trifling regulations which exist against them remain unattended to. A mulatto enters into holy orders or is appointed a magistrate, his papers stating him to be a white man, but his appearance plainly denoting the contrary. In conversing on one occasion with a man of colour who was in my service, I asked him if a certain *Capitam-mor* [Captain major] was not a mulatto man; he answered, "he was, but is not now." I begged him to explain, when he added, "Can a *Capitam-mor* be a mulatto man?" I was intimately acquainted with a priest, whose complexion and hair plainly denoted from whence he drew his origin; I liked him much. he was a well-educated and intelligent man. Besides this individual instance, I met with several others of the same description.

The regiments of militia, which are called mulatto regiments, are so named from all the officers and men being of mixed casts; nor can white persons be admitted to them. The principal officers are men of property; and the colonel, like the commander of any other regiment, is only amenable to the governor of the province. In the white militia regiments, the officers ought to be by law white men; but in practice they are rather reputed white men, for very little pains are taken to prove that there is no mixture of blood. Great numbers of the soldiers belonging to the regiments which are officered by white men, are mulattos and other persons of colour. The regiments of the line, likewise, admit into the ranks all persons excepting negroes and Indians; but the officers of these must prove nobility of birth; however, as certain degrees of nobility have been conferred upon persons in whose families there is much mixture of blood, this proof cannot be regarded as being required against the mulatto or mamaluco part of the population. Thus an European adventurer could not obtain a commission in these regiments, whilst a Brazilian whose family has distinguished itself in the province in former times will prove his eligibility without regard to the blood which runs in his veins. He is noble, let that flow from whence it may.

The late colonel of the mulatto regiment of Recife, by name Nogueira, went to Lisbon, and returned to Pernambuco with the order of Christ, which the Queen had conferred upon him. A chief person of one of the provinces is the son of a white man and a woman of colour; he has received an excellent education, is of a generous disposition, and entertains most liberal views upon all subjects. He has been made a colonel, and a degree of nobility has been conferred upon him; likewise the Regent [the later King João VI] is sponsor to one of his children. Many other instances might be mentioned. Thus has Portugal, of late years from policy, continued that system into which she was led by her peculiar circumstances in former times. Some of the wealthy planters of Pernambuco, and of the rich inhabitants of Recife, are men of colour. The major part of the best mechanics are also of mixed blood.

It is said that mulattos make bad masters; and this holds good oftentimes with persons of this description, who have been in a state of slavery, and become possessed of slaves of their own, or are employed as managers upon estates. The change of situation would lead to the same consequences in any race of human beings, and cannot be accounted peculiar to the mixed casts. I have seen mulattos of free birth as kind, as lenient, and as forbearing to their slaves and other dependents as any white man.

Marriages between white men and women of colour are by no means rare, though they are sufficiently so to cause the circumstance to be mentioned when speaking of an individual who has connected himself in this manner; but this is not said with the intent of lowering him in the estimation of others. Indeed the remark is only made if the person is a planter of any importance, and the woman is decidedly of dark colour, for even a considerable tinge will pass for white; if the white man belongs to the lower orders, the woman is not accounted as being unequal to him in rank, unless she is nearly black. The European adventurers often marry in this manner, which generally occurs when the woman has a dower. The rich mulatto families are often glad to dispose of their daughters to these men, although the person who has been fixed upon may be in indifferent circumstances; for the colour of the children of their daughters is bettered, and from the well-known prudence and regularity of this set of men, a large fortune may be hoped for even from very small beginnings. Whilst I was at Jaguaribe, I was in the frequent habit of seeing a handsome young man, who was a native of the island of St. Michael's. This person happened to be with me on one occasion when the commandant from the Sertam [*Sertão*: interior or backlands] was staying at my house. The commandant asked him if he could read and write, and being answered in the negative, said, "Then you will not do," and turning to me, added, "I have a commission from a friend of mine to take with me back to the Sertam a good-looking young Portuguese of regular habits, who can read and write, for the purpose of marrying him to his daughter." These kind [*sic*] of commissions (*encomendas*) are not unusual.

Still the Brazilians of high birth and large property do not like to intermarry with persons whose mixture of blood is *very* apparent, and hence arise peculiar circumstances. A man of this description becomes attached to a woman of colour, connects himself with her, and takes her to his home, where she is in a short time even visited by married women; she governs his household affairs, acts and considers herself as his wife, and frequently after the birth of several children, when they are neither of them young, he marries her. In connections of this nature, the parties are more truly attached than in marriages between persons who belonged to two families of the first rank; for the latter are entered into from convenience rather than from affection; indeed the parties, on some occasions, do not see each other until a few days before the ceremony takes place. It often occurs, that inclination, necessity, or convenience induce or oblige a man to separate from the person with whom he has thus been connected; in this case, he gives her a portion, and she marries a man of her own rank, who regards her rather as a widow than as one whose conduct has been incorrect. Instances of infidelity in these women are rare; they become attached to the men with whom they cohabit, and they direct the affairs of the houses over which they are placed with the same zeal that they would display if they had the right of command over them. . . .

I now proceed to mention that numerous and valuable race of men, the creole negroes; a tree of African growth, which has thus been transplanted, cultivated, and much improved by its removal to the New World. The creole negroes stand alone and unconnected with every other race of men, and this circumstance alone would be sufficient, and indeed contributes much to the effect of uniting them to each other. The mulattos, and all other persons of mixed blood, wish to lean towards the whites, if they can possibly lay any claim to relationship. Even the mestizo tries to pass for a mulatto, and to persuade himself, and others, that his veins contain some portion of white blood, although that with which they are filled proceeds from Indian and negro sources. Those only who can have no pretensions to a mixture of blood, call themselves negroes, which renders the individuals who do pass under this denomination much attached to each other, from the impossibility of being mistaken for members of any other cast. They are handsome persons, brave, and hardy, obedient to the whites, and willing to please; but they are easily affronted, and the least allusion to their colour being made by a person of a lighter tint, enrages them to a great degree; though they will sometimes say, "A negro I am, but always upright." They are again distinct from their brethren in slavery, owing to their superior situation as free men.

The free creole negroes have their exclusive regiments, as well as the mulattos, of which every officer and soldier must be perfectly black. There are two of these regiments for the province of Pernambuco, which consist of indefinite numbers of men, who are dispersed all over the country. These regiments are distinguished from each other by the names of Old Henriques and New Henriques. The name of Henriques is derived from the famous chieftain, Henrique Diaz, in the time of the Dutch war. I have heard some of the most intelligent of those with whom I have conversed, speak in enthusiastic terms of the aid which he gave to the whites in the struggle. I have seen some portion of one of these regiments in Recife, accompanying the procession of our Lady of the Rosary, the patroness of negroes. They were dressed in white cloth uniforms, turned up with scarlet, and they looked very soldier-like. They were in tolerable discipline, and seemed to wish to go through the duty of the day in the best manner that they were able; they acted with an appearance of zeal and the desire of excelling. Those of which I speak formed a finer body of men than any other soldiers which I had an opportunity of seeing in that country. On gala days the superior black officers in their white uniforms, pay their respects to the governor, exactly in the same manner that the persons of any other cast, holding commissions of equal rank, are expected to go through this form. These men receive no pay, so that their neat appearance on such occasions bespeaks a certain degree of wealth among them; neither are the privates nor any other person belonging to these regiments paid for their services. Some of the whites rather ridicule the black officers, but not in their presence; and the laugh which is raised against them is caused perhaps by a lurking wish to prevent this insulted race from the display of those distinctions which the government has wisely conceded to them, but which hurt the European ideas of superiority.

The creole negroes of Recife are, generally speaking, mechanics of all descriptions; but they have not yet reached the higher ranks of life, as gentlemen, as planters, and as merchants. Some of them have accumulated considerable sums of money, and possess many slaves, to whom they teach their own trade, or these slaves are taught other mechanical employments by which they may become useful. They work for their owners, and render to them great profits, for every description of labour is high, and that which requires any degree of skill bears even a higher comparative value than the departments of which a knowledge is more easily attained. The best church and image painter of Pernambuco is a black man, who has good manners, and quite the air of a man of some importance, though he does not by any means assume too much. The negroes are excluded from the priesthood; and from the offices which the mulattos may obtain through their evasion of the law, but which the decided and unequivocal colour of the negro entirely precludes him from aspiring to. In law all persons who are not white, and are born free, class equally; manumitted slaves are placed upon the same footing as persons born free. However, although the few exclusions which exist among the negroes are degrading, still in some instances they are befriended by them. They are unable, owing to their colour, to serve in the regiments of the line, or in any regiments excepting those which are exclusively their own; but by means of this regulation they escape the persecutions under which the other casts suffer during the time of recruiting. The officers and men of the Henrique regiments are so united to each other, that the privates and subalterns are less liable to be oppressed by any white man in office even than the soldiers of the mulatto regiments. Of these latter the officers, having a considerable tinge of white, sometimes lean towards the wishes of the *capitam-mor*, or some other rich white officer, instead of protecting his soldiers.

The men whose occupation it is to apprehend runaway negroes are, almost without exception, creole blacks; they are called *capitaens-do-campo*, captains of the field; and are subject to a *capitam-mor-do-campo* who resides in Recife, and they receive their commissions either from the governor or from this officer. By these they are authorized to apprehend and take to their owners any slaves who may be found absent from their homes without their master's consent. Several of these men are to be found in every district, employing themselves in such pursuits as they think fit, when their services are not required in that calling which forms their particular duty. They are men of undaunted courage, and are usually followed by two or three dogs, which are trained to seek them out, and if necessary to attack and bring to the ground those persons whose apprehension their masters are desirous of effecting. The men who bear these commissions can oblige any unauthorised person to give up to them an apprehended negro, for the purpose of being by them returned to his owner (see Fig. 29).

5.3. Four Classes of Blacks: The Observations of a British Clergyman in Rio de Janeiro (1828)

The following descriptions of four classes of black people encountered by the British clergyman, Robert Walsh, within hours of his arrival in Rio de Janeiro (see Document 1.9) reveal the diverse social and economic functions which black people could assume in Brazilian society, and so help to clarify the nation's complex racial attitudes. The first blacks Walsh saw in Rio's streets were slaves who, to his inexperienced eye, seemed little more than animals, were in fact treated worse than animals. Soon, however, he encountered other blacks who quickly altered his first impressions: well-dressed and disciplined black soldiers accompanied by a military band of their own regiment, shopkeepers, both slave and free, who had achieved some status and dignity, and finally a priest, who to Walsh seemed more devout and correct than his white associates. Walsh's impressions indicate how important it is to differentiate clearly between race relations and the physical treatment of slaves, if we are to reach sound conclusions regarding the nature of Brazilian society.

Source: Robert Walsh, *Notices of Brazil in 1828 and 1829*, 2 vols. (London: Frederick Westley and A. H. Davis, 1830), I, 134-141.

❧ [At the Alfandega, or custom house,] for the first time I saw the Negro population under circumstances so striking to a stranger. The whole labour of bearing and moving burdens is performed by these people, and the state in which they appear is revolting to humanity. Here were a number of beings entirely naked, with the exception of a covering of dirty rags tied about their waists. Their skins, from constant exposure to the weather, had become hard, crusty, and seamed, resembling the coarse black covering of some beast, or like that of an elephant, a wrinkled hide scattered with scanty hairs. On contemplating their persons, you saw them with a physical organization resembling beings of a grade below the rank of man; long projecting heels, the gastronimic [gastrocnemius] muscle wanting, and no calves to their legs; their mouths and chins protruded, their noses flat, their foreheads retiring, having exactly the head and legs of the baboon tribe. Some of these beings were yoked to drays, on which they dragged heavy burdens. Some were chained by the necks and legs, and moved with loads thus encumbered. Some followed each other in ranks, with heavy weights on their heads, chattering the most inarticulate and dismal cadence as they moved along. Some were munching young sugar-canes, like beasts of burden eating green provender, and some were seen near water, lying on the bare ground among filth and offal, coiled up like dogs, and seeming to expect or require no more comfort or accommodation, exhibiting a state and conformation so unhuman, that they not only seemed, but actually were, far below the inferior animals around them. Horses and mules were not employed in this way; they were used only for pleasure, and not for labour. They were seen in the same streets, pampered, spirited, and richly caparisoned, enjoying a state far superior to the negroes, and appearing to look down on the fettered and burdened wretches they were passing, as on beings of an inferior rank in the creation to themselves. Some of the negroes actually seemed to envy the caparisons of their fellow brutes, and eyed with jealousy their glittering harness. In imitation of this finery, they were fond of thrums of many-coloured threads; and I saw one creature, who supported the squalid rag that wrapped his waist by a suspender of gaudy worsted, which he turned every moment to look at, on his naked shoulder. The greater number, however, were as unconscious of any covering for use or ornament, as a pig or an ass.

The first impression of all this on my mind, was to shake the conviction I had always felt, of the wrong and hardship inflicted on our black fellow-creatures, and that they were only in that state which God and nature had assigned them; that they were the lowest grade of human existence, and the link that connected it with the brute, and that the gradation was so insensible, and their natures so intermingled, that it was impossible to tell where one had terminated and the other commenced; and that it was not surprising that people who contemplated them every day, so formed, so employed, and so degraded, should forget their claims to that rank in the scale of beings in which modern philanthropists are so anxious to place them. I did not at the moment myself recollect, that the white man, made a slave on the coast of Africa, suffers not only a similar mental but physical deterioration from hardships and emaciation, and becomes in time the dull and deformed beast I now saw yoked to a burden.

A few hours only were necessary to correct my first impressions of the negro population, by seeing them under a different aspect. We were attracted by the sound of military music, and found it proceeded from a regiment drawn up in one of the streets. Their colonel had just died, and they attended to form a procession to celebrate his obsequies. They were all of different shades of black, but the majority were negroes. Their equipment was excellent; they wore dark jackets, white pantaloons, and black leather caps and belts, all which, with their arms, were in high order. Their band produced sweet and agreeable music, of the leader's own composition, and the men went through some evolutions with regularity and dexterity. They were only a militia regiment, yet were as well appointed and disciplined as one of our regiments of the line. Here then was the first step in that gradation by which the black population of this country ascend in the scale of humanity; he advances from the state below that of a beast of burden into a military rank, and he shows himself as capable of discipline and improvement as a human being of any other colour.

Our attention was next attracted by negro men and women bearing about a variety of articles for sale; some in baskets, some on boards and cases carried on their heads. They belonged to a class of small shopkeepers, many of whom vend their wares at home, but the greater number send them about in this way, as in itinerant shops. A few of these people were still in a state of bondage, and brought a certain sum every evening to their owners, as the produce of their daily labour. But a large proportion, I was informed, were free, and exercised this little calling on their own account. They were all very neat and clean in their persons, and had a decorum and sense of respectability about them, superior to whites of the same class and calling. All their articles were good in their kind, and neatly kept, and they sold them with simplicity and confidence, neither wishing to take advantage of others, nor suspecting that it would be taken of themselves. I bought some confectionary from one of the females, and I was struck with the modesty and propriety of her manner; she was a young mother, and had with her a neatly dressed child, of which she seemed very fond. I gave it a little comfit, and it turned up its dusky countenance to her and then to me, taking my sweetmeat, and at the same time kissing my hand. As yet unacquainted with the coin of the country, I had none that was current about me, and was leaving the articles; but the poor young woman pressed them on me with a ready confidence, repeating in broken Portuguese, *outo tempo*. [sic.] I am sorry to say, the "other time" never came, for I could not recognize her person afterwards to discharge her little debt, though I went to the same place for the purpose.

It soon began to grow dark, and I was attracted by a number of persons bearing large lighted wax tapers, like torches, gathering before a house. As I passed by, one was put into my hand by a man who seemed in some authority, and I was requested to fall into a procession that was forming. It was the preparation for a funeral, and on such occasions, I learned that they always request the attendance of a passing stranger, and feel hurt if they are refused. I joined the party, and proceeded with them to a neighbouring church. When we entered we ranged ourselves on each side of a platform which stood near the choir, on which was laid an open coffin, covered with pink silk and gold borders. The funeral service was chanted by a choir of priests, one of whom was a negro, a large comely man, whose jet black visage formed a strong and striking contrast to his white vestments. He seemed to perform his part with a decorum and sense of solemnity, which I did not observe in his brethren. After scattering flowers on the coffin, and fumigating it with incense, they retired, the procession dispersed, and we returned on board.

I had been but a few hours on shore, for the first time, and I saw an African negro under four aspects of society; and it appeared to me, that in every one his character depended on the state in which he was placed, and the estimation in which he was held. As a despised slave, he was far lower than other animals of burthen that surrounded him; more miserable in his look, more revolting in his nakedness, more distorted in his person, and apparently more deficient in intellect than the horses and mules that passed him by. Advanced to the grade of a soldier, he was clean and neat in his person, amenable to discipline, expert at his exercises, and showed the port and being of a white man similarly placed. As a citizen, he was remarkable for the respectability of his appearance, and the decorum of his manners in the rank assigned him; and as a priest, standing in the house of God, appointed to instruct society on their most important interests, and in a grade in which moral and intellectual fitness is required, and a certain degree of superiority is expected, he seemed even more devout in his impressions, and more correct in his manners, than his white associates. I came, therefore, to the irresistible conclusion in my mind, that colour was an accident affecting the surface of a man, and having no more to do with his qualities than his clothes—that God had equally created an African in the image of his person, and equally given him an immortal soul; and that an European had no pretext but his own cupidity, for impiously thrusting his fellow-man from that rank in the creation which the Almighty had assigned him, and degrading him below the lot of the brute beasts that perish.

5.4. Official Acts Opposing or Outlawing Discrimination against Mulattoes and Free Blacks (1689 and 1849)

As the previous selections reveal, some blacks and mulattoes in Brazil enjoyed social advantages that were normally denied to their counterparts in the American South or even in free states of the North. Yet, as we have also seen, racial or color prejudice clearly existed in Brazil, and non-whites were often arbitrarily or even legally denied opportunities for schooling and other advantages which were freely granted to whites of similar economic circumstances. The following royal decree of February 28, 1689, uncovers one such act of discrimination—the refusal of Jesuit friars to admit mulatto boys to their school in Bahia—but also proves that on some occasions at least such discrimination was officially discouraged or even prohibited. The second document below, a decision of members of the Brazilian Emperor's Council of State, reveals the existence of de facto discrimination against non-whites in the nineteenth century, evidently again on the part of a Church body, and, once again, official rejection of such discrimination at a high level of government. Again, the contrast with the United States of the period is striking.

Sources: "Provisão de 28 de Fevereiro de 1689," in José Justino Andrade e Silva, *Collecção chronologica da legislação portuguesa compilada e annotada* (Lisbon, 1854-1859), x, 187; "Intelligencia do Acto Addicional na Parte Relativa as Assembléas Provinciaes," in *Relatorio da Repartição dos Negocios do Imperio* (Rio de Janeiro, 1857), p. 22.

❧ *A Royal Decree of 1689*

I the King make known to those who may see this my Order that concerning the petition sent to me by the mulatto youths of the city of Bahia to the effect that, possessing for many years the right to study in the public schools of the College of the Friars of the Company [of Jesus], the said Friars excluded them, and did not want to admit them to study in their schools, they being present in my Universities of Coimbra and

Evora, the color of the mulattoes not serving [there] as an impediment; having requested me to order the said Friars to admit [them] in their schools in Brazil, as they are admitted in the Kingdom [of Portugal], and having considered everything, including that which the Governor General of that State has told me concerning this request, it is to be desired that the Friars of the Company admit the mulatto youths for study.

A Decision of the Emperor's Council of State of 1849

Freedmen and free mulattoes. Any provisions which make hateful distinctions concerning mulatto citizens of Brazil or freedmen, such as excluding them from belonging to a religious brotherhood, etc., are unconstitutional. 18 September, 1849.

5.5. The Influence of Black and Mulatto Household Slaves upon the Character of the Brazilian Upper Class

It was customary, as we have seen, for upper-class Brazilian families to keep large numbers of slaves in their homes to serve their personal needs and perhaps to assure their neighbors that they were indeed people of substance. This practice resulted in intimate relationships between masters and servants which helped to mold the personalities of upper-class people and the whole nature of Brazilian society. The impact of household slaves upon the dominant class, especially female servants and their children upon the younger boys, is vividly described in the following selection from a book first published in 1894, which dealt with the need to establish a system of national education. Its author, a student of Brazilian literature, clearly based his opinions upon memories of a childhood spent among slaves. His thoughts may remind readers of the writings of the well-known Brazilian historian and sociologist, Gilberto Freyre.

Source: José Verissimo, *A educação nacional*, 2nd ed. (Rio de Janeiro, 1906), pp. 33-36, 50-51.

It is not possible to exaggerate the evils that slavery brought upon us. For three hundred years we lived like sloths from the labor, first of the Indian, then of the black. Let it be Brazil's destiny that so much time will not be needed to liberate us once and for all from this hateful institution, which, in response to history's unerring law of justice, requiring that each mistake carry its own punishment within it, even today

18. A Plantation Family and Their Servants

burdens and troubles us. Slavery not only eradicated and degraded labor; it consumed all the powers that were in us, which had already been weakened by climate and corrupted by heredity.

Once Indian slavery had been eliminated, the happy, carefree, and affectionate African, with the primitive morality of the savage, with the bitterness that belongs to those who are persecuted, intruded into the family, into society, into the home. He rocked the hammock of his mistress [*sinhá*], served as page to his young master [*sinhô-moço*], as attendant to his lord [*sinhô*]. As the nurse, the slave girl suckled every Brazilian generation; as the personal servant [*mucama*], she lulled them all to sleep; as a man, the slave toiled for every generation; as a woman, she surrendered herself to all of them.

There was not a household where there were not one or more young slave boys [*moleques*], one or more young servants [*curumins*], victims dedicated to the whims of the young master [*nhônhô*]. They were his horse, his whipping boy, his friends, companions, servants.

The girls, the young ladies, the mistresses of the house had their *mucamas* for the same purposes, usually creole girls or *mulatas*.

The depraved influence of this peculiar Brazilian type, the *mulata*, in the weakening of our character has never been sufficiently analyzed. "That leaven of national aphrodisia," as Dr. Sílvio Romero [a noted literary critic] calls her, was the ruin of our physical and moral manhood. Popular Brazilian poetry demonstrates this to us with its constant passionate preoccupation with the full force of her attractions and influence. The amorous poet, with his lascivious style, never tires of celebrating her charms, which he dissects minutely with his avid and burning desires. He sings of her sensuousness, her magic, as he puts it, with his ridiculous, eager, and intemperate language, her lust, her sorcery, her coyness, her coquettishness, her enchantments. She emphatically torments his inspiration, and the poets, with Gregório de Matos in the forefront, make her the heroine of their verses, employing the utmost frankness and sensuality.

In the family she is the young mistress's intimate companion and the young master's sweetheart. Thanks mainly to her, at fourteen years of age physical love holds no secrets for the Brazilian, initiated from the tenderest age in the provocative atmosphere that she creates around him, giving him his bath, dressing him, putting him to bed.

Weak because of climate, weak because of race, weak because of the precociousness of the reproductive functions, weak because of the absence of any labor, of any activity, the blood weak, the character without content, or cranky, and for this reason alone, inconsequential, the feelings ravished and abused, inflamed, undisciplined, ill-mannered in the

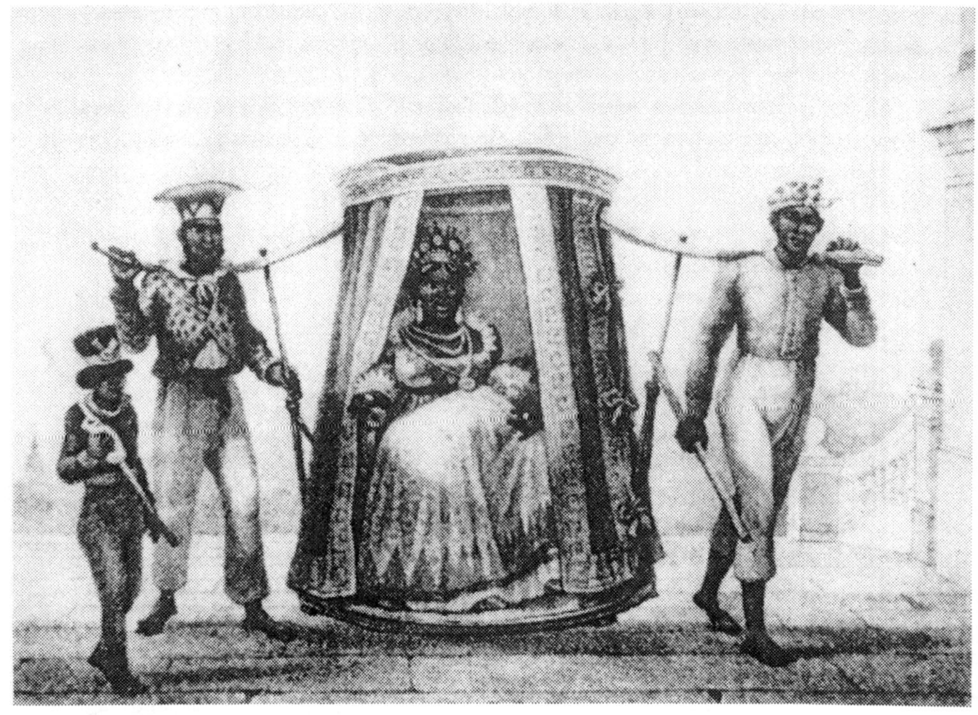

19. A Wet Nurse Taking a White Child to Church to Be Baptized

fullest meaning of the word—this is how the young Brazilian normally starts out his life. . . .

Until now the phenomenon, earlier mentioned, of having in every household a black boy or boys who were the playmates of the little masters [*sinhôzinhos*] and the victims of their roguish acts, a kind of whipping boy [*leva-pancadas*] against whom they concentrated their infantile fury, quickly corrupted their faculties to an extraordinary degree through a fusion of the black boy's poor upbringing and nasty habits and the bad, even depraved, instincts which were produced in the child by the pleasure, natural to him, which he took from striking somebody or something. His sensibilities were quickly blunted, not only the objective sensibilities, which cause us to feel something for others, but also the subjective sensibilities, which make us capable of feeling something for ourselves. The shameless black boy who pilfered, cracked jokes, wept, and sometimes while still in tears was forced to continue to play the game, obviously did not give the child a high impression of honor and dignity, and, since imitation has an important influence upon the development of a child's personality and moral inclinations, the result of this deadly familiarity was his assimilation of the black boy's own qualities.

On the other hand, the habit of giving commands from earliest childhood, far from strengthening character, demeans it, not only because it perverts the concept of authority, making it arbitrary and basing it upon privilege alone, but also because it suppresses the inclination to act independently and forces dependence upon outside energies.

5.6. Racial Conflict in Nineteenth-Century Maranhão

In the northern province of Maranhão a small population of European origin established itself thinly among a multitude of black slaves. The latter, responding (willingly or not) to the white man's sexual drives, unintentionally infused itself genetically into the dominating class. This rise of the mulatto in Maranhão did not occur, however, without conflict, brutality, and resentment. In fact, the racial discord in this region, where blacks so decisively outnumbered whites, seems to have been unusually bitter by Brazilian standards, as an entrenched elite tried unsuccessfully to maintain its racial "purity." The following excerpts from the personal memoir of João Dunshee de Abranches, a prominent writer and politician of Maranhão, gives some impression of the human costs of this struggle. Readers should be aware that persons descended from blacks and whites were frequently referred to as *cabras* or *bodes*, both of which mean "goat."

Source: João Dunshee de Abranches, *O captiveiro (memorias)* (Rio de Janeiro: Jornal do Comercio, 1941), pp. 50-51, 132-139.

❧ *To marry a goat* (this was the smutty expression that was used to stigmatize the mulattoes), or a *pardo*, a more genteel name that was also used for them, constituted an irreparable and permanent dishonor. The generation [that followed] remained forever *tainted*. In journalistic polemics, fatal were the references to those who were not of pure race or were unjustly accused of having *bellowed in their mother's womb*. Terrible satires about *Blockhead* [*Pascacio*] or *Smooth-Belly* [*Barriga-lisa*] or *Bald Ignacio* were popular in the province. Against Major Jacarandá, who did not hesitate in *O Apreciavel* to insult his enemies, they went so far as to order production of an engraving in Paris in which his soldierly head topped off the shaggy body of a goat. Because of his dark skin, the holder of the Chair in Geography at the Academy, Dr. Tiberio, was the target of the savage insinuations of his insolent students. On a certain day on the blackboard of his classroom they had written in bold characters: "Tiberio is a goat." The old teacher came into the room, looked with his legendary *lorgnon* at the rude inscription, and, with no sign of annoyance, picked up his chalk and retaliated: "Just like the rest of you." And then from atop his lecture chair he began at once to recite verses from the famous satire, *The Be-Goated One* [*A Bodarada*], commenting as he went with savage references to the parents and relatives of the authors of the cruel phrase. There were serious protests from the families, who considered themselves offended. The fact is that in São Luís there was a profound malice toward the race associated with slavery. Aluízio Azevedo summed up this prejudice very well in his novel, *O Mulato*. And greatly celebrated was the painful case of Gonçalves Dias, who finding himself rejected by the family of his very beautiful Anna Amelia because he was of mixed race, poured out his feelings in tender verses.

This instinctive aversion toward those with possible African blood in their veins reached such a level in the high and refined society of Maranhão in the period that it became a true obsession. It was generally believed that justice itself took a different attitude toward whites who became criminals. And this mistaken notion became so deep-rooted in people's minds that again and again I heard my *Black Mammy* [*Mãe Preta*] declare with complete conviction that not only the *whip*, but also the *pillory* and the *lasso* were for blacks alone. . . .

The slave system positively deadened people's hearts. The African blacks lived installed with the domestic animals in the houses where they served. Badly fed, plagued by harsh treatment, they were not permitted to rest, to sleep, or even to be sick. Day and night they toiled either for their masters or leased out to the public works. Generally speaking, the *yoked blacks* in São Luís had a monstrous appearance: forced to carry tons of merchandise on their shoulders and to serve as instruments for cutting enormous masonry stones, aside from being constantly infested with vermin, they became bow-legged and were seen with their bodies covered with hernias. Even then the so-called Dike stones were age-old proof of the painful martyrdom of those wretched carriers. . . .

The antipathy between the whites, especially the Portuguese, and the people of color did not cease with independence and the civilizing tendency that followed. Despite substantial and constant mixing, there was always a futile attempt to maintain a clear distance between the two races. In São Luís ladies of good families desperately struggled to avoid bastard offspring and to preserve pure blood among their children. However, their husbands were constant victims of the flesh's frailty. The

20. New Slaves

mixed girls of Maranhão were the most beautiful in the northern part of the country. Among the commercial people especially, almost all the innkeepers and clerks possessed a *second house*. This was known as keeping sweethearts [*amazias teúdas ou manteúdas*]. Second domiciles were in vogue, and with them counterfeit families [*familias postiças*], as the legitimate ones disparagingly called them. And in the same school it was common for natural sons to be classmates of legitimate ones. In the interior of the province, such alliances were even more damaging. Many planters boasted of being true nabobs. In Alto-Mearim, at an agricultural estate where I stayed some months after passage of the law of May 13 [the legislation of 1888 that ended slavery], I was entertained by a rich farmer who even then, without the least constraint, called my attention to a group of small dwellings in the vicinity of the family house, each one occupied by a concubine, his ex-slave, and respective heirs. And it was notorious in São Luís that in the Rosario Church, in the so-called Potter's Workshop [*Olaria*], a representative of a religious order had had more than two hundred children with his slave women, many of whom rose to the highest positions in the Empire.

The *Balaiada* [a widespread rebellion in Maranhão from 1838 to 1841], like all civil struggles, . . . aggravated the deplorable breakdown of customs even further. When the revolutionary movement broke out, panic overtook the rural populations. There was a general exodus from the villages and country estates. The slaves immediately took to the forests, rejecting slavery. The planters and their overseers, fearing the vengeance of the oppressed, rushed to seek shelter in the capital. Many abruptly abandoned wives and daughters in the countryside under the impression that, being women, they were less exposed to danger. Many of the latter, lacking the slightest instruction and brutalized by the licentious practices of the slave huts, quickly surrendered themselves either to the lust of the insurgents, because of fear, or they joined their favorite slaves. These rustic love affairs later gave rise to bloody and disgusting dramas. Everywhere there were frequent infanticides as a means of concealing lost virginity and adulterous acts. From the plantations nearest to São Luís, cloaked messengers arrived during the night in sailboats bringing newborn babies whom they cast into the streets near the beaches. The chronicles of the land preserved for generations the episode of the discovery in a single night of three abandoned girls, who, being adopted by illustrious families, were later notable ornaments of Maranhão society.

. . .

An abominable episode was that of the black man Amparo. A young woman who was married to a planter and belonged to one of the finest and most influential provincial families, fell passionately in love with one of her servants. The scandal quickly erupted. The ridiculed husband, pretending to leave on a trip to São Luís, returned to his plantation late in the night, and managed to capture the guilty man. The slave Amparo was then placed in stocks in a dark room where day after day he suffered hunger and thirst, until kinsmen arrived from the neighboring districts and from the capital. Meeting in a family council, in which titled men and prominent politicians took part, it was decided to send the adulterous girl to her maternal home in São Luís. As for her accomplice, he was stripped naked, and, after being cut to pieces with a lash, he was tied to a post in the middle of the pasture with his body daubed with honey, so that the mosquitoes would torment him until he succumbed to the deadly blows with which they had brutally mutilated him.

5.7. "Who Am I?" A Mulatto Ex-Slave Ridicules in Verse the Bigotry of His Racially Mixed Fellow Brazilians (1859)

An animosity toward mulattoes and other non-whites which existed to a considerable degree throughout Brazil was sometimes reflected in creative literature. Aluízio Azevedo's novel, *O Mulato*, mentioned in the previous selection, is probably the best-known example of this form of social comment. A brief and lesser-known example is the following poem written by the mulatto writer and abolitionist, Luís Gama (see Documents 8.20 and 10.9). Gama, the son of a Bahian gentleman of Portuguese descent and an African woman, was born free in Salvador, but illegally sold into slavery by his own father when he was only ten. Growing into manhood in the province of São Paulo, where, as a household slave, he learned to read and write, Gama fled from slavery, becoming a soldier, lawyer, editor, poet, and abolitionist. This poem, which uses the word "*bode*" or goat to refer to mulattoes just as "*cabra*" (also goat) was used (see previous document), was included in a volume of verses entitled *Primeiras Trovas Burlescas* (First burlesque rhymes) which Gama published in 1859 when he was twenty-nine. The original Portuguese version is appended.

Who Am I?

If black I am, or a *goat*,
it matters little.
For what should this denote?

Goats there are of every caste,
It's a species that's very vast.
Some goats are the color of ash,
some spotted,
some faded,
others mottled.
Black goats there are, *white goats*,
and let's be frank,
there are goats of little note,
and some of highest rank.
Rich goats, poor goats,
wise goats, prize goats,
and some wheeler-dealer goats.

Here in this good land,
everyone butts, everyone bleats.
Noble counts and duchesses,
wealthy damsels and marquises,
senators and deputies,
overseers and country lords,
lovely ladies proud,
flaunting their magnificence,
pompous princelings loud,
boasting their significance,
imperial dandies,
padres, bishops, cardinals, grandees,
poor folk, fine folk,
my kinsmen every bloke.
In each resplendent army coterie
one spots some high-born goaterie.

[QUEM SOU EU?

Se negro sou, ou sou bode
Pouco importa. O que isto pode?
Bodes ha de toda a casta,
Pois que a espécie é muito vasta. . . .
Ha cinzentos, ha rajados,
Bayos, pampas e malhadas,
Bodes negros, *bodes brancos*,
E, sejamos todos francos,
Uns plebeus, e outros nobres,
Bodes sábios, importantes,
E também alguns tratantes. . . .

Aqui nesta boa terra,
Marram todos, tudo berra;
Nobres Condes e Duquezas,
Ricas Damas e Marquezas,
Deputados, senadores,
Gentis-homens, veadores;
Bellas Damas emproadas,
Da nobresa empantufadas;
Repimpados principotes,
Orgulhosos fidalgotes,
Frades, Bispos, Cardeaes,
Fanfarrões imperiaes,
Gentes pobres, nobres gentes
Em todos ha *meus* parentes.
Entre a brava militança
Fulge e brilha alta bodança. . . .]

5.8. A Popular Verse Suggests Portuguese and Brazilian Attitudes toward Racial Mixing (1826)

Portuguese and Brazilian attitudes toward race are hinted at humorously in the following popular verse which a deputy representing Goiás, Raimundo José da Cunha Matos, read in the Brazilian Chamber of Deputies in 1826. "I believe that not one of us is so animated by the spirit of puritanism," he told his fellow deputies during a debate on the slave trade, "that he will fall into the great defect of our elders, who always wished to be gentlemen, although at the roots of their genealogical trees there was a Moor, a black, or a Jew." According to Cunha Matos, the Count of Castanheira, whose genealogy the verse allegedly outlined, was a favorite of King João III of Portugal. The original Portuguese version is appended.

Source: *Annaes da Camara dos Senhores Deputados* (1827), III, 16.

❧ Master John, a priest,
Of Barcellos a native son,
Had from one young Moorish lass
A good and likely son.
Pedro Esteves he was dubbed,
And honorably he lived,
And married with truest love

A lovely Indian miss.
From this, for we've nothing to hide,
Was born Maria Pinheira,
Mother of the mother of that great count,
Who was the Count of Castanheira.

[O mestre João sacerdote,
de Barcellos natural,
Houve de uma moura tal
Um filho de boa sorte.
Pedro Esteves se chamou,
Honradamente vivia,
E de amores se casou
Com uma formosa india.
Desta pois, nada se esconde,
Nasceu Maria Pinheira,
Mai da mai daquelle conde
Que é conde de Castanheira.]

5.9. A Renowned Brazilian Mulatto Encounters Prejudice in New York but Is Rescued by Brazilian Friends: A Contrast in Race Relations (1873)

While color prejudice certainly existed in Brazil, it was strikingly different from North American racism. As we have seen, Brazilian racial attitudes allowed friendliness and affection among people who were racially different but of a similar social rank, and Brazilians had less place in their system of values for the kind of discrimination and segregation that were normal in all parts of the United States. These differences between the two countries on the racial question are dramatized by the following excerpt from a diary written by the noted Brazilian mulatto, André Rebouças, during a visit to New York City in 1873. Rebouças was an economist, teacher, and engineer who is best known today for his abolitionist activities in the 1880s, but in 1873 he was honored by Brazilians mainly for his engineering accomplishments, which included the construction of important docks in Rio de Janeiro.

Source: André Rebouças, *Diário e notas autobiográficas*, ed. Ana Flora and Inacio José Verissimo (Rio de Janeiro: Livraria José Olympio Editora, 1938), pp. 245-246.

❧ *9 June* [1873]. At eight o'clock in the morning I disembarked at "White Star Docks." An investigation of my baggage took place there which was really more contrived than serious, and it was then sent on by the purser of the *Oceanic* to the Fifth Avenue Hotel. I went to the hotel with other fellow passengers in a coach belonging to the same company; there they said they had no more rooms and suggested another hotel. After some attempts, I realized that the reason I was being refused rooms was a problem of color. I obtained the address of the Brazilian Consulate and went there in a special coach.

At the consulate, fortunately, I met the old consul, Luiz Henrique Ferreira d'Aguiar, and the Minister, Carvalho Borges, who received me with great friendliness.

The son of the consul, an engineer, who at times had visited my assistant, José Americo, at the custom-house contruction office [in Rio de Janeiro], obtained a room for me in the Washington Hotel under the condition that I eat in my room and never in the restaurant.

The first room I had was a dirty little chamber on the third floor; later they gave me an apartment with a second room on the ground floor, No. 43, with a door that opened straight onto the square where Broadway begins.

The Washington Hotel once had the glory of receiving the immortal Washington; it was stylish for a few years, but today is a third-class hotel.

Upon my return to the consulate I met Lieutenant Captain Wandenkolk and several officers of the corvette *Niterói*. I made the acquaintance of the distinguished Brazilian, Dr. José Carlos Rodrigues, editor and owner of the *Novo Mundo* and *La América Ilustrada*. . . .

I spent the evening with Dr. Rodrigues. Color prejudice prevented me from attending the performance in the Grand Opera House.

I suggested to Dr. Rodrigues that he introduce into Brazil the magic lantern for advertising, like the one that functions at the corner of Broadway and Fifth Avenue.

10 June. In the morning I was obliged to take a bath in a barber shop.

SIX

"Peculiar Legislation": Slavery and the Law

THE BRAZILIAN legal expert, Augusto Teixeira de Freitas, wrote in his compendium of civil laws (*Consolidação das leis civis*, 3rd ed. [Rio de Janeiro, 1876], p. 35): "There are three kinds of property: movable effects, real estate, and stock holdings. Personal goods and chattels belong in the class of movable effects, and slaves are included among personal goods and chattels. Although it is accepted that slaves, as articles of property, are necessarily regarded as *things* [italics in original], they are not placed on an equal level with inanimate objects, and for this reason peculiar legislation applies to them."

The purpose of this part is to examine some of this "peculiar legislation." To some extent, of course, laws bearing on slavery are misleading to the student of Brazil, since enforcement was undermined by official corruption and the great authority of masters. In rural areas, as often as not, the real executive, legislative, and judicial powers were vested in the slaveholder himself, or delegated to his managers and overseers, and local judicial and peace-keeping officers often possessed little independent influence. Brazil was a nation where legal principles held an esteemed place in the minds of the elite, many of whom were lawyers as well as slaveholders. However, in real situations, when the interests of those same slaveholders were at stake, the law was easily bent, ignored, or violated.

The selections in this part nevertheless provide a glimpse into the legal web of restraints, privileges, and safeguards which were fashioned over the centuries to protect the master from his slave, the slave from his master, and the whole society from the institution of slavery itself. Some specific issues such as the question of slave marriages, the status of the slave *as* property, and the right of slaves to *hold* property are clarified here (see especially Document 6.1). Also included are examples of restrictive laws promulgated over several centuries which were intended to control and restrain slaves and other non-whites, and to punish them when they rebelled or disobeyed (see 2 through 7). Finally, two documents (numbers 8 and 9) offer important evidence concerning two controversial historical questions: whether a slave in Brazil could *demand* his freedom by offering his master his value or purchase price, as has been alleged; and whether a master had the legal right to abuse his female slave sexually on the basis of his right to her as property. The answer to this second question speaks volumes about the respect for the "moral personality of the slave," which was allegedly one of the factors making slavery in Brazil and Spanish America more humane than it was in other parts of the Americas.

6.1. "This Dark Blotch on Our Social System": An Analysis of the Legal Status of Slaves and Freedmen in Brazilian Society (1866)

The following essay by the legal historian, Agostinho Marques Perdigão Malheiro, is from a major study of slavery written in the 1860s. Based upon a deep knowledge of Roman and Luso-Brazilian law, this analysis contains authoritative discussions of the theoretical rights and responsibilities of slaveholders, the legal status of slaves and their peculiar place as people and property in Brazilian society, and, finally, the legal and civic status of freedmen.

To some extent the situation of the latter group will seem to contrast sharply with the status of free blacks in the United States. It must be cautioned, however, that the civil rights which Brazil's Imperial Constitution granted to freedmen in 1824 were in fact restricted to a small privileged minority. Few ex-slaves or freeborn descendants of slaves could have met the qualifications that the Constitution required of Brazilian citizens who wished to assume their political rights. To vote in primary elections, for example, Brazilian citizens, including freedmen, required a large annual income. In the United States blacks were denied their civil rights on grounds of race, the Brazilian poor of all colors—white, brown, black—by their poverty, ignorance, and low social status.

Source: Agostinho Marques Perdigão Malheiro, *Escravidão no Brasil: Ensaio histórico-jurídico-social*, 2 vols. 2nd ed. (São Paulo: Edições Cultura, 1944), I, 17-75, 95, 181-183; II, 123-124.

Neither our Constitution nor any of our laws regard the *slave* as belonging to the mass of the *citizens* for any purpose involving social, political, or public life, even if he was born in the Empire. Only *freedmen*, if they are Brazilian citizens, enjoy certain political rights and can exercise political responsibilities, as we will later show.

From the moment a man is reduced to the condition of a *thing*, from the moment he becomes the property of another person subject to his *power* and *authority*, he is regarded as legally *dead*, deprived of every *right* and possessing *no representation whatsoever*, as Roman Law previously established. Therefore, he cannot claim political rights, the rights of the *city*, in the phrase of the Popular King [the Etruscan ruler, Servius Tullius (578-534 B.C.), known for his influence on later Roman law], nor can he perform public functions. This is expressly laid down in various old Portuguese laws, and is contained in our present legal system in the form of unquestioned principles, which, despite this, are recognized as among the great evils resulting from slavery.

So complete is this incapacity that slaves among us are not even allowed to serve as recruits in the army or navy; nor can they exercise ecclesiastical responsibilities, either of a mixed nature such as those of a curate, or one of a purely spiritual character; on this point Canon and Civil Law are in full agreement. This legal principle, which *excludes slaves from the political community, from the exercise of any political right, from all participation in national sovereignty or public authority*, has been followed invariably in every ancient and modern nation where slavery has been introduced. . . .

Our ancient and modern laws formally denied and still deny to masters the power of life and death over the slaves; they grant them the right only *to punish them moderately*, as fathers may punish their children and teachers their students. If the punishment is not moderate, there is an excess which the law castigates as if the offended person were not a slave, and with very good reason.

Also, according to our law, brutal treatment authorizes the slave to demand that his master sell him, and in this case, as when masters wish to sell them as an act of vengeance, the Brotherhood of Saint Benedict was permitted to buy them, if they were fraternal members, for the purpose of setting them free.

If there is a reasonable fear that a master may mistreat his slave, he may be forced to sign a *security bond*.

Concerning mistreatment, even the Municipal Chambers had the responsibility to inform the General Provincial Councils of abuses and acts of cruelty practiced against slaves, suggesting ways to prevent them (Law of October 1, 1828). . . .

Our ancient laws reveal extraordinary provisions concerning slaves, such as applying the lash or torture as a means of forcing them to confess, branding them with a hot iron, mutilating parts of the body, excessive use of the death penalty, and other cruel punishments.

Torture, branding with a hot iron, brutal punishments, and similar acts, suitable only to barbarians, were absolutely and directly prohibited by the Constitution of the Empire, which was promulgated in 1824, and punishment with the *whip* was also abolished in that document. Concerning the latter, however, this was always understood to mean *except in the case of the slave*. Thus we find such punishments called for in the Penal Code, to be applied only to slaves, as was previously the case and as it has continued to be in subsequent legislation. It was also declared that a Justice of the Peace could not order the lashing of a slave unless he was properly tried in his master's presence.

This punishment, however, is not applicable to the freedman, even when he is only conditionally free, or is designated a *statuliber* [a slave conditionally freed by a testament], in accordance with Roman usage. The same should be understood concerning persons condemned to wear an iron, which is dealt with in Article 60 of our Penal Code. This same article, which orders that the slave be *surrendered to his master*, presumes that the condemned person was, is, and remains a slave. The freedman evidently ceased, however, to be one; and the *statuliber* is not properly and strictly a slave.

When he pronounces sentence, the judge has the duty to decide the *number* of lashes to be administered, as well as the manner and length of time that he is to wear the iron piece, and it is not legal to apply more than fifty lashes to the slave per day. This expedient must be carried out with real wisdom and humanity, so that it will not exceed a reasonable punishment and degenerate into a punishment more severe than the law intends, as it would be, for example, if death were to result.

According to the general rule contained in Article 60 of the Penal Code, the slave who incurs a punishment other than the death penalty or galley service, must be condemned to receive lashes and to wear an iron piece as commutation of the normal punishment. However, according to Article 311 of that Code, the commutation of temporary galley service to that of imprisonment with hard labor does not apply to the slave, even if there is a House of Correction in the vicinity. He remains condemned to the galleys. . . .

When there are offenses against a master or members of his family (his wife, descendants, or elders) residing in his company, or against his administrator or overseer or the women who may live with them, the punishment is specially determined by Article 1 of the exceptional law of June 10, 1835 [see Document 6.4]. Extraordinary reasons of public order, of the security of the citizens and their families, especially in agricultural areas, caused this law, which is contrary to the Criminal Code in this part, to be decreed.

Will this punishment be justified if the slave kills or wounds the master, administrator, overseer, etc., in self-defense? According to the provision of the Criminal Code in the general section which is not altered by the cited law, the answer appears to be yes. This must also be understood concerning any other causes that tend to eliminate guilt, as well as those that aggravate or attenuate guilt. . . .

In regard to trials, we should observe that there do not exist among us authorities, judges, or special courts that are expressly concerned with offenses committed by slaves. They are tried, sentenced, and judged in accordance with the crime and its circumstances, like other delinquents either freeborn or liberated, except for the modifications which will be dealt with later. As a rule, however, the general principles of penal law and the criminal process are applicable to slaves.

Is the extraordinary remedy of *habeas corpus* applicable to slaves? I understand that it is, if it is requested by a Brazilian citizen.

We must give attention to the legal exceptions and modifications that apply to slaves. They are the following:

1. The slave is not allowed to file a complaint by himself, but only through his master or through a Public Prosecutor, or, as a *miserable* person, it may be done for him by any citizen, if his master does not do so.

2. The slave cannot file legal complaints against his master.

3. He cannot give *sworn testimony*, but only informative testimony.

4. When a slave is a criminal or when he is accused of a crime, the trial judge has the responsibility to appoint for him a defender or guardian, if his master, as his natural guardian, does not agree to perform this function.

5. In cases of crimes covered by the law of June 10, 1835, as well as cases of rebellion or other crimes punishable by death, no appeal whatever is permitted, not even a general review.

6. In such cases an extraordinary session of the jury may be called to reach a judgment.

7. However, if the criminal is condemned to death, the punishment must not be carried out until the Moderating Power [the special power represented in the Emperor] has reached a decision concerning his appeal for clemency.

This exceptional legislation against the slave, especially as it affects his master, requires reform, specifically the use of the whip, the abuse of the death penalty, and the prohibition of appeals. These laws are not in compliance with scientific principles, nor has this excessive severity produced the results which were expected from it. The history and criminal statistics of the Empire have continued to record the same crimes, and the situation will only improve to the extent that customs are changed to the advantage of the miserable slave, making his captivity more tolerable, or less intolerable, and at last putting an end to slavery itself. This dark blotch on our social system has invaded our legislation and blackened some of its pages, whereas our Penal Code is otherwise one of the most perfect of modern times. . . .

Under penal law the slave, as the *subject* or agent of a crime, is not a *thing*, but a *person*, in the broad meaning of the word. He is a human being, a man, equal by nature to other free men whose qualities he shares. He is therefore responsible personally and directly for the crimes he commits. About this question there was never any doubt. However, when he is the *object* of a crime, a difference is recognized. The crimes of which he is personally the victim do not constitute a *personal crime*, but rather a *physical offense*, to be punished as such and with the offender obliged to indemnify the master. What is involved here is a question of *property*, whereas in the former case it was one of *personality*.

This does not mean, however, that the slave, while he is *property*, does not provide an opportunity for the commission of a crime, such as theft. On the contrary, since he himself is not offended, but only his master in his property rights, the crime is committed only against the latter, and so only against property. Thus stealing slaves is not simply theft. By law it is characterized as robbery; to sell someone else's slave or to alienate him as one's own property is fraud; and so it is with similar cases.

It must also be observed that no one may *provide a refuge* to a runaway slave, under threat of punishment if there is fraud or premeditated intent on the part of the person who grants him sanctuary. In every epoch and among all peoples this has been the case. Roman Law contains clear provisions concerning runaway slaves, and our ancient legislation enumerates a large number. . . .

Slavery is the cause of an even greater danger to the State and to public order requiring exceptional measures. In every country where this cancer has been introduced, the slave is looked upon not only as a *domestic* enemy, but also as a *public* enemy, always ready to revolt, to rise up against society. . . . Among us, one might say, slave rebellions have occurred from the moment slavery was first introduced into our country, to its great misfortune. The Indians always caused a great deal of trouble to the inhabitants and governments in their endless struggle to free themselves from the oppression and captivity to which they were subjected; this continued, in fact, until the law decreed their victory, freeing them from the scourge of their persecutors and exploiters. [A Portuguese law of June 6, 1775, freed all Indians in Brazil, confirming earlier laws. With the establishment of the Portuguese Royal Family in Brazil in 1808, forms of Indian servitude were reinstituted, but in 1831 Indian slavery was again abolished.]

The slaves descended from the African race, whom we still have among us, have resorted to armed struggle in the past and continue to do so, at times through their own resolve and at other times instigated by foreigners, in crises caused both by international and internal conflicts; this is a volcano that constantly threatens society, a bomb ready to explode with the first spark. Article 113 of the Criminal Code, judging this crime as one of the greatest seriousness, punishes it with extraordinary penalties [see Document 6.4]. . . .

Roman Law recognized and established the principle that *the slave has not had and does not now have a family*. Among slaves *marriage* did not as a rule exist, only *cohabitation (contubernium)*, a natural or de facto union. There was neither *kinship*, nor *marital power*, nor *paternity*. . . . Among us, unfortunately, the slaves live as a rule in illicit unions, both those in urban service as well as rural slaves; they are thus reduced to licentiousness, to the law of nature. It must be truthfully confessed that in some places, especially among the small planters, it is not unusual to see slave families made up of a husband, wife, and children. The Church, before which all people are equal, sanctions and legitimizes these marriages, despite the fact that for centuries slavery was an absolute impediment to matrimony. However, as a general rule, Civil Law grants these unions little practical effect, though it implicitly recognizes and sanctions the fact through its reception of the laws of the Church. Nevertheless husband, wife, and children remain the property of the master. . . .

The slave did not in the past and does not now acquire anything for himself; everything goes to his master. This was the principle of Roman Law, whether direct rights, property settlements, credits, legacies, inheritances, or personal possessions were involved, and this was true even when the master was unaware of the property or lacked interest in it.

[In Brazil, however,] the slave may make acquisitions under various circumstances. He may retain an inheritance of food, for example, or his independent possessions, his *pecúlio* The word *pecúlio* is used to refer to everything which the slave, with the express or tacit consent of his master, was permitted to administer, use, and earn, even when it included part of the master's own property. . . .

Among us no law guarantees the *pecúlio* to the slave; and even less its free disposal by means of a will or through inheritance, even when the slave is the property of the State.

Nevertheless, it is not unusual in rural areas to see slaves among us who cultivate land for themselves on their masters' plantations with their consent. The entire crop produced in this way is theirs; it becomes their *pecúlio*. Even in cities and towns some people allow their slaves to work like free people, nevertheless collecting from them a certain daily amount, with the excess being regarded as their *pecúlio*. Some are even allowed to live in houses which do not belong to their masters, possessing a great deal of personal freedom. . . .

From the earliest times our laws have recommended that everything should be in favor of freedom. The law even authorized the expropriation of a Moorish slave who could be traded for a captive Christian held in the power of Infidels. And, generally speaking, it recognizes that *against the general rules of law many things are constituted in favor of freedom*. It also recognizes, in principle, that slavery is *contrary to natural law; that the reasons in favor of freedom are stronger and of greater significance than those that justify slavery; that freedom is inherent in natural law; that proof is incumbent upon those who make demands against freedom, because the fullest legal presumption favors it; that in questions of freedom there is no jurisdiction*, that is to say, no power, that disallows the employment of any resource tending to favor freedom.

Other examples may be found in various laws and decisions. . . .

Since the slave is looked upon as a *thing*, subject to the authority (*dominium*) of his master, through a legal fiction he is subordinated to the general laws of property. Although he is a *man* or a *person* (in the broad sense), he is subject to his master's power (*potestas*) with its several consequences. This has been the case in every country. The Romans supply us with an abundant source of decisions in this respect.

The master has the right to obtain from the slave every possible advantage; that is, he can demand his services gratuitously in any way that appears most convenient to him. In recompense, he has the obligation to feed, clothe, and cure the slave, and may never be allowed to forget that in him there exists a human being.

Nevertheless, the master may not require criminal, illicit, or immoral acts from the slave [for a test case of this principle, see Document 6.9]. . . .

Through the property right which he has in his slaves the master can rent them, lend them, sell them, give them away, transfer them, bequeath them, use them as collateral, dispose of their services, and remove the fruits of slave property in cases in which he is not the unrestricted possessor. In short, he can exercise all the legitimate rights of an owner or proprietor. . . .

As property the slave can be an object of insurance. . . .

Today only slaves belonging to agricultural establishments can be mortgaged, and only if this is specified in the contract, and this can be done only in conjunction with other real estate to which slaves are looked upon as accessories, in the same way that animals are. . . .

As property slaves can be passed on by testament like other possessions of the deceased master, and taxes on inheritances and legacies are applicable to them in the same way.

As property slaves can still be sequestered, seized, confiscated, put up for security, placed on deposit, awarded, or sold to the highest bidder, subject to no conditions other than those which apply to the property constituted in them. The bidding is carried on openly, and in commercial deals it can be done by public auction. . . .

Slave status may be ended in the following ways: 1) through the natural death of the slave; 2) by manumission or enfranchisement; 3) by provisions of the law. . . .

Through manumission the slave is restored to his natural condition and state of manhood, to that of a *person*. He enters the social community, the *city*, as the Romans said, without any indication of his former slave status. It is then that he appears in society and before the law as a person (*persona*), being able under the law, properly speaking, to freely exercise his rights and activities like other citizens. He may establish a family, acquire a full right to property for himself, pass on a *legacy* even when dying intestate, make contracts, dispose of property through sale or trade or through his last will and testament; in other words, like the minor child who upon reaching adulthood acquires his *full freedom*, he can practice every act of civil life. He may even become a guardian or protector.

However, the law, responding to prejudices of our society, deprives the freedman of some of his rights in regard to *political and public life*. Those prejudices had their origin not so much in the former vile and miserable condition of the slave or in his ignorance, bad habits, and degradation, or because that status generally corrupted his spirit and morality. Rather it is the result of the more general prejudice against the African race, from which the slaves in Brazil are descended. Thus the freed Brazilian citizen may vote only in primary elections, and this only if he fulfills the legal conditions which other Brazilian citizens must fulfill to exercise that function. Thus he cannot become an elector, and he cannot hold any other position for which only persons having an elector's qualifications can be chosen. These include the offices of general or provincial deputy, senator, juror, justice of the peace, subdelegate, police delegate, public prosecutor, Counselor of State, Minister of Government, Magistrate, member of the Diplomatic Corps, Bishop, and similar positions.

However, if he is a Brazilian citizen, he is not prevented from becoming an alderman, because for this position it is enough to be an ordinary voter; consequently he may fill other offices from which he is not expressly or tacitly excluded because he lacks an elector's qualifications. The freedman, if he is a Brazilian citizen, may serve in the army or navy, either voluntarily or as a conscript. If he is a Brazilian citizen, the freedman is eligible for membership in the National Guard. He cannot, however, become an officer.

It can be seen, then, that concerning the exercise of political rights, public power, and national sovereignty, the position and status of the freedmen in our society are greatly restricted. . . .

In the churches the slave or person of color, among us, is at the side of the free man without distinction, as well as at the *altar of communion*; verifying the words of St. Paul: *neque servus nequer liber, vos omnes unum estis in Christo Jesu.*

In public vehicles no distinction is made for the brandmarks of slavery, or for color; the reasons for separation are others (public accommodation resulting from prices), which equally affect the free man.

In the United States this generally did not occur. But there the reason was not just slavery, but also race; this being a question which in Brazil is not taken into consideration by laws or customs. To be a person of *color*, even a black African, is no reason for not being somebody in our country, to be admitted into society, into families, into public vehicles, into churches in some places, into employments, etc.; moreover, the man of color enjoys as much consideration in the Empire as any other person to whom he may be equal; some have even occupied and now occupy the highest offices of the State, in provincial government, in the Council of State, in the Senate, in the Chamber of Deputies, in the Diplomatic Corps, in a word, in every kind of position; others have been and are now distinguished doctors, lawyers, illustrious professors in the highest scientific fields; to sum up, every area of human activity is completely open and free to him. It may perhaps be said that there are indications that he has had an exceptional degree of influence.

In the North American union public customs and even the laws concurred toward exclusion. People of *color* were not admitted into the schools. It was necessary to institute and create public conveyances especially for people of *color*. In hotels and inns and similar places people of color were rejected with loathing and contempt. [See Document 5.9.] In the church there was a corner reserved for them; and they were only admitted last of all to the altar of communion itself. Marriages between whites and persons of color were condemned. At a banquet, dance or meeting, even when held by the master of a household, the person of color was not permitted to take part along with whites. There was a profound separation, arising from a profound contempt for the African race and all their descendants, however light they might have been.

6.2. Legal Restrictions on the Activities of Slaves and Free Non-Whites in Portugal (1521, 1545, 1559, and 1621)

In Brazil slaves were often legally denied the right to engage in many kinds of common activities which the free population naturally regarded as their unquestioned prerogatives. "Not even their rude and simple pastimes," wrote the historian of Maranhão, João Francisco Lisbôa, in the nineteenth century, "not even the ornaments of their women escaped the implacable regulation of the crown." As the following brief royal decrees prove, such restrictions had already been imposed in Portugal at least as early as 1521, at a time when black slavery was still a negligible factor in Brazil. Significantly, some of these restrictions also applied to free non-whites, proving that in this early period such persons were also the victims of racial discrimination.

Sources: *Leis extravagantes colligidas e relatadas pelo Licenciado Duarte Nunez do Leão, per mandado do Muito Alto e Muito Poderoso Rei Dom Sebastião Nosso Senhor* (Coimbra, 1796), pp. 418-423; *Collecção chronologica de leis extravagantes posteriores á nova compilação das ordenações do reino publicadas em 1603* (Coimbra, 1819), I, 319.

The Banning of Weapons, 1521

Concerning slaves who carry weapons and are not in the company of their masters.

The said Lord ordered that any Moor or captive black, upon whom might be found a sword, dagger, or lance, not accompanying his master, or not being a black or Moor who customarily might accompany his master, is to pay five hundred *reaes* to whoever might capture him; and if his master does not wish to pay, he is to be whipped. According to a decree of July 8, 1521.

A Ban on Gambling, 1521

The said Lord ordered that any slave who might be found gambling in the Court or city of Lisbon be arrested and whipped at the foot of the pillory, where he would be given twenty lashes, or his master might pay instead thirty *reaes* to the person who arrested him, when he does not want him to be whipped. Decree of July 8, 1521.

Restrictions on Lodging and the Receiving of Goods from Slaves, 1545

The same Lord ordered . . . that from that time forward no male or female slave, either white or black, was to live in a house by himself. And if his master consented to it, he [the master] was to pay on each occasion ten *cruzados* [4$000], half to go to whoever accused him, and the other half to the public works of the city, and the slave man or woman was to be arrested and given twenty lashes at the foot of the pillory. Nor was any Moor or black, who might be a slave, either male or female, to receive or lodge in the houses where he lived any captive slave man or woman, nor might he keep any money or household goods, or anything else that the said captives might give him or bring to his house, nor was he to buy from them anything whatever, or to receive from them anything for any reason, under penalty for each offense of a fine of ten *cruzados* . . ., aside from the other penalties which the law and ordinances impose in such cases. Decree of February 1, 1545.

A Ban on the Playing of Musical Instruments and of African Dances, 1559

The King, our Lord, orders that in the city of Lisbon, and one league around it, there might be no assembly of slaves or dances or playing of musical instruments performed in their [the African] manner, either at night or during the day, on feast days or during the week, under penalty of being arrested, and each one of those who play instruments or dance is to pay a thousand *reaes* to whoever captures him, and those who do not dance and are arrested for being present are to pay five hundred *reaes*. And that the same prohibition be understood for free blacks. Decree of August 28, 1559.

Non-Whites Prohibited to Engage in the Craft of Goldsmith, 1621

It is good and it pleases me that under penalty of fifty *cruzados* for captives, no black, mulatto, or Indian, even if he be free, nor others of the kind, whatever their status, may learn or engage in the craft of goldsmith, either in this city of Lisbon, or anywhere else in the Kingdom; and the same penalty will be imposed upon anyone who teaches him or has him in his house to engage in the said craft, as the petitioners request. Decree of October 20, 1621.

6.3. Restrictions on the Activities of Slaves in Eighteenth-Century Brazil

The following decrees typify the restrictive legislation of the colonial period. The first two, which banned certain kinds of clothing or ornaments, originated in Lisbon and applied to Brazil as a whole. The third decree, which also applied to the entire colony, banned the carrying of certain weapons by slaves and revised the punishment which was to be imposed in such cases. The last two documents applied to São Paulo and the newly established Minas de Ouro (Minas Gerais) and dealt respectively with the problems of slaves' gambling and their possession of weapons in newly established and lawless mining camps.

The Banning of Lascivious Dress, 1709

Luis Cesar de Menezes, Friend. I the King greet you cordially. Having seen the petition which the officials of the Chamber of that city sent me concerning the licentiousness with which the slave men and women are accustomed to live and dress in my Overseas Conquests, going about at night and inciting the men with their lascivious apparel, I have decided to order you to enforce the ordinance as it concerns those who go about at night. And since experience has shown that from the apparel which the slave women use many offenses against Our Lord result, I order that you not allow the slave women to make use in any way of silks or of woven cloth or of gold in order that they may thus have occasion to incite to sin with the expensive adornments that they dress themselves with; and you will enforce this, my law, in all the Captaincies under your jurisdiction, ordering for this purpose that it be published and registered in the books of the Court of that State. . . . Written in Lisbon on September 23, 1709. King. Miguel Carlos. For the Governor General of the State of Brazil.

Source: Cited in full in Carlos B. Ott, *Formação e evolução étnica da cidade do Salvador* (Bahia: Tipografia Manú, 1957), II, 97-98.

A Prohibition of Certain Types of Clothing and Ornaments for Slaves and Free Blacks and Mulattoes, 1749

Chapter 9 of the Royal Proclamation of the 24th of May, 1749.

Having been informed of the great inconveniences which result in my conquests from the freedom of the blacks and mulattoes, the children of blacks or mulattoes or of black mothers, to dress in the same way as white persons, I prohibit the above, regardless of sex, and even if they have been liberated, or were born free, the use not only of all kinds of silk, but also of cloth of fine wool, of fine Dutch linen, and such fine cloth either of linen or cotton; and much less will it be legal for them to wear on their persons ornaments of jewelry, gold or silver, however minimal.

If after a month from the publication of this law in the administrative center of the district where they reside they should again wear any of the above, it will be confiscated from them, and for the first offense they will also pay the value of the same forfeited item in cash, or not having the money to satisfy the fine, they will be whipped in the most public place in the town, in whose district they may reside; and for the second offense, aside from the aforementioned penalties, they will remain imprisoned in the public jail until they may be exiled to the island of São Thomé for the rest of their lives.

Source: Cited in *O Americano* (Rio de Janeiro), November 7, 1849.

A Ban on Knives and Other Weapons, 1756

Dom José, by the grace of God King of Portugal and the Algarves, etc. Be it known to those who receive this my law that, having been informed that in the State of Brazil the mulatto and black slaves continue to use knives and other prohibited weapons, since the punishments imposed by the laws of March 29, 1719, and July 25, 1749, are not sufficient to restrain them: I hold it as beneficial that instead of the punishment of ten years of galley service imposed in the above-mentioned laws, the said black and mulatto slaves of the aforementioned State who violate those laws should receive the punishment of one hundred lashes, administered on the pillory, and repeated for ten alternating days, which will not be understood in regard to the blacks and mulattoes who may be free; because with these the established laws should be observed. Thus I order the President and Members of my Overseas Council and the Viceroy and Captain General of sea and land of the same State of Brazil, and all the Governors and Captains Major, as well as the Governors of the High Courts of Bahia and Rio de Janeiro, their judges and all the auditors, judges, justices, officials, and other persons of the said State that they comply with and keep this law, and have it complied with and executed in its entirety, exactly as it is written, and that it be published and registered in my High Royal Chancellery, and that in the same manner it be made public in the Captaincies of the said State of Brazil, and in each one of its districts, so that it may come to the notice of everyone, and nobody may allege ignorance, and that it also be registered in the said High Courts, and in the other places where such laws are customarily registered, this copy to be deposited in the Torre do Tombo. Lisbon, January 24, 1756. The KING.

Source: *Collecção chronologica de leis extravagantes posteriores á nova compilação das ordenações do reino publicadas em 1603* (Coimbra, 1819), IV, 476-477.

A Ban on Gambling in São Paulo, 1722

It having been reported to me that the slaves of the residents of this captaincy are in the habit of gambling, and that they gamble not only for money, but also for some pieces of gold and silver, which clearly is gathered by them, which not only is of great harm to their masters, but that they will steal what they can in order to gamble, and that it would be very convenient to put a stop to the damage which results: I order that from this time on all those who are found gambling in any place whatsoever should be immediately arrested, which will be done not only by the justice officers, but by any sergeant or soldier who may encounter them, taking them to the jail of this city or to the Corps of Guards, and those who are so arrested will receive on the first occasion a punishment of two hundred lashes on the pillory of this city; and on the second occasion they will be punished with the greatest demonstration available to my service, and this penalty will be incurred not only by the black men, but by any other type of slave who is found gambling; and so that this may be notorious to all and so that they cannot allege ignorance, I have ordered that this proclamation be hung out in the plaza of this city, and in the customary streets, and that it be made known to the regiment. São Paulo, February 5, 1722.

Source: Cited in Sebastião Ferrarini, *A escravidão negra na provincia do Paraná* (Curitiba, 1971), pp. 50-51.

A Ban on Weapons in Minas Gerais, 1732

Dom Lourenço de Almeyda of the Council of His Majesty, whom God protect, Governor and Captain General of the Captaincy of Minas de Ouro, etc.

Be it known to all those who receive this proclamation that, because I have been informed and received repeated complaints that the blacks of the district of Serro do Frio are going about fully armed committing murder and many other offenses, which must be stopped with the greatest care and diligence: I order by this my proclamation that no black or mulatto, either free or captive, may carry a defensive weapon of any sort whatever, not even the staffs which the blacks customarily carry, under penalty of two hundred lashes which will be given to them in the most public place in the [mining] Camp or Town, and two months in jail which will not be pardoned, so that their masters will also be encouraged not to permit them to carry weapons; and the weapons that are found on them will become the property of those who capture them. And only the black who is accompanied by his master or traveling with his written permission may carry a sword or musket, but even these blacks will be subject to the punishment referred to in this proclamation if they are found in possession of any other offensive weapon, aside from the sword and musket. And the General Auditor of the District and Captain Joseph de Moraes Cabral, and the common judges will carry out this proclamation without fail and with complete diligence, ordering that the justice officers, the soldiers, militia officers, and bush captains capture without fail every black found in possession of any kind of offensive weapon, who will be whipped immediately and forthwith. And so that it may come to the attention of everyone, I order that this decree be proclaimed to the sound of drums, and that it be posted in the most public places, and in the mining camps of the District of Serro do Frio, and that it be registered in the Offices of this Government and in the books of the Chamber of the District of Serro do Frio. Given in Villa Rica, the ninth of January, seventeen hundred and thirty-two. The Government Secretary, João da Costa Carneiro, set it down.

Source: *Revista do Archivo Público Mineiro* 7 (1902), 276-277.

6.4. Special Legal Provisions Concerning Slaves Promulgated in the First Years of the Empire

As Perdigão Malheiro pointed out in this part's first selection, many special laws dealing with slaves "blackened" Brazil's legal system. The following are examples of such laws promulgated during the first hectic decades following the establishment of Brazilian independence. As Perdigão Malheiro also noted, brutal physical punishments, including whipping, were banned by the Imperial Constitution of 1824, but this did not deter the authors of the new Criminal Code and other laws from specifically ordering lashing and other cruel punishments for slaves who committed crimes.

❧ *Decree of April 11, 1829, on the punishment of slaves who murder their masters*

Since the murders perpetrated by slaves against their own masters have occurred with great frequency, perhaps because of a lack of the prompt punishment which crimes of such a serious nature require, threatening public security as they do, and since the criminals involved in such crimes can never make themselves worthy of My Imperial Clemency, having now heard the opinions of My Council of State, I have decided to order, in conformity with Article 2 of the Law of September 11, 1826, that all sentences pronounced against slaves for killing their masters should be carried out without ascending to My Imperial Presence.

The authorities to whom knowledge of this law appertains should thus understand it and carry it out.

The Palace of Rio de Janeiro, April 11, 1829. With the seal of His Majesty.

Source: *Collecção das leis do Imperio do Brasil de 1829*, Part II, pp. 263-264.

21. Slaves Condemned to Galley Service

Provisions of the Criminal Code of 1830 concerning slaves

Art. 44. Criminals punished by galley service will be made to wear a shackle on one foot, with an iron chain attached, either when bound together or separate, and they will be employed in the public works of the province where the crime was committed, at the disposal of the Government.

Art. 60. If the criminal is a slave and incurs a punishment which is neither capital nor galley service, he will be condemned to punishment with a whip, and, after suffering this penalty, he will be surrendered to his master, who will force him to wear an iron piece for the period of time and in the manner decided upon by the judge.

The number of lashes will be fixed by the sentence; and the slave cannot be made to endure more than fifty lashes per day.

Art. 113. This crime (insurrection) will be regarded as having been committed when twenty or more slaves have combined to take their freedom by means of force.

Penalties. The leaders—death for the worst offenders; lifelong galley service for moderate offenders; fifteen years for minor offenders. For all others—lashes.

Art. 114. If the leaders of the insurrection are free persons, they will incur the same penalties imposed in the previous article on the leaders, when they are slaves.

Art. 115. Aiding, inciting, or counseling slaves to revolt, supplying them with weapons, munitions, and other means for the same person.

Penalties—imprisonment with hard labor for twenty years for the worst offenders; twelve years for moderate offenders; and eight years for minor offenders.

Art. 179. Reducing to slavery a free person who is in possession of his freedom.

Penalties—imprisonment for from three to nine years, and a fine corresponding to a third part of the time; however, the term of imprisonment will never be less than the period of unjust enslavement, plus one third.

Source: *Collecção das leis do Imperio do Brasil de 1830*, pp. 150-153, 163, 177.

The exceptional law of June 10, 1835

The Permanent Regency, in the name of the Emperor Dom Pedro Segundo, makes known to all the subjects of the Empire that the General Legislative Assembly has decreed, and it has sanctioned the following law:

Art. 1. The punishment of death will be suffered by all slaves, male or female, who kill by any means whatsoever, give poison, gravely wound, or commit any serious physical offense against their master, his wife, his descendants or forebears who may be living in his company, or against his administrator, or overseer or the women living with them.

If the wound or physical offense is light, the punishment will be lashes, in proportion to the circumstances, more or less aggravating.

Art. 2. When one of the crimes mentioned in Art. 1 occurs, or that of insurrection, or any other committed by slaves, for which the death penalty is applicable, there will be an extraordinary meeting of the district jury (if it is not in session) called by the Judicial Magistrate, to whom such instances will be immediately reported.

Art. 3. The Justices of the Peace will have cumulative jurisdiction in the entire municipality to judge such crimes, including the power to pass sentences and imprison offenders, and when they have reached their decision, they will send the case on to the Magistrate who will present it to the Jury as soon as it assembles.

Art. 4. In such crimes the imposition of the death penalty will be decided by two-thirds of the jury members; and for the others by a majority; and, if it is condemnatory, the sentence will be carried out without appeal.

Art. 5. All laws, decrees, and other provisions to the contrary are revoked.

Given in the Palace of Rio de Janeiro, the 10th day of the month of June, 1835.

Source: *Collecção das leis do Imperio do Brasil de 1835*, p. 5.

6.5. The Government of Bahia Orders Special Measures to Restrict and Control the Province's Slave Population (1822)

Restrictions on the activities of slaves were especially rigid during periods of turmoil and revolution, particularly when there was unusual fear of slave revolts. This was the case in 1822, at the height of Brazil's revolutionary struggle for independence from Portugal, when the Provisional Governing Council of the Province of Bahia, meeting in emergency session in the inland city of Cachoeira, passed the following emergency legislation. This law put local forces on special alert, prohibited slave assemblies and their possession of weapons, provided for the seizure and punishment of slaves found away from their places of work without their masters' permission, and ordered a special search for runaway-slave settlements and the arrest of any slaves who might be found in them.

Source: Doc. No. II-34, 10, 23, Seção de Manuscritos, Biblioteca Nacional, Rio de Janeiro.

❧ The Provincial Council of Government of this Province having learned through quite terrible indications and from the statements of certain authorities, that a slave uprising is being plotted, much desired and encouraged in the interior of the Recôncavo by the wicked Portuguese-European party, and the same Council being under obligation energetically to prevent any partisan outbreak, the only kind which might possibly occur during the present crisis, to the detriment of individual security: Orders in the Name of His Imperial and Constitutional Majesty, Dom Pedro I, Emperor and Perpetual Defender of Brazil, the following:

1st. That the Captains Major of the various Towns issue the most positive orders to the Captains and Officers of the regiments which they command to reconnoiter with escorts of armed militiamen all the districts where many slaves exist, severely prohibiting their meetings under the pretext of performing *autabaquis*, [a kind of African drum, or a dance accompanied by such a drum] and very scrupulously observing their conduct.

2nd. That the Captains Major by means of the Militia Officers, and the Judges by means of the Chiefs of Police make it known to all the Proprietors and planters under the responsibility of the Provisional Council that they not allow their slaves to have in the huts where they live muskets, lances, iron spears, scythes, cutlasses, swords, and knives, and furthermore that they not send their slaves anywhere without a written note, ordering at the same time that they not take with them any of the above-mentioned weapons.

3rd. That the militia escorts, and police on their rounds arrest any slave wandering along the roads, on the plantations, and in the forests, or without a note from his respective master, or, having a note, if he should be found with any of the weapons mentioned in the previous article; in the first case they should send the slave bound to his master for punishment, and in the second to the town judge, so that he may receive the punishment of a hundred lashes at the pillory, and later be turned over to his master independent of judicial justifications and other expenses and charges; however, the slaves who conduct wagons, beasts of burden, or who are carriers of provisions to the fairs and the town markets are excepted.

4th. That the Captains Major see to it that the forests, where it is believed that there may be shelters or quilombos [runaway-slave settlements], be searched, requesting the help of the militia units for this, if this becomes necessary, and seizing the fugitives found in them, who will be sent to the judge to receive punishment, as stated in Article 3.

5th. That the police patrols on their rounds in the towns and settlements seize all the black slaves who are wandering about without a note from their masters, or on the roads after nine o'clock at night, and send them bound to the judge to be punished with fifty lashes when they are not found with any of the weapons referred to in Article 2, and with two hundred if they are found with them; after which they will be returned to their masters in the same form determined in Article 3. The civil and military authorities to whom knowledge of this pertains will thus understand and enforce it, remaining responsible to His Imperial Constitutional Majesty for any lapses in the exact fulfillment of this salutary precautionary measure.

Meeting Hall of the Town of Cachoeira on November 28, 1822, with the signatures of the Ministers of the Provisional Council of Government.

Confirmed by the Official Jozé Albino Pereira.

6.6. The Province of Rio de Janeiro Restricts the Activities of Slaves, Free Africans, and Other Foreigners to Reduce the Threat of Slave Rebellion (1836)

The following law of the province of Rio de Janeiro restricting the rights and activities of slaves and free persons was promulgated in 1836 following a major slave revolt in Bahia (see Document 9.14) and at a time of general political unrest in the Empire. The municipalities of Niterói and Cabo Frio and the towns of Maricá and Magé are specifically mentioned, but it was also made clear in Article 3 that the provisions of these special ordinances were to apply to the entire province.

Source: *Legislação provincial do Rio de Janeiro de 1835 a 1850 organisado por Luiz Honorio Vieira Souto. Part I. Leis e decretos* (Niterói, 1850), pp. 93-96.

Decree No. 46 1836—No. 18—13th of May

Article 1. The ordinances of the municipal chambers of the cities of Nictheroy and Cabo Frio, and the towns of Maricá and Magé, concerning tranquility and public security, are confirmed and revised as follows:

ORDINANCE 1

Nobody may sell gunpowder or weapons of any kind without a license from the municipal chamber, and the latter will not be granted except to persons of the highest reputation, and even to these only after they have signed before the justice of the peace of the district where they reside a commitment not to sell the above-mentioned items to slaves, or even to suspect persons, with two credible witnesses who will guarantee their capacity and their compliance with the expressed commitment.

Violators will be punished with eight days in prison and a fine of thirty *milréis*. For every additional violation the jail term will be for thirty days and the fine will be sixty *milréis*. A slave violator will be punished with from one hundred to two hundred lashes.

If the person who has obtained the license is convicted of having sold gunpowder or arms to a slave or suspect person, he will be punished with eight days in jail and a fine of thirty *milréis*, and his license will be revoked and will never be granted to him again. The security witnesses will also be punished by fines of thirty *milréis* each.

ORDINANCE 2

It is absolutely forbidden to sell, give or lend, manufacture, repair, or arrange weapons of any sort whatever for slaves or suspect persons. Violators will incur the penalties declared in the first ordinance.

ORDINANCE 3

The owners, administrators, or cashiers of stores, coffee houses, taverns, or other public houses, whatever their nature, wherein are encountered gatherings of more than three slaves, not being able to prove that they are there with the purpose of making purchases ordered by their masters, will be punished with four days in jail and a fine of ten *milréis*, and with twice the amount upon the first recurrence; in the case of a second recurrence, they will be punished with thirty days in jail and a fine of sixty *milréis*, and their license to run an open public house will be revoked, and will not be renewed before the passage of two years.

ORDINANCE 4

Every slave who is encountered at night or on Sundays and holy days at any hour away from the plantation of his master, and if the latter lives in a town, away from the immediate vicinity of that town, without a written note from the said master, or members of their families, their administrators, cashiers, or overseers, or even from a neighbor when the master does not know how to read, the note stating that they have been sent out on some service, will be punished with from twenty-five to fifty lashes.

This provision will in practice be subject to necessary exceptions, whenever the circumstances and qualities of the slaves convince those charged with carrying it out that, despite their being found out without written notes, they are out in the service of their masters. The latter, because of some handicap or even through forgetfulness can often send them out without such a note: and especially if they are captives of persons who do not know how to write.

The slave found with weapons of any kind, even when out in the service of his master, will be punished with from fifty to a hundred lashes; and if he is found in the company of other slaves, all or most of them with weapons, he will be punished with two hundred lashes.

Exception is made for slaves who carry weapons, by order of their masters, which are not prohibited by law or by the ordinances of the municipal chambers, provided that in the written notes the type of arms they are carrying is indicated. The provision of the present ordinance does not include slaves who are mule or cart drivers, when they are carrying out the duties of their occupation.

Ordinance 5

No slave or freedman, foreign or national, may be employed in the profession of peddler or *pombeiro* [a slave who traveled for his master's profit], without a license from the municipal chamber, which he cannot receive unless he has presented an apt guarantee of his conduct, in the manner determined in the first ordinance; and even when having a license from the municipal chamber he may not remain on the plantations or farms without permission from the owners, administrators, or overseers. Violators who are freedmen, either nationals or foreign, will be punished with eight days in jail and a fine of thirty *milréis*, and with thirty days in jail and a fine of sixty *milréis* in case of recurrence. Foreign freedmen [so-called *emancipados* or free Africans], after being punished, will be obliged to sign a guarantee that they will immediately leave the municipality, under a penalty of thirty days in jail and a fine of sixty *milréis*, for each time they are found inside its territory.

Ordinance 6

Every person who in his house or residence, or in some other adjacent house, allows gatherings for dances or *candomby* [*candomblé*: religion of the Yorubas or their religious festival], in which outside slaves take part, will be punished with the penalties imposed in the fifth ordinance. The slaves who are arrested at such gatherings will be punished with from fifty to a hundred lashes.

Article 2. In every case dealt with in the above ordinances, the slaves, as soon as they have been punished, will be released at once and returned to their masters.

Article 3. The provisions of the preceding ordinances will be extended to all the municipalities of the province.

Article 4. All laws are revoked, etc.

6.7. Local Ordinances Bearing on Slavery from Six Provincial Law Collections (1833-1866)

During the nineteenth century Brazil's provincial legislatures promulgated municipal ordinances to regulate a host of local activities. Rooted in local concerns, these laws are an outstanding source of information on the Empire's social life. Among these restrictive or regulatory provisions were many intended for slaves alone. For example, many communities banned cultural activities associated with blacks such as drumbeating, African dances, and religious ceremonies; and slaves were forbidden to gamble, play certain games, beg, meet in public places, rent houses, engage in remunerative enterprises, or to carry on other activities which other people could freely engage in. On the other hand, some local laws were intended to protect slaves from brutal masters. The latter were sometimes compelled, for example, to provide their slaves with "decent" burial, to clothe them enough to avoid nakedness, or to stop loading them down in public with irons and chains.

Municipal laws, like those of the nation, naturally prescribed unequal punishment for the two legally differentiated elements of the population. Free violators paid fines or served brief jail sentences, but slaves, who normally lacked money and might even have welcomed a stay in jail, were usually condemned to lashes or *palmatoadas* (raps on the hands with an instrument called a *palmatória*). As will be seen here, these punishments were sometimes extraordinarily severe, amounting to as many as four hundred individual lashes.

The following examples of such legislation were selected from the provincial law collections of Espírito Santo, Santa Catarina, Minas Gerais, Pernambuco, Pará, and Maranhão.}

Town of Itapemirim, Espírito Santo, Law of June 7, 1841

Art. 13. Giving or selling poisonous substances, either natural or artificial, to anyone, the seller not being a druggist, and if the latter sells such a substance without a prescription from an approved and accredited professional, a fine of from ten to thirty *milréis*, and from two to ten days in jail; if a slave, the offender will suffer one hundred lashes.

Art. 59. To drive or to order driven through the town street carts or wagons without a guide, in addition to the wagon driver; to drive a cart or wagon, or to ride a horse inside the town at an abnormal speed, a fine of from four to eight *milréis*; if the rider is a slave and if his respective master is not liable for the fine, the former will suffer one hundred lashes.

Art. 61. Uttering indecent or obscene words in a public place, making gestures or assuming attitudes of the same nature, or drawing pictures or figures offensive to public morality, a fine of ten *milréis* paid at the jail; if a slave, the offender will be punished with fifty lashes.

Art. 62. The individual who publicly washes himself at any place in the river in front of the town or in its vicinity, in such a manner that he offends public morality, because he is seen by those passing by, a fine of ten *milréis*, and if a slave he will suffer fifty lashes.

Source: *Livro das leis da provincia do Espirito Santo*, Vol. 3 (Rio de Janeiro, 1841), pp. 30, 39-40.

City of Desterro, Santa Catarina, Law of May 10, 1845

Art. 38. From this time on assemblies of slaves or freed persons intended to form *batuques* are forbidden, as well as those which have as their purpose the supposed African royal ceremonies [*reinados africanos*], which they are accustomed to performing during their celebrations. All those in violation will be fined 4$000 *réis*, if free, and, not possessing the means to pay, 4 to 8 days in jail; and if slaves, and without their master's license, they will be punished in conformity with the law. The master who grants such licenses will be fined 4$000 *réis*.

Art. 39. Nobody may rent houses for slaves to live in independent of their masters; under penalty of paying a fine of 10$000 *réis*.

Art. 40. Slaves found gambling in the streets and plazas will be arrested and turned over to the police for punishment.

Art. 64. Anyone who shelters runaway slaves will be fined 20$000 *réis*, in addition to his responsibility to their masters.

Art. 83. The inhuman custom of having slaves buried wrapped in mats, and without a shroud, is forbidden under penalty of 4$000 *réis* fine. No person, however miserable he may be, will be carried to his grave without being wrapped in a shroud made of some kind of cloth.

Art. 86. The scandalous custom of nude persons exposing themselves on the beaches, in the rivers, or in fountains is forbidden. Anyone found in this condition, being free, will pay a fine of 4$000 *réis*; and if a slave he will be punished in the fashion of the police by the competent authority.

Art. 128. It is forbidden in any house of business to employ slave cashiers.

Art. 131. It will be permitted to slaveowners to commute the penalty of imprisonment of their slaves, at the rate of 500 *réis* per day, and in the same manner the pecuniary penalty will be commuted to that of imprisonment when the convicted persons are without the means to satisfy the former.

Source: *Leis da provincia de Santa Catarina de 1841 a 1847*, pp. 217-218, 224, 230, 241.

City of Diamantina, Minas Gerais, Law of March 26, 1846

Art. 41. Negro dances with hubbub and shouting [*batuques com algasarra*] which disturb the neighborhood are forbidden; penalty of one day in jail. . . .

Art. 45. All forms of gambling are forbidden to slaves and beardless youths; penalty of two days in jail.

Art. 46. Begging is forbidden for any purpose, penalty of thirty *milréis* fine; excepted are the Charity House [Misericórdia], the Brotherhoods of the Most Holy, and of Souls, and those which in their bylaws have a license to beg.

Art. 47. The merchant who buys from slaves, or suspect persons, anything of value, without being authorized by a note from a known person, will pay a fine equal to the value of the thing purchased, not exceeding thirty *milréis*, and imprisonment for four days; those who have in their possession goods stolen by slaves will suffer a fine of four *milréis*, and four days in prison.

Art. 48. Entering plantations without the owner's permission is forbidden; fine of four *milréis* . . . ; being a slave, the violator will be punished with fifty lashes in case his master does not pay the fine.

Art. 50. . . . If a slave is encountered inside plantations or in the houses of other persons, and he is suspect, he will be punished with fifty lashes, except as in Article 48.

Art. 78. It is forbidden to permit gatherings of slaves who are not making purchases in taverns or drinking houses. . . .

Art. 90. No license for a house of business will be granted to a slave, and if one is granted, his status having been maliciously concealed, the slave will be fined eight *milréis*, and the house of business will be immediately closed.

Art. 96. [*This article refers to penalties for violations mentioned in previous articles.*] If the person to be fined is a slave, and he does not possess the means to pay his fine, and his master will not pay it, his penalty will be commuted to lashes as follows: A fine of up to one *milréis*, to be commuted to twenty-five lashes; from more than one *milréis* up to four *milréis*, to fifty; more than four *milréis* up to ten *milréis*, to one hundred; more than ten *milréis* up to twenty *milréis*, to one hundred and fifty; more than twenty *milréis* up to thirty *milréis*, to two hundred; however, more than fifty lashes will never be given on a single day, and the guilty person will remain imprisoned until his punishment is completed.

Art. 97. The lashes will be administered in this city on the pillory, and outside it in the places which have been designated by the competent authority.

Source: *Livro da lei mineira. 1846. Parte 1ª, Folha No. 5*, pp. 41-43, 48-52.

Town of Itajubá, Minas Gerais, Law of 1853

Art. 99. Every form of gambling is prohibited to slaves in a public establishment licensed or unlicensed for this purpose, or in a business house or any public place; penalty of three dozen *palmatoadas*, and one day in jail. . . .

Art. 129. It is forbidden to dance *batuque* in the houses of the villages accompanied by loud noise either during the daytime or at night, in such a way that it disturbs the neighborhood: penalty of imprisonment for a day and the closing down of the meeting.

Art. 130. Negro dances [*quimbetes*] or royal ceremonies [*reinados*] which the slaves are accustomed to celebrate on certain days of the year are permitted, with the condition that they not be held at night, and with the payment of two *milréis* on each occasion: fine of eight *milréis*.

Art. 135. Anyone who purchases from slaves, or from persons who are not responsible for the administration of their own property, anything which they do not normally possess, unless it be authorized by an accredited person, will pay a fine equal to the value of the item purchased, with the provision that it not exceed the amount of thirty *milréis*, and one day in jail.

Art. 136. It is forbidden: Paragraph 1. To shelter runaway slaves without informing their masters within twenty-four hours, they being residents in the same place or within a distance of two leagues; within 48 hours if the distance is not more than four leagues; and so on progressively, counting two leagues per day.

Paragraph 2. To possess things stolen by slaves: a fine of four *milréis* and four days in jail.

Art. 138. It is forbidden to deal with gypsies in slaves and animals, unless they deposit a security pledge before the subdelegate. Gypsies are defined in this article as those persons who are considered as such and are in the habit of engaging in frequent trading and buying of animals and selling of slaves, and are not established residents of the district.

Art. 147. The slave found on a plantation or in a house belonging to others, who is suspect because he totally lacks a reason for being there, will be punished with two dozen *palmatoadas*.

Art. 174. It is forbidden to usurp, to fence in, to narrow, to encumber, or in any other way to destroy the highways, roads, bridges, or any public works: a fine of two dozen *bolos* [*palmatoadas*] for slaves, who will only suffer this penalty if they were not ordered to do so by their masters.

Art. 183. It is forbidden: Paragraph 1. To allow in drinking houses assemblies of slaves who are not making purchases.

Art. 198. To no slave will a license be granted for opening a business house, and when such a license is granted because the status of the slave was maliciously concealed, he will be fined four *milréis*, and in both cases the business house will be immediately closed. The license may be granted, however, if it is authorized by his master, who will take full responsibility.

Source: *Collecção das leis da Assemblea Legislativa da Provincia de Minas Geraes de 1853*, pp. 33, 38-39, 41, 46, ,50.

Ordinances applying to several towns and cities of Pernambuco promulgated from 1833 to 1843:

City of Recife, 1833

Title 10. Paragraph 2. Nobody may send slave men or women into the streets unless they are dressed with clothing which covers their bodies; these clothes must not be rags, under penalty of a fine of 640 *réis* paid by the master.

Paragraph 3. From this time on the games which the blacks and vagrants are accustomed to play on the streets, plazas, beaches, and stairways are forbidden; under penalty of suffering, those who are free, from two to six days in jail, and slaves from 12 to 36 *bolos*, administered in the same jail, later being turned over to their masters. This gradation in the level of punishment will be in proportion to the offenders' ages.

Paragraph 4. Every person who is encountered naked on the beach during the day or who is found taking a bath with his body uncovered without the required decency will suffer the same penalty stated in the previous paragraph, and in the same proportions.

Town of Nazareth, 1836

Art. 11. Every person who dirties the fountains, tanks, and lakes by washing clothes, horses, fish, or any other thing which might contaminate them, in the places where people go to get drinking water, will suffer a fine of 2$000 *réis*, or when he cannot pay the fine two days in prison, and being a slave 48 *palmatoadas*.

Art. 16. No person of this town or populated places in its district will leave garbage or filth which might contaminate the atmosphere, except in the places which have been designated for this purpose by the fiscal agents; violators will suffer a fine of 1$000 *réis*, or one day in jail, and, if a slave, 12 *palmatoadas*, aside from being made to remove the garbage to the designated place.

Town of Itamaracá, 1836

Art. 6. Screaming in the streets and in the churches, as well as public injuries, obscenities which offend public morality, *batuques* of the blacks at any hour, and boisterous diversions are forbidden: violators will pay a fine of 4$000 *réis* or will suffer 8 days in jail, and being a slave will receive 36 *palmatoadas*, and twice the number in case of recurrence.

Town of Cabo, 1836

Public Health. Art. 13. The inhuman custom of burying slaves wrapped in mats without a shroud is forbidden, under penalty of a fine of 4$000 *réis*.

Tranquility and Public Morality. Art. 1. Every shopowner who allows slaves to remain in his shop longer than the time needed to do their buying or selling, or who there allows meetings, dances, and drumbeating will be fined 4$000 *réis*.

Town of Serinhaem, 1836

Art. 3. Nobody may throw filth or garbage from the houses into the streets of this town or into those of the villages in its district; under penalty of a fine of 500 *réis* or one day in prison. If the violator is a slave, he will suffer a dozen *palmatoadas*.

Art. 11. Nobody may race on horseback inside the town or in the villages of its district; under penalty of paying, if free, a fine of 1$000 *réis* to the Council coffers, or 24 hours in jail, and captives will suffer three dozen *palmatoadas*.

Art. 17. Nobody may bathe himself or wash clothes, or anything else, in the public fountains; penalty of paying a fine of 500 *réis*. If the violator is a slave he will suffer two dozen *palmatoadas*.

Art. 23. Every person who apprehends runaway slaves, or in whose house or plantation they are receiving shelter, will deliver them at once to their masters, or to the competent district authority, under penalty of a fine of 20$000 *réis*, or eight days in jail; and in cases of recurrence 30 to 60$000 *réis*, or 15 to 30 days in jail.

Art. 39. Every tavernkeeper or any other person who allows meetings of blacks in his house at night, or any other individuals taking part in debauchery or drinking, with screaming and shouting which disturbs the neighborhood, will be fined the amount of 2$000 réis.

Town of Brejo, 1836

Art. 20. Shouting after hours is forbidden in the streets of this town, as well as *batuques* of any kind; violators will suffer a fine of 1$ reis, and 2 days in jail; and being a slave he will suffer 25 lashes, his master having the option of a fine.

Town of Olinda, 1840

Art. 28. Every butcher or seller of meat who when selling it falsifies the weight will be fined from 5$ to 20$000 *réis*, and will suffer from 2 to 8 days in jail; and if the violator is a slave, he will suffer aside from the jail sentence one hundred lashes.

Art. 49. Forbidden is every sort of public farce in which one or more individuals appear playing the roles of a priest or friar, dressed with church insignia, making a mockery of the functions of the sacred ministry; violators will suffer a fine of 10$000 *réis*, and if the violator is a slave he will suffer four dozen *palmatoadas*.

City of Victoria, 1840

Art. 13. No owner of slaves will permit the same to go about the streets of this city, or any other place where they may be seen, dressed in rags, and in such a way that they appear naked; under penalty of 1$000 *réis* fine paid by the owner of the slave who is thus encountered.

City of Goianna, 1843

Art. 12. Nobody may wash clothes and animals in the fountains which are used to supply drinking water for this city; free persons will pay 500 *réis* fine, and slaves will be arrested and taken at once to their masters to be punished; in case of recurrence the penalty will be doubled for free persons, and slaves will receive a dozen and a half *palmatoadas* in front of the jail.

Source: *Collecção de Posturas das Camaras Municipaes da Provincia de Pernambuco, decretadas pela Assembléa Legislativa Provincial de Pernambuco dos annos de 1836 a 1845* (Recife, 1845), pp. 5-7, 17-28, 32, 38, 41, 45, 54, 89-91.

Law of the province of Pará of December 16, 1852, regulating plantations and cattle ranches

Art. 33. It is against the law to purchase from slaves, or from free herdsmen, cattle, horses, meat, or hides, unless the seller presents a written order from his master, or landlord, in which are stated the name of the seller, the type, nature, marks, brand, and color of the animal which he is granted permission to sell, or the amount of meat, number of hides, their marks and brands.

Art. 63. He who violates the instructions in Art. 33, if he is apprehended, in addition to the penalties which would be incurred according to the general laws, and the loss of the object, . . . will suffer a fine of sixty *milréis* for each animal and ten *milréis* for each *arroba*, or for each hide which he buys outside the conditions there prescribed. In regard, however, to the seller, if he should be a slave, he will be punished with four hundred lashes, in the manner determined in the Criminal Code, and if he is free he will be arrested and taken to the respective police authority to be tried according to the law.

Art. 34. It is absolutely prohibited to set fire to fields belonging to others. . . .

Art. 64. Anyone who does not observe the provision in Art. 34 will be fined twenty *milréis*, and if he is a slave, will be punished with two hundred lashes in a public place.

Art. 66. Anyone who alters, marks, or mutilates another person's brand marks, in addition to the penalties which would be incurred by the general laws, will be fined thirty *milréis* for each mark or brand altered or mutilated, and if he is a slave he will receive three hundred lashes in a public place.

Art. 67. Every individual who catches horses or oxen used for riding or pulling wagons, intending to make use of them without the permission of their owners, may be arrested by any person who encounters him, and, being brought at once to the district police authority, will suffer, in addition to the penalties which would be incurred by the general laws, a fine of forty *milréis*. . . . If the delinquent is a slave, he will be punished with four hundred lashes in a public place.

Source: "Regulamento de 16 de Dezembro de 1852 para as fazendas e estabelecimentos de creação de gado da Provincia," *Collecção das leis da Provincia do Gram Pará*, Vol. 14, 1852, Part 2 (Pará, 1852), pp. 82, 89-90.

City of São Luís do Maranhão, Law of July 4, 1866

Art. 99. It is expressly forbidden for slaves to go about the streets of the city with neck-chains [*gargalheiras*], leg shackles [*grilhetas*], and other instruments of punishment. Those who are so encountered will be held by any of the fiscal employees who, after removing the said instruments from them, will deliver them to their masters, who will pay a fine of ten *milréis*, and double the amount in case of recurrence.

Art. 100. Slaves who, because they are old or for any other reason are not being made use of for their services, have been abandoned by their masters, or go about begging for public charity, will be taken by any of the fiscal employees who encounter them to their masters, who will pay a fine of ten *milréis*, and double the amount in case of recurrence.

Source: *Collecção das leis provinciaes do Maranhão* (Maranhão, 1866), pp. 84-85.

6.8. Could a Slave Acquire His Freedom against His Master's Will by Offering Him His Value? Two Legal Opinions and the Negative Decision of the Council of State (1853-1854)

Writers who have upheld the theory that Brazilian slavery was unusually mild and humane have pointed to the alleged ease with which slaves could achieve their freedom. Frank Tannenbaum (*Slave and Citizen*, pp. 54-56), for example, wrote: "From the sixteenth to the nineteenth century, slaves in Brazil, by reimbursing the original purchase price, could compel their masters to free them." This advantage meant, he believed, that "slavery under both law and custom had, for all practical purposes, become a contractual arrangement between the master and his bondsman. There may have been no written contract between the two parties, but the state behaved, in effect, as if such a contract did exist, and used its powers to enforce it. . . . Slavery could be wiped out by a fixed price, and therefore the taint of slavery proved neither very deep nor indelible."

The following three legal opinions, all dealing with the same incident, tend to refute Tannenbaum's optimistic assertions, at least in regard to the nineteenth century. The case in question was that of a municipal judge of Macapá, Pará, who in 1853 sought to divide up an inheritance of several slaves among a number of heirs, with the aim of granting freedom to one or more of them in exchange for their established value. Since one or more of the heirs opposed this procedure, thereby blocking the judge's efforts, the case was sent for an opinion to the provincial president, who sent it on to the local criminal judge, Francisco José Furtado. As Furtado wrote (Document A), the question was essentially the following: "Whether or not the slave may be freed against his master's will, by compensating him." Perhaps because Furtado recommended alterations in the law that would have benefited slaves, the case was then sent to the Crown's Legal Counselor in Rio de Janeiro, who wrote an opinion (Document B) that rejected Furtado's reforms and upheld the status quo. A final statement, which the Emperor endorsed, was then drawn up by the Justice Section of the Council of State (Document C).

Despite clear differences of philosophy and interpretation, all these legal authorities agreed that under existing Brazilian law a slaveowner or his heirs could not be forced to free a slave simply because the latter (or someone for him) was willing to pay for his freedom. There is clear evidence here that the practice was indeed recognized in Brazilian custom and common law, and even contained in older Portuguese law codes such as the *Código Filipino*, an early seventeenth century document drawn up by order of King Philip II of Spain (Philip I of Portugal). As a rule, however, slaves were clearly property, there was no "contract" between them and their masters, and their owners' rights were sacrosanct and upheld by the state and its legal representatives.

Source: From Decision No. 388 of December 21, 1855, in *Collecção das decisões do Governo de 1855* (Rio de Janeiro, 1855), pp. 454-462.

❧ A. *The Local Judge's Opinion*

Most Illustrious and Excellent Sir: I acknowledge receipt of Your Excellency's dispatch of the 6th of this month, in which you sent me two other letters from the Municipal Judge of Macapá and from the Judge of Orphans of this city, so that I might offer my opinion on the question contained in the two letters.

The question may be reduced to the following: "Whether or not the slave may be freed against his master's will by compensating him."

The practical solution to this question has been a negative one, invoking Paragraph 22 of Art. 179 of the Imperial Constitution [which fully guaranteed the right to property]; and it does not appear to me that any contrary decision has yet triumphed in the Higher Courts.

Thus, in a hypothetical case in which an attempt is made to free a slave, I believe the judge should resort to persuasive measures in the presence of the persons concerned, as was directed by Advice No. 2 of March 17 and July 29, 1830 (Nabuco Collection); and if there should be opposition from some of the heirs, with no intention to back down, in the case of a dividable inheritance the judge may order that the individual concerned be granted to the person who wishes to give him his freedom, receiving his value in return, as was allegedly the practice of the Deputy of the Municipal Judge of Macapá. However, if all are opposed, I see no remedy at all in favor of the slave, since it has been understood that, according to the Constitution, the master may not be forced to free a slave against his will, even when the latter offers his value.

I should not hide from Your Excellency the fact that I do not regard this interpretation of the Constitution as the best one, and that in fact it deserves the legal profession's criticism. And although I do not harbor the vain hope that my opinion will prevail, I will briefly state the principles upon which my [unfavorable opinion of the law] is based.

The Constitution absolutely guarantees the right to property; and yet, according to the above cited Paragraph 22 of Art. 179, necessity and public utility legitimize expropriation, and the law of September 9, 1826, specifies various cases in which [expropriation] may occur. However, since it does not specify the case in question, the slave has been denied the right to obtain his freedom by indemnifying his master, as long as the latter refuses this act of justice, humanity, and religion.

But this literal interpretation, protecting the master as it does so that he may carry out an act which is often motivated by nothing more than cruelty and bad character, is evil and clearly absurd. Moreover, it results in the equalization of one form of property—the human form—with irrational and material property. It is recognized that only by a fiction (of the abuse of force) can the slave be seen as a thing and as property, but, whatever the amplitude given to this fiction, it is not possible to grant the master the same broad rights over the two forms of property; and it is superfluous to point out that, while he can destroy his material property according to his whim and pleasure, he cannot destroy slave property without committing a crime.

Roman law, which at first granted the masters the—*jus vitae et necis*—over the slave, had to abolish this cruel law and to punish the killing of a slave by his master with the penalties imposed in homicide cases.

Like all rights, the right to property has restrictions inherent to the nature of that right, including all those that necessity and public utility impose. When dealing with property rights over human beings, these restrictions are more numerous; because man, even when enslaved, cannot be treated as if he were a senseless or irrational being. Thus it was that Legislation of ancient times, which were much less humane and philosophical than the present, allowed a slave to redeem himself from slavery against the will of his owner; and Paragraph 4 of the Ord. of Book 4, Title 11 [of the *Codigo Philippino*] serves as proof of this.

How, then, can it be imagined that our Constitution, which rendered such respect for the rights of man and all principles of philanthropy and Christian charity, was more barbaric and less humane in regard to the miserable slave than the laws made in much less enlightened times, in which the rights of man were unknown or not guaranteed? How can it be imagined that the law, which permits confiscation of the citizen's property even for beautification, does not permit it in order to grant freedom and to tear from captivity a person who, before natural and divine laws, is similar to himself? I cannot imagine it, and it seems to me that a literal interpretation, when it implies absurdity and evil, should be abandoned, and the spirit of the law should be followed, however much it may be in conflict.

Today, when all civilized nations see slavery as against the laws of reason and humanity and highly damaging to morality and human happiness, its continuation has no cause other than the impossibility of indemnifying all the masters, along with the risk of a sudden release into society and into the enjoyment of full freedom of thousands of individuals who are brutalized and degraded by slavery, and kept under control by a harsh discipline. None of these inconveniences are caused by gradual emancipation (to which the nation aspires, as laws and treaties attest), when the master is indemnified. Therefore I can see no reason why the question now under consideration should not be regarded as belonging among the exceptions of necessity and public good which, according to the Constitution, limit the right to property.

I will avoid collecting quotations to demonstrate that our legislators wish to end slavery gradually, and that they do not see this method as dangerous. It will not be inappropriate, however, to record that Resolution No. 30 of August 11, 1837, Art. 1, *in fine*, orders the liberation of all His Majesty's slaves who offer their value; that the same is done with those of the nation [slaves owned by the Brazilian state], Ord. No. 160 of October 30, 1847; and, finally, that the slaves armed by the rebels of Rio Grande do Sul [during the Farroupilha Revolution of 1835-1845] were expropriated. . . .

If for the expropriation of the slaves who served the Rio Grande rebellion there existed the highest and most powerful reasons of necessity and public utility, then in cases of partial emancipation there also exist reasons of necessity and public utility, and in the latter case there is no crime involved, as there is in the first.

It seems to me that our legislators have not passed laws dealing specifically with the matter under question because they perhaps feared the undisciplined spirit of our slaves, and possibly because they believed that a true philosophical interpretation might supplant the defect or legal omission.

I return the dispatches which accompanied that of Your Excellency, to which I have replied. God keep Your Excellency.—Pará, August 12, 1853.—Most Illustrious and Most Excellent Dr. José Joaquim da Cunha, President of the Province. From the Judge of First Instance of the 2nd Criminal Jurisdiction of the Capital, Francisco José Furtado.

B. *The Opinion of the Crown's Legal Counselor*

In regard to the questions here under consideration, no judge who knows and uses the provisions and doctrines of our legislation can have reason to hesitate, and he has no need to consult the nation's Constitution, which has nothing to do with the question; except if he wishes to invent or introduce new doctrines and with them to explain the most ancient laws, which have always been understood and practiced according to their letter and intention, . . . thereby bringing our legal system into a state of anarchy, and threatening all the personal and real rights of the citizens, which are based upon the same legislation, and upon the interpretation given to it, to the point that (and I am witness to this) provisions of our laws have been interpreted through the doctrines of the *Code Napoléon*.

When one keeps well in mind the dispositions of our laws received from Roman legislation, . . . it must be concluded that, with slaves considered in the category of inherited property, the heirs will have and exercise in them from the time of inheritance the same authority which was exercised by those whom they are succeeding through general inheritance, and since the latter were not obliged to free them during their lifetime, likewise the former cannot be forced to do so.

It is known to me that in the province of Bahia the practice was introduced in which, in the act of preparing the inventories, any slave could redeem himself when he offered his value. Although this is a fact, I am totally unaware of the basis of such a regulation, which, in my opinion, has no support in the laws which govern us.

What was always practiced and is still practiced in this province [Rio de Janeiro], and in all those subject to the Court of this city, is that any of the heirs, in the act of division, may require the appraisal of all the slaves so that some of them, according to their value, may be included in his quota to be freed, and this practice conforms with our legislation both ancient and modern, which favors the cause of freedom without offending individual rights. . . .

I will further point out . . . that, according to ancient provisions of the extinct Tribunal of Conscience [*Mesa de Consciência*, a royal council instituted by King João III to decide matters of conscience], some favors were granted to slaves which, by exception, contradict the doctrine and general practice which I have presented. While I was Superintendent of Absentee Properties in the jurisdiction of this city, and later in the district [*Comarca*] which comprises almost the whole province, I observed these provisions, and ordered them observed, by which it was decided:

1st. That whenever any slave belonging to the estate of absent persons, received by the Superintendency, offered his evaluation in favor of his freedom, or if anyone did so on his behalf, the offer was to be accepted, and his freedom granted at once.

2nd. That during auction sales it was to be legal for the slave to choose for his master anyone he might approve of among the bidders, and that the Superintendent was to accept that bidder's offer, even if others offered more.

C. *The Opinions of the Justice Section of the Emperor's Council of State*

In effect, we do not have any legal provision according to which the master can be forced to free his slave, and only the practice and provisions cited by the Crown's Legal Counselor established these favors in such a way that they did not offend the master's property right over the slave, consecrated in our laws and by the nature of our society.

The case under consideration contains two hypotheses. In the first, some of the interested persons agree to the emancipation. In the second they all oppose it.

This Section believes that in no case, when one of the interested persons opposes, can the price of the evaluation for conferring freedom be accepted directly from the slave or from a third (disinterested) person.

To this is opposed the property right which the heir, as the representative of him whom he succeeds, acquires by inheritance, as well as the principle that nobody can be forced to free a slave, because there is no law which requires this.

Obviously this is cruel, but it is a result of slavery. Reasons of State demand it, so that slavery will not become more dangerous than it is.

However, if one or more heirs agree to the liberation, and one or more oppose it, the solutions introduced by the practice mentioned by the

Crown's Legal Counselor are available. These solutions uphold the right of property, do not undermine the slave's feeling of obedience and subordination toward his master, and his dependency upon him which should be maintained, since the slave receives his freedom from a person who is also a master, and who has been transformed into the sole owner.

Dangerous examples cannot result from this.

If all the interested persons are opposed, the Section believes that it is not legal for the judge to accept the evaluation price or to confer freedom upon the slave by any means.

All of these interested persons together possess a full property right over the slave; they have exactly the same full and ample right over him which any other master possesses.

Thus, as the Section has already observed, the master cannot be forced to free the slave, because there is no law which requires him to do so, or which indicates, as would perhaps be desirable, the cases, conditions, means, and formalities with which this would have to be done. This is simply one of those matters about which no expedient should be allowed because of the danger involved. The law says nothing more.

Obviously it is very cruel to refuse the evaluation price of, for example, a slave who served his deceased master loyally and for many years, who accompanied him until his last moments, simply because the greed of his heirs opposed this.

An advantage granted in this way to long periods of service, to loyalty and good behavior could be useful.

But there is no law which establishes this in this case or in similar ones, and only by law may it be established, and by a law which would anticipate abuses.

This is the opinion of the Section. Your Imperial Majesty, however, will order what may be most just. Conference room of the Justice Section of the Council of State on March 6, 1854. Paulino José Soares de Sousa.—Caetano Maria Lopes Gama.—Viscount de Abrantes. The Palace, 18th of March, 1854. With the seal of His Majesty.—José Thomaz Nabuco de Araujo.

6.9. A Master Abuses His Adolescent Slave Girl: A Court Case of 1882-1884

Slaveholders, of course, had the legal right to possess and dominate female slaves as well as males, and so there was little the law, police, or even the Church could do to prevent them from committing acts of physical or sexual violence against them, despite the legal theory that masters could not force their slaves to commit criminal, illicit, or immoral acts (see Document 6.1). The following case against a slaveholder who physically abused his adolescent slave girl and the accompanying decision of the judges illustrate the point. Based upon fundamental tenets of Brazilian slave law, the arguments developed here, especially by the defenders of the master, clearly expose the human and moral contradictions inherent in legislation granting property rights over people. Significantly, the decision in favor of the master, a known molester of young black girls, was reached only four years before Brazilian slavery was abolished, indicating that the rape or molestation of slave women by their masters was essentially *legal behavior* for as long as slavery existed in Brazil.

Source: *O Direito* (Rio de Janeiro) 35 (1884), 103-118.

Deflowering of a slave woman by her master. Related questions

APPEAL.

Appellant.—Henriques Ferreira Pontes.
Appellee.—Prosecutor's office, for the slave girl Honorata.

COURT OF RECIFE.

Considering that the victim, Honorata, a twelve-year-old minor girl and slave of the accused, Henriques Ferreira Pontes, stated during an investigation carried out on August 18 of this year (folio 4) that about fifteen days before the questioning she was deflowered by the defendant, her master, this occurring on the occasion when he took her during the night from the house of Dr. Adolpho Wanderley, from whom he had just bought her, to his own residence; she further stating that before reaching his residence he took her to a room on the Barreira dos Milagres, which was the dwelling place of Tiburcio, also a slave of the accused, who was ordered to leave the room;

And considering that during the interrogation of Tiburcio, which also took place on August 18 (folio 8), he confirmed the statements of the victim, declaring that about fifteen days prior to that time the accused, his master, had come at about nine o'clock at night to his room on the Barreira dos Milagres, accompanied by the victim, with whom he went to bed in the same room, first ordering Tiburcio to leave and closing himself up inside with the offended girl, it being certain that it was only at about ten o'clock at night when Tiburcio saw them enter the residence of the accused;

Considering that the defendant was alone with the victim in the said room for about an hour, during which Tiburcio could hear nothing because of the falling rain; . . .

Considering that the testimony in folios 11 and 40 corroborates the victim's claim that her offender was the accused; . . .

Considering that the corpus delicti (folio 6), made on August 18, indicates that the deflowering was recent; . . .

Considering that the examinations demanded by the accused (folios 16 and 17), the first performed on August 20 and the second on August 26, revealed that the deflowering was recent and incomplete, since the hymen membrane was not completely dilacerated; and since it is the finding of the first examination that the deflowering took place ten to fifteen days prior to the date of the examination, which was the 20th, and the finding of the second that it occurred ten to fifteen days before the 26th, when the second examination was performed, . . . these times coincide more or less with the answers given by the victim and by Tiburcio, the slave of the accused, who stated on the 18th that the defendant was in the room with the victim about fifteen days prior to that time, the defendant's first act of copulation with the victim thus taking place on the 3rd;

Further considering that, even if the time of deflowering fixed by the doctors does not coincide exactly with that of the first act of copulation declared during these interrogations, this is because the accused copulated with the victim more than two times, the last on August 18. Therefore, since the penis of the accused is disproportionate in size to the victim's genital organs, which are still not developed, the latter resisted the new copulation, which obviously produced new damage, making it difficult to determine the time of the first act of copulation. Furthermore, because of the mentioned disproportion, the actual deflowering is still not complete.

Considering that the accused states in his petition (folio 14) that the victim was taken to his house on August 3, and considering that he does not deny in his own defense that he caused the deflowering, merely limiting himself to disclaiming the right of the court to take action in a case concerning a slave woman deflowered by her master, and therefore claiming that the inquiry should not have been opened and the public prosecutor should not have entered a complaint against him;

Considering that, even if this were true, the present inquiry and trial should proceed, because the crime they are concerned with is of the kind in which public justice is intended to function through the office of the prosecutor;

Considering that Art. 73 of the Trial Code provides that when the victim is a miserable person who, because of her circumstances, cannot bring an action against an offender, the public prosecutor has the responsibility, or any citizen the right, to lodge a complaint; it is self-evident that a slave is a miserable person in relation to her master when the latter is himself the offender, because, owing to the miserable condition which slavery brings about, the slave can bring charges against nobody, much less her own master when he is the criminal, and even less so, since Paragraph 2, Art. 75, of the same Code does not allow a slave to lodge a complaint against her master;

Considering that it would be the most horrible barbarity if the law allowed a master to commit every kind of crime against his defenseless slave;

Considering that since Art. 72 of the same Code grants to the master alone the right to lodge complaints for the crimes committed against his slaves, he being their legitimate administrator, it is perfectly clear that this right can only be exercised in the event of crimes committed against slaves by third persons, since it would be absurd for masters, when they themselves are the offenders, to lodge complaints against themselves, and in such cases the complaints will be appropriately lodged by the public prosecutor;

Considering that crimes committed against miserable persons are punishable, and that, since the law does not prohibit prosecutors from filing complaints against masters who commit crimes against their slaves, miserable people that they are, this trial comes under the provisions of our legal system, since the master cannot file a complaint against himself and the slave cannot be abandoned like an irrational thing, and since, moreover, the slave comes under the protection of Art. 266 of our Criminal Code;

Considering that our slaves are not equal under the law to the slaves of the Romans, and that they even have a certain personality, and that masters are even penalized for immoderate punishments carried out against them in violation of Art. 14, Paragraph 6, of our Criminal Code;

Considering that, if the law thus disposes in regard to punishments which, although immoderate, are nevertheless less serious and of less consequence than assaults upon chastity, the responsibility to punish the latter must not be evaded, even when the crime is committed by masters against their slaves, who cannot be regarded solely as things or irrational beings;

Considering that slaves possess so much personal honor that, in the opinion of our Criminal Code, nobody could deny the master's right to file a complaint against anyone who deflowered his slave woman; in spite of everything, honor or virginity is of interest to the peace of the community, and to important interests of the family, of society, and of public morality; . . .

For all these reasons I judge the complaint against the defendant, Henriques Ferreira Pontes, as valid, in light of the corpus delicti and the examinations, and I declare him to be in violation of Art. 219 of the Criminal Code and order him imprisoned and eligible for release on bail.

The clerk inscribes the name of the accused in the roll of the guilty and registers against him the respective orders for imprisonment; the costs to be paid by the same.

I set bail for the accused at 3:000$000.

Olinda, December 31, 1882.—*Hermogenes Socrates Tavares de Vasconcellos.*

Additional statement of Hermogenes Tavares de Vasconcellos written three weeks after the first

Sir: My indictment contained in folios 50 to 62 states my reasons for indicting the appellant.

I would now like to add that, in addition to other evidence, the minor age of the victim is proved by the two medical examinations which were required by the appellant, in which the four examining doctors avowed the victim's adolescence, the total lack of development of her genital organs, and the absence of hair and breasts, scientifically proving that the victim is ten to twelve years of age.

Sir: The appellant's lawyer has not lost the bad habit of inveighing against everything and everybody, and now he is attacking my opinions, accusing me of wishing to liberate other people's slaves and of inciting crimes against masters.

I will not stoop to reply, because I am accustomed to observing to what depths some people will lower themselves to earn their fees.

Sir: When four years ago I was chief of police, a young slave girl was brought to me by the police subdelegate of Bebiribe. She was a slave of the now deceased Mr. Boulitran, father-in-law of the appellant, and was in the appellant's personal service at that time. The subdelegate asked that some precautionary steps be taken against the appellant, who seemed determined to deflower the girl, or to have illicit relations with her. She, however, had refused, and had fled in alarm to Bebiribe.

I ordered that the father-in-law be informed of what the appellant was doing, and asked him to exchange the slave girl for another one, so that peace might return to his daughter's house. . . .

About two years ago the appellant was accused of deflowering a little

mulatto girl, and I still refused to indict him, not because I was not convinced of his guilt, but because the proof was weak and the witnesses at the inquiry contradicted each other concerning his culpability. I was indecisive, and so I did not indict. I was still not an abolitionist and only now have I become one, for which reason I have now indicted him, and also because this criminal must not forever be permitted to make a mockery of our laws.

I have neglected to mention one point. The actual crime of deflowering was only verified when the victim was brought to court to make an appeal for her freedom. At that time she reported her condition before the jury, which was then in session.

As the appellant's lawyer says, this crime was not used as a means of procuring the victim's freedom.

Olinda, January 22, 1883. *Hermogenes S. Tavares de Vasconcellos.*

Decision of the Court

The court, having listened to the evidence and having voted, supports the appeal against the charge contained in folios 50 to 62 which judged the appellant in violation of Art. 219 of the Criminal Code; the court has reached this decision because it regards the trial as null and void, since there does not exist in the documents any proof that Honorata, a slave woman, who belongs to the appellant himself and was deflowered by him, is a minor of seventeen years of age.

The costs to be paid from the municipal coffers.

Recife, May 11, 1883.—*Quintino de Miranda*, president. The winning vote was that of Counselor Queiroz Barros.—*Freitas Henriques.*—*Buarque de Nazareth.*

Further statement of Freitas Henriques

I, Freitas Henriques, voted against the basis for the decision because there exist among the documents no less than three examinations of the slave girl's person, and in every one of them the experts say that, in light of her physical condition, she cannot be older than eleven or thirteen years of age, the last two examinations having been signed by Drs. Augusto Trajano de Hollanda Chacon, Manoel Gomes de Argolo Ferrão, Tristão Henriques Costa, and Adriano Luiz Pereira da Silva. This information convinces me that, despite the lack of a certificate proving the slave girl's age, she is not yet seventeen.

Nevertheless, I voted against the appeal because I regard the trial as *ab initio* null and void for the following reasons: 1) . . . The inquiry which served to establish guilt was initiated ex officio by the subdelegate in respect to a crime in which public action is not admissible. Thus he acted without the competence positively required by the hypothesis in question, since Art. 41 of the Judicial Reference of November 22, 1871, permits only police authorities to open inquiries in cases of common crimes in which an accusation is proper, either the police themselves having knowledge of the matter, or at the request of an interested party, or in *flagrante delicto*, none of which was true in the case which we are considering. . . .

2. Because the inquiry and the resulting attempt to establish the appellant's guilt were based upon the declarations of the slave girl herself, given voluntarily without her master's knowledge or any suggestion to him that he should present himself to the authorities, despite the fact that this was a case in which *an accusation could not properly be made*, as though the slave girl possessed a juridic personality and could take part in a court case all by herself; and also because the statements of Tiburcio, who also belongs to the appellant, served as a basis for the inquiry, statements which in regard to the fact in question cannot merit any juridic value, both because of Ord. L. 3rd, Title 56, Paragraph 1, which denies slaves the right to testify against their masters or even to answer questions against them, and because of the letter and spirit of Art. 89 of the Code of Criminal Process, which does not permit slaves to testify against anybody, and even less so against their masters, particularly in reference to facts in which official proceedings are inappropriate.

Legally judges are only permitted to take information from slaves concerning complaints or accusations which are actually under litigation, and there was no accusation against anyone concerning the matter under consideration when those slaves responded to the interrogations. . . .

Despite the current ideas concerning the abolition of slavery in this country, which were dealt with in the documents, ideas which are most humanitarian and Christian, most legal and timely since passage of the law of September 28, 1871 [the Rio Branco or Free Birth Law], despite the fact that we do not have the same kind of legislation concerning slaves which the Romans had, as the judge declared in the appellee's statement; nevertheless, as long as slaves, regrettably, continue to exist in this country, it is obvious that the rights of the masters over their own slaves must always be regulated by special or peculiar laws, since this is not a question of equals before equals, and can never be so because of the particular nature of a society dominated by masters, because of the legal and moral superiority which masters have over their slaves, which was dealt with in the decision of the Supreme Court of Justice of August 22, 1866, in review No. 1890; in addition to the fact that in Paragraph 22, Art. 179, our Constitution guaranteed the full right of property. Concerning the servile element, our ancient legislation, which regards the slave as an article of property, still holds sway among us. They are included in the order of personal goods and chattels, without will, without a juridic personality, having as their only representatives their own masters. . . .

5. Finally, because in view of what has been revealed, I understand that the act of deflowering in the conditions given, although contemptible, escapes incrimination under Art. 219 of the Criminal Code if it does not involve free persons, especially when it is between a master and his slave woman, it being admitted and proved that the latter belongs to the appellant. It does not seem possible to me that the legislator of the Code article referred to above had such cases as this in mind, since the text does not so indicate. Furthermore, given the facts, the master would be forced to marry his own slave, she being in fact condemned by law as an article of property, or he would be condemned to banishment from the district where he resides and obliged to grant a dowry to the victim, despite the fact that according to our laws the slave's domicile is that of the master, or any place he decides upon, and the slave does not possess a will or juridic personality of her own, and is subject to the master's authority.

However repulsive these and other facts may be to good taste and public and private morality, however offensive they may be to the rights of others in a well-constituted and free society, to me they do not appear punishable, since they are not expressly referred to in any of the articles of our Criminal Code. . . .

If the legislator had intended to punish acts of deflowering practised by masters on their slave women under seventeen years of age with the penalties referred to in Art. 219 of the Criminal Code, giving public prosecutors the right to file complaints in these cases, on the grounds that the victims are *miserable persons*, it would follow that public prosecutors would have the same right to file complaints on behalf of slaves against their masters any time they committed some act which the Code classifies as criminal—if, for example, the master took something from the slave against his will, harmed him, insulted him with words, punished him, or threatened to punish him. The result of this would be thousands of trials and a serious threat to our society.

The slave's right to complain against his master is not incorporated into the Trial Code, and those who carry out its legal provisions cannot create this right by an act of will or extravagant interpretations.

If masters can be penalized for severe punishments which they inflict upon their slaves, it is because Paragraph 6 of Art. 14 of the Criminal Code regards as justifiable only the moderate punishment given by a father to his children, by masters to their slaves, and by teachers to their pupils. And in Paragraph 1, Art. 37, the Trial Code gives public prosecutors the right to press charges when slaves are physically injured, with the qualifications contained in Arts. 202, 203, and 204 of the Criminal Code. This is because of special legislation, and not because public prosecutors have the right to lodge complaints against masters in such cases.

I am among those who believe that as long as slaves exist in our country and as long as our legislation concerning them remains in force, masters cannot commit any crimes against their slaves other than those resulting from their authoritative power over them and from their right to punish, and that aside from these exceptions, masters cannot commit crimes against their slaves.

Deprived of civil rights, slaves do not possess a right to property, to freedom, to honor or to reputation. Their rights are reduced to the preservation and sustainment of their bodies, and only when masters attack one of these rights do they commit a punishable crime, which is not an offense, but rather a violation of a right!

[A new trial was held in 1884, and on April 25th of that year the Court of Recife again decided in favor of Henriques Ferreira Pontes, employing essentially the same arguments used by Freitas Henriques in the last document, while continuing to insist that there was no evidence that the girl was under seventeen.]

6.10. "And We Are the Best of Masters!" An Abolitionist Writes on the Legal System, Punishment, and the Extraordinary Power of the Master Class (1837)

As we have seen (Document 6.1), to advance the welfare of the slaves the Brazilian legal system imposed certain controls on brutal or misguided slaveholders. Owing to a large body of disparate laws which accumulated over the centuries, masters could not *legally* force their slaves to perform immoral acts, though there were obvious exceptions to this rule; they could not *legally* deprive them of life; they were *legally* obliged to feed, house, and clothe them and to grant them medical care, though the quality and quantity of such support was not specified; they were *legally* bound to maintain and protect them in sickness and old age, and during most of the nineteenth century they could not *legally* impose more than "moderate" punishment upon them. Nevertheless, as long as Brazilian slavery lasted, such laws or precepts were conspicuously violated, nearly always with impunity.

In the following excerpts from his important book on slavery which was published in 1837, the early abolitionist, F.L.C. Burlamaque, recognized this divergence between the law and the realities of Brazilian life and tried to explain it. Government granted slavemasters so much *de facto* power over their slaves, he believed, their dominance over them was so complete, and their class solidarity so firm, that the restrictions which government sometimes tried to impose could not be enforced. Finally, masters were so determined to maintain their supremacy that government, far from imposing fundamental reforms, hardly dared to alleviate slavery's most obvious abuses. Burlamaque's deeply felt statements verify the descriptions of harsh punishment contained in the next chapter and explain how such atrocities were possible.

Source: F.L.C. Burlamaque, *Analytica acerca do commercio d'escravos e acerca dos malles da escravidão domestica* (Rio de Janeiro: Typographia Commercial Fluminense, 1837), pp. 42-44, 100-103.

❧ As long as the principle continues to exist concerning slave property that anybody may do to his slave, or to his *thing*, whatever is not prohibited by law, it will be useless to try to put any limits on the masters' absolute power. For example, it may be possible to establish the number of lashes which a slave may suffer, either privately or inflicted by public authority; the food ration which he must have may be decided upon; or the days on which he should work for his master and those intended for rest, on which he may work for himself, may be regulated. However, since it is understood that the master may do anything that the law does not prohibit, the range of free will is so great that the established restrictions, instead of producing some benefit, may have the opposite effect. If punishment were prohibited to the master in one form, he would apply it in another; and the more restrictive the prohibition, so much greater must be his desire to mistreat.

Two methods come to mind for restraining punishment: the organization of police authorities to discover and punish minor offenses, and the establishment of juries to judge and apply penalties in cases of more serious guilt. But will this eliminate excessive punishment and clandestine abuse? Will the masters be satisfied with legally restrained punishments? Will this stop them from making their slaves go about naked, from imposing excessive labor upon them without giving them adequate food, from imprisoning them, and from inflicting a thousand other forms of oppression? It is said that if the masters commit such crimes, the laws will punish them, because the statutes which establish penalties for the slaves should also provide them to control evil masters. But how? What legal procedures should be followed during the trials? Who should be the witnesses? The slaves! For those who dared to testify, it would be a sorry day! Should the masters serve as witnesses? Which of them would want to press charges or testify in a trial in which the slave is the plaintiff and the master the defendant? Would a slave even dare to bring charges against his master? Slaves will never serve as accusers or as witnesses against their masters, unless we adopt the measure which the Roman legislators did, of previously freeing the slaves belonging to masters who are charged with capital crimes. . . .

In cases of mutilation, murder, or violence, the master would thereby lose his property right over his slave. But would our legislators dare to adopt this established principle of universal justice? Would the proprietors allow themselves to be subjected to it? Just the idea of permitting slaves to testify against their masters would arouse fury and terror among them. Just daring to speak of such an idea could be dangerous for the person who uttered it. If the masters really gave careful thought to this matter, however, it might seem less frightening to them, because if such a provision were put into practice, it would be as ineffective as all the other laws. Having very limited sophistication, the slaves are naturally improvident, and therefore if they were summoned to court they would probably tell the truth. However, this would happen only if masters were not able to intimidate them or to corrupt them with promises. Just as soon as they would arrive back at their masters' houses, rewards given for false testimony and punishments inflicted for honest statements would speedily teach them that, for a slave, there is neither good nor evil but only that which pleases or displeases the master; that it is a crime for them to speak the truth, and a duty to tell lies.

Clearly such a trial would be a complete travesty, and might even cause new abuse to the miserable slave, already mangled, mutilated, or collapsing from hunger. And there would be absolutely no way to legally restrain the acts of violence committed by masters, because in no way can their guilt be legally established. One cannot and should not rely on the testimony of white people; first because punishments are carried out only in the presence of slaves; and, secondly, because the proprietors make such a common cause among themselves against the enslaved race that they can never be expected to incriminate one another. This impossibility results from the nature of slavery itself. When a government establishes or sanctions slavery, by this simple fact it declares that the will and power of the masters will be the only law for the slaves, and that consequently their duty is to conform to that will and power. If later the same government wishes to impose new duties upon the slaves, to force new responsibilities upon them, it must protect them from every outside power and eliminate every element that makes it impossible for them to meet the new demands imposed upon them.

But how can such effects be obtained if the causes always go unchanged? Anyone hoping to suggest ways to improve the sad lot of the slaves will find himself, after giving the problem considerable thought, as perplexed as he was at the start, and he will finally recognize the uselessness of every thought that has entered his mind. . . .

There are only two ways to prevent evil and brutal behavior: persuasion or strong laws. Persuasion is certainly an effective weapon when it is well handled; but it must be remembered that it is really effective only during the first moments. After a short time has passed, the arguments are forgotten, but prejudice and habit always linger. If persuasion were always effective, the world would be a new Eden. How many stirring statements have been written and spoken in favor of virtue, and how many virtuous acts are there, and how many virtuous men and women? We can assemble all the logic of the great orators and the ancient and modern philosophers, but the strongest arguments will have no more effect than a grain of sand thrown in the ocean, when we are blinded by self-interest and bad habits.

Since persuasion is ineffective, only strong laws can rid society of the evils we so greatly fear. However, for a law to produce the desired effect, it is necessary, as we said, that the agents employed to enforce it are freely able to carry out the provisions contained in that law, and that they not encounter a force superior to their own, a force greater than the power of the laws and of the legislators themselves. We have seen that in a land of slaves and masters, all the laws which tend to control arbitrary acts of slaveholders are seen by them as infringements upon their rights, and that they will employ every measure to nullify the effects of coercive legislation. We have also seen that since punishment is generally dependent upon a trial, proof can never exist, because the judges and the witnesses are all against seeing an offender of their own race punished for misdeeds that they all commit. If there were a somewhat enlightened intermediate class among us, not owning slaves but also not miserable and dependent, it would then be easy to form a jury that would punish the violent acts and crimes of the masters; it would be easy to find witnesses and even accusers. However, such a class does not exist, because some of the individuals who belong to it temporarily soon find ways to enter the landholding class, and the rest vegetate during their entire lives in the deepest ignorance and misery.

In view of this, I confess ingenuously that I do not know how we can improve the conditions of that unfortunate race; because the will of the master is for the slave more unrelenting, more complete, and more powerful than all the good will or fine intentions of the public authorities; because in the end the will of the master is a law so powerful for the slave that it is sufficient to paralyze every other, those of religion, of morality, of government. . . .

If there were no other proof of the godlessness of the slaveowners, their lack of charity and pity toward the unhappy people whom providence has granted them would be proof enough. Not content with allowing them to go about naked, with making them live in unwholesome places exposed to harsh weather, providing them with the worst kinds of food, and these in amounts hardly sufficient to keep them from starving to death—not content with all this, they also lavish punishment and torment upon them at all hours and at every moment, with no restrictions or limits other than their own will or fancy.

In the cities and in the countryside, corporal punishment is so common that cracking instruments of punishment and the cries of their victims no longer arouse the attention of passers-by—so much are we accustomed to them!

The tendency toward cruelty which results from arbitrary power is encouraged by the fear which is inspired by the victims' desperation. In order to make men work, from whom they are constantly stealing the fruits of labor, they must resort to cruelty, and to prevent acts of revenge they must resort to more cruelty. To restrain the slave population, no other methods have yet been found, except stupidity, division, and terror.

In effect, the multiplication of the slaves, along with brutality and bad treatment, constantly threaten the security of their owners; their evil acts and their fears increase in the same proportion as the slaves increase, and since the low value of the slaves, resulting from their growing numbers, makes their survival seem less important, whereas it makes their maintenance more expensive, punishments and bad treatment increase in turn, along with the desperation of their victims. . . .

The cruelties of slaveowners would be unbelievable to us if we did not witness them every day. The least contradiction, the least delay, annoys them and makes them furious; and all end up finding the exercise of cruelty a kind of atrocious pleasure. . . .

Horrid punishments are common among us. Nevertheless, the false opinion has been propagated that we are the best of masters. If we are the most merciful, what must others be!

On the great plantations of northern Brazil it is shocking to witness the misery of the slaves, whose bodies, covered with wounds, clearly reveal the treatment of which they are the constant victims. In the provinces of Maranhão and Piauí, with which we are particularly familiar, "novenas," that is, whippings for nine successive days, are an ordinary form of punishment. The accused is fastened to a wagon and there receives two or three hundred lashes; the mangled flesh is then cut, and cayenne pepper and salt are applied to the wounds, on the pretense that this is a remedy required to prevent infection and gangrene. I know a man named Alvarenga in Piauí, who, when he wished to get rid of a slave, ordered him a "novena," and then exposed him in a sack to the burning sun, where the poor victim was further beaten until he died. The tourniquet, hand and neck stocks, thumbscrews, manacles, irons, pillories, and many other instruments of punishment are common on our plantations, and even in our cities they are not rare. It might be supposed that we inherited all these instruments of torture which were in use in barbarous ages and are worthy only of tyrants and the Inquisition; but this is not the whole story. The art of torture is much more advanced among us. To expose a slave for a whole night, tied to a stake, over an ants' nest, as is common in some provinces, or on a cross exposed to the stings of mosquitoes, as in Rio Grande do Sul, are refinements of barbarity peculiar to Brazil. And we are the best of masters!

SEVEN

"Shamefully Torn before Thy Eyes": Corporal Punishment

AS THE PERCEPTIVE Brazilian abolitionist, F.L.C. Burlamaque, wrote in 1837 (see Document 6.10), to make slaves work while stealing the fruits of their labor, cruelty was needed, and to prevent them from taking revenge upon those who inflicted this cruelty upon them, more cruelty was needed. In Brazil, as in the United States, the results of this situation were centuries of torture and brutality, examples of which are revealed in this part.

The cruelty of rural slavery "reached incredible extremes," in the words of the twentieth-century Brazilian writer, Arthur Ramos, including physical mutilation, punitive branding, and the widespread custom of lashing slaves for nine or thirteen consecutive nights (so-called *novenas* and *trezenas*). (See Ramos, "Castigos de escravos," pp. 79-103; José Alipio Goulart, *De palmatória ao patíbulo*.) Like its American counterpart, Brazilian slavery produced a complex assortment of punitive and restrictive devices to control slaves. Among the latter were numerous implements to imprison them or to impede their movement: shackles, handcuffs, wooden blocks or metal balls with attached chains, iron collars known as *gargalheiras* and *troncos* or stocks made of wood or iron which secured the arms, legs, or even the heads of slaves, rendering them defenseless against mosquitoes and other insects. Among instruments of persuasion or torture were thumbscrews (*anjinhos* or "little angels"), the *palmatória*, a wooden paddle used to strike the palms or knuckles of offending slaves, and the *libambo*, an iron loop affixed to the neck of known runaways, with attached metal hooks or even a large bell to hinder a slave's progress through a forest, or to alert pursuers to his presence. The contraptions of Brazilian slavery included the tin mask which was worn over the heads of slaves presumably to prevent them from consuming stolen sugar cane, from excessive drinking, or even from eating earth, a common but dangerous practice of Africans in Brazil and other New World countries.

Though the instruments of oppression were many and ingenious, in Brazil as in the United States the whip was the device most often used to inflict punishment upon slaves or to make them work. In fact, if there was an important difference between the ways this instrument was used in the two countries, it was in regard to the *number* of lashes that were normally inflicted. Whereas fifty, a hundred, two hundred, three hundred or more strokes were common and even legal during almost the entire history of slavery in Brazil (see Documents 2 through 8 in this chapter), in the United States, especially in such border states as Virginia and Maryland, it was often uncommon and even legally forbidden to violate the Biblical law which limited punishment of slaves to thirty-nine lashes—the result perhaps not of finer instincts in the United States, but of the greater cost there of replacing slave property. Attempting to persuade Brazilian masters to reduce the number of lashes they habitually inflicted upon their slaves, Father Manoel Ribeiro Rocha (see Document 7.2) cited the relevant passages from Deuteronomy and Paul's Second Epistle to the Corinthians. However, as Ribeiro Rocha's own words suggest, and many documents in this book tend to prove, during the entire history of Brazilian slavery lawmakers and interpreters of laws, the great mass of slaveholders, and even the Catholic Church itself generally ignored the Biblical injunctions that required them to reduce the number of lashes they imposed upon their slaves, "lest"—to cite the text of Deuteronomy itself—"thy brother depart shamefully torn before thy eyes."

7.1. The Governor of Grão Pará and Maranhão Informs the Portuguese King of Cruel Punishments Inflicted upon Indian Slaves (1752)

As the Brazilian legal historian, Agostinho Marques Perdigão Malheiro, wrote in the 1860s, ancient Portuguese laws contained extraordinary provisions concerning slaves "such as applying the lash or torture as a means of forcing them to confess, branding them with a hot iron, mutilating parts of the body, excessive use of the death penalty, and other cruel punishments." (See Document 6.1.) Obviously such punishments were not formulated at the Portuguese Court without considerable awareness of Brazil's conditions and without some expectation that slaveholders there were willing or even eager to adopt them. In fact, Portuguese kings and their councilors must have understood that Brazilian slaveholders were capable of going far beyond officially sanctioned levels of brutality.

The following letter, written in 1752 to King José I by the governor of Grão Pará, Francisco Xavier de Mendonça Furtado, indeed suggests that Brazilian slaveholders—not just a few but perhaps the large majority at certain times and places—were capable of inflicting almost unbelievable punitive excesses upon their slaves. Although the governor was mainly concerned here with the cruel treatment of Indians, his letter more than hints at the plight of blacks owned by masters of the kind who could inflict such atrocities upon a race of people whose slave status was often doubtful, who enjoyed generally more government and ecclesiastical protection than blacks, and who, in fact, during Mendonça Furtado's own governorship would be freed en masse by a royal decree of June 6, 1755.

Source: Instituto Histórico e Geográfico Brasileiro, *A Amazônia na era pombalina. 1° Tomo. Correspondência inédita do Governador e Capitão-General do Estado do Grão Pará e Maranhão Francisco Xavier de Mendonça Furtado* (São Paulo, 1963), pp. 304-306.

❧ Sir: In order to authorize brand marks on the blacks found in *quilombos* [runaway-slave settlements] in the state of Brazil, Your Majesty was pleased to proclaim the law of March 3, 1741 [providing for branding the letter "F," signifying *Fugido* or runaway, on a shoulder of each slave in a *quilombo*, and for cutting off an ear in the event of a second offense]. The officers of the Chamber of this city, having petitioned Your Majesty to allow that law also to be observed in the State of [Grão Pará e Maranhão] so that the punishments provided for in it might also be imposed upon slaves found in *mocambos* [another common term for runaway-slave settlements] in these districts, Your Majesty decided in con-

22. Common Punishments: The Block and Chain, the Neck Iron, the Tin Mask

sultation with the Overseas Council to order by the resolution of May 30, 1750, that this law be carried out here, branding slaves found in *mocambos*, but entirely forbidding that Indians captured in those *mocambos* be branded like the blacks in any way. This was made quite clear in a Provision of the Overseas Council dated May 12, 1751.

That punishment, which Your Majesty did not wish to impose upon Indians found in those *mocambos*, who were exempted from it by that same law, I find practiced here with a level of immoderation that is both brutal and scandalous.

It is the custom here among most of the inhabitants that when some of these Indians, whom they call slaves, run away or commit some other act which offends them, they order them bound, and with a red-hot iron or lancet, brutally incise the name of the supposed master on their chests. And, since the letters are often large, it is necessary for them to be written in two rows. The miserable Indians endure this torment without any human relief.

When I first saw one of them with this brutal, disgraceful, and scandalous lettering on his chest, I was filled with an appropriate sensation of horror. Intending to bring to trial the would-be master who had ordered it, I learned that he was dead. I then saw a great many of them [in this condition], and then people informed me that this was a quite normal thing. And since it was so prevalent that nobody was surprised by it, neither the governors nor the ministers forbade it, and it was in fact accepted and entirely known to them.

To prevent the people from convincing themselves that I also condoned continuation of this shocking offense, I not only began to criticize it, but also ordered into my presence every Indian who could be found with such lettering. And since many of them were free and found themselves in the power of their would-be masters, who possessed no more right to keep them in captivity than that very violence which accompanied their capture, I at once ordered them declared free.

Concerning those who were legally, or half legally, kept as slaves, or [held so] in conformity with the customs of the country, I ordered suspension of their legal slave status until I could bring the situation to Your Majesty's royal presence, so that I might make these people understand that, even if those Indians were in fact slaves, they could never possess that vicious liberty, especially when an explicit law exists in opposition to it.

I brought no further judicial proceedings against them because if I had started an examination or taken any additional action in the matter, those who would be found guilty would number only a very few less than the total number of inhabitants. Since the problem was so widespread, for the moment it seemed best to me to condemn and obstruct it as much as possible, making these people recognize the absurdity of what they were doing.

The practice had its beginnings in the ill-advised enthusiasm of one of the Troop Commanders who were ordered into the backlands to redeem some captive Indians. Not wanting to mix them up with those belonging to the Royal Treasury, he ordered all of them branded, and since these people had witnessed his example and are ignorant to an extraordinary degree, they started to imitate him, going beyond the single brand mark to an entire name.

Since this vicious custom has spread to most of the inhabitants and it is impossible to punish an entire people, and also because it is unjust to allow them to continue oppressing these Indians, it seemed to me that Your Majesty, if it should please you to do so, might promulgate a law here ordering that nobody may apply such lettering, not even a brand mark. And, in regard to the past, after scolding [the offenders] for the brutality they have inflicted upon [the Indians], it might please Your Majesty to pardon them for their crime and to relieve them of the punishment that they had incurred for committing such crimes, granting Indians found with such lettering their full freedom, and ordering every person possessing one of those Indians to have him appear at the Offices of this Government within a certain period of time, which in my opinion might well be four months. And at the end of that time, if one of them is found in slavery or has not been required to appear, the person in whose power he is found should receive the punishment that may seem just to Your Majesty in such a case. Your Majesty will order what seems proper. Pará, November 16, 1752.

7.2. "This Rustic Theology": A Catholic Priest Admonishes Slaveholders about the Cruel Punishment of Their Slaves (1758)

Published protests against excessive punishment became common in the second half of the nineteenth century, but even in the colonial period, when it was far more difficult to express controversial opinions in print, some objections were published. A notable example is the following excerpt from a book by a prominent Catholic clergyman and resident of Bahia, Father Manoel Ribeiro Rocha. Published in Lisbon in 1758, just six years after the governor of Grão Pará wrote his letter to the king (see previous document), this legal, philosophical, and theological reproof of the excesses of slavery has sometimes been regarded as early abolitionist literature, since it called for the liberation of children and improvements in the spiritual and temporal well-being of slaves. Ribeiro Rocha's appeals regarding punishment are further evidence of its extreme brutality in the colonial period and further proof that there was also strong, though probably isolated and largely ineffective, disapproval of such cruel behavior.

Source: Manoel Ribeiro Rocha, *Ethiope resgatado, empenhado, sustentado, corregido, instruido, e liberado* (Lisbon: Na Officina Patriarcal de Francisco Luiz Ameno, 1758), pp. 175-223.

❧ *Concerning Correction*

There is no doubt that the owners of slaves ought to punish them and correct their mistakes when they know through experience that their words alone are not effective. If a slave has a good character, he will rarely do anything wrong, and to correct him a scolding alone will be sufficient. However, if he is insolent or ungovernable, he will always behave badly, and when correcting him it will be essential to accompany scolding with punishment.

For these reasons human laws permit correction, reform, and punishment of serfs, slaves, and domestics . . . and this same obligation to punish is also contained in the fourth precept of Divine Law. . . .

To what extent this correction, disciplining, and Christian punishment is to be looked upon as praiseworthy is a most difficult question whose exposition we lack time to develop here. In Volume 9 of St. Augustine there is to be found the treatise *de bono disciplinae* in which the Holy Doctor, among other eulogies, refers to discipline as the mistress of Religion and true piety: *Disciplina magistra est religionis, magistra verae pietatis*. However, he then goes on to explain that he is referring here to discipline and prudent correction, punishment that neither shocks nor offends. . . . Therefore, if the slaves' punishment is to be pious and in conformity with the Christian religion, it must be administered with prudence, excluding all excessive roughness which might occur during the process. Punishment, then, ought to be well regulated in regard *to time*; well regulated in regard *to cause*; well regulated in regard *to quality*; well regulated in regard *to quantity*; and well regulated in regard *to method.*

First, for punishment to be well regulated *in regard to time*, it should not be immediately administered *in continenti* when the slave misbehaves or commits an offense. A period of time must be allowed to elapse, either long or short, depending upon the seriousness of the case and the incidental circumstances. The reason for this is that the mistake or offense will obviously be annoying to the master, and this will provoke him to anger; and punishment should not be administered with anger, but rather with gentleness and charity. Some delay is needed until the spirits have calmed down and the anger subsided. . . . Otherwise the furiousness with which the master punishes will arouse the anger of the punished slave, and the punishment will become unruly. Instead of following in the path of God's commands, the punishment will fall under the influence of the devil. . . .

In the second place, for punishment to be well regulated *in regard to cause*, there must be previous guilt. This is so because guilt is the reason for punishment in the first place, as St. Augustine says . . . ; and since there cannot be an effect without a previous cause, well-regulated punishment cannot exist where there is a lack of previous guilt. . . .

From which it may be concluded that if a slave does not give good cause, it will be a sin to punish him, and an abominable sin as well in the eyes of God. As Solomon says in Proverbs 17:15: "He that justifieth the wicked, and he that condemneth the just, both are abominable before God."

At Brazil's plantations, mills, and mines there are men who even today are so inhuman that their first act toward their slaves when they first appear before them after their purchase, is to have them severely whipped, with no cause other than their desire to do so, and they even boast of this as if to say that only they were born with the right to dominate slaves, and as if to make themselves feared and respected. And if their Confessor or another intelligent person objects and tries to raise some doubts in their minds, they reply that such a precautionary measure is reasonable to prevent the slaves under their control from behaving badly, so that from the outset they will conduct themselves correctly. They also add that once the slaves are theirs, the rule that each person can do with his own property what he likes, in conformity with his own understanding, goes into effect.

Let such masters or slaveholders understand that this rustic theology is the reverse of Christian theology, because Christian theology uniformly accepts as its first and unquestionable principle: If evil is not being done, good must result. Their backwoods theology tells them the opposite: that they can commit a wicked act now if the result in the future will be useful to them. Christian theology teaches that it is wrong to tell the smallest lie, even if it is certain to result in the conversion of the entire world. And the countrified theology of those petty despots dictates that they can commit the abomination and cruelty of punishing their guiltless slave, so that as a result he will be good in the future, and this with no certainty at all that this result is unquestionably achieved by such a method, nor even whether or not the new slave is undeniably bad.

Let them understand too that they may talk all they like about the legal principle that says that the owner may do with his property whatever he likes. However, few of them really understand this correctly, since what this really means is that each person may do with his property whatever he likes if the laws do not otherwise forbid it; and Divine and human laws, as previously stated, prohibit the punishment of servants without previous cause. This abuse, aside from being an abomination in the eyes of God, damages the commonwealth and implies injury and contempt for the human person, and the laws have taken all this into consideration, so that masters may be able to recognize that the slaves whom misfortune has placed under their subjection were constituted by nature on the same level of equality with themselves. . . .

In the third place, for punishment to be well regulated *in regard to quality*, it should not go beyond the *palmatória*, the switch, the whip, and shackles; because the other kinds of corporal punishment are condemned and prohibited in the domestic household. Therefore masters may not beat their slaves with large sticks, because this is cruel and inhuman. In all the above citations from Proverbs, when the punishment of domestic servants is mentioned, no word is used except *virga*, and this does not mean sticks and large rods, but rather the *palmatória* and also the young twigs from trees, which are thin switches like those of the quince tree, which are used in Europe, or the thin *cipós* or lianas, which we use in Brazil.

Similarly, when punishing with the whip, it is not proper afterward to incise the skin, or to prick the buttocks of the slaves, ordering such bleeding on the pretext of releasing the bruised blood which could become abscessed. It is true that the people who commit these acts are to be found at our plantations, mills, and mines, and that they are not men, but wolves and bears. This madness, this fierceness, this rage and brutality has descended from the human level to the beastly. . . .

The same level of cruelty, or even worse, occurs when, after whipping, they cauterize the bruises with drops of melted sealing-wax, and there are other similar torments which each of these monsters of arrogance (this is the source of all their excesses) conceives and carries out against these miserable slaves.

Let them understand that this and everything else their cruelty invents is prohibited to them by human and divine laws. . . .

In the fourth place, for punishment to be well regulated *in regard to quality*, it should be measured out in accordance with the level of guilt, in either greater or lesser amounts. . . . The Hebrews whipped St. Paul five times for the crimes or offenses which they imagined he had committed in preaching the Gospel, and in none of them did they exceed forty lashes. Rather, in order to avoid completing this number, they administered only thirty-nine lashes each time, as the Saint himself relates in 2 Corinthians, 11:24: "Of the Jews five times did I receive forty lashes, save one." And their reason for reducing the number is to be found in the laws of Deuteronomy, which state that for the worst possible offense punishable with the whip they might calculate up to forty, but they were not to exceed this number. As it says in Deuteronomy, 2-3: "And if they see that the offender be worthy of stripes: they shall lay him down, and shall cause him to be beaten before them. According to the measure of the sin shall the measure of the stripes also be. Yet so, that they exceed not the number of forty." And so that there would be no danger even of exceeding this number, they decided instead to reduce it.

And this is what slaveowners should also observe in regard to the volume of punishment, especially when using the whip. If the slave deserves three dozen lashes, punish him with two dozen only; and if he deserves two dozen, one and a half dozen will be enough; and deserving a dozen, commute his punishment to that of the *palmatoria* instead of the whip; so that, once the punishment has been justly determined by the nature of the error or offense, some part of the deserved punishment may always be reduced, as the Hebrews were accustomed to do, and as they did with St. Paul. . . .

Accordingly, the number of lashes which slaves receive ought not to be set at two hundred, three hundred, and four hundred, as is so commonly done at those plantations, mills, and mines, an abuse which not only is practiced with impunity but which no longer even seems strange there (it would seem even stranger, in fact, in such places, if such punishments were discontinued). Instead of this, the number of lashes should be set at twenty, thirty, and forty, and they would be well advised if when the most serious offenses are punished the forty lashes go unfinished. . . .

In the fifth and final place, if the punishment is to be well regulated *in regard to method*, it is essential that it not be excessive either in word or deed. Concerning deeds, punishment is excessive if the slave is beaten in the face, around the eyes, on the head, and about the private parts. Concerning words, punishment is excessive when, along with the normal words employed in scolding, other words are used which imply reproach, abuse, slander, and vilification. Above all, the owners of slaves should not beat them rudely on the head and on the irregular parts of the body, because they put themselves in danger of causing some permanent facial deformity, and of gravely threatening their health, and perhaps their lives. They will be behaving more like executioners than masters, and it will be as though they are using their authority to destroy them rather than moderate punishment to help them to mend their ways. . . .

The result of all this is that the slaves, hurt and offended, flee their master's place. Those who absent themselves in this way rarely reappear, despite the enormous effort and care which go into hunting them down, which happens every day. . . . And when they do not flee, they become enemies in their masters' households; because the slaves, if treated well and with love, even when punished for their improvement, are always our companions and good friends, as Seneca says; on the other hand, if we treat them barbarously and outrageously, they must become our domestic enemies, not because they willfully choose to be, but because we, with the bad will we show them, give them no alternative.

Again concerning *words*, when masters punish their slaves, they should not mix among their words of reproof others which are injurious or offensive, calling them by those disgraceful names which, unsuitable to my penpoint, are also inappropriate on their lips, since, to be honorable, the scolding of servants must not be injurious.

Even less should slaveholders, whether inflicting punishment or not, use curses and insults. This vice, which is so widespread and common in these Conquests, is disgusting and reprehensible, because the person who curses and harangues others with anger and evil intention is acting in direct opposition to the charitable manner expected of him, and thus he gravely sins. . . .

And in no case should we treat slaves with bitterness, anger, indignation, screaming, clamor, curses, and slander, because in the final analysis these slaves are our brothers and neighbors, whom we should not treat with such perversity. . . . As St. Paul says in the Epistle to the Ephesians, 4:31: "Let all bitterness and anger and indignation and clamor and blasphemy be put away from you, with all malice. And be ye kind one to another."

7.3. Advice on Plantation Punishment from an Agricultural Handbook (1839)

The following suggestions on plantation punishment contained in a practical handbook for the guidance of Brazilian planters and farmers may be usefully compared with the thoughts of Padre Ribeiro Rocha on the same subject (see previous document). Though writing nearly a century after Ribeiro Rocha's book was published, this author also deplored the use of abusive punishment and even torture in Brazilian society. Nevertheless, his thoughts on the master-slave relationship, his recommendations on the use of exemplary punishment to goad slaves to higher output, and his advice on the kinds of punishment to be administered under varying circumstances reveal him to have been far less humane and enlightened than the eighteenth-century priest. Neither author, it might be conjectured, had much effect on his contemporaries' thinking regarding the question of slave punishments.

Source: C. A. Taunay, *Manual do agricultor brasileiro* (Rio de Janeiro: Typ. de J. Villeneuve, 1839), pp. 11-14.

❧ Blacks are not bought so that their owners may have the pleasure of providing for them, or of watching them pass their time in leisure. Rather, they are acquired so that subsistence and profit may be extracted from their labor. The salary of these workers is paid in part with their purchase money, and the other part is paid daily when they are fed. Nevertheless, the black man, the passive part in this whole transaction, is naturally an enemy of every regular occupation, sometimes even preferring to fast and to give up every comfort rather than perform the labor which he should rightfully contribute in fulfillment of his contract, and only compulsion and fear can make him accomplish his daily tasks.

This compulsion is achieved through constant supervision, and fear is aroused in him by quick and certain punishment. . . . When we speak of labor, we do not mean the sluggish and indolent imitation of activity of those blacks who are left to themselves and waste away with hunger; the services performed by blacks imprisoned in the town jails provide a perfect example of this kind of work. By labor, rather, we mean the active and productive employment of all the body's powers, work that absorbs the slave's full attention, draws sweat from his whole body, and results in the completion of tasks as if by magic. This is the only kind of labor that achieves effects that correspond to the high cost of slaves. Such application on their part cannot be achieved without constant supervision, which, as we have said, requires the equivalent of military discipline, with the slaves assembled in groups or squads, with leaders or overseers who do not let them out of their sight for as much as a minute.

Fear, as we observed and proved, is the only way to force slaves to meet the responsibilities that their condition imposes upon them. . . . We have seen that constant supervision by the overseers, administrators, or masters is needed to make slaves work. However, this supervision would be a mere waste of effort without punishment, which should be moderately assessed, reasonably applied in a manner fitting the level of guilt and the delinquent's behavior, and executed in full view of all the other slaves; if done this way and with great solemnity, it will serve both to teach a lesson and to intimidate the others.

Whoeover observes these rules will see that it is not difficult to maintain the most rigorous discipline with very little use of the whip. In fact, excessive punishment, constantly repeated, far from correcting slaves, brutalizes them. Therefore overseers should not be allowed to punish immediately, except when slaves show signs of rebelliousness—the worst of domestic crimes. For this offense the maximum punishment should be applied later, whatever the immediate dose of punishment the culprit may have received when the crime was discovered. With this one exception, the overseers should be made to give a report of all offenses committed, along with their circumstances, to the administrator or owner, if he himself serves as administrator. After summary decisions, he should order the guilty slaves punished at the next assemblage.

The law ought to determine the levels of punishment and the instrument to be employed. The whip of one leather strand commonly called a *bacalhau* seems acceptable to us, and in our opinion fifty lashes with this device are sufficient to punish every crime for which the masters have been given judicial cognizance. The crimes which require greater punishment, such as constant running away, major thefts, disobedience, incorrigible drinking, rebellion against punishment, and others of the same nature, should be punished in the jails in the respective districts, at the request of the masters and with the approval of the justices of the peace, who will make summary decisions.

In regard to atrocious crimes such as murders, poisoning, armed rebellions, conspiracies leading to mass insurrection, etc., the law already requires that such cases come under the jurisdiction of the justices of the peace. Masters who, through greed or neglect, do not denounce such slaves, or help them to hide, will sooner or later regret such criminal complicity.

Our advice to every humane and reasonable master who encounters incorrigible slaves is as follows: after they have repeatedly suffered the maximum punishment and have not changed their ways, he should sell them without regard to financial loss, because the sale itself will serve to intimidate the others. They will know that the slaves who are sold away will fall into the hands of heartless and brutal masters.

For the most serious domestic crimes, and for the run-of-the-mill slave, fifty lashes will be sufficient. Anything above this number is more likely to arouse anger and revenge than to reform the slave, and even the repetition of this number of lashes should not be permitted except after an interval of one week.

Concerning stocks, pillories, manacles, and all the other countless instruments of torture—remnants of antique barbarity—which the government has already abandoned and which, through illogical or criminal neglect, it still tolerates in the hands of private persons, it is obvious that religion, humanity, and good sense urgently require that they be reduced to ashes. A prison for locking up mutinous or runaway blacks for a few days until there is a good opportunity to send them to the jails, and iron collars to humiliate lazy persons and habitual runaways in the eyes of their companions are all that should legally survive of that arsenal of torture machines.

The punishment of women and children should be in fitting proportion to their sex and lack of strength, and carried out at a place removed from the men. What we have said of the justice, moderation, and sang-

23. Plantation Punishments: The *Palmatória*, the Whip, and the Neck Iron for Runaways

froid which slaveholders require also applies in the case of these weaker and more docile slaves. The advice to sell incorrigible blacks is even more necessary in the case of black women of bad character who cannot accustom themselves to discipline.

What we have said here will be sufficient for masters and administrators who are reasonable and upright. As a result of their own experience and observation, such persons already practice the main principles which we have pointed out above; and if all slaveholders belonged to the same class, there would not be such a need for the government to intervene legislatively on the side of better treatment. They could entrust the lot of the slaves to the prudence, interest, and good character of heads of families, which was the custom in antiquity when paternal government existed in all its primitive simplicity. . . . As long as the purity of customs is maintained, along with patriarchal sincerity, there is little that is inconvenient about this system. However, when social life becomes more complicated, when luxury and greed overpower people, when wealthy proprietors gather in the cities to shine at court or to take part in politics, when the thirst for honors, pleasure, and wealth becomes a passion, it is then that the abuses of paternal absolutism and so many irresponsible domestic courts of justice spring up on all sides. It is then that tortures, afflictions, and acts of passion are conceived and carried out in the secrecy of the home. It is then that the gluttonous grow fat on the flesh of the slaves. It is then that the Roman matrons take delight in torment and blood, then that all the horrors and monstrosities are practiced which lust and cruelty inspire in minds depraved by pleasure. . . .

Today public protection is granted to the unborn child, and it accompanies him to the grave. Not even the European serf and the American slave are entirely abandoned, and the arbitrary treatment they suffer is the result of abuse and not of principles.

7.4. Lashes Inflicted upon Slaves at the Jail (*Calabouço*) in Rio de Janeiro (1826)

As observed elsewhere, masters could legally inflict only "moderate" punishment upon their captives. In cases, however, when slaves committed serious offenses supposedly requiring severe "correction," their owners could send them to the local jail (*calabouço*) where, under official direction, they were given corporal punishment, with no trial or other legal formalities required beyond the payment of a small fee.

The following document is taken from an accounting ledger kept at the Police Intendancy in Rio de Janeiro to record fees received from masters for the punishment of their slaves during the year 1826. Registered on only one day, the 2nd of January, 1826, these entries are typical of those recorded during the entire year. On this one day, for example, the Rio police received 4$640 *réis* in payment of 2,900 lashes, to be administered to sixteen slaves, including four women. Similarly during the entire month of January slaveowners paid 50$640 *réis* to the police for the infliction of 31,650 lashes upon some 170 slaves, including 37 women. For all of 1826 masters paid a total of 528$640 *réis* for this purpose, enough to pay for 330,400 lashes at the current rate of 1.6 *réis* per lash. The average number received was nearly two hundred, but many slaves received three hundred lashes, the maximum number per slave recorded during the year.

Source: Codex 385, Receita dos bilhetes de correção de escravos (Policia) 1826, Arquivo Nacional, Rio de Janeiro.

❧ This book will serve to record receipt of the bills of correction of slaves to be carried out in the year 1826, and which are numbered, . . . signed with the signature which I use [illegible signature] in conformity with Art. 2, Title 1 of the Accounting Plan of the General Intendency of Police, Rio de Janeiro, November 10, 1825 [illegible signatures].

JANUARY 2, 1826

1. Received by the Treasurer of the Intendancy Manoel José da Fonseca from Manoel Luis de Castro for 100 lashes for the slave Antonio — $160
   [Signed] Gomes
2. Rcd. from Manoel Luis de Castro for 100 lashes for the slave Geronimo — $160
   Gomes
3. Rcd. from Manoel Luis de Castro for 100 lashes for the slave Joaquim — $160
   Gomes
4. Rcd. from Manoel Luis de Castro for 100 lashes for the slave Manoel — $160
   Gomes
5. Rcd. from Cosme Damião de Caro for 200 lashes for the slave woman Maria — $320
   Gomes

6. Rcd. from João da Braga for 200 lashes for the slave Manoel $320
Gomes
7. Rcd. from José de Ribeiro for 400 lashes for the slaves João and Francisco $640
Gomes
8. Rcd. from João Antonio Machado for 200 lashes for the slave Manoel $320
Gomes
9. Rcd. from Manoel Fernandes for 200 lashes for the slave Antonio $320
Gomes
10. Rcd. from Luis Martins Lages for 300 lashes for the slave Jorge $480
Gomes
11. Rcd. from Father Antonio Teixeira for 200 lashes for the slave Francisco $320
Gomes
12. Rcd. from Jorge de Estrella for 300 lashes for the slave Evaristo $480
Azevedo
13. Rcd. from Anselmo dos Anjos de Menezes for 200 lashes for the slave woman Jozefa $320
Gomes
14. Rcd. from Geraldo Pires de Oliveira for 200 lashes for the slave woman Benedicta $320
Gomes
15. Rcd. from João Lopes dos Santos for 100 lashes for the slave woman Dionizia $160
Azevedo

7.5. "The Scene Was Deeply Afflicting": A Britisher Describes the Punishment of a Slave at the Rio *Calabouço* Early in the Nineteenth Century

The statistics in the previous document will be more meaningful if considered along with Figure 24 and the following description of the punishment of a slave at the same *calabouço* in Rio de Janeiro. Written by a British observer, James Henderson, who resided in Brazil some years before the Intendancy officials made their ledger entries, this description is one of many vivid and realistic glimpses of Brazilian slavery which Henderson published in his *History of Brazil* in 1821.

It is worth pointing out here that the British pastor, Reverend Robert Walsh (see Documents 1.9 and 5.3), who was in Rio in the late 1820s, learned of a man who, seeking personal revenge against a slave who had struck him, arranged to purchase the man and then had him so severely whipped at the *calabouço* that he was at last "sent in a mat to the burying ground of the Misericordia." (Walsh, *Notices of Brazil*, II, 357-358.) In effect, Brazilian law allowed him to use the public authorities themselves as his instrument of revenge.

Source: James Henderson, *A History of Brazil, Comprising Its Geography, Commerce, Colonization, Aboriginal Inhabitants* (London: Longman, Hurst, Rees, Orme, and Brown, 1821), pp. 72-73.

❧ The negroes are probably not used with more inhumanity here than in other colonies. In the interior they are treated much better than at Rio de Janeiro, where, in some instances, much cruelty is practised. For a trifling offence, they are sometimes committed to the charge of two or three soldiers, who pinion them with cords, and beat them in the most unfeeling manner along the streets, to the Calabouço, a prison for the blacks, where they are destined perhaps to receive a severe castigation before they are liberated. Their owners procure an order from the intendant-general of the police, for one, two, or three hundred lashes, according to the dictates of their caprice or passion, which punishment is administered to those poor wretches by one of their own countrymen, a stout, savage-looking, degraded Negro.

A gentleman obtained an order for the flagellation of one of his runaway slaves, with two hundred lashes. On his name being called several times, he appeared at the door of a dungeon, where the negroes seemed to be promiscuously confined together. A rope was put round his neck, and he was led to a large post, in the adjoining yard; around which his arms and feet were bound, while a rope secured his body in like manner, and another, firmly fastened round his thighs, rendered the movement of a single member wholly impossible. The black degradado set to work very mechanically, and at every stroke, which appeared to cut part of the flesh away, he gave a singular whistle. The stripes were repeated always upon the same part, and the negro bore the one hundred lashes he received at this time with the most determined resolution. On receiving the first and second strokes he called out "*Jesu*," but afterwards laid his head against the side of the post, not uttering a syllable, or asking for mercy; but what he suffered was strongly visible in the tremulous agitation of the whole frame. The scene was deeply afflicting, and it was to be regretted that the man who was capable of such fortitude should be in a condition that subjected him to so painful and degrading an infliction. He received the other one hundred lashes on the third day following, after which, a heavy iron chain to his leg, and an iron rivetted round his neck, from which a trident stood up above the head, by way of ornament, would be no pleasant appendages with which to pursue his usual labor.

7.6. "This, Then, Is Not a Crime": The Trial of a Coffee Planter Accused of Brutal Punishment (1878)

The following documentation of the trial of a coffee planter of Rio de Janeiro province, Joaquim Borges Rodrigues, accused of brutal punishment and other kinds of mistreatment, are a virtual catalogue of the kinds of abuses that were possible under a system of slavery which as late as 1878 still allowed almost unlimited personal domination. Ironically, the main defendant (three of his slaves, including an overseer, were co-defendants) published these trial documents as a means of exposing an alleged threat to the slave system and perhaps even of clearing his own name—in his mind a possibility, perhaps, since in spite of all the sordid evidence against him, he and his slave accomplices were acquitted, and their behavior was even condoned by judicial authority. Three documents are included: those comprising the accusations, the defense, and the judge's decision. Particularly revealing are Borges's philosophical comments in support of plantation punishment as the sole means available to slaveholders of forcing slaves to work and of maintaining order among them. To clarify the record, in his part of Rio de Janeiro province Borges Rodrigues was widely regarded as an exceptionally callous slavemaster.

Source: Joaquim Borges Rodrigues, *Processo Borges. Attentado politico contra a lavoura em Barra Mansa* (Rio de Janeiro: Typ. Universal de E. & H. Laemmert, 1879), pp. 39-55, 89-91.

❧ *The Accusations*

To the Illustrious Municipal Judge. Sir:

Last September 16 the slave of [Joaquim Borges Rodrigues] named Manoel, about 18 years of age, appeared before the police subdelegate of

24. A Public Whipping at the Praça de Sant'Anna in Rio de Janeiro

this city with an iron hook attached to his neck, and with a chain, also of iron, of about three fathoms in length, suspended from it. On his face there were signs of suffering, his body movements were impeded, and he stated that he had gone there to ask for help. From the questioning which followed and further careful investigation on the part of the police, it was learned that the victim, unable to perform his work, had hidden himself on the plantation, that at the end of three days he was captured, that on the 3rd or 4th of that month at the Desengano farm, by order of his master, he was stripped naked, tied to a stake, and whipped by the slaves André and Paulo, in the presence of the overseer, the slave Joaquim; that the order was for lashes administered with a two-thonged leather whip, that the strokes were numerous and uncounted, and that during the whipping the overseer, Joaquim, incited the others, telling them to beat him as long as he showed signs of life; that, finally, entirely mangled and severely hurt, he was assisted by Marcos Bernardino de Souza, a free man who intervened and prevented continuation of the punishment.

On the same day the victim was taken to his master's presence at the main plantation house. The latter ordered his hair cut along with the attachment of the previously mentioned iron neck piece and chain, and at the end of the chain a tree stump weighing about two *arrobas* [sixty-four pounds] was fastened. The victim was immediately taken back to the Desengano farm, with orders to continue his work, which was picking coffee; and in this condition, without receiving any medical care and incapable of labor, he wandered about the farm for about a week, at the end of which, because of the rain, in a state of suffering and with the tree stump having since been removed, he took refuge with the public authorities.

It appears that not long before this the victim had suffered the same kind of treatment for the same reason, and because of the lack of medical care, his wounds had become full of vermin.

The judicial inquest, as well as the police council's investigation, made by professionals of unblemished reputation and authority, revealed the existence of grave wounds, and the two physical examinations, also made by a group of specialists, confirmed this.

Not long ago the slaves Helena, Benedicto, Maria, and Luzia were punished in the same way, and, concerning the first two, there is physical evidence demonstrating that their wounds were grave.

If it is true that a master can inflict moderate correctional punishment on his slave, it is also certain that that punishment cannot exceed the legal limit, without degenerating into deplorable and criminal abuse subject to penalties; moreover, the Government's decisions of November

5, 1831, and August 11, 1836, stated that the whipping of slaves as punishment cannot exceed fifty lashes, and must never be inflicted all at one time.

And since this practice, which the accused Borges elevated to a regular system of conduct, deeply offends the precepts of religion, morality, and human rights, which every civilized society ought to defend, and constitutes crimes anticipated in Articles 2 and 5 of the Criminal Code, the undersigned offers the following listed testimony and requests that a trial be initiated against the accused and that an order of imprisonment also be written up.

He also requests that an examination be carried out to determine what signs may still remain of the cruel treatment practiced on the slave women, Luzia and Maria.

And since it has been revealed by the investigation that Joaquim Borges Rodrigues possesses about seventy slaves, some two-thirds of whom are of the feminine sex, and that on his plantation there are not more than three or four freeborn children [*menores ingênuos*, children freed by the provisions of the Free Birth Law of September 28, 1871], when it is well known that after passage of the Law of September 28, 1871, the number of children of slaves has increased on all the other estates, I request that a serious investigation be carried out, since there exists presumption of guilt to a high degree. . . .

Barra-Mansa, October 15, 1878. *The public prosecutor, Leonidas Marcondes de Toledo Lessa*. . . .

The Arguments of the Defense

The charge is complex. It contains various facts which require that the defense also be divided into several parts. . . .

THE WOUNDING OF THE SLAVE MANOEL

This is the capital fact which opened this trial. It is about this that the charges mainly deal.

Should the defendant, Joaquim Borges, answer to this charge?

Should the slaves Joaquim, Paulo, and André answer for him?

Let us look at the facts:

CONCERNING JOAQUIM BORGES

According to the declarations of the informants at the inquest and the sworn testimony of the witness Marcos—an important statement since Marcos was the only eyewitness—it is known that the punishment of Manoel was carried out at the Desengano farm.

25. Overseers Punishing Slaves

This place is about a league [four miles] from the Bom-Jardim plantation where the accused lives. On the day of the punishment the defendant was not at the Desengano farm, and so he did not attend the punishment and had not the least knowledge of it.

Therefore he cannot be accused of being the perpetrator of this punishment.

It could be alleged, however, that if Joaquim Borges did not punish, he nevertheless gave the order to punish

This objection is unacceptable, since Joaquim Borges did not directly and intentionally order the application of either severe or mild punishment.

Naturally he recommended to his overseer that, in the event the mulatto Manoel, who had run away, was found, he should be punished.

Now it is understood that this punishment should not be other than that which is customarily applied in such cases, that is, some lashes with a leather whip.

This is exactly what the testimony of folio 54 says when it states that the accused merely recommended that Manoel be given some *lambradas* or blows, which in popular speech corresponds to lashes or strokes with a whip.

It follows, then, that if there was excess, it should not be charged against Joaquim Borges, but rather against the overseers who, exceeding their orders, punished too much.

All that the accused Borges did was to order the wearing of the chain with the tree stump attached.

This, however, is merely a form of correctional punishment which the master may apply at his own discretion and which he is authorized to do by law.

This, then, is not a crime.

Concerning the Slaves Joaquim (the Overseer), Paulo, and André

It was these three who effectively applied the lashes to Manoel which caused the physical offenses to which the evidence refers.

However, do these blows constitute crimes in the strict sense of the law?

The evidence presented and the first physical examination qualified these offenses as serious.

However, the defendant Borges, not agreeing with this interpretation, asked Drs. Silveira Machado and Sant'Anna, distinguished physicians of this city, to examine the patient, and to state if he was entirely cured.

After a careful examination, they declared . . . that the patient was not only completely restored, but also fit to return to agricultural work. . . . [Other doctors examined Manoel, and, although there was disagreement about his condition, two of them claimed that the wounds had not produced a serious threat to his health.]

In conclusion, since this punishment was moderate, it was legal and innocent. Thus, neither the defendant Joaquim Borges nor his overseers are responsible for Manoel's punishment.

Helena's Punishment

None of the witnesses stated that the defendant punished this slave. . . .

Document no. 5 verifies that this woman was purchased in January of this year, which was not long ago, which demonstrates that these punishments were not inflicted during the period of time that this slave belonged to the accused.

This is in accord with document no. 5, where it is fully proved that this slave had brought signs of scrofula when she came from Macahé. At that time her skin was swollen and covered with eruptions and tumors, as normally occurs with this sickness, and these resembled marks of punishment.

In conclusion, the experts declare these marks to be old ones, and so they cannot have resulted from punishments inflicted by the accused, because it was only a few months ago that this slave came under his authority.

Benedicto's Punishment

The evidence from folio 22 divides this slave's punishments into old and new, and concludes that the former were immoderate and serious, and the latter moderate and light.

Now, in document no. 5 it was also shown that the slave Benedicto, who formerly belonged to Severino Francisco da Motta in Piraí, already had signs of punishment when he came under the authority of the accused, signs so numerous that they were visible from a distance.

Thus, these old punishments are those which the experts describe as serious; but the defendant cannot answer for them, because he did not cause them. . . .

The Small Number of Free Children (*Ingênuos*)

Questioned about this, the witnesses stated the following:

Marcos attributed the small number of children not only to the unequal ratio of males to females, but also to the fact that most of the slaves on the plantation of the defendant have come there only recently, so that they have not had time to procreate.

In his testimony, Francisco Silva attributed the small number of children not only to the hot milk of slave women exhausted from their work, but also to the amount of syphilis, with which these women are generally afflicted.

In his testimony Boaventura Nogueira da Silva attributed the small number of children to the great amount of work on the plantations and the women's lack of free time.

It can be seen, then, that the small number of children has been explained in various ways, all of them of an innocent nature or the result of fortuitous circumstances.

No one, however, claimed that this was caused by induced abortions or infanticide.

All the above conditions may be reprehensible or reason for censure, but none of them constitutes a crime, in the strict sense of the word.

General Considerations

Unfortunately, in our country agriculture depends upon slaves. However, the slaves, who do not and cannot possess ambitions and aspirations, do not work unless constrained to do so. Only when compelled by corporal punishment do they cultivate our lands. In the opinion of all the witnesses, punishments are indispensable.

If we were to regard the accused as criminals because they have punished slaves, there would be two possible conclusions: either all the planters would be criminals, or no punishments at all would be possible, however moderate they might be.

We say "however moderate they might be" because a few lashes, or even one, will cause bruises, which can result in tetanus or gangrene and bring about serious health problems and even death.

As long as we have slaves, our system of justice must guarantee this right to the masters, just as it must guarantee his right to his machines.

In a conflict between the master and the slave, in the present order of things our system of justice must take the side of the master, if the latter is not convicted of uncommon perversity or of premeditated murder. Otherwise the reins of discipline will go slack, and we will be incapable of holding back the waves of disobedience.

The defendant cannot be accused of perverse behavior or homicide because, on the contrary, all the witnesses say that he is hard-working, that he makes his slaves work well, and that he provides them with more than sufficient food and clothing.

Appealing to the conspicuous learning of the illustrious judge, to whom the peace of families and public order are confided, the defendant hopes that justice will be done and that this list of charges will be declared entirely lacking in foundation.

Barra-Mansa, November 23, 1878. *Joaquim Borges Rodrigues, and Joaquim de Oliveira Machado, defender of the accused slaves.*

The Judge's Decision

Having seen the evidence; . . .

Considering, in the light of the evidence presented, that Borges Rodrigues ordered the slave, and defendant, Joaquim, in his capacity of overseer at the Desengano farm, to punish with a few lashes the slave Manoel, who had repeatedly run away;

And considering that Manoel, though of minor age, is a person of bad character and a slacker in his work, so much so that he ran away twice; for which reason the order to punish him did not violate the law, but was rather a means of correcting him which is both indispensable and in general use on all the agricultural establishments;

Considering that when the fugitive Manoel was apprehended, the defendant Joaquim did nothing more than comply with his master's orders, inflicting punishment upon him;

Considering that the evidence does not reveal the number of lashes applied to this individual, it not being lawful, in fact, to claim excess or criminal abuse in cases of punishment with the whip, which the law allows to the masters;

Considering that the marks or wounds on Manoel's body were not of a serious nature, it being certain also that before thirty days had passed he was fully recovered and fit for work in the fields;

Considering that any punishment with a whip, however moderate, must leave some marks or stripes on the victim's body, in view of his youth and the sensitivity of his skin, which is less resistant than that of a grown man;

Further considering that, if the punishment administered by the powerful arms of André and Paulo had been prolonged and rigorous, the victim could not have survived, or at least would not have been able to walk an entire league, which is the distance from the Desengano farm to the Bom-Jardim plantation;

Further considering that, even if such punishment had in fact caused serious injury to his health (which incidentally is always more pronounced in the beginning because of the victim's physical reaction), and that nevertheless he was able to make the journey owing to despair or some supreme effort, this would not have been possible certainly on his return to Desengano when he was especially burdened and hindered by the iron at his neck, and the chain attached to the block of heavy wood.

. . .

Considering that, in any case, the defendant Joaquim was obeying the orders of his master, to whom he owes obedience, under pain of being punished himself, which fact precludes criminal intent, and puts him beyond legal sanction, since it was not proved that he exceeded the order which he received;

Considering, finally, that concerning the other slaves, Helena, Benedicto, Luzia, and Maria, there was a lack of proof, the evidence giving no firm basis for a clear condemnation, much less a sentence;

I judge the entire list of accusations with foundation, since they lack legal proof, and I deny recourse in regard to the defendants Joaquim Borges Rodrigues, André, and Paulo, and concede it in Joaquim's case, so that he may be released from prison where he now is; and I order removal of his name from the condemned list, as though he had not been imprisoned; the costs to be paid by the municipality. . . .

Barra-Mansa, February 20, 1879. *José Maria do Valle.*

7.7. Changing Attitudes: The Minister of Justice Cautions Provincial Presidents on the Dangers of Excessive Punishment (1861)

The most brutal forms of punishment were inflicted until the last years of slavery. Nevertheless, as slavery began to be widely recognized as both immoral and impermanent, brutality was more often criticized and therefore perhaps less common. Changing attitudes were reflected in the nation's laws. In the final decades of slavery, for example, the whipping of slaves who committed misdemeanors was often replaced by less damaging *palmatoadas*, or by a fine, or a few days in jail (see Document 6.7).

The following order of the minister of justice, dated June 10, 1861, is further evidence of moderating attitudes, as well as of the disastrous physical effects of traditional punishment.

Source: *Collecção das decisões do Governo de 1861*, p. 289.

❧ *Advice No. 365—Ministry of Justice—June 10, 1861. Ordering the judges to act with caution in the application of the punishment of whipping*

Most Illustrious and Excellent Sir: Since it is essential, as a way to reconcile the law's severity with humane principles, that the application of the penalty of whipping convicted slaves have as its sole aim the necessary punishment for the offense, without danger to life or prolonged and serious damage to the individual's health, His Majesty the Emperor

[Pedro II] wishes Your Excellency to recommend to the judges of your province the greatest caution in this regard, advising them to gradate the punishment to conform with the age and strength of the delinquent, because it is recognized, as physicians claim, that each time the number of lashes exceeds two hundred this is always followed by disastrous results; and that the application of punishment should be suspended as soon as the person, in the doctor's opinion, cannot endure it without danger.

God protect Your Excellency.—*Francisco de Paula de Negreiros Sayão Lobato*.—To the President of the Province of Rio de Janeiro.

The same as well to the Presidents of the other provinces.

7.8. A Government Report of the Deaths of Two Slaves Caused by Brutal Punishment (1887)

As the following selection shows, the government's order of 1861 to moderate slave punishments (see previous selection) was not always heeded. In fact, the cruel incident described here took place in the province of Rio de Janeiro, whose president had been specifically called upon just fifteen years before to take steps to avoid the whipping of slaves beyond their level of endurance. Significantly, the abolitionist, Joaquim Nabuco, denounced this incident in a series of newspaper articles, helping to bring speedy passage of a law the following October that banned the lashing of slaves as punishment in jails and other public establishments. This law, in turn, probably encouraged the vast runaway movement of 1887 which helped to bring a quick end to slavery less than two years later. (See Documents 9 through 11 in Part Ten.)

Source: *Relatorio do Ministerio da Justiça de 12 de Maio de 1887* (Rio de Janeiro, 1887), pp. 39-40.

❧ Rio de Janeiro. District of Parahyba do Sul. On July 27 [1886], while the slaves Alfredo, Thadeu, Benedicto, and Laurindo were being conducted to the plantation of their master, Domiciano Caetano do Valle, two of them died on the road.

Each of these slaves had been condemned to suffer 300 lashes; and the execution of the penalty began on the 21st of June and continued for six nonsuccessive days.

No doctor attended the application of the punishment, but on the second day a doctor was called, the individual Benedicto having manifested nervous disturbances; the doctor attended him, declaring that on June 26 the execution of the punishment might continue.

Each slave received three hundred lashes, fifty at a time, applied with the usual instrument of five strips of raw leather; and, the punishment having been completed, they were treated in the jail by a professional.

While being transferred on the road to their master's plantation, their wrists were tied with thin ropes, and in this way, joined in pairs, they were forced to accompany their guides, who followed on horseback, beating them on the way.

Alfredo and Benedicto died on the road, the doctor who examined the bodies declaring that they had succumbed to pulmonary apoplexy.

In order to carry out the exhumation and autopsy of the bodies, acts required to verify the cause of death, fourteen doctors were summoned. However, nine of these, making various excuses, refused to aid the cause of justice, and the others were unable to perform any work on dead bodies; as a result the examination did not take place.

The judicial inquest verified that the conductors of these slaves caused the deaths of Alfredo and Benedicto; and the public prosecutor of the district pressed charges against João Correia Ventura for having tied the victims' wrists, with their arms behind their backs, and for having beaten them in this condition, so as to force them to walk faster, thereby twice committing the crime of murder.

The establishment of guilt having been initiated, it ran its course, the accused having been sentenced twice to the penalties provided for in Article 193 of the Criminal Code, which, at the appeal, was confirmed by the lower judge of the district.

EIGHT

The Perils of Being Black

IN BRAZIL unwritten but well-accepted criteria determined who was likely to be a slave and who was likely to be free. As we have seen, a black skin, combined with African origin, was strong evidence of slave status, and most slaves, in fact, had black skins. Mulattoes or *pardos*, on the other hand, were more likely to be free *and to be thought of as such*, and, if still held as slaves, were more likely to be liberated than blacks, and to have their freedom respected. The standing of women was also slightly different from that of men. Evidence exists suggesting that a woman's chances of getting free were perhaps three or four times as great as those of a typical male, and her chances were further improved if her skin was light and her place of birth Brazil instead of Africa. To sum up, those persons most likely to be slaves in Brazil were black African males, and those most likely to be freed were light Creole females. Within this broad range, of course, there was much variety and flexibility, and there was much danger of re-enslavement.

It was with these facts in mind that the documents in this part were assembled. While they were intended to show that there was a genuine tradition of manumission in Brazilian society (see Documents 1 through 4) which established the foundations for large free black and mulatto populations, they will also prove that freedom did not come easily to dark-skinned people, as some have claimed, and that once it was achieved, it was by no means certain to last. This reality of oppression and disrespect for the rights of blacks and mulattoes contrasts sharply, in fact, with the well-known but exaggerated Brazilian reputation for benevolence and generosity.

In this regard, it is worth recalling that throughout Brazilian history countless thousands who were held as slaves were in fact legally free. This was true of Indians who were often held illegally as slaves in the colonial period and even in the nineteenth century. It was true of the many so-called *bens do evento*, blacks who for centuries were legally identified with stray cattle and other ownerless animals, and as such were subject to imprisonment, forced labor, and even the ultimate misfortune of being auctioned off as slaves (Documents 5 through 9).

The illegally enslaved included hundreds of thousands of Africans imported into Brazil after November 7, 1831, who, according to the law of that date were to be free the minute they set foot inside the country (see Document 10.8), but who generally remained in a state of servitude for the rest of their lives, along with their descendants. They included the so-called *emancipados* or "free Africans," some ten thousand or more blacks who were rescued from slave ships after 1818 and declared free by Brazilian courts or British-Brazilian mixed commissions, only to be consigned to prolonged periods of forced labor, or to be re-enslaved by the very persons appointed to protect them (Documents 11 through 14). They included, finally (and this by no means exhausts the list), many hapless children of slave women who, according to the Rio Branco Law of 1871, were born free, but whose "services" were placed in public auction in the final years of slavery (Document 15).

Included in this part are five selections dealing with the inter-provincial slave trade, a traffic in human beings which replaced the African slave trade in the mid-nineteenth century as a supplier of workers to the coffee plantations of southern provinces (Documents 16 through 20). These selections echo earlier revelations: property rights were more highly regarded than human rights; the health, dignity, and feelings of slaves were often of little consequence; and the free status of blacks and mulattoes and even obligations of kinship were easily and often violated.

8.1. An Unconditional Grant of Freedom (1851)

Most slaves who lived in Brazil died in slavery, but for individuals, especially mulattoes or other light-skinned people, liberation was a genuine possibility. Most often, perhaps, this occurred when a slave purchased his own freedom or another person did it for him, but it was not unusual for slaveholders to free favorite slaves, especially their own children or women who had served them or their children as wet nurses, or other household servants or favorites whose close personal relationship with the slaveholding family tended to invite such behavior. The following is an example of a voluntary and unconditional grant of freedom.

Source: Doc. 12, 4, 13, No. 77, Seção de Manuscritos, Biblioteca Nacional, Rio de Janeiro.

Letter of Freedom, granted in favor of the black man Manoel, of the Angola nation

No. 76

We the undersigned, Dr. Joaquim Caetano da Silva, a Brazilian citizen, and his wife Dona Clotilde Moinac da Silva, give freedom to our good slave Manoel, of the Angola nation, to enjoy all the rights and guarantees which the laws of our country bestow upon him. And so that it may be verified, documented and entirely clear, we grant him the present Letter, which will be registered in two of the notary offices of this Court, to be manifest for all time. Rio de Janeiro, first of December of eighteen hundred and fifty-one.

[Signed:] Dr. Joaquim Caetano da Silva
Clotilde Moinac da Silva

Witnesses [Signed:]
Dr. Francisco da Paula Menezes
Ignacio José Caetano da Silva
Dr. Fernando Francisco [illegible]

8.2. A Conditional Grant of Freedom (1827)

Recent research in Brazil has revealed that many, if not most, slaves who were freed by their masters were granted only conditional freedom, unless the act of liberation was the result of self-purchase on the part of the slave. Often this meant that the "liberated" man or woman was made to serve his "former" master for a stated number of years, or, perhaps more commonly, until the end of the master's life. The following letter of freedom which the historian, Vivaldo W. F. Daglione, discovered in an archive in the old mining town of Apiaí in southern São Paulo, aside from imposing conditions, threatened to revoke the freedom of the slave concerned, a nine-year-old boy named Cândido, in the event that he disobeyed his master or was ungrateful to him. Indeed, another document found by Daglione (not included here) written eleven years later following the death of Cândido's master, revoked the young man's freedom on grounds of ingratitude, a legal recourse of the owner's heirs which was based conveniently upon an old provision of Portuguese-Brazilian law.

Source: Vivaldo W. F. Daglione, "A libertação dos escravos no Brasil através de alguns documentos," *Anais de História* 1 (1968-1969), 131-134.

❧ Transcript of a letter of freedom which Antonio Pereira Freitas gives to a Mulatto Slave named Cândido, as stated below.

I, Antonio Pereira Freitas, state that among the properties which I possess is a Mulatto Slave by the name of Cândido, of more or less nine years of age, which slave I liberate and possess in a liberated condition from this day forward forever, with the declaration that he serve me while I live [and] that during this entire period of my life he not attempt to free himself by legal means, even if he possesses the money, since he is already free as a result of this my decision, and if at some time he should disobey me or show some ingratitude toward me of the kind stated in the laws, he will lose the freedom which I am granting him and will remain subject to enslavement to my person and heirs whom I may have, and I request His Majesty's justices to comply fully and rigorously with [what is contained herein]. Apiahy, 23 of August, 1827.

8.3. The "Liberation" of Eight Legally Free Children (1878)

The following letter of emancipation, one of a collection of such letters recently discovered in local archives in Minas Gerais, "liberated" eight children whose stated ages revealed that most or all of them were *ingênuos*, that is, children who had been born free as a result of the Rio Branco Law of September 28, 1871. Professor Marina de Avellar Sena, the original publisher of this document, suspected that these children, the offspring of four or five individual slave women, were the natural children of their "liberator." This is a real possibility, since most if not all of the children were mulattoes or *pardos*, and their mothers' master seems to have been particularly eager to assure their free status.

Source: Profa. Marina de Avellar Sena, *Cartas de liberdade* (Belo Horizonte: Promoção-da-Familia Editora, 1975), p. 76.

❧ Letter of Freedom conceded to Felix, Venância, Honório, Felícia, Inácia, Laurinda, Evaristo, and Manoel.

By the present [instrument] by me made and signed, I declare that I concede freedom from this moment on, as if they had been born free, to the following children of my slave women, to wit:

Felix, aged three to four years.

Venância, two years old, and Honório, three years old, *pardos* and children of Maria do Rosario, a Brazilian.

Felícia, seven years old, *parda* and natural daughter of Venância, a Brazilian.

Inácia, six to seven years old, Laurinda, five to six years old, Evaristo, two to three years old, *pardos* and natural children of Francisca, a Brazilian.

Manoel, two years old, *pardo*, natural son of Benedita, a Brazilian.

All of whom are enjoying their freedom as though they had been born free. The present document was made by my free and spontaneous will and so that it may last for all time I grant the Letter of Freedom to assure the rights of the same.

The plantation of Saudade on the twelfth of May of eighteen hundred and seventy-eight. Francisco Xavier Monteiro da Gama.

8.4. A Slave Petitions for Protection from His Master (1876)

One of two selections in this book written by a slave while still a slave (see also Document 9.12), this item was discovered by the historian Warren Dean in a São Paulo archive. According to Professor Dean, this was "the only document written by a slave discovered in a year of searching in Paulista archives."

Its content is largely self-explanatory, but some comments are needed. According to Dean, the original document included a clerk's notation that the writer was a slave named João who belonged to Dr. Luiz José de Melo e Oliveira (a planter), and that in November, 1876, he was in jail in the city of São Paulo. João wrote this letter seeking help in circumstances he described. Promised by his former master, one Colonel Ozoris, that he would be freed after ten years, he was instead sold to Melo e Oliveira after serving Ozoris for five years. Professor Dean observes that promises of eventual freedom were common, and often made to keep slaves at work long enough to assure profits. Such pledges were in fact traditional, going back at least to the eighteenth century (see Document 5.1), and obviously Ozoris's failure to keep his promise was not unusual. Equally rooted in tradition was Ozoris's offer to act as João's godfather, that is, to intercede with the new owner so that the latter would accept him back without punishment.

Dean concludes: "The police files reveal no further clue to João's fate. If he was given a chance to depose, those papers have strayed to other corners of the Archive. Probably he was not heard."

Source: Warren Dean, "A Slave Autograph, São Paulo, 1876," *Luso-Brazilian Review* 7 (1970), 81-83.

❧ I shall by means of this [letter] fall at your feet so that Your Excellency might out of charity look at this for me that I complain of to Your Excellency. Sr. Colonel Ozoris bought me, and when he bought me he told me that he bought me for only ten years and that afterward he would pass me my letter [of manumission]. This he said in front of two persons, saying that they would serve as witness of what he told me. But after serving him five years, he sold me to Sr. Doctor Luiz José de Melo e Oliveira. Since I did not know for how many years he sold me and now since he is maltreating me greatly—by myself therefore I came here [to the provincial capital] to ask him to take me back. He, not wanting to take me back, said to me that he would be my godfather, for me to return with my Master once again. Since I was not wanting to and he ordered me jailed. On account of this I appeal to Your Excellency asking for the love of God that you look at this for me, and thus I beg of your charity that you order me called into your presence so that I might better express myself. Here I remain waiting for Your Excellency to have pity upon me.

8.5. Disposing of Stray Blacks, Beasts, and Cattle (*Bens do Evento*) (1728)

As stated in the introduction to this part, it was by no means easy for free black people in Brazil to maintain their freedom, and sometimes the law itself seemed to be against them. According to traditional Portuguese law, stray animals and cattle, originally referred to as "property of the wind" (*bens do vento* or *evento*), could legally be seized by authorities and, if owners could not be found, sold at public auction. In 1853 the Viscount de Paraná, a member of the Imperial cabinet, wrote that *bens do evento* "are those properties which, without an owner, go wandering from place to place, or move as the wind moves, from whence comes the name." (See *Collecção das decisões do Governo*, 1853, pp. 105-106.)

The next five documents all concern this peculiar Portuguese and Brazilian legal concept which clearly jeopardized the precarious status of many ex-slaves and freeborn blacks and mulattoes. The first, a Royal Letter of 1728, is clear proof that, by at least the early eighteenth century, "slaves" had begun to be associated with beasts and cattle in this category of stray property, despite the moral difficulties involved, and this continued to be true until the last years of slavery.

Source: Archivo do Estado de S. Paulo, *Publicação Official de Documentos Interessantes para a História e Costumes de S. Paulo*, Vol. 18, Avisos e cartas regias, 1714-1729 (São Paulo, 1869), p. 246.

❧ Dom João, by the Grace of God King of Portugal and the Algarves on this side of the sea and on the other side in Africa, Lord of Guinea, etc.—I make known to you, Governor of the Captaincy of São Paulo, that for the convenience of my service the income derived from the slaves who are found without masters, like that from stray cattle [*gado do vento*], ought to be paid to my Royal Treasury, to remain on deposit until I have made a decision on this matter. . . . Done in Lisbon on the second of June of seventeen hundred and twenty-eight. Written by the secretary, André Lopes de Lavre.

8.6. The President of Rio Grande do Norte Regulates Disposal of *Bens do Evento* (1862)

During the nineteenth century both national and provincial governments passed legislation regulating the disposal and sale of *bens do evento*, both human and animal (for a national law, see *Colecção das leis do Imperio do Brasil*, 1859, pp. 452-453). Not only did such laws make homeless or unknown blacks coequal with stray beasts and cattle; they also overlooked the indisputable fact that some blacks and mulattoes might conceivably be free, and ought to possess the right to claim that freedom effectively.

The following regulations issued in 1862 for the disposal of *bens do evento* in the province of Rio Grande do Norte typify this kind of legislation.

Source: *Collecção das leis provinciaes do Rio Grande do Norte. Anno de 1862*, Part 2 (Rio Grande do Norte, 1862), pp. 13-16.

The president of the province, employing the power conferred upon him by Art. 24, Paragraph 4, of the Additional Act, and authorized by Art. 8 of provincial law No. 463 of November 24, 1859, orders that for the disposal of *bens do evento* the following regulations will be followed:

Chapter I. Concerning Bens do Evento

Art. 1. The following are regarded as *bens do evento*:

Para. 1. Beasts and cattle of any type found without identifying marks or brands, or when there is no information concerning who their owners may be, in conformity with Book 3, Title 93.

Para. 2. Runaway or abandoned slaves in the same circumstances as in Paragraph 1.

Art. 2. These properties will be deposited, evaluated, and sold at auction, and the proceeds from their sale will go to the fiscal stations, in conformity with this regulation.

Art. 3. If after three days of efforts and inquiries, the authorities who found or received the properties referred to in Art. 1 have not been able to identify their owners, they will have them transferred to the revenue office administrator or to the fiscal agent to undergo the proper legal procedures, under penalty of a fine of 30$000. . . .

Chapter II. Their Handling and Sale

Art. 4. As soon as he has apprehended or received any *bens do evento*, the administrator or fiscal agent will conduct them to the district judge, so that he may order his clerk to make a record of the properties seized with all explanations needed to avoid future disputes between private persons and the revenue office. . . .

Art. 5. As soon as the administrator or fiscal agent learns, or is informed, that someone has *bens do evento* in his possession, or if such properties are known to exist outside anyone's control, he will immediately take steps to have them seized, requiring the district judge to take all necessary actions for the accomplishment of their apprehension.

Art. 6. After they have been registered, the fiscal agent will post public notices summoning persons who may have a claim to these slaves, cattle, or beasts. These notices should contain a description of the property involved, with all marks and declarations, so that their identity may be verified, as well as the name of the person who found them, and the day, month, and place where they were found.

Art. 7. These notices will be published in newspapers wherever they may exist; one will be affixed to the door of the principal church and, through the medium of the police authorities, they will be proclaimed and affixed in all the populated places of the municipality, for a period of sixty days in the case of slaves and fifteen days in the case of beasts and cattle.

Art. 8. If within the period referred to in the preceding article, no one appears who is entitled to claim ownership of the *bens do evento*, the fiscal agent who holds them on deposit will deliver them to the district judge so that they may be sold in a single auction to the highest bidders. . . .

Art. 9. The auction will be preceded by the posting of a notice on the judge's door for a period of three days, and will take place without fail on the afternoon of the second Sunday after expiration of the period referred to in Art. 7. . . .

Art. 10. No bids will be accepted which are lower than the evaluations of property of identical quality and value in the latest inventories of the property of orphans and adults in the same jurisdiction; in such circumstances, there being no bids equaling the evaluations, this fact will be recorded, with all the circumstances noted, and the same properties will be turned over to the fiscal agent for private sale by him at prices never lower than those previously mentioned. . . .

Chapter III. General Provisions

Art. 13. If prior to the auction the owner of the slave, cattle, or beasts should make his appearance, he will identify the property and justify his possession of it before the fiscal agent, and if his right is recognized, the judge will order the object surrendered to him. . . .

Art. 18. Every three months the district judges will send the provincial treasury a report on the seizures and auctioning of *bens do evento* which have taken place in their respective jurisdictions under penalty, if failing to do so, of a fine of 30$000 imposed by the provincial treasury, subject to appeal to the provincial president.

Art. 19. All dispositions to the contrary are revoked.

Pedro Leão Velloso

8.7. A Public Notice of Human *Bens do Evento* Lodged in a Jail in Paraná (1857)

Provincial and national laws on *bens do evento* normally required that when such "property" was found, notices were to be posted and a certain time was to pass to allow "owners" to identify and make their claims. Meanwhile, human *bens do evento* were to be held in the local jail. The following notice, written in the capital of Paraná in 1857, is perhaps typical. In this case, significantly, two of the four persons involved were mulattoes who claimed to be free men, seemingly to little avail.

Source: Cited by Sebastião Ferrarini, *A escravidão negra na provincia do Paraná* (Curitiba: Ed. Lítero-Técnica, 1971), p. 56.

❧ The office of police makes known to the public that in the jail of the provincial capital are to be found the black man Fiel, who says he is a slave of Tristão Cardoso Menezes; the mulatto Graciano José dos Santos, who claims to be free and is the son of the mulatta Francisca, supposed slave of Cândido de Almeida, a resident of Guarapuava; the light mulatto Cândido, who claims to be free but who has been owned as a slave by D. Libânia Maurícia de Sá Ribas; and the black man Joaquim, who says he is a slave of Inácio Bueno, a resident in the place called Santa Izabel in the province of São Paulo. Those who believe they have a property right to the same should present their petitions to the chief of police, supplied with documents authenticating this right, it being certain that once the period specified by the law has passed, their fate will be that which the law provides for in these cases. Police Office of Paraná, in Curitiba, September 22, 1857.

8.8. An Auction of Human *Bens do Evento* in Rio de Janeiro (1867)

When *bens do evento* were not claimed, the next step was a public auction. The following notice of such a sale, which was to be held in Rio de Janeiro on July 13, 1867, was published in the government newspaper, *Diario Oficial*. As in the previous selection, the persons involved included both creoles and Africans.

Source: *Diario Oficial* (Rio de Janeiro), July 7, 1867.

❧ Dr. André Cordeiro de Araujo Lima, district judge of benefices and pious legacies in this Court of Rio de Janeiro and its precincts, by act of His Imperial and Constitutional Majesty D. Pedro II, whom God keep for many years, etc., etc.—I make known to all who may see this public notice that, by the terms of the regulation of June 15, 1856, there will be auctioned to the highest bidder, on the 13th of the current month of July, at the house doors of No. 101 Alfandega Street, at the close of the court hearings, the following slaves: Vicente, a Mozambique, valued at 100$000; Manoel, a mulatto from Minas Gerais, valued at 600$000; Gregorio, a creole, valued at 200$000; Miguel, a Monjolo, valued at 50$000; José, a mixed mulatto from Rio de Janeiro, valued at 600$000; Hilario, a creole who claims to be a Benguella, valued at 100$000; José, from Angola, valued at 300$000. These slaves have been classified as strays (*do vento*), since, having been detained in the house of correction, and the respective edicts having been published, nobody has yet appeared with the right to claim them. In order that this notice may come to everyone's attention, I order that it also be published in the newspapers. Given in the Court of Rio de Janeiro on July 5, 1867. I, Antônio José Hilarião Barata, temporary clerk, subscribe to it.—*André Cordeiro de Araujo Lima*.

8.9. A Lawyer Deplores the Legal Concept of Human *Bens do Evento* (1873)

As late as 1872 the legal concept of human *bens do evento* remained in full effect. On September 10 of that year, the minister of justice, Manuel Antônio Duarte de Azevedo, in response to an inquiry, wrote to the president of Pernambuco that the slaves regarded as *bens do evento* were not those who had been abandoned by their masters, who were free according to Article 6 of the Free Birth Law of September 28, 1871, but rather those found without knowledge of their masters' identities, in conformity with Article 85 of a government regulation dated June 15, 1859. Concerning such slaves, what had been determined in that regulation, and in other laws, was still to be observed.

This decision of the justice minister, duly published in the *Collecção das Decisões do Governo*, stimulated the following indignant arguments on the legal and moral problems associated with the concept of human *bens do evento*. Written as an article by a lawyer with some personal experience with this legal anachronism, this selection was published in an influential legal journal of Rio de Janeiro only fifteen years before the abolition of Brazilian slavery.

Source: D. F. Balthazar da Silveira, "Doutrina," *O Direito* (Rio de Janeiro) 1 (1873), 249-253.

❧ In the collection of laws and other dispositions of the year 1872 can be found Advice No. 318 of September 10, which still upholds the terrible idea which debases *man* to such a level that he is equalized with *things found on the loose* [*cousas achadas de vento*]!

And this at a time when there is so much talk about ending slavery, and at a time when the Golden Law reigns, which was promulgated on September 28, 1871!

Such an unexpected anachronism, such an *inflexible* evil, has stimulated my wish, already existing before, to reveal some humble thoughts aroused by my amazement at seeing upheld in the nineteenth century, in the so-called century of enlightenment, such a shameful doctrine.

Among the old *statutes* there is no regulation which includes slaves among *bens do vento* (today "*de evento*"), as is revealed by reading and combining Ordinance Book 2, Title 26, Paragraph 17, and Title 32, with Ordinance Book 3, Title 94.

And the same may be said of the *Repertorio das Ordenações* [Collection of ordinances] where it refers to stray property [*bens vagos*] as well as to beasts found on the loose [*bestas achadas do vento*].

And a reference to Ordinance Book 5, Title 62, and to Paragraphs 1 and 2 on runaway slaves, does not lead us to such a classification, does not order them to be confined and auctioned off. This, however, it does determine in regard to beasts and cattle in Paragraph 7, in which it orders that the Ordinance of Book 3, Title 94, be observed.

In legislation passed after the *Ordenações* we find the provisions of March 26 and April 3, 1720 (*Systema dos Regimentos*, Vol. 3, pp. 176-177), which order the district judge to confine slaves whose masters are unknown.

However, despite the severity of that epoch, despite the predominating attitudes, nobody is included in this designation except individuals clearly recognized as slaves, that is, those who said they were slaves but could not tell who their masters were, and whom it was not possible to regard as free, considering their recent arrival from the coast of Africa. This was a sad consequence of the hard necessity of their importation. At the present time such a case can no longer exist because, no matter how coarse the individual may be, he is able to tell whether he is a slave and to whom he belongs; and in such cases the general rule in favor of freedom ought to prevail. And with good reason, since every person is regarded as free by the principles of natural law, as is demonstrated by the Ordinances of Book 4, Title 11, Paragraph 4; Title 42; Title 61, Paragraph 1; the Decree of July 30, 1609; the Law of April 1, 1680; the Law of June 6, 1755, Paragraph 9, etc.

Slave status is never presumed, and so an individual who, because of his situation and circumstances, may arouse suspicion and attract the attention of the authorities, cannot and should not be considered a slave, unless he confesses it or it is proved in a legal way. Otherwise he is free.

If he confesses, or it is proved that he is a slave, he is returned to his master, who is responsible for any expenses that may be incurred.

And it cannot be denied that there are dangers which ought to be avoided, and that it is to the interest of all to prevent abuses and scandals. A person of black color or a mulatto who is suspected of being a slave is seized, but he is a deaf-mute or so feebleminded that he is like a brute. He cannot read, he cannot write, he doesn't know how to explain himself in any sure or certain manner. He is declared to be a piece of stray property [*bem do evento*] and is sold to the highest bidder!

Who can really be sure that he is a slave? On the contrary, he should be regarded as free, and the procedure of the authorities should be in conformity with this status.

When I was a judge in the Court of Pernambuco, I intervened in a trial which revealed to the public the scandal that involved the black man Manoel, who was married, a carpenter, and resident of the city of Recife. He was seized as a slave in an interior town and, despite testifying that he was a freedman, despite his claim that he had a certificate of emancipation, he was auctioned off as stray property.

And the most astonishing fact is that *interested persons* said that Manoel was a slave of the friars of St. Benedict, and instead of sending him to his supposed masters they proceeded to auction him off!

The black man's appearance and his profession aroused their greed.

Fortunately the Court of Pernambuco, by a decision of April 5, 1859, ruled in favor of the freedom of Manoel, who had been *less fortunate* in the judicial district of Rio Formoso.

But how can the harm, the torments, the beatings which he suffered be repaired?

I think it will be appropriate to recall the example which occurred when I exercised the post of judge in the capital of the Province of Maranhão.

While on circuit, a case was presented to me from the office of the purveyor based upon a letter, No. 13 of December 22, 1847, from the President of the Province, in which His Excellency had ordered the Municipal Judge of the 2nd District of the Capital to comply with Chapter 5 of the Regulation of May 9, 1842, in regard to four individuals: the *cafre* [Kaffir] Henrique; the *crioulo* [creole] José; the *pardo* [mulatto] Venancio; and the *cabra* [goat] Felix, who had been found among the Matteiros Indians and apprehended in 1846, not knowing a single word of the Portuguese language, not being able to offer information about themselves, having merely some evidence of having been carried off by the savages when they were still babies. They were looked upon as slaves, and as such *bens do evento*.

I ordered a delay in this trial and wrote at once to the president of the Province (on June 14, 1850), making him see how, according to legal principles, they should be regarded as free. The president fully informed the Imperial Government, and the latter declared that they should be regarded as free, and ordered that they be employed in the service of the port registry office. What is even more shocking, however, is that with the previously mentioned Golden Law in effect, this damned absurdity not only is not extinct, but there can appear the Advice of September 10, 1872, which is signed by a Minister who professes the ideas of conservatism, and whose learning is also recognized.

If that Law in its 6th article declares slaves of unclaimed inheritance to be free, as well as slaves abandoned by their masters, how can an evil which without question was always incompatible with the principles of freedom and civilization continue, and especially so since 1871!?

So much is being said, one hears so many cries in favor of freedom and progress, and a man can still be a *thing found on the loose*! . . .

Rio de Janeiro, September 16, 1873. D. F. Balthazar da Silveira.

8.10. The Precariousness of Freedom: The Statement of a Black Man Named John Eden (1843)

The following is a black man's personal account of his misadventures in Brazil dictated on board the British vessel *Crescent*, which in 1843 was docked in the harbor of Rio de Janeiro. The situations he described were not typical, since Eden was the slave of Englishmen (illegal under British law), had lived in Britain and spoke English, and so was more capable than most blacks in Brazil of seeking foreign assistance. Yet it gives some impression of what could happen in more typical cases: those of Africans or other blacks without contacts with foreign whites and with no knowledge of any legal rights they might possess.

Source: *British and Foreign State Papers*, Vol. 32 (1843-1848), pp. 261-262.

Statement of John Eden

I was a slave in the Brazils, and became the property of Charles Tross and Co., Arthur Moss being a partner in the same firm; shortly after, I became the sole property of Arthur Moss, the other partners giving up their rights to the said Arthur Moss. About 9 years afterwards, Mr. Moss gave me my freedom at the Consul's office at this place. Soon after Mr. Moss went to England in Her Majesty's ship *Spartiate*, who took me as his private servant. [Moss probably freed Eden because he could not legally take a slave to England. By setting foot there, Eden would in any case have become free under British law.] I was one year in England with Mr. Moss, still in the capacity of private servant.

On the 8th March, 1836, Mr. Moss returned to Rio de Janeiro on board Her Majesty's schooner *Spider*, bringing me with him as a free servant. [Under the Brazilian law of November 7, 1831, Eden would again have become legally free, even if at this stage he had been a slave, since, according to that law, any slave entering Brazil from abroad was legally free.] Sometime in August, 1839, I went to the Consul's office at Rio de Janeiro, and declared that some months after my return from England Mr. Moss sold me to a person residing in the mining district in the interior, where I remained about a twelvemonth. The same person brought me back to Mr. Moss, who sent me to Mr. Platt, a British resident at this place, from whose house I went to the Consul to claim his protection. I continued at Messrs. Platt and Reid's until about October, when I obtained a situation, on wages, on board one of the steamboats, as a free Negro. A month after I joined the steamer, I went on shore, with the master's leave; and shortly after landing, I was arrested by a "capitão de matto" (a bushranger for capturing runaway blacks) and was taken to the residence of Mr. Moss at Praia Flamingo, where I was put in irons, the next day sent to the House of Correction, and kept there at hard labour, in irons, for 6 months. I was then sold to Bernardino da Souza, a resident at St. Domingos, on the other side of the water, who came for me to the House of Correction, and kept me working as a slave during 4 months. On the 26th September, 1840, I succeeded in making my escape, and took refuge at the Consul's office, and was sent by the Consul on board Her Majesty's receiving ship, *Crescent*, for safe custody, till further orders from Her Majesty's Minister at this Court.

Dated on board Her Majesty's receiving ship *Crescent*, at Rio de Janeiro, this 27th day of March, 1843.

Witnesses:
M. Donellan.
Th. S.S. Gabriel.

his
JOHN X EDEN
mark.

I, the Undersigned, do hereby certify that the foregoing is a true copy of an original declaration made by a Negro, and to me produced under the signatures of Lieutenant Donellan, commanding Her Majesty's ship *Crescent*, and of Mr. Gabriel, the clerk on board said vessel.

ROBERT HESKETH

8.11. A Royal Decree Condemning "Free Africans" to Fourteen Years of Involuntary Servitude (1818)

The hazards faced by free blacks in Brazil are forcefully revealed by the experiences encountered by the so-called *emancipados* or *africanos livres* (free Africans), more than 10,000 African importees who were legally free, but kept in a state of de facto servitude, some for perhaps as long as half a century. The fate of these "free Africans," who should be distinguished from the much larger group of "free" persons who were landed in Brazil in violation of the anti-slave-trade law of November 7, 1831, will be revealed in the following five documents.

The peculiar status of the *emancipados* was the result of Great Britain's imposition in 1815 of a treaty to prohibit participation of Portuguese subjects in slave trading on the African coast north of the equator. In an Additional Convention of 1817, Britain and Portugal agreed that an international mixed commission, established at Rio de Janeiro to judge illegal traffickers in slaves, would also have the power to liberate Africans found aboard the ships which it condemned. These Africans were to be employed as "servants or free laborers," and each government pledged to guarantee the freedom of Africans consigned to it.

In compliance with this agreement, on January 26, 1818, King João issued a decree to enforce the partial slave-trade ban. The following excerpt from that decree established the government's system for dealing with liberated Africans which, though protective in spirit, condemned them to fourteen years of involuntary servitude.

Source: *Collecção das leis do Brasil de 1818*, p. 9.

❧ The slaves consigned to my Royal Treasury by the means prescribed in the above 7th article of the Mixed Commissions regulations, and all the other persons liberated in the manner described above, will be turned over to the custody of the district auditor's council, and, where this body does not exist, to that which is responsible for the preservation of the Indians, whose duties will be usefully increased.

Since it would not be correct simply to abandon them, they will be destined to serve as freedmen [*libertos*] for a period of 14 years in some public service, either for the navy, at the forts, in agriculture, or in the mechanical trades, whichever may be most convenient, being registered for this purpose at the various government posts. Or they may be publicly rented out to private persons of recognized integrity, who will sign a pledge to feed and clothe them and to teach them Christian doctrine and a craft or other suitable work. For the time stipulated [one year], these terms and conditions may be renewed as often as necessary until the above-stated period of 14 years is completed. However, this period may be reduced by two or more years for those freedmen who, by their fitness and good conduct, prove themselves worthy sooner of enjoying their complete right to freedom.

When they are destined for public service in the above-stated manner, whoever is in charge of the government post concerned will name an able person to sign the above-mentioned pledge, who will be responsible for the education and training of the freedmen. They will also have a guardian [*curador*], a person of recognized integrity, who will be named every three years by the judge and approved by the Privy Council of the Court, or by the Governor or Captain General of the province concerned. This official will have the responsibility to demand every measure which promotes the welfare of the freedmen. He will censure abuses, see to it that they are exempted from work at the proper time, and for their general welfare he will promote observance of everything which the law requires in favor of orphans, in so far as it may apply to them, and he will always be consulted when the above-mentioned judge issues any order that is relevant to their condition.

8.12. A Scottish Doctor Reports on the Mistreatment of "Free Africans" (1838)

The *emancipados* or "free Africans" may be divided into two groups: those taken at sea by ships of the British Navy, brought to Rio, and there freed by the British-Brazilian mixed commission, all prior to 1845, when that international court ceased to exist; and a smaller group consisting of Africans seized by Brazilian officials either on land or at sea and freed by Brazilian judicial authorities. Involved as it was in creating this category of Africans, the British government remained concerned for their welfare until 1864, when the Brazilian government at last decreed the full freedom of all *emancipados* who were then still alive. Reflecting this British interest is the following description of the mistreatment of Africans witnessed by Dr. William Cullen, a Scottish physician who was assigned to medical service in Rio during the 1830s. In this letter to a member of the House of Lords, Dr. Cullen gives the impression that every abuse against "free Africans" which Dom João's decree was intended to prevent was being practiced by that same array of officials whom the Portuguese king had assigned to protect them. Apparently even the British commissioners were exploiting the situation.

Source: *Class A. Correspondence Relating to the Slave Trade (1837-1838), Further Series* (London, 1838).

❧ It is quite common in Rio de Janeiro to hear all classes declaiming, particularly before strangers, against the disgraceful traffic [in slaves], as they call it; at the same time it is perfectly well known, that there is not a man amongst them who will not smuggle Africans into the country whenever an opportunity offers. . . . But the worst part of the matter is, that not one of the Africans is ever set at liberty. From the chicanery and perfidy of the Brazilian government, and the total want of efficiency on the part of the Mixed Commission, the condition of the Africans that are seized, is rendered a thousand times worse than if they had been allowed to remain in the hands of the smugglers. The smugglers would have sold them to persons who, generally speaking, would take care of them upon the same principle that domestic animals are cared for; whereas, from the indecision and negligence of the Mixed Commission, they are detained, unwholesomely crouched together, till their numbers are reduced by sickness, and the remainder are apprenticed for fourteen years, which ends in perpetual slavery. The individuals who obtain these apprentices are solely persons who have interest with the parties who hire them out, and it is an understood thing, that after a year or two not one of the Africans is ever heard of.

One half-year's hire is paid down when the apprentice is hired, and the party enters into an obligation to produce him when called upon by the Juiz dos Orfãos (Judge of Orphans), who is as great a rascal as any of the others; but the consequence of all this is, that the contracting party brings proof that his apprentice has run off, or that he is dead. This commonly takes place before the termination of the first year. A usual trick to which they resort is to produce a dead slave either from the Hospital or from the Misericordia [the Charity Hospital in Rio de Janeiro for the indigent poor], or from some of their friends who may have one that has died. A kind of inquest is held, and the apprentice is pronounced to have died a natural death. At other times they come before the judge with witnesses to prove that the apprentice has run off, as they have no lack of witnesses, who will swear to anything for a few patacs [*pataca*: a Brazilian silver coin worth 320 *réis*]. But as the Judges, Justices of the Peace, Clerks, &c. are all in collusion to defeat the purposes for which the Mixed Commission has been appointed, and as the members of it at Rio de Janeiro are certainly neglectful of their duty, it is as clear as the sun at noon, that the said Commission is no better than a dead letter. It has never rescued one African from slavery. In proof of this assertion I shall state facts, which show that the ill-timed and ineffectual interference of the Mixed Commission, instead of alleviating the sufferings of the poor Africans, has been productive of nothing but misery and death.

About the beginning of 1834 a small schooner (I think the name was the "*Duqueza de Bragança*") was captured by one of her Britannic Majesty's cruizers, and brought into Rio de Janeiro, having on board between three and four hundred Africans, mostly children; these poor creatures had suffered from their long confinement in such a small vessel, and it is believed a great many died on the passage. By the humanity of the late Admiral Sir Michael Seymour, . . . they were taken on shore and properly cared for; otherwise the mortality amongst them after landing must have been greater than it was. The Mixed Commission delayed giving judgement in the matter till the end of June, when they condemned the schooner, and adjudged the Africans to be free. But what was the destination of these free Africans. They were reduced by death to 288, all of whom were sent to the house of correction to work for the Brazilian government.

I called at this house of correction eight days after their arrival there, when 7 more had died, and there were then 35 sick, confined in a small room, lying on the floor, without bed or covering of any kind, with their heads to the wall, and their feet towards the centre, leaving a narrow path between the rows. A young Brazilian, calling himself a Surgeon, was paying them his daily visit at the time I called. . . . The same day I saw about one hundred of these children in an apartment on the ground floor, sitting all round on their heels, after the fashion of the country, and looking most miserable. I was glad to get away from the degrading sight, where human beings were treated much worse than dogs, and all this under the cloak of humanity. On the November following I again visited the house of correction, and learned that out of the 288 sent there in June 107 had died; and a great many more were sick. The Brazilian government at this time advertised to hire out the survivors on apprenticeships for fourteen years. Several gentlemen, both English and French, immediately applied, and were most desirous to

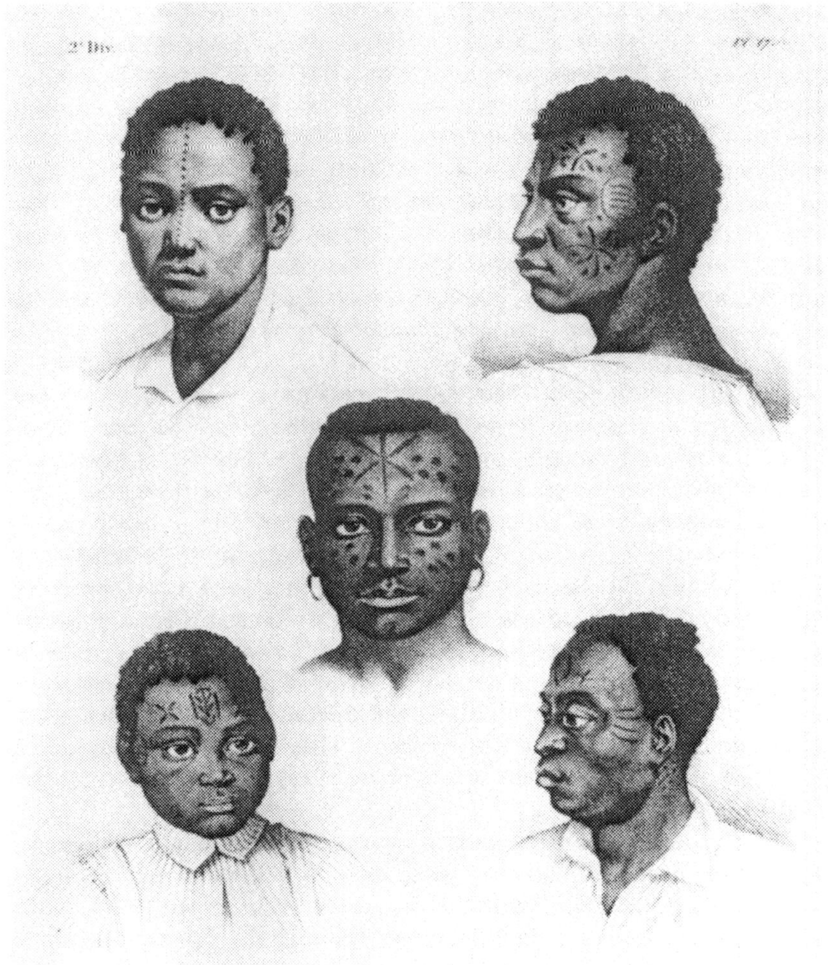

26. Mozambique Slaves

obtain, some one, and others two or more of these apprentices. Although numerous applications were made on the very day the advertisement appeared in the *Diario* [then the official government newspaper in Rio de Janeiro], not one was served but the parties themselves who had the hiring of them, and their immediate friends. The only Englishmen who obtained any were those belonging to the Mixed Commission. All the others were given to Brazilians and Portuguese. . . .

About the months of October or November, 1834, a British ship-of-

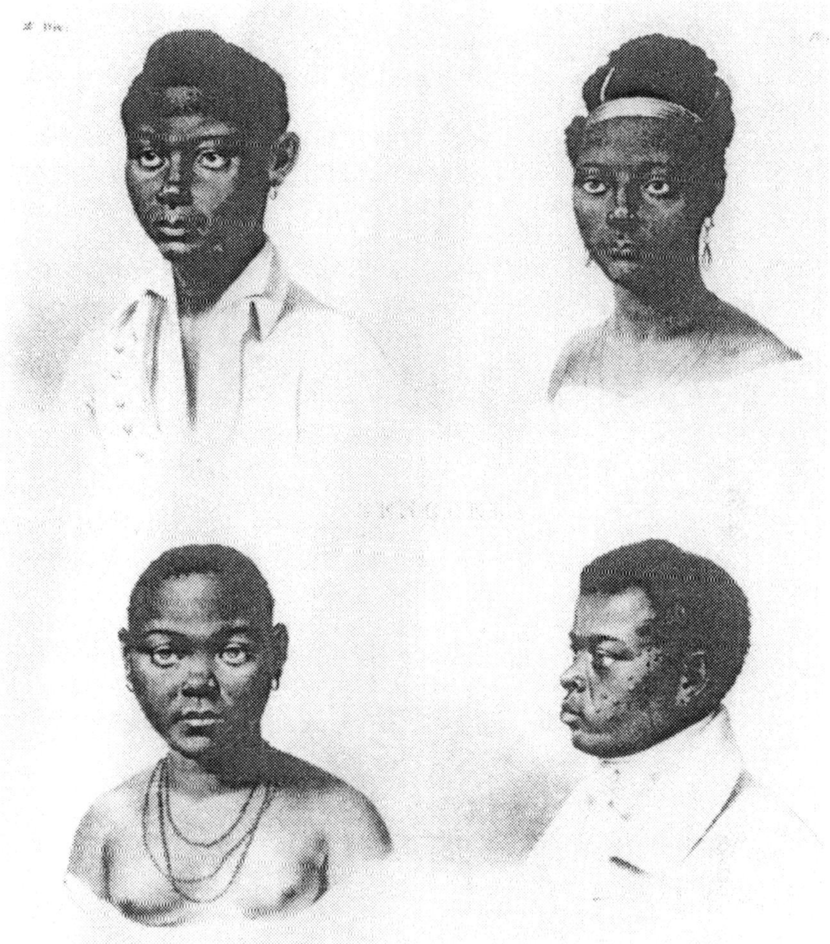

27. Benguela and Congo Slaves

war brought into the port of Rio de Janeiro a slaver, with about 400 Africans, who were landed by order of the Mixed Commission, and a guard, judged to be sufficient, placed over them. A few nights after they were put on shore, the guard was surprised in the middle of the night by a band of fellows, pretending to be justices of the peace, rigged out with ribbons, cocked-hats, &c., who carried off 200 Africans, and next day no traces of them could be found. Those that remained were taken to the House of Correction, and disposed of in the Brazilian fashion.

I remember an occurence, and although I have not note of the date of it here, yet it is, perhaps, worth mentioning. There were 30 negroes, more or less, conducted by a white man for the Praia Ibamingo, a short distance from the city, where they had been landed in the dusk of the evening, who were apprehended by some tide-waiters [customs officials], they considering them to be new blacks, which upon examination they actually found them to be. They likewise discovered them to bear the [brand] mark of His Excellency Senhor [Pedro de Araújo] Lima, the Regent, on their backs. After giving information of the seizure to the Justice of the Peace of the district where they were seized, the negroes, as well as the white man, were ordered by him to be put in a house of deposit, and the keys thereof to be lodged with himself, the said Justice of the Peace, till the following morning, when an examination should take place. All this was performed according to orders, and the Chief of Police acquainted therewith that same evening. Next day the competent judges assembled for the purpose of examining the captured; directions were given to call them in before the Tribunal, but behold! where were they? The messenger arrives and exclaims, "*Senhores, Senhores, a casa de deposito está vazia e as portas achei mesmo fechadas a chave*" (The place of deposit is empty, and the doors locked). The white prisoner and captured Africans had been let out by order of the Chief of Police, because the Africans belonged to the Regent [then acting head of state in place of the youthful Emperor, Dom Pedro II]. Nothing more was heard of them.

8.13. An Ex-Guardian of "Free Africans" Describes Their Treatment (1866)

The following account of the conditions of "free Africans" is by a Brazilian who was particularly qualified to write an opinion on the subject. This was the prominent legal historian, Agostinho Marques Perdigão Malheiro, who in the 1860s wrote a classic study of Brazilian slavery (see Document 6.1), from which this statement is taken. As this selection's style suggests, Perdigão Malheiro's interest in "free Africans" was not merely legal and scholarly. Having served earlier in his life as guardian (*curador*) of "free Africans" in Rio de Janeiro, he described their plight with the concern which results from personal experience, implying that a major cause of their mistreatment was their color.

Source: Agostinho Marques Perdigão Malheiro, *Escravidão no Brasil: Ensaio histórico-jurídico-social*, 2 vols., 2nd ed. (São Paulo: Edições Cultura, 1944), II, 70-72.

❧ The lot of these miserable people, both those working in towns and in rural areas, was in fact equal, or even worse, than that of the slaves. Belonging to the black race like the others, they were placed on the same level because of their color; but, not being slaves, they were not treated as well as the latter, or at best the same. Service and labor day and night; punishments; a lack even of necessities, or a scarcity of food and clothing; they slept on the ground in unsuitable places, exposed to disease; education was a dead letter. The children were cast into foundling homes in order to hire out their mothers as wet nurses, which caused the government to declare this prohibited by an order of April 11, 1846.

In cities the blacks were sent out to work or were employed in other profitable ways by private persons, not as the personal servants of those highest bidders, as they ought to have been according to the instructions. Black women, for example, were used mainly as wet nurses. To sum up, the free African was dealt with exactly like a slave. The abuse and scandal reached the extreme of substituting dead slaves having the same name for free Africans, in this way reducing the latter to slavery! And the children of free African women were baptized as slaves!

Loose living, vices, ignorance, an utter lack of moral and religious education, turned them into brutes. The grantees were careful only in extracting from them the greatest possible material advantage as instruments of labor, in exchange for a ridiculous and paltry price of 12$000 per year, which was the average bid for their services. Thus the grantees generally earned more in a month than they were required to pay in a year.

Truth requires the mentioning of some honorable exceptions among the grantees, who behaved in an honorable and Christian fashion. Generally speaking, however, they were concerned only with the extraordinary advantages to be gained from their services for such a pittance, which nevertheless they often failed to pay. They wished to live from the sweat of the free Africans exactly as from the slave. The best regulations were evaded through the spirit of profit, ever fertile and open to abuse.

8.14. An "*Emancipado*" Is Granted His Final Certificate of Freedom (1864)

This official document liberating an African named Cézar, was the direct result of the imperial decree of September 24, 1864, which ordered that all surviving *emancipados*, who decades before had been rescued from slave ships, were at last to receive their final letters of emancipation. This was not the first time, however, that Cézar had been freed. According to another document which accompanied this one (not published here) this Congo African, who was distinguished by a brand mark in the shape of a "V" on his left breast, had already been declared "free and emancipated" on July 26, 1838, to be employed as an apprentice for fourteen years. Although that apprenticeship had evidently lasted for more than twenty-six years, even as an old or middle-aged man Cézar was obliged by this final certificate of emancipation to register the place where he intended to live and the "honest occupation" with which he intended to support himself.

Source: Partially printed and partially handwritten document among Documentos sobre a repressão ao tráfico de africanos no litoral fluminense, in Secretaria de Educação e Cultura, Departamento de Difusão Cultural, Biblioteca Pública do Estado, Niterói, Rio de Janeiro.

Captain Francisco Xavier, Cavalier of the Imperial Order of Christ and of the Rose, Judge of Orphans *substituting* in This Imperial City of Nichtheroy, etc.

I make it known, in virtue of decree No. 3310 of September 24 which was communicated to me in a message from the Imperial Government of October 8, 1864, that the African *Cézar*, of the *Congo* nation, is emancipated. And whose characteristic features are in the margin. The same African having the full enjoyment of his freedom, being however obligated to declare in the police headquarters of this province the place in which he intends to reside, and the honest occupation from which he intends to live, and making such a declaration whenever he wishes to change his domicile. And as proof of his title I ordered the granting of the present certificate, which is signed by me. Given and granted in this imperial city of *Nichtheroy* the *12 of December of 1864*. And I *Pedro Henriques da Cunha Lopes*.

CHARACTERISTIC FEATURES
Height *56 inches*
Face *round*
Beard *none*
Color *black*
Eyes *large*
Nose *flat*
Mouth *ordinary*
Lips *ordinary*
Teeth *good*
Ears *small*
Hands and feet ordinary, the latter being small.

SPECIAL FEATURES
Lacks two teeth in the lower jaw. Has the mark V on his left breast.

8.15. The Services of "*Ingênuos*" (Freeborn Children of Slave Women) Are Placed in Public Auction (1882)

The Rio Branco Law of September 28, 1871, freed the children of slave women born from that date on, but their mothers' masters possessed the legal right to employ the "services" of these so-called *ingênuos* from the age of eight until the age of twenty-one, this right to their labor having been regarded as a way to compensate slaveholders for the costs of rearing free children. Although nothing was said in the law about the masters' right to *sell* these "services," the following letter from the abolitionist, Joaquim Nabuco (see Document 10.6), to the head of the imperial cabinet, Viscount de Paranaguá, shows that in 1882 those services were indeed placed in auction by at least one government official, along with Africans too young to have entered Brazil before 1831 (and therefore legally "free"), children too young to have been born into slavery, along with a host of crippled, diseased, and aged black people. Nabuco's letter communicates anger and dismay, but he of course knew that such abuses of black people's rights had long been practically routine.

Source: Joaquim Nabuco, *Cartas a amigos*, 2 vols. (São Paulo: Instituto Progresso Editorial, 1949), I, 76-78.

London, November 6, 1882

Most Excellent Counselor Paranaguá:

As a Brazilian citizen I judge it my duty to call Your Excellency's attention to a public notice of the purveyor's court [of the town] of Valença, dated September 22, 1882, and signed by the clerk, Gaudêncio Cesar de Mello. This notice, which was published in the *Jornal do Comércio* of October 7, invites offers for an auction of slaves and *ingênuos*, in which Africans under fifty years of age (when the law of November 7, 1831, *which was never revoked*, is fifty years old) appear alongside slaves of *ten years of age* (when the law of September 28, 1871, is already eleven years old), and alongside *ingênuos* only *a few days old*, placed in this way on sale as if this latter law had not been recorded in the legislation of Valença or did not exist among the laws of the State. Thus put on sale in this notice are, for example, "the services of the *ingênua* Georgina, black, 1 year old, daughter of Cândida, valued at 20$; the services of the *ingênuo* Benedito, creole, six months old, son of Damasina, valued at 20$; the services of the *ingênua* Orminda, a mulatta, three months old, daughter of Clara, valued at 20$000; the services of the *ingênua* Leonídia, a mulatta, a few days old, daughter of Alcina, valued at 10$000."

I do not know of a greater prostitution of justice than this notice from its beginning to its end! My hand shakes with indignation as I call the imperial government's attention to this judicial trafficking in *ingênuos*. The audacity of placing *ingênuos* only a few months or days old on public auction nearly makes one forget the audacity with which the local magistrates put up for auction Africans who (according to the recorded age which when stated in a notice of sale is bona fide information) were *necessarily* imported after the law which declared free all slaves who might enter the territory or a port of Brazil coming from outside. In this notice the following *slaves* are announced: "Marcelina, at 80$000; Manuel, creole, ten years old, son of Rosinha, valued at 700$000" (and two others). Can there be ten-year-old slaves in Brazil in 1882?

I will not call Your Excellency's attention to the following slaves: "Agostinho, black, 33 years old, leprous, valued at 300$000; Manuel, from Cabinda, 76 years old, blind, valued at 50$000; João, from Mozambique, 86, valued at 50$000" and others, because the written law was not violated in those odious aberrations of public morality, even though these unfortunate people might rightfully protest against our country, where lepers, the blind, and persons over 80 are auctioned off as *slaves* and the public authorities do not confine them to some public asylum. In what article of the law of September 28, 1871, are public auctions of *ingênuos* authorized, or the sale of their services?

The law of November 7, 1831, which abolished the traffic is revoked de facto; but the moment has come to demonstrate to the Government that this cannot be the fate of the law of September 28, 1871. We must stop this traffic in *ingênuos* which is beginning to appear. It is not by concealing scandals of this kind that this can be accomplished. That advertisement from Valença opens a very sad page in the history of Brazil and it is Your Excellency's responsibility to rip it out at once. If the sale of the ingênuos' *services* begins, with or without public notices, the world will soon regard the law of September 28 like any other monstrous lie which a nation resorts to in order to conceal a crime. The auction was scheduled for October 26, and by now it will already have taken place; nevertheless, the public authority will possess ways of pursuing the criminals and of rescuing the innocent. The question is the following: Can or cannot the *ingênuos* be sold? It is the responsibility of the Government to salvage the dignity of this entire immense class which was brought into being by the law of September 28. I write to Your Excellency with complete confidence in your intentions and I hope you will grant your full attention to the object of this letter.

Yours with the greatest consideration.

Your beholden friend and servant.

JOAQUIM NABUCO.

8.16. "This Very Barbarous and Inhuman Traffic": A Bahian Planter-Politician Seeks to Abolish the Inter-Provincial Slave Trade (1854)

After the African traffic was largely suppressed in 1851, the transporting of slaves for sale between the provinces, a trade long in existence, began to take on a growing importance, and increasing numbers of creole slaves from such provinces as Maranhão, Ceará, Pernambuco, Sergipe, and Bahia began to replace the declining African population on southern coffee plantations in such provinces as Rio de Janeiro, São Paulo, and Minas Gerais. In response to this growing movement, which was carried on overland as well as by sea, in 1854 a prominent member of the Chamber of Deputies from Bahia, João Maurício Wanderley (later the Baron Cotegipe), proposed a law to ban the sale or transportation of slaves over provincial borders or by sea from one province to another. As this speech in defense of his bill reveals, Wanderley was not motivated solely by humanitarianism. A more important reason for this legislation was the loss of manpower which northern provinces were suffering as a result of the "new traffic in human flesh," and the potentially disastrous effects of this loss upon northern agriculture. This document, while providing insights into the functioning and human consequences of this traffic, also reveals something of the attitude of the Brazilian planter class toward slaves as property. This is as true of the hostile or supportive comments which Wanderley's speech provoked among his colleagues as it was of his speech itself. This fiery afternoon debate is also clear evidence of the growing differences between northern and southern provinces on the question of slavery—the result in part of that very shift of the slave population which Wanderley tried but failed to stop. Wanderley's bill was rejected by the Chamber, and the traffic continued until at least 1881.

Source: *Annaes da Câmara dos Senhores Deputados* (1854), IV, 345-350.

❧ Mr. *Wanderley* (*Profound silence*): Mr. President, this session is already so far advanced, and the discussion of this bill so long delayed, that I have no hope that it can be approved in the few days that remain to us, even if it deserves the acceptance of the Chamber. I would not make a strong effort to defend it if I did not judge it my duty, as its author, to respond to two illustrious deputies [José Inácio Silveira da Mota, representing São Paulo, and Viriarto Bandeira Duarte, representing Mato Grosso], who have been moved by their consciences to oppose it. I believe, Mr. President, that the bill contains materials of urgent necessity

(*Hear! Hear!*), of great benefit to the Empire, and especially to the northern provinces.

A *Voice*: Not supported.

Many *Deputies*: Supported.

Mr. *Wanderley*: [The illustrious deputy from the province of São Paulo, Mr. Silveira da Mota] began by opposing the bill as unconstitutional. . . . [He] said that the bill attacked the right to property because it diminished the full right which any citizen has to dispose of his property, placing limitations . . .

Mr. *Silveira da Mota*: It kills the right to property.

Mr. *Wanderley*: The illustrious deputy now goes beyond what I attributed to him, because he now asserts that the bill kills the right to property. Mr. President, property cannot be destroyed by the laws emerging from this Chamber, but it can be restricted, and it has been, as the illustrious deputy himself recognized, quoting many laws that have done just that. The right to place limitations on property is not based solely on the property interest, as the honored member said; it is based mainly upon the interests of society and those of the state. When a society demands that the property right be restricted for the benefit of that society or of the state, obviously this limitation will not only be constitutional, but will also be based on every legal principle. (*Hear! Hear!*) . . .

Now, gentlemen, if this is true generally of property, what happens when we deal with property rights that are based upon an abuse? (*Hear! Hear!*) Does not society have the right to restrict that abuse, to act in such a way that it will be less harmful to that society? (*Hear! Hear!*) . . .

The illustrious deputy from Mato Grosso tells me: "I may use and abuse my property. This is one of the results of ownership."

Mr. *Viriato*: That is correct.

Mr. *Wanderley*: Yes, you may abuse your property in general, but you may not abuse your human property. (*Hear! Hear!*) If it is your understanding that you may abuse it to the point of destroying it, such an abuse could take you to the gallows. (*Hear! Hear!*) The illustrious deputy may destroy a house, may set fire to it without any interference; but if he does the same to a slave he will see what happens to him in the eyes of the law. (*Well stated.*)

Mr. *Viriato* makes a comment.

Mr. *Wanderley*: Whatever the meaning of the word "abuse" may be, what I am demonstrating is that the owners of that special or unique property are restricted in certain ways which cause all the arguments based on property rights which the illustrious deputies present to vanish into thin air. . . .

With this problem resolved, let me ask this question: Is this bill convenient, is it needed? The illustrious deputies from São Paulo and Mato Grosso say that it is not needed, that it is not convenient. It is against all economic principles, they say, it is unwise, and, finally, it is ethically unsound.

Mr. President, I am not sure whether it is the different local interests which we represent that causes us to judge this bill in such different ways, since I consider it as entirely in conformity with economic principles, extremely wise, and completely ethical. (*Many supportive comments.*)

Let us have a look. I don't need to tell the honored members, because they know, that almost all the agricultural production of the Empire is the result of slave labor . . .

Mr. *Ferraz*: Even in Maranhão.

Mr. *Wanderley*: . . . but that production differs according to the various localities, it being greater and more profitable in some places, and on a smaller scale and less profitable in others. Labor in the northern provinces, either because of the nature of their agriculture, which consists mainly of cane planting and sugar production, or because of the influence of their climate, is less productive than it is in the southern provinces, where slave labor applied to coffee cultivation is more advantageous. This state of affairs, gentlemen, creates a situation in which the sugar planters, or the farmers of the northern provinces, cannot compete with the planters of the south in the acquisition of the workers required on their properties. (*Hear! Hear!*) It is true that until now almost none of the great planters have disposed of their slaves, because they would lose the fixed capital employed in agriculture; however, gentlemen, observe that the field hands are diminishing in the north, as a result of mortality, at a rate of at least 5 percent annually, and that eventually the planters will have to turn to the cities to supply themselves with slaves, or to the small farmers, whose planting can be done by free workers. Take this source from them, and I can tell you that within a few years the north will find itself reduced to breeders of oxen! (*Hear! Hear! Various comments are heard.*)

I am told: "If you recognize that southern agriculture is more productive, then your bill is offensive to economic principles, since it prevents workers from finding employment in places where they will produce the greatest profit."

Gentlemen, I do not accept such arguments, and I am astounded that there are those who entirely forget the interests of their brothers, as they concentrate their attention solely on their own interests. Gentlemen, do you really want to see two or three provinces overflowing with wealth, while the rest are reduced to miserable Irelands? (*Hear! Hear! Lively objections.*) This is the strange reasoning of those who ignore the political interests of the Empire, and are impressed only by greater or lesser levels of production.

Mr. *Viriato*: We want to use scientific argumentation.

A *Deputy*: What science? That is science?! (*Comments continue.*)

Mr. *Wanderley*: It is true, gentlemen, that your production will increase, that you will enrich yourselves even further by drawing all the slave workers out of the north, but you will also enjoy another pleasure—that of observing an end to the production and wealth of the north. (*Hear! Hear!*)

Mr. *Oliveira Bello* [representing Rio Grande do Sul]: No one will get any pleasure out of that.

Mr. *Silveira da Mota*: What I can't understand is that the north is putting all its hopes in slaves.

A *Deputy*: And so why do you want them in the south?

Mr. *Mendes* [representing Maranhão]: And why do you come to us searching for children of eight and ten years of age? (*Comments continue.*)

Mr. *Wanderley*: Mr. President, it is not my intention to turn this into a violent discussion, but it is beyond my powers to control myself when I am dealing with a matter which, as I see it, concerns the fate of all the northern provinces. (*Hear! Hear!*)

Mr. *Silveira da Mota*: I opposed the bill with the greatest possible calm.

Mr. *Wanderley*: Mr. President, I have heard the following stated here: "Allow the slaves to leave the north, because as their numbers decline wages will increase, and as a result the industries in which they are employed will make greater profits." (*Comments are heard.*) My God! Where did the illustrious deputy from São Paulo ever get the idea that an industry which is not profitable when wages are low will become more profitable when wages are high?!!!

Mr. *Brandão* [representing Pernambuco]: This is a peculiar kind of economics. . . .

Mr. *Wanderley*: I have learned and I have always heard it said that the wage rate is the principal factor in the profits of any industry; the wages make up a portion of production expenses, and, the lower these are, the greater will be the profits. If the wages are low, you will see the profits increased; and by the same principle, when the wages are high, you will see the profits diminished and even disappear and carry with them the ruin of the industrious. . . .

The consequence of a radical change in the conditions of labor in the provinces will be political antagonism between the provinces of the south and the provinces of the north, because the latter, when they no longer have slaves, will insist that there be none in the south (*Hear! Hear!*); the provinces of the south will desire the opposite, and we will see springing up from this clash of interests among us the same dangers which have menaced the United States of America.

Gentlemen, the facts which are daily repeated before our eyes speak louder than the speeches of the illustrious deputies. It is horrifying to see Brazilian steamships flying the national flag and war pennant used to transport slaves from the north to the south. From the beginning of this year until the month of August, 2,700 slaves have been imported into the capital of the Empire coming from the northern provinces . . .

Mr. *Silveira da Mota*: It's a high figure!

Mr. *Dutra Rocha* [representing Rio Grande do Sul]: It's nothing, but with this happening every year we will see the result.

Mr. *Wanderley*: Last year two thousand and eighty-some slaves left the province of Bahia. . . .

Mr. *Viriato*: That's a blessing for Bahia.

Mr. *Wanderley*: It can be calculated, Mr. President, that the transportation of slaves from the north to the south is never less than 6,000 slaves annually . . .

A *Deputy*: From there on up.

Mr. *Wanderley*: The illustrious deputy has made a good point. Observe, too, that this is not exclusively the result of economic necessities. It is also the work of a strong association and a combination of new traffickers almost exactly like those who carried on the trade in Africa. (*Hear! Hear!*)

The constant emigration of slave workers from the north to the south of the Empire will cause a fall-off in production and will bring discontent to those provinces, because production augments wealth, and this is what brings civilization to a people, this is what makes a nation peaceful and satisfied. . . .

It has also been stated: "Your project is useless. In no way can you stop the movement of slaves from one province to another; the contraband will be carried on just as the African contraband was carried on." Gentleman, I have a conviction, which is perhaps not unfounded, and that is that laws are always enforceable when the authorities want to enforce them. (*Hear! Hear!*) If there is abuse, if there are violations, this in itself is a result of the social situation. Just because an individual or many individuals commit a criminal act, it does not follow that penal laws are useless; simply because the contrabandist manages to get 10 or 12 slaves through, it does not follow that there should be no prohibition. Besides, the contrabandists of the African coast had powerful interests in the illegal traffic, because the profits which they took from it were enough to cover all the expenses and risks of their speculations. They put 600,

800, 1,000 and more Africans on a ship which was bought for little more than a pittance; and, if that ship got through, the funds derived from the sale were enough to cover the previous expenses, and large profits were left over. Could a contraband trade be carried on today with the present high slave prices, and subject to the risks of a voyage to another province? What would be the advantage to the smugglers? What means could they use to corrupt so many officials, if someone in fact fears this kind of unethical behavior? I declare that I do not know of any. A few slaves could be gotten through illegally; but this evil would be very small in comparison with what we hope to prevent. . . .

Mr. *Silveira da Mota*: And what about the traffic overland?

Mr. *Wanderley*: Then you agree that the traffic by sea could be stopped?

Mr. *Silveira da Mota*: No, I do not agree.

Mr. *Wanderley*: Concerning the overland traffic, I will tell you that there are certain provinces such as Rio de Janeiro, Minas Gerais, and São Paulo, which have almost identical interests. Since there are rural properties along the borders of these provinces belonging to the same individuals, I will not hesitate to allow changes in the bill which would avoid the inconveniences that could result from an absolute ban, and I would permit planters to move their slaves about. But in other remote provinces an illegal overland traffic is impossible. How can 10, 12, or 20 slaves cross the provinces of Maranhão, Piauí, Bahia as far as Minas Gerais and not encounter in that huge expanse of territory someone who would ask them where they were going, someone who would ask to see their passports?

Mr. *Viriato*: They have already gone as far as Rio de Janeiro.

Mr. *Wanderley*: From where?

Mr. *Viriato*: From the province of Maranhão.

Mr. *Wanderley*: This was allowed. They were permitted to pass.

Mr. *Viriato*: They were runaways. . . .

A *Voice*: For that there are slave-catchers.

Mr. *Wanderley*: What I am certain of is that not a pound of coffee moves from the province of Minas to that of Bahia by way of the São Francisco River that does not pay duties, and so I believe that just as the passage of products can be prevented, it will also be possible to stop the passage of people. . . .

Mr. *Viriato*: Your Excellency does not understand me very well. Slaves passed out of Maranhão without paying duties . . .

Mr. *Ferraz* [representing Rio de Janeiro]: Some even to avoid confiscation by the public treasury.

Mr. *Wanderley*: It is possible that this has happened when there was no ban on transit to other provinces, but, even admitting that the law could sometimes be evaded, let me ask you this: how many murderers go unpunished? A huge number of them. And should we therefore regard criminal laws as useless and abolish them?

Gentlemen, the hour intended for this discussion has ended. I am going to conclude by responding to the final opposing argument of the illustrious deputy from São Paulo, the charge, that is, that the bill is ethically unsound.

Mr. President, it is true that the bill is ethically unsound. I did not even intend to improve the condition of the slaves in every respect, but from the point of view I am taking, it is entirely ethical.

Gentlemen, you do not know how the slave trade is carried on in the north. At the very beginning I explained to you that it was not the proprietors' natural tendency to give up their slaves. The sales are not normally made in order to meet some need, or to make better use of capital. Rather they occur as a result of repeated provocations and enticements. Here in the capital and in the provinces exist organized companies that send agents into all the towns and villages, even the least important ones. These agents go from door to door among the plantations. They offer the lure of high prices to the poor widow and the small farmer who owns one or two slaves . . .

A *Voice*: They even lure away the slaves themselves.

Mr. *Wanderley*: Yes, even the slaves themselves, telling them they will be happier. The small farmer who owns a slave from whom he makes a profit of 30 or 40 *milréis* and who serves him for the planting of food crops, figuring that he can get a better profit from the 700 or 800 *milréis* which he is offered, sells him. And what happens then? You might expect him to use this money productively, or to apply it to the improvement of his farm. No, gentlemen, the money is spent unproductively or turned over to some speculator who in those places is looked upon as a businessman, and this soon puts an end to everything. Thus the miserable farmer who had 1, 2, or 3 slaves with which he fed his family, finds himself deprived of them without any advantage to himself, and with harm done as well to his province, which is losing its workers. . . .

One also sees (and this is a terrible thing, gentlemen) children torn away from their mothers, husbands separated from their wives, parents from their children! Go to the Rua Direita, that *new Valongo*, and you will be offended and touched by the sight of so many miserable people. And this is happening in the capital of the Empire!

And that isn't all, gentlemen. As a result of all this, another kind of speculation has made its appearance in the north: the enslavement of free people . . .

Mr. *Aguiar* [representing Pará]: Exactly. And this is what is most lamentable.

Mr. *Wanderley*: Men to whom unfortunate mulatto or black children are entrusted have sold them. Others use violence to steal children and sell them! Incidents like these have occurred in my own province.

Mr. *Silveira da Mota*: Such things happen everywhere in the public marketplace.

Mr. *Wanderley*: What? Reducing a free person to slavery? Then, can a bill that tends to eliminate such immoral acts be looked upon as without ethical value?

Mr. *Silveira da Mota*: It won't bring an end to it. There will always be slave auctions.

Mr. *Wanderley*: The illustrious deputy is not listening. I am saying that this industry, this new speculation, this new traffic in human flesh (*Hear! Hear!*) which is searching in every town, every provincial center, for slaves to buy and to transport to the *new Valongos* of the capital, has brought about another type of immoral act: the tendency to reduce free persons to slavery. Something else happens. Many crimes committed by slaves in the provinces go unpunished, because the criminals are immediately withdrawn from the legal process and sent to be sold in the capital and in other places, where often worse crimes are perpetrated by them, because the families to whom they are sold are not aware of the vices and malicious character of these slaves. (*Hear! Hear!*)

Therefore, gentlemen, I believe that, even if this bill is not as complete as might be desired, even if it does not meet every need I had in mind, it nevertheless contains an immense usefulness which the Chamber of Deputies cannot reasonably reject. But whether the bill is passed or not, I am convinced that the idea is one that has been accepted in the whole northern part of the Empire (*many shouts of approval*); that the need for such legislation is felt in all the provinces which have imposed heavy taxes on the export of slaves without, nevertheless, stopping this traffic; that there is an almost unanimous outcry from all our great planters demanding a solution; and that it is necessary to give the most serious attention to an opinion which has been expressed by so many newspapers. (*Hear! Hear!*) I myself, gentlemen, not being very much given to sentimentality, confess that I am provoked, that I am horrified when I think of all the consequences of this very barbarous and inhuman traffic; let me repeat, a traffic more barbarous and inhuman than the traffic on the coast of Africa was before it. (*Many comments.*) I have concluded.

Voices: Very good. Very good.

The discussion is postponed because of the hour.

8.17. A Britisher Describes the Inter-Provincial Slave Trade of the 1850s

Despite evidence like that in the previous document, one writer, Herbert S. Klein, has sought to minimize the importance of the inter-provincial slave trade. Conceding that as many as 200,000 slaves were removed from one Brazilian region to another between 1850 and 1881, Klein argued that this "still means that the inter-regional trade was much less important than the Atlantic slave trade." The primary role of this traffic, he concluded, was "to supply *a relatively limited number* of *skilled slaves* to the southern markets." (Klein, *The Middle Passage*, pp. 95-120, italics added.)

To judge the real nature of this trade, however, other facts need to be emphasized. When compared with the 4,000,000 slaves thought to have entered Brazil from Africa during three centuries, 200,000 is not a very impressive figure; however, when the shortness of this period is considered, when it is realized that the figure of 200,000 does not include many thousands of slaves who were moved over shorter distances, and when it is remembered that the slaves involved were destined for a limited part of the country, at the expense of the rest of it, the figure of 200,000 becomes more impressive. It amounted, in fact, to about 6,500 per year, about half the annual average shipped to *all of Brazil* in the international trade—and it was approximately *half the total number* thought to have entered the United States through the entire international slave trade!

The effects of this traffic on the exporting provinces also need to be emphasized. If the figure of 200,000 is correct, this represents about 20 percent of the slave population of the slave-exporting provinces when the traffic began. Since two men were involved for every woman, moreover, it means that a much larger percentage of the male population was affected. In fact, this involuntary migration helped to create female majorities in all the northern provinces by the 1880s and large male majorities in many coffee-producing areas, and thus it divided many families and prevented the formation of many more. It also, of course, reduced the importance of slavery in the exporting provinces and thus the vested interest of those provinces in slavery and so helped to end it everywhere.

Finally, even if many of these migrants were skilled and urban, as Klein insisted, it is wrong to assume that coffee planters did not use them in agriculture. By 1872 more than 500,000 slaves were employed in agricultural labor in the coffee provinces, and only some 30,000 in the "manual or mechanical professions." In the last years of slavery even southern cities were major sources of slaves for the coffee zones, the slave population of metropolitan Rio de Janeiro dropping from about 47,000 in 1874 to only 8,000 in 1887. Some of these people obviously died or were freed, but many were clearly victims of the internal slave trade.

This traffic was rarely described. Fortunately, however, two such descriptions exist: that delivered before the Brazilian Chamber of Deputies in 1880 by Marcolino de Moura, an abolitionist from the province of Bahia (see Document 8.18), and the following description by the British consul at Recife, H. Augustus Cowper. The same humanitarian motivation revealed in Cowper's descriptions of slavery in Pernambuco (see Document 2.5) are once more strongly evident here.

Sources: *Class B. Correspondence on the Slave Trade . . . From April 1, 1856, to March 31, 1857* (London, 1857), pp. 246, 261.

❧ I cannot abstain from recurring to the subject of the coasting Slave Trade carried on in this Empire, that your Lordship's good offices may be exerted in defence of that race, which has suffered, is suffering, and I fear has yet to suffer, such unmerited and inhuman treatment.

One of the arguments advanced in favour of the African Slave Trade is, that the slaves are removed from a state of barbarism, to one of civilization and Christianity, and notwithstanding the practical untruth of this assertion, . . . I am willing to allow the argument such merit as it deserves.

But it can have neither weight nor place in discussing the coasting Slave Trade, which presents its naked and corrupt body to the view without a healthy or redeeming spot. Children are torn from their parents, parents from their children, the tie of husband and wife, which no man is "to put asunder," is severed like the Gordian knot, the tenderest feelings of our nature, the love of country, with its thousand associations of home, love, or friendship, are all violated and disregarded, and the unfortunate descendant of the African victim finds that, notwithstanding the Christianity and civilization of his new country, the wrongs of his race have been transported across the Atlantic to be perpetuated in him.

A very extensive and increasing trade in slaves, amounting to many thousands annually, is now carried on betwixt Rio de Janeiro and the northern provinces of Brazil; the traders make periodical visits and return with their unresisting victims, indifferent alike to the tears of the women and the curses of the men. Many of the young females are bought by these rascals for the express purpose of public prostitution in the capital: a case of this description fell under my own personal knowledge, when 2,400 *milréis* (nearly 300£.) were offered for twin sisters of fourteen years of age, which I am happy to be able to add their owner refused. A woman who had borne thirteen children, and thus considerably increased the means of her master, is now threatened with eternal separation from them, by being sold for the south by this same master; and a young mulatto man was thus recently sold by his own father, a Portuguese. It is unnecessary to multiply these cases of human suffering, well worthy of the touching humanity of a Beecher Stowe. . . .

The coasting traders have their establishments at the ports, and purchase their slaves from men of the lowest order, generally horse-dealers, who bring them down from the interior; this is the real source whence the coasting traffic is derived. Your Lordship may imagine the state of demoralization into which this trade, if encouraged or even permitted, will eventually plunge the rural population; man-stealing, the sale of children by their parents, and all the horrors of which we read as occurring in Africa, will be re-enacted here, and I am sure that Brazil has a greater interest in the suppression of this native trade than even that with the coast of Africa. . . .

To the honour of her legislators, however, a measure has already been proposed to render the export of slaves from one province to another illegal: I regret to add without success; but as reforms are usually tardy under Constitutional Governments, I do not despair of its final triumph. [This was the bill of João Mauricio Wanderley of Bahia, presented to the Chamber in 1854; see Document 8.16.] The Provincial Government, dreading the effects of the loss of labour which results from this continual drain upon their population, have enacted stringent laws to check it; in this province the export duty upon a slave has been raised to 200 *milréis* (about 22£.), and the number allowed to accompany their masters as domestic servants is strictly limited: the law is nevertheless evaded to a very great extent, so much so that duty was paid upon only 37 slaves during the whole of last year, and yet passports were granted to 606, who actually left the province during the same period; and it is notorious that as many as 70 have left by one vessel. I consider the real number of slaves annually exported from this Consular district to amount to 1,500. . . .

This is not a question of political rights, or even of social rights, but one of human rights. Could not a law be enacted guaranteeing to the slave the right of country? For to him there can exist no real difference betwixt a voyage of 2,000 miles from Pará to Rio de Janeiro, and one of 2,000 miles from the coast of Africa to Brazil. . . . Could not the law forbid the separation of man and wife, of parent and child, at least beyond the precincts of the province in which they reside? This would not only be an act of humanity, but of policy; it would dry the tears of thousands, and fill their hearts with contentment, and it would stop that drain upon the labour of the northern provinces which cannot fail to be shortly felt.

8.18. A Member of the Chamber of Deputies from Bahia Describes the Overland Slave Traffic (1880)

In 1880 the following description of the overland slave traffic was heard in the Chamber of Deputies during debate on another unsuccessful bill intended to stop the inter-provincial slave trade. The speaker, Marcolino de Moura, an abolitionist delegate from Bahia, claimed like Wanderley before him (see Document 8.16) that the traffic which he had witnessed in the interior of his native province was even more terrible than the slave traffic in Africa. In fact, however, his description is strongly reminiscent of Luiz Antonio de Oliveira Mendes's account of African overland marches written nearly a century earlier (see Document 1.3). In both cases slaves were chained together, moved in convoys, and forced to endure long treks sometimes beyond their powers. Moura's account of the mistreatment of encamped slaves also bears a powerful resemblance to Oliveira Mendes's account of the same nightly event in Africa.

Source: *Annaes da Câmara dos Senhores Deputados* (1880), v, 38.

❧ I call the attention of the noble president of the Council of Ministers to a bill which is now the order of the day, and I invoke his piety and patriotism in favor of it. I am referring to the bill that would ban the exportation of slaves from one province of the Empire to another. We are in need of a law to end this inhuman traffic which uproots thousands of unfortunate people to die far from their own country in the most painful captivity. Yes, far from their own country; because, gentlemen, the homeland of the slave is his birthplace, it is the locality where he lives, it is the narrow horizon of his dearest attachments.

Whoever has personally witnessed the convoys that cross the regions of our provinces, whoever has seen, as I have, the camping places of these death troops of tormented, innocent persons, among whom are women, children, and old men, has no other choice but to call the attention of the pious and patriotic members of this Chamber to this lamentable state of things which so dishonors our country. This iniquitous commerce has been having an effect upon me for a long time and may even turn me into a revolutionary. Not long ago in the heat of midday, I was passing through one of those desert regions of my native province; the sun burned white-hot. Suddenly I heard a confused clamor of approaching voices. It was an immense caravan of slaves destined for the fields of São Paulo. Among men with chains about their necks walked as many women, carrying on their shoulders their children, among whom were seen youngsters of all ages, the whole march being on foot, bloodying the hot sand of the roads. (*Sensation.*)

I wanted to run away from that painful sight, but I was immediately stopped by a sorrowful cry. It was the poor mother of two children who had fallen breathless by the roadside from the effects of the blazing sun. At night the appearance of one of these encamped convoys causes the strongest constitution, the hardest heart, to shake with horror. Around a huge bonfire the slaves lie extended without distinction of sex or age, and amid the clanging of irons, the wailing of the women and children, are heard the shouts of the guards testing the chains and imposing silence upon those who dare to complain. (*Sensation.*) But beyond the leaping shadows the most unrestrained vice. And if during the night one of those miserable slave women becomes a mother, the next day the march of the convoy is not interrupted, and the cherished fruit of her womb is condemned to die on the first or second day of travel, if it is not thrown before into some corner to die in abandonment. On this point we must insist, we must even cry out here, so that it isn't forgotten that these scenes which take place in the northern provinces degrade the soul of our nation. It is the traffic in its most horrendous form, and a liberal government cannot allow it to continue any longer without betraying the mission which has been confided to it. (*Hear! Hear!*)

Since that day I have sworn to fight this new traffic, which is a thousand times more horrible than that which might be carried on in the center of Africa and across the seas. (*Hear! Hear!*) I am an abolitionist, but I am not intransigent. In fact, I commit myself to the abandonment of my right to consider similar questions if this bill to extinguish the inter-provincial traffic becomes the law of the land.

8.19. Slaves Are Bought in Northern Brazil for Shipment to the South

Hundreds of brief advertisements like those that follow appeared in northern newspapers in the years from 1851 to 1881, revealing to potential sellers and to posterity alike that the slaves most in demand were young people of both sexes who would be adaptable to new conditions in the south and likely to contribute many years of valuable service on the coffee plantations of Rio de Janeiro, Minas Gerais, and São Paulo. Many of the young women undoubtedly ended up in the brothels of southern cities.

❧ SLAVE CONSIGNEES

At Rua Larga do Rosario, No. 22, slaves will be received to be sold on consignment, and for the account of their masters. Good treatment and quick sales assured, so that their masters will not suffer the smallest loss in their sale.

Diario de Pernambuco (Recife), July 27, 1858. Cited in Felix Lima Júnior, *A escravidão em Alagôas* (Maceió: Imp. Universitaria, 1975), p. 25.

SLAVES

In the Bazaar of Sampaio and Co. you will receive information about the purchaser of some slaves for Rio de Janeiro.

O Paiz (São Luís do Maranhão), October 25, 1879.

SLAVES

Both sexes will be bought. Preferred are those between 14 and 20 years of age, black color. Contact Fragoso and Co., 18 Praça do Commercio.

O Paiz (São Luís do Maranhão), December 12, 1879.

SLAVES

Both sexes will be bought in the Hotel do Porto, from 12 to 25 years of age; sellers will be pleased by the good prices paid.

O Paiz (São Luís do Maranhão), July 7, 1880.

SLAVES

Olympio and Brother will buy six slaves between 12 and 26 years of age; they will pay better than any other buyer, for a consignment to S. Paulo.

A Ordem (Baturité, Ceará), September 14, 1879.

8.20. Father Pompeu's Son

The following brief narrative deals with one of the cruel but perhaps inevitable consequences of the inter-provincial slave trade and of slavery itself: the selling of children by their own parents. Although this piece is nearly self-explanatory, it must be pointed out that its author, Luís Gama, was a prominent mulatto abolitionist, writer, and poet who in his childhood was himself illegally sold into slavery by his own father and shipped from Bahia to São Paulo. (See Documents 5.7 and 10.9.) Padre Tomás de Sousa Pompeu, the villain of this brief tragicomedy, was a priest, the author of several books on the geography of Ceará, and a senator from that province who opposed the Free Birth law of 1871. One of Gama's last writings, this short tale appeared in 1881 in *A Voz do Escravo* (The voice of the slave), an abolitionist newspaper of Pelôtas, Rio Grande do Sul.

Source: *A Voz do Escravo* (Pelôtas, Rio Grande do Sul), February 15, 1881.

❧ In 186 . . . His Excellency, Judge ——— of the High Court of Appeals, a native of one of the northern provinces, holder of high administrative posts, was staying as a guest on the plantation of Dr. ——— in the municipality of Mogi-Mirim in the province of São Paulo.

As the judge was standing at the window, a mulatto came across the long courtyard, and the judge exclaimed:

"What can Father Pompeu possibly be doing here?!"

"Father Pompeu?" retorted the proprietor.

"Yes, Father Pompeu himself, the senator."

Moments later the wealthy host showed his friend a magnificent thoroughbred horse. The same mulatto who had crossed the courtyard moments before was leading him by the bridle.

The distinguished guest fixed his eyes upon him, carefully examined him, and continued:

"It's perfect. He's younger, but in every other way he is the sculptured image of Father Pompeu!"

And then he asked:

"Where do you come from?"

"I'm from Ceará."

"From Ceará?! Worse yet . . ."

"Whose slave were you?"

"Senator Pompeu's."

"Where were you born?"

"In his house."

"And who sold you?"

"He himself."

The two friends exchanged meaningful glances, and the guest murmured: "How barbaric!"

NINE

"A State of Domestic War": How Slaves Responded

IN HIS BOOK, *New World in the Tropics*, Gilberto Freyre declared that in Brazil slave revolts were probably less common and less violent than in other parts of the Americas, and he went on to offer an explanation for this alleged difference that was quite as unfounded as the original premise. This comparative lack of antagonistic response on the part of slaves in Brazil, he suggested, was "perhaps because the treatment of slaves by the Portuguese, and later by the Brazilians, was less provocative of rebellion" (p. 76). As we have seen, however, the treatment that slaves endured in Brazil was nothing if it was not "provocative of rebellion," and the documents in the present chapter will prove that revolts and other forms of slave resistance were indeed both violent and common.

Many slaves in Brazil, hoping to survive and to avoid punishment, accustomed themselves to obey, to work, and to satisfy their masters' demands. Many others, however, especially the overpunished, the overworked, the underfed, the countless men and women without spouses and families who had little to lose, and those whose very existence was threatened by intemperate owners, did not submit to endless abuse. In fact, the historical record—not just the travelers' accounts which Freyre mentioned, but abundant archival evidence—proves that resistance to slavery was a constant characteristic of Luso-Brazilian slavery from the fifteenth century when the "Moors" of Africa fled and fought the Portuguese (see Document 1.1) until the late 1880s when tens of thousands of slaves abandoned plantations, encouraged by a powerful abolitionist movement (see Documents 9, 10, and 11 in Part Ten). An adviser to King João VI, writing in Rio in 1818, did not exaggerate when he described the relationship between Brazilian masters and their slaves as "a state of domestic war."

Resistance, of course, took many forms. Slaves obviously shirked hard work when they could, or performed it badly, the best proof of which was the liberal use of the whip and other kinds of coercive punishment which were normal features of Brazilian life. One of the common forms of resistance was physical retaliation, including attacks on masters, overseers, and members of their families. Desperate slaves also turned their violence upon themselves, taking their own lives or those of their children as a way to end their misery, at the same time depriving their masters of valuable property.

Less common, certainly, than individual acts of violence, but certainly as prevalent in Brazil as anywhere else in the Americas, were slave rebellions, both spontaneous plantation revolts and planned uprisings designed to achieve ambitious goals (see Documents 11 through 15 in this part and 4.9). As long as slavery lasted there was genuine fear among the slaveholding class that their captives were conspiring to revolt on a grand scale, to seize power, and to exterminate or drive them from the country. Particularly dreaded perhaps were Africans from the Mina coast—Yorubas, Ewes, Hausas, and Fulah or Fulani—all influenced to some extent by Islam and respected for their organization, leadership, and courage. Moslem slaves, or Africans influenced by that religion, were indeed responsible for most of the insurrections that broke out in Bahia in the first half of the nineteenth century, ending in the bitter conflict of January, 1835, in which slaves and masters fought in the city's streets (see Documents 13 and 14 in this part). Slave unrest was especially common when members of the dominant class were engaged in revolts or wars of their own. The great runaway settlements of Palmares (see Document 9.3) developed and thrived, for example, during the period of the Dutch intervention in northeastern Brazil (1624-1654), and slave uprisings were also common in the first half of the nineteenth century when Brazil was acquiring its independence from Portugal and elites in provinces like Bahia, Pernambuco, Maranhão, and Rio Grande do Sul were themselves at times in a state of rebellion.

Far more common, however, than armed uprisings, which were dangerous, hard to organize, and unlikely to succeed, was the simple alternative of fleeing the master's presence. Thousands of offers to reward the capture and return of runaway slaves which appeared in hundreds of newspapers over seven or eight decades are convincing proof that flight was a common solution to the slave's predicament (see Documents 2.1 and 9.1). Many who fled were quickly recaptured, but some found more permanent refuge in distant jungles and river valleys or in the vicinity of towns, villages, and other settled places where they could acquire necessities through purchase, barter, theft, or armed raids (see Documents 5 through 10 in this part). In the 1820s, for example, some of Brazil's major cities were virtually surrounded by such clusters of refugees, preying on plantations and travelers and trading with local merchants (see Document 9.6). Known as *mocambos* or *quilombos* (Kimbundu words for "mountain peak" and "capital" or "town" respectively), such runaway settlements were dispersed across the vast Brazilian countryside for as long as slavery lasted—proof enough that slaves in Brazil resisted their martyrdom and that, contrary to claims of a few modern writers and earlier apologists for slavery, their resistance was the logical response to the bitter realities they encountered.

9.1. Newspaper Advertisements Offer Rewards for the Return of Runaways

The problem of runaway slaves placed a permanent claim on the energies and assets of the slaveholding class. Loss of the slave's labor for weeks, months, or even permanently was merely the first and most obvious injury. Advertisements and rewards for his or her capture and return, salaries of policemen, soldiers and slavehunters, fees for punishment and cure or lodging at a local jail, outlays for arms, chains, *troncos, libambos*, and the other instruments of persecution and punishment, loss of livestock and other assets in raids by bands of fugitives, and the immeasurable toll of fear and lives lost were among the obvious costs. Few owners were without runaways listed on their slave rolls (see Document 2.12), and even slaves of the Imperial Family, presumably more fortunate than most, sought relief by running away. Of forty-seven persons, including children, who were listed as slaves at the Imperial plantation of Santa Cruz and at the Imperial Iron Foundry of São João de Ipanema in 1844, for example, no fewer than twelve, or slightly more than 25 percent, had left their place of labor without permission. (Oficios e outros papeis da casa imperial, 1801-1868, Arquivo Nacional, Rio de Janeiro, Codex 572.)

A major source of information about runaways are the multitude of advertisements which were published in newspapers throughout Brazil during the nineteenth century for the purpose of recovering lost slaves. The following notices, published from 1845 to 1872 in newspapers of several provinces, typify this kind of message in content and style. Telling much about the occupations, skills, clothing, punishments, and physical deformities of slaves, they also give clues to why they fled, how they gained and sometimes kept their freedom, what they did while absent, and the attitudes they assumed in the presence of white people.

❧ *100$000 Reward*

Fled on December 3 of this year from the plantation of Major Antonio de Campos Freire one of his slaves named José Antonio of the Benguella nation (though he says he is a creole) from 25 to 30 years of age with the following characteristics: short in stature, thin, well-made body, dark color, face rather long, pale jaw, almost no beard, lips rather full, round head, and is in the habit of going about with long hair, small eyes, long eyelashes, good teeth, nose medium large, speaks in a refined, humble, and insincere way, may have some old and small marks of punishment on his buttocks. He is a master blacksmith, also knows how to work with copper; also a master at killing ants with the bellows. He is accustomed to getting drunk and in that condition becomes violent. He took some work clothes, a poncho with a yellow lining, a firearm, a hat of rough straw; and whenever he runs away he usually claims to be free and changes his name. Whoever captures him and takes him to his master will receive 100$000 reward, in addition to expenses, which will be paid separately.

O Mercantil (Rio de Janeiro), January 13, 1845.

20$rs. to anyone who apprehends and takes to Rua da Alfandega No. 151 a slave women named Claudina, Mozambique nation, who fled on the 1st day of the current month, is thirty years old, regular height, strong, big breasts, with a mark under her left eye, has one of her fingers defective on her right hand. A protest is made against anyone who has hidden her.

O Mercantil (Rio de Janeiro), January 15, 1845.

Fled on September 30 of the current year a black boy {*moleque*} named Manoel, of the Megumbe nation, about 14 years of age, very thin over his entire body and face, with a shirt of Minas cotton and pants of the same; he is very talkative and is in the habit of joining the beggars, pretending to be needy. Whoever captures him and takes him to Rua do Rosario No. 117 will be well rewarded.

Diario do Rio de Janeiro, October 4, 1847.

Fled or was led astray a black girl {*moleca*} named Maria of the Caçange nation, who appears to be about 14 years of age and still does not have breasts, black color and thin, wore a dress of white calico with ribbons and pink flowers. The said girl was missing yesterday afternoon when she went to the Campo de Santa Anna to get water, and it appears that she was crying there because someone had stolen her water bucket. Whoever brings her to the Rua de Santa Anna No. 47B, upper floor, will be satisfactorily rewarded, or even someone who gives information about her so that her owner can get her back.

Diario do Rio de Janeiro, December 31, 1847.

Fled from Jaraguá from the custody of Mr. Mariz on the 21st of the current month the slave Izidoro, mulatto, 18 years old, tall, long hair; at the sugar mills of Garçatorta and Villa do Norte this slave has a father and relatives, it is very possible that he went to those places; he fled with manacles on his hands and should have some marks on his feet as a result of wearing irons for some days. We appeal to anyone who captures him to deliver him in Maceió to Mr. Antonio Teixeira Pinto in the Cambona, and he will be well rewarded. Maceió, December 22, 1855.

O Noticiador Alagoano (Maceió), December 30, 1855.

400$000 Reward

Fled on the 23rd of last month from the Tabocas sugar mill, Parish of da Luz, belonging to Francisco Antonio Cabral de Mello, five slaves whose names and features are as follows:

Joaquim, black, looks to be about 20 years of age, short, haggard body, and with no beard, has many marks on his feet of the *bicho* [tiny insect that lays its eggs under the skin, especially on the foot]; wore an iron ring on his neck, a new shirt of Bahia cotton, old pants, and a hat of old leather; it is supposed that he has gone to the vicinity of Limoeiro, from where he came in the custody of Dr. Nabor, who had bought him, and later, by his authorization, he was sold to me by the broker Souza in this market.

Marcellino, black, tall, haggard body, thin bearded face, looks about 35 years of age, wore blue pants and took along a striped pair, a jacket, a white shirt, and a straw hat.

Nicoláo, black, tall, full-bodied, looks about 22 years of age, took white pants, a striped shirt, and a new baize one. On his back he has marks of punishment, is a beginning carpenter.

Ezequiel, creole, very black, ordinary height, little beard, has some wounds on his lower legs, and looks about 25 years old, took along a cotton shirt, white pants and a blue pair, and a hat of rice straw. This black came from Pará.

João, mulatto, about 25 years old, rather tall and bearded, is a blacksmith, wore a straw hat, red striped pants, a cotton shirt, and also carried an old sword. This black came from Pará. Marcellino, Joaquim, and Nicoláo came from Maranhão.

Police authorities and slave-catchers are asked to apprehend these slaves, and whoever takes them to their master at the aforesaid sugar mill, or to Manoel Antonio Gonçalves, in the Rua do Cabugá, No. 3, will receive from him a reward of 400$000, or the amount corresponding to each one, in case they arrive separately.

Diario de Pernambuco (Recife), April 2, 1859.

Runaway Slave

Fled three months ago from the undersigned the slave Placido, about 25 years old, with the following distinguishing features: normal stature, dark skin, well-built, having scars on his back and being deaf. This slave belongs to Mr. Candido Augusto Ferreira. Presumably he is somewhere near São Bento in the immediate vicinity of the plantation of Captain Francisco Antonio Ferreira, where he has brothers.

We appeal to the police authorities and to the slave catchers to capture this slave, and whoever does so and delivers him in Vianna to the undersigned, or in São Bento to Captain Marianno Hermenegildo Nunes, or in Maranhão to Second Lieutenant Antonio Marcolino de Campos Costa, will be well rewarded. The advertiser protests against anyone who might have sheltered him. Vianna, September 28, 1862.

Caetano José de Mello

A Coalição (São Luiz do Maranhão), October 15, 1862.

200$000

reward to anyone who captures and brings to the Boa-Vista plantation in the district of Lorena, province of São Paulo, the mulatto Camillo, who ran away on the 14th of the present month and belongs to Major Manoel de Freitas Novaes.

Also will pay all expenses of the journey, etc., up to the time of delivery, the aforementioned mulatto having the following features: about 45 years of age, tall in stature, speaks with a high voice and always looks frightened, has some teeth missing in front and lettering on his forehead and on the palms of his hand which says: "Slave of Dona Fortunata," always wearing on his head a cap or handkerchief to hide the letters on his forehead. He wore trousers of woven cloth, a waistcoat of black cloth, a shirt of calico or shirt cloth, and a cloth jacket and poncho. He likes to boast that he is free. He is a master carpenter, sailor, and a coffee, cane, and hydraulic-works machinist.

There are reports that he passed through Sant'Anna de Sapucahy, where he said he was going to the province of São Paulo, meanwhile heading, I believe, toward central Minas.

All authorities and planters are asked to help capture the said slave, and not to trust the submissiveness with which he tries to deceive people of good faith in order to get away. There will also be a reward of 50$ to any person who captures him and puts him in jail, or gives an accurate report of him, protesting with the full rigor of the law against anyone who shelters him, his daily wage being worth 5$, as was stated previously in the complaint made in the city of Lorena. Lorena, March 16, 1872.—MANOEL DE FREITAS NOVAES.

Diario do Rio de Janeiro, March 24, 1872.

9.2. A Runaway Bookbinder, Fortunato (1854)

Similar in style to the previous advertisements, the following runaway-slave notice was printed as a small poster for distribution in Rio de Janeiro. In addition to the text, the original advertisement included an elaborate picture of a runaway black man carrying the traditional sack on a stick over his right shoulder. (See Fig. 28.) Interestingly, this poster was distributed by Eduardo von Laemmert, a noted publisher in Rio and author of a popular guide to the city which appeared in 1857. The "lazy" and "surly" slave in question seems to have worked as a bookbinder in Laemmert's establishment, and so the typesetter of this advertisement was probably one of Fortunato's fellow workers, perhaps himself a slave.

Source: Seção de Manuscritos, Biblioteca Nacional, Rio de Janeiro.

❧ *RUNAWAY CREOLE RS. 50$000 REWARD*

A runway since October 18, 1854, the creole slave named

FORTUNATO

of twenty years of age, lacking teeth in front, with little or no beard, short, strong, marked by the pox which he had a few years ago, he is very lazy, surly, speaks fast and with his mouth full, looking toward the ground; he is in the habit at times of going about wearing shoes, claiming to be free and saying that his name is Fortunato Lopes da Silva. He knows how to cook, to work as a bookbinder, and he understands labor in the country, where he was born. Whoever captures him, takes him to jail, and advises his master, Mr. Eduardo Laemmert, in the court, Rua da Quitanda No. 77, will receive a gratification of 50$000.

9.3. The Great Seventeenth-Century *Quilombo* of Palmares: A Chronicle of War and Peace

As stated in the introduction to this part, throughout the history of Brazilian slavery countless slaves sought release from servitude in runaway-slave settlements known as *quilombos* or *mocambos*. Certain features were common to these *quilombos*, whether they were tiny isolated clusters of huts or larger more permanent villages and towns. African culture, evident wherever slaves existed, could flourish freely in such places, although European, Christian, and Indian cultural influences were often strong. Safety from slave hunters was normally more dependent upon

CRIOULO FUGIDO.

RS. 50U000

DE ALVIÇARAS

Anda fugido, desde o dia 18 de Outubro de 1854, o escravo crioulo de nome

FORTUNATO,

de 20 e tantos annos de idade, com falta de dentes na frente, com pouca ou nenhuma barba, baixo, reforçado, e picado de bexigas que teve ha poucos annos, é muito pachola, mal encarado, falla apressado e com a bocca cheia olhando para o chão; costuma ás vezes andar calçado intitulando-se forro, e dizendo chamar-se Fortunato Lopes da Silva. Sabe cozinhar, trabalhar de encadernador, e entende de plantações da roça, donde é natural. Quem o prender, entregar á prisão, e avisar na côrte ao seu senhor Eduardo Laemmert, rua da Quitanda n.° 77, receberá 50U000 de gratificação.

28. Leaflet Advertising a Runaway Slave

favorable geography than upon weapons or tactics, but defense systems, sometimes elaborate and usually African in nature, were characteristic. Leaders were often chosen from among the bravest, wisest persons, some of whom were reputed to have been kings or queens in Africa, and in long-surviving *quilombos* leadership could become hereditary. Domestic animals, notably chickens and pigs, well-tended gardens, stores of food, and fishing and hunting equipment were common adjuncts, supplying fugitives with diets probably far better than those they had known on their masters' plantations. Often located near towns or plantations, *quilombos* at times maintained trade contacts with local merchants and other persons wishing to aid them or to profit from their plight. *Quilombolas* (the inhabitants of *quilombos*) often attacked nearby settlements or plantations to acquire supplies or women. Both to re-enslave them and to eliminate the danger they represented, government forces, bush captains (*capitães-do-mato*), or bands of volunteers often carried out raids against them, resulting in numerous reports of expeditions which are the principal source of information about them.

The following selection is an account of a network of runaway settlements and strongholds which together were known as Palmares, literally "palm groves." These settlements were established in the backlands of northeastern Brazil in the early seventeenth century, and during the long wars against Holland grew and thrived. This narrative is particularly fascinating for the account it gives of a peace treaty entered into in 1678 by one Gangasuma (Ganga-Zumba), the king of Palmares, with the Portuguese governor of Pernambuco. This pact, which recognized the freedom of blacks born in Palmares, was similar to treaties of metropolitan governments made with black fugitives in Mexico, Venezuela, St. Domingue, Jamaica, and elsewhere in the Americas. Unfortunately, peace between the Portuguese and the runaways was not permanent. In 1690 a new campaign was begun against the settlements, the principal stronghold was surrounded and captured in 1694, and resistance ended the following year with the capture of the *zumbi* or war chief, who was later executed.

Published in the *Revista do Instituto Histórico e Geográfico Brasileiro* in 1876, this chronicle of war and peace was written in the late seventeenth century by an unnamed writer. The original manuscript (Codex CXVI-2-13) was found in the Biblioteca Pública in Evora, Portugal.

Source: Pedro Paulino da Fonseca, "Memoria dos feitos que se deram durante os primeiros annos da guerra com os negros quilombolas dos Palmares, seu destroço e paz aceita em Junho de 1678," *Revista do Instituto Histórico e Geográfico Brasileiro* 39 (1876), Part 1, 293-321.

❧ In a palm forest sixteen leagues northeast of Porto Calvo existed the *mocambo* of the Zambi (a general or god of arms in their language), and five leagues farther north that of Acainene (this was the name of the king's mother, who lived in this fortified *mocambo* about twenty-five leagues northeast of Porto Calvo, and which they called the Acainene Compound, since it was fortified by a wall of earth and sticks).

To the east of these was the *mocambo* of the Wild Canes [Tabocas], and northeast of this one that of Bambiabonga. Eight leagues north of Bambiabonga was the compound called Sucupira; six leagues northward from this the Royal Compound of the Macaco [monkey], and five leagues to the west of this the *mocambo* of Osenga. Nine leagues northwest of the town of Serinhaem was the compound of Amaro, and twenty-five leagues northwest of Alagôas the palm forest of Andolaquituxe, the Zambi's brother.

Among all these places, which were the largest and best-fortified, there were others of less importance and with fewer people. It is widely believed that when blacks were first brought into the captaincies of Brazil they began to live in these Palmares, and it is certain that during the period of Dutch rule their numbers greatly increased.

They called their king Gangasuma (a hybrid term meaning "great lord" composed of the Angolan or Bunda word "ganga" and the Tupí [Indian] word "assú"). This king lived in a royal city which they called Macaco. This was the main city among the other towns or *mocambos*, and it was completely surrounded by a wall of earth and sticks.

The second city was that known as Sucupira (later the camp of Good Jesus and the Cross founded by Fernão Carrilho). Here lived the Gangasona, the king's brother. Like the latter, all the cities were under the command of rulers and powerful chiefs, who lived in them and governed them.

Sucupira, the war command center where the confederation's defense forces and sentinels were trained, was also fortified, but with stone and wood. Nearly a league in length, it contained within its boundaries three lofty mountains and a river called Cachingi, meaning "an abundance of water."

Before the restoration of Pernambuco from Dutch rule, twenty-five probing expeditions were sent into the area, suffering great losses but failing to uncover the secrets of those brave people. . . . The first was that of Captain Braz da Rocha Cardoso with six hundred men. Little was accomplished by this expedition because of the difficulties of the terrain, the roughness of the trails, and the impossibility of transporting equipment over unknown country. It merely served to show what would have to be overcome in future attempts.

Later came the expedition of Colonel Antonio Jacomo Bezerra, which did them some damage, and those of various other leaders. . . . Outstanding among them, not only for the bravery they exhibited during encounters and skirmishes but because they served at their own expense, were Tibaldo Lins, Christovão Lins, Clemente de Rocha, and José de Barros, all residents of Porto Calvo.

All this occurred during the governorship of Francisco Barreto, who, recovering the captaincy from Dutch rule with the surrender of Recife in January, 1654, immediately undertook a campaign against Palmares, since for him these internal enemies were just as harmful and more barbaric and dreadful than the former. . . .

From March, 1657, to January, 1674, the date that Captain D. Pedro de Almeida assumed the governorship of the captaincy, it was for no lack of effort that victory was not achieved, because all the governors until that time more or less dealt with the problem. However, the obstacles encountered by the governors made unbeatable those whose bravery alone would not have sufficed to protect them. The army's best fighters, the most experienced leaders of the war against the Dutch, were at once employed for this purpose, with immense effort and suffering, but very little achieved.

The inhabitants of Alagôas, Porto Calvo, and Penedo were constantly under attack, and their houses and plantations robbed by the blacks of Palmares. The blacks killed their cattle and carried away their slaves to enlarge their *quilombos* and increase the number of their defenders, forcing the inhabitants and natives of those towns to engage in fighting at a distance of forty leagues or more, at great cost to their plantations and risk to their own lives, without which the blacks would have become masters of the captaincy because of their huge and ever-increasing numbers.

This was the situation in January, 1674, when D. Pedro de Almeida took possession of the captaincy and at once attempted to pursue the conquest. . . . He prudently made all the necessary preparations for the first undertaking, assigning the expedition to Major Manoel Lopes Galvão, whose valor, enthusiasm, and experience offered the greatest promise of success.

By September 23, 1675, Major Manoel Lopes was in Porto Calvo with 280 men, including whites, mestizos, and Indians, to attempt the action, and on November 21, after two months of preparation, they entered the wilderness where their labors and dangers were enormous and constant.

On January 22, 1676, they reached a well-garrisoned and populous city of more than two thousand houses, and after more than two hours of bitter fighting, with bravery displayed on both sides, our men set fire to some houses, which, being of wood and straw, quickly burned, turning the place into an inferno. The great fear which then possessed the blacks forced them to flee, and regrettably they abandoned the city. The next day, gathered at another place and with terror still reigning among them, they were again attacked, suffering considerable losses. . . . Many were killed or wounded in those two encounters, the others seeking refuge in the forests.

The nearby towns and villages immediately experienced the effects of these great victories; the terrible lesson forced many of the *quilombolas* to go in search of their old masters, since they no longer felt safe in that wilderness. . . .

D. Pedro de Almeida, satisfied with the results obtained, and wishing to take advantage of the experience acquired and the demoralization in which Major Manoel Lopes had left them, decided to commit new forces to the enterprise. To accomplish this he sent an invitation to Commander Fernão Carrilho, who was then in Sergipe and had become famous for the work he had accomplished in destroying the *mocambos* of the blacks and the villages of the Tapuia Indians who infested the backlands of Bahia. Accepting the honorable invitation, the latter left for Pernambuco with some of his relatives and dependents. . . .

D. Pedro, active and enterprising and gifted with intelligence, wisdom, and shrewdness, had given very careful attention to how this war was to be carried out, certain mistakes of past efforts serving him as correctives to assure success in future ones. . . . Taking great precautions, he told Fernão Carrilho that his most successful strategy would be to establish and maintain a fortified camp inside Palmares; and since it appeared impossible to inhabit that dense and nearly impenetrable forest because of the climate and the great lack of provisions which could not be supplied from the surrounding area, he took every necessary precaution, ordering the needed provisions to be supplied from nearby towns, so that nothing would be lacking to those who would be stationed in the projected camp.

Without delay Fernão Carrilho left for Porto Calvo where he was expected by the people who had assembled from the other parishes, which, according to orders, should have been 400 men; but only 185 were there, including whites, mestizos, and Indians of the people of Camarão [famous Indian commander in the war against the Dutch]. . . . Despite the dangers and the known and expected problems, on September 21, 1677, the expedition set out on its march from the town of Porto Calvo for the interior forests of Palmares. Accompanying it until it entered the forests were Commander Christovão Lins and his brother Tibaldo Lins, along with those who were most experienced in those marches and those most interested in its success.

Commander Fernão Carrilho then spoke to the troops, telling them the following: "that numbers neither added to nor reduced the courage of valiant men; that only bravery itself made a soldier determined; that, while the multitude of the enemy was large, it was a multitude of slaves whom nature had created more to obey than to resist; that the blacks fought as fugitives, and they were hunting them down as lords and masters; that their honor was endangered by the disobedience of the black slaves; their plantations insecure because of their robberies; their lives placed in great jeopardy by their impudence; that no one among them fought for another man's property, and all defended their own; it being a great disgrace for every Pernambucan to be whipped by those whom they had themselves so many times whipped; . . . that if they destroyed Palmares they would have land for their farms, blacks for their service, and honor and esteem for themselves; and that, if he had taken this great task upon his shoulders, not being a resident of those captaincies, it was for the service of His Highness alone, and for the sake of obedience to the governor, D. Pedro de Almeida. . . .

Having thus spoken, his reasoning being accepted with a good spirit by everyone, Carrilho entered the forest in search of the Acainene Compound, a fortified *mocambo* 25 leagues northwest of Porto Calvo, where the king's mother lived, for whom the *mocambo* had been named. So impressed were the men by the magic words of Carrilho that each one thought of himself as invincible.

As soon as the blacks knew of their presence, they quickly abandoned the city, still in the state of terror inspired by Major Manoel Lopes. On October 4 our men attacked the fugitives with such force that they killed many and captured nine, but the king's mother was not found among them either dead or alive.

Not only did they gain advantages from the enemy's losses of a strong city and a large number of men; this victory also served to furnish our side with guides and information. From the prisoners it was learned that the king, Gangasuma, with his brother, Gangasona, and all the other rulers and main chiefs were at the compound called Sucupira, which was then serving as a stronghold where the king waited to engage us in battle. This *mocambo* was 45 leagues from Porto Calvo.

It appeared to Carrilho that to establish his camp under the best conditions it would be desirable to capture a more centralized position, and so Sucupira became his objective. . . . Intending to take advantage of the latest successes, on October 9, equipped with the needed supplies, Carrilho set out toward the Sucupira Compound over open forest trails.

After a great expenditure of effort, our men found the *mocambo*, and when they spotted it from a distance they moved silently and with great caution to avoid being discovered. Eighty men then went out again to explore the site and to verify the existence of a stockade, and they returned with news that the terrorized blacks had set fire to the city, which even in ashes revealed its greatness. When Gangasuma had received the news carried by the fugitives from Acainene that Fernão Carrilho was about to pursue them there, he found it preferable to sacrifice the city to fire rather than place his own people in danger.

As soon as this occurred . . . our men took possession of the site, and there Carrilho established his camp, giving it the name "Bom Jesus e a Cruz" [Good Jesus and the Cross], fortifying it in the best possible way with batteries of cannon. [After some successes on the part of the fugitives, the reinforced expedition achieved another important victory, killing and capturing many blacks, including the field commander, General Gangamuiza, whom they executed along with other male prisoners.] The king, who had also been present at the beginning of the battle, had fled with the few people he could rescue from the carnage. . . .

News of such a fortunate and magnificent action brought elation to the camp. Wisely taking advantage of this and prudently ignoring the deed practiced against the prisoners in order to keep the unanimous support of his men, Commander Carrilho sent Captains Estevão Gonçalves and Manoel da Silveira Cardoso with a new levy of fifty fresh soldiers in pursuit of the king and the other fugitives.

After 22 days of hard campaigning in that wilderness, on November 11 they received news that the king, Gangasuma, was with Amaro in his *mocambo* nine leagues northwest of Serinhaem. This same Amaro, celebrated for his bravery, impudence, and insulting behavior, was also greatly feared by our men, and he had made himself known by his incursions into the surrounding towns. He lived separated from the others as an independent ruler. His *mocambo*, which was known by his name, was fortified by high, thick palisades extending the length of a league and containing more than a thousand inhabited houses.

In this *mocambo* the fugitive king believed himself to be safe, but even there he could not escape the vigilance and tenacity of our men who were ambitious for glory and motivated by their comrades' example. Divided into two groups, they marched with the intention of besieging the site by closing up the single entrance to the *mocambo*. Fortunately or unfortunately, however, before the entrance area could be occupied, the blacks, aware of our men's intentions, began to evacuate the compound, but not before our men attacked. Many of them were killed and wounded on the ground, and 47 were captured, among whom were two free black women and a little mulatto girl, the daughter of a noble resident of Serinhaem who had been seized at that place. Also captured were Anajuba, two of the king's children named Zambi and Jacainêne, the former a man and the other a woman, and others numbering about twenty, among them children and grandchildren of the king. Among the dead were Tucúlo, a son of the king, Pacasâ and Baûbi, powerful chiefs among them. So greatly frightened was the king that he fled from our furious attack, and so badly disorganized that he left behind a gilded pistol and a sword, and he was also reported wounded. . . .

This great event brought total disorganization to the blacks, who had lost any hope that they could remain any longer in those places, since they had lost their principal leaders, including the most capable and feared among them, and found themselves weakened and surrounded on all sides. . . .

D. Pedro received news of all this at exactly the moment that Commander Carrilho and Major Manoel Lopes reached Recife; and taking this news into consideration as well as the views of the two distinguished leaders, whose judgment was highly regarded, he concluded reasonably that the *quilombos* of Palmares had been destroyed, and the remaining blacks were wandering about aimlessly, scattered in disorder. He therefore devised a plan to summon them to him and to offer them peace as a way to achieve complete pacification.

From conception of this plan to its realization, little time was lost. The governor selected a young ensign who was accustomed to those marches and completely familiar with those backlands to search for the leaders and tell them that Commander Carrilho was prepared to return and destroy what was left of them and would not leave a single enemy alive; that if they wanted to live in peace with whites he would promise them, in the name of the king, total peace and good treatment, and he would grant them a specified place for their dwellings and land for their gardens; and their women, children, and grandchildren who were prisoners and slaves would be returned to them, and they would remain in their positions of leadership. The one whom they referred to as king would remain commander of all those who had been born in Palmares, and these would be granted the privileges pertaining to the vassals of the king of Portugal, to come under the protection of our arms, and to serve our colors, when conditions might require this, all those who were born in freedom to remain exempt from slavery. . . .

King Gangasuma, having been informed of this or having judged by his own experience that he could no longer resist, or fearing further setbacks, or for other reasons which we cannot determine, accepted D. Pedro's offer; and on June 18, on a Saturday afternoon, on the eve of the day on which the parish church of Recife celebrated the feast of St. Anthony of Lisbon, the ensign who had undertaken the assignment entered the plaza accompanied by two of the king's sons and ten more of the most important blacks of those *quilombos*, who had come, in conformity with the offer made to them, to prostrate themselves at the feet of D. Pedro. They had been sent by King Gangasuma to render vassalage in his name, to ask for peace and friendship, and to tell him that only he had been able to achieve that which so many other governors and so many principal chiefs had attempted and never achieved: their conquest; that they would submit to him and subject themselves to his rule; that they did not desire any more war, and were only trying to save the lives of those who remained; that they were without cities, without sources of food, and, worse yet, without their wives and children; and that D. Pedro might do with them what he wished. . . .

The appearance of those barbarians caused amazement, because they came naked, and with their natural parts alone covered. Some wore their beards in braids, others wore false beards and mustaches, and others were shaved, and nothing more. All were husky and powerful, armed with bows and arrows, and carrying only one firearm. One of the king's sons rode a horse, because he still bore an open bullet wound which he had received during the fighting.

All prostrated themselves at D. Pedro's feet, striking their palms together as a sign of surrender and to acknowledge his victory. They asked for peace with the whites, as their king had ordered them to do, which was his decision and that of all the other rulers who had thus far escaped our resolute fury.

D. Pedro de Almeida received them with great pleasure, and not wishing the glory for such an outstanding achievement for himself alone, he entrusted them to the new governor, Ayres de Sousa, so that he would also have a part to play in the realization of this great event. They also prostrated themselves at his feet, telling him that they wanted no more war; that their king had sent them there to ask for peace and harmony with the whites; that they had come humbly to submit to his will and command. They wanted commerce and trade with the Portuguese residents, and aspired to be vassals of the king and to serve him in every way which he required, asking only freedom for those born in Palmares, promising that they would return all those who had fled from our towns and plantations, that they would themselves abandon Palmares and go to live in a place designated for their gardens and dwelling places.

Great was the pleasure with which Governor Ayres de Sousa received them, and extraordinary was his delight at being so highly esteemed by those enemies. He treated them with great courtesy, spoke to them gently, and promised to do everything for them. He ordered them to be dressed and adorned with yellow ribbons, which pleased them greatly. All the people applauded the success of D. Pedro and the benevolence of Ayres de Sousa. . . .

The governor then wished to have them baptized so that they might begin to enjoy the benefits of peace under divine influence; and since the blacks themselves wished to receive baptism, it was wisely decided to take advantage of this opportune occasion so that they might pledge themselves with utmost seriousness to the purpose for which they had come. A solemn mass was sung, and the vicar of the parish church rose to the pulpit and gave deserved thanks to God, repeated praise to St. Anthony, and to the governors the compliments they had earned. . . .

The blacks greatly admired everything they saw, were very pleased with the sumptuousness of the church and impressed with the greatness of the governors, with the multitude of people, and with their friendliness.

The next day Governor Ayres de Sousa convoked a council of all the leading men to decide how they might best guarantee the peace which they hoped to establish. In the presence of D. Pedro, the members of the city council, of the high judge, Lino Camello, the royal treasury officer, João do Rego Barros, and Commanders Manoel Lopes and Jorge Lopes Alonso, the governor asked them to advise him concerning the petition of the king of Palmares in which he asked for peace, freedom, land for settlement, and the return of their wives and children. D. Pedro de Almeida, who had originated and directed this entire business, who had investigated and weighed all the problems and advantages of that acquisition, delivered a speech on the question, skilfully outlining his opinions. The others eagerly supported his views, which were the following: that they agree to make peace with the king of Palmares, acknowledging his obedience; that they [the blacks] be granted the site where they would choose to settle, a place suitable for their dwellings and their farms; that they must begin to live there within three months; that those born in Palmares would be free; that they were to return all the runaways who had come from our populated places; that they would have commerce and friendly trade with the whites; that they would acquire the privileges of the king's vassals; that they would remain obedient to the orders of the government; that their king would continue as commander of all his people; and that the wives of the king and all the other rulers would be returned to them. There being some doubt among the members of the council that King Gangasuma would have sufficient power to dominate another rebellious runaway who lived at a distance from his *mocambos*, his son responded that the king would be able to manage all of them, and if some of them were insubordinate and insolent and resisted their subjection, he would conquer them, and he would provide guides to our forces so that they might be overcome. And he immediately indicated the place which they regarded as most suitable for their settlement, which was an extensive forest situated in the headwaters of the Rivers Serinhaem and Formoso, which they called "Cacaú," where there was no lack of palm trees to provide them with food. With these matters clarified, the peace was agreed upon, the desired site was granted, and the council ended its meeting. And Governor Ayres de Sousa ordered that everything be recorded, so that the blacks could take with them in writing what the council had decided, and thus they were sent away in the company of a regimental major.

These are the happy events which took place in the immense region of Palmares, which would have had a great impact upon the entire country if the wisdom and good will of the new governor of the captaincy had been equal to those of his predecessor.

9.4. "White Man Won't Come Here": A Twentieth-Century Folk Memory of Palmares

As stated in the introduction to 9.3, the peace treaty between the blacks of Palmares and the Portuguese government was soon violated, and the struggle resumed. Despite eventual defeat, however, the Palmares legend survived into modern times, not only among historians, but even among the backland descendants of the runaways themselves.

The following account of a black folk festival of Alagôas was written by a local scholar, Alfredo Brandão, early in this century and reprinted by the noted student of black history and culture, Arthur Ramos. This festival, variations of which were widespread in the part of Alagôas where the Palmares settlements had once existed, is an indication of the powerful impression which they had upon the local consciousness, and evidence too that the Palmares communities were not totally eradicated in the late seventeenth century, as history would have it. According to Ramos, who witnessed a similar festival in the Alagôan town of Pilar, none of the participants with whom he spoke had any knowledge of the historical Palmares, and yet they had just impressively reenacted life in the *mocambos* along with the battles that had led to their collapse. In the process, they had revealed a strong sympathy for their unknown ancestors and a healthy contempt for their ancestors' enemies, both of which, remarkably, had survived in local tradition for two and a half centuries.

Source: Arthur Ramos, "O auto dos quilombos," *Revista do Instituto Arqueológico, Histórico e Geográfico Pernambucano* 37 (1941-1942), 202-207.

❧ The popular tournament known by the name of *quilombo* is a festivity that is tending to die out, not only in Viçosa, but also in other localities of the region.

It remains, meanwhile, a purely Alagôan festival recalling one of the most important events of our history—the Palmares war—and ought to be preserved not only for love of tradition, but also because this type of diversion never loses its fascinating qualities, and is even superior to the old-fashioned and exhausting contests of horsemanship.

The *quilombo* tournament took place on the day of the patron saint. At dawn, in a corner of the plaza, a palisade structure was set up and romantically festooned with palm fronds, banana stems, and various green branching trees brought there during the night. From the branches hung flags, flowers, and bunches of fruit. In the center of the palisade two thrones of woven sticks and leaves were constructed. The one on the right was occupied by the king, who wore a doublet and white breeches and an embroidered blue cloak, and had on his head a golden crown and a long sword thrust into his sash. Around him black men dressed in blue cotton danced to the sounds of *adufos, mulungus, ganzás* [percussion instruments of African origin] and tambourines, ecstatically singing the following couplet:

> Black man rejoice.
> White man won't come here.
> And if he does,
> The devil take him.
>
> [Folga negro
> Branco não vem cá
> Se vier
> O diabo há de levá.]

Later the men let loose a din of warlike shouts, playing their instruments with ever increasing excitement. At the sound of hunting horns the blacks dispersed to sell their nightly plunder. This loot was represented by oxen, horses, sheep, chickens, and other domesticated animals which had been brought secretly to the *quilombo* from various houses. The sales were made to the actual owners, who generally paid the sellers one or two hundred *réis*. At about ten o'clock in the morning the king, at the head of the black men, went off to search for the queen, a little girl dressed in white who, in the midst of a great deal of bowing, music, and flowers, was led to the vacant throne. The festivities, the dances, the singing, and the warlike shouting continued until noon, when the first *caboclo* spies appeared [*caboclo*: formerly a descendant of whites and

Indians, now generally a poor rural inhabitant or even a treacherous person]. The latter, wearing only breechcloths and headbands of feathers and grass, arrived armed with bows and arrows. They emerged cautiously, attempting to locate the enemy's positions through the foliage.

With much shouting the black men prepared themselves for battle.

Soon all the *caboclos* came into open view with their king, wearing a yellow cloak and a sword, in the vanguard. They marched singing and dancing the *toré*, a savage dance accompanied by music from crude and monotonous instruments, including young bamboo canes, split reeds, and rolled-up palm leaves. The battle took place on the plaza in front of the *quilombo*, and after many skirmishes and simulated retreats and attacks, the king of the *caboclos* managed to subjugate the king of the blacks, and to gain possession of the queen.

At that moment the church bells began to ring, fireworks began to spin noisily in front of the church, and, in the midst of screaming children, the black men, defeated by the *caboclos*, retreated to the center of the *quilombo* which was then besieged and destroyed. The festival ended with the sale of the blacks and the delivery of the queen to one of the leading men of the village, who, in order to cut a good figure, had to grant lavish rewards to the victors.

9.5. "The Armadillo's Hole": A Predatory *Quilombo* Near Bahia (1763)

More typical in regard to size than Palmares was the *quilombo* known as Buraco do Tatú (Armadillo's Hole), a settlement in a jungle region near the city of Bahia which harbored perhaps two hundred people at the time of its destruction in 1763. The following letter sent to Lisbon by the members of the provisional government of Bahia describes this *quilombo*, the predatory activities of its inhabitants, and its elimination. Among the sixty-one persons seized in this settlement, thirty-nine were branded with an "F," which signified "*Fugido*" or runaway, in compliance with the royal order of March 3, 1741. Six of the leading captives, who were judged guilty of crimes more serious than merely living in a *quilombo*, were sentenced to severe public whippings and to long periods of galley service. (For a modern version of the layout drawing mentioned in the text and an analysis of this *quilombo*, see Stuart B. Schwartz, "The *Mocambo*," pp. 313-333. For a reproduction of the original plan, see A.J.R. Russell-Wood, *The Black Man in Slavery and Freedom in Colonial Brazil*, Plate 10.)

Source: Doc. No. 6449, Arquivo de Marinha e Ultramar, Lisbon. Cited in full in Pedro Tomás Pedreira, *Os quilombos brasileiros* (Salvador: Editora Mensageiro da Fé, 1973), pp. 129-131.

❧ Most Illustrious and Excellent Sir: The entirely reasonable complaints which came repeatedly to the attention of the government from the residents of the farms and plantations in the forests up to two leagues distance around this city, the frequent damage done to them by the slaves living in those forests, emerging from them to commit robberies and damage on the plantations, attacking the homes of the inhabitants of those places, stealing their cattle and other stock; appearing on the roads to strip travelers of their clothing and money, mainly black men and women who come to the city daily with produce grown in their gardens, returning on the same or following day with the profits from those sales; carrying off to the *quilombo* by force the black women who were most attractive to them; and, finally, entering the city streets at night to supply them with gunpowder, shot, and the other kinds of equipment needed for their defense; having contacts with the city blacks and those of the countryside, and even with some whites who feared they would be murdered in their isolated homes, or that their crops would be destroyed—all these reasons moved the government to seek precise information about the existence of such a "*quilombo*" and the true extent of its strength.

Having acquired authentic information, the government fully verified the existence of the *quilombo* called Buraco do Tatú [Armadillo's Hole], that it was established twenty years ago, and that it was made up of a large body of blacks, and that it would be dangerous to approach it because of its location and the existence of an abundance of covered pits filled with many sharpened stakes, a plan of which is being sent to Your Excellency so that you may have some impression of the layout of the *quilombo*.

Of all the precautions which the government was obliged to take, the most essential was to ask people experienced with those forests to give information about the traps and pitfalls which they had prepared there, in order that the *quilombo* could be reached without great loss of life and damage to the men, since otherwise the subjugation of those blacks would have been impractical. Without much difficulty, guides were found who were willing to join the expedition, which was sent out with Indian soldiers taking part, notably auxiliaries from the pacified village of Jeguiriça in Jaguaripe, and with a number of other men suitable for that incursion.

With these people a corps of 200 persons was formed, with some grenadiers present to make use of the grenades, all armed with the provisions of war and food supplies needed for the duration of the incursion. They were ordered not to desist from fighting and not to retire from the forests until they had destroyed the *quilombo*, captured the blacks, killed those who resisted, investigated the nearby forests, burned the huts and traps, and filled in the ditches; all of which was in fact accomplished to the fullest extent possible, given the circumstances.

Sixty-one blacks, both males and females, were captured, taken to the jail, and delivered over to the Judge of the Criminal Court to be examined and punished as the law provides for those guilty of their offense. They were at last sentenced, as the enclosed certificate indicates, from which it may also be seen that their masters were fined in just proportion for a total of 245$493 *réis* which the Royal Treasury had spent for the purchase of the supplies provided for the people who took part in the incursion. May God protect Your Excellency.

Bahia, January 14, 1764. Signed: Colonel Gonçalves Xavier de Brito e Alvim, Chancellor José Carvalho de Andrade, Friar Manoel de Santa Inês, Archbishop.

9.6. The Police Chief of Rio de Janeiro Suggests Ways to Eliminate *Quilombos* Near the City (1824)

The following letter from the police chief of Rio de Janeiro, Estevão Ribeiro de Rezende, to the Brazilian minister of justice deals with the problem of *quilombos* and runaway lawlessness which in 1823 and 1824 were causing unusual alarm in the Brazilian capital. At that time, with the violence and weakened authority which accompanied Brazil's independence struggle, thousands of slaves, aided by army deserters, had established themselves in numerous settlements in the mountains and forests surrounding the city of Rio, creating an emergency which even the members of the first Brazilian Constituent Assembly found time to discuss. (See *Annaes do Parlamento Brasileiro: Assembléa Constituinte. 1823* [Rio de Janeiro: Typographia de Hyppolito José Pinto e Cia., 1876-1884], v, 178.) In the present selection the police chief recommended unorthodox emergency measures for dealing with the *quilombos* which the government quickly sanctioned.

Source: *Collecção das decisões do governo, 1824*, pp. 196-197.

29. Bush Captain with a Captured Runaway Slave

Most illustrious and excellent Sir:

Day after day in this city and its neighborhood there is an increase in the number of runaway slaves who join the many others in the various *quilombos* which exist in the sierra and forests of Tijuca and the surrounding region. Because of the assaults they commit on the roads and even within this capital city, these fugitives are causing ever-increasing danger to public security.

I have ordered assaults against some of these *quilombos* with a police squad and another force whose assistance I asked for, along with soldiers of the militia, but all has been in vain. Such attacks are never undertaken without a great deal of alarm and confusion, and when the assault begins the blacks (and the deserters who live among them) have already been informed and have abandoned the place where they were thought to be hiding out. As long as expeditions are launched with military fanfare, they will always be given this kind of warning. The reason for this is that, both day and night, the fugitives carry on a regular trade with tavern-keepers and other black men and women of this city, who transport and sell the stolen goods which the fugitives acquire from country houses and from highway robbery. Moreover, as long as they are carried out by ordinary soldiers, these attacks can never accomplish anything except to frighten the blacks and drive them away, because it is not practical for booted, uniformed, and armed men to penetrate into those steep, lofty mountain jungles, caves, and grottoes where the blacks hide out and move about with total freedom.

The so-called bush captains, which the town council appoints, are worthless, and every day there are complaints against them. The title given to them by the council serves more as a license to steal than to promote the public good. Many have been arrested for stealing slaves, whom they sell to Minas Gerais, in league with gypsies. The evil is growing and must eventually be stopped. I have been informed that there are *quilombos* with a considerable number of slaves, and even freedmen and deserters.

In Minas Gerais, and mainly in the Serro do Frio, there are foot soldiers and bush captains who make their living by pursuing diamond smugglers and runaway blacks, people who can penetrate mountainous jungles because of their use of leather clothing which protects them from briers and thorns. It would be most advantageous if a dozen of these men were allowed to come here, released by the government of Minas Gerais from their regular employment, bringing along their weapons and clothing. The provincial Finance Committee could order that they continue receiving the salaries which they earn there, and aside from that they might also be given 400 *réis* per day while in residence here, paid from police coffers, in addition to the amount provided for in the Regulations for the capture of slaves in *quilombos*, and finally houses where they could live (which might be a storehouse of the kind which the police themselves possess). Thus, picked and able men could come here to be employed each day in entering the forests and destroying *quilombos*, and even capturing runaway blacks in the city and its suburbs, in accordance with the orders they would receive from the Chief of Police. I am convinced that in a few months we would be able to eliminate the *quilombos*, establish public security, and protect the private interests of proprietors and slaveholders, and such advantages are obtained only through expense and sacrifice.

To indemnify part of the expenses of the police in this work, each master might be required to pay 4$000 in the act of receiving any slave captured in a *quilombo*.

If this plan, for which I beg Your Excellency's support, is worthy of delivery to His Imperial Majesty's presence, and deserves his Imperial Sanction, it will be essential to submit the necessary orders to the provincial government of Minas Gerais, recommending utmost speed and careful selection.

Rio, December 18, 1824.—To the most Illustrious and Excellent Clemente Ferreira França.—From Estevão Ribeiro de Rezende.

9.7. "All the Huts Were Burned": The Destruction of *Quilombos* Near Rio de Janeiro (1876)

The following police report of attacks on *quilombos* carried out in 1876 in a swampy region of Guanabara Bay near the imperial capital reveals a pattern of conditions and events much like those depicted in previous *quilombo* documents. The settlements were old; they were located in remote places but with easy access to a nearby urban area; they were well defended; their inhabitants carried on various enterprises, including agriculture; and they maintained trade contacts and friendly relations with free neighbors. The now familiar hostility toward the *quilombolas* is also clearly evident.

Source: "Relatorio apresentado ao Illm. e Exm. Sr. Conselheiro Francisco Xavier Pinto Lima, Presidente da Provincia do Rio de Janeiro, pelo Chefe de Policia, Dr. Luiz de Hollanda Cavalcanti de Albuquerque," in *Relatorio . . . do Rio de Janeiro apresentado no dia 22 de Outubro de 1876* (Rio de Janeiro, 1876).

The Police Delegate of the County of Estrella, Colonel Joaquim Alves Machado, aided by Faustino Gonçalves Vieira, administrator of the plantation called Mosquito, accomplished the arrest of 23 runaway slaves on several successive days in the month of June. These were found in the two *quilombos* known as Quilombo Grande and Quilombo do Gabriel, the first also known as Bomba, located in the district of Iguassu. On this occasion ten of the mentioned slaves of the *quilombo* of Bomba escaped or fled.

Continuing his efforts to capture the rest and to extinguish the *quilombo*, the same Delegate set out on the night of July 7, for the Parish of Pilar, accompanied by a notary, soldiers, and civilians. From there, on the following morning, he went up river with the aim of posting himself at a point near the entrance of the *quilombo*, and he sent another force of men to the Inhomerim River, to a point where they met a black man named Tiburcio, who offered them assistance.

Despite certain adversities and incidents which might have thwarted the expedition, the Police Delegate did not lose hope. Taking every precaution to prevent the slaves from hearing of his presence, which was known in the Parish of Pilar, a center of support for the runaways, on the 9th he managed to achieve the purpose of the expedition, capturing three of the slaves, the others to the number of six getting away. Even so, with much difficulty, another was captured, the rest entering the mangrove forest.

Continuing the campaign, the Police Delegate set out for the dwelling places of the runaways, for which he used one of the prisoners [as a guide], since the black man, Tiburcio, was still pursuing the others with the soldiers.

Despite the great distance of those dwelling places and the strategic trails full of traps, ruses, and defenses, they managed to arrive at their destination. There they found eight huts, more or less regular in shape, covered with the straw of cocoanut palms and with walls of joined sticks, one of which was not inhabited, since it served as the tomb of Joaquim Bunga. There they also found an insignificant sugar cane field, and a place used as a cemetery, where there were three graves. One of the skeletons . . . was uncovered, and it was recognized that it was the skeleton of the black man Aleixo.

All the huts were burned. In the first settlement five firearms, two swords, two axes, and two scythes were confiscated; and in the second a canoe, a loaded hunting musket, axes, scythes, hoes, a fishing net, some carpentry tools, and 64 containers of good firewood.

Those *quilombos*, which were very old, were located in a vast mangrove forest, with an outlet to the sea on one side which allowed easy communication with the city of Rio de Janeiro, from where many people came to supply themselves with firewood. On the land side they were bordered by various plantations, with few inhabitants, such as those of the Benedictine Friars. There the runaway slaves found a secure shelter as a result of the vast forests and lack of people willing to inhabit such places where, aside from everything else, communications are difficult.

In exchange for food and rum, given to them by those who went there to get wood—such mangrove forests furnish the best that is supplied to the city of Rio de Janeiro—the slaves cut the wood to fill the boats, whose owners took advantage of this profitable trade and always warned them when there was reason to suspect that the authorities were trying to capture them.

Thus the two *quilombos* of Bomba and Gabriel have been eliminated, and the said Police Delegate, Colonel Joaquim Alves Machado, deserves praise for the methods he used and the zeal he employed to accomplish such a satisfactory result.

9.8. The Destruction of *Quilombos* in Maranhão (1853)

The rugged, jungle-covered river valleys of the northern provinces of Pará and Maranhão were particularly suitable for the establishment and preservation of runaway settlements, and some of the more isolated areas were havens where blacks established themselves in relative security and survived for generations. The following document, a report of the president of Maranhão to the provincial assembly delivered in 1853, describes the destruction of such isolated *quilombos*. At least one of these settlements, founded more than forty years before, was playing a significant and perhaps long-established economic role in the region at the time of its destruction, probably sheltering persons who had never experienced personal servitude.

This document, like some of the previous ones, reveals as much about the master class as it does about the slaves. Although some of the blacks captured in these *quilombos* had been born and had lived in de facto freedom, and although their legal ownership would have been hard if not impossible to prove, the provincial president, adopting a rancorous style, referred to them as "merchandise" and "bandits" and announced his intention to recommend to their "masters" that they be deported from the province. He also revealed that a significant reason for attacking these *quilombos* was to open a fertile, underdeveloped territory to new agricultural settlement.

Presidential reports similar to this one on *quilombos* and their eradication were especially common during the nineteenth century in the provinces of Pará, Maranhão, Pernambuco, Alagôas, Sergipe, and Espirito Santo.

Source: *Relatorio do Presidente da Provincia do Maranhão o Doutor Eduardo Olimpio Machado, na abertura da Assemblea Legislativa Provincial, no dia 1 de Novembro de 1853* (Maranhão, 1853), pp. 7-8.

❧ As you know, the main location of the *quilombos* of fugitive slaves is the district of Tury-assú, though some of little importance exist in the district of the Upper Mearim. I will not take time to demonstrate the need that existed to free that district from the yoke of the *quilombos*; it is sufficient to point out that they kept it constantly under the threat of an uprising which would inevitably have spread to the Alcântara and Viana districts; that they placed both property and the personal safety of its inhabitants in danger; and that they rendered inaccessible a territory that was otherwise extremely fertile and suitable for various types of agriculture.

I will limit myself instead to informing you that last June 18 the needed military force under the command of Captain Guilherme Leopoldo de Freitas left this capital well supplied with the equipment essential for the destruction of those *quilombos*. The following August, having reached his destination—the plantation known as Jussural in the district of Parauá from where several trails fanned out toward the *quilombos*—Captain Freitas was able to destroy those settlements, after wisely and carefully taking every necessary precaution. These included the *quilombos* of the Maracassumé mines and of Cris-Santo, which were reputed to be the principal ones and those causing the greatest anxiety. The *quilombo* of the mines was situated on the banks of the Maracassumé River, and the one that had as its king the renowned Cris-Santo, who somehow was killed, existed for more than two years between the Parauá and Maracassumé Rivers. The king of the *quilombo* of the mines, named Epiphano, is also dead.

The slaves who inhabited the first of these *quilombos* supported themselves from the yield of the mines, which they traded in Santa Helena and other places for food, ammunition, and dry goods. They had gathered themselves together in a regular village, and they maintained relations with peddlers and people of nearby population centers. Those who inhabited the second *quilombo* lived isolated from one another in camps located in the depths of the forests, cautiously avoiding all contact with outsiders and supporting themselves exclusively through agricultural labor.

Despite the most positive and repeated recommendations of this government, and Captain Freitas's efforts to comply with them, it was not possible to avoid bloodshed entirely, because the blacks, well-armed and supplied with ammunition as if they had been warned beforehand, offered a formal and desperate resistance lasting several hours. Reporting on this engagement in a statement of August 23, Captain Freitas said that ten blacks were killed at the battle site, and that several more were seriously wounded, and since the latter fled into the heart of the forest, they most likely suffered the same fate. Among the soldiers who took part in the expedition, only two of the police guards were seriously wounded, fortunately both surviving, and thirteen soldiers of the 5th Infantry Battalion received light wounds. In the skirmish of August 10, forty-six slaves were captured and are now safely in prison, along with a tolerable number of weapons and ammunition.

The population of the *quilombos* may be estimated at about 200 slaves, 98 of whom are out of action, that is, those who were captured, those who died, and those who have surrendered themselves voluntarily to their masters. In regard to the others, left as they are to their own means and harassed by various expeditions which are now pursuing them, it must be assumed that they will decide to give themselves up. The gardens and shelters of those bandits were completely destroyed.

Enlightened by the lesson they have just received, I am certain that, despite the long de facto freedom in which they have lived (since 1811), they will not quickly gather again in *quilombos*; especially if, as I intend, a military colony is established in that wild, far-off region to prevent their reestablishment.

In view of the information which has been presented to me, there is no question but that the blacks were encouraged in their attempts to resist by some merchants who carried on trade with them. You are aware of the great necessity of providing an example which will root out such dangerous commercial relations. The following persons, who were the ones most involved, have been arrested: Marcellino José da Costa Ramos, Isidoro Francisco de Oliveira, Theodoro Sudré, and Mariano Gil.

Since, when masters attempt to justify a claim to their slaves, fraud may arise if the proceedings are held before local authorities; and since it will be helpful to the peace of mind of slaveholders if these slaves—so long affected by habits of independence and idleness—are sold outside this province, I have ordered that all the slaves captured in *quilombos* are to be sent to this capital. When they arrive I will speak to their masters and suggest to them that the exportation of that merchandise is the solution that will best benefit their interests.

Having received reports that on the banks of the Gurupi River a formidable *quilombo* existed composed of slaves, deserters, and Indians, I suggested to Captain Freitas that he make the required investigation, and that he should destroy the *quilombo* if its existence should be confirmed. Having seriously looked into the question of the alleged *quilombo*, Captain Freitas informs me that its existence is questionable, or that at least it is not as large as popular tradition had made it seem. Nevertheless, since the detachment was assembled at the Maracassumé mines, I ordered it to carry out a scouting operation along the shores of the Gurupi at the point where tradition has placed the *quilombo*.

Not long ago a force of thirty soldiers under the command of Lieutenant José Guilherme de Almeida, joined by some civilians, set out to attack some *quilombos* existing in the heart of the Upper Mearim district. This important assignment was entrusted to the zeal and enterprise of the district judge and the police delegate of Coroatá, with whom the lieutenant will come to an understanding.

9.9. "A Sort of Enchanted Land": *Quilombos* of the Amazon Valley in the 1850s

The following descriptions of remote *quilombos* in the region of the Amazon Valley and the several campaigns which the provincial government of Pará launched against them are taken from three separate reports to the British Foreign Office by one Mr. Vines, who was British consul in Belém. This selection is clear evidence that some slaves managed to achieve permanent freedom by fleeing to a *quilombo*, especially in the huge jungle-covered regions of Maranhão, Pará, and Amazonas.

Sources: *British and Foreign State Papers*, Vol. XLIV (1853-1854), pp. 1241-1243; *Class B. Correspondence with British Ministers and Agents in Foreign Countries and with Foreign Ministers in England, Relating to the Slave Trade. From April 1, 1855, to March 31, 1856* (London, 1856), pp. 234-235; ibid. *From April 1, 1855, to March 31, 1857* (London, 1857), p. 230.

❧ JANUARY 28, 1854

There have been known to exist, for several years, settlements of runaway negroes; one at Santarém, about 1,300 miles from this port, where upwards of 1,000 fugitive slaves are located, amongst the mountains and swamps in the vicinity of the villages of Parinha and Monte Alegre, and near the town of Macapá, are encampments from whence fugitives easily escape to Cayenne. Within 60 miles of the city of Pará [Belém] a settlement has been formed on the river Mujú, from which a female slave was recovered a few weeks ago; she had escaped during the insurrection of 1835, and reappeared with a large family; and within a circuit of 2 leagues of Pará are many fugitive slaves.

The sites of these encampments appear to be carefully chosen to guard against a surprise attack.

The fugitives are said to be industrious in the cultivation of rice, mandioca, and Indian corn, and in the manufacture of charcoal. They make canoes and barcoes, or small sailing vessels, which are used for the interior trade. They carry on a traffic with the inferior class of tradesmen in the neighbouring towns, exchanging the produce of their labour for certain necessaries, such as gunpowder and shot, cloth and soap, &c. Some of them are frequently known to venture into the city of Pará at night, where they have occasionally been taken and claimed by their owners, who endeavour to sell them, but find generally much difficulty in doing so, the freedom of their wandering life unfitting them for slavery.

The situation of these encampments being naturally difficult of access, and the connivance afforded the fugitives by parties trading with them, have rendered the repeated attempts to capture them abortive.

JANUARY 28, 1856

In reference to the settlements of fugitive slaves in the Amazonian districts, which I had the honour to mention to your Lordship in my annual Slave Trade Report, under date of 28th of January, 1854, as having baffled all attempts of the military authorities here to disturb them, I regret that I am obliged to report to your Lordship that they have recently succeeded in discovering two large encampments at Mucajubá and at the River Trombetas, and in capturing 45 slaves, who were brought to the prison of this city, and delivered to their owners or their heirs.

On the night of the 7th of September last, a detachment of forty soldiers, under the command of a Captain and Lieutenant, left Pará to effect the destruction of the Mocambo (Settlement) of Mucajubá, in the district of Aycaraú, about fourteen miles from this city, it having been reported that the fugitive negroes encamped there, had attacked the canoes of several planters, and had committed depredations on some of the neighboring estates. The detachment disembarked secretly, and lay concealed in the woods near to the paths by which the fugitives were supposed to leave their settlements. One negro being captured, was forced to show the best pass by which to enter the lake or swamp on which the encampment of Mucajubá was situated, which occupied several hours in reaching, sometimes wading through water up to the waist, and occasionally being obliged to swim; on arriving at the first house, a discharge of fire-arms from it killed one soldier and wounded some others. The expedition then returned, having captured two negroes, but returned to the locality on the 11th of September, being reinforced by fifty soldiers and four officers, and thirty-two soldiers of the National Guard; with this company they succeeded in reaching the lake, on the banks of which the Settlements are situated, on which they embarked in small canoes, and after twenty-eight days' bush-fighting, they captured 45 fugitive slaves, took twenty-seven canoes belonging to the negroes, and destroyed seventeen houses, many of which are reported to have been substantially built dwellings. These Settlements, for they extended over two or three leagues, had never before been visited, except by fugitive slaves; they consisted of little villages, well inclosed and entrenched, containing a population roughly calculated at between 1,000 and 2,000, having large tracts of land under cultivation with the mandioca plant.

Another detachment of forty soldiers, under the command of a Captain, left Pará to destroy the Quilombo of Trombetas, a famous Settlement, over fifty years old, and which hitherto had been deemed inaccessible to military enterprise, and looked upon by the slave population as a sort of enchanted land. The mouth of the Trombetas is about 450 miles distant from Pará, and its source is said to be close to British Guiana; on the landing of this detachment, a captured negro gave such an account of the difficulties and dangers of the journey to this settlement, that thirty-three out of forty soldiers, refused to accompany their captain, and he and seven soldiers proceeded in search of it; after nine days' wandering through dense forests, they reached the settlement, which they found deserted and burned by the negroes, who had broken up their ovens and utensils for making farinha of mandioca. About three leagues from the Quilombo of Trombetas exists a tribe of white Indians, of the Uariquena nation, who being on friendly terms with the fugitive slaves, are supposed to have given them notice of the intended attack.

JANUARY 21, 1857

The fugitive slave settlements, mentioned in my dispatch of the 28th of January, 1856, continue to be maintained, notwithstanding every effort of the Government against them. I am told that some of them have removed their cantonments to more distant and inaccessible positions; and that the authorities of this province, despairing of any successful foray against them, have resolved not to molest them, unless they should attempt piratical excursions upon the navigable part of the Amazon and its confluents.

9.10. The Captured Residents of a Runaway-Slave Settlement Are Claimed as Slaves but Freed by a Legal Decision (1877)

During the last decades of slavery judges and other officials, influenced by abolitionist ideas, were ever more likely to reach decisions favorable to black fugitives if the facts stood clearly against the demands of the masters. The following decision of a judge in Belém, Pará, concerning the fragile claim of would-be heirs to sixty-two blacks seized in a *quilombo* in the Amazon Valley, most of whom "had never known a master," is evidence of this more liberalized attitude. Moreover, it is further proof that at least in the more rugged parts of Brazil slaves could not only achieve permanent escape from slavery by running off to a *quilombo*, but that they could successfully pass this precarious de facto freedom on to their descendants.

Source: *O Direito* (Rio de Janeiro) 17 (1878), 284-286.

❧ *The Recoverers*: The Baron of Santarém and others.
The Recovered: The *quilombolas* from Curuá, district of Alemquer, Raymundo, Severino, and others.

Sentence

The Baron of Santarém, José Joaquim Pereira Macambira, Mauricio José Pereira Macambira, José Pereira Macambira, and Mathias Affonso da Silva, the heirs of the late Dona Maria Margarida Pereira, requesting that the *quilombolas* coming from Curuá, numbering 62 persons, who were arrested by the police, be recognized as their slaves; to this purpose they state in their bill of complaint that they are the heirs of the aforementioned Dona Maria Margarida Pereira, and that among the properties left at the time of her death were the slaves Manoel, Raymundo, Manoel Severino, Maria Eva or Té Maria, Archangela, Maria Barbara, Maria Domingas, Maria de Nazareth, Maria Paulina, Maria Benta, and Maria Joaquina, all of whom were fugitives when she passed away.

They further state that the same slaves were duly registered, and, in effect, form a portion of the runaway slaves from Curuá (documents in folios 12 to 23).

And, finally, that the other claimed slaves, according to the documents in folio 34, are the children and grandchildren of those slave women, but were not registered because they were born in the *mocambo* of Curuá, in Alemquer.

With the document in folio 12 the plaintiffs duly proved that they are the legitimate heirs of Dona Maria Margarida; with this same document they also proved that, when the inventory of Dona Margarida's property was made, a list of runaway slaves was presented in court by the person in charge of making the inventory, which included ten slaves whose names correspond to those which have been mentioned; that, furthermore, these slaves were registered in 1872 with the additional declaration that they were runaways, and that it was believed that they had children, the number and names of whom were unknown, since all of them had been born in the forests of the Quilombo of Curuá, as stated in the registration contained in folios 50 and 52.

Up to this point the plaintiffs have merely proved that the aforementioned Dona Margarida possessed 10 slaves with names identical to those mentioned in the second article of the bill of complaint; concerning the other 52 slaves whom they claim, nothing is clear in the documents except the simple and vague assertion, made in the registration, that those slaves had children.

It therefore remains to be proved:

1. That the slave women referred to in the bill of complaint and mentioned in the registration are in fact the same people.

2. That the other claimed slaves are their offspring.

To prove these capital points of the case, the plaintiffs offered the documents in folios 34 and 66.

The first of these documents is a list of questions and answers heard before the chief of police, in which some slave women replied that they were known by names identical to those of the claimed slave women; that they were born in the Quilombo of Curuá; that they had children; but that they had never had masters.

These declarations are not sufficient to prove identity; that the names are the same is not significant, since nothing would be easier or more natural than that the names of those ten black fugitives should be the same as those of others among the hundreds who over a period of decades inhabited the *mocambo*; so much more so because not even their slave status is clear, since they were unknown, were born in Curubá, and had lived there in a state of freedom.

And so unconvinced were the plaintiffs themselves of the adequacy of this proof that they offered a second document from folio 66, which is a transcript of the inquest which was required by the district of Santarém.

This inquest was carried out at a time and place other than that set, as is noted in folios 64 and 65; in any case, it does not in any way establish additional proof.

Six witnesses were questioned; and none of these provided any positive evidence concerning the recognition and identity of the claimed slaves, whom they did not in fact know, since it was many years ago that the slaves of the deceased Dona Margarida ran away; and the witnesses stated only vaguely and incompletely concerning them that some *quilombolas* from Curuá had declared before the chief of police that they were the slaves of Dona Margarida; but they did not say precisely that it was the defendants who had made that declaration, whereas the opposite is indicated by the cited document from folio 34, in which, in response to questions, the defendants stated that they had never known a master.

Finally, those witnesses merely proved that many years ago—more than fifty, according to some—a number of slaves belonging to the aforementioned Dona Margarida ran away; however, concerning the recognition and identification of the claimed slaves, they prove absolutely nothing.

Based on the documentation and the foregoing facts, I judge the plaintiffs' action to be groundless, and charge the costs to them; and I order that the freedom of the defendants be recognized, and that they be released from the prison where they are now being held.

Belém, March 26, 1877.—*J. F. Meira de Vasconcellos.*

9.11. Slaves of Minas Gerais Plot Revolt (1719)

In the early eighteenth century the captaincy of Minas Gerais was a newly settled region of far-flung gold mining camps where slaves greatly outnumbered whites. As elsewhere in Brazil, the white race brutally dominated the black, but the new mining districts lacked the security and discipline of the older coastal zones. The region's peculiar conditions seem to have brought some temporary alterations in the traditional master-slave relationships, encouraging masters to grant their workers exceptional privileges and responsibilities, and inspiring a high spirit of rebelliousness in the slaves, based upon their understanding that their greatly outnumbered masters were not omnipotent.

These are the impressions given at least by the following letter of Count Pedro de Almeida, captain general of Minas Gerais, to King João V. In this document the count reported a conspiracy to rebel involving slaves in widespread parts of the captaincy inspired in part, he thought, by the indulgent policies of the region's slaveholders. Seeking to advise

the king, he deplored the masters' easygoing attitudes and urged adoption of more restrictive policies to discipline the restive slave population.

Source: Cited in full in José Alipio Goulart, *Da fuga ao suicídio (Aspectos da rebeldia dos escravos no Brasil)* (Rio de Janeiro: Conquista, 1972), pp. 284-286.

❧ In a letter of June 13 of last year I informed Your Majesty of the unrestrained life style of the blacks in this mining region, especially the runaways who, gathered together in *quilombos*, dare to commit all kinds of offenses without fear of punishment. I also called Your Majesty's attention to the great importance of this question, because it seemed to be reasonably well founded that the blacks might possibly carry out operations similar to those of Palmares in Pernambuco, encouraged by their large numbers and the foolhardy attitudes of their masters. Not only do the latter trust them with all kinds of weapons; they also conceal their acts of insolence and their crimes (even those perpetrated against themselves) to avoid the risk of losing them if they should be seized by the agents of Justice. The harm caused by this situation seems without remedy, as I pointed out to you in that same letter, owing to the absence of preventive measures and the great carelessness which has always been characteristic of this situation.

With the passage of time my fears have been verified. No longer satisfied merely to harass us from the *mocambos* which they control in various places, and have always held despite the great efforts I have made to destroy them, the blacks now aspire to an even greater enterprise. And, although this is an ambitious undertaking, it is not beyond their powers, if we consider their large numbers compared with the number of whites, and if God does not use their barbarousness to block their success, with the many gross errors they commit when seeking to maintain the secrecy of their plans.

Having entered into a conspiracy to rebel against the whites which involved most of the blacks of these mines, they attempted to establish contacts with one another by means of various secret agents who went from one place to another over a vast area attempting to arrange a general revolt. They had decided that their first attacks would take place on Maundy Thursday of this year. With all the white men occupied in the churches, they reasoned, they would have time to break into their houses and attack the whites, pitilessly exterminating them. A few days before Holy Week those blacks began to quarrel among themselves, because it was the intention of one nation to impose its rule upon the rest, and the secret was therefore revealed in the Rio das Mortes district, where, along with news of the revolt, it was learned that the blacks of that district had named for themselves a king, a prince, and military leaders. I had already decided that this was probably some black nonsense, when another message arrived from a place called Furquim, a dependency of this city two days travel from here, and six or seven days travel from Rio das Mortes. This message outlined circumstances like those reported in the message from Rio das Mortes, and so it began to be clear to me that this was indeed a very serious situation.

I immediately decreed the necessary preventive measures, including the arrest of all the suspected blacks in the several places. And conscious of the fact that on the hill of Ouro Preto there were also suspicious circumstances suggesting that the blacks who lived there were also involved in the conspiracy, and that that was where the greatest danger existed, I went to Vila Rica and ordered two companies of soldiers to ascend the hill to hunt for weapons. None were found, however, either because none in fact existed, or because they had hidden them in some concealed underground places which the blacks of that hill inhabit. I then decreed a strict ban on the possession by blacks of weapons of every kind, at the same time imposing rigorous punishments upon them and upon their masters. I also ordered that extra precautions were to be taken on Maundy Thursday, the day appointed for the uprising, ordering that all weapons were to be stored in secure places where blacks would not have access to them, and that any weapons left by their owners in their houses should have their gunlocks removed, and should be concealed where the blacks could not find them. And because the blacks in Rio das Mortes, a district less populated by whites, had displayed greater self-confidence than elsewhere, openly threatening the whites with remarks about the date of the uprising, I ordered Lieutenant General João Ferreira Tavares to go there to arrest all blacks he thought were guilty, and to investigate the conspiracy. This he diligently did, arresting and sending to this city the so-called kings of the Mina and Angola nations and others who were allegedly chiefs and military leaders of the rebellion.

. . .

Since all these preventive measures were taken before the date determined by the blacks for their first attacks, and since many guilty black men and women were imprisoned, and others punished, the problem ceased to exist. The sedition was extinguished, and the country returned to its former tranquillity. However, since we cannot prevent the remaining blacks from thinking, and cannot deprive them of their natural desire for freedom; and since we cannot, merely because of this desire, eliminate all of them, they being necessary for our existence here, it must be concluded that this country will always be subjected to this problem. This is not, in fact, the first rebellion that the blacks have planned;

already in times gone by they have had such intentions. And because their multitudes, in comparison with the number of whites, give them courage; and because the whites place too much trust in them, failing to correct them despite repeated instances of unfaithfulness; and because, by merely looking about them they can see the haven offered to them by the immense forests, the defenselessness of the towns, the absence of soldiers to defeat them or pursue them into the forests, they gain courage enough to attempt anything; and their boldness is a disgraceful result of their prejudiced opinion of the white men. Their self respect grows because of the fear the whites have of them, a pride which, whether arising from the negligence of the whites or the scorn of the blacks, always has unpleasant and ugly consequences. Everywhere we look we find a certain lewdness accompanying their pride, which brings discredit to the inhabitants of this country. And it seems to me that there should be some mature reflection on this matter, and that Your Majesty should consider its importance along with the measures that should be employed in the future to prevent the harmful consequences which could easily result from the kind of evil we have just witnessed. Once decisions have been arrived at, Your Majesty might adopt the most useful policies.

May God preserve Your Majesty's Royal Person for many years.

Vila do Carmo, April 20, 1719. *Count Dom Pedro de Almeida.*

9.12. "The Slaves' View of Slavery": A Plantation Rebellion Near Ilhéus, Bahia, and the Rebels' Written Demands for a Settlement

The following two documents were discovered by the historian Stuart B. Schwartz in the Arquivo Público do Estado da Bahia and published in both Portuguese and English in the *Hispanic American Historical Review*. The first is a letter which a royal magistrate addressed to the governor of Bahia giving an account of a slave rebellion on a large sugar plantation near Ilhéus in what is now southern Bahia. This letter goes on to tell of the seizure of the rebels which followed a violent engagement, the sale of most of them to distant Maranhão, and the imprisonment of their leader, the *cabra* Gregorio Luís, who was kept in a jail in Salvador for some sixteen years prior to the date of the magistrate's letter. Far more remarkable than this letter, however, is the second document, a peace proposal which the rebels drew up and sent to their master prior to their seizure to inform him of the conditions under which they would return to work. Written probably by Gregorio Luís, the "most astute" among the rebels, these proposals tell us much about slavery from the point of view of its victims: the conditions under which they labored and the amount of work required of them, both men and women, their clothing, their sources of food, the activities that brought them income, their ethnic conflicts, their pleasures and pastimes, and much more. As Professor Schwartz suggests, the circumstances under which this document was written and the proposals it contains make it extraordinary and perhaps unique in the annals of Brazilian slavery.

Source: Stuart B. Schwartz, "Resistance and Accommodation in Eighteenth-Century Brazil: The Slaves' View of Slavery," *Hispanic American Historical Review* 57 (1977), 69-81.

The Royal Magistrate's Letter

Illustrious and most Excellent Sir:

The Supplicant Gregorio Luís, a *cabra*, finds himself a prisoner in the jail of this High Court where he was sent by his master, Captain Manoel da Silva Ferreira, resident on his *engenho* called Santana in the district of the Town of Ilhéus; there coming at the same time with him, as I remember, some fifteen or sixteen other slaves. These were sent to the merchant José da Silva Maia, his commercial agent, so that he could sell them in Maranhão while the Supplicant came with the recommendation that he be held in prison while the Court of that district prepared the charges so that he could be given exemplary punishment. Taking a preliminary investigation of the Supplicant, I have determined the following facts. The above-mentioned Manoel da Silva Ferreira being master and owner of the aforesaid *engenho* with three hundred slaves, including some of the Mina nation, discovered the majority of them in rebellion refusing to recognize their subordination to their master. And, the principal leader of this disorder was the Supplicant who began to incite among them the partisan spirit against their master and against the Sugar Master. The Supplicant was able with a few of his followers to kill the latter and until now none know where they buried him. Taking control of part of the *engenho*'s equipment, they fled to the forest refusing not only to give their service or to obey their master, but even placing him in fear that they would cruelly take his life. For this reason the *engenho* has remained inactive for two years with such notable damage that its decadence is dated from that time forward, and, moreover, these damages added to the danger that the rest of the slaves might follow the terrible example of those in rebellion. Thus the majority of the slaves persisted divided into errant and vagabond bands throughout the territory of the *engenho*, so absolute and fearless that the consternation and fright of their master increased in consideration that he might one day fall victim to some disaster.

Matters being in this situation, the rebels sent emissaries to their Master with a proposal of capitulation contained in the enclosed copy [see next document] to which he showed them that he acceded: some came and others remained. The Supplicant as the most astute was able to extort from him a letter of Manumission which was granted at the time without the intention that it have any validity, at the same time he [the Supplicant] sought the District Judge who entering the *engenho* with eighty-five armed men sought out the house of his Master: The latter who could not now confide in the principal leaders of that uprising took advantage of a stratagem of sending the Supplicant Gregorio and fifteen others with a false letter to the Captain Major of the militia, João da Silva Santos, who was in the Vila of Belmonte, telling them that they would receive from him some cattle and manioc flour for the *engenho*. Arriving at the said Vila all were taken prisoner with handcuffs despite the great resistance that they made almost to the point of much bloodshed. They were finally conducted to the jail of this High Court as I have said, that is, the Supplicant as the prime mover to be held until his charges were seen and the others with orders to the aforementioned merchant to be sold to Maranhão as they were.

Twice there had been required from this court an order to be sent the investigation or any other charges against the Supplicant and until now they have not arrived.

I must also tell Your Excellency that the Master of the said *engenho* has on repeated occasions recommended with the greatest insistence that the Supplicant not be released from prison except by a sentence that exiles him far away because if he is freed he will unfailingly return to the *engenho* to incite new disorders, that may be irreparable.

That which is reported here seems to me enough to give Your Excellency a sufficient idea concerning the Supplicant and the reasons for his imprisonment. God Protect Your Excellency. Bahia 22 of January of 1806. The Desembargador Ouvidor Geral do Crime.

Claudio José Pereira da Costa

The Slaves' Proposals for Peace

TREATY PROPOSED TO MANOEL DA SILVA FERREIRA BY HIS SLAVES DURING THE TIME THAT THEY REMAINED IN REVOLT

My Lord, we want peace and we do not want war; if My Lord also wants our peace it must be in this manner, if he wishes to agree to that which we want.

In each week you must give us the days of Friday and Saturday to work for ourselves not subtracting any of these because they are Saint's days.

To enable us to live you must give us casting nets and canoes.

You are not to oblige us to fish in the tidal pools nor to gather shellfish, and when you wish to gather shellfish send your Mina blacks.

Make a large boat so that when it goes to Bahia we can place our cargoes aboard and not pay freightage.

In the planting of manioc we wish the men to have a daily quota of two and one half hands [*mão*, a measurement of quantity still used in backland Brazil] and the women, two hands.

The daily quota of manioc flour must be of five level *alqueires* [about thirteen liters to an *alqueire*], placing enough harvesters so that these can serve to hang up the coverings.

The daily quota of sugar cane must be of five hands rather than six and of ten canes in each bundle.

On the boat you must put four poles, and none for the rudder, and the one at the rudder works hard for us.

The wood that is sawed with a handsaw must have three men below and one above.

The measures of firewood must be as was practiced here, for each measure a woodcutter and a woman as the wood carrier.

The present overseers we do not want, choose others with our approval.

At the milling rollers there must be four women to feed in the cane, two pulleys, and a *carcanha* [*calcanha*: a woman who swept the *engenho* and did other chores].

At each cauldron there must be one who tends the fire and in each series of kettles the same, and on Saturday there must be without fail work stoppage in the mill.

The sailors who go in the launch besides the baize shirt that they are given must also have a jacket of baize and all the necessary clothing.

We will go to work the cane field of Jabirú this time and then it must remain as pasture for we cannot cut cane in a swamp.

We shall be able to plant our rice wherever we wish, and in any marsh, without asking permission for this, and each person can cut jacaranda or any other wood without having to account for this.

Accepting all the above articles and allowing us to remain always in possession of the hardware, we are ready to serve you as before because we do not wish to continue the bad customs of the other *engenhos*.

We shall be able to play, relax, and sing any time we wish without your hindrance nor will permission be needed.

9.13. Slaves Rebel in the Captaincy of Bahia (1814)

Black rebellions or plots to revolt were especially common in Bahia in the first half of the nineteenth century, no less than eleven such incidents coming to light between 1807 and 1835 in the city of Salvador and the surrounding plantations. This unrest, extraordinary even by the standards of Brazilian slavery, has sometimes been explained by the immense number of Africans, often followers of the Moslem faith, who were brought to Bahia from the so-called Mina Coast, including modern Nigeria and Dahomey, and concentrated in cities like Salvador to work as servants or *prêtos de ganho*. Such urban slaves had opportunities to observe their masters' weaknesses, to recognize their own strength, and to learn about such outside events as the black revolution in Haiti, increasing their will to cast off oppression. Moreover, their gatherings for entertainment or religious worship, which were not always prevented, gave them opportunities to plan strategy and to enlarge their vision of the dazzling potential consequences of a successful rebellion.

The following petition, sent in 1814 to the prince regent, Dom João, by merchants and citizens of Bahia, describes the mass unrest of the black population at that time and the spreading revolt in the nearby interior which threatened the capital itself. This uprising and the growing "insolence" of the city's slaves were blamed on the weak policies of the governor, the Count dos Arcos, who was looked upon by many residents of Bahia as too friendly to blacks.

Source: Cited in full in Carlos B. Ott, *Formação e evolução étnica da cidade do Salvador*, 2 vols. (Bahia: Tipografia Manú, 1955, 1957), II, 103-108.

❧ With the deepest respect the principal merchants and other residents of this city of Bahia, full of great anguish and concern, wish to describe for Your Royal Highness the shocking catastrophe and provocations which have taken place here, and to request humbly the prompt measures that this deplorable state of affairs requires for the security of their lives, honor, and property.

It is notorious that some three or four years ago the blacks tried to rebel and murder all the whites, and, having in earlier years launched attacks on two occasions, at dawn on February 28, only a league from this city, they attacked a third time, displaying even greater boldness and causing even more damage than they did on the other occasions. These attempts, Sir, are clear proof that, unless serious steps are taken, the day will come when they will completely accomplish their purposes, and we will become the victims of their rebellion and tyranny.

The question is not whether this would be possible, or whether it might be difficult, because the deciding factor is the degree of power on both sides. This is enormously to our disadvantage, since, according to the population lists compiled in this city in the time of the Most Excellent Count da Ponte, it can be calculated that there are twenty-four to twenty-seven blacks for every white or mulatto, and here we include only those in the city. Outside it the situation creates a sense of horror. We need only to recognize that there are 408 plantations, including those growing sugar, tobacco, and subsistence crops, and that, estimating one hundred head to a plantation, this comes to 40,800 blacks, whereas there are not more than six whites or mulattoes per plantation, if in fact that many. It is sometimes argued that they are of different nations and so unable to unite their forces. Well, the opposite has happened in the present revolt, in which, aside from Hausas [an ancient people from Nigeria and the Sudan much influenced by Islam], those of the Nagó [Yoruba tribesmen from Nigeria], Calabar [various groups from eastern Nigeria], and other nations are involved. And so it must be, because the desire to free themselves is common to all, and although there are some in fact of better character who find such behavior undesirable, they are forced to agree with the majority for fear of being killed, and the recent events are the best proof of this.

The rebels started out at Manoel Ignacio's warehouse, moving from there to Itapuã and to the Joanes River with the intention of joining up with blacks from other plantations and farms, and crying out: "Freedom! Long live the blacks and their King, and death to whites and mulattoes!" And they killed all the black women and a black boy who did not want to join them.

It is perfectly clear that they are a large force and that the white and mulatto side must therefore suffer defeat. Even ignoring the present dire facts, nobody with good sense can doubt that the fate of this captaincy will be the same as that of the island of Saint Domingue [Haiti], and for two reasons. First, because of the enormous advantage they have in numbers, and this in a people accustomed to hardship, and so barbarous that when they attack they do not fear death, since in their countries they kill for pleasure, and they have the superstition that they will return to their kingdom [after death]. They even commit murder to satisfy unimportant feelings, or because of false pride, and many in this rebellion have been found hanged in the forests of the Rio Vermelho. And the second reason for reaching that conclusion is the relaxation of customs and lack of civility which are commonly observed in this city because of the many liberties that have been granted to them, and for which reason insults are constant, white women being shamelessly attacked in the streets, and others threatened.

They have even seized prisoners from the hands of justice. This happened last December, for example, to the customs officials who, along with another policeman, both so-called *guerreiros* [warriors or professional bearers of arms], conducted a black man who had been arrested inside the customhouse. Going up the street known as "Escadinhas do Palacio" [Palace Steps], they were met there by a group of blacks of the sort who normally hire out their services at the customhouse dock. Cutting the ropes that bound the prisoner, they released him, threatening the two officials with knives, and all this went entirely unpunished. This and even worse must be expected where punishment is absent, and, in fact, the time has come when masters are actually rebuked by the government for applying it, even when they do so reasonably, more attention being given to the blacks' complaints than to the arguments of the masters, and this is known as "humanity and Brazil's golden age." This, however, is how things are for the blacks, who are granted humanity's privileges, while we are treated with inhumanity, aside from many other trials that afflict us every day.

What is most amazing in this lamentable and disastrous situation is the government's indifference. Not satisfied with a policy of inaction over a period of forty days, it even permits and recommends in its first and only order of the day during that time that the blacks be allowed to entertain themselves with their dances in the two plazas named Barbalho and Graça, places as dangerous for a gathering as any that exist, without considering what they might do there, and when in fact, in the present circumstances, not even three should be allowed to talk together. In payment for the barbarousness with which they treated people in the places they burned, where the houses numbered over 150, and the people killed more than a hundred, it is even suggested in this first order that interference with the *batuques* which might be performed elsewhere should be carried out with great moderation. Perhaps we should ask them on our knees not to dance the *batuque* and not to convert this country into a new Mina Coast, as they have been doing up to this time. . . .

Having learned of the rebellion from Captain Manoel Ignacio, one of the officials played down the news as though it were some unlikely deception, and only very reluctantly did he agree to let thirty soldiers go out. These marched very slowly and with orders to treat the blacks most gently and courteously, when, as he already knew, they had burned the captain's properties and murdered part of his family, he himself escaping only because he was then in this city. Since on their arrival there they encountered a large number of blacks and since they did not have an order to use violence against them, they came back, asking for reinforcements. However, when these reinforcements arrived there it was already far too late; the slaves had already marched on to Itapuã where they caused great damage and loss of life, the establishment of João Vaz de Carvalho having suffered a great deal of damage. All of this would have been avoided if a sufficient number of troops had been sent out at once, or even if those who went had had orders to attack them and force them to surrender, thus preventing their march. They did nothing, however, and it was only the men who arrived from Torre and other unseasoned militiamen who managed to kill and capture some and force others to flee. Finally, fate allowed us to escape, and so it remains for us to make this plea for help.

Failure to establish firm principles spoils these people; fear and rigorous punishment are the only way to make them behave correctly. Since their *batuques* have been allowed (they are in fact banned by statutes), and since they have been permitted to dress themselves up in royal costumes, crowning themselves with pageantry and public ceremony, and paying homage to one another, gathering together to play a kind of single-stringed instrument resembling a *guzla*, and agitating the city [the instrument was probably the *berimbau*, which is still used in Bahia today to accompany the athletic male dance called *capoeira*]—it is since all this has been permitted that we have witnessed most of the acts of violence and disobedience. The murders that they have committed cause bitter tears to flow and will continue to do so in the future. One such murder was that of the merchant, Luis Antonio dos Reis, our friend, who up to his death was with his wife. She witnessed the brutal act, and, although beaten, managed to escape. They burned more than a hundred houses, even killing innocent children, and the evil now continues in other places. In Iguape, Cachoeira, and Itaparica, the blacks of Gonçalo Marinho Falcão, Rodrigo Brandão, and Francisco Vicente Viana have run away and revolted, and all these owners of sugar plantations have fled to this city, where they now are. Every day blacks run away from this city, but the government lacks information about them because their masters do not report them.

Just a few days ago a black man belonging to the British consul dared to go to the place called Pedreiras, where there was an allotment of new blacks bought by Antonio Ferreira Coelho and his partner Domingos José de Almeida Lima for shipment to Maranhão. There this black urged them to revolt, arguing that there were very few whites and that already they had killed a large number of them. He told them not to go on board the ship, but to stay and assist the rebels, that they would soon become masters of everything, etc., all of which was witnessed by one of the Gangó blacks who had been placed in charge of the others, and after they had beaten him they drove him away. All of this, Sir, and many other facts are Gospel truth, about which Your Majesty can easily inform himself. In the light of all this, what is most disheartening is the total lack of action and precautionary measures.

The Powder House, an important place which is very much exposed to danger, was guarded during the tenures of former governments by a large body of sentries, but since this government arrived here this force has been reduced to a patrol of eight inactive recruits, and they are all located in the middle of a forest surrounded by *quilombos* of blacks. In the same way all the guard units of the city were reduced when this government arrived, the arsenal, for example, having been left with an insignificant patrol of eight men. In the present circumstances, the weapons there should have been passed out to the militia companies so that they would be ready in the event of an attack upon the city, which the blacks had planned to carry out. However, the weapons remained inside the arsenal, and can be used now only against us, because (even forgetting the confusion and delay that must occur in getting the weapons to them) the soldiers' quarters are so far away from the arsenal that before they will be able to receive them they will be killed on the road.

Finally, gatherings of blacks can be seen at night in the streets as before, conversing in their language and saying whatever they like, and with constant whistling and other signals. They are so impertinent that even in our language they blurt out their reasons for putting off the day of their planned revolt. They know about and discuss the disastrous occurrences that took place on the Island of Saint Domingue, and one hears mutinous claims that by St. John's Day there will not be one white or mulatto alive.

It is in these very sad circumstances, in which danger could not be more immediate, that we trust that Your Majesty will provide the speedy remedy which the seriousness of the situation requires, sending enough soldiers to induce respect and fear among this flood of blacks, because they are such that no matter how numerous the line troops of this city may be, they will never be enough.

Furthermore, it is our opinion that the pernicious commerce in slaves should be banned, and the greatest vigilance and severity should be established concerning those already here, who by themselves constitute an exorbitant number. The arrival of married white couples from Portugal and the Islands should be encouraged; because of their poverty, these workers will seek employment and will be even more useful to the agriculture of this country than the blacks. Motivated by their wages and winning the affection of their masters, they will accomplish more than a superior number of blacks, since the latter are made to serve by force and without the least advantage to themselves. And we request any additional measures which Your Highness regards as useful, and we solicit all this prostrate before your throne, hoping that our just complaints will be attended to. It will be beneficial if steps are taken while fate still gives us the opportunity, because once we have rejected it, it will be useless to lament the time that will have been lost. Moreover, Your Highness will have lost a realm, and we our lives, honor, and properties.

All these facts are accurate, and there are many other important ones which we have omitted in order to avoid excessive repetition. We swear this before the Sacred Evangelists, and Your Majesty should know that whoever states the opposite, denying the great danger that exists, is seriously in error.

The King's favors produce order.

9.14. Soldiers and Africans Clash in Bahia's Streets (1835)

Probably the best-known urban slave revolt in Brazilian history is the one that took place in Bahia on the night of January 24-25, 1835. The following report from the city's chief of police to the provincial president, written while the violent events were still fresh in his mind, suggests the determination and even desperation of the blacks, both free and slave, whose long-planned insurrection was revealed by informers just before it was scheduled to begin. An especially interesting aspect of this rebellion, revealed here as well as in other documents, was the significant part that religion played in it, notably Islam. Also exposed here are the beginnings of the white community's retribution which, before it ran its course, had brought five executions, the deportation of hundreds of free Africans, and severe corporal punishment. The latter consisted in some cases of more than a thousand lashes applied at the legal rate of fifty per day, Sundays excluded, with frequent respites of a week or less. The punishment of a slave named Pacífico, to cite an example, began on the tenth of April, continued through May, and ended at last on the twelfth of June.

Source: Cited in full in José Carlos Ferreira, "As insurreições africanas da Bahia," *Revista do Instituto Geográfico e Histórico da Bahia* 10 (1903), 107-115.

❧ Illustrious and Excellent Sir:

Although Your Excellency has been informed of the events which took place on the night of the 24th and 25th of this month and thereafter, it is nevertheless my duty to prepare a brief account of what has come to my attention so that Your Excellency may be able to best decide on the measures that should be adopted for the tranquillity of the province.

When Your Excellency received the extraordinarily fortunate warnings on the night of the 24th that the Africans, particularly the Nagôs, would revolt at dawn, setting fires at various points in the city and attacking the guardhouses, the justices of the peace went into the streets and called upon the citizens to join the police. Soldiers and guards immediately took up their weapons, and the regular units sent to various places men who were capable of suppressing any initial uprising on the part of the blacks.

Having received Your Excellency's message at about eleven o'clock at night, I inspected several places, gave some orders, and then went to the Ladeira da Praça where, according to the reports, many of the insurgents were to have been assembled in some houses. There I found the justices of the peace of the two cathedral districts with some citizens and municipal police who were searching some of those places.

In compliance with your orders, and recognizing that there was no danger in the center of the city where the police barracks and guardhouses are located, and with everything in a state of readiness, having made some requisitions which I considered important, I headed straight for the cavalry barracks, which I found on the alert. Ordering a cavalry guard to follow me later to the Largo do Bomfim, I hurried immediately to that place while the soldiers were mounting up, fearing that any delay could be disastrous for so many unarmed families who were near the sugar mills and separated from the forces of the city and so in the worst possible location for such an attack. I had hardly given some orders tending to reduce the danger when a cavalry patrol arrived at full gallop to inform me that some Africans had attacked at various points in the city.

With this news, I ordered a municipal police detachment of eighteen men who were in Bomfim that, in the event of danger, they should make the families go into the church and lock themselves in, defending themselves from any attack until I could come to their aid. Returning to the cavalry barracks at three o'clock in the morning, I found it prepared, with one force mounted and the other on foot, along with some men of the National Guard. The latter withdrew into the building to defend the entrance and to fire on the Africans from the windows, while the cavalrymen waited for the attack in the plaza below.

Within a few minutes some fifty to sixty of them appeared on the scene armed with swords, lances, and even pistols and other firearms. Encountering pistol and rifle fire from the barracks windows, they advanced furiously, causing the cavalry to break up in pursuit of them to prevent their escape by way of the Noviciado road. At this moment the cavalry commander, Captain Carvalhao, who awaited them dismounted, was wounded and forced to withdraw.

As I and some horsemen again charged the Africans at the barracks door, the latter began to disperse, with the two groups of cavalry in pursuit of them. Meanwhile, more Africans appeared, and with the rest of the cavalry absent, I entered the barracks, from which the firing continued for another quarter of an hour, until they were all overcome. This was accomplished mainly by the mounted cavalry who bravely charged them, forcing them to leap into the sea or to hide in the nearby hills which are covered with underbrush. They left seventeen dead behind, others wounded and captured, aside from many who were drowned or, having been wounded, lost their lives among the waves. I have been informed that several of these have been found in various places.

With the danger reduced, knowing that the rest of the city was free from attack, and fearing an assault on the village of Bomfim, I went there with the cavalry. . . . There I remained until I was certain that there was no movement at all at the nearby sugar plantations. Returning to the cavalry barracks as dawn was approaching, I found forty men there from the frigate, whom Your Excellency had sent me. I ordered sixteen of these to embark for Itapagipe, and there they stayed until calm had been reestablished.

Later I learned from reports that while the justice of the peace, following up a private tip, was attempting to search a house near Guadalupe on the Ladeira da Praça, a mulatto woman showed reluctance to open the door to him, claiming there was nobody there. Since he was prepared to break his way in, she opened the door, but just then another door inside was seen closing. With growing suspicion, the Commander of the Regulars, Lieutenant Lazaro Vieira do Amaral, entered the hallway in the direction of the closed door, when suddenly, at a signal given allegedly by the mulatto woman, the door opened, a shot was fired from a blunderbuss from within, and a group of about sixty blacks came forth armed with various weapons, mainly swords, scattering the small, unsuspecting force and gravely wounding Lieutenant Lazaro and others who stood in their way.

This group then headed toward Nossa Senhora d'Ajuda in the Largo do Teatro, where it was met by a volley fired off by eight Regular Guards commanded by the adjutant of the same unit. These soldiers were dispersed by the Africans after five of them had been wounded. From this place the blacks ran with a great deal of shouting to the Rua de Baixo killing and wounding people on the way, allegedly including two mulattoes. From there they went straight to the artillery barracks, perhaps with the intention of joining the group from Victoria, as was later verified. Near the barracks they killed a National Guard sergeant named Tito from the 2nd Battalion, who was escorting a justice of the peace seeking help from the fortress, but had stayed a bit behind to take a shot at them.

Afraid to attack the artillery barracks, they returned by the same road, and soon they made contact with the other group coming from the Victoria area. These had crossed the new fortress road, despite some shots that were fired from there. Now united, they went to attack the Regular Army barracks where there were only twenty-two soldiers, the rest having been sent to several other places. After an exchange of fire there in which two soldiers were killed and others wounded, the barracks gate being closed, they headed toward Barroquinha, arriving a second time at Nossa Senhora d'Ajuda. From there they went toward the school, attacking the retreating guardsmen. Some shots were fired there by a group of Regular Army reinforcements who happened to be at that place. There they also killed an Artillery soldier who had come to take away an image of the Saint. Before falling wounded, he defended himself courageously, killing one with a single shot and wounding many others. While descending the Baixa dos Sapateiros, they killed a mulatto and, I am told, a second one as well, continuing toward Coqueiros, as I have already informed Your Excellency. After the damage which was done to them in this last place, they never reassembled, and this was the only time that they were not on the offensive. . . .

I should also inform Your Excellency that the mulatto woman of the house where the blacks were found and her husband are under arrest. There are reasons to suspect that they are co-conspirators or sympathizers.

From the cavalry barracks to the fortress of São Pedro many dead and wounded Africans have been found, but few were captured during the attacks. I calculate the number of dead found in all the places, including those found along the shore, at fifty. However, in addition to these, there were the wounded ones, who will certainly not escape death, considering the seriousness of their wounds and the length of time which elapsed before they were treated. These are in the hospitals where I ordered them sent, and the dead are in the Sea Fortress. In the morning some were found in the nearby forests with bullet or sword wounds, and some of these tried to escape using disguises.

At six or seven in the morning six blacks belonging to João Francisco Ratis suddenly came out of his house armed with swords, pistols, and daggers and dressed in battle apparel, in their fashion, and after setting fire to their master's house they ran toward Agua de Meninos and were quickly killed on the way. It can be assumed that these blacks were also in on the conspiracy but were unaware of the early morning events, since the sixty in the house near Guadalupe were forced to begin their attack prematurely.

I have given the necessary orders for the search of every house where Africans are living, without any exceptions, and the result will be sent to Your Excellency at the proper time. Your Excellency may already be assured, however, that the revolt was planned long ago with an unbreakable secrecy, and with a design superior to that which we might expect from their brutishness and ignorance. Generally speaking, almost all of them can read and write in unknown characters which are similar to the Arabic used among the Ussás, who now evidently have made an alliance with the Nagôs. The Ussás are the nation which in earlier times rebelled on several occasions in the province, having later been replaced in this by the Nagôs. Teachers exist among them who give lessons and have tried to organize the insurrection, in which many free Africans, even rich ones, were also involved. Many books have been found, some of which, it is said, must be religious precepts derived from the mingling of sects, mainly the Koran.

What is certain is that religion played a role in the rebellion, and the leaders managed to persuade the miserable people that certain papers would save them from death. For this reason many of these have been found on the dead bodies and in the rich and exquisite vestments which were found during some of the searches and probably belonged to the leaders. It was also observed that many of the rebels were the slaves of Englishmen and were better armed. These facts should probably be attributed to the lesser amount of constraint in which they are held by these foreigners, who are accustomed to living with free people.

According to information I have received, in addition to the deaths of the National Guard sergeant, the artilleryman, four mulattoes, and two Regular Army soldiers, many others were wounded, and some gravely.

There is no doubt, Sir, that if we had not been prepared by the warnings, the end result would have been the same, although the destruction would have been much greater. Therefore, to increase our security, it will be useful to reward the black women who gave us the warnings, granting them their freedom, if they do not already possess it, or a reasonable compensation.

Precautionary steps are still being carried out enthusiastically, and in all the districts procedures are being followed to discover any guilty persons who may still exist, in order to make effective examples of them for the other Africans. To best achieve this, I have tried to establish procedures everywhere in a uniform and regular manner. After such events, it is quite natural that there should be abuses, and these have taken place to such an extent that they completely justify the many well-founded complaints. Soldiers are arresting, beating, wounding, and even killing slaves who, under their masters' orders, are going into the streets. I have reported this matter to Your Excellency and have taken every preventive measure which is available to me.

Otherwise peace has returned, and we will now have time to establish measures, by legislative means, so that it will not be necessary to fight such people a second time, especially free Africans. Almost all the latter, while enjoying their freedom, bear the stigma of slavery, and their presence is in no way profitable to this country.

Bahia, January 29, 1835. To the Most Illustrious and Most Excellent President of the Province. (Signed)—*Francisco Gonçalves Martins*, Chief of Police.

9.15. Insubordination, Assassinations, Rebellions, Conspiracies, and Runaways: A Report of the Minister of Justice (1854)

Often ended by plantation "justice" rather than by public authorities, much local violence on the part of slaves was never described on paper. Nevertheless, some rebellions, conspiracies, and acts of insubordination created terror in the general population or aroused the interest of a local official, and as a result they were described in police reports or even in the messages of the justice ministers which were read each year before august gatherings of the General Assembly. The following selection is made up of excerpts from a ministerial report written in 1854 by José Tomás Nabuco de Araújo, a noted statesman of the Empire, member of several Liberal Party governments, and father of the abolitionist, Joaquim Nabuco.

Source: *Relatorio da repartição dos negocios da justiça apresentado na segunda sessão da nona legislatura pelo respectivo Ministro e Secretario de Estado José Thomaz Nabuco de Araújo* (Rio de Janeiro, 1854), pp. 1-6.

❧ In August about fourteen armed slaves assembled on the "Lavagem" sugar plantation, in the district of Páo do Alho in the province of Pernambuco, with the intention, as they themselves said, of demanding from their masters the restoration of [freedom from labor on] holy days, which has been abolished by the Holy Father. However, what they actually did at that assembly, which did not increase in size, was to atttack and rob the house of one Agostinho Tinoco, a resident in that area. This incident, coinciding with reports of other meetings planned in Santo Amaro de Jaboatão, inspired terror everywhere, and it was soon supposed that there existed a vast plot to rebel, centered in the capital and with ramifications on the sugar estates. The energy and precautionary measures which the authorities took have reestablished peace and confidence. The fourteen slaves were arrested by the police and severely condemned by the jury of Páo do Alho. . . .

In June, almost all the slaves, amounting to eighty, of the Fazenda da Serra, belonging to Francisco Ignacio Botelho, in the municipality of São João d'El-Rei [Minas Gerais], fled to that city to request their freedom from the authorities. The energy and quick action of the police, as well as the presence of a sizable force sent to that place by the provincial president, prevented the terrible consequences which that rebellion might have caused. The frightened population was put at ease, and the mutinous slaves were controlled and restored to order.

On the night of Good Friday a slave belonging to Father Joaquim Pereira de Barros appeared before the judicial magistrate of the district of Taubaté [São Paulo] to report that on the night of April 16 to 17 the slaves of the municipalities of Taubaté and Pindamonhangaba planned to revolt, taking advantage of the feast of St. Benedict, which, with the tolerance of their masters, many of them are in the habit of celebrating. The details which the slave offered revealed a well-premeditated plan, and his accusations appeared authentic. In these circumstances the authorities of the two municipalities acted swiftly to implement the necessary measures for public salvation, aided by the inhabitants of those communities who at once contributed their services, aware of the danger that threatened them all.

The slave quarters of the various plantations, where weapons intended for use in the rebellion were thought to exist, were searched, and some firearms and a large quantity of barbed arrows with poisoned tips were found. The slaves who were pointed out as the leaders fled as soon as the authorities appeared, but sixty suspects were arrested. The judicial examinations to which some of the slaves responded, which coincided with each other in nearly every detail, confirmed the existence of a plot to rebel. According to the police investigations, only two of the many prisoners could be regarded as leaders, and only ten as accomplices.

It is worth pointing out that as soon as the provincial president was informed of this situation, he took every step within the range of his authority, and today I can tell you that those municipalities, freed from the fear of the immediate danger they faced, are enjoying peace and tranquillity.

In January, in the district of Carangola, municipality do Presidio in Minas Gerais, the planter José de Lanes Dantes Brandão and his son-in-law, Manoel José Ribeiro, were murdered by their slaves. After the crime was committed, the slaves returned to the plantation house intending to kill the family, who were saved, however, by four workers who came to their rescue, barring the doors and resisting with firearms until they were relieved by the police. The latter arrested a *cabra*, who was a personal and intimate servant of the unfortunate Lanes, along with nine other slaves who were perpetrators of this crime. . . .

In the district of Barbacena in the province of Minas Gerais on the plantation of Commander Mariano Procopio Ferreira Lage, the overseer was barbarously murdered by his slaves, who numbered more than a hundred. . . .

The main *quilombo* of runaway slaves existing in the province of Maranhão, known as the *quilombo* of Maracassumé [see Document 9.8], was entirely destroyed, ten slaves having been killed at the point of conflict, about the same number having been gravely injured, and forty-six taken prisoner. Among the forces of legality, two police guards were seriously wounded, and three soldiers of the 5th Infantry Battalion slightly wounded. The destruction of this *quilombo*, which for so long has kept the inhabitants of those places in a state of terror, and which, as a nucleus of insurrection, might have been disastrous to public order, is an important achievement for which the worthy president of Maranhão deserves praise. Steps were taken to prevent the establishment of new *quilombos*, and to punish the slaves and the persons who traded and maintained contacts with them, who, for the most part, were Portuguese.

TEN

"The Noblest and Most Sacred Cause": The Abolition Struggle

THE ABOLITION of Brazilian slavery was a long, complicated process which did not have its beginnings in Brazil itself, but rather in such places as Britain, France, New England, and the French Caribbean colony of Saint Domingue. Philosophical opposition to slavery emerged in Europe and North America in the late eighteenth century, and practical responses to this problem included abolition by the French National Assembly in 1794, bans on slave trading by Britain and the United States in 1807 and 1808, the ending of slavery in New York, New England, and other northern states early in the nineteenth century, and the abolition of slavery in British colonies in 1833. By the latter date, anti-slavery activity in the United States was already creating a national crisis which would end in civil war, and a massive slave revolt in Saint Domingue, beginning in 1791, had long since transformed that sugar-producing colony of France into America's first independent black state. Even Chile, Argentina, Uruguay, and Mexico, whose slave populations were small, had abolished the institution as part of their revolutionary struggles against Spain, and other Spanish American countries, with the exceptions of Spain's "loyal" colonies of Cuba and Puerto Rico, were soon to follow.

In contrast, until the Portuguese crown established itself in Rio de Janeiro in 1808 with the help of British naval power, the Luso-Brazilian world maintained a business-as-usual attitude toward slavery and the slave trade. While numerous writers and politicians criticized slavery in other countries, the few published works on the subject which emerged from Portuguese presses in this age of revolution either defended the traffic in response to international opposition, or limited themselves to criticizing the waste and brutality of slavery, stopping short of opposing it directly. As British opposition to the international slave trade mounted after 1808, the Portuguese government in Rio was forced to agree with Great Britain in three separate treaties (1810, 1815, and 1817) to limit Portuguese slave trading in Africa to territories of Portugal south of the equator. Nevertheless, slave trading continued to be looked upon in Brazil as essential to her economy and way of life, and, with a few notable exceptions (see Document 10.1), few persons publicly opposed it. The slave trade was in fact legally abolished in 1831, owing more to British pressure than to internal opposition, but the traffic continued illegally until 1851, when it was at last suppressed.

It was only in the mid-1860s, in part because of events in the United States, that the need to reform slavery itself—and eventually to end it—was at last recognized at the highest levels of the Brazilian government (see Document 10.3). In 1871, after years of agitated public debate both inside and outside the General Assembly, a reform bill was at last passed into law (see Documents 4 and 5). This Free Birth or Rio Branco Law, which was popularly expected to bring a gradual end to slavery by eliminating its last source of renewal, was received with great fanfare and jubilation, and in the minds of many Brazilians it seemed to end the need for additional reforms. Thus for the next eight or nine years after its passage, opposition to slavery was at best scattered and ineffective.

In 1880, however, a new and far more powerful abolitionism emerged, setting off one of the most remarkable social struggles in Brazilian history (see Documents 6 through 8). Some of the most stirring episodes of this conflict took place in such northern provinces as Ceará and Amazonas, where most of the slaves had been freed by 1884, but it was during the culminating phase of the struggle centered in the province of São Paulo that the slaves themselves became most involved. Encouraged by abolitionists, in late 1886 tens of thousands of black workers began to abandon São Paulo's plantations (see Documents 9 through 11), and this runaway movement soon spread to nearby provinces and then virtually to every part of the country. Thus, by early 1888 slavery had all but collapsed nationwide, and the Brazilian Assembly had little alternative when it met in May, 1888, but to pass a law to end it (see Document 10.12).

The abolitionist movement was a splendid chapter in Brazilian history, but it did not by itself end Brazilian slavery. This was the result, rather, of a number of interrelated developments which undermined the institution during most of the nineteenth century. These included: 1) international rejection of slavery which ended the African traffic in mid-century and eliminated the main source of Brazil's captive workers; 2) the gradual decline of the slave population after 1850, mainly owing to an excess of deaths over births; 3) the interprovincial slave trade, which concentrated slaves *and the defenders of slavery* into the southern coffee provinces of Rio de Janeiro, Minas Gerais, and São Paulo; 4) abolition of slavery in the United States, which helped inspire a national policy of gradual emancipation through "free birth"; 5) a slow but persistent erosion of pro-slavery opinion after 1865, especially in cities and poorer provinces, helping to bring on a powerful anti-slavery movement in the 1880s; and 6) the resistance of the slaves themselves, which reduced the efficiency of slavery and culminated in the massive runaway movement of 1886 to 1888, the final death blow to a labor system that had existed for nearly four hundred years.

10.1. "Perhaps No Nation Ever Sinned More against Humanity than Portugal": Brazil's First Prime Minister Fires an Opening Salvo in the Struggle against Slavery (1823)

Despite the pro-slavery consensus which lasted in Brazil until the 1860s, some Brazilians spoke out early against the slave trade and even slavery itself. One of these was the first prime minister of independent Brazil, José Bonifacio de Andrada e Silva, who in 1823 wrote the lucid essay on slavery from which the following excerpts are taken. Newly independent in 1823, Brazil was under British pressure to abolish the slave trade, and to some extent this essay owes its existence to that situation. Nevertheless, José Bonifacio was himself a product of the Enlightenment who had spent decades in Europe studying and teaching at major universities and associating with some of the Continent's finest minds. Returning to Brazil in 1819 after a thirty-six year absence, he was prepared by intellect and experience to recognize slavery's effects upon his country, to grasp the fallacies of pro-slavery arguments, and to prepare a comprehensive plan to end the slave trade, improve the living conditions of existing slaves, and begin a process leading toward eventual abolition and full incorporation of black people into the nation.

José Bonifacio's analysis and proposals were never read before the first Brazilian Constituent Assembly, as they were intended to be, because the Assembly was closed down in November, 1823, and José Bonifacio was forced into exile. Nevertheless, this essay was soon published in Europe in Portuguese and English, providing future abolitionists with powerful, well-founded arguments and serving as an opening salvo in the long anti-slavery struggle.

Source: "Representação à Assembléia Geral Constituinte e Legislativa do Imperio do Brasil sobre a escravatura," in *O pensamento vivo de José Bonifacio*, ed. Octavio Tarquinio de Sousa (São Paulo: Livraria Martins Editora, 1944), pp. 39-66.

❧ I am a Christian and a philanthropist, and God gives me the strength to lift my weak voice in the midst of this high assembly on behalf of the cause of justice and sound policy, the noblest and most sacred cause which can inspire generous and humane hearts. Legislators! do not fear the cries of sordid interest. It is your duty to travel fearlessly the road of justice and political rebirth, but we must also move with caution and wisdom. . . .

How can there exist a liberal and lasting Constitution in a country constantly inhabited by a huge multitude of brutalized and hostile slaves? Let us therefore begin at once this great work for the expiation of our ancient crimes and sins. Yes, we must not only be just, but also repentant. We must prove before God and the rest of mankind that we are sorry for all we have done over the centuries contrary to justice and religion, that we are moving forward in harmony with the precept *of not doing unto others that which we do not wish done unto us*. We must end those robberies, devastations, and wars which we foment among the savages of Africa. The thousands and thousands of blacks who die suffocating in the holds of our ships, packed together more tightly than bales of merchandise, must no longer come to our ports. Once and for all these countless deaths and martyrdoms, which we inflicted and still inflict in our own territory, must come to an end. It is time, and more than time, that we put a stop to a traffic so barbaric and butcherlike, time too for us to eliminate gradually the last traces of slavery among us, so that in a few generations we may be able to form a homogeneous nation, without which we will never be truly free, respectable, and happy. . . .

Indeed, gentlemen, perhaps no nation ever sinned more against humanity than the nation of Portugal, of which we were formerly a part. The Portuguese have constantly gone about devastating not only the lands of Africa and Asia, as Camões testified, but also those of our own country. The Portuguese were the first people since the time of Prince Henry who made it a branch of legal commerce to seize free people and to sell them as slaves in European and American markets. Even today some forty thousand human beings are each year torn from Africa, deprived of their homes, of their parents, their children, and brothers, transported to our shores without the slightest hope of ever again breathing their native air, and destined to toil throughout their entire lives under the cruel lash of their masters—they, their children, and their children's children for all time to come!

If the blacks are men like us, and do not constitute a separate race of irrational beasts; if they think and feel as we do, what a picture of sorrow and misery must they present to any sensitive and Christian person! If an animal's groans arouse our pity, how is it possible for us not to feel a certain charitable sadness at the hardships and misfortunes of the slaves? Such is the effect, however, of habits, and such the effect of greed, that men can watch tears flow from other men's eyes without shedding a drop of pity or concern. Greed, however, does not feel or think like reason and humanity. In order to repel the accusations justly raised against it, greed invented and still uses a thousand specious arguments to serve as its apology. It claims that to bring slaves from Africa is an act of charity, because in this way these wretched people avoid falling victim to despotic chieftains. It also claims that, if these slaves did not come here, they would be denied the light of the Gospel which every Christian must work for and spread. It says that these unhappy people move from a burning and terrible climate and country to a mild, fertile, and pleasant land. It asserts, finally, that since criminals and war prisoners are condemned to immediate death by the barbaric customs of their country, they are given an advantage when they are bought, since their lives are saved, even if they remain in captivity.

Wicked and foolish men! All these arguments would have some value if you yourselves went to Africa to search for blacks to give them freedom in Brazil, and to establish them as colonists. But to perpetuate slavery, to make these unfortunate people more unhappy than they would be if some of them were executed by the sword of justice, or even to provide reasons for the continuation of these horrors is most obviously an open crime against the eternal laws of justice and religion. And why do the children of those Africans also remain slaves? Did they commit crimes? Were they captured in war? Did they move from a bad climate to a better one? Did they pass from the darkness of paganism to the light of the Gospel? No, certainly not, and yet, according to you, their children, and the children of those children should be forever condemned. . . .

If the owners of blacks in Brazil would at least treat those wretches more humanely, I would not excuse them, of course, but I might have more understanding for their blindness and injustice. However, the free inhabitants of Brazil, and particularly the Europeans, are not only on the whole deaf to the voices of justice, and to the precepts of the Gospel, but are even blind to their own financial interests, and to the domestic happiness of their own families.

Indeed, immense amounts of capital are sent out each year from this Empire to Africa; and immense amounts of capital are used inside this huge country to buy slaves, who then die, get sick, become useless, and, in any case, perform little actual labor. The useless extravagances of slavery can be seen in our towns and cities, which, if they gave up their wasteful habits, could manage well enough with only a few needed servants. What kind of an education can families be receiving, when they are served by these miserable people, devoid of honor and religion—female slaves who prostitute themselves to the first man who approaches them? In this life, however, everything has its price. We tyrannize over our slaves and reduce them to brute beasts, and they pass on to us all their vices and immoral habits.

And in truth, gentlemen, if the morality and justice of a people are based partly upon their religious and political institutions, and partly, if I may so put it, upon the domestic philosophy of each family, what sort of image can Brazil offer, if we consider her from these two points of view? What religion do we have, notwithstanding the beauty and sanctity of the Gospel, which we profess to follow? Generally speaking, our religion is a system of superstitions and anti-social abuses; our clergy, generally ignorant and corrupt, are the first to make use of slaves, and they amass them so as to enrich themselves through trade and agriculture, and, in many cases, to establish with the unfortunate female slaves a Turkish harem. As long as the slave trade continues, our families will not possess education or enjoy its advantages; until then nothing can familiarize them with the knowledge and love of virtue and religion. Wealth and more wealth, scream our pseudo-statesmen, our buyers and sellers of human flesh, our ecclesiastical bloodhounds, our magistrates—if we can bestow a title so honorable upon persons, mostly open to bribery, who wield the powers of justice merely to oppress those unfortunate people who cannot satisfy their greed or contribute to their prosperity. Under these conditions, gentlemen, how can justice and virtue prevail, how can good customs flourish among us? When I enter into these sad thoughts, I lose almost all hope of ever seeing our Brazil one day regenerated and happy, since it appears to me that the order of human vicissitudes is entirely inverted in Brazil. Luxury and corruption sprang up here before civilization and industry; and what can be the chief cause of such an alarming phenomenon? Slavery, gentlemen, slavery, because the man who relies upon the daily earnings of slaves lives in idleness, and idleness inspires every other kind of vice.

Blind greed claims, however, that the slaves are necessary in Brazil, because the people here are weak and lazy. This is clearly a lie. The province of São Paulo, before the establishment there of sugar mills, had few slaves, and nevertheless its population and agriculture grew every year, and it supplied many other maritime and interior provinces with corn, beans, flour, rice, bacon, pork, etc. . . .

Besides, once we have put an end to the abominable method of farming which so speedily destroys our forests and ravishes our land, once we have introduced the improvements of European agriculture, doubtlessly with few workers, and with the use of plows and other farming implements, our agriculture will develop quickly, our plantations will be consolidated, and the land, the more it is worked, the more fertile it will become. Wise and provident nature provides the necessary means for the advancement of society in every part of the globe, and no country requires foreign and involuntary workers in order to acquire culture and prosperity.

Moreover, the importation of fresh Africans into Brazil does not increase our population, and it only serves to hinder the development of our industry. To prove the first assertion, it is enough to look carefully at the census taken five or six years ago, where it will be seen that, despite the arrival in Brazil, as I have said, of nearly forty thousand slaves per year, the increase in this class is either nil, or of very little consequence; almost all die either of hardship or of desperation, and yet they cost us huge amounts of capital, which are forever lost, and they do not even return the interest on the money employed.

To prove the second assertion, that slavery hinders the development of our industry, it is enough to recall that the masters who possess slaves live for the most part in idleness, because they are not driven by hunger or poverty to perfect their industry or to improve their agriculture. Besides, since slaves continue to be employed, to the exclusion of others, in agriculture and in the crafts, even when poor foreigners come to establish themselves in the country, experience shows that in a short time they stop working the land with their own labor, and just as soon as they can acquire two or three slaves they give themselves up to idleness and sloth, with exaggerated notions of haughtiness. The crafts are not improved, and machines—those great labor-saving devices—are scorned, because of the extraordinary abundance of slaves in the towns. Rage rises up in me, or amusement rather, when I see twenty slaves busy transporting twenty sacks of sugar, which could be carried in one or two well-constructed wagons drawn by two oxen or a pair of mules.

Agriculture in Brazil, carried on with the use of raw and lazy slaves, does not yield the profits which ignorant and conceited men falsely imagine. If we calculate the present cost of acquiring the land, the capital employed in the slaves who must cultivate it, the value of the farm tools with which each of these slaves must work, the food and clothing, illnesses real and imagined, their cure, the many deaths caused by bad treatment and desperation, the repeated flights to the forests, to *quilombos*, it becomes clear that the profit from agriculture must be very small in Brazil, despite the immense fertility of the soil. . . .

These are not the only evils which accompany Brazil's vast system of slavery, because the state itself is damaged even more. If the landowners did not possess an excessive number of slaves, they themselves would make use of lands already opened up and cleared of forests, which today are abandoned and lie fallow. Our forests, rich in woods for civil and maritime construction, would not be destroyed by the murderous axe of the black man, and the devastating flames of ignorance. The peaks of our mountains, constant sources of rainfall and fertility for the lands below, the creators of electrical circulation, would not be left bare and scorched by the burning heat of our climate. . . .

Society's first source of strength is justice, and its principal object is the happiness of mankind; yet by what sort of justice does a man steal another man's freedom, and worse yet, the freedom of this man's children, and of his children's children. It may perhaps be said that to favor the freedom of the slaves is to launch an attack against property. Gentlemen, do not deceive yourselves. The right of property was sanctioned for the good of all, and what benefit does the slave receive from the loss of all his natural rights, from his transformation from a *person* into a *thing*, to use the phrase of those skilled in the law. It is not, in fact, the right of property that they wish to defend, but the right of force, for, as a man can never be converted into a thing, likewise he cannot become property. If the law must defend property, much more must it defend the personal freedom of human beings, who cannot be the property of anyone, without an attack on the rights of Providence, which made men free and not slave, and without subverting the moral order of society, which means the strict observance of all the duties set down by nature, religion, and sound policy. . . .

Let us therefore put an end once and for all to the disgraceful African traffic. However, since not everything can be accomplished with this step, it is also necessary to initiate serious measures to improve the lot of the existing slaves, such reforms to be regarded as a step toward their future liberation.

The laws ought to establish these measures, if they indeed recognize that the slaves are men created in God's image. And if the laws consider them fit for penal legislation, why should they not also be worthy of civil protection?

I repeat, however, that I do not want to see slavery abolished suddenly. Such an event would be accompanied by great evils. In order to emancipate slaves without injury to society, it is necessary first to make them worthy of freedom. Reason and law require that we convert them gradually from vile slaves into free and active men. When that has been accomplished, the inhabitants of this Empire will also be altered from the generally cruel people that they are in this regard into just and Christian human beings, gaining much with the passage of time, putting dead capital, which is absorbed by the use of slaves, into free circulation, liberating families from domestic examples of corruption and tyranny, from their enemies and the enemies of the State, who today are without a country of their own, but who can become our brothers and compatriots.

The evil has been done, gentlemen, but let us not constantly increase it. There is still time to make amends. Since we are compelled by reasons of policy to tolerate the existence of the present slaves, once the cruel slave trade has been ended, we are obliged to work first toward their gradual emancipation. Before we have accomplished the liberation of our free country from this cancer, which will require time, let us reduce the slaves' suffering, let us aid and increase all their domestic and civil advantages; let us instruct them in the fundamentals of the true religion of Jesus Christ, and stop teaching them mummeries and superstition. By all these means we will convey to them all the civilization they are capable of in their degraded condition, while robbing them as little as possible of the dignity of citizens and human beings. This is not just our duty; it will also be greatly to our advantage, because by allowing them the hope of one day becoming our equals in the rights they possess, and by beginning to enjoy at once the freedom and nobility of the soul, which only vice can rob us of, they will serve us with loyalty and love; from enemies they will be turned into friends and protegés. Let us be kind and just, gentlemen, and then we will feel in our hearts that there is no pleasanter situation than that of a kind and humane master, who lives content and without fear among his slaves, as if in the lap of his own family, who admires and enjoys the enthusiasm with which these unfortunate people anticipate his desires and obey his commands, observes with joyful pleasure how husbands and wives, children and grandchildren, healthy and active, satisfied and cheerful, not only cultivate his lands to increase his wealth, but come to him voluntarily to offer the fruits of their gardens, of their hunting and fishing, as to a tutelary god. . . .

Finally, gentlemen, I will offer you the articles which may provide the basis for a new law which I desire. Discuss them, amend them, expand them according to your wisdom and sense of fair play. . . .

A Project of Law on Slavery

Art. 1. Within four or five years the African slave trade will entirely cease, and during this interim period twice the existing duty will be paid on each male slave imported; on the female slaves, however, only half will be paid, so as to encourage marriages.

Art. 2. Every slave sold after the publication of this law, whether coming from Africa or already in Brazil, will be publicly registered, and in this registry the price for which he was sold will be set down. . . .

Art. 3. When slaves, whose selling price has not been registered, are liberated, a legal evaluation will be established by two sworn arbitrators, one of whom will be named by the master, and the other by the competent public authority.

Art. 4. When these evaluations are made, consideration will be given to the number of years the slave has been held, the kinds of service he has performed, the state of his health, and his age. For example, children up to one year of age will be evaluated at only one-twelfth of the value of a grown man; those from 1 to 5, at only one-sixth; those from 5 to 15, at two-thirds; those from 15 to 20, at three-fourths; from 20 to 40 at the full price; and from there upward the value will decrease in proportion.

Art. 5. Any slave, or anyone on his behalf, who offers his master the value for which he was sold, or of his evaluation, will be freed at once.

Art. 6. But if the slave, or somebody on his behalf, cannot pay the entire price, as soon as he has offered one-sixth of it, the master will be required to accept it, and he will grant one day free each week, and thus more days in proportion, as he receives the sixths, up to the total value.

Art. 7. The master who emancipates slaves gratuitously may retain the freedmen in his service for five years as a reward for his generosity, without paying him a daily wage, but only his food, medical care, and clothing. . . .

Art. 8. Every master who frees an old or incurably sick slave will be made to feed, clothe, and provide him with medical care during his lifetime, if the freedman lacks a means of providing for himself; and if he does not do so the freedman will be housed at the hospital or workhouse at the master's expense.

Art. 9. No master may sell a male slave who is married to a slave woman unless at the same time he sells the wife and children under twelve to the same buyer. The same provision applies to the unmarried slave woman and her children of that age.

Art. 10. All free men of color who lack a skill, or an assured way of making a living, will receive from the state a small grant of land for farming, and they will also receive the assistance needed to establish themselves, the cost of this to be paid back over a period of time.

Art. 11. Every master who carries on a sexual relationship with a slave woman, or who has had one or more children by her, will be obligated by law to free the mother and children, and to see to the education of the latter until the age of fifteen.

Art. 12. The slave is legal owner of his savings, and may by inheritance or donation, leave them to whomever he wishes, in the event that he lacks clear heirs; and if he dies intestate, and without heirs, the Charity Fund will become the heir.

Art. 13. The master may not punish his slave with lashes, or in any other cruel manner, except on the public pillory of the city, town, or village, having first obtained a license from the police magistrate, who will determine the punishment according to the nature of the offense. . . .

Art. 14. Any slave who proves before the police magistrate or the Provincial Council for the Protection of Slaves that he has been cruelly mistreated by his master has the right to seek another master; but if he has been maimed or barbarously mutilated, he will be immediately freed by law.

Art. 15. Slaves may testify in court, not against their masters, but against other persons.

Art. 16. Before the age of twelve slaves must not be employed in labor which is excessive or harmful to their health; and the Council will assure the execution of this article for the good of the State and the masters themselves.

Art. 17. Also, the Councils for Protection of Slaves will determine in each province, according to the nature of the work there, the hours of labor, and the food and clothing of the slaves.

Art. 18. The slave woman during pregnancy, and for three months thereafter, will not be made to perform hard and strenuous work; in the eighth month she will be employed only in housework; after giving birth she will have one month to convalesce; and for one year after this she will not work at a great distance from her child.

Art. 19. The slave woman who, having given birth to her first child, again becomes pregnant, will have an additional hour of rest beyond the established hours, aside from what has been determined above; and so on as she has more children; when she has given birth to five children, she will be liberated, but required nevertheless to obey and live with her husband, if she is married.

Art. 20. The master may not prevent the marriage of his slave men with free women, nor with his own slave women, once the former have agreed to live with their husbands, or when the latter freely wish to be married.

Art. 21. The Government is authorized to take the necessary measures to force owners of mills and large plantations to have at least two-thirds of their slaves married.

Art. 22. It will also establish every measure for assuring that slaves are instructed in religion and morality, from which it will derive the great advantages not only of eternal bliss, but also the subordination and necessary loyalty of the slaves.

Art. 23. The Government will try to convince the parish priests and other clerics, who possess means to support themselves, that religion requires them to grant freedom to their slaves, and not to add to the number of these unfortunate people.

Art. 24. So that the workers required by agriculture and industry will not be lacking, the Government will promote the active execution of the police laws against vagrants and beggars, especially if they are men of color.

Art. 25. In the manumissions carried out with the Charity Fund, mulattoes will be preferred over other slaves, and creoles over those from the Coast.

Art. 26. The day when these manumissions take place will be a day of solemn celebration with the participation of the civil and ecclesiastical authorities.

Art. 27. As a reward for their kindness and sense of justice and religion, every master who frees eight slave families, and grants them lands and the needed tools, will be looked upon by the Government as a person highly esteemed by the Fatherland, and will have the right to solicit favors and public distinctions.

Art. 28. In order to stimulate a fondness for labor among the slaves, and their greater domestic happiness, the Government will create in all the Provinces savings funds, like those existing in France and England, where the slaves may deposit the pecuniary products of their labor and industry.

[Art. 29 provides that the Charity Fund for freeing slaves is to be financed by ecclesiastical fees, pious legacies, unclaimed inheritances, income from religious brotherhoods and Church properties, and other similar sources. Art. 30 authorizes the Fund to receive and make use of donations and legacies. Art. 31 establishes a High Council for the Protection of Slaves in each province, and Art. 32 creates local committees in towns and villages to deal with related matters on the local level.]

10.2. A Defense of the Slave Trade in Response to British-Inspired Abolitionism (1823)

At about the time that José Bonifacio was writing his essay on the slave trade (see previous document), the *Diario do Governo* of Rio, an official journal still controlled by José Bonifacio's government, reprinted an article from the London-based Portuguese-language newspaper, *Correio Brasiliense*. This was a liberal journal published from 1808 to 1822 by the Brazilian-born writer, Hipólito da Costa, who, based as he was in England, sometimes took moderately progressive stands on the slave-trade issue.

The following selection is an indignant reply to the *Correio Brasiliense* article by a reader of the *Diario do Governo*, who, in responding to arguments of slave-trade critics abroad, expressed views which were common among Brazilians: British opposition to slave trading was economically motivated; the traffic was essential to the Brazilian economy and good for the Africans concerned; blacks could only be made to work if kept in a state of slavery; natural development of Brazil's slave population was not possible; and European immigrants could not quickly or easily replace African workers in Brazil. To this anonymous writer, it was even conceivable that God had created Africans for the specific purpose of laboring on Brazilian plantations.

Source: *Diario do Governo* (Rio de Janeiro), April 22, 1823.

❧ *To the Editors*:

Among the several excerpts from the *Correio Brasiliense* of last December, which you have published, there is to be found in No. 79 of the aforementioned *Correio* an article that deals with the abolition of slavery in Brazil. The English, covering their charming policy of self-interest with the sacred mantle of human welfare, have known how to insinuate deftly certain ideas, apparently philanthropic, to achieve a purpose which they so greatly desire: that is, the annihilation of slavery all over America; and their efforts have not been without some success. After the publication of the analysis of the justice of the commerce in slaves from the coast of Africa, written in French by the scholarly José Joaquim da Cunha de Azeredo Coutinho (whose loss Brazil so greatly regrets), the whole world knows that the slave trade, far from being barbarous, as ordinarily depicted by the friends of humanity, is legitimate and useful to those same Africans, who, through the mild captivity they experience among us, escape that other tyrannical servitude to which they are condemned by their conquerors, and often death itself. With the arguments thus demolished which the philanthropists so well know how to use to color their canvas, it is entirely clear that their aim is either to delay the progress of America or to encourage the circulation of money, in this way to increase the consumption of the commodities which the [countries of America] import. But, putting all this aside, let us examine the harmful effects which the extinction of slavery would bring to Brazil, despite the opinion of the *Correio Brasiliense* that this same slavery is the greatest obstacle to the development of Brazilian industry.

We will not go so far as to claim that the wealth of a country consists, as some assert, only in the existence of many workers; but it is certain that without such workers agriculture, industry, and navigation cannot exist. Brazil is one of the most precious portions of the Universe; yet what will this avail us if she is without workers who can make the admirable fertility of her soil useful? What we see here of agriculture, mining, and industry we owe to the African workers who annually enter our ports. Stop this commerce and we will suddenly see everything reduced to the most deplorable state of misery.

We do not doubt that many persons in Europe can easily erase from their minds this formidable obstacle. They would argue that since there exist in Brazil a large number of slaves (and these have no way to subsist except by their own labor), and since, furthermore, a population is more prolific in a condition of freedom than in captivity, Brazil would continue to have the same number or perhaps even more workers for her service, even if slavery were entirely eliminated. These are beautiful theories, but the real situation is quite different. African slaves are generally rude, soft, and lascivious. Only the goad of slavery can rouse them from the profound inactivity in which they live. Free of that goading, they will return to their natural apathy. However, since they will have certain needs, there will be robberies and murders, and when these unfortunate people find themselves greatly pursued, they will penetate into the interior. There, surviving on fruits and jungle animals and covering themselves with skins, they will suffer the same destiny as this country's native population.

Many persons who are fooled by the activity which they observe among liberated persons, by their diligence and love of labor, believe that the inactivity of the slaves is the result of their lack of personal interest in what they are doing. However, this is not the case. Freed persons do not develop that activity *after* their liberation; quite the contrary, their manumission is normally *the result* of that activity.

Concerning natural procreation, we would like to suppose that it might be achieved, but this is absolutely impossible due to the bad moral state they are accustomed to, which cannot be remedied in any way. And would we even want expansion of this population?

Since, as we have demonstrated, and as all who have lived in this country know, without slavery it is impossible to make use of African labor, which Brazil so greatly needs, we might consider turning our eyes toward Europe, to attempt to attract immigrants from the Old World to the New. In fact, this idea, so presented, seems advantageous to Brazil and easy to put into practice. It seems advantageous because in this way Brazil might acquire a hard-working population, educated and healthy; easy to put into practice, because Nature's astonishing fertility in this country seems to invite Europeans to leave the ungrateful lands they inhabit and to avail themselves here of the liberalities America offers. However, this project presents obstacles, one of which is perhaps invincible. When the Author of Nature drew from nothing the precious continent of Brazil, it seems that through an act of His special Providence he also created just opposite Brazil in the interior of Africa men who were deliberately constructed to serve on this continent; men who in the heart of summer, when any European would want to envelop himself in snow, seek out the sun and gather about a fire to warm themselves. In fact, it would be difficult, if not completely impossible, for Europeans to accustom themselves to work exposed to the fiery rays of the sun in a large part of Brazil.

This being accepted as the most important reason why we cannot depend upon the services of Europeans, at least during the years required to acclimatize themselves, there are other reasons which merit some attention, and one of these is the extraordinary difference in the kind of labor performed here. Today the farmers of Europe live in a rural habitat which is shaped and pruned; they labor greatly, in fact, tilling their lands, which bring them little profit. However, that labor is mild, and it shares something of the agreeable quality which the poet divulges in his descriptions of bucolic living. This is not true in Brazil, where nature is virgin, where the colonist must chop down frightful forests before he can build his hut and plant his crop. Brazil's agriculture requires men who possess self-confidence and a kind of grand design which is very different from that which Europeans are accustomed to, with their vision of small landholdings into which almost all their native land is divided. Add to all this that the majority, or more correctly, all the Europeans of the class we are referring to, come to Brazil attracted by the hope of buying a slave to help them make their living. It is thus clear that, with slavery abolished, there would be one less reason for them to emigrate.

Such is the immense damage that the abolition of slavery would bring to Brazil, considering the present reality. We do recognize, however, that the elimination of slavery is essential if we are to improve public morality, the low state of which is no small obstacle to the progress of the nation. Nevertheless, it seems to us that this task must be achieved over a period of time rather than through an act of legislation. Stimulate European immigration, let these immigrants branch out and mix with the families of this country, let them propagate and produce, and within a few years we will have workers in abundance. The slaves will become useless, and the slave trade will cease all by itself. On the other hand, to pass laws intended specifically to abolish slavery appears to us a mistake which can bring many terrible results.

Dear Editors, I ask that you provide a place in your paper for this humble production of some idle moments of your

REGULAR READER

10.3. Proposals for Gradually Abolishing Slavery (1865)

Under great pressure from Britain, Brazil suppressed the slave trade in 1850 and 1851, but for more than a decade thereafter little was done to ameliorate slavery, and few Brazilians opposed it publicly. After slavery was ended in the United States, however, a barrage of articles, pamphlets, and books on the question were published in Rio, and in the Assembly legislators began to propose reforms, some of them outspokenly encouraged by the Emperor, Pedro II, himself. Some of these were significant, such as the proposal to abolish slavery outright on some future date (never enacted), or the free-birth bill favored by Pedro (adopted in 1871). Others, however, seemed mainly intended to increase the supply of agricultural labor, or to eliminate slavery's harsher aspects in order to reduce foreign criticism and prolong its existence.

In the following letter to the secretary of the British and Foreign Anti-Slavery Society, Louis Chamerovzow, Aureliano Cândido Tavares Bastos, an abolitionist and Chamber member from Alagôas, summed up the most important of these ideas and added some of his own. In the process he revealed something of the current political and social situation, the decline of slavery, for example, in some regions of the country, and the growing importance of free labor in those same areas—notably Amazonas, Rio Grande do Sul, and much of the northeast. Tavares Bastos, in fact, anticipated the provincial development of abolitionism, which was particularly powerful and effective in those same regions. In the forefront of the anti-slavery movement in 1865, his own cautious opinions portended a lengthy and difficult abolition process.

Source: First published in *Jornal do Comércio* (Rio de Janeiro), 1865, reprinted in Agostinho Marques Perdigão Malheiro, *A escravidão no Brasil: Ensaio histórico-jurídico-social*, 2 vols., 2nd ed. (São Paulo: Edições Cultura, 1944), II, 356-361.

❧ I believe you will appreciate seeing here an outline of the measures that are most often suggested for abolishing slavery soon, or at some more remote time.

These fall into two groups: direct and indirect.

The indirect measures to be taken, which are those most generally welcomed, some of which are even recommended in official documents, would bring about abolition by stages. These I will outline in the order in which, slowly and with adequate intervals, they would be adopted:

A. The prohibition of the public sale of slaves in auctions or judicial sales.

B. A ban on the separation of members of the same family. [In 1869 the Brazilian Parliament banned public slave auctions and separation by sale of a husband from his wife or a child under fifteen from his mother.]

C. Assistance to the slave who seeks his freedom, or compulsory manumission imposed upon the master in certain cases.

D. A ban on the possession of slaves by ecclesiastical corporations.

E. Emancipation of the so-called slaves of the nation, that is, those existing on plantations or establishments belonging to the government. At the present time the government possesses 1,468 slaves, of whom 851 are to be found on the plantations in the province of Piauí. The sale of such establishments has at times been proposed, but it would be a gross injustice to sell the slaves of the nation along with those properties. They should be emancipated. [The "slaves of the nation" were freed by Article 6 of the Free Birth Law of 1871.]

F. A ban on possession of slaves by foreigners in Brazil.

G. Prohibition of employment of slaves in certain urban industries, or imposition of a progressive tax on slaves in cities, increasing the tax according to the number of slaves that each master owns.

These measures are recommended as a way to promote movement of slaves from the cities into agriculture. Generally they are suggested as a means of facilitating the planters' acquisition of field hands, while the need for urban workers is to be met by free persons, native or foreign. It is recognized that the spectacle of the cities dispensing with servile labor and initiating an exclusive system of free labor will be most helpful to the cause of emancipation. . . .

H. Abolition of the coastal traffic in slaves, which is carried on from province to province. Nobody denies that this traffic is inhuman, immoral, and pernicious. More than that, it is a disastrous donation to the southern provinces, whose farmers compromise their own interests through insatiable purchases of slaves on credit. That traffic, moreover, causes the slow depopulation of the northern provinces, whose harsh climate does not favor European immigration. The coastal traffic deprives the north of an acclimatized population, accustomed to the kind of labor performed there.

I. A ban on the movement of slaves from one province to another by any means and under any pretext. [This was done by the so-called Sexagenarian Law (Saraiva-Cotegipe Law) of 1885 which freed slaves over sixty-five.]

J. A ban on the transfer of slave property by gift or sale. The only kind of transfer to be permitted would be through inheritance. Slavery would thus be virtually transformed into serfdom.

Having reached this point, we find ourselves near the border line dividing the preparatory, preliminary, or supplementary measures from the direct measures. I repeat what I said above, that is, that such measures cannot be accomplished simultaneously, but can only be done gradually and slowly, advancing with perseverance and with the respect due to interests formed upon the present [social] base. I will say the same thing for the direct measures: for the same reasons these are also more or less [to be achieved] in the remote future.

It is not conceived that any of them should be introduced suddenly, shaking the society at its foundations.

Recognizing this limitation, I will point out the two main systems of direct action which are competing for preference:

A. Emancipation of all slaves after a fixed period, that is, thirty or fifty years. Those who advocate this also believe that the state should not be made to pay an indemnification, since it guarantees the present owners a long period before emancipation.

B. The liberation of the womb, that is, the recognition of the freedom of each newborn baby. Those who propose this idea believe that this law should be passed at once and be carried out quickly. Slavery would thus end with the present generation. Supporters of this measure believe that the state should demand that the slaveholders feed and educate the newly declared freeborn children, and that the masters should be compensated by the temporary servitude of these children until they reach the age of eighteen or twenty. [These were, of course, the main provisions of the Free Birth Law of 1871, which gave masters the right to the labor of freed children until the age of twenty-one.]

To these main plans I venture to add the following proposals:

C. The gradual abolition of slavery by province, beginning with those bordering neighboring countries, and with those with the fewest slaves. In the former, emancipation of the slaves should occur at once with indemnification; in the others, within a reasonable time, without indemnification.

The provinces of Amazonas, Pará, Mato Grosso, Rio Grande do Sul, Santa Catarina, and Paraná, which border on neighboring countries (French, British, and Dutch Guiana, Venezuela, New Granada, Peru, Bolivia, Paraguay, the Argentine Republic and Uruguay), in none of which slavery is permitted, represent for this very reason permanent threats to the internal peace and defense of the Brazilian State.

In the last war, carried out against the government of Montevideo, and in the present war with Paraguay [the so-called War of the Triple Alliance or Paraguayan War of 1864 to 1870], the leaders of the enemy forces have constantly tried to incite the slaves of Rio Grande do Sul to revolt; and nobody doubts that this tactic, however barbarous it may be, would, if successful, bring down the worst disasters upon us. Slavery in the frontier provinces is indeed a very serious element of military weakness.

In the last war (1864) the government of Uruguay sent agents to arouse the slaves of Rio Grande do Sul. In Cruz Alta, Taquari, and other places there were, as a result, attempted revolts. The Uruguayan leaders, Múñoz and Aparicio, in their invasion of that province, announced that they had come to free the slaves. The last report of the Minister of Justice attributed the attempted rebellions of Taim and Taquari to the maneuvers of the Uruguayans.

Furthermore, in peacetime the fleeing of slaves to neighboring territories, and similar facts, promotes conflicts among the authorities and causes bitterness to enter into some of our international questions. Not long ago there were reports from the north of the flight of slaves from the upper Amazon to the territory of French Guiana, or to the contested territory of Amapá.

The discussions for the extradition of slaves escaping across the frontier of Rio Grande do Sul, the disputes that this has aroused, the series of protests of the Uruguayan regime directed against the Brazilian government which were renewed in 1864, the difficulty in complying with the treaties of extradition, the bad feelings caused by their execution, and the abuses of the people of Rio Grande who hope to preserve slavery on their estates in Uruguay masked by employment contracts for enormous periods (ten, fifteen, or twenty years)—these are all realities that should lead toward abolition of slavery in that great southern frontier province.

In fact, Rio Grande do Sul is exactly the province that could first dispense with slaves. [A popular anti-slavery movement broke out in Rio Grande do Sul in 1884, freeing most of the 60,000 slaves of the province in a matter of months.] As in Santa Catarina, a true prolongation of Rio Grande, the climate there is much milder than that of the other provinces, and less harsh than that of the Rio de la Plata. Rio Grande is the garden of South America: there agricultural labor, in agricultural colonies, is almost exclusively exercised by free men. Although the slave population of the province amounted in 1859 to 73,749 among 229,747 free persons . . . , it must be noted that, with the exception of certain counties, the proportion of slaves to the whole population is minimal. Moreover, a flow of [European] immigration is now well established to that part of the Empire.

Another border province, Amazonas (where the Indian is the field worker, boatman, and house servant), possesses scarcely 851 slaves among a free population of 39,408 souls, according to the official statistics of 1863. . . . The ratio is one slave to forty-six free persons or a little more than 2 percent. [In 1884 an enthusiastic abolitionist campaign led by the provincial president ended slavery in Amazonas.]

Santa Catarina, Paraná, and Espírito Santo also possess few slaves.

Aside from this there are provinces that do not border foreign territory, such as Ceará, where slaves are found at a ratio of one to every fourteen free persons, according to the statistics of Senator Pompeu. Agriculture in Ceará is almost exclusively practiced by free workers, says our friend, Dr. Lafayette [Rodrigues Pereira] in his presidential report of 1864; and he adds that, despite elimination of the [Atlantic] traffic, the income of Ceará has not declined, but has in fact increased. [A powerful antislavery movement developed in Ceará in 1880 and 1881, all but ending slavery there in March, 1884.]

In that same province, as in Rio Grande do Norte, Paraíba, Alagôas, and even Pernambuco, free wage-workers are employed in field labor, mainly in growing cotton and even sugar cane, and on a scale that promises to grow.

Much the same thing is true in the interior of Maranhão. This is the northern province which for many years has been distinguished by its men of letters; one might say the most literary province of Brazil. In the circle of poets, journalists, writers, and politicians of that province, emancipation is commonly favored.

Its eminent men advocate emancipation. Not long ago the Viscount Jequitinhonha quoted a written opinion of Mr. Furtado (a senator from that province and ex-President of the Council) in which the noble senator argued with true intellectual superiority that the slave could be freed against the will of the master, by indemnifying him. [See Document 6.8 for Furtado's statement.] This opinion was written in 1853, when Mr. Furtado held the office of criminal judge in Pará. It states frankly that gradual emancipation does not present serious inconveniences, and that the country aspires to it.

If it were proper for me to quote opinions that have not been publicly expressed, I would have the pleasure of naming other gentlemen of that province, no less worthy of the consideration and recognition of those who support wholesome social principles.

It remains for me to point out one more proposal:

D. Annual liberation by the State of a number of female slaves (the preference for the female sex is easy to understand). The number so freed should be sufficiently higher than the annual excess of births over deaths in order to accomplish two related aims: obstruction of the growth of the slave population and its gradual year-by-year decline.

These measures would be slow and costly, but nevertheless effective in a certain period of time, more or less remote, depending upon the number of manumissions each year. . . .

The question which occupies me is the most serious among those now confronting the Brazilian intellect. In this matter too much oratory is as damaging as indifference; still more damaging, however, is fear.

Certainly the government that would propose moving firmly toward this goal—the emancipation of labor—would find itself entangled in a web of problems. It is easy in such a situation to lose balance and to call for violence, as the means of cutting the knot; however, it is more worthwhile to prepare a logical solution, even if it should be a slow one. . . .

And the Omnipotent One, who placed this mountain of slavery into Brazil's path, will inspire her sons with the courage required to remove it.

Such is my belief and hope.

I am, sir, yours most respectfully, etc.

Tavares Bastos.

10.4. "Slave Property Is as Sacred as Any Other": A Chamber Member Opposes Free-Birth Legislation (1871)

The main solution to the "servile question" which the emperor, Dom Pedro II, decided to pursue in the 1860s was the "liberation of the womb," that is, the freeing of the newborn children of slave women. During the Paraguayan War (1864-1870) the monarchy tried at intervals to prepare the nation for this reform through official speeches and publications, but when it became clear at war's end that the Crown was at last seriously promoting rapid passage of a free-birth law, powerful opposition materialized at once in parliament and in the press. Despite this resistance, Dom Pedro remained committed to free birth and to the other provisions of this legislation, which together were intended to improve Brazil's reputation abroad and to begin the difficult process leading to total abolition. To advance this reform, on March 7, 1871, after months of political maneuvering, the emperor appointed a Conservative Party cabinet headed by Viscount Rio Branco, a noted diplomat and politician from Bahia who was sympathetic to a free-birth law and possessed the talent, prestige, and conservative credentials needed to steer a bill through a reluctant parliament. The long debate on this bill, which began on May 12 and ended with its triumphal passage on September 28, 1871, was one of the most dramatic and hard-fought battles in Brazilian parliamentary history (for a copy of the Free Birth or Rio Branco Law in

English in its final form, see Robert Conrad, *The Destruction of Brazilian Slavery, 1850-1888* [1972], pp. 305-309).

The following excerpts from a speech delivered in the Chamber of Deputies on July 21 by an opponent of this legislation, José Inácio Barros Cobra of Minas Gerais, typifies the strong views held by many of the bill's adversaries. Barros Cobra was especially hostile to the free-birth provision, which he saw as a simple violation of the slaveholder's right to property. Although he claimed that Brazilians were "naturally generous" and that Brazilian slavery was "mild," this legislator, like some of his colleagues, warned the Chamber of Deputies that many of the children who would be freed if the bill was passed would be abandoned or allowed to die because their mothers' masters would not be motivated by a proprietary interest in their survival. The same opinion was expressed by Senator Cristiano Ottoni at about the same time (see Document 2.11).

Source: *Annaes da Camara dos Senhores Deputados* (1871), III, 249-263.

❧ Mr. *Barros Cobra*: Mr. President, Your Excellency and this chamber should recall that the nation experienced displeasure and tremendous shock when the first word regarding the solution of this grave question was spoken in parliament. (*Hear! Hear!*)

In 1867, for the first time, the Speech from the Throne called the attention of the legislative body to the solution of the great problem of the servile element. At that time, not only the press, but also the opposition in this chamber and in the Senate, rose as one man to reject and condemn the unheard-of irresponsibility with which, at that critical and difficult time, that delicate, complicated, and dangerous question was raised. Both political parties, Conservative and Liberal, . . . employed the same language, and with one voice rejected that rash endeavor.

The government was forced to yield before the clear will of public opinion; not only was no legislative bill initiated in the 1867 session, but likewise the Speech from the Throne of 1868 no longer requested a solution to the servile problem; it limited itself to stating that the matter continued to be the object of serious study on the part of the government.

This form of expression contained in the 1868 Speech from the Throne brought tranquillity to the nation, and this tranquillity was confirmed and consolidated when, on July 16 of that year, the Conservative Party, which during difficult days had so vigorously struggled against the unwise statement of the cabinet of August 3 [, 1866], was called to power. (*Very good!*)

The country did not believe, gentlemen, that the Conservative Party, whose outstanding past was so well known, would, once it was in power, use language different from that which it employed while in opposition; the country did not even imagine that the ideas of this party, once it reached the heights of power, would undergo such a profound change, so that that controversial and dangerous question could so soon again be brought before this parliament. . . .

Gentlemen, it is true that in this country there exists a point of view that demands a solution to the great problem of slavery. The existence of this opinion is undeniable in the abstract, in principle; fortunately there is not one Brazilian who wishes the permanent preservation of slavery in the Empire; in this sense there is unanimous agreement: the cause of abolition is definitely decided upon.

To the honor of the Brazilian Empire, we do not need to overcome the difficulties, prejudices, and animosities against which the legislators of France and the United States had to struggle; the natural generosity of the Brazilian character, the religious spirit and the principles of morality and civilization decided the theoretical question a long time ago.

But, if we can be proud of the existence of that unanimous opinion in respect to the humanitarian and civilizing idea, there is no doubt that public opinion does not reveal itself equally in favor of the ideas contained in the government's bill, or in favor of the solution that it calls for. . . .

No, gentlemen, this country, which had lulled itself to sleep in the shadow of the total confidence that it had placed in the government, which reposed serenely in the security that the Conservatives inspired; this country, which believed that a cabinet drawn from the Conservative Party, would never forsake the principles and the traditional wisdom of that party, does not want, cannot want, must not want that unwise solution. It is for this reason that, since the presentation of this ill-advised proposal, since the public has become aware of the method set forth in the solution, truly aroused fears, threatened rights, ardent and concerned patriotism, the science of politicians and statesmen, the ordinary wisdom and good sense of the citizens, all have combined and have sprung up to fight and condemn this rash enterprise. (*Very good!*)

When we attempt to solve this great question, we should not be motivated by abstractions, philosophical concepts, or sentimental inspirations, but rather by the high and venerable interests that are associated with it and that constitute the foundations of Brazilian society (*hear! hear!*); much may be said, much may be desired in this regard, but a study and practical knowledge of our circumstances and of what can reasonably be done are what should guide us, in order that we may go forward securely. (*Hear! Hear!*) Gentlemen, I reflected very serenely about how we might most conveniently solve this important problem, which demands full attention and challenges the deepest meditation. I considered it with total calm, far from my legislative responsibilities, and with my mind uncluttered by other concerns. Momentarily the idea of freeing the womb seemed an acceptable method (to this chamber I confess the feelings of my inner conscience); however, further thought convinced me that this idea, which at first glance is so appealing, is the most dangerous way to go in this country. (*Hear! Hear!*)

History, that great preceptress of experience, shows us that almost all the nations that tried to abolish slavery gradually did not achieve this, but were instead forced to rush headlong and disastrously toward total abolition; this was the experience of England, France, and Portugal herself. A contrary example, such as that of the United States, may be mentioned; but none of those states had a tenth of the slave population which we have, and so cannot constitute an argument in favor of the government's bill. [This is not true; to cite just one example, in 1860 Georgia had a slave population of 462,000, more than any Brazilian province during that country's entire history.]

The illustrious special committee asked in their report: "What reasons do we have to fear that in our country things will go differently from the way they did in countries where, after experiencing the same exaggerated fears, the same transformations were brought about?"

But those countries did not find themselves in circumstances identical to ours; they did not possess the number of slaves that we unfortunately possess, nor was agriculture almost the sole basis of their private and public wealth; nor like us did they have a free population spread out over an immense territory and, in terrifying contrast, a slave population concentrated in the main production centers. These different circumstances call for different ways to cure the evil. (*Hear! Hear!*) . . . Brazil's circumstances in this regard are very special, and we must not lose sight of them.

The servile institution unfortunately appeared as a main element of our social organization, and for three long centuries it sank deep roots into our laws and soil; it represents immense and important capital investments, and almost the only instrument of agricultural labor. Agriculture is practically our only industry, and so almost the only source of our wealth and public revenue, of our prosperity and credit; as a result, the interests associated with slavery are extensive and complex; they are the interests of the entire society that relies upon them.

Almost all the other nations found themselves in quite different circumstances; slavery was localized in the colonies, at great distances, and therefore its abolition could have no effect upon the metropolises. Even in the United States the difference was great, because also there slavery was localized in the southern states, which made up a small part of the republic; so that the solution to the problem there, if fatal to the South, did not damage the greatness and general prosperity of the republic. Besides, those countries were energetic and rich, with resources sufficient to overcome the crisis, and agriculture was not practically the only source of income; and, most important, none of them chose the least opportune moment, the most critical combination of circumstances, as our government did, to attempt to abolish slavery. (*Hear! Hear!*) . . .

Mr. President, from all the known methods leading toward emancipation, the government's bill selected as the best solution that of liberation of the womb, or, more accurately, the liberation of those born from the date of the law, with indemnification of the masters of those same newborn children, once they have reached the age of eight. Depending upon the masters' choice, this indemnification will be either monetary, that is, in the form of bonds valued at 600$ each, maturing in thirty years, with a 6 percent annual interest rate, or they will take the form of the freed children's services until the age of twenty-one.

This solution, which the government and the bill's supporters have called the wisest and most agreeable solution, is, I repeat, the most dangerous of them all (*hear! hear!*); and, saying this, I am not guided by reason alone, but also by the example of other nations who were forced to make similar reforms.

In all those nations this measure had to be followed at once by others more decisive, which precipitated the final solution to the crisis. And why should this not be so? Do we not observe that the mere introduction of this proposal has already brought agitation and that, still more important, the enforcement of such a law will arouse false expectations among the slaves, desires for freedom, optimistic feelings of impatience which will become a source of great dangers and, who can predict? of great catastrophes for the society and for the slaveowners. (*Hear! Hear!*)

Do we not see also that, with this measure, we throw open the door to the demands of the impatient propagandists, who will prove ever more difficult to control as they attain more and more concessions? With this step forward, the national and foreign philanthropists will not be satisfied; they will want something more, and their foolishness, along with the certain intensification of the desires and strengthened hopes of the slaves, must lead us along a road that we do not wish to travel.

To me it appears that all these considerations deserve to be measured and evaluated, so that we will not march toward complete national disaster which will entail a threat to our institutions themselves. . . .

30. Propaganda against the Free Birth Law of 1871: The Blindfolded Figure Symbolizes Agriculture (*Lavoura*) Menaced by the Hand of the Government Lighting the Powder Keg of the "Servile Element"

Mr. President, Article 2 of the bill now under discussion forsees a situation that constitutes one of the defects of the bill's main idea, which has been pointed out by the opposition: the abandonment of the liberated minors by their patrons.

Mr. *Gama Cerqueira*: Hear! Hear!

Mr. *Barros Cobra*: Doing justice to the generosity and natural humanity of the Brazilian character, I do not expect the law to produce a slaughter of innocent children. But, when the present interests of the masters are not sufficient to prevent a huge mortality among the newborn slaves, it can be seen as obvious that, with this great incentive lacking, the mortality will be much greater.

Concerning abandonment, however, it may be anticipated that it will take place on the greatest imaginable scale; since the promised indemnification is not adequate, as I will demonstrate, and because it is dependent upon many chance events and circumstances, there will be a complete loss of the incentive that otherwise would encourage masters to accept the efforts and burdens involved in rearing and educating the children of the slave women, along with the loss of the latter's services during the time they are burdened with pregnancy and motherhood. The law cannot, must not, rely upon charity, which is certainly a very beautiful thing, but cannot be relied upon when legislating for human beings. And what will the government do, with what methods and resources is it prepared to provide for at least half of the children who are born each year, that is, twenty or thirty thousand, according to the least exaggerated claims? The organizations [intended to care for the children] which are mentioned in Art. 2 have not been established, and when they are they will be a very small remedy compared with what will be needed.

Yet this is not the principal or even the greatest defect which I find in the bill; there are others which I request permission to examine quickly.

Above all, I must point out that the bill, as now conceived, is unconstitutional: 1st, because it disrespects the right to property; 2nd, because it grants political rights to a class which, according to the Constitution, cannot possess them.

However unjust, inhuman, and absurd the domination of one man by another, that is, slavery, may be, it is certain that this condition was legally established by civil law, which created and regulated the master's property right over the slave. Therefore, for good or for evil, slavery became a legal institution among us more than three centuries ago, authorized and protected by law and strengthened by its antiquity, and therefore slave property is as sacred as any other, though illegitimate in principle.

The law cannot impose upon the present generation the expiation of a guilt which was not its own, and in which the state itself is an accomplice. It is enough to remember that the present owner of a slave was not the owner in the past and may not be in the future; he found this property established in the society into which he was born, and he obtained that property by purchase, trade, or inheritance, by some means, that is, for legally acquiring property. Therefore, this property is as sacred as any other, and to deprive the owner of it is a violent and evil act.

Appreciating the truth of these principles, the Speech from the Throne always called for respect for property as an essential condition for slavery reform; in its preamble to the bill, the government makes that guarantee, and the illustrious committee, straying from the realms of philosophy and religion to deny this principle, at last recognized it in chapters 8 and 14 of its written evaluation, and proclaimed the need for indemnification, *without which, it says, to suddenly wrest the slave from the master would be an act of unqualified violence.*

However, once the fact is accepted that slavery is legal, if not legitimate, equally legal is the right to ownership over the present slaves, as well as ownership of the slave womb and the children who may emerge from that womb. Our national law, the Portuguese as well as the Brazilian, always honored and acknowledged the Roman principle *partus sequitur ventrem*, and it was constantly and uniformly respected by the legal wisdom of our courts. Therefore the fruit of the slave womb belongs to the owner of that womb as legally as the offspring of any animal in his possession. However much this conclusion may offend our humanitarian feelings, it is undeniably logical and in conformity with law.

It is claimed that the right to unborn slaves does not yet exist because it is not confirmed by current possession. But, gentlemen, if in reality the material fact of birth and the effective and true possession of the fruit of the womb have not yet come into being, there is undeniably an acquired right to that fruit which is as valid as that of a tree's owner to the fruit that that tree may produce; there is a perfect identity of conditions.

However, the government's bill attacks and disregards this right, proclaiming the freedom of children of slave women born from the date of the law, and thereby expropriating from the citizen that which is legally in his possession, without prior compensation in compliance with the Constitution.

In fact, gentlemen, the bill refers to indemnification, but, whether it means monetary indemnification or indemnification through the services of the person freed, I look upon both of them as unreal and in no way sufficient. (*Hear! Hear!*)

Concerning monetary indemnification, we see that the child's master is not given an equivalent amount of money, or an amount over which he has full and free enjoyment and the right of disposition; he is to receive merely a thirty-year bond which represents nothing more than nominal capital and cannot be regarded as real indemnification, not even for the expenses of rearing the children.

Mr. *Gama Cerqueira*: Hear! Hear! It amounts to 36$ a year, while in many places a doctor's visit costs more than that.

Mr. *Barros Cobra*: Aside from the fact that, in the final analysis, the indemnification is reduced to 1:080$000 paid in thirty annual installments of 36$, an amount which, if we consider the long period over which the payments are to be made, is equal to a slave's labor for two or three years, if indeed that much.

Passing on to an analysis of indemnification through services, supposing that a patron chooses it, . . . what does he receive? In the name of indemnification, he receives exactly the thing that he would obtain from his slave anyway, and for which he has a right to be indemnified.

The slave born of a slave woman, who belongs to her master in virtue of principles sanctified in civil legislation, represents capital and is an instrument of labor; however, it is understood that the value of the slave is precisely dependent upon the services that he can perform (*hear! hear!*); nobody would want an unused slave for the mere joy of possessing him. The capital here is represented by the instrument of labor, whose value is in direct proportion to the greater or lesser usefulness which as such he can render; in just the same way that the price of a slave is more or less, depending upon his capacity and fitness for work.

This being the case, which seems to me undeniable, it is entirely obvious that the intention here is to indemnify the masters with the identical thing that belongs to them by law, and which they cannot be deprived of without receiving full compensation. There is, however, a single difference: they are granted the use of the individual for thirteen years, a usufruct which, according to law, would otherwise belong to them for as long as the slave might live. It seems to me, therefore, that the right to property, sanctified and guaranteed by the Constitution of the Empire, which cannot be taken from the citizen of Brazil without prior indemnification, is in this case confiscated without any indemnification whatsoever, or with a false indemnification, which amounts to the same thing. . . .

Mr. President, I will now turn to an examination and evaluation of the bill's main provision, always assuming that the law may be carried out without serious disturbances and disorders which are unfortunately much to be feared. The bill imposes upon the masters the obligation to rear and care for the children of their slave women until they are eight years old. I will not consider the problem of how this obligation will be enforced, and how compliance will be regulated. I will examine it from another angle.

It is known that, thanks to the generous and humane character of the Brazilians, slavery among us is so mild that the condition of our slaves is greatly preferable to that of the working classes of some European countries; on the largest agricultural establishments, order and subordination are maintained entirely by means of a prudent system of constant and severe discipline, in which careful preventive measures ordinarily make repression unnecessary. Once the proposed law is enforced, that system cannot be maintained, and it will be seriously and dangerously undermined by the simultaneous existence in those establishments of slave parents and free children, not as an exceptional or accidental situation, but as a regular and permanent reality, and by the unavoidable meddling of the authorities responsible for enforcement of the law. This situation will awaken in those who remain slaves a dangerous impatience and a terrible hopelessness which must shatter all ties of subordination and respect for their masters. . . .

And how should the patrons deal with the freed persons who remain on their properties? If they are required to rear and educate them and to treat them as free persons, this will bring great problems and cannot be achieved, since the discipline of the slaves will be upset by this new element remaining among them, irritating them because of their status and arousing insubordination among them, particularly if the authorities must enforce compliance with that responsibility and interfere for that purpose on those establishments. On the other hand, if the freed people must continue to live on their patrons' agricultural establishments in conditions identical to those of the slaves, brought up, treated, and maintained in perfect equality, they will become an inconvenience and a permanent danger, they will react, provoke disorders, and how can this be avoided or prevented?

Furthermore, these freed people, who will remain in the houses or on the establishments of their patrons, receiving the same status and treatment as the slaves, living among the latter and bound to them by family ties, at the age of twenty-one will enter into society infected with all the vices of slavery, ignorant, brutalized, despising work, with no education whatsoever, with no comprehension of human dignity, which only freedom awakens. What future is being prepared for our society which thirty years after the law goes into effect will annually receive into its bosom at least 30,000 freedmen, 30,000 new citizens—illiterate, emerging from a brutalizing captivity—but *ingênuos* nevertheless, possessing, that is, full political rights. Will this not be a cause of anarchy, a permanent source of grave perils and tremendous misfortunes? . . .

Public order, security, the peace and tranquillity of families, conditions even more sacred than the right to property, will obviously be upset and constantly threatened; and the government will lack even minimum resources to protect and reassure them. We, those who live in the large cities, normally have around us a large free population, which reduces our fears. We are protected by the government and by the armed forces, who are quick to come to our aid at the smallest disturbance; but those who live on the agricultural estates in the backlands of the Empire, which is as large as Europe, find themselves in a different situation; there families exist made up of three or four people, who live among hundreds of slaves in places far from any center of population. (*Hear! Hear!*).

Gentlemen, continuous or gradual emancipation by indirect methods, aside from being the easiest way, is also the one which will serve us best for the accomplishment of this most important reform. . . . To endeavor by means of a well-synthesized system of indirect measures, to aid and encourage private initiative, to facilitate manumissions, to establish an emancipation fund as large as possible, and meanwhile to undertake a careful and complete census of the slave population, to encourage and favor agriculture, to provide for a substitute of slave labor by free labor; this is our great mission, a difficult one obviously, but more meritorious than raising the banner of the slaves' redemption above the ruin and destruction of the nation. (*Hear! hear!*) By the wise and continuous application of this combination of measures, in less than twenty years, without threatening public order, without a significant setback to our wealth and production, the abolition of slavery could be achieved, because by then the slaves will be diminished [by deaths and emancipation] to a third of their present number. . . .

I thank the Chamber for the attention with which it has honored me, and ask your pardon for having abused your patience for so long. (*Very good; very good.*)

The speaker is complimented by many of the honorable deputies.

10.5. "As If It Were a Crime to Be Born" A Mulatto Senator Passionately Defends the Free-Birth Law (1871)

On September 5, 1871, near the end of the long debate on the Rio Branco Law, Dr. Francisco Salles Torres-Homem, a political writer, outstanding parliamentarian, and senator representing the northeastern province of Rio Grande do Norte, took the Senate floor to support the bill and to respond to its opponents' arguments. In his powerful speech, parts of which are included here, Salles Torres-Homem reminded the nation of the illegal foundations of much of Brazil's slavery and the peculiar nature of slave property, brilliantly challenging the theory, supported by legislators like Barros Cobra, that masters were the legitimate owners of the unborn children of slave women (see previous document). Himself the son of a black woman and one of the few Brazilian mulattoes to enter the General Assembly, he expressed attitudes that reflected his origins. For example, the senator opposed granting masters indemnification in the form of bonds or the freeborn children's labor for thirteen years, in exchange for raising those children until the age of eight. The true burden of caring for those infants, he argued, would be borne by their mothers—not by the masters to whom the law intended to grant indemnification.

Source: *Discussão da reforma do estado servil na Camara dos Deputados e no Senado, 1871*, 2 vols. (Rio de Janeiro: Typographia Nacional, 1871), II, 282-297.

❧ Mr. *Salles Torres-Homem*: Mr. President, it is with great emotion that I join the debate on the cabinet's bill dealing with the servile condition, an extraordinary question in which the highest considerations of moral order and material interest combine to give it an importance without equal among all those problems that have occupied the attention of the representatives since free government was first established in this country. . . .

Gentlemen, after a long age of obscurity and blindness in which all of us were involved, there came a time when the institution of slavery appeared before the conscience of the Brazilian people as it really is, enveloped in a new light which illuminated every aspect of the tragedy, producing in our minds and sentiments a gradual revolution which has never ceased, which has constantly moved forward, acquiring new strength along the way.

Mr. *F. Octaviano*: Hear! Hear!

Mr. *Salles Torres-Homem*: It was this moral revolution that twenty years ago effectively contributed to the successful suppression of the traffic, which neither the cruisers nor the resources of the world's first maritime power had been able to suppress [a reference to Britain's long campaign against the international slave trade]. That revolution is the same one which today raps on the doors of parliament demanding an instant completion of the work of civilization.

There were two ways to perpetuate slavery . . . : the [Atlantic] traffic and reproduction, that is, the bearing of children. The power of public opinion which destroyed the first of these ways will destroy the second, because both are equally nefarious and inhuman.

Far away in the African backlands where all is silence, the traffic seized the savage pagan's son, a victim of barbaric wars of which we took no notice, to transport him to the emporium of toiling flesh. The other process is no less evil; new creatures whom fate chooses to send to this world are waylaid at the very door of life, and there impressed into slavery, though born on the same soil, close to the same hearth, before God's temple, surrounded by the spectacles of freedom, which made their hardship and degradation even more difficult to bear! This is piracy carried on about the crib, in the waters of God's authority, and in the immediate view of a Christian people! . . .

I will turn now, Mr. President, to a consideration of the bill's contents. This bill cannot be fully understood and evaluated except in the direct light of the principles that inspire it, the necessities upon which it is based, and the purposes for which it is intended. If, as its enemies claim, it had no other design but to obey a sentimental impulse and to realize a shallow philanthropic dream, giving us a nobler aspect before the world; then, however generous our motives, the bill might appear hasty and ill-timed, keeping in mind the interested groups who desire and demand measures with slower and less clear results.

However, if its purpose is to prevent a relapse into one of the most terrible outrages ever to disgrace the human species; if its aim is to restore to our civilization the laws of God and nature and to uproot the evil that impedes our development, far from having the defects earlier mentioned, it might instead be denounced as timid and incomplete, as a plan that arranges compromises with poorly conceived interests, to the neglect of justice and human rights. . . .

If [the slaveholders] are asked why the legislator who can reform and amend the laws cannot amend laws that deal with property, they will doubtless reply that property is inviolable because it is based upon natural law that existed before civil law, and is derived from an immutable principle of justice, which sanctifies and affirms for each man the fruit of his own labor, a principle without which society could not exist. We are thus transported to the realm of law and justice, where the rational basis for the inviolability of property in general is indeed to be found.

But, gentlemen, if it is proved that ownership of a human being, far from being founded upon natural law, is on the contrary its most monstrous violation, if instead of being supported by justice it is sustained only by the evil of coercion and force, then the alleged basis of the inviolability of that special property disintegrates and disappears; and the law that supported it is seen as nothing more than an error, or a social crime, and is subject to amendment like any other law that does violence to the nation's interests.

Now, Mr. President, I should not have to demonstrate before this august assembly that intelligent creatures, endowed like us with noble qualities, facing the same destiny, should not be compared, from the point of view of property, to the colt, the calf, the fruit of the trees, and to the living objects of nature that are subject to human domination. An absurd, detestable doctrine! The beings with whom we are concerned do not yet exist; the dust of which their bodies will be composed is still scattered over the earth, the immortal souls, which will endow them with life, still repose in the lap of the creative power, serene and free, and already the monstrous slavocrat claims them as his property, already he usurps them from God's domain for the hell of slavery. (*Very good.*)

Listening to [pro-slavery petitioners] speak so loudly about property rights, one is surprised that they have so soon forgotten that the greater part of the slaves who work their lands are the descendants of those same people whom an inhuman traffic criminally introduced into this country with an affront to laws and treaties! They forget that during the period from 1830 to 1850 more than a million Africans were thus surrendered to our agriculture, and that to obtain that quantity of human cattle it was necessary to double and triple the number of victims, strewing their blood and their bodies over the surface of the seas that separate this country from the land of their birth. (*Very good!*)

And since human and divine laws were trampled upon in this way, how can such laws be invoked to support the future enslavement of the children and grandchildren of the victims of that hateful commerce?

The petitioners also oppose the indemnification, which they would like to see increased to a price equal or even superior to that of the child, to whom they possess no claim whatsoever. What is the purpose of the indemnification? The costs, it is said, of bringing up the children.

But these unfortunate people are nursed by their mothers, nourished by the crumbs of coarse food which their mothers help to plant and harvest: the milk from the maternal breast given to her own child, the mother's sweat that allows them to survive and covers their nakedness, this is what the masters will possess to sell to the treasury!

Mr. President, I regret that this provision is included in the bill; it blemishes it just as it disgraces the proprietors, because it appears to be designed as a safeguard against their barbarity; there is concern that they will abandon the children to hardship and death, if their inhumanity is not offset and controlled by their greed. However, even in this case, it is not gold that rightfully should be given to such men; it is the Gospel that they should receive, so that they may learn to comply with their sacred duties of charity toward the children of those people who labor endlessly and without pay to produce their masters' wealth and that of their descendants. (*Hear! hear!*)

Meanwhile the petitioners insist that they favor the reform, that they do not argue with the necessity of it, but only disagree on how to achieve it. Let's take a look at the terms that they agree to.

They accept the reform, without the freedom of the newborn; without the indemnification, which does not represent the whole value of the slave; without the slave's right to his personal savings; without obligatory manumission; without the protective intervention of the public authority to prevent the law from becoming a fraud; without the essential precautions against abuse; without any rest whatsoever from the prisons of captivity; without the immediate implementation of the law, and with no implementation for as long as a complete slave census has not been taken; without, finally, anything that directly or indirectly, at a distance or near at hand, may be contrary to their habits or cause them the least discomfort! (*Hear! hear!*) Otherwise they are in complete agreement. (*Laughter. Very good.*) Incomparable reformers.

How sad it is that they have not been well understood. They accept the reform with the condition that Roman legal regulations regarding slavery are to be retained in all their genuine and classic purity. . . .

Mr. President, one of the most distinguished members of the other chamber, for his talents and prospects, did not hesitate to praise the benefits of the institution of slavery and to deplore the fact that the government was trying to put an end to an arrangement essential to the production of the country's wealth. I might reply that the production of wealth is not the single and paramount aim of society, which is not made up only of creatures who are born, consume, die, and are buried in the furrows of the earth which nourishes them, that their destinies are higher, their circumstances, needs, intrinsic makeup, and civilization more complex.

But, moderating my argument in the face of opposition and granting the production of wealth all the importance it deserves, I will add that here, like everywhere else, in antiquity as in modern times, slavery was and should be recognized as a powerful source of backwardness and degeneration. . . .

Gentlemen, the secret of wealth lies not only in the variety of climates, in the soil's fertility, in natural advantages; it is to be found mainly in the innermost being of each person, in his energy and talents, and in the laws that protect and develop him. (*Hear! hear!*) The moral order creates the material order in its own image. Brazil, visibly held back by slavery on the road to prosperity, will not soar off into the future of greatness and opulence to which it is destined, except when on its free soil no plant grows moistened by the sweat and blood of the slave. (*Hear! hear!*) . . .

Those thousands of women who during the course of three centuries have so often cursed the hour of their motherhood and blasphemed Providence, seeing the innocent fruit of their bodies condemned to perpetual slavery, as if it were a crime to be born, will now raise their arms and their prayers toward heaven invoking the divine blessing upon those who granted them control over their own wombs. (*Very good.*) These grateful demonstrations of poor, afflicted people are of greater consequence than the curses of the shameless wealthy (*hear! hear!*); they outweigh the attacks of the powerful who did not understand how to obtain wealth except through the degradation and suffering of those who so much resemble them! (*Very good; very good.*)

The speaker is congratulated and praised by various senators.

10.6. "We Are Seeking Our Country's Highest Interests": An Abolitionist Analyzes Slavery and Calls for a Break with the Past (1883)

For some years after passage of the Rio Branco Law the anti-slavery movement was nearly dormant. However, as it became clear that most children "freed' by the law remained de facto slaves, that one of the law's key creations, the emancipation fund, was freeing few persons, and that otherwise the plan to end slavery gradually was not achieving great results, a new group of anti-slavery leaders suddenly appeared to initiate an entirely new phase of the anti-slavery struggle. In 1879, the young Pernambucan, Joaquim Nabuco, began making anti-slavery speeches in the Chamber of Deputies, and the following year, supported by a few colleagues, he introduced a bill to ban some of slavery's harsher features and to abolish it completely within ten years. His ideas brusquely rejected in the Chamber, Nabuco then turned to propaganda, organizing the Brazilian Anti-Slavery Society in September, 1880, and publishing a short-lived monthly newsletter, *O Abolicionista*. In that year journalists in Rio and other cities, notably the young mulatto José do Patrocinio (see Document 10.8), began to establish an abolitionist press, and newly formed emancipation clubs began holding regular meetings.

This outburst of anti-slavery activity aroused a powerful reaction among slaveholders, and, owing in part to this angry response, the new movement quickly declined. By 1881 most anti-slavery clubs were inactive, and late that year Nabuco himself was defeated in a bid for reelection, after which he sailed for England into self-imposed exile. It was during his residence abroad that Nabuco wrote his anti-slavery book, *O Abolicionismo*, from which this selection is drawn. In this work he brilliantly analyzed the effects of slavery upon Brazilian society and the nature of the abolition struggle. This selection includes a penetrating examination of Brazilian slavery as it existed in 1883 and a final appeal to Brazilians to make an abrupt break with the past and to begin a new era of reform and progress.

Source: Joaquim Nabuco, *Abolitionism: The Brazilian Anti-Slavery Struggle* (Urbana: University of Illinois Press, 1977), pp. 85-96, 164-173.

❧ Since the law of September 28, 1871, was passed, the Brazilian government has been trying to make the world believe that slavery has ended in Brazil. Our propaganda has tried to spread to other countries the belief that the slaves were being freed in considerable numbers, and that the children of the slaves were being born *entirely* free. Slave mortality is an item which never appears in those fraudulent statistics, behind which is the philosophy that a lie spread abroad allows the government to do nothing at home and to abandon the slaves to their fate.

The record of manumissions—highly creditable to Brazil—dominates the official picture and obscures slave mortality, while crimes against slaves, the number of Africans still in bondage, the hunting down of fugitive blacks, the fluctuating price of human flesh, the rearing of *ingênuos* in slavery, the utter sameness of our rural prisons, and everything unbecoming, humiliating, and bad for the government are all carefully suppressed. . . .

The Brazilian people, however, understand the entire matter. They know that after passage of the law of September 28 the life of the slaves did not change, except for those few who managed to redeem themselves by begging for their freedom. It is essential that we outline the condition of the slave today as it appears before the law, before society, before justice, before the master, and before himself, so that it will not someday be said that in 1883, when this book was written, abolitionists no longer faced the traditional slave system but another kind of slavery, modified for the bondsman by humane, protective, and comparatively just laws. I will sketch this picture of our slavery with strokes perhaps too rapid for a topic so vast.

Whoever arrives in Brazil and opens one of our daily newspapers finds there a photographic image of modern slavery more accurate than any painting. If Brazil were destroyed by a catastrophe, one issue of any of our great newspapers chosen at random would adequately preserve forever the forms and qualities of slavery as it exists in our time. The historian would need no other documents to re-create its entire structure and pursue all its effects.

In any issue of any major Brazilian paper—with the exception, I understand, of those of Bahia, where the press of the capital ceased the publication of slave advertisements—one would find, in effect, the following kinds of information which describe completely the present condition of the slaves: advertisements for purchase, sale, and rental of slaves in which invariably appear the words *mucama, moleque, bonita peça, rapaz, pardinho, rapariga da casa de familia* [black servant girl, black boy, pretty piece, boy, little darky, girl for family service] (free women advertise themselves as *senhoras* in order to differentiate themselves from slaves); official announcements of slave sales, a queer kind of document, of which the latest example from Valença is one of the most thorough [see Document 8.15 for Nabuco's criticism of the government's sale of slaves and *ingênuos* at Valença, Rio de Janeiro province]; advertisements for runaway slaves accompanied in many papers by the well-known vignette of a barefoot black with a bundle on his shoulder, in which the slaves are often distinguished by the scars of punishment they have suffered and for whom a reward is offered, often as much as a *conto* [1,000 *milréis*], to anyone who can catch him and bring him to his master—an encouragement to the bush-captain's profession; rather frequent notices of manumissions; stories of crimes committed by slaves against their masters, but particularly against agents of their masters, and of crimes committed by the latter against the slaves, barbarous and fatal punishments which nevertheless comprise only a very small part of the lordly misuse of power which occurs, since this kind of abuse rarely comes to the attention of authorities or the press, owing to a lack of witnesses and informers willing to testify to this kind of crime.

One finds, finally, repeated declarations that slavery among us is a very mild and pleasant condition for the slave, better for him, in fact, than for the master, a situation so fortunate, according to these descriptions, that one begins to suspect that, if slaves were asked, they would be found to prefer slavery to freedom; which merely proves that newspapers and articles are not written by slaves or by persons who for one moment have imagined themselves in their condition. . . .

The provisions of our Black Code are very few. Slavery is not indentured servitude which imposes a certain number of specified responsibilities upon the servant. It is the possession, domination, sequestration of a human being—his body, mind, physical forces, movements, all his activity—and it only ends with death. How can we define in legal terms what the master can do with the slave and what the slave cannot do under the supervision of his owner? As a rule the master can do *anything*. If he wants to shut the slave up inside his house forever, he can do so. If he wants to prevent him from establishing a family, he can do so. If the slave has a wife and children and the master desires that he neither see them nor speak to them, if he decides to order the son to whip the mother, if he wishes to usurp the daughter for immoral purposes, he can do so. Imagine all the most extraordinary injuries which one man can inflict upon another without killing him, without separating him by sale from his wife and children under fifteen, and you will have what slavery is *legally* among us. The House of Correction, in comparison with this other condition, is a paradise. Excluding thought of the crime of condemning an innocent person to imprisonment as an example to others—which is worse than the fate of the most unfortunate slave—there is no comparison between a system of fixed obligations, of dependence upon law and its administrators, and a system of proprietary subjection to a person who can be a madman or a barbarian.

Concerning the slave's civil capacity, according to the law of September 28, 1871, he is allowed to form a *pecúlio* [personal liberation fund] which he may derive from gifts, legacies, inheritances, and, *with the consent of his master*, from his labor and personal thrift. But application of this law depends entirely upon the master, who owns the slave and everything the slave possesses, in a country where the protection of bondsmen by the courts is neither spontaneous nor effective. Concerning the family, it is forbidden, under penalty of invalidating the sale, to separate a husband from his wife or a child from his father or mother, except when the child is over fifteen (Law no. 1,695 of September 15, 1869, Article 2). [Nabuco seems not to have known that a provision of the Rio Branco Law had lowered the age of the child who could be separated from a parent by sale from fifteen to twelve.] But a wedding depends upon a master's authorization, and if he is not allowed to separate a family by sale, he can break up that family whenever he desires and for as long as he likes by a simple command.

To recapitulate, I will sketch in broad strokes what slavery is *legally* in Brazil in 1883:

1. The present bondsmen, born before September 28, 1871, and today at least eleven and a half years old, are slaves until they die, *exactly* like those of earlier generations. The number of these, as will be seen, is more than a million.

2. Whoever is subject to slavery is compelled to obey without question every order received, to do whatever he is told, without the right to demand a thing: neither pay nor clothing, improved food nor rest, medicine nor change of duties.

3. The man so enslaved has no duties—to God, to his mother and father, to his wife or children, or even to himself—which the master *must* respect and allow him to perform.

4. The law does not fix maximum hours of labor, a minimum wage, rules of hygiene, food, medical treatment, conditions of morality, protection of women. In a word, it interferes as much in the organization of the plantation as it does in the supervision of draft animals.

5. There is no law whatever which regulates the obligations and prerogatives of the master; whatever the number of slaves he may possess, he exercises an authority over them which is limited only by his own judgment.

6. The master can inflict moderate punishment upon slaves, says the *Criminal Code*, which compares his authority to the power of a father; but in fact he punishes at will, because justice does not penetrate the feudal domain. A slave's complaint against his master would be fatal, as it has been in practice, and in fact the master is all-powerful. The attitudes of today are what they were in 1852. It is as dangerous now, and just as useless, for a slave to complain to the authorities as it was then. To accuse his master, the slave requires the same will power and determination that he needs to run away or to commit suicide, particularly if he hopes for some security in his servitude.

7. The slave lives in total uncertainty regarding his future; if he thinks he is about to be sold, mortgaged, or pawned, he has no right to question his master.

8. Any person released from the House of Correction or even confined within it, however perverse he may be, whether he be a Brazilian or foreigner, can own or buy a family of respectable and honest slaves and expose them to his whims.

9. Masters can employ female slaves as prostitutes, receiving the profits from this business with no danger of losing their property as a result, just as a father can be the owner of his son.

10. The state does not protect the slaves in any way whatsoever. It does not inspire them with confidence in public justice but instead surrenders them *without hope* to the implacable power which weighs heavily upon them, morally imprisons or constrains them, arrests their movement, and in short destroys them.

11. The slaves are governed by exceptional laws. The use of the lash against them is allowed, despite its prohibition by the Constitution.

Their crimes are punished by a barbaric law, that of June 10, 1835 [see Document 6.4], the sole penalty of which is execution.

12. The belief has been spread throughout the nation that slaves often commit crimes in order to become convicts, in this way escaping from slavery, since they prefer the chain gang to the plantation, as Roman slaves preferred to fight wild beasts, in the hope of achieving freedom if they survived. For this reason a jury of the interior has absolved criminal slaves to be restored later to their masters, and lynch law has been carried out in more than one case. Here we have slavery as it really is! Death by suicide is looked upon by the bondsman as the *cessation of the evils of slavery*, imprisonment with hard labor such *an improvement of his condition* that it can be *an incentive to crime!* Meanwhile we, a humane and civilized nation, condemn more than a million persons, as so many others were condemned before them, to a condition alongside which imprisonment or the gallows seems better!

13. Not all the powers of the master, which, as we have seen, are practically without limit, are exercised directly by him, absent as he often is from his lands and out of contact with his slaves. Instead, these powers are delegated to individuals without intellectual or moral education, who know how to command men only by means of violence and the whip.

It is odd that masters who exercise this unlimited power over their human property look upon the law's least intervention on behalf of the slaves as intolerable oppression. The resistance of our agricultural community to that part of the law of September 28 which granted the slave the right to accumulate his own *pecúlio*, and to use that fund to acquire his own freedom once he had saved it, proves that not even this crumb of freedom was willingly dropped from their table. The planters of Bananal, for example, whose names indicate that they represent the agricultural families of São Paulo as well as those on the borders of Rio de Janeiro province, stated in a petition to the Chambers: "*Either property exists with its essential characteristics, or it decidedly does not exist*. Forced liberation, with the various measures relating to it, is armed vengeance which threatens every home, every family, the destruction of agriculture, the death of the nation." Significantly, when an attempt was made in the Council of State to give slaves the right to possess their own savings, the Marquis of Olinda declared, "*We are not creating ethical law*." . . .

It is said that among us slavery is mild and the masters are good. The truth is, however, that all slavery is the same, and the goodness of the masters depends upon the resignation of the slaves. Whoever would try to compile statistics on crimes committed either by slaves or against them, whoever would inquire into slavery and hear the complaints of those who suffer it would see that in Brazil, even today, slavery is as hard, barbarous, and cruel as it was in any other country of America. By its very nature slavery is all this, and when it stops being this it is not because the masters have improved. It is because the slaves have resigned themselves totally to the destruction of their personalities. . . .

What this system represents we already know. Morally it is the destruction of every basis and principle of religious or positive decency—the family, property, social harmony, humanitarian aspirations. Politically it is slavishness, the degradation of the people, the disease of bureaucratism, the languishing of patriotism, the division of the countryside into feudal domains, each with its own penal system, its own seat of judgement, beyond the reach of police and courts. Economically and socially it is the temporary prosperity of one class alone, and this class decadent and constantly in a state of renewal. It is the elimination of accumulated capital through the purchase of slaves, the paralyzation of each potential separate unit of national labor, the closing of our ports to immigrants who look to South America, the exaggeration of the social importance of money however acquired, contempt for all those whose scruples make them unfit to engage in our materialistic competition or cause them to fall behind in that competition. It is the sale of noble titles, the demoralization of authority from the highest to the lowest level, the inability of persons worthy of leading their country toward a higher destiny to rise to authority because of the people's reluctance to support their defenders, their disloyalty to those who sacrifice themselves on their behalf. And the nation, in the midst of all this demeaning of character, of honest labor, of quiet virtues, of poverty which would rise above its condition with clean hands, is, as was said of the southern states, "enamored of her shame." . . .

None of the great national causes which produced as their heroes the greatest spirits of humanity ever had better reason to exist than ours. Let every true Brazilian become the instrument of that cause. Let the young people, from the moment when they accept the responsibilities of citizenship, swear to abstain from the purchase of human flesh. Let them prefer an obscure career of honest labor to amassing wealth by means of the inexpressible suffering of other human beings. Let them educate their children—indeed, let them educate themselves—to enjoy the freedom of others without which their own liberty will be a chance gift of destiny. Let them acquire the knowledge that freedom is worth possessing, and let them attain the courage to defend it. . . .

The abolitionists include all those who believe in a Brazil without slaves, all those who anticipate the miracles of free labor, all those who suffer *slavery* as a detested vassalage imposed upon the entire nation by some and in the interests of some. They include those who now gasp in the foul air which slaves and masters freely breathe—those who do not believe that Brazil, with slavery gone, will lie down to die, as did the Roman in the age of the Caesars because he had lost his liberty.

This means that we are seeking our country's highest interests, her civilization, the future rightfully hers. But, between us and those who are blocking the path, who will win? This, indeed, is the very enigma of Brazil's national destiny. Slavery injected fanaticism into her bloodstream, and she is now doing nothing to grasp control of her fate from those blind and indifferent forces which now silently lead her on.

10.7. A Municipal Chamber of São Paulo Gives Its Opinions on the Slavery and Labor Questions (1885)

By 1884 abolitionism was achieving unprecedented gains. In March of that year a popular movement allegedly freed the last slave in Ceará, and in a brief period from March to June the 1,501 slaves registered in the huge province of Amazonas were systematically freed by an enthusiastic population, led by the provincial president. In Rio Grande do Sul, the borderland province that Tavares Bastos thought might end slavery first (see Document 10.3), an enthusiastic movement freed two-thirds of the province's 60,000 slaves in a matter of months. In Rio the same revulsion for slavery was displayed in public demonstrations, as local committees tried to free slaves in selected urban areas, imitating the strategy used with great success in Ceará.

In June, 1884, the emperor reacted to this situation with the appointment of a new Liberal Party cabinet. On July 15 this ministry, headed by the Bahian senator, Manoel Pinto de Souza Dantas, proposed a law to grant unconditional freedom to all slaves reaching the age of sixty. This so-called Dantas Bill, like the Rio Branco Law before it, set off an intense national debate, inspiring a senator from São Paulo, Joaquim Floriano de Godoy, to submit a questionnaire to the municipal chambers of his province, presumably to help him decide how to vote on the Dantas Bill. The following reply to Godoy's questionnaire from the municipal chamber of Franco do Imperador typified the thinking of planters of that province on the Dantas reform and the problem of agricultural labor. These local leaders opposed freeing sixty-year-old slaves because to do so implied the government's right to free any slave without compensation, regardless of age, and it was thus a violation of the right to property.

Source: J. Floriano de Godoy, *O elemento servil e as camaras municipaes da provincia de São Paulo* (Rio de Janeiro: Imprensa Nacional, 1887), pp. 155-160.

❧ Most Illustrious and Excellent Dr. Joaquim Floriano de Godoy, Respected Senator of the Empire for the province of São Paulo.
Sir:

This Chamber has given its deserved consideration to the request for advice which Your Excellency, responding to feelings of true patriotism, addressed to the Municipalities of this province concerning the momentous problem of the servile element.

And, having studied the matter, it now submits to Your Excellency's high appreciation the sum of its observations:

Should bill no. 48, presented by Counselor Dantas to the Chamber of Deputies, be adopted?

Among its other harmful provisions, the renowned bill of July 15 orders in its first article the liberation of sixty-year-old slaves without indemnification.

Obviously such a provision openly injures the right to property which is fully guaranteed by Art. 179, Paragraph 22, of the Political Constitution of the Empire, as well as by the law of September 28, 1871.

Counselor of State Paulino de Souza recognized the following dilemma in his written opinion delivered at the conference of July 25 of last year: "Either the servile element is legal property or it is not. If it is legal property, expropriation requires indemnification under every conceivable circumstance. If it is not legal property, the power to free the slaves older than sixty is unquestionably extended to those under fifty, forty, thirty, and twenty, and under such a hypothesis, if the legislator is logical, he must decree simultaneous and immediate abolition." And he continues: "If the liberation of sexagenarians is decreed without indemnification, servile property is legally demoralized and has no legal basis in the minds of the population, since it has none in the mind of the legislator."

Mr. Affonso Celso made the following valuable observations: "With your permission, I am obliged to point out that the decreeing of unrecompensed liberation of the slaves who reach the age of sixty will be harmful to those same slaves. Plunged into a state of idleness because of a lack of asylums, and incapable of easily earning their living because of their indolence and lack of strength, they will die of misery or personal misfortune. They will find themselves, on the other hand, removed from the places where they had lived, frequently far from their poor homes and their companions of many years, precisely in the last phase of their lives when their need of love, care, and the solace of friends and relatives is greatest. It is not an advantage, but rather an injury, which will be done to them.

"These disadvantages of the bill, seen from this angle, are not the only ones; others appear when it is studied from the legal point of view.

"When it is decreed that the slaves reaching a certain age will enter into their full freedom, what will be the status of the younger ones, according to law? They will no longer be slaves, but will become *statu-liberi*; that is, persons who have acquired freedom, who already possess that right, of which they can not be deprived, the effectiveness of which, nevertheless, remains dependent upon a condition of time."

In regard to the same question, Counselor Vieira da Silva made this lucid statement: "The old slaves are not entirely useless on the plantations. Like the children, they perform services which, if not done by them, would have to occupy able-bodied persons.

"Aside from this, the measure undermines the principle recognized by the law of September 28, 1871, of slave property and indemnification. The slave possesses in his old age, as when he is sick, the right to be cared for, clothed, and fed by his master. What good is freedom if, old and sick, he can no longer work?"

Nor should we argue, as the newspapers of unrestrained abolitionism have done, with the example of cultured nations, and especially those of Europe, because such arguments are counterproductive.

France, with 250,000 slaves in its overseas colonies, decreed indemnification payments totalling 214,000,000 francs, that is, eighty-five thousand *contos de réis*.

Your Excellency has observed that Sweden paid 250,000 francs for the liberation of the few slaves which it possessed on the island of St. Bartholomew.

And the United States, which proclaimed emancipation en masse, as an immediate consequence suffered the memorable War of Secession, which for years ruined and bled that great republic. [This, of course, is inaccurate; slavery ended in the United States as a *result* of the Civil War.] As one of our distinguished legislators said, the violation of a property right, once decreed, is an open door to the violation of all property rights.

Therefore, this Chamber's reply to Your Excellency's question must be entirely negative. The Dantas Bill on the servile element should not be adopted.

In the case of rejection:

2ND.

Will it be desirable to fix a date for granting the extinction of the servile element, or would gradual extinction be preferable?

The setting of a date should be rejected from the outset, because it has the effect of misleading the slaves who, by the very nature of the situation, would be free before that date arrives, with great harm to the agricultural interests and the security of property.

The setting of a date, however reasonable it may seem, would bring incalculable disadvantages, and experience cries out against such a measure.

Yes, gradual extinction is indeed better, as established by the law of 1871.

3RD.

Should the law of September 28, 1871, be kept unchanged?

It would not be wise to change the golden law, which alone, faster than may be imagined, will end slavery among us. By conserving the status quo of the law of September 28, this Chamber believes, the problem of abolition has been resolved without disturbance, without revolution, without assaults on property, without contempt for law.

4TH.

If neither of these proposals is accepted, what measures should be adopted to solve the problems of emancipation?

Essentially answered by the reply to the third question.

5TH.

Can free national workers satisfactorily fill the gap created by acts of emancipation?

This is a very complex question which requires much effort and patriotism. National colonization is certainly preferable to foreign, especially since European immigration does not come to our shores, because of the errors of the government, which does not know how or does not want to attract it. Concerning foreign colonization, this Chamber agrees with the resolution taken by the last Agricultural Congress held in the Court in July of last year: the immigration of Chinese workers appears to be in harmony with the interests and needs of agriculture, because, considering the nature and realities of labor, those workers will bring to Brazil an advantage identical to that which Asian workers produced in other regions where slaves existed.

There is no lack of workers in this country; they are superabundant in the cities, towns, and villages. How to attract these armies of idle people to agricultural labor is what must be considered, because such efforts will tend to put the native Brazilian to work. The situation of the *ingênuos* has been almost totally ignored. A compulsory labor law for the *ingênuos* and freedmen is a requirement of public order; and to this should be added the severe corrective remedy of agrarian penal colonies.

The substitution of the slave worker by the free is a question of vital concern to the nation. Abolitionism does not solve this problem, but seeks merely to unleash upon the literate and hardworking classes the mindless mass of a million ignorant and often bloodthirsty slaves. They live for today and forget tomorrow. This is the future of our fatherland.

Such a substitution will be achieved only by means of corrective measures, which the government should initiate, with the aim of moralizing the *ingênuos* and freedmen and establishing the national worker on the soil by means of a reasonable contract, so that rural labor may be transformed but not disorganized.

God keep Your Excellency for many years. Palace of the Municipal Chamber of Franco do Imperador, in extraordinary session on the 14th of February, 1885.

The President, *José Theodoro de Mello.—Francisco Lucas Brigagão.—Antonio Flavio de Castro.—Alvaro de Lima Guimarães Junior.—José Garcia Duarte.—Thomaz José da Motta.*

10.8. The Mulatto Editor and Abolitionist, José do Patrocinio, Condemns the Government's Slavery Policy (1885)

In May, 1885, the Chamber of Deputies rejected the Dantas Bill intended to free slaves reaching sixty, and a new "Liberal" cabinet headed by Senator José Antônio Saraiva introduced a watered-down project to replace it. Instead of freeing elderly slaves outright as the Dantas Bill would have done, this new bill provided that slaves turning sixty were to compensate their masters for their freedom with five more years of unpaid labor. Just four days after the government submitted this legislation to the Chamber, the mulatto editor and abolitionist, José do Patrocinio, lashed out at Saraiva and his bill in the following editorial, one of a series of articles entitled "Semana Politica" (Political week) which, under the pseudonym "Proudhomme" Patrocinio published in his newspaper, *A Gazeta da Tarde*. In this editorial Patrocinio concentrated on a single section of the Saraiva Bill: that which ordered a new national registration of slaves to replace that carried out after passage of the Free Birth Law of 1871.

What Patrocinio found most objectionable was Saraiva's removal of the requirement (contained in the Dantas Bill) that each slave registration include the individual's birthplace (*naturalidade*) and parentage (*filiação*). As Patrocinio suggested, these were important items of information, since hundreds of thousands of people then held as slaves were in fact descendants of Africans illegally imported into Brazil after 1831, who were therefore legally free—a freedom that would have been revealed if their "masters" had been forced to state where they were born and who their parents were. This selection goes beyond these questions of the day to include startling revelations drawn from Patrocinio's own childhood experiences and memories of his slaveholding father.

Source: *A Gazeta da Tarde* (Rio de Janeiro), May 16, 1885.

Political Week

I have just read the speech with which Ernest Renan received Ferdinand de Lesseps [the builder of the Suez Canal] into the French Academy. It was necessary for him to justify the widsom and correctness of the great assembly for having admitted into its bosom the immortal Frenchman whose works were carved into the rocks of the isthmuses. . . .

When I had finished reading Renan's speech, I came back down to earth as I remembered that I had to write about Mr. Saraiva's government! Life's sad experiences! To cease observing the great figure of a man who opens great highways to humanity, to look instead upon an individual who once again would open up new trails to the convoys of the traffic in human flesh! . . .

Before beginning my study of the GREAT STATESMAN [here Patrocinio was sardonic], the GREAT MINISTER OF GOVERNMENT, and of the GREAT BILL, which I must do, I would like to compare one of the articles of his bill with one from the [Dantas] bill of July 15 [, 1884].

Article 1 of [Saraiva's] bill states: "A new registration of all slaves existing at the date of the law will be carried out throughout the Empire, specifying the name, color, sex, parentage, *if it is known*, occupation, age, and value, estimated by the method set forth in Article 2." [A scale of values followed in the bill.]

Article 1, Paragraph 2, of the Dantas Bill states: "The government will order that a new registration of the slaves be carried out with a declaration of the name, color, age, marital status, *birthplace, parentage*, aptitude for work, and value, estimated by the means set forth in Paragraph 2 of this article."

The GREAT STATESMAN is mainly respected and celebrated for his honesty. In the political balance he has been granted this accolade of honor. However, Article 1 of the great bill stands here before us to call this reputation to account.

The capital point of the slavery question is its challenge to the legality of existing slavery. Abolitionist propaganda claims that today's slavery is the product of piracy and has proved this with the book of history in hand. An honest legislator does not have the right to ignore this point, which is at the heart of the controversy. Either Mr. Saraiva is convinced that the origin of slavery is legal, and thus ought not to deny to the written record its most certain element; or he believes the opposite, and so by dispensing with the birthplace and parentage in the registration, makes himself an avowed accomplice of the criminals whom Minister Souza França ordered punished as of May, 1831, as violators of Article 179 of the [criminal] code, which [dealt with] reducing free persons to slavery.

Let's accept His Excellency's entire bill; let us not question the indemnification for enslaved persons of sixty years of age, of their purchase [with five more years of labor] of their right to die, which until now cost them nothing. Let's not waste time calculating the financial mistake which orders that, in a land of permanent deficit spending, assets of the state are to be diverted to the benefit of a class which [has been] an accomplice in the crime of violating the laws and treaties of that same state. We will limit ourselves to the question of honor; we wish only to challenge the foundations of Mr. Saraiva's reputation. However hard His Excellency may try to justify himself for having turned such an article into an open point of debate, history's inflexible justice will condemn it.

Even now, as I am writing, God has seen fit to make me the victim of a deep sadness. I went out to reexamine a list of free Africans [see Documents 8.11 through 14] who [earlier in the nineteenth century] were confided to the care of persons of the highest reputation; Africans who, having been made captives, had been guaranteed their freedom by the state. This is not the first time that I have turned the pages of this sad document, in which the names of persons of great importance in our history appear. But one name had escaped me. It was the name of a priest of Jesus Christ, of a titular canon and preacher in the Imperial Chapel, a man decorated with the Orders of the Rose and of Christ, vicar of the ecclesiastical district of Campos, confessor of the Bishop of Rio de Janeiro, and, at that time, provincial deputy for this province: Bachelor João Carlos Monteiro.

This name is that of my father!

I must inform Mr. Saraiva that [the Africans held by my father] were reduced to slavery, that on many occasions I heard one of them trembling and repeating in a deeply moving chant this accusing stanza, coarse with the intelligence of the underdog, a verse which until today has agitated my sleep and will continue to do so until in some way I can make up for my father's crime:

"The white man is greatly honored.
He drinks no rum,
but makes the freed black toil for him
until he's numb."

[Branco é muito honrado
Não bebe catambá,
Mas faz zi negro forro
P'ra zelle trabaiá.]

I saw in the house where I grew up, aside from the unhappy Arsenio, many other Africans who were unquestionably of the same origin; from them my father's slaves were derived, and these grew to a total of ninety-two persons. Because of the death of their master, these wretched people were sold to pay the debts of the very man who had enslaved them.

And [on the list], along with my father's name, are those of the fathers of many of today's noblemen, including that of one who must be a kinsman of Mr. Paulino de Souza [a leading pro-slavery politician from Rio de Janeiro province], who in 1871 introduced obstacles to including the slaves' birthplace and parentage in the registration, and whose arguments have probably once again been influential in favor of continuing the system of concealing this most wicked of crimes.

This name is Bernardo Belisario Soares de Souza.

An honorable legislator who understands his country's history, who has prepared himself to solve a problem of the moral and economic importance of the servile question, who knows that there were years in which the criminal importation of [Africans] amounted to 50,000 (1846), 56,000 (1847), 60,000 (1848), and who knows that from 1831 to 1852 this figure grew to about 600,000 Africans, as demonstrated by the official statistics of Euzebio de Queiroz [the justice minister most associated with abolishing the slave trade]; who knows that of these Africans only 1,027 were freed (the figure put forward by Pereira Pinto); such an honorable legislator would have no alternative but to demand that the slaves' birthplace and parentage be included in the registration. Mr. Saraiva cannot run away from this: either he is a man of honor and, like Mr. Dantas, demands the recording of the slaves' birthplace and parentage in the new registration, at the cost otherwise of their liberation; or he does not require this and so consents to allow the impartiality of history to place him side by side with those earlier legislators who justifed the commerce in free men on the grounds of the violence of the English cruiser.

I do not wish to finish without calling Mr. Saraiva's attention to Renan's words: "Human progress is not the task of men who do not have the courage to involve themselves in great actions. This is the task of the bold, of those who defy the interests of the moment in the name of the permanent interests of law and science."

PROUDHOMME

10.9. An Ex-Abolitionist Recalls the Anti-Slavery Struggle in São Paulo (1918)

In 1885 the Brazilian Assembly passed the bill known as the Saraiva-Cotegipe Law, essentially the legislation which José do Patrocinio had criticized (see previous document). Abolitionists generally opposed this law as retrogressive, but for months after its passage it seemed to diminish their enthusiasm for rapid change. Seen in the light of later events, however, it seems more probable that the movement was merely pausing to take stock of the situation and to prepare the next phase of the struggle. In any case, before the end of 1886 that new phase had clearly begun. More violent and less beholden to legality than earlier abolitionism, the new efforts which began in late 1886 were concentrated in the key coffee-producing province of São Paulo to which tens of thousands of slaves had been sent in previous decades from other provinces, and where opposition to the anti-slavery movement had been correspondingly intense.

The following document, the personal reminiscences of a Paulista abolitionist, is one of the most important descriptions of the movement in that province. While it deals briefly with early phases of abolitionism in São Paulo, it emphasizes the last dramatic months of the struggle during which the slaves themselves heroically abandoned their masters' plantations, contributing enormously to the collapse of slavery in 1888. Usefully too, this narrative also refers to a little-noted aspect of the movement, participation of women and women's organizations and their efforts to free female slaves, especially the young and those of childbearing age. This document—somewhat condensed here—was written some thirty years after abolition and was first published in the newspaper *O Estado de São Paulo*, on May 13, 1918.

Source: Antônio Manoel Bueno de Andrada, "A abolição em São Paulo," *Revista do Arquivo Municipal* (São Paulo) 77 (1941), 261-272.

❧ For about ten years after promulgation of the merciful law of the free womb the abolitionist movement had declined in intensity throughout the country. The pleasure of victory had cooled the energy of action.

Never, however, did the real abolitionists, the intransigents, regard their humanitarian aims as fully achieved by the certainty that never again would a Brazilian be born a slave.

At various points in Brazil men of will, spirit, and courage worked tirelessly for the complete elimination of slavery.

In my time the young men of the Polytechnical Academy in Rio de Janeiro, led by the beloved and immortal Viscount of Rio Branco, were all in favor of abolition. In São Paulo, Luís Gama fought endlessly as a propagandist and as a lawyer for the freedom of the slaves. [See Documents 5.7 and 8.20.]

At the higher level of politics in São Paulo there were many partisans of the good cause, but few who dedicated themselves to it in a practical manner. Among the latter I am proud to include my father, Counselor Martim Francisco Ribeiro de Andrada, who, as Minister of Justice in the Cabinet of August 3 [,1866], that of Zacarias, used his influence to include for the first time in the Speech from the Throne, that is, in the political program of the cabinet, the necessity of solving the problem of the extinction of slave labor. Ostracized by his party but true to his beliefs, the ex-minister continued working for the realization of his ideas, in the defense of which he had lost power.

To free my testimony of partiality, I will recall among the services performed by him only this: the founding of a ladies' society for the emancipation of slave girls (1870).

My mother, Dona Ana Bemvinda Bueno de Andrada, was chosen to preside. Many members were enlisted, each contributing 2$000 per month. Then twelve years of age, I was one of the collectors of those monthly fees. The association, which was called the Emancipadora, redeemed many young girls; some of them married and established families who today are living in prosperity.

I recall that Ferreira de Menezes and Salvador de Mendonça, then editors of *Ipiranga*, organ of the Liberal Party of São Paulo, supported the Emancipadora with enthusiasm; along with the student, Aureliano de Oliveira Coutinho.

Thus many influential politicians in São Paulo opted in favor of the emancipation of the servile element, but the popular chief of propaganda, its boldest apostle and fighter was unquestionably Luís Gama.

With clear purpose I use the term fighter [*lutador*], because the word well defines the abolitionist efforts which he put forward in that difficult situation.

Luís Gama lived on his meager lawyer's income. He had no other support. His dedication to the enslaved people consumed his time and repelled wealthy clients. Such considerations did not deter him. Gratuitous service in favor of liberation became his law-office specialty. His polemical struggles in favor of freedom were incessant, and some aroused public opinion. For example:

During the year 1871 a millionaire Portuguese died in Santos—one Neto. The inventory of his property aroused a considerable demand among heirs and business associates. Included among the spoils were more than one hundred slaves; Luís Gama, on what grounds I do not know, intervened in the case, making a plea for the liberation of the slaves. A tenacious and exhausting battle ensued, creating an enormous scandal, but he was victorious. From his noisy triumph in the celebrated "Neto trial," there were two results:

The number of cases of this kind grew rapidly. All were assigned to the great defender of the oppressed. He never rejected a single case. And, achieving one victory after another, the liberal lawyer managed to reduce extraordinarily the price of the so-called "letters of liberty.". . .

The influence of Luís Gama grew day by day, and consequently his circle of action and his exhausting labors. In the end the robust nature of the fighter was affected by his excessive effort. The decline of the giant was rapid.

When he died [in 1882] nobody could assume his humanitarian responsibilities in the same way. No abolitionist could bring together at that sad moment all the qualities needed in the legal struggles and in other spheres to defend with the same success the cause of freedom. Some had debating experience; others the same dedication; one understood the situation and enjoyed the support of others; another had the free time, but none encompassed the extraordinary qualities of the leader whom death had stolen from us.

Nevertheless, among the most fervent initiates of abolitionism was included an exceptional man. In fact, Dr. Antônio Bento de Souza e Castro was a person of unique qualities. Occupying an exceptional position, with ties to the wealthy, rich himself, a follower of conservative doctrines, a stern and frigid ex-judge, he seemed the living antithesis of Luís Gama. However, one quality common to both brought them together: a deep and outraged aversion to the system of slavery.

While the supreme leader lived, [Bento] followed him loyally and politely, with the same dedication shown by the others. However, when we no longer possessed the former, he spontaneously focused the confidence of the rest, putting himself at the head of the movement. Destiny favored us in her choice.

Antonio Bento, born, educated, and trained in law in the capital of São Paulo, was known by everybody and knew everybody. His appearance attracted attention, his figure could be recognized at a distance: rather tall, with dark eyeglasses, a large abundant black "cavaignac," he wore a wide-brimmed hat, and frequently went about wrapped in a large black cape. He knew the history of São Paulo in its smallest details, and yet in his conversations with great people and small, although a bit sardonic, he never embarrassed anyone. Generally well-liked, he was able to expand the popular agitation which had already developed around the problem of the extinction of the servile element. On the other hand, he was a judge, knew how to plead a case, and so could succeed the great patron of the slaves in the legal arena.

For some time after that the abolitionist action continued in the courts. But the speeches of Rui Barbosa [noted abolitionist and liberal statesman from Bahia] and the propaganda of [José do] Patrocinio [see previous document] profoundly arousing all the social classes, attracting to the abolitionist ranks new and numerous contingents, little by little dislocated the struggle for freedom from the restrictive sphere of the law toward that of revolutionary agitation.

Around Antonio Bento, aside from the companions of Luís Gama, new popular groups assembled.

He ably understood how to make use of older and recent elements.

At the Confraternity of Nossa Senhora dos Remedios, which is the property of a church located in the center of the city, he began bringing together all the strands of the net in which the slave system of São Paulo would be ensnared. In the huge building, headquarters of that Confraternity, are large rooms which he used to establish the printing office of a newspaper of bold and effective propaganda, *A Redenção*. [Redemption.]

In the *Redenção* offices the brothers of the Rosary met almost daily with the other abolitionists. It was a revolutionary club. Some discussed ideas, brought in news; others wrote articles; one recalled some useful expedient; others introduced new followers; almost all left voluntary contributions.

Soon the organization divided itself into two groups, which, though joined by a common aim, were distinguished by useful capabilities: the intellectuals of the party and the men of action, those of the latter group becoming known by the name of "Caifazes of Antônio Bento."

As soon as it was known that on some agricultural establishment the slaves were treated harshly, they organized a true plan of action to free them from the power of their master. At the beginning of this revolutionary process, they struggled against great difficulties. To make [the slaves] flee the plantation was not the greatest of their difficulties, since, once they had arrived at the capital it was not always easy to hide them from the police investigations or from the searches of the "bush captains."

The conquering wave of abolitionist ideas quickly inundated the heart and mind of the inhabitants of the city of São Paulo and principally of the city of Santos. So that the troops of slaves brought from the plantations by the "caifazes", guided by the latter two centers, gradually, with greater ease, were hidden away and sheltered. A message from Antônio Bento was enough to accomplish this.

From the church of Remedios the revolutionary plot spread to many interior cities. From the most important rural centers Antônio Bento and the editors of *A Redenção* received information and proposals for the redemption of the slaves.

In Campinas, Amparo, Casa Branca, and other points of apparent slavist domination existed groups of persons who, with great caution, conspired as true "caifazes." Where, however, abolitionism won over every mind and produced an admirable unity of opinion was in the city of Santos.

Once a slave had managed to set foot on the streets of that port, he was in fact free; and more and more they found paid work loading and unloading coffee.

With the purpose of encouraging the exodus of the enslaved toward free soil, the inhabitants of Santos established in a high valley of the city a new district, a special dwelling place for runaway slaves, which took the picturesque name of "Quilombo de Jabaquara."

The invading current grew, and in a short time the two cities were saturated with that strange element. Antônio Bento then set out on a most original revolutionary path. He arranged with some planters, whose fields had already been depopulated, to receive slaves who had left other masters. Each worker from outside would receive from his new employers the daily wage of 400 *réis*. The process, without entirely upsetting the agricultural economy, freed hordes of slaves and interested many planters in the victory of our ideas. I myself took some of those planters to confer with Antônio Bento. The law of May 13 [, 1888] found more than a third of the plantations of São Paulo worked by slaves who had left other plantations. It was a beautiful idea.

Such, in rapid strokes, was the development of abolitionism in São Paulo under the direction of Antonio Bento. Nevertheless, some events stand out from the general action, scenes I am determined to recall, not only because they reveal the energy of the "caifazes," but because in that period they produced a sensation.

One excessively brutal master made martyrs of his slaves. One of them, the black man Antônio, was suspended for many days from a ceiling by an iron chain which was wrapped around his neck, so that the unfortunate man supported himself on the floor only by the tips of his toes. He increased the suffering of his slaves by wounding the palms of their hands with the point of a knife.

The "caifazes" managed to bring the martyr to São Paulo. *A Redenção* had violently protested. When he arrived in São Paulo Antônio Bento organized a procession of all the brothers of the Confraternity dos Remedios. An impressive performance. Between the platforms of the saints, suspended on long staffs, appeared instruments of torture: iron collars, chains, yokes, whips, etc. In front, beneath the livid image of Christ crucified, walked the unfortunate slave, numb and tottering. Never have I attended such a sad and suggestive ceremony. The impression of the city was profound! The police did not dare to impede the march of the popular mass. The multitude followed silently. All felt deeply moved, except the unfortunate martyred black man, who was maddened by his pain.

The bold and solemn originality of the brothers of Nossa Senhora dos Remedios cooled the moral force and spirit of the angriest slaveholders. From that day on the doors of the city remained open to the hordes of fugitives. Our leader had achieved a decisive victory. . . .

I will end these notes with an account of the sinister events that took place in the Santo Amaro Pass on the very eve of total emancipation.

From the neighborhood of Capivarí fled a large group of captives, some one hundred persons including full-bodied men, women, old people, and children, led by a black man named Pio. They marched toward the city of Pôrto Feliz. Police units surrounded them on the road. They resisted and dispersed their attackers. In the full light of day, marching calmly and self-possessed, they passed through the streets of the city. Farther on, two or three victorious skirmishes with the police. With his men defeated, the police chief asked for an army detachment. Under the command of Second Lieutenant Gasparino Carneiro Leão, fifty cavalrymen set out to surround and stop the determined rebels. Already at this time the National Army had refused to serve as "bloodhounds," as slave hunters. Lieutenant Gasparino, a young man with a generous spirit, did not conceal his abolitionist views. He set out on the disgraceful expedition with the intention of not pursuing the unfortunate slaves, but in the vicinity of Santo Amaro, from the top of a hill, he spotted the slaves, who from the opposite side were descending toward the bottom of the pass. The commander sent out a corporal, also an abolitionist, to advise the slaves to disperse into the forests. The corporal dismounted and set out on foot. The leader of the fugitives, the black man Pio, ignoring the sympathetic intentions of the soldier, attacked him and killed him with a blow of a scythe. The soldiers, in spontaneous reprisal, shot the black man. Despite the excitement of the moment, the abolitionist officer did not permit the slaughter of the frightened wanderers. He returned to São Paulo, responded to a military court, and was unanimously absolved.

The slaves continued their painful journey toward the city of Santos, and on the edge of the Serra do Mar, among the mountains where the Cubatão flows, they were hunted like wild beasts. The bush captains and the police killed men, women, and children without pity. Less than twenty fugitives were able to reach Santos.

The body of the black man, Pio, which was brought to São Paulo, was opened up at police headquarters. The official report showed that he had not eaten in more than three days!

Thus, the autopsy revealed that this black leader, who had defeated organized forces, who had marched with a commanding presence through wealthy towns, was suffering from hunger at the very moment in which he gave his life for the freedom of his race.

10.10. "Ceasing to Consider the Slave a Mere Laboring Machine": A Paulista Senator Calls for Quick Solutions to the "Servile Question" (December, 1887)

The wholesale abandonment of São Paulo's plantations brought a fundamental change to the provincial labor system and a giant step forward for abolition. Threatened with a total loss of their black field hands at a time when coffee was bringing excellent prices in world markets, by mid-1887 many Paulista planters had begun to free their slaves, with the provision that they serve them for a specified period of time, normally three or four years. Such promises of future freedom were not sufficiently appealing, however, to prevent more thousands from taking to the roads. Thus, by late 1887 the slaves' own rejection of slavery had so undermined the labor system that slaveholders who only months before had opposed further reforms were now, like their province's namesake, St. Paul, abruptly changing sides.

Responding in the only way they could, in late 1887 a group of fifty-one planters and representatives of 156 more—owners together of some

7,000 slaves—met in open session in the city of São Paulo to establish a provincial "Liberating Association" (Associação Libertadora). This organization had two purposes: 1) to promote liberation of every slave in the province by the end of 1890; and 2) to modify the labor system in order to keep the freedmen at work during the transitional period from slavery to unconditional free labor. The following speech, abbreviated here, was read at that meeting by the prominent Conservative senator, Antônio Prado. A leading opponent of abolitionism only a few months before, Prado had suddenly become an important advocate, nationally as well as locally, of rapid emancipation.

Source: J. Floriano de Godoy, *O elemento servil e as camaras municipaes da provincia de São Paulo* (Rio de Janeiro: Imprensa Nacional, 1887), pp. 621-627.

❧ This meeting of planters to decide on the liberation in a brief time of the slaves existing in the province of São Paulo constitutes a fact of great importance in our social life. Whatever its results may be, history must register it as eloquent proof of the influence that the ideas of liberty and justice exercise in the destiny of peoples.

It was not long ago that, for the planters, the word "liberty," when used in reference to the slaves, was a genuine cause of fear. At that time, when necessity demanded a consideration of the facts concerning the servile element, ideas were exchanged in secret and behind closed doors. Today it is with open doors, in the home or in the public plaza, with full public knowledge, that the liberation of the slaves is being discussed and decided; today, in short, it is the planters themselves who are meeting for this purpose.

If it had been necessary to demonstrate the need of a prompt and definitive solution to the servile question, the fact that I have just related would alone have sufficed. However, in this question now being considered by the planters, to discuss it is to resolve it. Such is the purpose of this meeting.

The association that we are seeking to organize is dedicated to two principal aims: 1st., to achieve the total liberation of the slaves existing in the province in a period of three years, that period to end on December 31, 1890; 2nd., to promote a modification of the system of agricultural labor on the plantations, in order to make certain that the freedmen will remain there, at least during the transitional period, thus avoiding the disorganization of labor.

I believe I faithfully express the views of the province's planters when I state that the period of three years for the elimination of slavery in the province is a sufficient time to achieve the transition from servile labor to unconditional free labor. If doubts may arise in this respect, it is in regard to the desirability of setting a shorter period, or of introducing immediate and unconditional liberation.

It must be observed, however, that setting a date for ending slavery does not imply an obligation to prolong it until the end of that time. The association which we will establish is an association of propaganda; therefore, if the economic conditions of agriculture, or other unforeseen circumstances, recommend or demand a shorter period or even immediate and unconditional liberation, our forces will converge toward that purpose. Thus interpreting the establishment of a three-year period for the total elimination of slavery, we satisfy the aspirations not only of those who wish to accelerate the emancipation movement, but also of those who would like to moderate it. A voluntary granting of conditional liberation by the planters, or their willingness to freely set a termination date, independent of any clause for the granting of additional services, would dispense with the association's need to intervene by means of organized propaganda. . . .

The usefulness of the association we are about to establish, and which is intended, by means of organized propaganda, to extend to all the slaves the benefits that some enjoy, is obvious. However, the association does not propose merely to promote the full freedom of the slaves existing in the province. Its objective is also to counsel and encourage the creation of a system of labor that is appropriate for keeping the freedmen on the plantations, avoiding the disorganization of labor. The disorganization of labor caused by the slaves' abandonment of the plantations, or by a general disturbance of public order, is what particularly concerns the planters of São Paulo. Therefore, it is that side of the question that most interests the association.

Many planters responded as follows to our circulars: Guarantee to us the labor of the freedman, and we will liberate our slaves at once. We all recognize the impossibility of the absolute guarantee which some planters desire, but reason and good sense call for measures which inspire an assurance that we can retain the freedman's labor.

What are those measures?

I will state my opinion as frankly as possible. The liberation of the slaves, whether conditional or without a clause providing for additional labor, does not by itself resolve the economic problem that concerns agriculture. Experience shows that that measure, unaccompanied by other provisions, does not assure the permanence of the freedman at work. It is natural for him to wish to enjoy the rights of freedom which he expresses by running away.

What, however, does logic call for? That the planter immediately grant him the enjoyment of those rights, rewarding his labor with a salary and modifying the labor system itself, reducing the hours of work, totally abolishing punishment, giving him better food and clothing, ceasing, finally, to consider him a mere laboring machine. I am convinced that these measures will produce the desired result. Other measures will be needed to assure the performance of labor, but these are dependent upon government; thus obligating the association to study them and to prepare relevant petitions.

Let us not fool ourselves, however, about the seriousness of the situation that we find ourselves in, because what we are dealing with here is a social and economic reform, and for such reforms to succeed without a great disruption of public order and without a huge sacrifice of the interests connected with the status quo, much wisdom is needed, and, particularly, a great deal of determination and firmness in the adoption and application of the procedures for action.

Note, however, that the dangers of inaction will be even greater, and perhaps insuperable. The events that have recently taken place in some of the districts of the province are there to demonstrate the dangers of the situation, which might have been avoided if the measures that I have mentioned had been attempted at the proper time. The disorganization of agricultural labor threatens to spread over the entire province, producing results more to be feared than those caused by any natural disaster. Under such circumstances, it would be more than ineptness, it would be madness to stand with crossed arms and watch the sad spectacle of the abandonment of the plantations, the ruin of crops, and perhaps the destruction of properties. I therefore urge that we face the difficulties of the situation, whatever the price.

Now in these moments of social crisis, a primary condition for the effectiveness of any measure of salvation is that it be strengthened in its application by a unity of forces. This is how the association will be useful. The number of planters who have already accepted the idea that unites us here, the importance of the responsible citizens who are sponsoring this meeting, the irresistible power of the emancipation movement, and the support of public opinion—all assure the success of the aims of the Liberating Association.

Unfortunately, in the province of São Paulo, there are still laggards in this question, but the obstacles which they represent to the work of emancipation as we all desire it—carried out, that is, by the planters themselves—are insignificant compared with the difficulties created by the anarchists and speculators.

It is to be regretted that the patriotic initiative of the planters of São Paulo, and this eloquent demonstration of the power of their forces to overcome the difficulties of the situation, are opposed by the disturbers of order or those who speculate upon the fate of the unhappy slaves, who, deceived, leave the work of the plantations, where in peace they could enjoy the advantages and rights of their new condition, to be abandoned on the public roads, consigned to misery and hunger, the first penalties of their black ingratitude toward their ex-masters. And all this is done in the name of freedom, morality, and religion!

Gentlemen, in the province of São Paulo, the advantages of free labor are no longer discussed; they are testified to by many years of experience. But even when it was possible to doubt free labor's capacity for preserving the system of large agricultural properties and our main agricultural product, we should have acclaimed it for rendering impossible the continuation of slavery, to which at this very moment it is delivering its final death blow. (*Hear! hear! very good.*)

10.11. "Hours of Bitterness and Terror": A Planter's Account of the Ending of Slavery in São Paulo (March 19, 1888)

The following private letter from a Paulista planter and former slaveholder, Conselheiro Paula Souza, to an abolitionist member of the Chamber of Deputies, César Zama, was written on March 19, 1888, at a moment when the planter class of São Paulo was breathing a sigh of relief following the liberation of most of the province's slaves without a collapse of their economy and traditional ways of doing things. An intimate and dramatic account of that transformation from the point of view of a former opponent of abolitionism only recently converted to that cause, this letter was correctly recognized by its recipient as an important historical document, and so was offered to the press for publication. It appeared in the Conservative Party newspaper, *A Provincia de São Paulo*, on April 8, 1888, a little more than a month before the emperor's daughter, Princess Isabel, sanctioned the "Golden Law" that ended Brazilian slavery.

Source: *A Provincia de São Paulo* (São Paulo), April 8, 1888.

Remanso, March 19, 1888.

❧ My dear Zama,

I wrote not just one letter to you while you were campaigning for reelection in the 13th district, but two. By now you must have received the second one. I thought of writing a third to you to congratulate you on your victory; but I didn't, because the great amount of work I have recently had has taken all my time.

I'm going to give you some news that should please you, and at the same time some information concerning free labor.

Since the first of January I have not possessed a single slave! I liberated all of them, and bound them to the property by means of a contract identical to the one that I have with the foreign colonists and that I intend to have with those whom I will hire. You can see that my slavocratic tendencies are moderate and tolerable.

I joyfully inform you that my new colonists have not yet given me the least reason for complaint. I am living happy and content among them, and they shower me with attention and respect.

I granted them total and unconditional freedom, and in the short speech which I made to them when I passed out their letters, I spoke to them of the grave responsibilities that freedom imposed upon them, and I spoke some words to them that came from my heart and were completely different from those that I had prepared for the occasion. From the literary point of view it was a total fiasco, because I also wept. I ended up granting them a week to make the arrangements that would suit them best, while at the same time informing them that my place would always remain open to those among them who wished to work and behave themselves.

With the exception of three, who went to search for their sisters in São Paulo, and of two others, including an *ingênuo*, who joined their father, whom I freed ten years ago, all stayed with me, and they are the same whom I find about me, and with whom I am now happy and content, as I said above.

And now to the information that will benefit the planters in the north, who soon will be faced by that social necessity: the total and immediate emancipation of the slave.

Tell the others in your province not to fool themselves with a half-measure of freedom in the hope of not disorganizing work that has already been started. With conditional liberation they will get nothing from the slaves. They want to feel free, and to work under a new system only, and with total responsibility.

Conditional liberation, even with a very short period of continuing obligations, does not have any effect upon those people who have been tormented by such a long captivity. They suspect—and with reason in regard to some—that that kind of freedom is a mere trick to keep them in that slavery from which circumstances have now freed them. They work, but lazily and with a poor attitude. The body functions, but not the spirit.

When they are completely free they cause a bit of trouble, but in the end they establish themselves at one place or another. What does it matter? What difference does it make if my ex-slaves go in search of another patron, if at least they work, and others come to take their place!

We here in São Paulo have a complete experience with the matter and a total understanding of every form of liberation. There is only one reasonable and profitable kind of freedom, and that is total, immediate, and unconditional freedom. The liberated people must themselves take responsibility for the error of leaving the place where they were slaves. It is obvious that there are masters who have lost all their workers, and the only reason for this is that they did not deserve to possess them. But the great majority will be settled someplace within a month.

I have excellent examples in my own family. My brother freed all that he owned. Some of these left and looked for work at some distant place. A week later they came to me, or to my brother himself, and they reached agreements with us, bringing unfavorable impressions of the vagabond life which they had led during that week.

So as not to annoy you further with such matters, let me sum up by saying that during the month of February we endured hours of bitterness and terror in this province, witnessing the most complete disorganization of labor imaginable.

The whole body of workers deserted the plantations, which were almost all abandoned! I do not exaggerate when I say that 80 out of every 100 were deserted, while the blacks went to the cities or followed wicked seducers. Sadly we wondered what was to become of us.

Little by little they grew tired of roaming about, and in turn the seducers grew weary of providing for them without any advantage to themselves, and today, March, all are more or less settled. Understand that when I say "all," I am excluding proprietors with bad reputations. These, in fact, will be eliminated and replaced by the force of circumstances, and the agricultural system will not miss them.

It is possible that there will be some loss of fruit to the present coffee crop. However, the crop is so large that this loss will not be important, and will be mostly compensated for by the benefits of freedom. Something else that you should tell your fellow provincials is that they are laboring under a serious error when they imagine that they will suffer great damage through the loss of slave property.

You will remember that my major argument as a pro-slavery man was that the slave was the only force we could count on for constant and indispensable agricultural labor, and that if we could always rely upon free workers I would willingly give up the slaves.

Anyone who argued in this way could be considered a pessimist, but not obstinate.

Very well, your people should give up this fear. Workers are not lacking to those who know how to find them. First, we have the slaves themselves, who do not melt away or disappear, and who need to live and feed themselves, and, therefore, to work, something they will understand in a brief time.

Then we have an enormous body of workers whom we did not count upon. I do not mean the immigrant, who today is seeking us in abundance; I refer to the Brazilian, a sluggard yesterday, living upon the scraps of slave labor and the benevolence of the rural proprietor, whom he served in the capacity of a hanger-on, a hired gunman, or in some other way. Today this Brazilian devotes himself heroically to labor, either because it has become more respectable with the advent of freedom, or because he has been denied his former options. This is what we are witnessing today.

Concerning myself, I have gathered many of them together, fearful that in the present circumstances I will not be adequately supplied with workers.

Many people who were living from four hills of beans and a quarter of corn are now appearing for work in the coffee fields, and cheerfully at the coffee drying grounds, and those I have hired have established their quarters perfectly well in the old slave buildings. It is true that mine are good ones; but they were built in the shape of a quadrangle—until now a hated arrangement.

It remains the same, except without the lock, and today they even prefer the quadrangle, because they gather their provisions inside it without fear of damage from their animals. My quadrangle is a large courtyard surrounded by clean, white houses, whose doors I now intend to open toward the outside.

Your fellow provincials must also know that free labor is not as expensive as it seemed at first. This point was my greatest surprise in the transformation that we are passing through.

As I told you, with my ex-slaves I have the same contract that I had with my colonists.

I give them nothing and sell them everything, even their supplies of cabbage or milk.

Understand that I am only doing this to teach them the value of labor, and so that they will understand that they have only themselves to depend upon, and never for personal profit, since only one visit from the doctor, whom I am paying, costs me much more than all the cabbages I possess, and all the milk my cows produce.

In any case, this ration of cattle or milk, the cattle that I slaughter, the produce that I buy wholesale and sell them retail, and cheaper than in the cities, are almost enough to pay for the costs of labor.

None of this was understood under the system of slavery!

There goes the second sheet of paper, and I am still on the same topic! But this topic does in fact deserve the full attention of the people of Bahia, who soon will find themselves face to face with the problem which not long ago caused me such fears for the future. They should not hesitate, they should emancipate and establish contracts. In the production of sugar cane the method will be even more advantageous for the owner than in the production of coffee. I have at the far side of a pasture a small cane-producing property which belongs to my sister, very good for this region but probably inferior to those of Bahia. I took charge of the place, and from it my little sister derives proportionally more profit than I do on my coffee plantation of 250,000 trees!

Enough, you will scream! All right, enough. From here I welcome an embrace from the abolitionist, Zama, for the slavocrat, *Paula Souza*.

10.12. "Slavery Is Declared Abolished" (May 13, 1888)

The law that ended slavery seems an appropriate final selection for this book. Brief and uncomplicated when compared with earlier slavery legislation, this law, sanctioned by the Princess Regent Isabel on May 13, 1888, brought an end to legal slavery, without, of course, eliminating the enormous human problems that slavery had implanted in Brazil over the centuries, including the de facto servitude that survived chattel slavery in much of rural Brazil. Nor, of courses, did it eradicate the cultural enrichment that millions of black Africans involuntarily carried to Brazil, one of the few positive effects of a labor system that in almost every other respect stands as a blot on the history of human relations.

Source: *Extincção da escravidão no Brasil (Lei No. 3353 de 13 de Maio de 1888) Discussão na Camara dos Deputados e no Senado* (Rio de Janeiro: Imprensa Nacional, 1889), p. 93.

❧ *Law No. 3353 of May 13, 1888. Declares slavery in Brazil abolished.*

The Princess Imperial Regent, in the name of His Majesty the Emperor Dom Pedro II, makes known to all subjects of the Empire that the

General Assembly has decreed, and she has sanctioned, the following law:

Art. 1. From the date of this law slavery is declared extinct in Brazil.

Art. 2. All provisions to the contrary are revoked.

She orders, therefore, all the authorities to whom the knowledge and execution of this Law belong to carry it out, and cause it to be fully and exactly executed and observed.

The Secretary of State for the Departments of Agriculture, Commerce and Public Works, and *ad interim* for Foreign Affairs, Bachelor Rodrigo Augusto da Silva, of the Council of His Majesty the Emperor, will have it printed, published, and circulated.

Given in the Palace of Rio de Janeiro on May 13, 1888, the 67th of Independence and of the Empire.

PRINCESS IMPERIAL REGENT

Rodrigo Augusto da Silva. . . .

CHRONOLOGY OF IMPORTANT EVENTS

1095 Beginnings of Portuguese independent existence under the House of Burgundy.

1139 Afonso I becomes king of an independent Portuguese monarchy.

1267 Portugal gains control of the Algarve, consolidating its national territory.

1415 Portuguese capture Ceuta in North Africa, initiating era of overseas expansion.

1425 Portuguese colonize Madeira.

1443-44 Portuguese initiate direct seaborn slave trade with West Africa.

1445 The Azores are colonized by Portuguese settlers.

1479 Treaty of Alcaçovas between Portugal and Castile gives Castile the Canary Islands and confirms Portugal's rights in Africa and the Atlantic islands.

1493 Pope Alexander VI grants Portugal all lands east of a line 100 leagues west of the Cape Verde Islands, Spain to receive all lands west of that line.

1494 Treaty of Tordesillas moves the papal demarcation line 370 leagues west of the Cape Verde Islands, placing all of Africa and eastern Brazil within Portugal's sphere of influence.

1500 Pedro Alvares Cabral, on a voyage to India, reaches the Brazilian coast and claims the land for Portugal.

1501-30 Navigators explore the Brazilian coast and Portuguese and French merchants establish temporary trading posts for the collection of brazilwood.

1532 First permanent Portuguese settlement in Brazil is established at São Vicente, in what is now the state of São Paulo.

1534 System of hereditary captaincies is established in Brazil to encourage exploration and colonization.

1537 Pope Paul III prohibits the enslavement of Indians, including those of Brazil.

1539 Duarte Coelho, *donatário* of Pernambuco, requests a license from King João III to import slaves from Guinea.

1549 Thomé de Souza, first governor general of Brazil, establishes the city of Salvador da Bahia.
Beginnings of organized African slave trade to provide workers for the newly established sugar industry.

1551 A bishopric is established at Bahia.

1554 Father Manoel da Nóbrega establishes a Jesuit school at Piratininga, at the present site of the city of São Paulo.

1555 French colony of France Antarctique is established on the island of Villegaignon in the harbor of Rio de Janeiro.

1559 A royal decree allows the transportation of African slaves to Brazil to work in the sugar industry.

1565 Portuguese settlers under Estácio de Sá establish the city of Rio de Janeiro.

1567 French colonists are expelled from the region of Rio de Janeiro.

1570 King Sebastião I bans enslavement of Brazilian Indians except when captured in a just war.

1578 King Sebastião I dies in battle in North Africa and is succeeded by his uncle, Cardinal Henrique, last ruler of the Aviz dynasty.

1580 The Spanish Hapsburgs establish control over the Portuguese kingdom and indirectly over Brazil and other Portuguese colonies.

1595 Philip II of Spain bans the enslavement of Brazil's Indians.

1605 Runaway slaves begin to establish the *quilombos* (runaway-slave settlements) of Palmares which last until their destruction in 1695.

1612 French establish a colony at São Luís do Maranhão while Portuguese settle nearby Ceará.

1615 Portuguese seize Maranhão from the French, broadening their control over northern Brazil.

1616 Portuguese establish the city of Belém, Pará.

1624 Dutch attack and capture Salvador da Bahia but are driven out the following year.

1630-54 Period of Dutch conquest and colonization of Pernambuco and other parts of northern Brazil, ending after a long armed struggle.

1640 Portugal reestablishes her independence under the Braganza dynasty, ending sixty years of Spanish domination, the so-called "Babylonian Captivity."

1648 Portuguese colonize Paraná, setting the stage for further southern expansion.

1664 King Afonso VI issues a decree to prohibit overcrowding on Atlantic slave ships.

1684 King Pedro II issues new regulations intended to reduce crowding and high mortality in the African slave trade.

1695 The *quilombos* of Palmares are attacked and subdued.

1695-99 Paulistas discover gold in Minas Gerais, beginning a gold rush and an era of colonization and development in the region.

1722 Gold is discovered in Goiás and Mato Grosso.

1729 Large diamond deposits are discovered at Tejuco (the modern Diamantina) in Minas Gerais.

1737 Beginnings of colonization of Rio Grande do Sul.

1750	Treaty of Madrid between Spain and Portugal recognizes de facto Portuguese control over regions west of the Tordesillas line.
1755	The Marquis of Pombal bans the slave trade to Portugal, but encourages the traffic to Brazil with creation of the commercial company of Grão Pará and Maranhão.
1759	Jesuits are expelled from Portugal and Brazil.
1763	Viceregal capital is established at Rio de Janeiro.
1775	A new ban on the enslavement of Indians in Brazil.
1777	Treaty of San Ildefonso between Spain and Portugal establishes Brazil's western and southern boundaries, consolidating the country in roughly its present form.
1789	Revolutionary conspiracy known as the Inconfidência Mineira denounced in Minas Gerais.
1798	"Revolt of the Tailors," a revolutionary conspiracy involving free mulattoes and slaves, is uncovered in Salvador da Bahia.
1807-08	The Portuguese royal court is transferred to Rio de Janeiro under British naval escort.
1808	Brazilian ports are opened to world trade. The first newspapers are published in Rio de Janeiro. Prince Regent Dom João reestablishes forms of Indian forced labor.
1810	In a treaty with Britain Dom João agrees to eventual abolition of the slave trade, and to prohibit the traffic at once to Portuguese subjects in non-Portuguese territories in Africa.
1815	Portuguese government in Rio agrees in a treaty with Britain to forbid participation of Portuguese subjects in the slave trade north of the equator. Brazil is proclaimed a kingdom equal in status to Portugal and the Algarve.
1816	With the death of Queen Maria I, Dom João is crowned King João VI of Portugal, Brazil, and the Algarve.
1817	A Liberal revolt breaks out in Pernambuco but is quickly suppressed. In an Additional Convention with Britain King João VI agrees to measures to enforce the partial ban on the slave trade.
1818	King João VI decrees measures for the protection and employment of free Africans (*emancipados*), providing that they be put to work in government establishments or hired out to private persons, their apprenticeship to last for fourteen years.
1821	After a liberal revolt in Portugal, King João VI returns to Lisbon, leaving his son, Dom Pedro, behind in Brazil as regent.
1822	Dom Pedro declares Brazilian independence from Portugal (September 7) and is crowned Emperor Pedro I of Brazil (December 1).
1823	A general constituent and legislative assembly meets in Rio de Janeiro in May to write a constitution.

Pedro I dissolves the constituent assembly in November and exiles some of its principal leaders.

1824 Pedro I promulgates an imperial constitution.

Revolts break out in various northern provinces.

1826 In a treaty with Great Britain the government of Pedro I agrees to outlaw the slave trade three years after the treaty's ratification by the two governments.

1830 The slave trade to Brazil becomes illegal (March 13).

1831 A liberal revolt forces the abdication of Emperor Pedro I (April 7) in favor of his five-year-old son, Dom Pedro.

A three-man regency is chosen to rule on the young Pedro's behalf.

The General Assembly passes a law (November 7) declaring the freedom of all slaves entering Brazil from that day on.

The General Assembly abolishes Indian slavery in Brazil (October 27).

1832 After a brief decline, the African slave trade, now illegal, is renewed.

1834 An Additional Act liberalizes the Constitution of 1824, giving more power to the provinces and creating a one-man regency.

1835 A major slave revolt breaks out in Salvador da Bahia but is quickly suppressed.

Farroupilha Revolt begins in Rio Grande do Sul, ending with the reincorporation of the province into the empire ten years later.

1837 Conservatives reassume power under the regency of Pedro de Araújo Lima.

1839 The British Parliament passes the Palmerston Bill authorizing British naval vessels to seize all Portuguese ships found transporting slaves or equipped to do so.

1840 Dom Pedro's majority is declared and he assumes the crown as Emperor Pedro II.

1845 The British Parliament passes the Aberdeen Bill, giving British naval vessels authority to seize Brazilian slave ships wherever they might be found.

1850 Under British pressure, the Brazilian General Assembly passes the Queirós Law (September 4), again abolishing the African slave trade to Brazil and specifying means of enforcing the law and punishing its violators.

1851 The African slave trade to Brazil virtually ends, but is quickly replaced by an inter-provincial slave trade.

1864 The Brazilian government grants final liberation to all free Africans (*emancipados*) (September 24).

1865-70 Brazil, Argentina, and Uruguay fight and defeat Paraguay in the War of the Triple Alliance.

1866 A government decree grants freedom to government-owned slaves who agree to serve in the Brazilian Army.

1867 In his annual Speech from the Throne, Emperor Pedro II urges the General Assembly to give consideration to the slavery question at an appropriate time.

1869 The General Assembly passes a law (September 15) banning public slave auctions but allowing judicial sales of slaves for settling estates; the same law prohibits separation of married couples by sale, or the separation of children under fifteen from their parents by sale.

1871 After a long and intense national debate the General Assembly passes the Rio Branco Law (September 28) freeing the newborn children of slave women and otherwise reforming the slave system.

1879 Joaquim Nabuco, newly elected to the Chamber of Deputies, reopens the slavery question in the General Assembly.

1880 A powerful anti-slavery movement emerges in Rio de Janeiro and other parts of Brazil.

An effective anti-slavery press appears in Rio and other cities.

Joaquim Nabuco, André Rebouças, and others establish the Brazilian Anti-Slavery Society (September 7).

The provincial assemblies of Rio de Janeiro and Minas Gerais pass laws in December to restrict importation of slaves from other provinces, followed by the assembly of São Paulo the following month.

1881 A popular anti-slavery movement breaks out in the northeastern city of Fortaleza, Ceará, where crowds demand and achieve an end to the shipment of slaves from the province to southern plantations.

José do Patrocinio acquires the *Gazeta da Tarde* and makes it the principal anti-slavery newspaper in Brazil.

1882 José do Patrocinio travels to Ceará in October and is present there as a systematic program of provincial liberation begins. A major slave revolt breaks out near the city of Campinas, São Paulo.

1883 An Abolitionist Confederation is created in Rio de Janeiro, uniting seventeen anti-slavery organizations representing at least five provinces and the imperial capital.

André Rebouças and José do Patrocinio publish the "Manifesto" of the Abolitionist Confederation.

In Europe Joaquim Nabuco publishes his anti-slavery classic, *O Abolicionismo*.

1884 Powerful anti-slavery movements in Ceará and Amazonas virtually end slavery in the two northern provinces.

Abolitionists of Rio Grande do Sul free a majority of the province's slaves.

Liberal government of Senator Manoel Pinto de Sousa Dantas proposes liberation of all slaves reaching the age of sixty (the Dantas Bill).

1885 The Dantas government falls following a no-confidence vote (May 4).

A revised version of the Dantas Bill, the Saraiva-Cotegipe Law, is passed by the General Assembly (September 28), freeing slaves sixty and older, though with the obligation to serve their masters without pay for five more years, or until the age of sixty-five.

1886 The General Assembly passes a law banning whipping as punishment for slaves in public establishments (October 16). A popular anti-slavery movement develops in the port of Santos, and the Paulista city becomes a haven for runaways.

1887 Thousands of slaves abandon the plantations of São Paulo, encouraged by abolitionists, forcing slaveholders to free their slaves en masse.

Led by Marshal Deodoro da Fonseca, the Brazilian Army officially requests relief from the task of hunting down and subduing runaway slaves.

1888 As slaves abandon plantations, the slave system crumbles throughout much of Brazil.

The Golden Law (Lei Áurea) abolishing slavery is passed by both houses of the General Assembly and sanctioned by the Princess Regent, Isabel, on May 13.

1889 The Empire of Dom Pedro II is overthrown and a republic is established (November 15), in part owing to the perceived roles of Dom Pedro and his heiress, Princess Isabel, in the abolition of slavery.

GLOSSARY OF PORTUGUESE, AFRICAN, AND BRAZILIAN TERMS

Africanos livres (*emancipados*). Africans illegally subjected to the slave trade who after 1817 were declared free by British-Brazilian mixed commissions or Brazilian courts; many, however, becoming de facto slaves.

Agregado. See *morador*.

Aguardente (*cachaça*). Strong rum normally made of sugar-cane juice.

Alqueire. Dry measurement of about thirteen liters; also a land measurement in Brazil ranging from about six to twelve acres.

Ama de leite. Wet nurse; often a slave woman purchased or rented to suckle children of the privileged.

Angú. Manioc or corn flour boiled in water.

Anjinhos. Literally "little angels"; thumbscrews for punishing or torturing slaves.

Arroba. Measurement of about thirty-two pounds.

Bacalhau. Literally "codfish"; whip of one or more leather thongs used to punish slaves.

Balaiada. Popular uprising and civil war in the province of Maranhão, 1838-1841.

Barracão. Barracoon, a barrack or temporary shelter for slaves on the African coast.

Batuque. African dance usually accompanied by drums.

Bens do evento (singular: *bem do evento*). Stray animals or blacks assumed to be slaves, who were imprisoned, later to be returned to their masters or sold in public auction.

Bicho do pé. Small insect laying eggs under the skin of animals or people, often on a slave's unprotected foot.

Boçal. See *negro boçal*.

Bode. Male goat; like the word "*cabra*," term often used to refer to a mulatto.

Bolo. See *palmatoada*.

Caboclo. Offspring of a white with an Indian.

Cabra. She-goat; like the word "*bode*," term often used to refer to a mulatto.

Cachaça. Sugar-cane rum.

Cadeirinha. Sedan chair for transporting passengers, usually carried by slaves.

Cafres. Kaffirs, peoples of eastern and southern Africa.

Caifazes (singular: *caifaz*). Radical abolitionist followers of Antônio Bento in São Paulo who urged slaves to flee their masters' estates during the last years of slavery.

Calabouço. Town jail where criminals and runaways were imprisoned and punished.

Calcanha. Slave woman who swept a sugar mill or did similar tasks.

Candomblé. Religion of the Yorubas of West Africa or their religious festival.

Candomby. Variation of *candomblé*.

Canjica. Corn-flour porridge.

Capitão-do-mato. Professional slave-hunter.

Capoeira. Athletic game or dance engaged in by young blacks, often with the use of razors or knives; like *candomblé* and other African customs, often forbidden.

Carimbo. Instrument used to brand slaves, or the mark it produced.

Carne seca. See *charque*.

Carurú. Edible green plants, or a dish prepared from them.

Catinga. Body odor often associated with blacks.

Charque. Dried or salted beef, an important product of Rio Grande do Sul, often an important part of the slave diet.

Chicote. A whip.

Cigano. A gypsy.

Código Filipino. Portuguese law code of 1603 in full use in Brazil until 1823 and in partial use thereafter; included laws on slavery and the slave trade.

Conto. Currency denomination of 1,000 *réis*, written 1:000$000.

Cria. Young animal, often a colt or filly; term also popularly used to refer to the children of slave women.

Crioulo (feminine: *crioula*). Creole, a black born in Brazil.

Cruzado. A coin worth 400 *réis*.

Curador. Public official assigned to guard and protect orphans, slaves or freed persons, including *Africanos livres*.

Curumin. Word of Indian origin meaning "servant."

Elemento servil. Literally "servile element," a popular euphemism for the slave population in the last years of slavery.

Emancipado. Free African. See *Africanos livres*.

Engenho. Sugar mill or sugar plantation.

Farinha. Flour; in Brazil often manioc or corn flour.

Farroupilha Revolt. So-called War of the Ragamuffins in Rio Grande do Sul, 1835-1845.

Fazenda. Plantation or farm.

Fazendeiro. Owner of a *fazenda* or plantation.

Feijões (singular: *feijão*). Beans.

Feijoada. Traditional meal of black beans and meat, often served with rice and rum.

Feitor. Overseer or foreman on a plantation.

Free Birth Law. See *Rio Branco Law*.

Fubá. Corn or rice flour.

Funidor. Backlander in Africa who engaged in hunting and buying slaves.

Gargalheira. Iron collar worn by slaves, especially convicted runaways.

Ingênuo (feminine: *ingênua*). In Roman law, a freeborn person; specifically in Brazil the offspring of a slave woman born free according to Article 1 of the Rio Branco Law of September 28, 1871.

Irmandad. Religious brotherhood.

Ladino (feminine: *ladina*). An African with some knowledge of the Portuguese language and culture and of Christianity; as opposed to a *negro boçal*, a newly imported African without such knowledge.

Lavoura. Cultivation of the soil, the agricultural industry.

Lavrador. In northeastern Brazil, a landless and dependent tenant farmer or sharecropper.

Lei Áurea. Golden Law of May 13, 1888, which abolished slavery.

Lei do Ventre Livre. Law of the Free Womb. See *Rio Branco Law*.

Libambo. Iron chain used in Africa and Brazil to confine slaves, especially during transport; also an iron neckpiece worn in Brazil by recaptured runaways.

Liberto (feminine: *liberta*). A slave who had been liberated.

Macambo. See *mocambo*.

Mãe prêta. Black mother; often affectionate term for a female servant or wet nurse who suckled and cared for the children of a patriarchal family.

Mamaluco (feminine: *mamaluca*). Offspring of a white with an Indian, a person of mixed racial origin.

Mandioca. Manioc or cassava.

Mesa de Consciência. Royal council instituted by King João III of Portugal (1521-1557) to reach decisions on moral questions.

Milréis. One thousand *réis*, written 1$000.

Mineiro. Inhabitant of the captaincy or province of Minas Gerais.

Misericórdia. See *Santa Casa da Misericórdia*.

Mocambo. A runaway-slave settlement. See *quilombo*.

Moleque. A black boy.

Morador. Literally "resident"; term designating a squatter or poor farmer on a large estate who was allowed to live there under certain conditions.

Mucama. A black lady's maid or personal attendant.

Mulato (feminine: *mulata*). A mulatto, the offspring of a white and a black.

Muleque. See *moleque*.

Negro boçal (plural: *negros boçais*). "Raw" or unacculturated African newly arrived in Brazil; as opposed to a *ladino*.

Negro de ganho. See *prêto de ganho*.

Nossa Senhora do Rosario. Our Lady of the Rosary; in Brazil the patron saint of black slaves.

Novena. Prayers or devotion carried on over nine days; in Brazil, slave punishments inflicted over a period of nine days.

Palmares. A group of seventeenth-century slave settlements in northeastern Brazil.

Palmatoada. Stroke inflicted on the hand with a *palmatória*. A *bolo*.

Palmatória. Wooden paddle used to strike the hands of school children and slaves as a form of punishment. See *palmatoada*.

Pardo (feminine: *parda*). A mulatto or a person whose skin was dark brown.

Pataca. A minor Portuguese coin often valued at 320 *réis*.

Paulista. An inhabitant of São Paulo.

Peça. Literally "piece;" in slave-trade parlance, a term designating a slave of a certain size and weight.

Pecúlio. Personal possessions; specifically the property a slave was allowed to hold, officially recognized by the Rio Branco Law of September 28, 1871.

Pombeiro. A slave who traveled for the profit of his master.

Prêto de ganho (also *negro de ganho*). Black slave whose master allowed him to work independently or hire himself out to others, with the obligation to give his master a stipulated sum of money.

Quilombo. Runaway-slave village or settlement.

Quilombola. Inhabitant of a *quilombo*.

Real (plural: *réis*). Monetary unit. See *milréis*.

Reinado africano. In Brazil, a ceremony or celebration in which individuals were chosen to rule symbolically as monarchs.

Rio Branco Law. Complex legislation passed into law on September 28, 1871, freeing children of slave women born on and after that date, and otherwise reforming the slave system.

Roça. Small plot of land granted to slaves to produce food for their own consumption or for sale.

Rua. Street.

Santa Casa da Misericórdia. Religious brotherhood established in various Brazilian cities offering social services, including medical care, to all social and racial groups.

Saraiva-Cotegipe Law. Law of September 28, 1885, which freed slaves of sixty and older, with the condition that they serve their masters five additional years without pay, or until they reached the age of sixty-five.

Senhor de engenho. A sugar mill owner.

Senzala. Group of huts or other buildings housing slaves on a plantation.

Sertanejo. Backlander or rustic.

Sertão. A sparsely populated region of the interior, especially in northeastern Brazil.

Sinhá, sinhô, sinhôzinho. Corrupted forms of *senhor, senhora*, and *senhorzinho*; terms of address used by slaves for members of the master class.

Soba. Angolan or Kimbundu term for a local chief or judge.

Tangosmão. A hunter of slaves or slave dealer in Africa.

Toré. In Alagôas, a warlike dance performed to the sound of fifes, trumpets, and other instruments during festivals recalling the *quilombos* of Palmares and their destruction.

Trezena. Prayers or devotion performed for thirteen consecutive days prior to a saint's feast day; in Brazil, slave punishments carried out over thirteen days.

Tronco. Wooden or metal stocks used to imprison and punish slaves or other offenders.

Tumbeiro. A slave ship; or a person who hunted slaves in parts of the African interior.

Valongo (*Rua do Valongo*). A street in Rio de Janeiro where slaves were concentrated and sold.

Vaqueiro. A cowboy, especially in northeastern Brazil.

Zumbi. An African war chief; title sometimes used by *quilombo* leaders.

SELECTED BIBLIOGRAPHY

Abranches, João Dunshee de. *O captiveiro (memórias)*. Rio de Janeiro, 1941.

Almada, Vilma Paraíso Ferreira de. *Escravismo e transição: O Espírito Santo (1850-1888)*. Rio de Janeiro, 1984.

Andrews, George Reid. *Blacks and Whites in São Paulo, Brazil, 1888-1988*. Madison, Wis., 1991.

Bastide, Roger, and Florestan Fernandes. *Brancos e negros em São Paulo*. 2nd rev. ed. São Paulo, 1959.

Bastos, A. C. Tavares. *Cartas do solitario*. 3rd ed. São Paulo, 1938.

Benci, Jorge, S. I. *Economia cristã dos senhores no governo dos escravos (livro brasileiro de 1700)*. 2nd ed. Proto, 1954.

Bethell, Leslie. *The Abolition of the Brazilian Slave Trade: Britain, Brazil, and the Slave Trade Question, 1807-1869*. London, 1970.

Boxer, C. R. *The Dutch in Brazil, 1624-1654*. New York, 1973.

———. *The Golden Age of Brazil, 1695-1750: Growing Pains of a Colonial Society*. Berkeley, 1962.

———. *The Portuguese Seaborne Empire, 1415-1825*. London, 1969.

———. *Race Relations in the Portuguese Colonial Empire, 1415-1825*. Oxford, 1963.

Burlamaque, Frederico L. C. *Analytica acerca do commercio d'escravos e acerca dos malles da escravidão domestica*. Rio de Janeiro, 1837.

Cardoso, Fernando Henrique. *Capitalismo e escravidão no Brasil meridional: O negro na sociedade escravocrata do Rio Grande do Sul*. São Paulo, 1962.

———, and Octávio Ianni. *Côr e mobilidade social em Florianópolis: Aspectos das relações entre negros e brancos numa comunidade do Brasil meridional*. São Paulo, 1960.

Carneiro, Edison. *Antologia do negro brasileiro*. Rio de Janeiro, 1967.

———. *O quilombo dos Palmares*. 3rd ed. Rio de Janeiro, 1966.

Carreira, Antônio. *As companhias pombalinas de navegação, comércio e tráfico de escravos entre a costa africana e o nordeste brasileiro*. Porto, 1969.

Christie, William D. *Notes on Brazilian Questions*. London, 1865.

Conrad, Robert. *Brazilian Slavery: An Annotated Research Bibliography*. Boston, 1977.

———. "Nineteenth-Century Brazilian Slavery." In Robert Brent Toplin, ed., *Slavery and Race Relations in Latin America*. Westport, Conn. 1974.

Conrad, Robert Edgar. *The Destruction of Brazilian Slavery, 1850-1888*. 2nd ed. Melbourne, Fla., 1993.

———. *World of Sorrow: The African Slave Trade to Brazil*. Baton Rouge, La., 1986.

Costa, Emília Viotti da Costa. *Da senzala à colônia*. São Paulo, 1966.

Curtin, Philip D. *The Atlantic Slave Trade: A Census*. Madison, Wis., 1969.

Davis, David Brion. *The Problem of Slavery in Western Culture*. Ithaca, New York, 1966.

Dean, Warren. *Rio Claro: A Brazilian Plantation System, 1820-1920*. Stanford, Cal., 1976.

Debret, Jean Baptiste. *Voyage pittoresque e historique au Brésil*. 3 vols. Paris, 1834, 1835, 1839.

Degler, Carl N. *Neither Black nor White: Slavery and Race Relations in Brazil and the United States*. New York, 1971.

Dornas Filho, João. *A escravidão no Brazil*. Rio de Janeiro, 1939.

Eakin, Marshall C. *British Enterprise in Brazil: The St. John d'el Rey Mining Company and the Morro Velho Gold Mine, 1830-1860*. Durham, N.C., 1989.

Eisenberg, Peter L. "Abolishing Slavery: The Process on Pernambuco's Sugar Plantations." *Hispanic American Historical Review* 52 (1972), 580-597.

———. *The Sugar Industry in Pernambuco, 1840-1919: Modernization without Change*. Berkeley, 1974.

Ewbank, Thomas. *Life in Brazil; or a Journal of a Visit to the Land of the Cocoa and the Palm*. New York, 1856.

Fernandes, Florestan. *The Negro in Brazilian Society*. New York, 1969.

Fonseca, L. Anselmo da. *A escravidão, o clero e o abolicionismo*. Bahia, 1887.

Freitas, Décio. *Palmares: A guerra dos escravos*. 4th ed. Rio de Janeiro, 1982.

Freyre, Gilberto. *O escravo nos anúncios de jornais brasileiros do século XIX*. Recife, 1963.

———. *The Mansions and the Shanties: The Making of Modern Brazil*. New York, 1963.

———. *The Masters and the Slaves: A Study in the Development of Brazilian Civilization*. New York, 1946.

———. *New World in the Tropics: The Culture of Modern Brazil*. New York, 1963.

———. *Order and Progress: Brazil from Monarchy to Republic*. New York, 1970.

Furtado, Celso. *The Economic Growth of Brazil: A Survey from Colonial to Modern Times*. Berkeley, 1963.

Galliza, Diana Soares de. *O declínio da escravidão na Paraíba, 1850-1888*. João Pessoa, 1979.

Genovese, Eugene D. *From Rebellion to Revolution: Afro-American Slave Revolts in the Making of the New World*. New York, 1979.

———. *Roll, Jordan, Roll: The World the Slaves Made*. New York, 1972.

Girão, Raimundo. *A abolição no Ceará*. Fortaleza, 1956.

Godoy, J. Floriano de. *O elemento servil e as camaras municipaes da provincia de São Paulo*. Rio de Janeiro, 1887.

Gorender, Jacob. *A escravidão reabilitada*. São Paulo, 1990.

———. *O escravismo colonial*. 5th ed. São Paulo, 1990.

Goulart, José Alipio. *Da fuga ao suicídio (Aspectos da regbeldia dos escravos no*

Brasil). Rio de Janeiro, 1972.

———. *Da palmatória ao patíbulo (Castigos de escravos no Brasil).* Rio de Janeiro, 1971.

Goulart, Mauricio. *A escravidão africana no Brasil: Das origens à extinção do tráfico.* 3rd ed. São Paulo, 1975.

Graham, Richard. *Britain and the Onset of Modernization in Brazil, 1850-1914.* Cambridge, 1972.

———. *Patronage and Politics in Nineteenth-Century Brazil.* Stanford, Cal., 1990.

Graham, Sandra Lauderdale. *House and Street: The Domestic World of Servants and Masters in Nineteenth-Century Rio de Janeiro.* Cambridge, 1988.

Harris, Marvin. *Patterns of Race in the Americas.* New York, 1964.

Henning, John. *Red Gold: The Conquest of the Brazilian Indians.* London, 1978.

Ianni, Octavio. *As metamorfoses do escravo: Apogeu e crise da escravatura no Brasil meridional.* São Paulo, 1962.

———. *Raças e classes sociais no Brasil.* 2nd rev. ed. Rio de Janeiro, 1972.

Karasch, Mary C. *Slave Life in Rio de Janeiro, 1808-1850.* Princeton, 1987.

Klein, Herbert S. *African Slavery in Latin America and the Caribbean.* New York, 1986.

———. *The Middle Passage: Comparative Studies in the Atlantic Slave Trade.* Princeton, 1978.

Knight, Franklin W. *Slave Society in Cuba during the Nineteenth Century.* Madison, Wis., 1970.

Libby, Douglas Cole. *Transformação e trabalho em uma economia escravista: Minas Gerais no século XIX.* São Paulo, 1988.

Lima, Lana Lage da Gama. *Rebeldia negra e abolicionismo.* Rio de Janeiro, 1981.

Lombardi, John V. "Comparative Slave Systems in the Americas: A Critical Review." In Richard Graham and Peter H. Smith, eds., *New Approaches to Latin American History.* Austin, 1974.

Luna, Luiz. *O negro na luta contra a escravidão.* Rio de Janeiro, 1968.

MacLachlan, Colin M. "African Slave Trade and Economic Development in Amazonia, 1700-1800." In Robert Brent Toplin, *Slavery and Race Relations in Latin America.* Westport, Conn., 1974.

Maestri Filho, Mário José. *O escravo no Rio Grande do Sul: A charqueada e a gênese do escravismo gaúcho.* Porto Alegre, 1984.

———. *A servidão negra.* Porto Alegre, 1988.

Magalhães, Raymundo. *A vida turbulenta de José do Patrocinio.* Rio de Janeiro, 1969.

Malheiro, Agostinho Marques Perdigão. *Escravidão no Brasil: Ensaio histórico-jurídico-social.* 2 vols. 2nd ed. São Paulo, 1944.

Marchant, Alexander. *From Barter to Slavery: The Economic Relations of Portuguese and Indians in the Settlement of Brazil, 1500-1580.* Baltimore, 1942.

Menucci, Sud. *O precursor do abolicionismo no Brasil (Luiz Gama).* São Paulo, 1938.

Miller, Joseph C. *Way of Death: Merchant Capitalism and the Angolan Slave Trade, 1730-1830.* Madison, Wis., 1988.

Moraes, Evaristo de. *A campanha abolicionista (1879-1888)*. Rio de Janeiro, 1924.

Mörner, Magnus. *Race Mixture in the History of Latin America*. Boston, 1967.

Morel, Edmar. *Vendaval da liberdade*. Rio de Janeiro, 1967.

Mott, Maria Lucia de Barros. *Submissão e resistência: A mulher escrava na luta contra a escravidão*. São Paulo, 1988.

Moura, Clovis. *O negro: de bom escravo a mau cidadão?* Rio de Janeiro, 1977.

———. *Os quilombos e a rebelião negra*. São Paulo, 1981.

———. *Rebeliões da senzala: quilombos, insurreições, guerrilhas*. Rio de Janeiro, 1972.

Nabuco, Carolina. *The Life of Joaquim Nabuco*. Stanford, 1950.

Nabuco, Joaquim. *Abolitionism: The Brazilian Anti-Slavery Struggle*. Urbana, 1977.

———. *Minha formação*. Rio de Janeiro, 1900.

Nelson, Thomas. *Remarks on the Slavery and Slave Trade of the Brazils*. London, 1846.

North, Douglass C. *The Economic Growth of the United States, 1790-1860*. New York, 1966.

Ott, Carlos B. *Formação e evolução étnica da cidade do Salvador*. 2 vols. Bahia, 1955, 1957.

Pang, Eul-Soo. *In Pursuit of Honor and Power: Noblemen of the Southern Cross in Nineteenth-Century Brazil*. Tuscaloosa, Ala., 1988.

Prado, Júnior, Caio. *The Colonial Background of Modern Brazil*. Berkeley, 1967.

Queiroz, Suely Robles Reis de. *Escravidão negra em São Paulo (Um estudo das tenções provocadas pelo escravismo no século XIX)*. Rio de Janeiro, 1977.

Ramos, Arthur. "Castigos de escravos." *Revista do Arquivo Municipal* (São Paulo) 47 (1938), 79-103.

———. *As culturas negras*. Rio de Janeiro, 1972.

Rebouças, André. *Agricultura nacional*. Rio de Janeiro, 1883.

———. *Diário e notas autobiográficas*. Rio de Janeiro, 1938.

Reis, João José. *Rebelião escrava no Brasil: A história do levante dos Malês (1835)*. 2nd ed. São Paulo, 1981.

Ribeiro, João. *História do Brasil*. 19th ed. Rio de Janeiro, 1966.

Rodrigues, José Honório. *Brazil and Africa*. Berkeley, 1965.

———. *Independência: Revolução e contra-revolução*. 5 vols. Rio de Janeiro, 1975.

———. "A rebeldia negra e a abolição." In *História e historiografia*. Petrópolis, 1970.

Rugendas, Johann Moritz. *Malerische Reise in Brasilien*. Paris, 1835.

Russell-Wood, A.J.R. *The Black Man in Slavery and Freedom in Colonial Brazil*. New York, 1982.

———. *Fidalgos and Philanthropists: The Santa Casa da Misericórdia of Bahia, 1550-1755*. Berkeley, 1968.

Salles, Vicente. *O negro no Pará sob o regime da escravidão*. Rio de Janeiro, 1971.

Santos, Maria Januária Vilela, *A Balaiada e a insurreição de escravos no Maranhão*.

São Paulo, 1983.

Santos, Ronaldo Marcos dos Santos. *Resistência e superação do escravismo na província de São Paulo, 1885-1888*. São Paulo, 1980.

Sayers, Raymond S. *The Negro in Brazilian Literature*. New York, 1956.

Scarano, Julita. *Devoção e escravidão: A Irmandade de Nossa Senhora do Rosário dos Pretos no Distrito Diamantino no século XVIII*. São Paulo, 1975.

Schwartz, Stuart B. *Sugar Plantations in the Formation of Brazilian Society*. Cambridge, 1985.

Scott, Rebecca J., et al. *The Abolition of Slavery and the Aftermath of Emancipation in Brazil*. Durham, N.C., 1988.

Skidmore, Thomas E. *Black into White: Race and Nationality in Brazilian Thought*. New York, 1974.

Slenes, Robert Wayne. "The Demography and Economics of Brazilian Slavery: 1850-1888." Ph.D. dissertation, Stanford University, 1976.

Stein, Stanley J. *Vassouras: A Brazilian Coffee County, 1850-1900*. Cambridge, Mass., 1957.

Tannenbaum, Frank. *Slave and Citizen: The Negro in the Americas*. New York, 1963.

Toplin, Robert Brent. *The Abolition of Slavery in Brazil*. New York, 1972.

———. "Upheaval, Violence, and the Abolition of Slavery in Brazil: The Case of São Paulo." *Hispanic American Historical Review* 49 (1969), 639-655.

Toplin, Robert Brent, ed. *Slavery and Race Relations in Latin America*. Westport, Conn., 1974.

Verger, Pierre. *Flux et reflux de la traite des nègres entre le Golfe de Bénin et Bahia de Todos os Santos du XVII*[e] *au XIX*[e] *siècle*. The Hague, 1968.

Viana Filho, Luiz. *O negro na Bahia*. 2nd ed. São Paulo, 1976.

Walsh, Robert. *Notices of Brazil in 1828 and 1829*. 2 vols. London, 1830.

INDEX

CPSIA information can be obtained at www.ICGtesting.com
Printed in the USA
BVOW07s1155060914

365541BV00002B/71/P